Writer's and Illustrator's Guide to Children's Book Publishers and Agents

2002–2003

Who They Are! What They Want!

And How to Win Them Over!

ELLEN R. SHAPIRO

PRIMA PUBLISHING

Published by Prima Publishing, Roseville, California. Member of the Crown Publishing Group, a division of Random House, Inc.

ISBN 0-7615-2515-7
ISSN 1536-1497

02 03 04 BB 10 9 8 7 6 5 4 3
Printed in the United States of America

First Edition

"Frog, you are looking quite green."
But I always look green," said Frog. "I am a frog."
"Today you look very green even for a frog," said Toad.
"Get into my bed and rest."
Toad made Frog a cup of hot tea. Frog drank the tea, and then he said,
"Tell me a story while I am resting."
"All right," said Toad. "Let me think of a story to tell you."

—ARNOLD LOBEL

For Steven,
Who always tells me stories (even when I'm not resting).

* * *

And for all I know he is sitting there still, under his favorite cork tree, smelling flowers just quietly.

He is very happy.

—MUNRO LEAF

And for Jonathan Cooper,
who now, surely must be very happy.

Contents

Part Two
Directory of Publishers and Editors 77

Part Three
Literary Agents and Artist Representatives 445

Acknowledgments

Never in my experience as a writer have I encountered a group so generous and helpful as those in the children's book universe.

To the authors, illustrators, and editors who bent over backwards to share their knowledge with me and offer kind words of support: I thank you. To all those who contributed articles and who gave their time to be profiled (there were so many generous contributors, and each is recognized separately within the body of this book): There isn't thanks enough for your generosity of time and spirit. Special appreciation is due to Laura Backes for her forthright generosity and her goodwill. And to Jennie Dunham, a superlatively busy agent who nonetheless contributed enthusiastically in three separate sections of this book: Thanks for all of your time and conscientious effort. Thanks also to Edie Weinberg, who for no other reason than pure kindness regularly took time out from her schedule to make suggestions and offer contacts when I came knocking. Once again, at the close of a Prima project, I thank Jamie Miller and Ben Dominitz, who coaxed me into the project and realized it was for me even before I did. And to Shawn Vreeland and the rest of the team at Prima, from editorial to design: Thanks for the great effort and for turning this manuscript into the resource it promises to be.

Special thanks to my cousin Stephanie, who hooked me up with authors and illustrators, to my cousin Jane, to my brothers Michael and Jonathan, to my father and my mother-in-law Penny, who knew when to intrude and when to lay low, and to my mother for instilling a love of children's books in me shortly after I emerged from the womb. Thanks also to Margot and Curry for providing exactly the right amount of distraction at precisely the perfect time, every time, and to Eric, who at the last moment swooped in to help with the procrastination. And, as always, to my husband Steven, my best friend, my best editor, my best office assistant, and my best entertainer: There will never be thanks enough.

PART ONE

How to Get Published

INTRODUCTION

Publishing Secrets of the Pros

Ellen R. Shapiro

If you decided to write for children because you thought it would be easier than writing for adults, think again. Though children's books are shorter than adult books, all the rest of the evidence points to one thing: They're harder to write, and perhaps even harder than that to illustrate. But writing and illustrating children's books are also two of the most rewarding endeavors imaginable, and they can be done if you follow a few important, professionally tested and proven guidelines.

In this part, with the help of a great team of experts, I've sought to cover all the bases of the children's publishing process: From practical advice about selling your work, to important tips on the craft of writing, to information of specific interest to "creatives" (artists/illustrators, who of course will also benefit from the other articles in this section), to discussion of legal issues, to a presentation of the pros and cons of the phenomenon on everybody's mind right now: electronic publishing.

Though most of this book is about how to sell your writing, it goes without saying that the single most important thing you can do to sell your work is to write well. Many different elements go into writing a good story, and though I can't include them all here, I've included a selection of articles about some of the most important elements of the craft of writing for children.

The experts who have contributed articles to this section of the book are the best of the best. They are teachers, successful authors, consultants, lawyers—and they know how to get children's books published, and published well.

- Linda Arms White, editor of *Author to Editor: Query Letter Secrets of the Pros,* who teaches writing around the country through Children's Authors' Bootcamp, gives a definitive rundown (with real-world examples) of the most important documents you'll create in the process of selling your work: cover letters, query letters, and book proposals.

- Laura Backes, publisher of *Children's Book Insider: The Newsletter for Children's Writers* and author of *Best Books for Kids Who (Think They) Hate to Read* (Prima Publishing), who contributed several essays here, provides an essential presubmission checklist. In other pieces, she discusses the superimportant question of how best to research the market. She also offers advice on the craft of writing, in the areas of character development and classification of age groups.
- Susan Salzman Raab, author of *An Author's Guide to Children's Book Promotion* and the principal of Raab Associates (an agency that offers marketing consulting, telecourses, and publicity services for companies and individuals looking to market children's and parenting books and products), tells how to make your work stand out through an effective marketing strategy.
- Mary Anderson, author of 30 novels for middle readers and young adults, teaches how to work with dialogue.
- Alexander Steele, acclaimed author and dean of faculty at the excellent Gotham Writers' Workshop in New York, gives a breakdown of the types of animal characters that appear in children's books.
- Deborah Perlberg, also with the Gotham Writers Workshop, gives her take on the essential craft of revision.
- David Niles, retired professor of illustration at Rhode Island School of Design (RISD), with 28 years of freelance illustration in Boston and New York and 20 years of teaching at RISD under his belt, tells how to assemble a winning portfolio and, in another essay, discusses the best strategies for getting a rep.
- Talented illustrator Phyllis Pollema-Cahill shares the essential survival guide for showing your portfolio in New York City.
- Top-flight publishing attorney Lloyd L. Rich discusses some of the intricacies of different types of publishing contracts and steers you to sources where you can learn more.
- Veteran writer Moira Allen, author of *Writing.com: Creative Internet Strategies to Advance Your Writing Career,* gives the definitive rundown on the pros and cons of e-publishing.

What I hope you'll notice through all these essays is the seriousness and conscientiousness with which the authors treat their subject matter. I cannot thank them enough for their time and effort. There's a lot of subtlety of opinion expressed herein, and also many references to important works of children's literature. Take the time to follow this advice and all the leads, and you'll no doubt be rewarded.

Please feel free to send comments or corrections to ellen@writechild.com and visit www.writechild.com for updates and further information.

From Author to Editor—Writing Cover Letters, Query Letters, and Proposals That Work

LINDA ARMS WHITE

You've labored over your manuscript for months, maybe years. Finally, your polished, spell-checked, one-of-a-kind manuscript is finished. It meets the general industry standards for word length and/or number of pages for its genre. You've set the manuscript to cool, reread it, and polished it again. It is as good as you could ever make it. You'd go so far as to say it's brilliant! Now what?

It's Time to Approach an Editor. But How?

To get an idea, sit for a moment in an editor's chair. You have been hired to produce great books that sell well, have a long shelf life, and, you hope, win awards that multiply already high sales. While you are in the publishing business because you love rich images, tantalizing words, and moving stories, you understand your books must significantly add to the company's bottom line or you will be sitting in the park reading to the pigeons. Your workdays are spent with purchased manuscripts. You work with and sometimes coddle authors; you edit their manuscripts, coaxing precise thoughts, actions, and images from each word; you research illustrators for each book, then prepare presentations hoping to sell your choice to the acquisitions team. You labor to contract the artist, often having to start all over again. You shepherd each project on each list from purchase to finished book. You may be working on five lists at any one time. And you attend meetings—acquisitions meetings, marketing meetings, editorial meetings, lunch meetings with agents—endless meetings. You are tired. Your eyes hurt. And your body would give anything to get out of that chair and move!

But still, you have a list several years out you must fill. There is no shortage of manuscripts. Since writers began using computers and printers, you have received hundreds of manuscripts each month. How can you find the jewel in that pile? When will you find time? The only time left is on the train to and from work, over the weekend, or at your son's baseball practice.

First, you must manage that slush pile. You're not sure how—yet. Some editors you know have stopped accepting unsolicited manuscripts altogether; some accept only from agents who represent authors; some accept manuscripts only in October and April, using the remaining months to work through the manuscripts received. But for now, you are one of a dwindling list of editors who still look at everything sent to them. You'll take home the pile or maybe stay at the office all weekend and sort it out. Some of this stuff has been here for six months, and it's time the authors had a decision. Having read submissions for years, you know exactly what you are looking for.

Open the top envelope. First sentence doesn't grab my attention? It's unlikely the story will. Out. Next envelope. Letter doesn't look professional. Words are misspelled, including my name. Out. Third envelope. This letter says it's a nonfiction book. We only publish fiction. Out. This one's a YA (young adult). We don't publish them, either. Out. You can size them up in 10 seconds. (Ten seconds!) Editors say that's how much time many submissions get, in part because 95 percent of the submissions are unsuitable for one reason or another. Back in the writer's chair, your job is to figure out how to get that editor's attention—how to make your submission stand out. You'll get her attention for sure if you send bribes such as candy or if you fill your envelope with confetti celebrating the anticipated sale, but it won't be the kind of attention you want. The only way to get that attention is to do your job and do it better than most other authors whose submissions are in that stack.

You've Got 10 Seconds!

How will you best use your 10 seconds? If you were in the editor's chair, what would it take? First, the submission must be appropriate in genre, subject, and style to what your house publishes. It must follow the company's guidelines. You'd like it if your name were spelled correctly. Your tired eyes would find a concise letter with lots of white space and an easy-on-the-eyes font—like Courier—with 10 characters to the inch, refreshing.

As we've seen, *your submission can get in the top 5 percent simply by being appropriate*. Do the research. Start with a trip to your local library and bookstore. Study the books on their shelves. Which publishers publish material similar to yours? Ask children's librarians whether they would allow you to look at those publishers' catalogs, which are usually kept in an office for staff use. Or order a catalog and author or illustrator guidelines for yourself. These are generally available for an SASE. Many publishers also have Web sites where guidelines and other helpful information can be found. Information about publishing companies is listed in resource books such as the one you are holding. Here, you can find out to whom you should send your manuscript or artwork, the type of material they are interested in, and the number of projects they purchase each year. Make sure you are researching in current resource books as changes abound in the publishing industry. Once you have chosen the company you will send to, you may want to call the company to ask if the editor listed is still the one you should address and double-check the spelling of his or her name.

In resource books you will also find the form in which the company accepts submission. Do they want to see a complete manuscript, an outline or synopsis with sample chapters, a query, or a proposal? *Send exactly what is requested.* Anything else will likely be a waste of time and postage.

No matter what shape they want your submission to take, the first thing the editor sees will be a letter. Everything in that letter counts—spelling, punctuation, content, and presentation. The letter's first sentence must be compelling enough to get her to read the next sentence. That sentence, if intriguing, will lead her through the paragraph. That paragraph determines whether the editor reads the second; and it, the third. Your letter is crucial. If it isn't top-notch, she will never see the first paragraph of your carefully crafted manuscript.

Cover Letter, Query Letter, or Proposal—Which Do I Use?

Though they are similar, each has a specific purpose.

A cover letter is used to "cover" the manuscript. It asks the editor or agent whether they would be interested in the accompanying material. It is sent along with a manuscript to houses where unsolicited manuscripts are accepted or with a manuscript that has been solicited as a result of a query.

A query letter is the first step to getting your work in the door at publishing houses that do not accept unsolicited manuscripts. It is similar to the cover letter, except it is sent alone. In one perfect, polished page, it must persuade the editor or agent to allow you to send your finished manuscript or an in-depth proposal for a book or series.

A proposal is a more in-depth look at a project, either fiction or nonfiction. It is also used for proposing series ideas. Accompanied by a cover letter, it details the project, outlines chapters, contains sample chapters, and tells something about the author. It consists of many pages.

Whatever type of letter your project requires, it is your representative—your sales tool. It must convince the recipient that your book needs to be published, that you are the one to write it, and he or she is the one to publish it. Let's look at each of these in more detail so you can use your 10 seconds for all they're worth.

Soaring Cover Letters

A cover letter is a business letter introducing a particular piece of writing, which accompanies the letter, to an editor or agent. It should be concise, informative, and professional. *Professional* does not mean stuffy. This letter is your representative, so let your own personality come across.

The letter should contain all the necessary information—and nothing more.

Cover letters are typed and single-spaced, written in standard business form. They are printed on plain white, 8 1/2 by 11-inch paper unless you have personal business letterhead, in which case you may want to use that. Ideally, the letter is no longer than one page. The more white space on the paper, the more inviting a busy editor will find your letter.

Begin the cover letter with a paragraph that states what you are submitting. It should include the title of the piece, the genre, and the approximate word count. Usually, nothing more needs to be written about the manuscript as it will be enclosed in the envelope and will speak for itself. However, in some instances you may want or need to impart more information—such as to alert the editor to the timeliness of your topic, provide important exclusive source information, or let the editor know that photos are available.

In the next paragraph, tell why you have chosen to send your material to that editor or publishing house. Perhaps your manuscript fits with a series they publish, you particularly like the way a book similar to yours was illustrated, or you read in a named resource that she was looking for magazine features such as yours. All this establishes the fact that you have some knowledge of the industry.

Finally, tell a bit about yourself, but only what is pertinent to the project. If your background gives you some expertise in the field about which you have written, state that. If you have publishing credits in the field or genre, state that. One short line about your professional writing affiliations can let the editor know you take your writing seriously. If you have none of these things to tell, omit this paragraph altogether. Always, keep a positive tone to your letter.

The packet you send will include your cover letter, the completed manuscript, synopsis and sample chapters, or proposal, plus a self-addressed stamped envelope large enough and with sufficient postage for the return of the entire package.

Why Did This Letter Work?

- The first paragraph explains why Anna sent her submission where she did, but it also informs the editor that she has done her research.
- Paragraph 2 explains that she would like to illustrate her own book, but, if the editor prefers a different illustrator, it is not a deal breaker. The editor hears "realistic and easy to work with."
- Having no publishing credits is usually thought to be a negative, but in the last paragraph, which could have been omitted, Anna gives it a positive slant. She shows she's not a "dabbler" and, better yet, lets her determination and spirit show appropriately.
- Notice the only mention of the book was the title. There was no need for more as the short, picture book manuscript accompanied the letter. Leaving that information out gave a clean, inviting look to the letter.
- Anna Grossnickle Hines sold this manuscript, and many more since. It all started with this letter.

Triumphant Query Letters

Remember our paper-logged editor? Frustrated editors everywhere have sought ways to decrease the number and size of those manuscript stacks. The largest and least profitable

A Winning Cover Letter

Author's Name
author's street address
author's city, state, and ZIP
author's phone / fax

October 15, 20XX

Editors' Name
Editor's Title
Publishing Company
Editor's Mailing Address
Editor's City, State, and ZIP

Dear [editor's name here]:

I recently attended the Northern California Booksellers Association Book Show where I was very impressed with some of the books on your list. I also had the opportunity to meet your rep for this area, [rep's name here]. With his encouragement, I am sending a manuscript for a picture book titled *For Real Pretend.*

Also enclosed is a rough dummy and copies of two finished illustrations. Obviously, I am interested in illustrating as well as writing and would be happy to send the original art and to develop more samples. However, if you like my story but would prefer to have it illustrated by someone else, that is also acceptable to me.

Though I have not yet published, I am a serious writer of children's fiction, picture books through middle grade. I have been receiving encouragement from editors and believe that I will one day be successful in this field.

Thank you very much for your time and consideration.

Sincerely,

[Author's Signature]

Anna Grossnickle Hines

stack has always been that slush pile. So, more publishing houses each year hang out the "no unsolicited manuscripts" sign. Many writers think this means doors are closed to them, but that is not the case. It only means you must ask the editor whether he or she is interested in seeing your project. This is done with a query letter. If the editor wants to see more as a result of your query letter, your project has become a solicited manuscript.

A query letter is a business letter asking permission to send the project described in the letter. The query letter is sent without an accompanying manuscript. So, in addition to all the things cover letter does, a query letter must convince the editor she'd like to look at your project.

For some projects, it makes sense to start with an excerpt from the text you hope to send. Chose a dramatic passage in which something incredible is revealed or there is intense action. Think of this as the trailer you see on television ads for movies. Find an excerpt that draws the editor in and leaves her wanting to know more.

The first paragraph of the letter itself must hook the editor's attention just as the first paragraph of your manuscript must. That hook should be in the tone of the manuscript you want to submit—whether rollicking, somber, humorous, or whatever it may be. In a couple of sentences, tell the plot of your story. Many people write this as they would write a book cover flap, drawing the reader in. Unlike the cover flap however, don't keep the editor guessing. Tell the high points of your plot in a sentence or two. That's hard to do. Plan to take your time and do it well. Remember those 10 seconds. If you don't sell your story and yourself in this letter, that's all the editor will ever see—your letter. Do this with carefully prepared facts and polished work, no hype.

The remainder of the query letter will have the same information a cover letter would—the nature of what you want to submit (genre, word count, title), why you chose to send to them, and pertinent information about yourself.

One editor who still takes unsolicited manuscripts tells how much she likes query letters. When the mail arrives, she says, the manuscripts are placed in the slush pile for later perusal, but the queries are opened that day, read, and decided on. If a self-addressed stamped postcard has been enclosed, she can comment or check the appropriate box and get it back in the mail. If the project is not something she can use, she is finished with it, and in just a few days, the author knows he or she can mail the manuscript to another editor who might find it is just what he is seeking. If, however, the editor wants to see the entire manuscript, the author will mark the envelope "requested material" when he or she sends the manuscript, and it will be placed in the "solicited" manuscript pile, which will be dealt with long before that slush pile.

When you send your query letter, enclose a business-sized, self-addressed stamped envelope for the editor's response.

Why Did This Query Letter Work?

- The letter opens with an engaging overview of the story, giving a sense of the characters, their needs, and the tumultuous conditions in which they live. It shows tension and conflict, two things needed to sustain interest.
- Paragraph 3 gives title genre and word count of the manuscript she would like to send, orienting the editor. However, in this instance, there are three other selling

A WINNING QUERY LETTER

Author's Name
author's street address
author's city, state, and ZIP
author's phone / fax

Date

Editors' Name
Editor's Title
Publishing Company
Editor's Mailing Address
Editor's City, State, and ZIP

Dear [editor's name here]:

Maria, a nine-year-old girl living in a village in El Salvador, is looking forward to her market holiday with her father as a chance to escape from the worries at home. But as Papa explains the turmoil between the government soldiers and the guerrillas, Maria realizes it won't be easy to bring home everything the family needs. They have only a few items to trade and no cash money to spend. When Papa briefly leaves Maria and her teddy bear with the last of their goods, the girl makes up her mind to find a way to make a good trade.

A Bear for Miguel is a 1150-word, four-chapter historical fiction beginning reader designed for your I Can Read Books, based on studying a number of titles in the series. My father emigrated from El Salvador as a teenager, and most of our family still lives there. This story reflects the day-to-day life of many of the people of El Salvador during the guerrilla war, and it was inspired by letters from my grandmother and family stories.

I am a member of the Society of Children's Book Writers and Illustrators and the recipient of their Magazine Merit Award for Fiction for my first historical novel for children, *The Ghost Cadet.* My articles and stories for children regularly appear in such magazines as *Cricket, Highlights for Children, Child Life, Children's Digest, Story Friends, Junior Trails, On the Line,* and others.

May I submit *A Bear for Miguel* for your consideration? Should you be interested in publishing this manuscript, I would look forward to working with you and your editorial staff on revision as required.

Thank you very much for your attention. I look forward to hearing from you, and I enclosed a SASE for your convenience in replying.

Sincerely,
[Author's Signature]
Elaine Marie Alphin

points—the author has researched and is familiar with the series she submits to; she has family connections to the story, giving her immediate and dependable access to resources and information; and letters exist from the time—original sources available to no one else.

- Paragraph 3 tells us she is a serious writer. While she has been published in magazines and even won some awards, the author feels that wasn't as persuasive as her membership in the Society of Children's Book Writers and Illustrators. That tells the editor the author has made an investment of time and money in a professional organization and considers herself professional.
- The fourth paragraph briefly states she understands there will be revisions and looks forward to working with the rest of the team to make it the best book possible. An editor appreciates her knowledge and understanding.

Victorious Proposals

A proposal is a sales tool that describes and outlines or summarizes a yet-to-be-written project. It is used for fiction and nonfiction, books and magazines, series and single titles.

In as few words as possible, a proposal maps the project you have in mind. It lays out the idea, shows its tone and style, and evaluates its commercial appeal. If the editor is interested, it allows him to have input into the project in which you will be partners and that he will represent to his publishing company before you begin to write.

Before the proposal is ever mailed to any editor, it has already proven itself valuable to you, the writer. It has allowed you to organize your thoughts, make sure there is enough material for the project, and decide whether you have enough interest to complete the project. It then lets you see whether there is industry interest in the project before you invest months or years writing it.

A proposal usually consists of an introduction, a chapter-by-chapter outline or a synopsis, and a few sample chapters.

An **introduction** has three parts—an overview of the project, the resources needed to finish the book, and an author bio.

The overview begins with a "story line" that tells the story in a few succinct sentences. Briefly explain your project. As always, begin with a hook to pull the reader (in this case, the editor) into your project. The overview is your chance, in limited space, to explain exactly what your project is in a way that will convince the editor that the subject or story should be published. Include the title, genre, and the word count you envision. Tell of any expertise or particular interest you may have in the topic or story, and be sure to tell of access you have to any experts in the field, especially if they might be enlisted to write an introduction or promotional material. List any back matter you will include—glossary, bibliography, index, and so forth. Show that you've done your homework by describing the market for the project—who will buy it—and tell of any markets outside the usual public and school libraries and bookstores. List any competing material while telling how your project will be different from all the others.

Also describe resources you will need to finish the book. Will you need to travel? Will you need to purchase tools or equipment? Will there be telephone expenses for interviews? Will you have to pay for permissions to use some material or photographs to illustrate the project? Give your best, educated estimate as to what it will cost to complete the project. Give, also, an idea of how long it will take to write the project once you get the go-ahead.

Finish the overview by telling briefly about the author. Write this section in the third person. Tell, in descending order of importance, what qualifies you to write this project. Include anything in your background and any expertise as it applies to the subject. Tell of any publishing credits. At the end, if it feels appropriate, state your passion for this subject or story in the first person.

The **chapter-by-chapter outline,** written in prose for nonfiction or the **synopsis** for fiction, shows the editor you have thought your idea through, that there is suitable material for your project, and that your organizational structure will work. Think of the nonfiction outline as a table of contents with notes. It should read well (though it does not have to be beautiful, lyrical writing) and give the editor a comprehensive look at the project. Devote anywhere from a few sentences to a page to each chapter. Use a well-chosen chapter title, and then let your outline read like one. You may find the following format works well for you. "This chapter analyzes . . . . It starts when . . . . The next section describes . . . . At the end of the chapter . . ." Each book will be different and dictate its own format. Let it flow naturally.

A synopsis is generally one or two pages that capture the characters and action of the story in the tone in which it will finally be told.

Sample chapters show your ability to move from outline to the finished text. Unless you have specific reason not to, it's wise to send the first few chapters in order. This is your chance to prove you have what it takes to actually write this project. If your book has an introduction, you may choose to send it along with your one or two sample chapters. If the book or work has no chapters, send what amounts to about ten percent of the book.

Remember, *you are in charge of what goes into your proposal.* You know your material. You know its selling points. You know what intrigued and drew you to it. Convey these things the best way you can in your proposal.

To mail the proposal, gather these pages, paper clip them together with a cover sheet, and slip them into the right pocket of a pocket folder. If you are published, put clips or copies of a smattering of that work into the left pocket of the folder. Label the front, add your cover letter, and mail it along with an SASE to your selected editor.

Why This Proposal Worked

- The proposal has a professional, well-organized look. The editor will believe the author knows how to put a project together.
- The proposal has been well thought out. In addition to covering the topic in a fun and innovative way, the author tried to anticipate questions the editor might have and to answer them before they were asked.
- The author targeted the proposal well, knowing this was exactly the type of project the company was looking for. By taking the time to develop a well-planned proposal, she was able to take advantage of that fact.

Pages from a Winning 10-page Proposal

A Proposal for

Cooking on a Stick:
Campfire Recipes for Kids

by

Linda White
Author's Address
Authors' City, State, and ZIP
Author's phone and fax numbers

TABLE OF CONTENTS

INTRODUCTION

Overview

Food always tastes better when it's cooked outdoors. Any outdoor meal is a special event, and young picnickers and campers like to share in the cooking. By keeping the equipment to a minimum, the recipes simple and fun, and the child a safe distance from the fire, young cooks can help prepare food for themselves and their families.

Under supervision, young adventurers will learn to make a campfire and know when it is ready to cook kid-appealing, nutritious foods with captivating names like Snail on a Stick, Honey Bear's Delight, Ants in a Log, and Naturalist's Pouch. Readers will learn how to use long straight sticks as skewers, forked sticks as toasters, and other sticks combined with foil to make a forest skillet and a reflector oven. Each of the recipes, some with variations, are formulated to be healthy, tasty, quick, and involve minimal cleanup. They include alternate cooking methods for children who don't yet have the patience to stand by the fire long enough to finish cooking their feast.

Rikki Raccoon hides in the rocks and bushes, gently whistling suggestions and safety reminders to young cooks.

Cooking on a Stick: Campfire Recipes for Kids is a 48-page picture book for readers 6 to 10 years of age. It guides the young child through the steps necessary to become a successful outdoor cook on the first try. The book has a forest theme, so it can be illustrated in field-guide style enhanced by woodland animals. For example, the borders around the "Ants in a Log" recipe could feature a fox or bear playfully batting at a trail of ants parading into a hollow log. The illustrations would be effective in either pen-and-ink or full color. An index will be included.

The market for this book consists of boy and girl outdoor enthusiasts and all those who purchase books for them. It can be sold to school and public libraries, through bookstores, scouting programs, and outdoor shops.

Cooking on a Stick: Campfire Recipes for Kids can be the first of a series of cookbooks for children, including *More Campfire Cooking* (for older camp cooks), *Mountain Man Cooking, Chuck Wagon Cooking, Cooking on the Frontier,* or the first of a series of outdoor books including *Camping, Outdoor Exploring, Tracking,* and many more.

I have found no books that would be in direct competition with the elementary presentation of Poke it on a Stick, Stick it in a Pocket. A few juvenile books are available on outdoor cooking, all much too advanced for the 6- to 10-year-old age group. The manuscript will be finished three months after receipt of the advance.

(continues)

ABOUT THE AUTHOR

Linda White grew up in a camping family. Her children have grown up the same way. All, even the youngest, have been encouraged to do their share of the camp cooking.

Linda has sold a picture book, *Too Many Pumpkins,* to Holiday House. It is scheduled for publication in the fall 1996. She has sold stories to *Highlights for Children* and written, under contract, for D. C. Heath's classroom magazine *Images.* Her two screenplays have each won writing awards.

Linda is a member of the Society of Children's Book Writers and Illustrators, having been on the board of directors of the Rocky Mountain chapter for the past three years and president last year. That experience has given her many connections that will be helpful in promoting the book.

Linda White lives in a log house with her husband and the youngest of their four children just outside Loveland, Colorado, where deer, red foxes, raccoons, and great horned owls share their property.

OUTLINE OF THE BOOK

A Note to Parents 1 page

This front matter page will stress the fact that this is an adult-supervised cookbook but that recipes and equipment have been simplified for the safety and success of the young child. It will also suggest some simple equipment to help the child make and gather before the picnic or camping trip that will simplify on-site cooking.

Campfires 3 pages

This section talks about where campfires can be built and how to build one and know when it's ready for cooking. Campfire safety and cooking cleanup are also explained.

Helpful Cooking Equipment 4 pages

Using fire tongs and oven mitts is suggested here. Cooks are then shown how to make simple wire stick holders. Some meals take a while to cook. These racks can be placed on either side of the campfire to hold cooking sticks over the fire. The use of various sticks and foil for cooking is explored.

Poke It on a Stick 5 recipes, 6 pages

Recipes that can be cooked on a stick held over a campfire are presented here. Examples: Snail on a Limb (made with Beary Basic Biscuit Mix presented in this section or with a purchased biscuit mix), Porky in a Poke, and Cozy Cave.

Stick It in a Pocket 7 recipes, 10 pages

Here, cooking food in a foil pocket, either on the stick or in the coals, is explained, and recipes for cooking in the pocket are presented. Examples: Bird's Nest Breakfast, Wh-o-o's Chili? Ants in a Log, Honey Bear's Delight, and Hibernating Bananas.

Cook It on a Forest Skillet 3 recipes, 4 pages

A forked stick covered with heavy foil can become a skillet. Bucky Burgers and Bandit's Stuffed Fish are some of the things that can be cooked on the skillet.

Bake It in a Naturalist's Oven 3 recipes, 4 pages

A quick oven can be made with heavy foil stretched over a twig framework near the fire. Making and using the oven are described here. Porcupine Meatballs and Foxy Pizza are two of the recipes.

Tasty Side Dishes and Snacks 6 recipes, 6 pages

This section has some no-cook recipes. When combined with those in the other sections, they can complete the meal. Most can be made ahead of time. Examples: Walking Salad and Gorp.

Index 2 pages

BOOK SAMPLES

A Note to Parents

A child cooking near a campfire requires adult supervision at all times.

Any outdoor meal is a special event, and young picnickers and campers always want to share in the cooking. By keeping the equipment to a minimum, the recipes simple and fun, and the child a safe distance from the fire, young cooks with adult supervision can help prepare food for themselves and their families.

The recipes and equipment in this book have been simplified for the safety and success of the young cook. Ingredients require little cutting, cooking requires little cleanup. The day of the picnic or camping trip will be more fun for everyone if as much preparation as possible is done ahead of time. Sticks

(continues)

and equipment can be gathered, the simple equipment on page 000 can be made, and some of the ingredients can be mixed.

Sample Recipes

RECIPE FROM POKE IT ON A STICK SECTION

Snail on a Limb
In a medium bowl, add 1 cup of water to 3 cups of Beary Basic Biscuit Mix (or store-bought biscuit mix). Add more water, a little at a time, if needed to make a sticky dough.

1. Roll a handful of the mixture into a "snake" shape.
2. Wrap "snake-shaped" dough in a spiral around your cooking stick.
3. Hold dough low over hot coals (but not touching them). Turn as the dough cooks. It's ready when it is golden brown all over.

Pull off the end of the stick and eat as is or put butter and jelly in the hole, or ham and cheese. Makes 4.

Caterpillar in a Cocoon
Push a hot dog onto the end of your cooking stick. Cook over coals until bubbling, then follow directions for Snail on a Limb above.

Rikki Raccoon says "Try adding a slice of cheese, too."

RECIPE FROM COOK IT IN A POCKET SECTION:

Honey Bear's Delight

1 apple, cut in pieces
Handful of raisins
Half a handful of chopped nuts
3 marshmallows
Honey in squeeze bottle

Tear off a 10-inch piece of heavy-duty foil. Put apples, raisins, nuts, and marshmallows on foil. Drizzle honey on top. Fold foil into a pocket (see page 000), and use fire tongs to place pocket in hot embers. Cook 20 minutes, open, and enjoy.

Rikki Raccoon: "Careful, it's hot!"

- As the author said, from her experience, backed up by research, there was need for this book and no competition.

Why Don't I Hear Back?

No matter how perfect your submission, days, weeks, months, and—dare I say it—years can go by with no word from the editor. We imagine our envelope has slipped behind a file cabinet where a mouse now calls it home, or it was left on the subway where someone picked it up and has submitted it elsewhere under his or her own name, or it is has been presented to the acquisitions meeting, everyone loved it, and a contract is being issued at this very moment. What really happened? We have no way to know, but most likely, it has to do with the fact that the editor is overwhelmed, overworked, and paper logged. Our job, however, as a professional author, is to find out.

If three or four months have passed with no word, unless the publisher's guidelines say you shouldn't expect to hear back for a longer period, it's time to follow up. Phone calls, e-mails, and faxes might alienate an editor you don't yet have a working relationship with. So, once again, craft a letter.

Explain that on ___ date you sent a query/manuscript/proposal entitled _________ and that you would like to check on its status. Enclose a self-addressed stamped postcard for the editor's reply. And always, thank the editor for considering your project.

Hopefully, whatever and wherever your project is, it will be located. Then, you'll be glad you took the time and the care to craft the perfect letter. You'll have used your ten seconds for all it's worth.

Submission Checklist

- ❑ My return address includes my name, address, phone number, and e-mail address so the editor can contact me if they are interested in my project.
- ❑ The letter is addressed to the proper editor, whose name is spelled correctly.
- ❑ The letter is concise, polished, and written in a business format.
- ❑ The letter has been written with as much care as was used in crafting my manuscript.
- ❑ The one-page letter contains no more than three or four paragraphs and as much white space as possible.
- ❑ My letter sounds professional, much like any other job application.
- ❑ I have used Courier typeface at 10 characters to the inch (12 point).
- ❑ I have checked my spelling and grammar.
- ❑ I have enclosed an SASE large enough for the return of my material (just in case it's necessary) or for the editor's response.

Linda Arms White is the editor of *Author to Editor: Query Letter Secrets of the Pros* published by Children's Book Insider (www.write4kids.com). An award-winning author of books for children (*Too Many Pumpkins*, *Comes a Wind*, *Cooking on a Stick: Campfire Recipes for Kids,* etc.) and adults, she teaches writing around the country through Children's Authors' Bootcamp.

This article was excerpted and adapted from *Author to Editor: Query Letter Secrets of the Pros*, which features 30-plus actual contract-generating book proposals, cover letters, and query letters from the files of successful children's authors.

Before Submitting, Apply This Final Checklist to Your Work

LAURA BACKES

You've worked for months on your manuscript, and it's finally done. And this time, you did it right. You outlined the book before you began writing, you carefully sketched out the characters, giving them depth and substance. You even took each chapter to your writer's group and incorporated all (well, many) of their suggestions. Now you can breathe a sigh of relief and prepare to send the manuscript off to publishers.

But before you lick the stamps on your queries, consider one more step: the final revision. This happens after you work out the plot twists, after the dialogue and description are well in place. The final revision waits until you're so saturated with your book that you can't bear to look at it again. But this is a good thing; you've passed the point where you're in love with your words and are apt to be more objectively critical. And you may find flaws in your work that can mean the difference between rejection and publication.

It's wise to set the manuscript aside for at least a week, or longer, if possible. In the meantime, do something else. Read; start another project; go on vacation. When you're ready, return to your manuscript with an open mind and a fresh eye.

Here are some things to look at when conducting your final revision. Think of this as the polishing stage; you're working with what you've got and making it shine.

FICTION

- ❑ *Plot.* Do the events of the story lead naturally from one to the next? Is the turning point on page 50 the logical outcome of everything that's happened on pages 1 through 49, or did you have to manufacture the tension so your characters would end up where you wanted them to be? It's often difficult for authors to judge the flow of their plots because they know the story so well. If you have any doubts about a specific plot point or scene, apply these two tests: First, *try lifting the scene from the story*. Does the plot directly before and after the missing scene unravel? It should. If it doesn't, the scene wasn't necessary in the first place. Second, if you suspect the scene feels contrived rather than a natural extension of previous events, *ask yourself what needs to happen earlier in the story to make this scene believable*. Perhaps you need to foreshadow the action or expand the role of a character to give the scene credibility. Is there any "downtime" in the story? Slowing the pace is acceptable in middle grade and young adult fiction, and sometimes necessary for the reader (and the characters) to take a breather and absorb everything that's happened. But less action does not mean less story. Have you used this downtime to develop your characters (providing character background or showing a character's motivation through dialogue and thoughts; allowing your character to contemplate the situation and how it affects his or her life; introducing secondary characters and implying how they'll impact the story)? Quiet places in a book can also heighten tension, especially in mystery or suspense stories. When characters are locked in a dark, abandoned house, the reader knows something spooky is probably just around the corner.

- ❑ *Characters*. Are your characters true to themselves? Everyone can (and should) display a wide array of emotions, but how a character acts on those feelings should be consistent with the way you've developed his or her personality. Show thoughts and feelings through precise examples. Gestures, mannerisms, even what a character has for lunch can provide a snapshot of a person that doesn't intrude on the story's flow.
- ❑ *Clean up the dialogue*. Early drafts are often cluttered with dialogue tag lines ("he said"; "she answered") that get in the way of what's being said. If it's clear who is doing the talking, the tag lines aren't necessary. Make sure the tag lines add to the conversation, not just reiterate the spoken words. "'Where is Dad going?' wondered Jack" is redundant; "'Where is Dad going?' Jack whispered" adds an element of suspense to the same dialogue.
- ❑ *Description*. It takes a light touch to get the right amount of description in your novel. You want the reader to have a clear sense of time and place but not stop the story cold. It's best if descriptions are sprinkled throughout the story, detailing items as your main character would see them. She might be annoyed when the dust on Front Street dirties her new petticoats as she walks to her cousin's house for tea. This tells the reader something about the landscape, fashion, and family dynamics in your book without your coming right out and saying it. One of the most noticeable overuses of description is when the author physically describes each character as he or she enters the story. Unless your main character is meeting this person for the first time, physical appearance would probably go unnoticed. However, the main character might comment on a new hairstyle or outfit. Give the reader enough information so the people, setting, and events can be easily visualized, and no more. Don't account for every small action of each character, unless those

actions play a vital role in the plot. On the other hand, no description (especially of the setting) leaves the reader floating with nowhere to ground the story.

- ❑ *Check for clichés.* As you're scanning your descriptions and dialogue, be on the lookout for clichéd phrases. While "strong as an ox" might adequately describe your character, it's not likely to leave much of an impression on your reader. We remember best those phrases we've never heard before.

NONFICTION

- ❑ *Organization.* Does the information unfold in a logical way throughout the book? Have you presented the most general information first so your reader will have the necessary background to understand the specifics? In good nonfiction, each chapter builds on the groundwork laid in the previous chapters. Even biographies show the route the subject took to arrive at the accomplishments that made him or her famous.
- ❑ *Tone.* Whatever the topic, the author must choose a particular slant to the material. This slant helps determine the tone and style of the text. If you've chosen a light, humorous look at your subject, don't lapse into long passages of dry facts. At the same time, a serious approach loses impact if the author suddenly throws in a few knock-knock jokes. The tone should be consistent throughout the manuscript. If you're using an upbeat, informal style in nonfiction, you can put particularly funny anecdotes or zany facts into a sidebar. This keeps the humor in the book without interrupting the flow of the text.
- ❑ *Quotes.* Whether quoting a person or a written source, the quotes should serve to enhance the surrounding information and give it credibility. As with dialogue in fiction, the quotes provide additional information, not just reiterate what you've stated in the text. Check that your quotes are specific and to the point. And avoid paraphrasing general information with "experts say . . . ." Editors and readers want to know exactly who these experts are and what they're telling us.
- ❑ *Quantity of information.* When writing nonfiction it's tempting to throw in every interesting fact you uncover. However, not all these facts will necessarily have a place in your book. If the organization of the material feels off, see whether you've digressed from the point of the book simply to utilize all your research. Make sure that the amount of information you cover is appropriate for the age of your audience. If you've gone into too much detail, remove some of the content and save it for another book. If certain juicy tidbits beg to be included but don't fit neatly into the body of the main book, consider using sidebars or boxes that separate the supplementary facts from the rest of the text.

It's hard to postpone submitting your manuscript while you take the time to do a final revision, but it will pay off in the long run. Ultimately, a few days of work now can save you months of rejection slips down the road.

Laura Backes is the publisher of *Children's Book Insider: The Newsletter for Children's Writers* and author of *Best Books for Kids Who (Think They) Hate to Read* (Prima Publishing). For more information about Children's Book Insider (CBI) and access to a complete library of free "how-to" information for children's writers, visit www.write4kids.com. You can also receive information about CBI by calling (970) 495-0056.

Why Authors Need to Know the Market

LAURA BACKES

Your job as a writer is to write. And as long as you create a solid story or a well-researched, interesting nonfiction book, you have nothing to worry about. Any editor who knows what she's doing would be thrilled to publish your work.

If that's what you think, consider the recent experience of one new author. She has a contract for a nonfiction book on a very specialized subject with a publisher who doesn't ordinarily do children's books. She had gotten the contract based on an outline and sample chapter, but when she submitted the first several chapters of the book, the publisher was disappointed. Though the chapters she wrote followed the outline and style of her proposal, the publisher was worried that the book was too heavy for kids. Would children really read nonfiction with so much information? The author got off the phone and went to work, not on revising her manuscript, but on making a case for her book. She collected articles on writing nonfiction, as well as nonfiction articles she had written for children's magazines. She tore out some pages from children's publishers' catalogs that described recently published nonfiction books. She wrote a long letter stating that she was well read in children's literature and knew the market, and she also came up with ideas on presenting the information in a more kid-friendly way without sacrificing content. Then she mailed off the packet to the publisher and waited.

A few days later the author got another phone call. The publisher was convinced, and the book is on track again. "But," said the author, "was I glad I studied the market and could authoritatively tell him that juvenile nonfiction is hot!" Learning how to write is only half your education as an author. If you ever want to get your books published, you have to know what sells and why. Here are other reasons to learn the current state of the children's book market:

To improve your own writing. The style of saleable fiction changes with each generation. What was appealing when you were a child may sound too didactic today. Plots

Ways to Keep Up with Market Changes

Reading reviews in trade journals like *Publishers Weekly* and *The Horn Book* is important, but don't stop there. *Publishers Weekly* also tracks industry changes such as mergers and the formation of new companies. You can get much of this information on the magazine's Web site: www.Publishers Weekly.com. The editorials and articles in *The Horn Book* often deal with general trends in writing and children's publishing.

The Children's Book Council's Web site (www. cbcbooks.org) has a listing of all its members (go to "Publishers Page"). This includes a brief description of each publisher's list and whether the publisher is taking unsolicited submissions. Links to publishers' Web sites are provided, and the site is updated every couple of months.

Newsletters such as *Children's Book Insider* and the bimonthly *Society of Children's Book Writers & Illustrators Bulletin* (sent to members; see the organization's Web site at www.scbwi.org) give current market information.

Joining a children's writing message board is a great way to network with other writers and trade information. There's one on CBI's Web site, write4kids .com.

Attend a writing conference at least once a year. Chatting with writers, agents, and editors is one of the best ways to keep on top of what editors are looking for, current trends, and the direction publishers are heading.

are faster paced, story lines are more realistic, and often the vocabulary is simpler in modern children's books than those written 20 or 30 years ago. There are also categories that didn't exist when we were kids; easy readers, for example, have boomed in the last 10 years. Nonfiction is presented in an entertaining way, with the illustrations and design of the book often being an important extension of the information.

Knowing what's hot can also help you make a sale. While following specific trends often doesn't guarantee success (the trend will probably be over by the time your book comes out), understanding the general direction of the industry can give you ideas on what to write. Young adult (YA) fiction is getting popular again, so now's the time to get back to that YA novel you abandoned five years ago when no one wanted new fiction for older readers. Nonfiction for all ages is in great demand. Historical fiction, especially for younger readers, is needed. By attending writing conferences and browsing through publishers' catalogs (free from the publisher for a SASE, or ask your librarian whether you can look through the catalogs in the library), you can get a sense of what publishers are excited about this season.

To write to fill gaps. Books from the current season's offerings are always prominently displayed in major bookstores and featured in reviews (good review sources to scan on a regular basis are *Publishers Weekly, The Horn Book,* and *School Library*

Journal, found in most libraries). As you touch base with the market, do you notice anything missing? Are there no folktales from South America? Are there several new books on the Revolutionary and Civil Wars, but nothing about the wars from the 20th century? Librarians and teachers are also gold mines of information about gaps in the market that need to be filled.

To target submissions. This, of course, is the biggest reason to know the market. Sending your manuscript to a publisher who is looking for the kind of book you're writing is *one of the most important steps you can take toward selling your work.* But knowing who publishes what is just the beginning. You also need to keep track of each publisher's changing needs and staff fluctuations. It sounds overwhelming, but if you spend your time wisely, you'll stay on top of what you need to know. Use the resources listed in the sidebar to help keep you abreast of market changes.

Knowing the market helps in every phase of the writing process. Authors who understand this are the ones who are most successful at writing what editors are looking for and at placing their work with publishers.

Laura Backes is the publisher of *Children's Book Insider: The Newsletter for Children's Writers* and author of *Best Books for Kids Who (Think They) Hate to Read* (Prima Publishing). For more information about Children's Book Insider (CBI) and access to a complete library of free "how-to" information for children's writers, visit www.write4kids.com. You can also receive information about CBI by calling (970) 495-0056.

Researching the Market

LAURA BACKES

Editors always plead with authors to research the market before submitting manuscripts. This makes sense—it cuts down on the number of inappropriate submissions an editor may receive, and presumably it will lower the chance of a manuscript getting rejected.

But how, exactly, does one research a market that produces thousands of new products each year? I suggest a systematic, three-part approach that works for both book and magazine publishers. This involves studying a publisher's overall list, individual books or issues, and writers' guidelines. It doesn't matter which part you do first as long as you cover all three. Illustrators can use this same system to research potential illustration markets and then send for artists' guidelines.

OVERALL LISTS

Book publishers have seasonal lists. A magazine's "list" is composed of a year's worth of issues. To get a sense of what each publisher does, read industry newsletters, attend writers' conferences, and consult books on children's book publishing (many of which are published annually or biennially to remain current). Note which publishers cater to the audience for whom you want to write, in both age group and subject matter. Send for these publishers' catalogs, generally free with a 9 by 12-inch, self-addressed stamped envelope with two to four first-class stamps (bigger publishers = bigger catalogs). For magazines, get the most recent issue and then study back issues at the library. Many publishers also have Web sites that feature their current lists, though I find it's easier to study and compare material if you have a hard copy.

But what if you receive several catalogs from large publishers and they all look the same? Then it's time to read the fine print and find the differences. Does HarperCollins seem to have an abundance of fiction picture books for ages 5 to 8 ? Then they might not be buying much for this age group for the next couple of years. Has another publisher just debuted a line of nonfiction chapter books? Maybe your chapter book on whales is just what they need. Do certain publishing giants tend to repackage classics from known authors rather than books from new writers? Pick another publisher who isn't afraid to feature new talent. Narrow down your number of potential markets.

Individual Books or Issues

Go to a bookstore or library and actually hold books from your potential publishers in your hands. Look at the vocabulary and sentence structure, the style of writing, the pacing of picture book stories. For magazines, note length and subject matter of fiction and the slant on nonfiction topics. Though you don't want your book to be just like someone else's, it must fit in with the overall taste of the editors from each company, and the general tone of a publisher's list. Narrow down your markets once again.

Writers' Guidelines

Now it's time to send a self-addressed stamped envelope to each publisher asking for writers' guidelines. Follow the submissions procedures in the guidelines exactly. If you submit a manuscript or query letter more than a month after receiving guidelines, call the publisher to verify that it is still open to submissions.

Once your manuscript is in the mail, try to put it out of your mind and start writing something else. And be assured that all your research means your work is most likely headed to where it will be eagerly read.

Go with Your Feelings

Sometimes, in the course of your research, you'll get a general feeling about a publisher. When this happens, go with your gut.

I just got off the phone with the editorial department of a large house. I had picked up its writers' guidelines at a conference, but they were very sketchy (instructions on how to format the manuscript, but nothing on the types of books needed). So I thought I'd call to get more information. After 20 minutes of trying to get past an army of surly receptionists—each of whom gave me a different number for the children's editorial department and then either disconnected me or transferred me to the voice mail of someone on vacation—I managed to sneak through and actually speak to a human being. She was a retired editor working part-time from home who just happened to be in the office today, but by that time I didn't care. She said she thought they were taking unsolicited submissions, but since the department had been without leadership for the last month, she couldn't be certain. I hung up convinced that if I had a manuscript to submit right now, this publisher would not be on my list.

Laura Backes is the publisher of *Children's Book Insider: The Newsletter for Children's Writers* and author of *Best Books for Kids Who (Think They) Hate to Read* (Prima Publishing). For more information about Children's Book Insider (CBI) and access to a complete library of free "how-to" information for children's writers, visit www.write4kids.com. You can also receive information about CBI by calling (970) 495-0056.

Hunting Readers in a Bunny-Eat-Bunny World

SUSAN SALZMAN RAAB

Children's publishing has been called a bunny-eat-bunny world, but anyone who has seen the rabbit in *Monty Python and the Holy Grail* knows that can be a scary thought. In fact, the children's book business is tough to break into and, once published, publishing for children is a hard way to make a living. One reason is that it looks deceptively easy—after all, how hard can it be to write (or illustrate) a 32-page picture book with far less text than most school term papers? Then, the common notion is that once you publish, you visit a few schools, get the word out among parents you know, and agree to autograph at some bookstores. Not so.

One difficulty is that kids are a tough audience to reach because of the various adults in their lives who serve as gatekeepers. Parents, teachers, librarians, booksellers, editors, publishers, and sales reps are just some of the people who have to like your book before it gets placed in the hands of a child. That's the reason that many of the best children's books appeal to both adults and kids (think of *Winnie-the-Pooh, The Wizard of Oz, Charlotte's Web,* and *The Very Hungry Caterpillar*). This publishing challenge is compounded by the facts that children's books are often expensive to produce (especially if they have four-color art or special formats), they appeal to specific age groups, and there's a lot of competition for what is a small market compared with that of adult books.

The good news is that there's a lot of room for creativity in marketing, as well as in writing and illustrating for children, and it's never too early to start. Everyone who considers your book, from the slush pile reader to the editor to the bookstore buyer, needs to decide whether your book has potential to succeed in the marketplace, and, from your query letter onward, you should be prepared to explain why it will.

A good place to start building your case is at a good library or bookstore, where you can compare your idea with other books already out on the same subject or for the same age group. Ask yourself these questions: How is my story different? What special perspective do I bring to this topic? What can be done (in tone, format, or illustration) to enhance the story for young readers?

Consider whether the book is timely or topical. Does it have potential for specialty markets or foreign sales? Have you included special features, such as activities, fact sections, or other elements that should be highlighted when the book is promoted? What about your background? Do you have special knowledge of the subject matter, if the book is nonfiction, or do you have an interesting story to tell about how you got the idea for a fictional story? Whether your book is an ABC book, a humorous chapter book for middle graders, a gritty young adult novel, or a fact book about grizzly bears, you should be able to identify why it's unique or special. Then you should work to make sure key decision makers are told.

Start by discussing the book's features and your hopes for marketing with your editor. He or she will be the person who champions your book to others in the publishing house. Don't be shy about providing more information and ideas than you're asked for, and make sure your editor knows you're willing to work hard to ensure the book's success. Ask what other authors have done to help make their books a success. Get as clear a picture as possible about the specifics of what will be done in-house, and ask who you can be in touch with as the marketing, publicity, and sales to schools, bookstores, and libraries evolve.

Get to know the publicist who will be handling your book and offer your help. Tell them who you think should receive copies of the book (include any media contacts, booksellers, librarians, and teachers you know who you think would take a personal interest in spreading the word about your book). Don't be shy about asking, but do be selective. Identifying 10 influential contacts is better than asking to have the book sent to a large list of people who won't matter. The publisher is more likely to cooperate with you if you are respectful of their time and resources.

Once you've identified what the publisher will do, it's time to assess where best to spend your time. Start by playing to your strengths. If you're a good speaker and you like working with kids, look for opportunities to speak at schools and libraries. Many authors and illustrators help support their publishing careers by speaking at schools where they are paid honoraria to do one- or multiday presentations and workshops. These visits often provide opportunities to sell books either in advance or during the day of the visit for autographing. The honorarium for such visits can run from a few hundred dollars to more than $1,000 dollars per day. If you're better with adults, see whether you can make presentations at teacher conferences. This is a good way to have impact in the school market, which is still a key component of the children's book business. If you're comfortable on radio, in front of a camera, or speaking with the press, look for media interview opportunities and concentrate your efforts on doing publicity.

Get to know other authors and illustrators, and ask what marketing strategies have worked for their books. An excellent resource for networking and information is the Society of Children's Book Writers and Illustrators (www.scbwi.org), which provides opportunities to network with other authors and illustrators as well as with editors, art directors, and others working in publishing. A number of author groups also meet online. A good place to start is the Writer's Chat on America Online.

Know that many first-time authors and illustrators mistakenly believe that their work is done once their book is accepted for publication. You'll have a head start if you know that getting published is just the beginning and that to succeed, you'll need to work hard on behalf of your books to help them sell.

Susan Salzman Raab is the author of *An Author's Guide to Children's Book Promotion* and principal of Raab Associates, an agency that offers marketing consulting, telecourses, and publicity services for companies and individuals looking to market children's and parenting books and products. She is marketing adviser for the Society of Children's Writers and Illustrators and is a trade journalist and a frequent speaker at industry conferences. Her company's Web site, www.raabassociates.com, provides articles, tips, and other information for those interested in children's book marketing.

Speak Easy: Developing Realistic Dialogue

MARY ANDERSON

Being an incurable "nosy Parker," I love including lots of dialogue in my books. One of the main reasons I think it's of interest to young readers is its voyeuristic aspect. In a way, it's like listening in on someone else's conversation—something I readily admit I do constantly. I can't take a ride on a bus or stop in a coffee shop without eavesdropping on other people's chatter, no matter how ordinary it may seem. Who knows whether a brief snatch of that conversation may not generate a new story idea?

A reader can find out so much about characters from their dialogue, and it can be a far more interesting way of delivering information than through narrative. Through a character's diction (word choice) and syntax (sentence structure), the reader can discern where the characters come from, their ethnic background, their attitude toward life, personal point of view, and many more details without having to go into a lengthy narrative. Young readers don't like lengthy narratives.

Frankly, neither do I. When I pick up a book and see that it has page after page of narrative with no break within the text, I get the message it's going to be a rough read. Children can be easily put off by a book that seems to require too much effort. But when I glance through the pages and notice lots of open space interspersed with blocks of dialogue, I'm much more readily pulled into the story. Purely technically speaking, breaking up your narratives with dialogue will help your young reader stay involved in your story. It will make it look more like a "fun" book rather than a textbook. Kids have to read enough textbooks during their school years, so we want to make their leisure reading as much fun as possible.

Personally, I don't feel you really know your characters until you hear them speak. Everyone has something distinctive about the way they communicate to others. Two characters placed in a similar situation will not only feel differently, they'll also respond differently, so dialogue should be an integral way of moving your story along and revealing your character's motivations. Here's a good test of how well you know your characters, their attitudes, and opinions: Walk them through a real-life situation and ask yourself, "What would so-and-so have to say about this?"

Ideally, you should know your characters well enough to do this. The actress Joanne Woodward once said she knew how to portray a character as soon as she could figure out what kind of hat she wore. I know my characters when I can intuit what they'll say in any given situation. You'll get to the heart of your fictional characters when you can hear their voices in your mind and be able to give their thoughts words.

What about regional dialogue? Should it be used? Well, if you're writing a historical piece set in another time or a story about a certain ethnic group such as the Amish, you must acknowledge the fact that people did and do speak differently. A regional dialogue, such as that used in the Uncle Remus tales, can be charming if a child has an adult to read it aloud, but it can be quite daunting trying to read it on one's own. My advice is to use it sparingly. Include just enough to add flavor and uniqueness to your characters.

And what about contemporary speech—fad words and phrases that go in and out of style? If this is an important aspect of your character, make sure you are using the in phrases of the time or the moment. Having one of your characters set in the 1960s say "groovy" or "cool" may have demonstrated how hip he was then, but these same phrases may make your characters laughable or unbelievable now. The most obvious way to avoid using the wrong contemporary phrases is to have personal contact with children. If you don't have kids of your own within the age range for whom you're writing, go listen in on them.

Which brings me back to one of my favorite pastimes: eavesdropping. Listen to kids on their bus rides home. Lend an ear at the local coffee shop or pizza parlor. You might even come up with some juicy story ideas. I have!

Mary Anderson has written 30 novels for middle readers and young adults.

Characters Give Fiction a Firm Foundation

LAURA BACKES

If you've read much how-to material on writing children's fiction, you probably know that ideally the plots evolve from the characters. But what does this mean?

In good fiction, the main character is the foundation of the story (the exception to this would be board books and some event-driven picture books for toddlers). Who that character is, what he or she likes and dislikes, and how the character reacts when faced with the circumstances of the story all affect the twists and turns of the plot. And the story's resolution will be a natural fit because only this character would ride out these events in this particular way. If you begin with a specific plot idea and know the ending you want to convey to the reader before you have your main character in place, you'll almost always wind up with a lesson instead of a story. Plugging a character into a preexisting series of events and then manipulating that character toward your desired outcome is a sure route toward rejection.

But if you're itching to get your manuscript under way, how much character development do you need to do? It's always a good idea to brainstorm character traits until you can see the person in your head and hear him talk. If you know more about your character than you put in the book, the depth of her personality will be implied through her dialogue and actions. And if you truly understand what makes your character tick, he'll move through the story on his own. You'll just have to follow along and write down what happens.

Some authors create detailed biographies of their main characters and key elements of their secondary characters' lives as they connect to the life of the main character. Others simply brainstorm, letting random thoughts take them in unexpected directions. Or they write letters to themselves from their main character, allowing that character's voice to emerge. Use whatever works for you.

Here is a checklist of major points to keep in mind when developing fictional characters:

Picture Books: Points to Remember

- ❑ The story revolves around one main character who has a problem that can be stated in one sentence.
- ❑ Whether the character is an animal, child, or adult, he or she must have the perspective and outlook of a child four to eight years old.
- ❑ The reader should like the main character, but that character doesn't have to be perfect.
- ❑ Often the character's flaws provide humor or tension that fuel the plot.
- ❑ Though the character can ask the advice of adults, he or she should ultimately solve the story problem on his or her own. This often involves the character discovering hidden strengths or gifts, or simply mustering the courage to be him- or herself. As a result, the character grows in some way by the story's end.

Common Mistakes

- Characters who have no depth and therefore are predictable.
- Characters who have adult concerns or who approach a situation from an adult's perspective.
- Characters who were created by the author to teach a lesson to readers and therefore have no child appeal.

Easy Readers: Points to Remember

- ❑ Main characters should be the age of the reader (grades 1–3) or be adults or animals who have the concerns, emotions, and perspective of this age child.
- ❑ Though characters are well developed, they have one or two outstanding traits that fuel the plot (they take everything literally, they like to play practical jokes, they sneeze when they're embarrassed, etc.).
- ❑ This outstanding trait must be shown to the reader through action and dialogue.
- ❑ The main character (and one friend, if appropriate) must solve his or her dilemma by means found within the child's everyday world (i.e., without adult intervention).
- ❑ Humor is key, for both characters and plots.

Common Mistakes

- Characters who rely too much on inner thoughts and emotions to convey their personalities (easy readers are written in very concrete visual terms—action and dialogue—with no description and very few abstract thoughts or feelings).
- Characters with whom children in grades 1 through 3 can't relate or empathize.

- Characters with no sense of humor.
- Characters without a personality "hook" on which the plot can hang.

Chapter Books: Points to Remember

- ❑ Characters are ages 8 to 11 and realistically portray the feelings, thoughts, emotions and perspectives of children in grades 2 to 4.
- ❑ Characters have two or three outstanding traits that fuel the main plot, but also several other characteristics that play a part in the story. A 9-year-old girl may play the violin and love practical jokes, but she's also afraid of spiders, likes to draw, and has a secret crush on her new teacher.
- ❑ Characters may be portrayed through their feelings more than in easy readers, but the story is still told mainly through action and dialogue.
- ❑ Characters are beginning to discover and appreciate their own strengths, and they are forming strong opinions about the other people in their lives.
- ❑ Family and peer groups are equally important. Kids usually have one or two best friends but often socialize with larger groups.

Common Mistakes

- Characters who are one-dimensional or have no unique attributes.
- Characters who have no friends or interactions outside of their families.
- Dialogue that sounds too "young" for the character.
- Characters who don't have strong ideas, likes and dislikes, or opinions (these can all change during the story, which is a way to show character growth).
- Characters who don't clearly inhabit that time between early elementary school and middle school: kids are comfortable with the school routine and are coming into their own personalities, but they're not yet concerned with dating or conforming to a peer group.

Middle Grade: Points to Remember

- ❑ Main characters are 9 to 13 years old, and they embody the concerns and life experience of a child this age.
- ❑ Whether characters are animals, fantasy creatures, or children who live in another time, they are experiencing timeless issues that affect today's children.
- ❑ Characters are defining and developing their roles within their family and peer groups.
- ❑ Characters experience a full range of emotions, have a rich inner life, and can be concerned with other issues related to the plot that form subplots. Secondary char-

acters play a bigger part in middle-grade novels and so should be well developed with complex personalities.

Common Mistakes

- Main characters who are too young (middle graders like to read about kids a year or two older than themselves).
- Dialogue that's dated (unless the book takes place in the past) or stiff or sounds like the idealized speech of an adolescent.
- Stories that aren't complex enough. This usually results from characters who lack depth.
- Characters without strong emotions, or several bland characters in a book who can't be differentiated from each other.

Young Adult: Points to Remember

- [ ] Main characters are at least 12 years old but rarely older than 17.
- [ ] Characters (regardless of the time period of the story) are living through events and concerned with issues relevant to the lives of today's teens.
- [ ] Teenage characters must ring true. They should be authentic and complex and come from the teenage perspective.
- [ ] Even if the story is humorous, the main characters are coming of age in some way. They are learning to see the world differently; they're thrust into an adult situation for the first time; they're finding out how they fit into the larger world outside their families; they're discarding long-held views and developing new ones.
- [ ] Plots don't need to be completely wrapped up at the end of the book, but the reader should have a sense of how the main character has changed through the story and the direction his or her life will now take.
- [ ] Secondary characters are very important and often provide important subplots or plot twists.

Common Mistakes

- Main characters who are too young or who are really middle-grade characters in teenage bodies.
- Character problems or concerns that aren't sophisticated enough or that smack of "middle school" as opposed to "high school."
- Unrealistic dialogue, or dialogue that sounds like it came from an adult.
- Too much adult or parental involvement in teenage character's lives. Though the teen's relationship with his or her parent can be a major subplot, it should be somehow connected with other issues going on in the teen's life. The character resolves his or her independent problems first and then brings those resolutions home.

Books to Study

Picture books: The *Arthur* series by Marc Brown (Little, Brown); *Stellaluna* by Janell Cannon (Harcourt); *The Mixed-Up Chameleon* by Eric Carle (Philomel); *Froggy Gets Dressed* by Jonathan London (Puffin); *Officer Buckle and Gloria* by Peggy Rathmann (Putnam); *Comes a Wind* by Linda Arms White (DK Ink)

Easy readers: *Nina, Nina Ballerina* by Jane O'Connor (Grosset All Aboard Reading); *It's Not Easy Being a Bunny* by Marilyn Sadler (Random House Beginner Books); *The Golly Sisters Go West* by Betsy Byars (Harper I Can Read); *Mr. Putter and Tabby Pour the Tea* by Cynthia Rylant (Harcourt)

Chapter books: *Cam Jansen and the Mystery of the Stolen Diamonds* by David A. Adler (Puffin); *Flat Stanley* by Jeff Brown (HarperTrophy); *Amber Brown Is Not a Crayon* by Paula Danziger (Little Apple); *The Time Warp Trio* series by Jon Scieszka (Puffin); *Chocolate Fever* by Robert Kimmel Smith (Yearling)

Middle Grade: *Tuck Everlasting* by Natalie Babbitt (Farrar, Straus & Giroux); *On My Honor* by Marion Dane Bauer (Yearling); *Charlie and the Chocolate Factory* by Roald Dahl (Puffin); *Harriet the Spy* by Louise Fitzhugh (Harper); *Bunnicula: A Rabbit-Tale of Mystery* by Deborah and James Howe (Aladdin)

Young Adult: *The Outsiders* by S. E. Hinton (Puffin); *Catherine, Called Birdy* by Karen Cushman (Harper); *The Giver* by Lois Lowry (Laurel-Leaf); *Homecoming* by Cynthia Voight (Fawcett)

- Not enough going on in the teen's life outside of home/family (unless the lack of friends or other activities is a major plot point).

Laura Backes is the publisher of *Children's Book Insider: The Newsletter for Children's Writers* and author of *Best Books for Kids Who (Think They) Hate to Read* (Prima Publishing). For more information about Children's Book Insider (CBI) and access to a complete library of free "how-to" information for children's writers, visit www.write4kids.com. You can also receive information about CBI by calling (970) 495-0056.

Animals: Handle with Care

ALEXANDER STEELE

Animals are frequently featured in children's literature. Kids tend to like animals, and I think they even identify with them.

But beware. Using animals in your children's book, if you don't know what you're doing, is a sure way to end up in the vast zoo of unpublished authors. The matter is more complex than you might think. There are actually three basic ways to handle animals in storytelling, and you should be clear about which method you are using.

Anthropomorphic In an "anthropomorphic" animal story, the animals act mostly just like humans. They may wear clothes, walk on two legs, live in houses, eat with silverware, go to school, try to break into publishing, and so forth. Many famous children's books employ this device, from *The Wind in the Willows* to the *Babar* series to *The Cat in the Hat*. You, however, should avoid this device. Why? It is so overdone by wannabe authors, it makes editors and agents want to throw up. Probably half the children's book submissions they get are anthropomorphic animal tales, and probably half of those tales feature alliterative titles, such as *Roberto the Raccoon* or *Clarissa the Cat*. If you absolutely must write this kind of story, it had better be spectacularly unique.

Semirealistic In the semirealistic animal story, the animals act mostly like real animals. They don't wear clothes or go to school. But they have certain human qualities. *Charlotte's Web* is a famous example. The animals live in a barn; they eat animal food; they are somewhat at the mercy of their human owner. Yet they converse with each other and have recognizably human emotions and thoughts. Then again, who's to say that animals don't converse and have such thoughts and emotions? In this type of story, the animals usually appear perfectly normal to the humans, who cannot see inside the animals' secret world. Other examples in this category include *The Story of Ferdinand* and the

Black Beauty series. The semirealistic method is done far less than the anthropomorphic method and can be an interesting way to probe the mystique of animal life. The trick is to lay down the reality rules and treat them consistently.

Realistic. In the realistic animal story, animals are portrayed with total realism. They do nothing that a real animal might not do. They can, however, be intriguing and vivid characters. Examples include *My Side of the Mountain*, *Shiloh*, and the *Black Stallion* series. Here the protagonist will most likely be a human who interacts with one or more animals. The human perception is needed to tell the story. Though it's not impossible to use a realistic animal as a protagonist, it is very difficult to do without cheating. Sooner or later, the animal would probably need to understand human language and that would move things into a semirealistic animal story. In addition to being done less frequently than the other methods, the "realistic" animal tale operates under the wise assumption that animals are plenty fascinating just the way they are.

No matter which method you employ, you should be specific about your reason for choosing certain animals. In *Horton Hears a Who*, why did Dr. Seuss make Horton an elephant? Because it's a story about sensitivity. Horton finds a teeny-tiny speck of dust, which he suspects might house a teeny-tiny being. The story gains power from the fact that Horton is an elephant, the most gargantuan creature on land. Dr. Seuss had a specific reason for choosing his animal, and so should you.

Animals, in both real life and children's literature, must be handled with infinite care. Doing so will help you break free of that unpublished author zoo.

Alexander Steele has written numerous books for the WISHBONE series and, under a pseudonym, for a famous series about two teenage detectives who are brothers. He is the cofounder of Squibbler, which develops children's stories for the computer medium. He teaches children's book writing for Gotham Writers' Workshop (www.gothamwritersworkshop.com), where he is also the dean of faculty.

The Difference Between Middle Grade and Young Adult

LAURA BACKES

It's often difficult for writers to know whether they're creating a middle grade novel (ages 8–12) or a book for young adults (12 and up), also commonly abbreviated YA. Because many of the themes and situations are similar for the two age groups, authors go by the age of the main character: If the protagonist is under 12, it's middle grade; over 12 means young adult. But the differences are more complicated than that.

The author of the true, classic middle grade novel does not worry about vocabulary choices or simple sentence structure; once children are ready for these books, they are good readers. Middle grade novels are characterized by the type of conflict encountered by the main character. Children in the primary grades are still focused inward, and the conflicts in their books reflect that. While themes range from friendship to school situations to relationships with siblings and peers, characters are learning how they operate within their own world. They are solidifying their own identity, experiencing the physical and psychological changes of puberty, and taking on new responsibilities all within the boundaries of their family, friends, and neighborhood. Yes, your character needs to grow and change during the course of the book, but these changes are on the inside. Middle grade readers are beginning to learn who they are, what they think. Their books need to mirror their personal experience.

Charlotte's Web, the classic middle grade novel by E. B. White, is a perfect example. Wilbur the pig is threatened by his world: He's worried that once he grows up, he'll be sent to the butcher. And while his friend Charlotte saves Wilbur from death, the book is really about the meaning of true friendship and how Wilbur gains confidence and self-esteem. A Newbery winner, *The View from Saturday* by E. L. Konigsburg, is about four children and their sixth grade teacher as they compete in the regional Academic Bowl.

But the competition is a backdrop for the individual journeys each child takes on the path to becoming a team and how they help their teacher find her own place in the world. The real victory is how each of the five main characters goes through some inner struggle during the book and ends up in a better place.

Characters are also a key element to young adult novels, but these books often have more complicated plots than those for middle grade. Protagonists experience an internal change, but this change is triggered by external events and fits into a bigger picture. They begin to step outside themselves and see how they influence, and are influenced by, the larger world. They go beyond their backyard and encounter adult problems for the first time.

In Suzanne Fisher Staples's novel *Dangerous Skies*, 12-year-old Buck Smith is suddenly made aware of the racial hatred and prejudice entrenched in his small southern town when his best friend is a suspect in a murder investigation. By the end of the book, Buck has lost his innocence, and his eyes are opened to the ethical shortcomings of his family and the neighbors he has known all his life.

The age of the main character and length of the manuscript are still a rough guide in determining the audience (middle grade manuscripts tend to be 100 pages or shorter, with young adult books being longer, though this is not always the case), but the kind of conflict the characters encounter is a better measuring stick. Many publishers have created a new young adult category for ages 10 to 14, for books that bridge the gap between middle grade and young adult, and have designated novels with older themes as ages 15 and up. The story, rather than the character's age, delineates the audience, as in Carolyn Coman's *What Jamie Saw* (a 1996 Newbery Honor Book). The book features a 9-year-old protagonist, but the subject of domestic abuse prompted the publisher to give it an age range of 10 and up. As an author, it's your job to decide who you want to reach with your book—elementary kids, junior high, or high school—and then create characters and conflicts accordingly. Regardless of genre—science fiction, mystery, historical, or contemporary—if your characters are learning about themselves and the world in the same way as your readers, your audience will find you.

Laura Backes is the publisher of *Children's Book Insider: The Newsletter for Children's Writers*, and author of *Best Books for Kids Who (Think They) Hate to Read* (Prima Publishing). For more information about Children's Book Insider (CBI) and access to a complete library of free "how-to" information for children's writers, visit www.write4kids.com. You can also receive information about CBI by calling (970) 495-0056.

The Honorable Art of Revision

Deborah Perlberg

Lucky you! You were inspired, you worked hard, and now you're the proud possessor of a *completed* first draft manuscript. Congratulations! But, where do you go from here? You revise. I often hammer at this point because most beginning writers are so proud of finishing a story (deservedly so!) that they can't bear the thought of changing a single word. But seasoned writers know that most of writing is revising, and any writer should expect to write draft after draft.

Sound daunting? It is. But make it easier on yourself. First, get your manuscript read. Form a writer's group; snag your next-door neighbor; inflict your book on family and friends. After they've read it, demand their true opinions. Of all the questions you should ask, the most important one is "What did I actually write?"

What story do your readers think you're telling? Is it the same story you intended to tell? Did you write what you intended to write? If not, be comforted by the fact that you have a whole first draft of wonderful material to pilfer from and build on. Nothing you write is ever written in vain.

What is the feeling readers get from your story? Is it the feeling you were aiming for? Do they react to your main characters the way you wanted them to? How would they summarize the plot? The underlying theme? What worked well? What needs attention? Did they enjoy reading it? Be prepared to hear more than you bargained for. Not everyone is a writer, but most everyone is a reader, and readers are critics. Detach! Be objective! Try not to take it personally. It's a rare, rare story that gets everything right the first time. Feel free to disagree with others in your mind, but listen to what they say.

At this point, you'll have a rough idea of the shortcomings of your manuscript, and (thankfully!) a rough idea of how to fix them. Where do you start? I envision the revision process as a series of four concentric rings.

The Outermost Ring: The Story's Theme

What is the *overall* point of your story? What premise or moral will be illustrated by the events you've constructed? You can apply this test to any level of children's book. And remember, it's okay to think in terms of broad clichés: Don't judge a book by its cover; it takes courage to go against the crowd; you don't appreciate what you've got until someone takes it away; Mommy and Daddy are usually right. Whatever. If you find, to your horror, that your story completely lacks an underlying theme or that it wanders aimlessly (even though your plot events are fresh, imaginative, howlingly funny, and hauntingly poignant), don't despair. Through the magic of revision, you can *go back* and put in a theme.

Often, writers pick a theme without consciously knowing it. You might need your readers to discern your underlying message. Chances are, however, that your writing reflects personal themes of deep meaning to you: a child's need for strong parents; the value of friendship; the pain of jealousy. Remember: An underlying theme is important even if you're writing a harmless, guileless story about The Day Little Ducky Got Wet. Maybe Ducky learned to listen to Mama and bring his boots along; maybe he learned that an ounce of prevention is worth a pound of cure. The last thing you want is for readers to say, "Great story, but what's the point?"

Ring 2: Character

Plot springs from character. (Or it should!) Did your main character *change* and/or *grow* during the course of the story? Did this *growth* illustrate your main point or underlying theme? Be honest; be ruthless. Perhaps your main character didn't change or grow. Think of Peter Rabbit, who disobeys Mum, invades Mr. MacGregor's garden, barely escapes with his life, and returns home to suffer the loss of his dessert and a dose of dreaded chamomile tea. Will incorrigible Peter obey Mum next time? Doubtful. But, hopefully, readers have learned that being disobedient (or foolhardy) brings its own punishment.

Ring 3: Your Plot

The plot supplies the stages of the journey, so the next ring to examine is plot. What scenes have you devised to illustrate your character's journey? Are they satisfying in themselves? Are they placed with a sense of rising conflict, rising tension, and final resolution?

Pulling the Rings Together

Theme, *character*, and *plot*. To me, these are the three main rings to address. Within those, at the core of your work, are those pesky things we call *chapters*, *scenes*, *paragraphs*, *sentences*, and *words*.

The most damning (and most frequent) comment I scribble on manuscript margins is "Nothing happens in this scene!" Series book publishers require full chapter-by-chapter outlines before a story is approved. Why? To make sure that something happens in each chapter. An event that forwards the plot and brings the story to its inevitable conclusion. Review your chapters (or, for picture books, the main story events) to make sure that something significant occurs in each chapter or segment, something that either expands character or forwards the plot. Yes, it's tempting to indulge in a brief interlude of reverie or blissful description every now and then, but your poetic efforts will be wasted if readers skip ahead to see what happens next. We've all done that, haven't we? So keep it meaningful; keep it moving. Ditto for scenes within chapters: something should happen in each scene.

By this time, you're either sick of your own work, or obsessively poring over each perfect paragraph, each scintillating sentence, each wondrously brilliant word. That's fine. Revising gives you the chance to get the most mileage out of every element of your story. Yes, it's hard work.

Beginning writers often ask questions about point of view. How should they decide whether to write in first person or third? Your instincts may help you choose a voice appropriate to the age group you're writing for. But remember that youngest readers have trouble with the first-person point of view; they get confused about who "I" is. And most middle grade books are also written in third person. But as readers get older, first-person stories become more attractive. Still, I usually advise authors not to worry about point of view in a first draft. You'll know your story more intimately when you've finished, and, most likely, the best point of view will make itself obvious. Or who knows? Maybe you'll devise some groundbreaking, point-of-view-shifting style that no one's ever thought of before!

A Word about Rhyme

The same advice holds. Rhyming stories also need to have a theme or an underlying idea to keep the "plot" moving. They also have an extra requirement: Be strict with your rhyme scheme!

As author, you'll hear the rhythm of your words in your head; but ask someone else to read the piece out loud, and you may hear a completely different rhythm. Your job is to hone your language so tightly that there's no risk of readers mutilating your beautiful rhyme scheme.

The Last Word

Above all, never be afraid to tear the work apart and begin again. That's the true meaning of revision. If your frustration level is too high to even consider this, *set the work aside*. I know, we all read about first-time wonders who sit down and six weeks later produce an instant bestseller. May this happen to each and every one of us! In the meantime, you can't replace the value of good old hard work, and revision, revision, revision.

Deborah Perlberg, writer, editor, and editorial consultant, currently enjoys teaching at New York's Gotham Writers Workshop (www.gothamwritersworkshop.com), where her students soon learn to revise, revise, revise. She's hard at work on a book teaching how to construct successful plots for children's books. Watch for it!

Portfolio: Your Magic Book

DAVID NILES

To further your goals as a creative (that's what the industry likes to call us: creatives), we need to establish a visual link between ourselves as artists and those with whom we wish to share our talents: our clients. To do this, however, requires skills that spring from a number of important factors:

- A clear understanding of who you are and what you do.
- The ability to create a visually ordered design that clearly communicates who you are and what you do.
- And through this to achieve your major goal, which is to get the kind of work you love to do.

This leads to the obvious conclusion that what we are talking about seems to be a physical object common to us all in the business: It's known as your "book." Its physical form is varied, from the conventional zippered plastic case with acetate pages to the custom-designed presentation box with your name embossed in gold on leather.

For want of a better word, we call it *portfolio*. As "portfolio," it is obviously a selection, a compendium of your best efforts with examples of your very best creative efforts on every page. It is really the lifeblood of your presentation to the world, and it must have a quality of impact and individuality that will remain after you have walked out the door.

I can look back over the number of years during which I looked at literally hundreds, if not thousands, of portfolios. I can particularly remember some that stood out in my mind as innovative, outstanding, and original, above and beyond the rest of the pack. And I can also remember a few that were outstanding for other reasons—all of the worst reasons.

Let that be a lesson to you in respect to your "book." Though you make an effort to show only your finest work, it's undeniable that anything less than this will probably be the ones they'll remember, no matter how great you think you are. As a matter of fact, an art director once told me that the thing that always sticks out in her mind once a portfolio has walked out the door is not the best piece she has seen but the worst!

Now, to be sure, *content* is the real issue, and though presentation is also a key factor, don't ever allow the packaging, no matter how fiendishly clever you may think it to be, to overpower the contents. Don't do what a young woman did to show her work: Her portfolio was an alligator case with brass fittings and lock, and all the while I expected an absolute blaze of talents once she opened it. I was shocked to discover what was obviously an embarrassing display of ineptitude.

The rules of thumb to remember are these:

- Impact counts.
- Less is more.
- Where excellence is required, pretty good, or even average, is totally worthless.
- So you can see that for we average folk, there's a lot of hard work ahead.

Your portfolio's role is that of communicating to your prospective client that this new work of yours is not only something they want but also something they *need* and can't possibly get from someone else. This something new has to be a unique and fresh visual approach, done with absolutely flawless execution. Carefully conceived, clear, well designed, uncluttered, and limited in number—probably no more than 10 to 12 strong pieces, each one of which has a solid impact.

I am simply amazed at the number of illustrators who still haven't figured out that a portfolio is very simply a design problem. It must have a unity consistent with any good piece of design. And this unity must have variety to be truly effective. Certainly if it has unity without variety, it will bore them out of their minds; if it has variety but lacks unity, then it will be totally chaotic—a quality unthinkable for any portfolio of creative work.

The whole should be absolutely greater than the sum of its parts: flow, rhythm, and pacing have to be your concern, as well as an ability to structure the pages as part of an essential grid design.

Portfolio General Rules of Thumb

- ❑ Start strong; end strong.
- ❑ A title page with your name and perhaps a small piece of artwork can set the tone for the book.
- ❑ Vary sizes through the book.
- ❑ Generally, no more than one image per page. Exception: spot illustrations that can be arranged systematically on one page.
- ❑ Don't let a horizontal on one page face a vertical on the opposite page. If horizontals and verticals are necessary, then try to keep from mixing them on the same spread of two facing pages.
- ❑ Keep black and white in one section and color in another section of the portfolio, unless there is a distinct need to use this device to show how diverse you are.

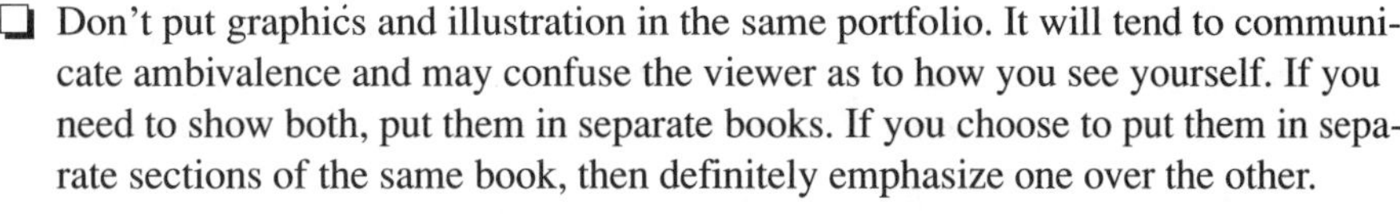

- ❑ Don't put graphics and illustration in the same portfolio. It will tend to communicate ambivalence and may confuse the viewer as to how you see yourself. If you need to show both, put them in separate books. If you choose to put them in separate sections of the same book, then definitely emphasize one over the other.

- ❑ Above all think smaller, rather than larger. If your best originals are the same size as the Sistine Chapel ceiling, have some quality reproductions made.

YOUR OPTIONS

- Originals
- Tearsheets
- Slide transparencies (in plastic sheets, 20 per sheet, or in a loaded tray ready for showing.)
- Larger chrome transparencies (either 8 by 10 or 11 by 14)
- Custom color prints
- Laser color photocopies

A NOTE ON ORIGINALS

Showing original art is often necessary if you have nothing else to show; however, most art directors do not expect to (or want to) see originals. Remember that originals are vulnerable to damage, or even loss, so it makes sense to find other ways to show the work.

The other aspect of showing only originals has to do with so-called drop-off days. In this case, your portfolio is out of commission while it sits in someone's office waiting to be viewed. With a portfolio made of photo replications or various kinds of copies of original works, you can afford to have more than one portfolio to use, which means that when you do drop-offs at one place, you've still got a book to show at others.

This is a key point that needs emphasis. If you have one portfolio that contains, say, 12 pieces of original work, you're essentially limited to one call per client with this book. You certainly aren't going to go back with the same portfolio again. To schedule another appointment with the same prospect some time later, you need another different portfolio all ready to go. So, in effect, you have *two portfolios of work*: Book A and Book B, each containing 10 to 12 pieces. This way, a quick callback is possible, and you don't end up scrambling to put another book together after you've shown your one and only book to all the prospects on your list. This, obviously, doesn't preclude the fact that you're continuing to generate additional portfolio pieces.

As you see prospects with your work, your marketing eye will be looking for clues to what prospective buyers liked as well as what they need, which may give you a firm idea of the kind of work you need to generate and show them a second time around.

Every portfolio call you make should be logged in your presentation log, noting that on a given date at Such and Such Advertising Firm you showed X pieces to Mr. Z. Therefore, when Mr. Z calls you back for another review, you show him new and different work—because you know what he's already seen.

When you have downtime—time when you aren't working on a paid project—this is prime time for you to work on new stuff. *The worst thing you can do is to show someone the same piece or pieces they've seen before*. Their assessment of you will immediately drop.

Quality: The Real Issue

The most important factor of all is *quality*. Edit mercilessly: "When in doubt, take it out!" And I don't care how much it hurts to withdraw that favorite piece: *Do it anyway*. Ten great pieces will be fondly remembered and revered, 20 fair ones will be forgotten, but 10 really inferior pieces will probably be remembered for all time: "Oh, yeah—he's the guy who did that portfolio of really miserable portraits."

In addition, it's well to pay extreme attention to those pieces that impress your prospect. (It also doesn't harm your case to ask them what might be eliminated, to improve the portfolio.) When a particular piece really scored, I would note it and send them a c-print or a color copy in a file folder with my name, phone number, and address for their file.

An even more valuable tool is to have something you can leave behind, such as a printed piece or a promotional card. An option to this approach is to send something a few days later with a note of appreciation. With some people, this really wins points and tends to emphasize you as an individual. Most people don't take the time to do this. It is good promotional practice.

The Content

If you're after freelance assignments, you need to create a portfolio that focuses and speaks with a single voice. Veteran artist Seymour Chwast puts it this way: "I tell my kids what not to include." Don't show a little of everything—a type sample, a life drawing, a silk-screen print, two sketches, and a few photo collages. Instead, project confidence in the kind of work you want to do, by showing that work.

Tailor the book to a specific aim. It shows the way you think!

Finally, be sure that each work displays evidence of copyright notice (on the rear of the piece is okay). If you're a guild member (Graphic Artists Guild, Society of Children's Book Writers and Illustrators, etc.), it's often very effective to place your guild sticker somewhere in the inside of the book. Also, your portfolio case (or box, or container—whatever it is), should be labeled with your name, address, and phone number, so that when it gets buried in that pile of droppings—I mean drop-off—it's origin will still be evident.

Recap in a Nutshell

- ❑ The portfolio items are limited in number: 10 to 12 pieces.
- ❑ Speak in a single voice if you're planning to freelance.
- ❑ Keep the size manageable. Oversize originals should be photographed or reduced and shown at smaller size.

- ❑ Show consistency of skill, concept, and style.
- ❑ Only your very best work should remain in the book. After you edit it with savage intensity, show no mercy; take no prisoners. When in doubt, you know what to do.
- ❑ Rhythm and flow are all-important. No visual roadblocks. Think of it as very much like designing a picture book.
- ❑ Keep the work developing, so that your portfolio will keep growing and never stagnate. Repeat business comes from a strong evidence that your work is vital, lively, and constantly growing.

Whew!

David Niles is a retired professor of illustration at Rhode Island School of Design (RISD), with 28 years of freelance illustration in Boston and New York and 20 years of teaching at RISD. He now writes on illustration and design career issues. He lives in Massachusetts. This essay originally appeared on the Web site The Drawing Board for Illustrators (www.members.aol.com/thedrawing), authored by Theresa Brandon, children's book illustrator, and David Niles.

Showing My Portfolio in NYC

PHYLLIS POLLEMA-CAHILL

In May 2000, I spent four days in New York City showing my portfolio to children's publishers. I started by sending written requests for appointments in January to 20 publishers who already had my samples on file. I wrote again in March and enclosed a sample of my work. Not all were prompt in responding, so in late April I started making calls. I was able to meet with nine publishers and drop my portfolio off at seven more.

I had several objectives in making the trip: To show publishers my newest samples, to meet them in person and hopefully come across as someone they'd like to work with, and to strengthen the possibility of them calling me with assignments. In addition to new samples, I brought a couple they'd already seen, hoping they'd recognize them and make the connection that I'd been sending them my work for some time already. Following are some points I found helpful.

REQUESTING APPOINTMENTS

Start early and avoid the dates of national conferences by checking the trade journals. Have the publisher's catalog and be familiar with its line. See only those publishers who have expressed an interest in your work. It would be wasteful of their time (not to mention very disappointing to you) to invest the time, energy, and money only to be told, "Your work isn't appropriate for our line."

With your written request for an appointment, enclose a sample illustration and a self-addressed stamped postcard for their response. Suggest a date and time. Don't schedule appointments any closer than one and a half hours apart. I tried grouping appointments by location but found it rarely works. Call to confirm appointments one to two weeks beforehand. Try calling early in the morning to get through to a person instead of voice mail. Also confirm that you have their correct address (including the floor), the cross streets, and correct side of the street.

In Advance

Get a subway map and study it thoroughly. Walk or run and climb stairs to get in good physical shape (really!). During my trip I walked about five miles a day, plus stairs, and it was exhausting. Get a good detailed map showing street numbers. Photocopy the section you need and mark the exact location of your appointments in a contrasting color. Type up your schedule with the contact name, title, address, directions, and phone numbers. Society of Children's Book Writers and Illustrators (SCBWI) has a New York Buddy program that is very helpful. They will send you a list of affordable hotels and restaurants, plus the buddy you're assigned can give you advice and moral support.

Transportation in the City

The most difficult part is getting around the city. Traffic can be awful and the sidewalks congested. Buses and taxis are often slow. The subway proved to be the fastest way to get around, but it takes time to figure out. Rides cost $1.50 one-way, but buy a Metrocard instead, which gives a discount for multiple rides and can be used for the subway and bus. Consider bringing your spouse or a good friend. My husband helped me get from appointment to appointment and was very supportive. If you have a question, New Yorkers are very helpful.

What to Bring

Travel light. I use a small portfolio that holds 12 standard-size color photocopies and my resume with a list of my published work. I labeled the photocopies with when and where they were published. I also carried a separate case with extra photocopies, printed books and tearsheets, a credit card, phone card, some cash, my schedule, a city map, and a subway map. Bring a dummy book if you don't have printed books. A compass is very helpful to show you which direction to head when you step out of the subway stairwell. Don't forget an umbrella if rain is forecasted.

What to Wear

Absolutely, positively wear comfortable shoes with cushioned soles. After the first day I quickly resorted to black tennis shoes. Dress casually in layers. Wear clothes that don't show dirt that you might pick up from public transportation.

The Appointments

Allow 45 minutes of travel time between appointments. Find your appointment location at least 15 minutes early and sit in a café, drink something, and relax. Don't expect to be asked into your appointment exactly on time. I waited up to 30 minutes and in two instances was stood up. Receptionists can tell you how to pronounce names properly. I thought I would be nervous but wasn't. At that point, I'd done all I could to prepare, and now it was time to enjoy meeting new people. Give the art director or editor your portfolio, and let them page through it at their own pace. Offer them samples to keep that you've prelabeled with your name, address, and phone number. *Ask whether they know of anyone else who might be interested in your work.*

Appointments generally last 15 minutes. I had a couple that were 30 to 45 minutes and consider those to have been the most promising. Many remembered my logo and illustrations I'd sent them. Take notes immediately afterward to help you remember the person, what was said, questions asked, and ideas about how you could follow up. Write them a thank-you note as soon as you can.

Drop-Off Portfolios

Some publishers only see portfolios on a drop-off basis. You usually drop them off at the front desk, mailroom, or messenger center before noon and pick them up after 2:00. I prepared three drop-off portfolios using cheap, plastic folders. In the front plastic window, I placed a sheet with my name, address, phone number, and a very brief note thanking them for reviewing my work and instructing them that the samples in the back pocket were for them to keep. I also included blank lines where I wrote in the name of the art director, when I would pick up the portfolio, and space for them to write comments. Bring an extra drop-off portfolio in case of loss or damage. In one case the art director was out sick. In other cases my portfolio was seen by an assistant rather than the person to whom I had addressed it. They will often enclose a letter giving you feedback.

Last Impressions

What was the end result of my visit? I'm waiting to find out. I've talked to illustrators who received contracts while in New York. I felt it was promising that two publishers talked with me about upcoming projects. It was a good experience to meet them in person. I hope that by making the trip it shows my determination and commitment.

If I go again, I will definitely allow more time between appointments, send my drop-off portfolios through the mail from home and spend my time in New York for in-person appointments only, and wear the most comfortable shoes possible.

Phyllis Pollema-Cahill has illustrated many magazine stories and several picture books, including *Free to Learn* and *God's Big Story*. To learn more about her and her work, visit www.phylliscahill.com.

Getting a Rep

David Niles

To any artist with career aspirations, getting a rep seems to offer great possibilities. However, we too often hear people voice the opinion that getting a rep is the most direct route to success. So let's look at the problem and see whether it's really all that simple. You may discover that getting an agent to represent you and your creative work isn't as easy as you expect it to be.

When the moment arrives and you've made the decision to start looking for that magical rep to open the door to your successful career, wait just a moment and recognize an essential truth. This is a large industry—some would say overcrowded—and so intensely competitive as to stagger the imagination. Many artists and illustrators are out there seeking their place in the industry, and there's a lot of noise. In the large publishing centers such as New York, Boston, Chicago, and Los Angeles, among others, there is strong evidence of busy reps influencing what goes on there. One must believe that being an artists representative is, in itself, a burgeoning profession. The truth of the matter is that there really aren't enough good reps to go around. Of those actively engaged in repping creatives, a surprisingly low percentage of them are really good at what they do.

If you spend some time flipping through the talent directories, you'll see the names of many reps and the work of those they represent in full living color. It's also pretty easy to be deluded into believing that everyone who's making it out there has a rep. Not necessarily so.

First, let's consider why artists might seriously consider getting an agent to represent them and their work. It's clear that busy artists need to spend as many hours as possible producing their work in the studio. Balancing this need with the other side of freelancing (i.e., selling your work through portfolio calls to prospective clients, to say nothing of tending to a host of other professional needs outside the studio and working half the night), getting your own rep seems a natural step to take. So why not place your career into the hands of someone who really knows the marketplace and is experienced in the selling and marketing of creative work? Many illustrators who seem to find it difficult to face the realities of self-employment, and deal directly with clients, are convinced that having an agent is an utter necessity. However, you must be convinced of one thing: Of the thousands of successful illustrators in the professional field today, a considerable number of them have never used a rep at any time in their careers.

For one thing, reps are expensive. On average they can take at least a 25 percent commission on all the work they generate for you, sometimes even more. As I indicated before, the rep can be out selling while you are producing your work for the clients your rep establishes. Even though the best reps in the industry possess considerable skill in negotiation, marketing, and sales presentations, some reps can be extremely high-priced pickup and delivery services. If that's all you need, you will be taken to the cleaners if you're paying 25 percent for such menial services.

So let's put all this together:

- Good reps are hard to find.
- Most reps, good and bad, won't take on someone without quality work and top experience as well as a strong client list.
- Reps will not take you if your work isn't related to the market segment they cover. In other words, don't expect a rep who sells to corporate clients to be willing to sell your picture books around town.
- The best reps are not in the business to develop your career from square one. Rather, they are more interested in broadening your already strong career position.
- Look at the artists an agent already represents. If the rep has a strong reputation in the field you wish to work for, this could be a positive sign.
- Your present clients are often in a good position to recommend a rep to you.
- A rep won't be interested in you if already representing someone with a style similar to yours.
- Look seriously at your portfolio. Is it generally pretty good? In most cases, that won't be good enough to impress any rep in the business. Pretty good isn't good enough.

It's natural for anyone seriously considering a freelance career in children's book illustration to conclude that a good rep can boost a career beyond measure. Developing your work because of its unique style is one thing, but ultimate success comes from work that is highly competitive within its chosen market. So it's easy to understand that many folks without experience think that reps make an artist's life pure gold. Finding a rep—that is, finding a good rep—may be such a complex problem that it might create tougher times than facing life without one.

Your rep must have a personality that matches yours. If there's going to be a successful relationship between the two of you, there must be an agreement on mutual goals. Again, looking at this from a slightly different perspective, the curious thing about getting an agent is that one can never predict how well the two of you will work together until you begin! Most artist–representative relationships are contract based, which includes a trial period after which a long-term agreement is possible. So this creates a set of conditions that tests the way you and your rep interact with day-to-day pressures and how mutual trust can be encouraged to grow.

It's interesting to note that years ago, one rarely encountered any female artist's reps, but today, particularly in the children's book industry, there are many—not surprising when one considers that the majority of children's book editors are women.

So remember that it's a mistake to seek a rep before you've had some experience developing your own career, which often means that you must exhibit extraordinary talent before any rep will even consider becoming your agent.

If you feel unsure of yourself in working directly for clients and feel that if you get a rep, you won't ever have to, you are doing it for all the wrong reasons. A rep is not meant to fill the role of therapist or protector. In addition, talk with your colleagues. If they rave about a certain rep being a "cool guy" even though most clients resent his arrogance, will he be the one to solve your career problems?

On the other hand, if you do find a strong prospect, spend a lot of time talking about mutual goals before you even think of looking at a contract on paper. If this person was referred to you by your cousin's brother-in-law who roomed with him at Williams, don't blunder into a deal without getting all the answers. In the end, ask all the appropriate questions and read every single six-point word thoroughly, before you even consider signing that contract!

Carol Bancroft & Friends
121 Dodgington Road
Bethel, CT 06801
(203) 748-4823
Web site: www.carolbancroft.com

Cornell & McCarthy
2-D Cross Highway
Westport, CT 06880
(203) 454-4210
Web site: www.cornellandmccarthy.com

HK Portfolio, Inc.
666 Greenwich Street
New York, NY 10014
(212) 675-5719
Web site: www.hkportfolio.com

Liz Sanders Agency
16 Phaedra
Laguna Niguel, CA 92677
(949) 495-3664
Web site: www.lizsanders.com

The Penny & Stermer Group
East Coast: (212) 505-9342
West Coast: (520) 708-9446
Web site: www.pennystermergroup.com

David Niles is a retired professor of illustration at Rhode Island School of Design (RISD), with 28 years of freelance illustration in Boston and New York and 20 years of teaching at RISD. He now writes on illustration and design career issues. He lives in Massachusetts. The article originally appeared on the Web site The Drawing Board for Illustrators (www.members.aol.com/thedrawing), authored by Theresa Brandon, children's book illustrator, and David Niles.

Publishing Contracts: Special Cases You Need to Know About

LLOYD L. RICH

The author/illustrator could be involved in many types of publishing contracts for any given project. The most important is the book publishing contract between the publisher and the author/illustrator because it defines the scope of the author's/illustrator's and publisher's interests and governs their respective rights and obligations in the specific project. This topic, however, is best discussed in book-length sources that fully discuss the publisher–author/illustrator agreement. [*Editor's Note:* Please see the "Other Resources" appendix, at the end of the book, for a list of books about publishing law and contracts.]

This article briefly explains the importance of a written publisher–author/illustrator agreement, but the balance will discuss other important, but less written-on, publishing contracts that may be needed by the author/illustrator to complete and publish the project, such as one for a collaborator, writer, illustrator, or photographer who may be contributing creative material to the project. The importance of these contracts is that each particular contract also defines the scope of the parties' respective interests as well as their rights and obligations in their particular undertaking with respect to the project.

THE WRITTEN PUBLISHER–AUTHOR/ILLUSTRATOR AGREEMENT

Although the publisher–author/illustrator agreement has traditionally been a written contract, this has not always been the practice with contracts between collaborators or freelancers. A written and not an oral contract should exist for the following reasons:

- An oral contract could lead to problems if the parties have a disagreement regarding the specific terms of their contract or whether in fact a contract actually exists.
- The Copyright Act requires all transfers of copyright ownership and exclusive licenses be incorporated in a written document that has been signed by the copyright owner or her or his agent.
- A state law requirement, commonly known as the Statute of Frauds, provides that there must be an executed written document for any agreement that cannot be completed within one year from the effective date of the agreement.

Collaborator Agreement

Collaboration or coauthor agreements may be more important in children's publishing than in any other publishing genre. This is because, especially with illustrated children's books, the specific project will require one individual to write the text and a second to illustrate the text. When this situation occurs and if the author and illustrator desire to be recognized as coauthors and co-copyright owners of the work, then they should formalize their arrangement in a written collaborator agreement.

The "joint authorship" doctrine of the Copyright Act provides for the sharing of copyright ownership and its exclusive rights. *Joint authorship* is defined as a work prepared by more than one author "with the intention that their contributions be merged into inseparable or interdependent parts of a unitary whole."

Under existing law, it will be presumed that the following joint authorship principles will apply to the coauthors' work if their work is a joint authorship work:

- Each coauthor will own an equal ownership share in the work. This will occur even if one of the coauthors contributed a greater quantity of the work than the other coauthor.
- Each coauthor will own an "undivided" interest in the entire work. This means that when the publishing project consists of illustrations and text, the artist and the author will each own 50 percent of the entire work and not just their own specific contribution. Thus, the author who has written the text would no longer own all of the text but would instead now be considered the owner of 50 percent of the text and artwork, and vice versa for the illustrator.
- Either coauthor, without the permission of the other coauthor, may grant nonexclusive rights to use the work to a third party. However, a coauthor may only grant exclusive rights to the work to a third party when she or he has obtained the coauthor's prior consent.
- Each coauthor has a duty to account to the other coauthor for any profits obtained from her or his exploitation of the work.
- A coauthor has the right to assign or bequeath her or his ownership share in the work to a third party or heirs.
- Each coauthor will be entitled to equal authorship credit for the work upon its publication.

A joint authorship legal relationship could exist, even when there is no written agreement, as long as the coauthors had the intent to create a work of joint authorship.

Therefore, if the coauthors want to modify the joint authorship principles as enumerated here, or if they want to include other clauses in their agreement, such as one that describes each of the respective coauthor's specific responsibilities or what happens if one of the coauthors fails to complete her or his work on the project, then they will need a written collaborator agreement.

Freelancer Agreements

Two types of freelancer agreements may be used by the author/illustrator for those situations in which a freelancer is contributing creative material to the project, such as artwork or photographs. The first, and usually more favorable, contract for the author/illustrator is a *work made for hire* contract. This contract provides that the author/illustrator owns all the rights in the freelancer's creative work, including copyright ownership, and therefore provides complete control over how the author/illustrator can use the work. The Copyright Act requirements must be satisfied for this type of contract to be valid. The requirements are as follows:

- The work is specially ordered or commissioned by the author/illustrator;
- the work fits into one of the nine categories of work enumerated in the Copyright Act, and
- there is a written agreement between the author/illustrator and freelancer specifically stating that the work was created as a work made for hire. Furthermore, it is highly recommended that the parties sign this agreement before the freelancer commences with the creation of the work.

The second type of contract is an *assignment of rights* contract. This type of contract is generally more limited in scope than a work made for hire contract because the freelancer usually remains the copyright owner of her or his creative work and only grants the author/illustrator limited rights to use the work—for example, in the print edition of the book. Any other use by the author/illustrator would require that additional compensation be paid to the freelancer.

The importance of written publishing contracts cannot be understated. It only takes one contract problem—whether it is a dispute over the terms of an oral or written contract or the fact that a written contract is not valid and thus unenforceable—to cause authors/illustrators difficulties that might have an adverse impact on their publishing projects. Therefore, authors/illustrators should endeavor with as much certainty as possible that their investment in each publishing project is protected by a proper publishing contract that meets their specific needs, and above all, that would be enforceable if it becomes necessary in a court of law.

Note: This article is not legal advice. You should consult an attorney if you have legal questions that relate to your specific publishing issues and projects.

Lloyd L. Rich is a Denver attorney specializing in publishing, intellectual property, and Internet law. He has more than 30 years of publishing experience as a publisher and attorney and represents print, electronic, and multimedia publishing companies on matters, including intellectual property management and protection, contract preparation and negotiations, copyrights, trademarks, acquisitions and divestitures, new product development, licensing, and distribution. He can be reached at 1163 Vine Street, Denver, CO 80206; phone: (303) 388-0291; fax: (303) 388-0477; e-mail: rich@publishingattorney.com; Web site: www.publaw.com.

Electronic Publishing—E-Books for Children?

MOIRA ALLEN

You've been searching for a publisher for your children's book, to no avail. You believe in your project but know better than to seek subsidy publishing. Where can you turn?

According to some authors, the answer may be electronic publishing. E-books for children? It's not as far-fetched as it may sound. As Karen Wiesner, author of *Electronic Publishing: The Definitive Guide*, points out, "Kids are extremely computer-literate, and statistics state that 65 percent of American homes have computers. Kids younger than five may be using computers as skillfully (or more so) as their parents."

Children's author Leta Nolan Childers agrees: "It's an absolute natural. What I've discovered since my books for children were published electronically is that kids who might not otherwise find interest in reading—on a computer or not—enjoy the experience because they become part of it. It takes the reading experience a step beyond just suspension of disbelief to inclusion in the story."

The Basics of Electronic Publishing

Today's commercial e-publishers are working hard to correct the impression that e-publishing is a dumping ground for unpublishable manuscripts. Reputable e-publishers screen submissions for quality and marketability just like print publishers; many accept less than 10 percent of submissions. Books are always reviewed, edited, and proofread before publication. Nor do writers pay a "fee" to be published; reputable publishers work on a royalty basis. (Any e-publisher who charges a fee for publication is considered a subsidy publisher—even if it tries to tell you differently!)

E-books are offered in a variety of formats, including HTML and PDF. They may be delivered on disk or CD-ROM, as a file that can be downloaded or transmitted by e-mail, as a file that can be transmitted to a handheld electronic reader, or as a file that must be accessed online. Most e-books are sold through the publisher's Web site, though they are also available through most online bookstores (e.g., Amazon.com and Barnes and Noble). Distribution through traditional bookstores is still limited, but because e-books have ISBNs, they can be ordered through any book outlet.

One of the advantages for children's literature is the ability inexpensively to include multimedia features, such as animation, sound, and hyperlinks. "Animated pictures can be really exciting for children," says Wiesner. "Consequently, children's picture books, toddler books, and books for older children are all viable in this market. Other e-publishers are doing a whole spectrum of innovative children's ideas—storybooks, activity books, coloring books. I just heard of an author who writes children's stories for the age group of about 12. His story has links to sites all over the Web that the kid follows, like an interlocking puzzle. The area, Wiesner notes, is wide open—especially for original, innovative ideas.

Advantages of E-Publishing

Electronic publishing can offer several advantages over traditional print publishing:

- **Better chances of acceptance.** "E-publishing is opening the doors for a lot of new authors," says Mary Wolf of Hard Shell Word Factory. "It is also a home for those great books that fall between the cracks with New York publishers." Issues such as length may be less important, and books needn't be as tightly "categorized" to fit the requirements of bookstore shelves.
- **More control.** "Writers have greater freedom with characters and plot, more 'say' in revisions, and more input in cover art and sales blurbs," says Wolf. For a children's author, this can mean better opportunities to both write and illustrate one's own text, and even to provide other media inputs, such as audio elements.
- **Higher royalties.** Because the costs of e-publishing are significantly lower than print publishing, authors typically receive a far higher share of revenues. Royalties range between 20 and 40 percent. Most e-publishers also pay royalties quarterly rather than annually or semiannually.
- **Author-friendly contracts.** Most e-publishers ask only for electronic rights, leaving the author free to market print rights elsewhere. In addition, most e-publishing contracts are renewable rather than indefinite. Thus, instead of tying up an author's work until it goes "out of print" (a meaningless term in e-publishing), either party usually has the option to renew or terminate the contract at the end of a specified period (usually a year). Most reputable e-publishers post their contracts online, so an author can review terms before submitting. (*Beware of any publisher who posts an incomplete contract or one that states that key details are negotiated "individually."*)
- **Shorter response times.** Most e-publishers attempt to respond to submissions within two to four months, although response times are lengthening in the higher-volume firms. "We used to have a four- to six-week turnaround time," says Marilyn Nesbitt of DiskUs Publishing, "but we get so many submissions now that this is changing. Still, we try to keep a manuscript no longer than four months."

- **Faster publication.** "It takes a book almost two years to go to print with a traditional publisher," says Bonnee Pierson of Dreams Unlimited. "We can do it in a matter of weeks." Most e-publishers tend to publish within three to six months of acceptance, allowing time to generate advance reviews and publicity. Some publishers have a backlog, however, and are scheduling release dates several months from now.
- **Multimedia options.** An e-book can include a host of nonprint elements, such as music, graphics, animation, audio, or interactive features. "I'm allowed to create interactive stories and insert surprises here and there that I couldn't do if the books were published in the traditional manner," says Childers. External links can also add to a book's educational and entertainment value.
- **International availability.** "Readers in Australia can buy the book the same day it's released in the United States," says Pierson. "They don't have to wait for export or foreign rights negotiations." (Authors should note, however, that this could influence one's ability to sell international rights to another publisher.)
- **Lower prices.** "The books are much cheaper; therefore, people may be more willing to buy," says Wiesner. "I attended a conference recently, and people were just grabbing up the children's e-books: 'My grandkids will love these! And they're affordable!'"
- **Longer "shelf life."** Since it costs little to keep an e-book in "stock," a book doesn't have to sell thousands of copies to remain available. As long as sales remain "good" (by e-book standards), most e-publishers are willing to keep a title in inventory.

Disadvantages of E-Publishing

Unfortunately, electronic publishing also poses some disadvantages that deserve consideration:

- **Lower sales.** Marilyn Nesbitt of DiskUs Publishing points out that "at this point, e-publishing won't make you as much money as if your book were traditionally published." According to Mary Wolf of Hard Shell, sales of 500 are considered good for a title. At present, according to Wiesner, children's books seem to be doing about as well as any other genre in this regard. Publishers and authors agree that for a book to be successful, an author must devote considerable effort to its promotion.
- **Lack of availability in bookstores.** Though e-books are generally available through online bookstores, they are hard to find in traditional stores. Though all e-books can be ordered by their ISBN, this isn't the same as being "on the shelf," where casual book browsers can find them.
- **No advance.** Some genre organizations consider a book "commercially published" only if an advance is paid, which means that e-books may not meet certain organizations' membership requirements or qualify for industry awards.
- **Fewer reviews.** While some publications (especially online) review e-books, many traditional review sources don't. "They're still under the impression that we're not selling 'real' books," says Pierson. Karen Wiesner agrees: "I doubt too many metropolitan newspapers would consider e-books at this time." Nor are e-books likely to be reviewed in major book and library trade publications, such as *Kirkus Reviews* or *Editor and Publisher*.

- **Limited formats.** At present, there is no single "standard" format for e-books, which means that readers may need different software to read products from different firms. Some e-books are formatted only for Windows. However, more and more publishers are moving toward formats such as PDF, which can be read by Adobe Acrobat for Windows or Mac.
- **Lack of security.** Many authors avoid e-publishing out of fear of piracy, and indeed, there is little to deter someone from buying an e-book and distributing an unlimited number of copies. However, most e-publishers say they have experienced little problem.
- **Consumer reluctance to read "online."** While the popularity of e-books is growing, many consumers are still reluctant to buy a "book" that must be read onscreen or printed on one's own paper. In the case of children's books, this can be an added disadvantage: While you may be willing to take your laptop onto the porch for a casual "read," you're probably not going to let your five-year-old use it to read an e-book in the sandbox or treehouse. Children love to lug books around with them, and this simply isn't possible with an electronic book. Nor can one print off books with multimedia elements (e.g., audio or animation) or hyperlinks.

Should You or Shouldn't You?

E-publishing is itself in the "toddler stage" and experiencing the growing pains of a new industry. Technological advances continue to shape that industry; for example, the impact of hand-held readers is still difficult to predict. "I believe it is only a matter of time before e-books are accepted just as print books," says Nesbitt. "Electronic publishing is really the wave of the future." At the same time, it isn't difficult to find authors and publishers who disagree.

One thing is clear: *It is a choice to be made only after careful consideration of the pros and cons*. Never rush into any form of publishing out of desperation or excessive haste to be published. Instead, think carefully about the message you want to impart with your book—and whether that message might, indeed, work best in an electronic medium. If the answer is yes, then welcome to the future!

Commercial Electronic Publishers That Publish Children's Books

This list is by no means exhaustive, nor should it be taken as a specific endorsement of the publishers listed.

Antelope Publishing—http://www.teleport.com/~writers/books/index.html

DiskUs Publishing—http://www.diskuspublishing.com

The Fiction Works—http://www.fictionworks.com

Hard Shell Word Factory—http://www.hardshell.com/child.html

INFOCIS Publishing—http://www.infocis.com/e-books.html

Main Publishers—http://www.mainstudios.com/mp.htm

New Concepts Publishing—http://www.newconceptspublishing.com

Yahoo's Guide to Electronic Publishers—http://dir.yahoo.com/Business_and_Economy/Companies/Publishing/Electronic_Publishing/

Moira Allen has been writing professionally for more than 20 years. Her most recent book, *Writing.com: Creative Internet Strategies to Advance Your Writing Career,* has just been released from Allworth Press; learn more at her "Tips for Writers" site at http://www.tipsforwriters.com. To find out more about the authors mentioned in this article, visit Karen Wiesner at www.eclectics.com/karenwiesner and Leta Nolan Childers at www.geocities.com/Paris/Cathedral/8168/index.html.

PART TWO

Directory of Publishers and Editors

Directory of Publishers and Editors

About the Directory of Publishers and Editors

Ellen R. Shapiro

The *Directory of Publishers and Editors* has three elements: (1) book publisher listings; (2) magazine listings; and (3) interviews with a diverse group of authors, illustrators, and editors. Although the first two of these categories appear to the naked eye as endless pages of listings, and of course they are quite detailed, they are also windows into the likes and dislikes of all the major book and magazine publishers in the industry. Reading them for content, as opposed to just using the listings as a source of names and addresses, will present a picture of the overall business of writing for children that would be impossible to view any other way.

Understanding the Book and Magazine Publisher Listings

The goal of this book is to be the most comprehensive, reliable, and up-to-date resource for children's writers and illustrators. One important requirement for that kind of accuracy is to use only information that comes directly from the publishers. Thus, each of the hundreds of publishers listed here received a survey form requesting detailed information about all aspects of the business, as well as submission guidelines and other materials. Most responded enthusiastically (some required a gentle nudge or two), and their responses are included here in their entirety (with only occasional, minor editorial modifications for the sake of clarity and consistency—such as putting all comments in the third person) so that you can read exactly what they want you to know. The language belongs to the publishers—there has been no editorializing in the assembly of these listings. Thus, much can be learned by paying close attention to the tone and nuance of each entry. A publisher that says "please" and conveys an overall sense of enthusiasm in these listings may be more likely to display that same attitude in dealing with authors.

Sometimes, publisher survey responses have been supplemented with information obtained from follow-up interviews and correspondence, as well as the publisher's publicly available guidelines and corporate informational materials. In some cases, a publisher did not reply to the survey in time for this book's deadline, but it is nonetheless listed. If that company has chosen to make its submission guidelines and other information about the company public, whatever important information is publicly available is included here, organized in response to the relevant survey queries (annoying quotation marks have for the most part been dispensed with, but please know that everything herein comes directly from the publishers). If not, in a very small minority of cases, only name, address, and basic information are listed.

All publishers listed here are, as of press time, actual publishers in the traditional sense of the word: They will pay to publish your book. These are not self-publishers or other variations of publishers that require an author to pay to publish a book. Not every publisher listed here, however, will accept an unsolicited, unagented manuscript or submission of illustrations. Such publishers are listed here so that you as a writer or illustrator can avoid wasting postage and time on submitting manuscripts and art that simply will not be read (or, if you are an agent, these listings may apply to you). Remember, this book is a cooperative effort between authors and publishers—the idea is to save everybody from wasting time. So please don't submit anything in violation of what you read here; it will only widen the already unpleasant rift between writers and the publishing industry. For advice on finding an agent or rep, who can perhaps submit to a wider range of publishers than a writer or artist acting alone, see the many articles on agents and art reps in this book.

There has been, especially of late, a trend toward consolidation in both the book and magazine industries. Some magazine companies now publish as many as thirty-six different magazines, and some book publishers have dozens of imprints (subsidiaries). In some cases, the imprints function as independent companies, and the common ownership is merely a corporate financial arrangement. But in other cases the imprints are heavily affected by their parent companies. In an effort to keep things clear, the listings include information as to the corporate structure, where it is known, of each publisher mentioned. In some cases, where it made particular sense to do so, listings have been combined; but for the most part each imprint or magazine is treated separately.

At least for the current edition of this book, only print publications and publishers are listed (though the occasional online publication is listed if it is transitioning one way or the other). Many online outlets exist for your writing and artwork—both in online magazines and in the new world of e-publishing—but the rapidly shifting sands of this emerging sector make information obsolete almost as soon as it is gathered. The decision not to include these types of outlets in this book, however, should not be interpreted as a value judgment. Indeed, online and electronic sources can be excellent for beginning and experienced writers and illustrators alike, and it is inevitable that this will become more true as time goes on. (It's not always necessary or even wise to start at the top; many will have an easier time starting with online outlets and smaller magazines before moving up to the larger periodicals and book publishers.) For a discussion of e-publishing, see the piece in Part I of this book. For tips on finding online outlets for your writing and artwork, see the Internet appendix at the back of the book.

Other information you'll see in each listing should be relatively self-explanatory. After basic address, contact, corporate, and editorial staff data, there are descriptions of the publisher's needs, preferred forms of contact, policies regarding unsolicited manuscripts and queries, simultaneous submissions policies, terms for writers and illustrators, submission guidelines (either how to obtain them or, if they're straightforward, a statement of the actual guidelines), and illustration and photography policies. This is a resource guide for professional writers and illustrators, so some technical language is employed. If you're unfamiliar with any technical publishing terms, the glossary contains complete explanations.

Some of the publishers listed here will not accept an unagented, unsolicited submission of any kind—neither a manuscript nor art nor even a query. Nonetheless, because this book is intended for a range of authors and artists, some of whom have professional representation, these publishers are included. At the same time, the entries for these publishers are shorter, because they are less relevant to the typical user of this book.

Every attempt has been made to keep the entries in this book reliable and current, including modifications literally made as the manuscript was on the way to the printer. Still, given the volume of precise data contained herein and the speed with which the industry changes, some of this information will inevitably become outdated quickly. In particular, bear in mind that more and more publishers are coming online each day, and many of their Web sites contain up-to-the-minute guidelines and other relevant information for authors (though some make an effort to hide this information deep within their sites or don't provide it at all). When you get serious about making a submission, it makes sense to go online for the particular publisher's very latest guidelines, or, if they're not available electronically, you should send for them by mail.

If you come into possession of any newer and more accurate information than what you find in this book, please don't hesitate to send an e-mail to ellen@writechild.com, and the changes will be reflected in the next revision of this book. In the interim, check www.writechild.com for news and updates.

Lessons of the Publisher Listings

Perhaps the most significant element of each publisher entry is the "tips and comments" section, where most publishers took the opportunity to give their insiders' views of how to get on their good sides. And despite an amazing diversity of publishers, time and again hundreds of publishers said many of the same things on their surveys. Some of those are well worth mentioning here:

1. The most common plea by far, of nearly every publisher listed here was, Get to know the publisher's guidelines very, very well before you submit any work. In literally hundreds of telephone interviews, surveys, and follow-up e-mail discussions, publishers

complained bitterly of authors wasting everybody's time with inappropriate submissions that don't conform in any way to the required submission guidelines. As an author, I know how frustrating it is to deal with publishers' delays that sometimes amount to stonewalling. And as a former publishing company employee—at two of the largest publishing houses in the world—I know that some of the blame for disorganization and irresponsible handling of manuscripts falls squarely on the publishers. But at the same time I also must acknowledge that authors contribute more than their fair share to the backlog by putting publishers in the unenviable position of having to read work that is simply not right for the house. This kind of behavior helps nobody. So please, take the time to read the entries here carefully. Take them seriously. And if they ask that you pursue further information before making a submission, please do so before you submit anything. That means read not only submission guidelines but also many representative samples of a publisher's output, be it books or magazines. To be a good writer, first be a good reader. If every prospective author takes only one lesson away from this entire book, let this be it.

2. Another piece of ultrasensible but oft-disregarded advice is this: Read children's books. I'm glad you bought this book, I really am, but the truth of the matter is that this book is only the second most valuable weapon in the arsenal of a prospective children's author. The most potent weapon is other children's books. Too many authors are willing to read fifty reference books about writing for children, without ever picking up a single children's book. But your real teachers should be the great children's authors, past and present—the past, to learn from the masters, and the present, to learn what today's kids are reading (they're quite different today than you and I were as children, and they won't buy the same types of books we bought).

3. Some of the publishers' advice seems incredibly straightforward and obvious, yet it never ceases to amaze me how many reports I hear of writers failing to follow a few very basic and near-universal technical procedures. Primarily, these are as follows: Always include an SASE (self-addressed stamped envelope) with carefully measured and sufficient postage for return of a manuscript, notification of a decision, or whatever you want mailed back to you. Publishers will simply throw out anything not accompanied by an SASE. In addition, never send your originals of anything, no matter what. I must confess I'm guilty of violating this rule—once. When I was getting started in photography (I both write and photograph travel and reference guides for adults), I sent originals of some photographs of a trip to France to a magazine that had asked for the submission on spec. Because it was a short-notice thing, I didn't have time to get the slides copied, and I was so desperate to be published that I wasn't going to let that be a sticking point. So even though I knew better, I sent my originals. Needless to say, I never saw them again—and they were never even published. Injustice, yes; but there's nothing I or anybody can do about the reality of things getting lost. So make copies. Lots of them.

4. It should go without saying that you should only ever submit your best work. Publishers don't exist as free critiquing services for rough drafts. This is about to buy or not to buy. Don't expect help or even compassion from a commercial book or magazine publisher. So don't submit work that you aren't completely satisfied with or that you don't

absolutely love. And as a corollary, many publishers gave the sage advice that you should write what you're good at writing—not what you think a publisher wants to read (they can see right through that ploy).

5. Many publishers have requested that authors not pester them by phone. Certainly, a first follow-up inquiry should be made by mail in most cases—and not for a generous period of time. An unwanted phone call may make it through to an editor, but chances are it won't make that editor any more favorably disposed to liking your manuscript or (just as important) you.

6. Know your target age group, and write or illustrate for that group. If you use vocabulary or a style that's inappropriate for that group, your manuscript or illustrations may never see the light of day.

7. Don't use a shotgun approach. Authors often have no choice but to make multiple, simultaneous submissions—it's the reality of the business—but there are simultaneous submissions and there are simultaneous submissions. Rarely is one manuscript right for a hundred different publishers. Far better to submit the right thing to the right place than to submit the wrong thing to a hundred places.

8. And finally, on the bright side, many publishers know your pain. Many people working in publishing companies are also writers, and ultimately they all work on behalf of writers. So take the advice many of them gave: Never give up; never surrender. Believe in yourself and your work, be patient, do all the right things, and—perhaps just when you've almost given up hope—something will happen for you.

About the Author, Illustrator, and Editor Profiles

Throughout this section you will find profiles of authors, illustrators, and editors: real people who have published real children's books and magazine articles.

Writing can be the most rewarding career imaginable, but it can also be the most difficult and trying. My own early experiences as a writer couldn't have been more disheartening. I tried to become a writer under the best possible circumstances: I had worked in book publishing and therefore had many contacts. I saved up plenty of money so I could live for a year and truly devote myself to writing full-time. I had no kids, and my husband supported my effort 100 percent. Through my contacts and my experience, I knew a lot more than most writers starting out could ever hope to know. Yet I published absolutely nothing for more than a year. Not one word of my writing was purchased by anybody; and not a single photograph, either. I got a few of the proverbial "good" rejections (those that include a kind and encouraging handwritten note in addition to the form rejection letter), but nothing panned out. I had a few terrible experiences where publishers strung me along, gave me hope, and then abandoned me—leaving me disheartened and depressed (as bad as it's ever going to get for you, that's how bad it was for me). But ultimately, when I least expected it, I got an acceptance on one of my pieces, and overnight

I had an article and a full photo spread in a major national magazine, and another, and another, and then I was a columnist for an additional publication and work was coming to me. Before I knew it, a publisher (this one) made an approach to me about doing a reference book. And a second one. This is my third in less than two years.

When I got the opportunity to do this book, the first thing I thought about was how I could help aspiring writers and illustrators get over the emotional hurdles nearly every one of us experiences when getting started. So I decided to include interviews with authors and illustrators who have made it, so you can see the different paths they took.

I've tried to select a great group of people and also a varied group: Young and old, beginners with one book and veterans with 150 (really), with different styles and target audiences, and from many different cultural backgrounds. I let them tell their stories in their own words—sometimes at great length (that's why this book is in such small type). Everyone has a unique story, and I think you'll find them all fascinating and inspiring (not to mention fun), but there's one thing you can learn from every one of them: Be persistent. They were persistent (except for a few lucky dogs for whom it was easy), and that's a big reason why they succeeded. They had talent, but much talent will go unrecognized without persistence. Luck helps, too, but over that you have no control.

At the same time, persistence as an undirected force is only worth so much. You should spend your persistence wisely. That's where the more practical parts of this book (the listings, the down-to-brass-tacks advice) can help.

I've also included interviews with several editors and art directors, so you can get their unique perspectives on the world of children's writing and illustrating. After all, these are the people who will decide whether or not to buy your work, so you should pay careful attention to what they have to say.

One other thing you'll see in both the profiles and the publisher listings: There's a lot of contradictory advice out there (do/don't submit manuscripts and illustrations together; do/don't use an agent or rep; etc.). While this may appear confusing, it should actually be viewed with optimism. There is no one path, no right answer for everybody. You're an individual, not a statistic. In the end, you must decide to do what's right for you and your particular abilities.

I sincerely wish you the best of luck.

Please feel free to send comments or corrections to ellen@writechild.com and visit www.writechild.com for updates and further information.

SECTION ONE

Book Publishers

ABDO Publishing

4940 Viking Drive, Suite 622
Edina, MN 55435
(800) 800-1312
(952) 831-1632 (fax)
E-mail: info@abdopub.com
Web site: www.abdopub.com

Description: Book publisher including ABDO & Daughters, Checkerboard, and SandCastle imprints, all nonfiction.

Description of nonfiction titles: SandCastle is a library of nonfiction books for the beginning reader. Reading difficulty is graduated over three levels. The books incorporate basic concepts of the phonics and integrated language methods of reading instruction. Checkerboard Library includes books at two reading levels: grades 2 to 3 and grades 3 to 4. The text is supported with striking photographs. Fast Facts sections, maps, time lines, and simple diagrams encourage readers to learn from several formats of information. The ABDO & Daughters books are at a midrange elementary reading level: grades 4 to 5. Photos, graphics, and illustrations enhance the text to encourage the reluctant reader. Elements such as tables of contents, glossaries, bibliographies, and indexes allow students to become familiar with nonfiction book conventions.

Recent nonfiction titles:

Do You Wonder? (series: simple answers to everyday questions)

Baby Animals (series: basic facts about popular animals)

Opposites (series: a variety of comparisons made with common objects and experiences)

Bears (series: explores the wide variety of the world of bears. Each book discusses a different species, taking a close look at the characteristics, habits, and environments of each.)

Awesome Athletes (series: from Brett Favre to Sheryl Swoopes, ice skating to golf, this series has something for all readers. The personalities, talents, and hard work of many different athletes are brought to life in these biographies.)

Submission guidelines: Write with an SASE for guidelines.

Book Publishers

Abingdon Press

201 Eighth Avenue S.
Nashville, TN 37203
(615) 749-6384
(615) 749-6512 (fax)
E-mail: paugustine@umpublishing.org

Corporate structure/parent: United Methodist Publishing House.

Description: America's oldest theological publisher, serving the Christian community with quality resources.

Established: 1789.

Key people:

Children's editor: Peg Augustine

Abrams Books

100 Fifth Avenue
New York, NY 10011
www.abramsbooks.com

Corporate structure/parent: Harry N. Abrams, Inc.

Description: Publisher of art and illustrated books.

Established: 1949, started publishing children's books in 1986.

Recent nonfiction titles: Three major bestsellers for children by author/illustrator Graeme Base: *Animalia*, an alliterative alphabet book, which has over one million copies in print; *The Eleventh Hour,* a mystery story told in rhyme, which has over 750,000 copies in print; and *The Sign of the Seahorse,* a rhyming underwater adventure story with a first printing of 400,000.

The First Impressions series offers art books for young readers. Featured are biographies of such artists as Leonardo da Vinci, Rembrandt, Vincent Van Gogh, Mary Cassat, and Pablo Picasso.

Preferred form of submission/contact: If you have a proposal, please send your idea in as much detail as possible *via e-mail* only.

Submission guidelines: Send e-mail proposals to submissions@abramsbooks.com. If Abrams is interested, you will be contacted for further information.

Tips and comments: Abrams specializes in high-quality art and illustrated books. Abrams does not publish works of fiction.

Absey & Co.

5706 Root Road, Suite #5
Spring, TX 77389
(281) 257-2340

E-mail: abseyandco@aol.com
Web site: www.absey.com

Description: Book publisher.
Key people:
Editor in chief: Trey Hall (also acts as acquisitions/submissions editor)
Accepts unsolicited/unagented: Yes.
Submission guidelines: Include a brief cover letter, a chapter-by-chapter outline, an author's information sheet (including relevant qualifications and previous publishing experience), one or two sample chapters, and an SASE for return of materials and/or response.

ACTION PUBLISHING

PO Box 391
Glendale, CA 91209
(323) 478-1667
(323) 478-1767 (fax)
Web site: www.actionpublishing.com

Description: Publisher of the Scott E. Sutton series of rapid learning materials.
Key people:
Publisher: Michael Metzler

ADDISON-WESLEY

1 Jacob Way
Reading, MA 01867
Web site: www.aw.com

Corporate structure/parent: Includes the imprints Addison-Wesley, Longman, Benjamin Cummings, and Allyn & Bacon.
Description: Educational publisher, textbooks.
Accepts unsolicited/unagented: Yes.
Submission guidelines: Write with SASE or visit Web site for guidelines. For submissions, please include (all of which are detailed in the guidelines) a prospectus and outline; a brief description of your book (in one or two paragraphs describe the work, its approach, and your purpose in writing such a text); outstanding features; pedagogical features (will the book include summaries, examples, cases, questions, problems, etc.?); supplements (do you plan to provide supplementary material such as a teacher's manual, study guide, etc.?); level; a statement as to whether the material has been class-tested; your background; please attach a copy of your vita; the competition; the market; the outline (the outline provides an overview of the entire work—it is a road map guiding both the reviewer and the publisher along your specific point of view); sample chapters

(submit three chapters); additional information (please see our guidelines). Address to Discipline Name, Submissions Editor.

ADVOCACY PRESS

PO Box 236
Santa Barbara, CA 93102
(805) 962-2728
(805) 963-3580 (fax)
E-mail: advpress@impulse.net
Web site: www.advocacypress.com

Corporate structure/parent: Girls Incorporated of Greater Santa Barbara.

Description: Publishes illustrated children's stories incorporating self-esteem, gender equity, and self-awareness concepts.

Established: 1983.

Key people:

Acquisitions/submissions editor: Laura Webster

Description of fiction titles: Children's books that promote self-awareness, gender equality, and life skills.

Recent fiction titles:

Shadow and the Ready Time by Patty Sheehan; illustrated by Itoko Maeno (family values and parenting)

Kylie's Concert by Patty Sheehan; illustrated by Itoko Maeno (learn about threats to the environment, endangered species, standing up for what you believe, and using one's unique talents to make a difference)

My Way Sally by Penelope C. Paine; illustrated by Itoko Maeno (how learning to be a leader can change things for the better)

Description of nonfiction titles: Curriculum and workbooks that promote self-awareness, gender equality, and life skills.

AFRICA WORLD PRESS

PO Box 1892
Trenton, NJ 08607
(609) 844-9583
(609) 844-0198 (fax)
E-mail: awprsp@africaworld.com
Web site: www.africaworld.com

Description: Book publisher focusing on Africa and African American life.

Key people:

Editor: Kassahun Checole

ALADDIN PAPERBACKS

1230 Avenue of the Americas, 4th Floor
New York, NY 10020
Web site: www.simonsayskids.com

Corporate structure/parent: Simon & Schuster.

Description: General interest publisher (picture books, beginning readers, chapter books, novels, nonfiction).

Established: 1972.

Key people:

Publisher: Brenda Bowen

Editorial director: Ellen Krieger

Executive editor: Stephen Fraser

Art director: Debra Sfetsios

Acquisitions/submissions editor: Address correspondence to Manuscript Submission Editor

Books per year and description: Nearly 200 books per year, mostly fiction.

Percentage by first-time authors: Small number, since 75 percent of titles are reprints from hardcover imprints. However, Aladdin is always looking for new authors.

Seeks: Chapter books and chapter book series; beginning readers (fiction and nonfiction); mysteries.

Accepts unsolicited/unagented: Yes.

Description of fiction titles: Accessible.

Recent fiction titles:

King of Shadows by Susan Cooper (a time-travel fantasy where a boy meets Shakespeare)

The Folk Keeper by Franny Billingsley (a coming-of-age fantasy based on the selkie legend)

Hard Love by Ellen Wittlinger (a contemporary novel of first love)

Preferred fiction titles: Looking for mysteries, chapter books.

Description of nonfiction titles: Curriculum tie-ins; fun, accessible titles.

Recent nonfiction titles:

Black Frontiers by Lillian Schlissel

How to Find Lost Treasure in All Fifty States (and Canada, Too!) by Joan Holub

Preferred form of submission/contact: A query letter is fine. Sometimes a manuscript saves time, since Aladdin can tell right away whether it is right for them or not.

Time to reply: We try to respond within a few weeks.

Time to publish: 18 months.

Accepts simultaneous submissions: Yes. It is always preferable, of course, to have an exclusive submission.

Number of illustrators used annually: Many.

Desired illustrator qualifications: A range of styles. Commercial, accessible.

Prefer manuscript/illustration packages, or separate: Separately.

Include with illustrator query: Samples.

Time to reply: Within a few weeks.

Purchases freelance photography: Not usually.

Terms for writers: Usually 6 percent for paperback; negotiable for established authors.

Terms for illustrators: Flat fee for chapter books and covers; advance against royalty for beginning readers. Royalties split evenly with authors.

Submission guidelines: Obtain by writing to manuscript submissions editor.

Tips and comments: Take a look at the kinds of books Aladdin publishes. Submit only what seems appropriate. The biggest error in submissions is an author (or agent) sending a manuscript or proposal that is completely inappropriate for the list.

ALBERT WHITMAN & COMPANY

6340 Oakton Street
Morton Grove, IL 60053-2723
(847) 581-0033
(847) 581-0039 (fax)
E-mail: mail@awhitmanco.com
Web site: www.awhitmanco.com

Description: Publisher.

Established: 1919.

Key people:

Editor in chief: Kathleen Tucker

Art director: Scott Piehl

Books per year and description: Albert Whitman & Company publishes approximately 30 books per year for the trade, library, and school library market.

Seeks: Picture book manuscripts for ages 2 to 8; novels and chapter books for ages 8 to 12; nonfiction for ages 3 to 12; art samples showing pictures of children.

Accepts unsolicited/unagented: Yes.

Recent fiction titles:

Haunting at Home Plate by David Patneaude
Dirt Boy by Erik Jon Slangerup
Pumpkin Jack by Will Hubbell

Recent nonfiction titles:

Is a Blue Whale the Biggest Thing There Is? by Robert E. Wells
I'm Tougher Than Asthma! by Alden R. Carter and Siri M. Carter
Guns: What You Should Know
Small Steps: The Year I Got Polio

Preferred form of submission/contact: Enclose a brief cover letter. Include a self-addressed stamped envelope (SASE) for a reply. If you would like your work to be returned to you, please make sure the postage and size of your SASE is sufficient. Label the outside envelope of your submission to indicate whether a query or a full manuscript is enclosed. Please do not use e-mail or fax to send your work.

Time to reply: Three to four months on manuscripts. Queries, if labeled appropriately, are usually answered within six weeks.

Accepts simultaneous submissions: Yes. But if you are sending your manuscript elsewhere, please advise in your cover letter.

Meet Henry Cole

Illustrator

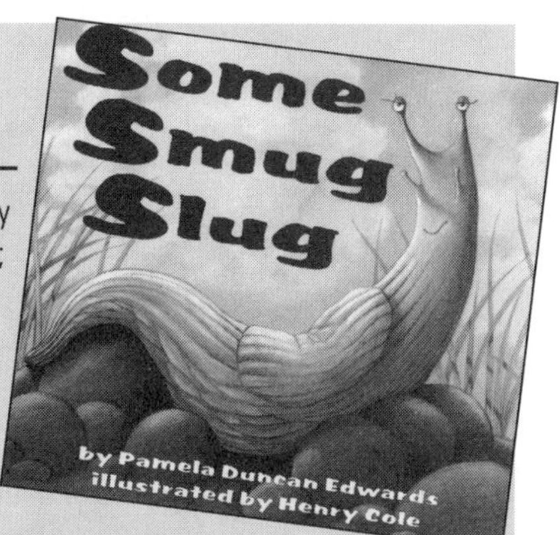

Henry Cole has illustrated 26 books for the elementary audience, including: *Jack's Garden* (Greenwillow, 1995); *Some Smug Slug* by Pamela Edwards (HarperCollins, 1996); *Livingstone Mouse* by Pamela Edwards (HarperCollins, 1996); *Little Bo* by Julie Andrews Edwards (Hyperion, 1999); *Moosetache* by Margie Palatini (Hyperion, 2000); and *Clara Caterpillar* by Pamela Edwards (HarperCollins, 2001). He was born in Virginia, sometime in the 20th century. He has a B.S. from Virginia Tech in forestry. Before he became a children's book illustrator, he was an elementary science teacher, for 16 years.

How did you get your first book published?

When I worked as an elementary science teacher, we would have guest children's book authors and illustrators come to the school to speak. Each time we had one of these visitors, I would think, "That's what I want to be doing more than anything else in the world!" I had a couple of ideas for stories and made up a dummy of one of them, and some sample illustrations for another one, and, with the names of a couple of editors in New York, set up appointments to see them. The first idea was taken right away, and the second publisher gave me a manuscript to look at, to "see if I was interested in illustrating it." Interested?! That's all I wanted in the world to do! That was in the fall of 1993, and my first books started coming out the spring of 1995. That's a pretty typical length of time, as it takes a while to get a book out. It was tough getting up the nerve to call and make appointments, and I was all sweaty palms and dry mouth when I went to see editors the first time. Also exhilarating and exciting. I loved teaching, and I think it gave me insight into children and the way they think. I miss being in the classroom, but now I do many school visits to schools all around the country. Each time I do I think, "This is exactly what I wanted!"

Did you have an agent when you published your first book?

I do not have an agent. I was lucky to find a publisher on my own, and each project has led to other projects, so I have not (yet) needed an agent to find work or push my stuff around editors' desks.

Are you still with your first publisher?

I work on projects with six or seven different publishers now, including my first one. It is nice working with different editors, art directors, and designers because you learn so much from each one.

Do you have any advice, in terms of finding a publisher, for an illustrator starting out?

Wear comfortable shoes! Make connections; ask people questions; don't be too shy. Most folks like giving advice or offering help. It helps to know people, so get involved in the children's book publishing world by taking classes, going to literature conferences, and seeing whether visiting authors are presenting at local schools or bookstores. Talk to them. If you have children, volunteer

continues

at their school library and check out all of the books! Of course, when starting out, don't hesitate to take on any project they hand you.

Do your write the text for the books you illustrate?

I have written the text for two books, but most projects I work on are written by other authors. The two I've written were sold "as a package." The author I work with most was a librarian at the school where I was science teacher, so we have been colleagues and friends for a long time. Sometimes we submit things jointly. Other times an editor will just call me up or e-mail me or stop me at a conference and ask whether I am interested in a particular manuscript.

What procedures do you follow when you work?

With a pile of work to do, I must be disciplined and schedule myself. I get up early and work late. I love scheduling my own time. Big fantasy: To have a big stretch of time to work on my own projects and not have stuff pile up.

Where do you get your ideas?

It sounds cliché, but I get ideas from watching and listening all around me. Also, I had a pretty interesting childhood and grew up on a farm with great older siblings; they are very creative people, and so I always had super role models to look up to.

Did you pursue any formal training, or was it just a question of practice, or something else?

I studied the "Ologies" in college: ornithology, ichthyology, dendrology, aquatic entomology, and so on. But I always liked to draw so practiced all the time as I doodled all the time. In fact, when I got into teaching, I would notice that some students were always doodling on the margins of their papers instead of (I thought) listening to me. It took me a while to realize that those kids were just like me—that they could doodle and listen at the same time. In fact, they could listen better when they had a pencil in their hands doodling!

Anything you really wish somebody had told you when you started out?

It's a competitive world out there. Remember the comfortable shoe thing. Editors are people, too. And have fun with it!

Prefers manuscript/illustration packages, or separate: Send color photocopies, tear sheets, slides, or other reproductions, but do not send originals. Will keep samples unless you enclose an SASE for their return. If you have an online portfolio, you may send the address of your site. Be sure to type "Portfolio" in the subject line of your e-mail. Please send the address only—do not send file attachments of any kind.

Time to reply: Will contact you if interested in seeing more work.

Submission guidelines: Please send submissions to the attention of Kathleen Tucker, editor in chief. Please adhere to the following guidelines for submissions: *Story text* need only be presented in a typed and double-spaced manuscript. Given this format, most picture book manuscripts should be less than eight pages. Other formats—such as storyboards, dummy books, layout suggestions, and illustration ideas—are unnecessary. Please do not include them unless you are a professional artist. Illustrations are not needed. When Whitman publishes a manuscript, it prefers to choose an artist whose style it feels best complements the story. *Novels*: Whitman prefers that you send a query letter with three sample chapters first. Whitman publishes very few novels, so please bear in mind that the competition is particularly fierce. At this time, Whitman is not seeking manuscripts or writers for the Boxcar Children Mysteries series. *Nonfiction*: You may send the entire manuscript if it is picture book length (see above for picture book guidelines). For any work that is longer, please send a query letter first. Whitman will consider biographies but prefers ones that are not fictionalized.

Alef Design Group & Torah Aura Productions

4423 Fruitland Avenue
Los Angeles, CA 90058
(323) 585-7312
(323) 585-0327 (fax)
E-mail: misrad@torahaura.com
Web site: www.torahaura.com

Corporate structure/parent: Alef Design Group and Torah Aura Productions are sister companies publishing Jewish materials for the trade market and educational settings.

Description: Book publisher.

Key people:

Acquisitions/submissions editor: If you have any questions, they may be directed to Jane Golub at (888) 574-7355.

Books per year and description: To this date, Alef Design Group has published 31 works in the juvenile (ages 8–11) and young adult (ages 10–14) categories, as well as for the adult nonfiction shelf.

Seeks: At this time Alef Design Group is only considering manuscripts in the juvenile fiction and adult nonfiction category. They do not publish picture books of any kind.

Accepts unsolicited/unagented: Yes. Alef Design Group and Torah Aura Productions are currently open to unsolicited manuscripts submitted exclusively to them.

Preferred fiction titles: At this time Alef Design Group is only considering manuscripts in the juvenile fiction and adult nonfiction category. *Does not publish picture books of any kind.*

Preferred nonfiction titles: Torah Aura will only consider materials for classrooms or teacher education.

Preferred form of submission/contact: Manuscripts should be typed and submitted in their entirety if possible. If not, please send an outline and a writing sample.

Time to reply: A note from the editorial staff will be sent on receipt of manuscript, and if, on first review, the manuscript seems not to fit the company's needs, the manuscript will be returned at that time. If the manuscript seems to be something of interest to the companies, they will hold it until the next editorial meeting. Meetings take place twice a year, in October and February.

Time to publish: Both Alef Design Group and Torah Aura have a two-year backlog of materials to be published before new materials will be produced.

Accepts simultaneous submissions: No.

Prefer manuscript/illustration packages, or separate: Does not publish picture books of any kind.

Submission guidelines: Write with an SASE for guidelines.

Tips and comments: Make a copy of your manuscript before sending, as the companies cannot be responsible for submissions lost in the mail. Please be sure that your name, address, and telephone number appear on at least the first page of your manuscript as well as in your cover letter. Please submit you manuscript to either Alef Design Group or Torah Aura Productions at the address above. Please enclose a self-addressed stamped envelope with sufficient postage attached (not a check or cash) for the return of manuscript. Books are available through Barnes & Noble, Borders, and Amazon.com. Torah Aura Productions is an educational publishing house, specializing in materials for Jewish Sunday and afternoon school programs. Torah Aura materials are distributed through catalog sales to educational settings. Torah Aura has more than 300 titles in its current catalog.

ALFRED A. KNOPF AND CROWN BOOKS FOR YOUNG READERS

201 E. 50th Street
New York, NY 10022
(212) 782-5623
Web site: www.randomhouse.com/kids

Corporate structure/parent: Random House, Inc.

Description: Book publisher.

Accepts unsolicited/unagented: Yes.

Description of fiction titles: Completely varied and original.

Preferred titles: Please study and familiarize yourself with as many Knopf BFYR titles as possible before putting pen to paper. Looking for original material presented in a fresh and compelling voice.

Preferred form of submission/contact: Do not send the only copy of your manuscript (we cannot be held responsible for loss or damage to the material). Do not send disks; we will review a hard copy of material only. Do not send check or cash for postage; postage must be glued on the envelope that will be returned containing your letter. Do not send manuscripts by fax or by e-mail. Cannot acknowledge receipt of the manuscript or guarantee personal responses or response times.

Time to reply: Within six months of receipt.

Include with illustrator query: For artist/illustrator submissions please contact the Art Department at (212) 940-7600 for information. Do not send original art.

Tips and comments: Review as many Knopf and Crown children's books as possible before submitting your work to so that you will have a better understanding of Knopf and Crown's publishing needs. Books may be viewed in New York City at The Children's Book Council, 568 Broadway, New York, NY 10012, or in your local library or bookstore. All manuscripts must be accompanied by a self-addressed stamped envelope for their return. Do not send original art.

ALL ABOUT KIDS

6280 San Ignacio Avenue, Suite C
San Jose, CA 95119
(408) 578-4026
(408) 578-4029 (fax)
Web site: www.aakp.com

Description: New independent book packager and producer, established 1999, planning to publish 20 or more young readers picture books per year, with many by new authors.

ALLEN & UNWIN

PO Box 8500
St Leonards, NSW 1590
Australia
(61 2) 8425 0100
(61 2) 9906 2218 (fax)
E-mail: frontdesk@allen-unwin.com.au
Web site: www.allenandunwin.com

Description: Publisher.
Established: 1976.
Recent fiction titles:
Bungaloo by Katrina Nannestead; illustrated by Steven Axelson
Dorothy the Dinosaur and the Magic Shell by Bentley Jonathan
The Emperor & the Nightingale by Fiona Waters and Paul Birkbeck
Whoever's Heard of a Hibernating Pig? by Shen Roddie and Eleanor Taylor
Recent nonfiction titles:
The ABC Book of Kids in the Kitchen by Helen Martin
Inside the Australian Ballet by Diana Lawrenson
Tips and comments: Allen & Unwin is Australia's leading independent book publisher and distributor of an extensive range of quality Australian and international books. Its children's books are published under the Allen & Unwin imprint, and it publishes across a wide range, including picture books, beginner novels, novels for 10- to 12-year-olds, young adult fiction, activity books, and the nonfiction True Stories and Discoveries series. Many of Allen & Unwin's children's books are award winners.

ALLOYBOOKS

Penguin Putnam BFYR
345 Hudson Street
New York, NY 10014
Web site: www.penguinputnam.com/about/children/puffin.htm

Corporate structure/parent: Penguin Putnam.

Description: AlloyBooks is a result of Penguin Putnam's groundbreaking partnership with the leading Web site for teens, Alloy.com.

Established: 2000.

Key people:

Publisher: Tracy Tang

Books per year and description: AlloyBooks released its first four books in August 2000. AlloyBooks will release more original nonfiction titles and launch a new teen fiction series.

Accepts unsolicited/unagented: At this time most Penguin Putnam Inc. imprints do not accept unsolicited manuscripts. If you would like your work to be considered for publication by a major publisher, Penguin Putnam Inc. recommends that you work with an established literary agent.

Description of fiction titles: Innovative fiction and cutting-edge design.

Description of nonfiction titles: In-your-face nonfiction and cutting-edge design.

Recent nonfiction titles:

Slam (a unique poetry anthology)

DIY Beauty (a cool do-it-yourself beauty guide)

Dreams (a funky dream interpretation manual)

Any Advice? (a book packed with advice for teens from Alloy.com's advice experts)

Allyn & Bacon

160 Gould Street
Needham Heights, MA 02494
Web site: www.ablongman.com

Corporate structure/parent: Addison-Wesley.

Description: Educational publisher; textbooks.

Established: 1868.

Accepts unsolicited/unagented: Yes.

Preferred form of submission/contact: Always interested in hearing about new ideas for textbooks. Please see guidelines for detailed submission requirements.

Submission guidelines: Write with an SASE or see the Web site for exhaustive guidelines on preparing for manuscript submission.

Alyson Wonderland

6922 Hollywood Boulevard, Suite 1000
Los Angeles, CA 90028
Web site: www.alyson.com

Corporate structure/parent: Alyson Publications.

Description: Book publisher.

Established: 1990.

Accepts unsolicited/unagented: Only considers solicited manuscripts.

Recent titles:

Daddy's Roommate by Michael Willhoite (gay issues)

Heather Has Two Mommies by Lesléa Newman; illustrated by Diana Souza (gay/lesbian issues)

Preferred titles: Will consider book queries with gay, lesbian, and/or bisexual themes. Alyson usually does not publish books of poetry (poems may be submitted for anthologies). Does not consider individual short stories or poetry.

Preferred form of submission/contact: Please send a query letter detailing your novel's plot or your nonfiction idea. You must indicate whether this is a simultaneous submission (i.e., you have submitted elsewhere). Give a summary of the book, a chapter outline if you have it, approximately how many words, and what qualifies you to write this particular book. If you are querying a children's book, please send with illustrations or indicate that you have an illustrator. No sample chapters at this stage.

Time to reply: Each query will be reviewed and a response sent to you within two to four months of its receipt. Please do not call to check on the status of your submission.

Accepts simultaneous submissions: Yes, but you must indicate whether this is a simultaneous submission (i.e., you have submitted elsewhere).

Tips and comments: Alyson Publications is the leading publisher of books by, for, and about lesbians, gay men, and bisexuals from all economic and social segments of society and of all ages, from children to adults. In fiction and nonfiction format, Alyson books explore the political, legal, financial, medical, spiritual, social, and sexual aspects of gay, lesbian, and bisexual life and the contributions to and experiences in society of our community.

American Bible Society

1865 Broadway
New York, NY 10023
(212) 408-1305 (fax)
Web site: www.americanbible.org

Description: Book publisher focusing on books with spiritual/religious/Biblical themes.

American Girls Collection

8400 Fairway Place
Middleton, WI 53562
(608) 836-4848
(608) 828-4768 (fax)
Web site: www.americangirl.com

Corporate structure/parent: The American Girls Collections is Pleasant Company Publications' historical fiction imprint.

Description: Publisher.

Established: 1995.

Books per year and description: Historical fiction.

Seeks: Pleasant Company Publications publishes books for girls in the 8 to 13 age range and welcomes submissions from authors and agents in the fields of historical fiction, contemporary fiction, and nonfiction. Pleasant Company Publications seeks manuscripts for its forthcoming contemporary fiction imprint. Novels should capture the spirit of contemporary American girls and also illuminate the ways in which their lives are personally touched by issues and concerns affecting America today. Looking for thoughtfully developed characters and plots, and a discernible sense of place. Will also consider manuscripts and queries for other historical fiction.

Accepts unsolicited/unagented: Yes. Fiction manuscripts should be 100 to 200 typewritten pages, double-spaced. Please submit the entire manuscript.

Description of fiction titles: Historical fiction and also moving toward contemporary fiction for young girls aged 8 to 12, reading level for grades 3 to 5.

Recent fiction titles: *Historical fiction:* The books in this collection tell the stories of six American girls who lived long ago, including Felicity (1774), a spunky, spirited colonial girl full of energy and independence; Josefina (1824), a Hispanic girl whose heart and hopes are as big as the New Mexico sky; Kirsten (1854), a pioneer girl of strength and spirit who settles on the frontier; Addy (1864), a courageous girl determined to be free in the midst of the Civil War; Samantha (1904), a bright Victorian beauty, an orphan raised by her wealthy grandmother; Molly (1944), who schemes and dreams on the home front during World War II. Through their adventures, readers learn what things about growing up have changed and what things—like families, friends, and feelings—have remained the same. Not seeking unsolicited manuscripts for this collection.

Recent nonfiction titles:

Groom Your Room: Terrific Touches to Brighten Your Bedroom

Super Slumber Parties

Oops! The Manners Guide for Girls

The Care and Keeping of Friends

Preferred form of submission/contact: Send entire manuscript.

Time to reply: Please allow 12 to 16 weeks for response.

Tips and comments: Readers are girls in the formative years, girls who dream big dreams. Mission is to encourage that dreaming and to reinforce each reader's self-confidence, curiosity, and self-esteem as she prepares to navigate adolescence in the years ahead. All contemporary fiction submissions will be automatically considered for the Pleasant T. Rowland Prize for Literature for Girls.

AMIRAH

PO Box 541146
Flushing, NY 11354
(718) 321-9004
E-mail: amirahpbco@aol.com
Web site: www.ifna.net

Description: Publishes fiction, educational material, multicultural material for children and young adults with a spiritually uplifting application.

Atheneum Books for Young Readers

1230 Avenue of the Americas
New York, NY 10020
(212) 698-1295
(212) 698-2714 (fax)
Web site: www.simonsayskids.com

Corporate structure/parent: Simon & Schuster.

Description: Book publisher.

Established: 1924.

Key people:

Associate publisher and vice president: Ginee Seo, Atheneum

Editorial director, Anne Schwartz Books: Anne Schwartz, Atheneum

Editorial director, Richard Jackson Books: Richard Jackson, Atheneum

Senior editor: Caitlyn Dlouhy, Atheneum

Acquisitions/submissions editor: Caitlyn Dlouhy, senior editor, Atheneum

Books per year and description: Approximately 100 trade titles a year, from books for the youngest reader, through chapter books, through middle grade, to young adult.

Percentage by first-time authors: 10 percent.

Seeks: Books that are innovative, beautifully written, and aren't afraid to take chances.

Accepts unsolicited/unagented: Yes.

Description of fiction titles: Stories that break from the norm, ones that take chances, try to do something new. They tend to have characters with distinctive voices.

Recent fiction titles:

Dovey Coe by Francis O'Roark Dowell

Postcards to Father Abraham by Catherine Lewis

All That Remains by Bruce Brooks

Preferred fiction titles: Not looking for series or books that are "Babysitter Club" types. Not looking for books that are derivative (i.e., Harry Potter redo's). Looking for books that are exceptionally well crafted, with a distinctive voice and great characterization.

Description of nonfiction titles: Publishes very little nonfiction.

Preferred nonfiction titles: Not looking for nonfiction.

Preferred form of submission/contact: A query letter is best.

Time to reply: Tries to respond in three months or less.

Time to publish: A novel could be published within a year of acceptance. A picture book is less predictable as it really depends on when the finished artwork is completed.

Accepts simultaneous submissions: Yes, as long as made aware that the submissions are simultaneous.

Number of illustrators used annually: 15 to 20.

Desired illustrator qualifications: Someone with a fresh eye and fresh approach, who can develop great characterization visually, and who can bring more to the work than just a mirroring of the text.

Prefer manuscript/illustration packages, or separate: Only accepts manuscripts with illustrations from authors who are equally talented artists and vice versa. *If you are not an artist, do not submit art with your manuscript.* The same applies to artists who are not writers.

Include with illustrator query: Several samples of animals and children, as most picture books include one or the other, or both. It's also helpful to see several consecutive pieces featuring the same cast of characters—for instance, take a favorite fairy tale and illustrate several spreads.

Time to reply: Approximately two months.

Purchases freelance photography: Very rarely.

Submission guidelines: Send in a request with an SASE.

Tips and comments: Take a look at the types of books Atheneum publishes—that will give you a good sense of the kinds of projects Atheneum likes. Don't send artwork with your manuscript! Don't try to write toward particular trends; write about what you know best.

August House Publishers, Inc.

PO Box 3223
Little Rock, AR 72203-3223
Web site: www.augusthouse.com

Description: Book publisher.

Seeks: Editorial mission focuses on world folktales and the art and uses of storytelling. For the general trade line, interested in acquiring books pertaining to folklore, folktales, and storytelling. For the children's picture-book line, seeking single-story manuscripts that feature traditional folktales. For the audio line, not soliciting recordings released under other labels for distribution. The primary purpose of August House Audio is to produce audio adaptations of previously published books that pertain to storytelling or folklore. No audition tapes for third-party voice talent, since most of our authors work as performing storytellers. Storytelling resources published in four formats: picture books; folktale collections; instructional/how-to books; and personal story collections.

Accepts unsolicited/unagented: Yes.

Description of fiction titles: Has published fiction in the past, but not now acquiring such titles. Does not publish poetry, westerns, romance novels, science fiction, fantasy or horror, technical books, how-to books, memoirs, or autobiographies.

Preferred form of submission/contact: August House does not accept book proposals or editorial inquiries *by e-mail or telephone*.

Time to reply: Please allow at least 12 weeks for responses to query letters and proposals, and 16 to 18 weeks for responses to manuscripts should you be invited to submit yours. If at any time you want your manuscript returned, please drop a note to the editorial department. Will acknowledge receipt of manuscripts immediately by postcard if a self-addressed stamped postcard is provided with submission. (Cannot without great difficulty acknowledge a previously submitted manuscript by phone, as manuscripts are stored in more than one location.) If you've received acknowledgment, please don't call to check on progress.

Accepts simultaneous submissions: August House will read manuscripts being simultaneously submitted to other publishing houses.

Prefer manuscript/illustration packages, or separate: Separately. August House considers submissions of artwork separately from submissions of text, even if proposed for the same work. Never send an original work or irreplaceable copy as a submission. Send duplicate slides, photocopies (either color or B/W), or other such samples as are replaceable at minimal expense.

Include with illustrator query: Freelance illustrators may submit portfolio samples to the art department. Send to attention of Art Director, August House, PO Box 3223, Little Rock, AR 72203.

Time to reply: Unless art samples are submitted with a book proposal, they are usually filed for future reference. If you prefer that your samples be returned, please so indicate in a brief cover note and enclose a self-addressed stamped envelope large enough to accommodate your artwork without damage. Submissions not accompanied by such an envelope will not be returned. For prompt notification of receipt, enclose a self-addressed stamped postcard with a place for initials and date. Unless art samples are submitted with a book proposal, there will customarily be no reply to the sender if no immediate need for artwork of the type submitted is anticipated. This should not be interpreted as a lack of possible future interest.

Tips and comments: Please correspond in writing. No manuscript submissions or book ideas accepted by appointment, and the office is not designed for drop-in traffic. Phone calls are usually ineffective and result in disruptive bouts of telephone tag. If you need to follow up your submission with additional information, please drop a postcard to the editorial department. If you have a question that is not addressed here, please indicate it by query letter. Please be aware that August House cannot offer critiques of manuscripts it chooses not to publish, nor can it offer advice on how to get started writing a book, how to find a ghostwriter or collaborator, or how to find a publisher if August House can't use your manuscript. Biographical data are especially helpful in considering proposals and manuscripts.

A/V Concepts Corp.

30 Montauk Boulevard
Oakdale, NY 11769
(631) 567-7227
(631) 567-8745 (fax)
E-mail: info@edcompublishing.com

Description: Educational book publisher with primary focus on classic literature, science, math, and language.

Baker Book House

PO Box 6287
Grand Rapids, MI 49516
(616) 676-9185
(616) 676-9573 (fax)
E-mail: submissions@bakerbooks.com
Web site: www.bakerbooks.com

Description: Baker Book House Company is a leading evangelical press publishing books in many fiction and nonfiction categories, including children's books.

Bantam Books

1540 Broadway
New York, NY 10036
(212) 354-6500
Web site: www.bdd.com

Description: Book publisher.

Accepts unsolicited/unagented: If you wish to submit your work for consideration by Bantam and are unagented, send a query letter.

Preferred form of submission/contact: Query should be no more than three pages, covering the basics of your characters, what the conflict is that they face, and how your plot develops. Please don't submit sample chapters or a complete manuscript until requested.

Time to reply: It usually takes eight weeks to receive a response.

Tips and comments: Review the titles Bantam has published during the past several years by bestselling authors. Unfortunately, Bantam cannot give comments on any submissions. Be sure to include a self-addressed stamped envelope; Bantam cannot respond to queries that are not accompanied by return postage. Bantam is constantly searching for the stars of tomorrow. If you write a great book, Bantam will buy it!

Barefoot Books Ltd.

PO Box 95
Bristol BS30 5BH
United Kingdom
Web site: www.barefoot-books.com

Description: Book publisher.

Established: 1993.

Seeks: Most projects are developed by staff.

Accepts unsolicited/unagented: As a small publishing house, Barefoot often receives more manuscripts in a week than it can publish in a year. Most projects are developed by in-house staff, but if you have a manuscript of no more than 2,000 words that is appropriate for Barefoot, please send it via regular mail, attention Submissions Department.

Description of titles: Barefoot's approach is "less is more"—Barefoot aims to be selective in what it publishes and to make sure that every project has enduring value as well as lots of child appeal. Barefoot's commitment is to bring art and story to today's children in a way that encourages their own creativity and honors the diversity and wealth of the many traditional cultures of the world. Barefoot believes that these cultures have important messages to offer about our place in the web of life, so many titles introduce new and ancient perspectives on the world we share.

Recent titles:

Cleo the Cat by Caroline Mockford (Barefoot Beginners; age range: 1–6; pre-K–1)

How Big Is a Pig? by Clare Beaton (Barefoot Beginners; age range: 2–6; pre-K–1)

Making Minestrone by Stella Blackstone (Barefoot Beginners; age range: 4–8; pre-K–3)

Include with illustrator query: If you wish to submit illustrations, please send a representative range of full-color print samples or high-quality color copies via regular mail to the same address, together with information on your professional background. All submissions must be accompanied by return postage and packing. We cannot take responsibility for returning unsolicited material that does not include return postage and packing.

Tips and comments: Barefoot Books is an independent children's publisher dedicated to creating better books for children. In less than 10 years of publishing, Barefoot has a reputation for producing some of the finest picture books in the world. From small beginnings—the company started in 1993 with no staff—Barefoot has grown into a robust international business with a team of 28 working out of busy offices in the United Kingdom and the United States.

Barnaby Books, Inc.

3290 Pacific Heights Road
Honolulu, HI 96813
Web site: www.BarnabyBooks.com

Description: Publisher, focuses on children's literature with Hawaiian and Pacific Rim themes.

Books per year and description: Barnaby is a small press, publishing no more than one title per year.

Accepts unsolicited/unagented: Yes.

Recent fiction titles:

The Three Little Hawaiian Pigs and the Magic Shark by Donivee Martin Laird; illustrated by Carol Ann Jossem

Maui and His Magical Deeds by Kats Kajiyama

Hau Kea and the Seven Menehune by Donivee Martin Laird; illustrated by Carol Ann Jossem

Meet Edie Weinberg

Art Director

Edie Weinberg has worked on hundreds of books over her career, mostly for very young children from infants up to nine years old. In her current job as art director of Cartwheel Books, Scholastic Book Group, she's involved in 200 books in various stages at any given time. She's worked on the I SPY series, which started in 1990 and continues still. She's also worked on many titles featuring Clifford: The Big Red Dog. This is a series that started long before her time but continues with classic 8 by 8 picture books, many novelty formats, and TV tie-in books now that Clifford has his own TV show. A particular favorite book of hers is *Clifford's Schoolhouse,* a large-format, die-cut, lift-the-flap book. Another large-format lift-the-flap book that she loves is *The Great Golden Easter Egg Hunt,* featuring flaps and punch-out eggs that you collect through the book and put in an Easter basket at the end. Another favorite is *The Happy Book,* a touch-and-feel novelty book that the company created from scratch, rather than the norm through a packager.

Edie was born in Far Rockaway, New York, in 1960, though her family moved to New Jersey when she was two months old and she considers herself a Jersey girl. She has a B.F.A. in communication design from Parsons School of Design. She always wanted to work on books, and through them and their affiliation with The New School, she created her own minor in publishing. Before her current job, she was a freelance designer at Clarion Books, a staff designer at Dutton Children's Books, a staff designer at Dell Books, and assistant art director at Grosset & Dunlap. She's been at Cartwheel since 1990—11 years.

As an art editor/director, what do you look for in a children's book, and in a potential artist?

In a book I look for eye-catching, appealing artwork, something young and fun and colorful. From a potential artist, the same but also a sense of style, whether its mastery of a medium or just a particular graphic sense.

Do you have any advice for an artist starting out in the children's book field, in terms of how to get a book published?

Don't give up! I know it's frustrating, but I always say if talent and a strong portfolio are all that's needed for a successful illustration career, there'd be a lot of happy and satisfied creative people out there. But we all know that's just not the way of the world. We all know it's not just talent. I have over 30 feet of art samples in my office filled with samples from talented illustrators. A great deal of it is luck and finding the right place. I really do look in those files from time to time, but the majority of projects are not assigned that way.

Find a way to make your samples stand out. I recently got a folded circus tent filled with small samples of different characters. It's fun, but the work itself was not my favorite and it shows me the illustrator was not aware of a current dictum: the circus doesn't sell; it just doesn't have the cachet it used to when I was a kid (no one runs away to the circus any more!). So, even with cleverly conceptualized samples, they can help you hang out on the art director's desk for a while, but ultimately it's the work that will get that decision made.

Humor is always good to include/show off. There is an illustrator who has been sending me hilarious samples for years (Terry Sirrell). He finally got an assignment last year. The humor made me chuckle every time I went past his samples. Reillustrating scenes from familiar tales is also a good way to help your images stick in the art director's brain. A few scenes to show you can manage continuity of character is also helpful. The sad truth is there's no magic formula; just keep plugging away doing good works, and hopefully it will be rewarded with rewarding assignments.

Sometimes submitting a dummy is a good way to get your stuff seen by editorial as well. Even if it's rejected, it could come back with "Maybe they'd be good for this other project I haven't told you about yet."

Do you prefer that artists have reps when they come to you with a book idea?

I'm willing to work with agents, but as far as I'm concerned it's no guarantee of quality. The only time when I seek out an agent is when I have a large licensed property that needs a lot of art at once. I find it does simplify things for me to go to that one entity and have them help keep track of who's doing what and keeping them all on schedule. For the most part I'm willing to work directly with individual illustrators or through their agent.

Do you have any advice, in terms of finding an art rep, for an illustrator starting out?

Find someone who believes in you and your talent and who you feel comfortable working with. Keep in mind this is not a prerequisite for getting work, so don't feel you have to sign up with someone right away—it will be worth the wait.

Do authors and illustrators usually approach you together, or do you approach an illustrator when you have a project in mind?

When a book comes as a package deal [text and illustrations], it usually is through editorial. If they're paired already before they hit my desk, it makes my job that much easier. It's not a necessity at all, though again, it can be a good way to get your work considered, to get into the editors' radar even if ultimately the project doesn't happen.

What, in your opinion, makes an illustrator easy to work with?

Many of the illustrators I work with are truly wonderful to work with. They are creative individuals who are usually so happy to be working they're on their best behavior. An important thing to keep in mind is that getting a book published is truly a team effort. That means many people get to put their two cents in. An illustrator who is willing to make adjustments, and not negotiate each request for change, is wonderful. An illustrator who meets the schedule they agreed to (and often my schedules are really short!) is golden! If I could magically modify behaviors, meeting deadlines would definitely be the change I'd make.

Do you recommend formal training for children's book illustration, or do you think it's a question of practice, or of natural ability?

Formal art training is invaluable though not necessary for some styles/looks. I don't think the training needs to be in "children's books"; I think the best children's books training is to go to stores and see what's out there, what's selling.

Is there anything else you'd like to say to aspiring authors and illustrators of children's books?

Don't give up, but don't give up your day job!

BARRON'S EDUCATIONAL SERIES

250 Wireless Boulevard
Happauge, NY 11788
(800) 645-3476, ext. 259

Description: Book publisher.

Established: 1942.

Key people:

Publisher: Ellen Sibley

Acquisitions/submissions editor: Wayne Barr

Accepts unsolicited/unagented: Yes.

Description of fiction titles: Mostly juvenile books like *The Tickly Monster* and *Chunky Farm* books.

Recent fiction titles:

The Tickly Monster by Andrea Doering; illustrated by Sue King
Chunky Farm Cow, illustrated by Emily Bolam
Chunky Farm Sheep, illustrated by Emily Bolam

Description of nonfiction titles: Focus on student test prep books. Also many books on animals, arts and crafts, and new age subjects.

Recent nonfiction titles:

Turtles: Animals of the Oceans (series) by Judith Hodge and Susan Brocker
Living in Space by Felicity Trotman; model by Eli Butler (text with cardboard model)
The Giant Panda by Carol Amato and David Wenzel

Preferred form of submission/contact: Query, unless the children's book manuscript is short enough.

Time to reply: Up to three months.

Time to publish: If the book is already written and edited, approximately six months.

Accepts simultaneous submissions: Yes.

Number of illustrators used annually: Many freelancers.

Desired illustrator qualifications: Unique style.

Prefer manuscript/illustration packages, or separate: Accept them together, or separately.

Include with illustrator query: Resume and samples.

Time to reply: One month.

Purchases freelance photography: Yes.

Terms for writers: Royalties with $3,000 advance against the royalties.

Terms for illustrators: Flat fee that is variable depending on the project.

Submission guidelines: Call or write for guidelines.

Tips and comments: Proofread your submissions before you mail them. When you write for children, make sure that you are targeting your age group. Children at different ages read at different levels and have different comprehension. Be sure to keep that in mind when you put pen to paper, and indicate on the submission the age group for whom you are writing.

Beach Holme

2040 W. 12th Avenue, Suite 226
Vancouver, British Columbia V6J 2G2
Canada
(604) 733-4868
(604) 733-4860 (fax)
E-mail: bhp@beachholme.bc.ca
Web site: www.beachholme.bc.ca

Description: Book publisher with primary focus on historically based works set in the Pacific Northwest and northern Canada.

Bean Sprouts

8121 Hamilton Avenue
Cincinnati, OH 45231
(513) 931-4050
(513) 931-0590 (fax)
E-mail: customerservice@standardpub.com
Web site: www.standardpub.com

Corporate structure/parent: Standard Publishing.

Description: Book publisher of Children's Christian books, Sunday school curriculum, vacation Bible school materials, and other Christian education resources.

Established: 1866.

Key people:

Publisher: Mark Taylor

Books per year and description: Approximately 60, including picture books, board books, and coloring books.

Percentage by first-time authors: Approximately 10 percent.

Seeks: Picture books; juvenile picture series.

Accepts unsolicited/unagented: Yes.

Description of fiction titles: Must be real-life but child-friendly situations that incorporate clearly stated Christian values.

Recent fiction titles:

Lost in the Store by Clare Mishica (little girl gets separated from her mother in a store, but she prays to God and remembers the advice her mother gave her about what to do if she ever gets lost)

Tell the Truth, Tyler! by Jodee McConnaughay

Can God See Me? by Jodee McConnaughay

Preferred fiction titles: Not looking for fantasy, fairy tales, or science fiction

Description of nonfiction titles: Primarily Bible stories or creation science books for kids and devotional stories.

Recent nonfiction titles:
God Made Outer Space by Heno Head, Jr.
Hurry Up Noah! by Patricia S. Mahany

Preferred nonfiction titles: Not looking for nonfiction submissions right now.

Preferred form of submission/contact: Write or call for writer's guidelines.

Time to reply: Up to three months.

Time to publish: Usually within 18 months.

Accepts simultaneous submissions: Yes.

Number of illustrators used annually: Approximately 10 to 15.

Desired illustrator qualifications: Drawing ability—likes to have a variety of styles and approaches to select from as well as samples of good color sense and layout.

Prefer manuscript/illustration packages, or separate: Prefers separately but no objection to viewing art with the basis (text) for the scene or illustration.

Include with illustrator query: Samples—good samples to keep on file for editors to review for upcoming projects.

Time to reply: Responds when interested in the artists' work.

Purchases freelance photography: Some.

Preferred photography: Variable by project.

Terms for writers: Variable by project.

Terms for illustrators: No set terms at this time.

Submission guidelines: Writers can call (513) 931-4050, write (with an SASE), or look on our Web site for guidelines.

Tips and comments: Send only samples that can be kept on file—artwork is not returned.

Behrman House

11 Edison Place
Springfield, NJ 07081
(973) 379-7200
(973) 379-7280 (fax)

Description: Publisher focusing on Judaism and Jewish history, culture, holidays, and ethics.

Benchmark Books

99 White Plains Road
Tarrytown, NY 10591

Corporate structure/parent: Marshall Cavendish Corporation.

Description: Benchmark is the school-and-library imprint of Marshall Cavendish, publishing books for children in grades K to 8.

Established: Cavendish established in 1975; Benchmark, 1994.

Key people:

President: Albert Lee

Benchmark editorial director: Kate Nunn

Art director: Jean Krulis

Acquisitions/submissions editors: Senior editor: Joyce Stanton; editors: Angela Catalano and Douglas Sanders; assistant editor: Molly Morrison

Books per year and description: Approximately 120 curriculum-related topics: social studies; science; American and world history and cultures.

Percentage by first-time authors: Approximately 5 percent.

Seeks: Series only; no single titles. Look for relationship to curriculum or high interest

Accepts unsolicited/unagented: Yes

Description of nonfiction titles: Strong narratives with high accuracy.

Preferred nonfiction titles: Looking for quality. Series ideas often generated in-house. No publishing for niche markets; rather, the company seeks an interesting angle on a mainstream topic.

Preferred form of submission/contact: By query letter, with a writing sample or outline.

Time to reply: 90 days at the outside.

Time to publish: Accepts the concept for a series, not completed manuscripts. About two years from time contract signed.

Accepts simultaneous submissions: Yes.

Number of illustrators used annually: Very few. Relies mostly on photographs.

Desired illustrator qualifications: Mostly cartographers and scientific illustrators. Looking for appeal and accuracy.

Photography: The company uses photo researchers, who rely on freelancers and archives for photos. Editors do not review photographers' work.

Terms for writers: Mixture of flat fee and royalty, which is based on the net price of the book.

Terms for illustrators: Illustrations tend to be single pieces of art—usually flat fee.

Submission guidelines: Send query letter and sample of work. Will not respond to e-mail queries.

Tips and comments: Check out the Web site. Be familiar with both the company's market and its publishing history. Talent as a writer or illustrator is only part of the picture. You need to become savvy about the world you wish to become a part of. Learn about different publishers. Send queries to the right people.

BENEFACTORY

925 North Milwaukee Avenue, Suite 1010
Wheeling, IL 60090
(847) 919-1777
(847) 919-2777 (fax)
Web site: www.readplay.com

Description: Publishes true stories about real animals in partnership with the Humane Society of the United States and the National Wildlife Federation.

Berry Books

425 West Schrock Road
Westerville, OH 43081
(614) 898-5630
E-mail: CPaulson@BerryBooks.com
Web site: www.berrybooks.com

Description: Children's Berry Books are about fun, food, fiber, and related products that we all need but that most people take for granted. The literature focuses on the vast world of agriculture.

Recent fiction titles:

The Making of Strawberry (Kathy and Joe decide to help save the family corn crop from pesky crows by creating a scarecrow.)

Strawberry Meets Rex (Rex the crow injures himself while trying to steel food from Strawberry the friendly scarecrow.)

An August Game (Strawberry and Rex have a contest to look for things that you see or do on a farm that begin with the letters of the alphabet.)

Maude's Ice Cream (A dairy cow's fantasy written in rhyme)

Bess Press

3565 Harding Avenue
Honolulu, HI 96816
(808) 734-7159
(808) 732-3627 (fax)
Web site: www.besspress.com

Description: Publisher with a focus on children's literature with Hawaiian and Pacific Rim themes.

Established: 1979.

Seeks: Bess Press specializes in textbooks on Hawaiian history, language, culture, and science; Pacific history and culture; Asian and Pacific languages; and reference works. Curriculum materials are primarily used at the K to 12 level. Bess Press also publishes general interest titles about Hawaii including children's books in the following categories: Elementary, intermediate, high school, and college textbooks about Hawaii and the Pacific; trade books (children's, cookbooks, guidebooks, etc.) about Hawaii; and introductory Pacific language materials

Accepts unsolicited/unagented: Yes.

Recent fiction titles:

The Musubi Man: Hawai'i's Gingerbread Man, illustrated by Pat Hall

Sumorella: A Hawai'i Cinderella Story, illustrated by Esther Szegedy

Let's Call Him Lau-WiliWili-HumuHumu-NukuNuku-NukuNuku-Apua'a-'oi-'oi by Tim Myers; illustrated by Daryl Arakaki

Too Many Curls by Marilyn Kahalewai and Karen Poepoe

Recent nonfiction titles:

Hawaii's Royal History, rev. ed. by Helen Wong and Dr. Ann Rayson

Preferred form of submission/contact: Manuscript for shorter books; outline and sample chapter for longer submissions.

Time to reply: Tries to respond within three to four weeks.

Submission guidelines: Please submit hard copy and self-addressed stamped envelope. For longer books, send an outline and sample chapter. It is not necessary to send illustrations, but if you do, Bess Press prefers photocopies.

Tips and comments: Please see our catalog or Web site for a listing of individual titles now in print.

Bethany House Publishers

11400 Hampshire Avenue South
Minneapolis, MN 55438
(952) 829-2572 (fax)
Web site: www.bethanyhouse.com

Description: Evangelical book publisher.

Seeks: Only series fiction, no stand-alones.

Recent fiction titles:

Three Cousins Detective Club (series)

Mandie Books

Girls Only

Bloodhounds, Inc.

Also partner with Focus on the Family to bring their Kidwitness Tales; the Christy Miller series.

Recent nonfiction titles:

What Children Need to Know When Parents Get Divorced

What's with the Mutant in the Microscope?

Bethany Backyard titles:

Janetter Oke's Animal Friends

The Wonderful Way Babies Are Made

Preferred form of submission/contact: Address the proposal to the attention of the Youth Department, and include a self-addressed stamped envelope if you wish your material returned. No submissions via e-mail or fax. Send a clearly typed, double-spaced synopsis of the book and the first three chapters. Be sure to keep a copy for yourself; Bethany cannot be responsible for lost or damaged submissions. Include a brief description of your writing experience, religious background, and educational credentials.

Time to reply: Within 12 weeks.

Submission guidelines: Write with an SASE or check the Web site for guidelines.

Tips and comments: Bethany House is an evangelical publisher of books in a broad range of categories, from preschool to adult. As the premier publisher of youth fiction in the Christian market, the list contains many bestselling series. No unsolicited proposals for full-color picture books. No cartoons, biographies, poetry, or short stories. Nonfiction manuscripts should fall between 20,000 and 40,000 words for middle readers and 30,000 and 40,000 words for teens. *Before you send your manuscript*: Is the language appropriate for the intended age group? Have you checked your facts? Is the plot too complex? Too simplistic? Is the theme realistic and meaningful to today's youth? Are there books in the market similar to your idea? If so, what makes yours unique? Does your main character have a clearly defined goal he or she is trying to achieve? Does your story build to a natural, effective climax? *Do your homework*: Familiarize yourself with the company and what types of books are published. Study the catalog and your local Christian bookstore shelves to determine where there might be a need. (To obtain a copy of the Bethany catalog, send an 11 by 14-inch self-addressed envelope with five first-class stamps affixed.)

Beyond Words Publishing, Inc.

20827 N.W. Cornell Road, Suite 500
Hillsboro, Or 97124-9808
E-mail: info@beyondword.com
Web site: www.beyondword.com

Description: Book publisher.
Established: 1983.
Key people:
Publisher: Richard Cohn
Editor in chief: Cynthia Black
Director of the Children's Division: Michelle Roehm
Acquisitions/submissions editor: Barbara Mann, Children's Acquisitions
Books per year and description: Four to six young adult nonfiction books a year and two to four picture books a year.
Percentage by first-time authors: About half of titles come from first-time authors.
Seeks: Looking for kid's advice books, nonfiction books written by kids, and picture books.
Accepts unsolicited/unagented: Yes, but no e-mail submissions are accepted.
Description of fiction titles: Fiction titles limited to picture books. Categories covered in the past include multicultural stories/themes, historical fiction, folktales, fairy tales, and other stories that are inspiring to children.
Recent fiction titles:
Abbie Against the Storm by Marcia Vaughan
Picture Book (historical fiction)
She Is Born by Virginia Kroll
All Ages Picture Book (celebrating the birth of a daughter)
Preferred fiction titles: Looking for original and creative children's stories.

Description of nonfiction titles: Nonfiction titles encourage kids to go for their dreams. In the past, have published advice books and career books for kids.

Recent nonfiction titles:

Girls Who Rocked the World 1 & 2 by Amelie Welden and Michelle Roehm

Throw Like a Girl by Shelley Frost and Ann Troussieux

The Girls' Life Guide to Growing Up by Karen Bokram and Alexis Sinex

Preferred nonfiction titles: Looking for nonfiction advice books for kids.

Preferred form of submission/contact: A writer can send a manuscript or proposal with a cover letter. Optional: Authors can also include market research/publicity ideas on a separate page.

Time to reply: Three to six months.

Time to publish: One to two years.

Accepts simultaneous submissions: Yes.

Number of illustrators used annually: Five to 10 illustrators.

Desired illustrator qualifications: Looking for black-and-white illustrations for our nonfiction books and color illustrations for picture books.

Prefer manuscript/illustration packages, or separate: Accept manuscript/illustration packages.

Include with illustrator query: Color copy samples of an illustrator's work submitted with a query letter.

Time to reply: Typically, one to three months.

Purchases freelance photography: No.

Submission guidelines: Call or visit the Web site for guidelines.

Tips and comments: Learn more about the company by visiting the Web site to see whether your work would be a good match. Research is the key—browse through some of the books and familiarize yourself with the house style.

BLACKBIRCH PRESS, INC.

260 Amity Road
PO Box 3573
Woodbridge, CT 06525
(203) 387-7525
(203) 389-1596 (fax)
E-mail: staff@blackbirch.com
Web site: www.blackbirch.com

Description: Publisher.

Accepts unsolicited/unagented: Only from previously published authors.

Description of fiction titles: Publishes a very small number of fiction titles, all of which are picture books for ages 5 to 8.

Recent fiction titles:

Monsieur Thermidor by Richard Kidd

Salt-dough Sculptures by Lindsey Kidd

The Lonely Wizard written and illustrated by Helmut Kollars

Recent nonfiction titles:

THE LIBRARY OF FAMOUS WOMEN series (awe-inspiring women who've changed the world)

NOTORIOUS AMERICANS AND THEIR TIMES series (some of the most-hated, most-feared figures in U.S. history)

OLYMPIC GOLD! series (the incredible stories behind the world's greatest Olympic athletes)

EyeOpeners! (all about animal vision)

LIFE IN THE SEA series (exciting underwater adventures in science)

NATURE CLOSE-UP series (easy-to-do projects and cool experiments)

Preferred nonfiction titles: 95 percent of titles are nonfiction series and run 4,000 to 8,000 words in length.

Preferred form of submission/contact: *Nonfiction:* Resume and brief description of your qualifications plus a brief synopsis—less than one page. *Fiction:* Full manuscript (which doesn't need returning), with resume and cover letter.

Time to reply: Multiple months. Please do not call to "check in."

Terms for writers: Advance/royalty basis.

Submission guidelines: Prefers not to have to return submissions.

BLUE SKY PRESS

555 Broadway
New York, NY 10012
(212) 343-6100
Web site: www.scholastic.com

Corporate structure/parent: Scholastic Inc.

Description: Publisher of hardcover children's fiction and nonfiction.

BOINGO BOOKS

12720 Yardly Drive
Boca Raton, FL 33428

Description: Book packager. Handles children's books but only through publishers. Does not accept queries or manuscripts.

BOYDS MILLS PRESS

815 Church Street
Honesdale, PA 18431
(570) 253-1164
Web site: www.boydsmillspress.com

Meet Larry Rosler

Editorial Director

Larry Rosler is the editorial director at Boyds Mills Press. He has worked on more than 150 titles for preschool through young adult, such as *The Always Prayer Shawl* by Sheldon Oberman and illustrated by Ted Lewin; *Barn Savers* by Linda Oatman High and illustrated by Ted Lewin; *How God Fix Jonah* by Lorenz Graham and illustrated by Ashley Bryan; *Merry Christmas, Old Armadillo* by Larry Dane Brimner and illustrated by Dominic Catalano; *Rio Grande* by Peter Lourie. He was born in Newark, New Jersey, on April 19, 1951. He has a B.A. in communications from Seton Hall University. Before his current job, he was assistant to the director of school and library programs at Henry Holt and Company, assistant to the editorial director at Henry Holt and Company, and worked in a bookstore for a couple of years.

As an editor, what do you look for in a children's book and in a potential author?

Something fresh and inventive (but not trendy), informative and entertaining; novels with substance and picture books with staying power.

Do you have any advice for an author starting out in the children's book field, in terms of how to get a book published?

Writers starting out should consider writing from their hearts and write the story they need to tell. If they follow a trend, they're bound to be left behind. The current trend quickly becomes yesterday's news. Meeting editors through conferences and workshops also can be helpful, as well as participating in writing groups. And, of course, read the best in children's books and the best in literature in general.

Do you prefer that authors have agents when they come to you with a book idea?

At Boyds Mills Press, all manuscripts receive equal consideration, whether agented or not.

Do you work with illustrators?

At Boyds Mills Press, we normally approach the illustrator after we've found the manuscript. We're happy to consider joint ventures, but aspiring writers and illustrators should be cautious of these types of collaborations. If either of the collaborators' work appears amateurish, it can sink the book. At the outset, I think it's wiser to go it alone.

What, in your opinion, makes an author easy to work with? Difficult to work with? If you could magically modify the behavior of all authors, what would you have them do to make your job more pleasant? How about for illustrators?

I'm not sure it's a matter of making an editor's job more pleasant. It has more to do with helping the writer make his or her book the best it can be. The editor may have some insights into how that might be accomplished. It's easier to work with a writer who's willing to consider suggestions.

continues

Some writers are resistant to change, and that can make the process a struggle. I think the same applies to illustrators.

Do you recommend formal training for children's book writers, or do you think it's a question of practice or of natural ability?

I think some people are born with a talent for narrative, just as some are born with a talent for music. But talent needs to be developed, and that's the value of practice and study.

Corporate structure/parent: Highlights for Children, Inc.

Description: Book publisher of quality books for children.

Established: 1990.

Key people:

Publisher: Kent Brown Jr.

Editorial director: Larry Rosler

Manuscript coordinator: Beth Troop

Books per year and description: 25 picture books; 4 books of poetry; 4 novels; 10 nonfiction.

Percentage by first-time authors: 5 to 10 percent.

Seeks: Quality books with fresh ideas and subject matter and real literary merit. Genres of interest include picture books, middle-grade and young adult novels, nonfiction and poetry collections.

Accepts unsolicited/unagented: Yes.

Description of fiction titles: The best way to gain insight into the types of books published is to visit the Web site.

Recent fiction titles:

Cat on Wheels by Larry Dane Brimner (picture book)

Mr. Beans by Dayton O. Hyde (novel)

An Alligator Ate My Brother by Mary Olson (picture book)

Preferred fiction titles: Looking for stories with fresh ideas. No fantasy or romance. Avoid well-worn themes.

Description of nonfiction titles: The best way to gain insight into the types of books published is to visit the Web site.

Recent nonfiction titles:

See the Stars by Ken Croswell

Mississippi River by Peter Lourie

What's Opposite by Stephen Swinburne

Preferred nonfiction titles: Looking for general interest nonfiction but *not* material that is more appropriate for the educational market.

Preferred form of submission/contact: Authors may send the entire manuscript; however, if it's a novel, they may wish to query first. Be sure to include an SASE for a reply.

Time to reply: 30 days.

Time to publish: It is variable based on needs and/or illustrator availability.

Accepts simultaneous submissions: Yes.

Number of illustrators used annually: Varies.

Desired illustrator qualifications: Artists who can creatively interpret picture book text and transfer ideas into lively art that children will enjoy.

Prefer manuscript/illustration packages, or separate: If the author/artist is experienced in children's publishing, willing to review a manuscript with accompanying illustrations. Otherwise, prefers to review them separately.

Include with illustrator query: Resume and samples.

Time to reply: Varies.

Purchases freelance photography: No.

Terms for writers: Rates vary.

Terms for illustrators: Rates vary.

Submission guidelines: Make requests for guidelines in writing. Be sure to enclose a letter-sized SASE.

Tips and comments: Study the company's books. Don't assume that because the list includes a certain book on a certain topic, more of the same will be wanted. Writers may want to emulate the *style* of the company's books but not necessarily the subject matter. Study the various styles of our artwork. If you feel your style fits with it, send some samples to be kept on file. *Do not* send manuscripts that are more suitable for the adult market.

CALVIN PARTNERSHIP, LLC

40 Ardmore Road
Ho-Ho-Kus, NJ 07423-1008
(201) 670-8412
(201) 670-0464 (fax)
E-mail: jahelka@attglobal.net

Description: Children's book publisher.

Established: 1998.

Key people:

Partners: Alvin R. Jahelka and Carole S. Ford

Books per year and description: Four per year, for preschool (ages 1 to 5).

Percentage by first-time authors: 100 percent.

Accepts unsolicited/unagented: No manuscripts.

Description of fiction titles: Preschool-appropriate.

Preferred form of submission/contact: Query.

Time to reply: One week.

Accepts simultaneous submissions: No.

Number of illustrators used annually: One.

Desired illustrator qualifications: Fun, interesting characters .

Prefer manuscript/illustration packages, or separate: No packages.

Include with illustrator query: Samples.

Time to reply: One week.
Tips and comments: Calvin Partnership's books entertain and teach.

Candlewick Press

2067 Massachusetts Avenue
Cambridge, MA 02140
(617) 661-3330
(617) 661-0565 (fax)
Web site: www.candlewick.com

Corporate structure/parent: Walker Books, UK
Description: Independent children's book publisher.
Established: 1991.
Key people:
Publisher: Karen Latz
Executive editor: Mary Lee Donovan
Editorial director: Liz Bicknell
Editor: Gale Pryor
Associate editors: Kara LaReau and Cynthia Platt

Books per year and description: 150 to 200 new titles annually: picture books, fiction (middle grade and YA), novelty books, board books, poetry, nonfiction, easy readers, Brand New Readers.

Percentage by first-time authors: Approximately 10 percent; Kate DiCamillo, Matt Tavares, and Tobin Anderson are all first-time authors Candlewick has published.

Seeks: Text that meets current standards—or exceeds them. No one who is unfamiliar with the list should submit material.

Accepts unsolicited/unagented: Yes, but do your homework. *Education* (i.e., prepping yourself) *is the key* to a successful manuscript!

Description of fiction titles: Literary; cutting-edge; excellent. List is small and deliberately so.

Recent fiction titles:
Because of Winn-Dixie by Kate DiCamillo
The Brimstone Journals by Ron Koertge
Fire, Bed, and Bone by Henrietta Branford

Preferred fiction titles: Not looking for formulaic, highly plot-driven novels that lack voice, authenticity, or engaging characters.

Description of nonfiction titles: Original, quirky, high-production values. Some series (e.g., *Read and Wonder*), but mostly single titles.

Recent nonfiction titles:
Vision of Beauty by Kathryn Lasky; illustrated by Nneka Bennett
Castle Diary by Richard Platt; illustrated by Chris Riddell
Art of Science by Jay Young; illustrated by a selection of artists
Kennedy Assassinated by Wilborn Hampton
It's So Amazing! by Robie Harris; illustrated by Michael Emberley

Preferred nonfiction titles: Looking for passion, vision, fascinating subject matter, a unique voice, and personal experience.

Preferred form of submission/contact: *Novels:* Send a query letter with pertinent details of the novel and the author's experience to "Manuscript Submissions." *Picture books:* Send manuscript with cover letter to "Manuscript Submissions." *Please enclose an SASE for return of materials!*

Time to reply: Six weeks to three months.

Time to publish: If it is not illustrated, within 18 months; if illustrated, it varies based on the artist's schedule.

Accepts simultaneous submissions: Yes.

Number of illustrators used annually: Approximately 50.

Desired illustrator qualifications: A fresh approach; ability to extend a story. Illustrators include Jules Feiffer, Chris Raschka, Vladimir Radonsky, Rosemary Wells, Elisa Kleven, Laura Kuasnosky, Scott Nash, P. J. Lynch, Kevin Hawkes, Lucy Cousins, and Anita Jeram.

Prefer manuscript/illustration packages, or separate: Separately, unless both the author and illustrator are extremely committed to one another—and extremely talented.

Include with illustrator query: Resume, samples, and tear sheets.

Time to reply: Six weeks to three months.

Submission guidelines: Call; there is a recording set up to answer guidelines questions. Or go to the Web site.

Tips and comments: *Do your research!* Borrow Candlewick books from your library or look at them in bookstores. Observe what kinds of books Candlewick publishes to decide whether yours meet the company's standards and would fit well on the list. *Candlewick is very discriminating!* Candlewick currently receives more than 12,000 manuscript submissions a year and looks at each one. Do not abuse this service by sending inappropriate materials or ones that do not meet the company's standards. Do not complain when you receive a form letter of rejection. Do not telephone to inquire where your manuscript (among the other 11,999) may be. Do take writing very seriously, as seriously as Candlewick does.

CANDY CANE PRESS

535 Metroplex Drive, Suite 250
Nashville, TN 37211
(615) 333-0478
(615) 781-1447 (fax)

Corporate structure/parent: Ideals Publications

Description: Book and magazine publisher; *Ideals* magazine (six issues annually); Candy Cane Press (children's books); holiday/historical books for adults.

Established: 1944.

Key people:

Publisher: Patricia Pingry

Books per year and description: Variable; stories usually center around holidays and biblical characters.

Seeks: Board books/picture books for children on a growing number of subjects.

Accepts unsolicited/unagented: Yes.

Description of fiction titles: No fiction for children.

Description of nonfiction titles: Children's books have story lines centered around holidays, some historical events, and Bible stories.

Recent nonfiction titles:

The Story of America's Birthday

The Story of the Ten Commandments

(Some titles are translated and sold in Spanish.)

Preferred nonfiction titles: 200 words for board books; 1,000 words for picture books; variety of educational subjects.

Preferred form of submission/contact: Manuscript with an SASE. *No query letters.*

Time to reply: Six to eight weeks.

Accepts simultaneous submissions: Yes.

Prefer manuscript/illustration packages, or separate: No illustrations with manuscripts.

Include with illustrator query: Tear sheets.

Purchases freelance photography: No.

Preferred photography: Photos centered around themes of the seasons (for *Ideals* magazine).

Terms for writers: Purchases one-time North American rights only. Payment policy is $0.10 per word for poem published.

Terms for illustrators: Variable depending on the project.

Submission guidelines: Send SASE with request for guidelines.

Tips and comments: Familiarize yourself with the company's publications before submitting manuscripts. Request writer's guidelines first! Please submit only tear sheets of previously published illustrations. Media preferred are watercolors, gouaches, oils, colored pencils, pen and ink, and pastels.

Carolrhoda Books, Inc.

241 First Avenue N.
Minneapolis, MN 55401
(612) 332-3344
(612) 332-7615 (fax)
Web site: www.lernerbooks.com

Corporate structure/parent: Lerner Publishing Group.

Description: Book publisher.

Established: Established in 1969, Carolrhoda Books features critically acclaimed and award-winning picture books, nonfiction, and fiction titles for children in grades K to 6.

Key people:

Acquisitions/submissions editor: The submissions editor for Carolrhoda Books is Rebecca Poole. An SASE is required for all submissions. *No phone calls, please.*

Books per year and description: Only one or two picture books each year.

Seeks: Carolrhoda Books publishes high-quality fiction and nonfiction for children ages 4 to 12. The company specializes in nonfiction: biographies, photo essays, nature and science books, beginning readers, and books published in series. Looking for nonfiction that is interesting and entertaining as well as informative. Also publishes some fiction for ages 7 to 10 and some historical fiction for ages 8 to 12.

Accepts unsolicited/unagented: Yes.

Preferred titles: Unique, honest stories that stay away from unoriginal plots, moralizing, religious themes, and anthropomorphic protagonists. In both fiction and nonfiction, Carolrhoda is especially interested in new ideas and fresh topics. Carolrhoda likes to see multicultural themes. Make sure your writing avoids racial and sexual stereotypes. Carolrhoda does not publish alphabet books, textbooks, workbooks, songbooks, puzzles, plays, or religious material.

Preferred form of submission/contact: Prefers completed manuscript, but will accept an outline and sample chapters for longer biographies or fiction.

Time to reply: Allow two to six months for a response (response time is generally three to four months). You will be notified of a decision regarding your manuscript at the earliest possible time. Please do not expect a personal response from an editor, as time does not permit this. If you would like confirmation that your manuscript has been received, please send a self-addressed stamped postcard.

Prefer manuscript/illustration packages, or separate: You do not need to send art with your submission as Carolrhoda generally commissions its own artists, but if you are sending art samples, do not send originals.

Include with illustrator query: Samples.

Submission guidelines: Carolrhoda accepts requests for guidelines and catalogs year-round. Do not address these requests to Ms. Poole. Please address requests to Guideline Request and send a business-sized SASE. To receive both a catalog and guidelines, write to Catalog Request and send a 9 by 12-inch SASE with $3.20 postage.

Tips and comments: The best way to familiarize yourself with the list is to study the catalog or find Carolrhoda books in the library. For a catalog, send a self-addressed 9 by 12-inch envelope with $3.20 in postage. Submissions are accepted in March and October *only*. Submissions received in any month other than March or October will be returned *unopened* to the sender. Lerner Publishing Group does not publish alphabet books, puzzle books, song books, textbooks, workbooks, religious subject matter, or plays.

Cartwheel Books

555 Broadway
New York, NY 10012-3999
(212) 343-4404
(212) 343-4444 (fax)
E-mail: eweinberg@scholastic.com

Corporate structure/parent: Scholastic, Inc.

Description: Book publisher.

Established: 1920.

Key people:

Publisher: Bernette G. Ford

Acquisitions/submissions editors: Grace Maccarone; Jane Gerver; Sonia Black; Liza Baker

Books per year and description: 200 titles in jacketed hard covers, novelty books, board books, and original paperbacks.

Percentage by first-time authors: 25 percent.

Seeks: Fun and young. A new take on classic themes such as color or the alphabet.

Accepts unsolicited/unagented: Yes.

Description of fiction titles: Picture books.

Description of nonfiction titles: Picture books.

Preferred form of submission/contact: Send query, manuscript, or writing samples to the editorial department.

Time to reply: Variable.

Time to publish: One to two years.

Accepts simultaneous submissions: Yes.

Number of illustrators used annually: 125.

Desired illustrator qualifications: Good samples/portfolio showing young lively kids, cute fuzzy animals.

Prefer manuscript/illustration packages, or separate: Either. Together is fine.

Include with illustrator query: Samples, tear sheets, or personal portfolio. The art department likes to meet with prospective illustrators.

Time to reply: One to two months.

Purchases freelance photography: Yes.

Preferred photography: Usually after good people shots—candid, unposed, and natural.

Terms for writers: Advance against royalties; 5 percent total to be split between the author and the illustrator.

Terms for illustrators: Advance against royalties; 5 percent total to be split between the author and the illustrator.

Submission guidelines: Write with an SASE and request guidelines.

Tips and comments: Don't give up!

Chelsea House Publishers

1974 Sproul Road, Suite 400
Broomall, PA 19008
(800) 848-BOOK
E-mail: Sales@ChelseaHouse.com
Web site: www.chelseahouse.com

Description: For over 30 years, Chelsea House has been a quality publisher of nonfiction books for children and young adults.

Recent nonfiction titles:

African American Answer Book by Richard S. Rennert (six volumes including *Arts and Entertainment* and *Biography*)

20th Century Pop Culture by Dan Epstein (six volumes including *The Early Years to the Forties* and *The Fifties*, *The Sixties*, etc.)

Chariot Books

4050 Lee Vance View
Colorado Springs, CO 80918
(719) 536-3271
(719) 536-3269 (fax)

Corporate structure/parent: Chariot Victor Publishing.

Description: Book publisher. Chariot Books is the imprint for children's books, ages 1 through 12, focusing on books that help children apply their faith to life, build Christian character, and instill values.

Accepts unsolicited/unagented: No unsolicited manuscripts.

Description of titles: Chariot books go primarily to the family and the home, rather than to the church. Each book helps readers better understand themselves, their relationship to God, and/or the message of the Bible. Chariot publishes Bible story and information books, fiction, nonfiction, devotionals, and occasionally activity books.

Preferred form of submission/contact: Query letter with an SASE should be addressed to the editorial assistant. Chariot Victor Publishing assumes no responsibility for unsolicited material.

Tips and comments: Before writing for Chariot Victor Publishing, become familiar with the type of books the company publishes. They can be found in bookstores throughout the United States and Canada.

Charlesbridge Publishing

85 Main Street
Watertown, MA 02472
(617) 926-0329
(617) 926-5720 (fax)
E-mail: tradeeditorial@charlesbridge.com
Web site: www.charlesbridge.com

Description: Book publisher.

Established: 1980.

Books per year and description: Picture books in fiction and nonfiction. Fiction books include adventure, concept, contemporary, multicultural, and history. Nonfiction books include animal, biography, healthy, history, multicultural, and science.

Seeks: Charlesbridge Publishing has three imprints: *Charlesbridge, a* nonfiction imprint (focus on appealing and educational nature, science, and social studies); *Talewinds* (lively, plot-driven picture books); and *Whispering Coyote* (cozy, fun stories, in whimsical verse or prose).

Accepts unsolicited/unagented: Yes but they must be *exclusive submissions.*

Recent fiction titles:

Otto's Rainy Day by Natasha Yim (Talewinds imprint)

Firefly Night by Carole Gerber (Whispering Coyote imprint)

Recent nonfiction titles:

Hail to the Chief by Don Robb (Charlesbridge)

Preferred form of submission/contact: Please send submissions to the submissions editor. All submissions envelopes and cover letters must be marked "Exclusive Submission." Send complete manuscript; no queries, please.

Time to reply: Three months.

Accepts simultaneous submissions: No.

Number of illustrators used annually: Five to 10.

Prefer manuscript/illustration packages, or separate: Prefer to review manuscripts and illustrations separately but will review them together—each element should be able to stand on its own.

Include with illustrator query: Send samples and tear sheets. *No original artwork, please.*

Time to reply: Reply only if interested in the artist's work.

Purchases freelance photography: Not usually.

Submission guidelines: Write for a copy of guidelines and please include an SASE.

Chicago Review Press, Inc.

814 N. Franklin Street
Chicago, IL 60610
(312) 337-0747

Description: Book publisher.

Established: 1973.

Key people:

Publisher: Linda Matthews

Acquisitions/submissions editor: Cynthia Sherry

Books per year and description: Eight books; all activity related for children of all ages.

Percentage by first-time authors: 25 percent.

Seeks: High-quality activity books.

Accepts unsolicited/unagented: Yes.

Preferred form of submission/contact: Send a query letter or short proposal with an SASE.

Time to reply: Four to eight weeks.

Time to publish: 12 to 18 months.

Accepts simultaneous submissions: Yes.

Number of illustrators used annually: Six.

Prefer manuscript/illustration packages, or separate: Separately.

Include with illustrator query: Samples and tear sheets.

Time to reply: Replies only if interested.

Purchases freelance photography: Occasionally.

Preferred photography: Buys photos only when looking for a particular image or subject, so it is very variable.

Terms for writers: It works on a sliding scale and varies from one writer to the next. A general guideline would be: 7½ to 12½ percent sliding scale and $2,000 to $6,000 advance.

Terms for illustrators: Work-for-hire contracts only. Rates vary based on the project

Submission guidelines: Request by mail with an SASE.

CHILDREN'S BOOK PRESS

2211 Mission Street
San Francisco, CA 94110
(415) 821-3080
(415) 821-3081 (fax)
E-mail: cbookpress@cbookpress.org
Web site: www.cbookpress.org

Description: Nonprofit publisher of multicultural and bilingual picture books for children.

Established: 1975.

Books per year and description: Two children's picture books per year.

Seeks: Multicultural literature for children.

Accepts unsolicited/unagented: Only those that fit into the scope of the company's editorial guidelines.

Description of fiction titles: Short bilingual fiction stories or poetry books for children.

Recent fiction titles:

My Very Own Room/Mi propio cuartito by Amada Irma Pérez; illustrated by Maya Christina Gonzalez (Five little brothers, two parents and a house full of visiting relatives make a young Mexican girl feel crowded—she loves her family but how can she get a little space of her own?)

Angels Ride Bikes and Other Fall Poems/Los ángeles andan en bicicleta y otros poemas de otoño by Francisco Alarcón; illustrated by Maya Christina Gonzalez

Preferred form of submission/contact: A writer may send a manuscript *by mail only*.

Time to reply: Eight to 10 weeks. Please *do not* make inquiries during that time.

Time to publish: Up to 18 months.

Purchases freelance photography: No.

Submission guidelines: Send an SASE to Children's Book Press. Can also provide guidelines by e-mail, in which case you should send your request via e-mail to cbookpress@cbookpress.org.

Tips and comments: Review editorial guidelines and study current titles *before* submitting anything. The company has a very specific focus, and only publishes one book per season. The editors *almost always* seek out the authors and artists with whom they wish to work. Despite this, the company receives countless unsolicited submissions on a daily basis, which is really a waste of time *and* money for so many aspiring authors and artists. The bottom line is this: If your manuscript or art samples do not meet with the guidelines, they will be returned to you *without review* (and that's only if you include an SASE), so save yourself a great deal of time, energy, and frustration and do your homework first. Submit your manuscript or art only when you're confident that you're on the right track.

Children's Press

Grolier Publishing
90 Sherman Turnpike
Danbury, CT 06816
(203) 796-2605
(203) 797-3899 (fax)
Web site: www.publishing.grolier.com

Corporate structure/parent: Grolier Publishing.

Description: Children's Press books have shown, to the delight of tens of thousands of readers, that information, education, and entertainment are inseparable.

Established: 1945.

Books per year: Over 300 books per year.

Seeks: Children's nonfiction and early readers.

Accepts unsolicited/unagented: No.

Description of nonfiction titles: Known primarily for highly successful geography series, biographies, and True Books series, Children's Press publishes some 300 titles a year on a broad range of subjects for children from preschool through junior high.

Recent nonfiction titles:

¿Dónde está Max? by Mary E. Pearson
¿Qué está arriba cuando estás abajo? by David F. Marx
A Day with Firefighters by Jan Kottke
A Day with Paramedics by Jan Kottke
Basketball: Outside Shooting by Bill Van Gundy
Bear Attacks by Patrick J Fitzgerald
Colonial Life by Brendan January

Preferred form of submission/contact: Please query with an SASE.

Submission guidelines: Write with an SASE for guidelines.

Child's World

PO Box 326
Chanhassen, MN 55317

(800) 599-READ
(952) 906-3940
Web site: www.childsworld.com

Description: Educational publisher, curriculum based.
Established: 1968.
Accepts unsolicited/unagented: No.
Tips and comments: The goal of The Child's World is simple. The Child's World wants all young children to enjoy reading educational books.

CHINA BOOKS & PERIODICALS, INC.

2929 Twenty-fourth Street
San Francisco, CA 94110
(415) 282-2994
(415) 282-0994 (fax)
E-mail: info@chinabooks.com
Web site: www.chinabooks.com

Description: Publisher, importer, and distributor of books from and about China.
Established: 1960.
Key people:
Publisher and president: Chris Noyes
Editor in chief: Greg Jones
Books per year: One to two per year.
Percentage by first-time authors: 50 percent.
Seeks: Relating to China only—history, mythology, folktales, myths, and so forth.
Accepts unsolicited/unagented: Yes.
Description of fiction titles: Chinese fiction only—history, mythology, folktales, myths, and so forth.
Recent fiction titles:
Moon Maiden & Other Stories
Preferred fiction titles: Not actively looking right now.
Preferred nonfiction titles: Titles of interest to parents who have adopted children from China.
Preferred form of submission/contact: Query with a sample chapter. Include SASE.
Time to reply: Two to three months.
Time to publish: Within one year.
Accepts simultaneous submissions: Yes.
Purchases freelance photography: No.
Terms for writers: Negotiable and variable.
Submission guidelines: Go to the Web site at www.chinabooks.com.
Tips and comments: Make sure your work has a strong China interest (no general Asia); request the catalog or check out the Web site to see what kinds of books are featured.

Christian Ed. Publishers

9230 Trade Place
San Diego, CA 92126
(858) 578-4700
(858) 578-2431 (fax)
Web site: www.christianedwarehouse.com

Description: Bible curriculum publisher.

Established: 1951 (as Christian Workers Services Bureau).

Key people:

Publisher: David Malme

Acquisitions/submissions editor: Dr. Lon Ackelson, senior editor

Books per year and description: 96 publications for two- and three-year-old curriculum through high school curriculum.

Percentage by first-time authors: 40 percent.

Accepts unsolicited/unagented: No, all writing is by assignment only.

Description of fiction titles: Fiction is by assignment only. To fit specific themes and word counts for a specific age level. Fiction appears in Take-Home Papers.

Preferred fiction titles: Age-appropriate writing to guidelines.

Accepts simultaneous submissions: Yes

Number of illustrators used annually: Six or more.

Desired illustrator qualifications: Simple, black-and-white line drawings of people and patterns. The ability to send files in Adobe Illustrator PC or Mac.

Prefer manuscript/illustration packages, or separate: Separately.

Time to reply: Two to three weeks.

Purchases freelance photography: No.

Terms for writers: $0.03 per word.

Terms for illustrators: $10 per illustration

Submission guidelines: E-mail (from Web site) or write with an SASE.

Tips and comments: Please follow guidelines carefully. Observe the age group for which you are writing. Stay within word count.

Christian Publications/Horizon Books

3825 Hartzdale Drive
Camp Hill, PA 17011

Not accepting unsolicited manuscripts at this time.

Chronicle Books

85 Second Street, 6th Floor
San Francisco, CA 94105

(415) 537-3730
(415) 537-4460 (fax)
E-mail: frontdesk@chronbooks.com
Web site: www.chronbooks.com/Kids/index.html

Description: Book publisher.

Key people:

Acquisitions/submissions editor: Please submit manuscripts and queries to address above.

Seeks: Chronicle Books specializes in high-quality, affordable books for children (and adults) and children.

Accepts unsolicited/unagented: Yes. In some categories prefers the entire manuscript; in others, prefers a query with supporting information. Please see below for more detail.

Preferred form of submission/contact: Should include a cover letter giving a brief description of the project and what is included in the package; your proposal, including outline, introduction, illustrations list, sample captions, and text/sample chapters (approximately 30 pages of text); sample illustrations or photographs (duplicates rather than originals); a market analysis of the potential readership for the book, including title, publisher, and publication date of all similar books, with an explanation of how your book differs from each; and author/illustrator/photographer biography that includes publishing credits and credentials in the field. If desired, include a self-addressed stamped blank postcard for acknowledgment of receipt of manuscript. For fiction, *please submit the entire manuscript*, not a query letter.

Prefer manuscript/illustration packages, or separate: Together. Please see guidelines below.

Include with illustrator query: If you are interested in having your design, illustration, or photography work considered for use, please send a few nonreturnable tear sheets or samples (color copies are fine), labeled with your name, address, and phone number. Samples will be kept in reference files. If you wish to send original art, slides, photographs, you must enclose a self-addressed stamped envelope if you want the items returned. Please understand that you do this at your own risk as the company accepts no liability for unsolicited materials lost or damaged in transit or on the premises.

Time to reply: If a suitable project for your talents arises, you will be contacted at that time to schedule a portfolio review. Do not send your portfolio (original art) unless you have made specific arrangements with one of the in-house designers.

Purchases freelance photography: Please see above.

Tips and comments: Do your homework—read as many children's books as you can, and familiarize yourself with the kinds of books the company publishes. If you are interested in receiving one of the most recent Children's books catalogs, simply send an e-mail to frontdesk@chronbooks.com. Don't forget to specify which catalog (children's) you would like and your mailing address. *Please note:* Chronicle Books does not publish romances, science fiction, fantasy, westerns, or other genre fiction.

Mission statement: "Inspired by the enduring magic and importance of books, our mission is to create and distribute exceptional publishing that is instantly recognizable for its spirit, creativity, and value. This mission also informs our business relationships and endeavors be they with customers, authors, vendors, or colleagues."

Meet Grace Lin

Illustrator and Author

Grace Lin has written and illustrated many books for ages two to nine: *The Ugly Vegetables* (Charlesbridge Publishing, fall 1999); *Dim Sum for Everyone!* (Knopf, summer 2001); *Olvina Flies* (Henry Holt, spring 2002), *Kite Flying* (Knopf, summer 2002), and *Kevin's Seasons* (Charlesbridge, forthcoming; and has illustrated *Round Is a Mooncake* (Chronicle, fall 2000); *Where on Earth Is my Bagel* (fall 2001); *Red Is a Dragon* (Chronicle, fall 2001); *Favorite Foods* (Compass Point Books, fall 2001); and *The Jade Necklace* (Tradewind Books, forthcoming). She was born in New Jersey on May 17, 1974. She got her B.F.A. at the Rhode Island School of Design (RISD), majoring in illustration. Before she became a children's book illustrator and author, she was a giftware designer, a beer menu designer, and a file girl, and then worked retail at a children's bookstore (Curious George Goes to Wordsworth in Harvard Square) before finally being able to support herself with book work. By far, working at the bookstore was her favorite (though lowest-paying) job. She learned about all the books that came out—what publisher printed which books and what sold. Not only was she immersed in her passion (children's books), she also got to research the field, which helped her quite a bit when she began her quest to find publishers.

Most of her books have a strong Asian slant. There is a reason for this. She grew up in upstate New York in a predominantly Caucasian community. While the people were very welcoming, she always felt strangely isolated being the only Asian in the classroom, the only Asian in the school photo. Because of this, early on, she turned to books as friends. However, one of the things that always bothered her about these books was that there were no people like her in them. The few books with Asian characters were usually folktales, set in an ancient time—nothing a completely Americanized Asian girl could relate to. Now that she is older, she still loves books. She loves them so much that now she creates them. And one of the things she always keeps in mind when she starts a project is the child that she once was and the hunger she had for a character she could relate to. That's probably why most of her books are Asian themed and why publishers come to her with Asian-themed stories. They are the books she wished she had when she was young.

How did you get your first book published?

After graduating from RISD, I moved to Boston and panicked. I had just graduated from an art school and felt like I had no prospects for any kind of financial security. I loved children's books, I dreamed of being a children's book illustrator; but people kept telling me how impossible it was, how little money, and so forth. I sent a few mailers out and heard very little response. One response was from an editor named Harold Underdown. He didn't say much, just, "like your work, keep sending samples." While that was encouraging, I was still jobless and needed to pay my rent. Finally, I got a job at a small giftware company designing confetti and mugs and T-shirts (the most famous slogan was "Did anyone tell you you're terrific today?"). I worked in a cubicle, in front of a computer, 9 to 5. It was a far, far cry from my paints and my dream, but I clung to the security.

Then, after about a year and a half of working there, the company was taken over. They were closing down the Boston branch and locating everything to Kalamazoo, Michigan. I was laid off and given a severance package. I seized the opportunity. With this severance I would finally try to make my dream come true. Now, I would try full force to make it in the children's book world. I sent out hundreds of mailings. No response.

As my severance was ending, and as I began to doubt myself, Harold Underdown, the editor who had liked my work from two years ago, contacted me. He had just accepted a job as senior editor at Charlesbridge Publishing, he told me. He had always liked my work and now he was finally in a position to do something with it. Did I have any story ideas? And, even though I didn't have anything, I said, "Yes, I do. Would you like to meet and see them?"

We set up a meeting, and I went to the computer and wrote. It was like magic—the story came out of me like water from a faucet. It was a simple, true story. It was about me, my mother, and the Chinese vegetables she used to grow and the embarrassment I had felt over our differences. I wasn't trained as a writer, but I think there was something in the story that connected, because for once, everything seemed to fall into place. I showed the story to Harold, and he enthusiastically liked it. He had me rewrite it twice, once in third person and another with more children. But, in the end, it was the original version that was used and was to become my first book *The Ugly Vegetables.* So, in a way it took me one day to create *The Ugly Vegetables.* But in another way it took over two years.

Do you have any advice, in terms of finding a publisher, for an illustrator starting out?

First, have a strong style that you are comfortable with, you enjoy, and you are confident about. That is the most important thing. You must love what you do—it'll show in your work! Second, research your market. Learn that Lee & Low specializes in multicultural books and Little, Brown uses agented material. Compile a list of places that fit your style, that do the books you want to do. Third, send off the best mailers you can afford. Make them epitomize your personality and style. Never send anything that makes you look like an amateur or less than the talented professional you are. Fourth, after you've heard some responses from your mailers, set up some appointments and make the rounds with your portfolio in New York City. It is so important for you to put a face with the name and for them to put a face with the art. It will make your work stand out that much more to them. Also, if you have any dummy books you will get an immediate reaction from them. You will know, within minutes, whether or not your book may work for them. Which is much better than waiting for them to get it through the slush.

When I first graduated, I sent queries to publishers about some of my manuscript/illustration packages. One editor responded and asked to see some of them. I sent them off with a big "Requested" written on the envelope, and I was very excited. Months passed and I heard nothing. A year passed and I gave them up for lost. By this time, I had reread them and realized how poor they were. I was too humiliated to inquire about them because they were that bad. Another six months passed and I began setting up appointments in New York City to show my work around. One appointment was with this editor. At the meeting she looked at me, slightly red-faced and said, "I've always liked your work. I remember inquiring before about some your stories. I'm embarrassed to say I still haven't gotten around to them." Which shows you how backed up her slush pile was!

Lastly, but most important—be confident. Remember, that everything is subjective, and a rejection does not determine your work's worth. On one of my trips to New York City I brought around a dummy book. At one house, the editor looked at it and handed it back to me with almost a look of

continues

disgust. "I don't like this book at all," he told me, "I just can't stand this kind of book." I was completely, completely disheartened. Of course this book was horrible, I thought, I can't believe I thought it was good. I'm going home and burning it and no one is ever going to see it again. I had one more appointment and in the middle of the meeting (since the editor was being so nice), I changed my mind and decided to show it anyway. And, she loved it. I got a contract for it almost immediately. The lesson here is obvious: Believe in yourself and your work. One person's trash is another's treasure.

Do your write the text for the books you illustrate?

Some of my books I've written and illustrated. Those books, I present as a package. This is a black-and-white sketch dummy book and sometimes color photocopy of a finished piece from the book. Usually, if the house doesn't find the book suitable for them, they keep the art sample on file just in case a different story that suits my style comes up. For books that I've illustrated only, the publisher is the contact. Usually, it is an editor who has liked my work in the past and has found a story that suits my style. I never have much contact with the authors.

Where do you get your ideas?

Ideas come to me from everywhere. I carry a sketchbook, and sometimes a phrase or a picture hits me and I write it down. I'm always thinking, "That's a great idea for a children's book!" For example, my roommate came home one day with a story of how UPS had messed up the spelling of her name. Alvina had been changed to Olvina. And I thought, "What a great name for a chicken character!" (Olva means egg in Italian by the way). Immediately, I pictured how she would look—slightly lost, polka-dotted dress. Couple this with an event at the bookstore: "Do you have any books about airplanes?" a woman asks. "I'm bringing my child on a plane for the first time, and I want a story to prepare him." "I don't think we have any story-type books," the clerk says.

And then the light bulb flashes! Olvina is a chicken. She is a bird that can't fly—the only way she could ever fly is on an airplane. Kids could be prepared to fly by Olvina's experience—ta-dah! And *Olvina Flies* is born.

Another book is born as fast as this: "Let's go out for dim sum," I said to a good friend of mine. "What's dim sum?" she asks me. And the next book by Grace Lin is *Dim Sum for Everyone!* Not all my ideas are good, however. Like a photographer, I figure if I take enough pictures a couple of them will be great.

Did you pursue any formal training, or was it just a question of practice, or something else?

I went to RISD and majored in illustration. At RISD, I was not the most promising student. I was not the cream of the crop. But, what I did have, which has made me more successful, is the passion and drive to become the best illustrator I could be. I didn't really come into my own in terms of mastery of style or confidence until a couple years after RISD. I like to think of myself as a late bloomer. So, honestly, I feel formal training, practice, and talent help, but passion is what makes it.

Anything you really wish somebody had told you when you started out?

Be patient, be confident, and love what you do. Children's books is a hard market. But I think it is completely worth the challenge.

Clarion

215 Park Avenue South
New York, NY 10003
(212) 420-5889
(212) 420-5855 (fax)
Web site: www.houghtonmifflinbooks.com/trade/

Description: Trade book imprint of Houghton Mifflin.

Clear Light Publishers

823 Don Diego
Santa Fe, NM 87501
(505) 989-9590
(505) 989-9519 (fax)

Description: Multicultural book publisher focusing on Native American middle readers and young adults.

Concordia Publishing House

3558 S. Jefferson
St Louis, MO 63118-3968
Web site: www.cph.org
Guidelines: www.cph.org/html/manuscript.htm

Description: Publishes Gospel-centered picture books for ages 4 to 7 and series fiction, *but is not accepting new proposals at this time.*

Cook Communications

4050 Lee Vance View
Colorado Springs, CO 80918

Description: Christian book publisher.

Coteau Books

401—2206 Dewdney Avenue
Regina, SK S4R 1H3
Canada
(306) 777-0170
(306) 522-5152 (fax)
E-mail: coteau@coteaubooks.com
Web site: coteau.unibase.com

Description: Coteau Books is a literary press, publishing children's and young adults "chapter books" (with the exception of picture books) with literary merit.

Established: June 1975.

Seeks: Juvenile fiction.

Accepts unsolicited/unagented: Yes. But Coteau publishes only authors who are Canadian citizens.

Recent fiction titles:

Angels in the Snow by Wenda Young (Fifteen-year-old Nicole has spent half her life wanting to ask her mother why she left when Nicole was seven. Now, she's going to get the chance, if she's got the courage to travel from small-town Nova Scotia to Nagano, Japan, and spend time with the woman who is at the same time a stranger and a bittersweet memory.)

Buddy Concrackle's Amazing Adventure by Chris McMahen (Come along with 10-year-old Buddy and his family for a tasty tale about the open road and keeping an open mind.)

The Cherry-Pit Princess by Lynn Manuel (Dagny and Megan are friends, but can they be best friends? Can they help Aunt Allie get all her Bing cherries picked and save her orchard before it's too late?)

Preferred form of submission/contact: You may send the full manuscript or a sample (3–4 stories or chapters; 20–25 poems) accompanied by a self-addressed envelope of appropriate size, stamped with sufficient postage to either send a reply as to the company's intentions, or to return the entire manuscript should it be declined, if that is your wish. Or you may send a sample that is a maximum of 20 pages by e-mail, as an attached file, in the Mime protocol (for PCs) to coteau@coteau.unibase.com. Please also include a curriculum vitae specifying previous publications. If your manuscript is accepted, be prepared to submit it on 3.5-inch floppy disks, in Microsoft Word 6.0 format, if at all possible.

Accepts simultaneous submissions: No.

Submission guidelines: Write with an SASE, e-mail your request or go to the Web site.

Cricket Books

20 Battery Park Avenue
Asheville, NC 28801
(828) 236-3097
(828) 236-3098
E-mail: contactus@frontstreetbooks.com
Web site: www.frontstreetbooks.com

Corporate structure/parent: Front Street Books.

Description: Publisher.

Established: 1999.

Key people:

Publisher: Stephen Roxburgh

Editor in chief: Marianne Carus

Books per year: 12.

Percentage by first-time authors: Believes in new voices; half of authors are previously unpublished.

Seeks: Front Street/Cricket Books publishes quality chapter books and middle-grade novels for children ages 7 to 12 to encourage a lifetime enjoyment of reading and an appreciation for literature. Fantasy, realistic fiction, and humor are the main components of the list. For twenty-five years Cricket Magazine Group has published the best of the best in its award-winning magazines, and it applies that same expertise to Front Street/Cricket Books.

Accepts unsolicited/unagented: Front Street is willing to consider unsolicited manuscripts.

Description of fiction titles: Picture books reflect the joy, spontaneity, and energy of infants and toddlers. Middle-grade chapter books address the various settings and activities of school-age children. Young adult fiction often deals with children in crisis, children at risk, and offers hope and succor, however difficult the subject.

Recent fiction titles:

Mop to the Rescue
Oh No, It's Robert
There's a Kangaroo in My Soup
Casebook of a Private (Cat's) Eye
The Boy Trap
Eleanor Hill
The Shadowed Unicorn
Running on Eggs
Two Suns in the Sky
That's Ghosts for You
Write Me If You Dare!
How I Survived My Summer Vacation

Preferred form of submission/contact: Please enclose a dated cover letter so that there is a record of your name and return address. Unsolicited materials will not be returned unless you provide a self-addressed stamped envelope. If there is no SASE included, it will be assumed the materials can be discarded. Unable to return manuscripts to destinations outside the United States. Do not send submissions as e-mail attachments. Submissions sent in this manner will be automatically deleted. *Fiction:* If under 100 pages, submit the complete manuscript. If over 100 pages, submit one or two sample chapters and a plot summary. Will request the balance of the manuscript if interested. *Poetry:* Please send a selection of no more than 25 poems that are representative of your work. Will request more if interested. *Anthologies:* Will only consider anthologies of work by various authors if accompanied by a detailed proposal and permissions budget. *Nonfiction:* A detailed proposal and sample chapter will suffice. *Other:* Whatever it takes to give a sense of the project.

Time to reply: All submissions are considered in the order they are received. This is a time-consuming practice and your patience is requested.

Accepts simultaneous submissions: Discouraged but tolerated.

Prefer manuscript/illustration packages, or separate: *Picture books:* Not currently accepting texts only for picture book manuscripts. Will accept picture book texts accompanied by artwork. If you are the artist, or are working with an artist please include the manuscript, a dummy, and a sample reproduction of artwork rendered in the manner and style representative of the final artwork. *Do not send original art.* Cannot be held responsible for damaged or lost materials.

Tips and comments: Current catalog is available online at www.frontstreetbooks.com; familiarize yourself with the list before making submissions. If the decision on your submission is negative, you will receive a form rejection letter. This procedure enables the company to reduce the time it takes to respond to submissions, time that can be devoted to reviewing more submissions.

CROCODILE BOOKS

46 Crosby Street
Northampton, MA 01060
Web site: www.interlinkbooks.com/About_Interlink.html

Corporate structure/parent: Interlink Publishing Group, Inc.

Description: Book publisher. Crocodile Books publishes high-quality illustrated children's books from around the world.

Established: 1987.

Accepts unsolicited/unagented: Yes, but only those that are already illustrated.

Description of fiction titles: Titles published under this imprint include quality picture books for preschoolers, as well as fiction and nonfiction books for children ages three to eight.

Time to reply: Up to three months.

Prefer manuscript/illustration packages, or separate: Only accepts manuscript/illustration packages.

Tips and comments: Become familiar with the kinds of books the company publishes. Request a catalog; order them; buy them from local booksellers or directly from the publisher; read them at your local library. Write for a complete catalog of illustrated children's books or call at (800) 238-LINK. Please, do *not:* send a full manuscript unless requested; send anything without an SASE (that includes adequate postage); send queries via fax or e-mail (they will *not* be answered); send poetry or plays (doesn't publish any); call about the status of a query unless the company has requested the manuscript and you have not heard back for at least three months.

CROSSWAY BOOKS

1300 Crescent Street
Wheaton, IL 60187-5800
(630) 682-4785 (fax)

Corporate structure/parent: Crossway Books is a division of Good News Publishers.

Description: Book publisher.

Seeks: Especially want to publish fiction in the youth/juvenile category.

Accepts unsolicited/unagented: Queries only. Please include a self-addressed stamped envelope that will hold the materials that you send so that your submission materials can be returned to you in the event that they cannot be used.

Preferred fiction titles: Not interested in issues novels; end-time or prophecy novels; short stories or anthologies; biblical novels (set in Bible times); fantasy/science fiction; romance novels; horror; mystery, western, and supernatural novels.

Preferred nonfiction titles: Looking for issues books—books that typically address the critical issues facing Christians today in our personal lives, families, communities, and the wider culture; books on the deeper Christian life—in general, these books seek to provide a deeper understanding of Christian truth and its application to daily life. Many of these involve the exposition of Scripture; others are more topical and systematic. Books in this category could include biblical teaching, the application of the Bible to Christian growth, evangelism, devotions, and so on. Not interested in nonfiction titles pertaining to end-time or prophecies; sermons; exposés of well-known Christians; personal experience or true stories; poetry; or art books.

Preferred form of submission/contact: Query letter. Please send a synopsis (one to two pages, double-spaced) and no more than two chapters. No submissions of entire manuscripts. Please include a self-addressed stamped envelope that will hold the materials that you send.

Time to reply: Allow four to six months for your submission to complete the review process. All inquiries as to the status of a submission should be made by letter or fax only.

Tips and comments: Please do as thorough a job of research and writing as possible before submitting your manuscript. If possible, have a professional proofreading service look over your manuscript for grammar, punctuation, and spelling errors. Please do not send outlines or tables of contents only. These will tell the reviewer little about the manuscript's content, nor will they give the reviewer any knowledge of your writing skills. A chapter-by-chapter synopsis is preferred. All submissions must be neatly typed and double-spaced, with pages numbered consecutively. Send a photocopy, not the original. Computer printouts are also acceptable, preferably printed by a laser printer. Please use only white bond (no texture) paper. On the first page of the submission, please include your name, address, telephone number, and an approximate total word count for your entire manuscript. *No electronic submissions.*

Dandy Lion Publications

3563 Sueldo, Suite L
San Luis Obispo, California 93401
(800) 776-8032
(805) 544-2823 (fax)
E-mail: dandy@dandylionbooks.com
Web site: www.dandylionbooks.com

Description: Educational publisher.

Established: 1980.

Seeks: Materials should be educational activities, exercises, games or instructional procedures to be used with above-average, creative students or as supplements to the basic curriculum.

Accepts unsolicited/unagented: Yes.

Description of nonfiction titles: Educational materials for classroom use.

Recent nonfiction titles:

Red Hot Root Words by Dianne Draze

Analogies for Beginners by Lynne Chatham

The Great Chocolate Caper, A Mystery That Teaches Logic by Mary Ann Carr

Preferred form of submission/contact: Manuscript or outline with sample selections.

Submission guidelines: When submitting sample pages (as opposed to a complete manuscript), please also include an explanation of the scope and sequence of the entire text; approximate number of pages; answers to the following questions: What are the specific objectives of your material? For what grade would this be appropriate? What format do you suggest? How would the material be used in the classroom? Where would these materials fit in the curriculum? Are these materials designed to teach skills usually taught by basal textbooks or intended to supplement standard material? Do you know of any material similar to the ones you propose that are currently published? Though review pages may be submitted, usually the entire manuscript must be reviewed before a contract will be issued. Any contracts that are issued based on a partial text are done so with the condition that if the completed/revised manuscript is not acceptable, the contract may be revoked.

Tips and comments: When submitting, bear in mind that the texts should be accomplishing the following objectives: Enrich or extend the regular school curriculum; expose students to topics that are not part of the regular curriculum in terms of the topic itself, the extent or the way in which the material is handled, or the age level at which it is introduced; develop higher-level thinking; encourage independent study; be activity oriented and multisensory, integrating and cognitive, affective, creative, intuitive, and physical whenever possible; give students opportunities to deal metaphorically with ideas and information; create challenging activities by using questions that are open-ended and/or based on higher levels of thinking; be a striking combination of interesting subject matter coupled with challenging activities.

DANIEL WEISS ASSOCIATES, INC.

33 W. 17th Street, 11th Floor
New York, NY 10011

Description: Book publisher.

Key people:

Acquisitions/submissions editor: Jennifer Klein, editorial assistant

Books per year and description: Love stories.

Seeks: Love stories.

Accepts unsolicited/unagented: Yes.

Description of fiction titles: Love stories—romance novels.

Preferred fiction titles: Love stories are the young adult romances of the nineties. They are individual novels about the wonder and excitement of first love and the roller-coaster ride of being part of a couple. The stories can be told in the first or third person. The role of the boy is essential in these books. He must be a solid, three-dimensional character with dreams and plans of his own. The overall feel of the series is classic and romantic, yet modern, fresh, and forward looking. The emphasis is solidly on the romance between the boy and a girl, and the conflict that threatens to keep them apart. These stories contain no sex but are full of tender, touching, and even thrilling moments. Heavy on plot and fast-paced, these books must have well-developed, three-dimensional characters.

Preferred form of submission/contact: Will consider completed manuscripts accompanied by a detailed plot synopsis, or a detailed outline and partial manuscript (two to four chapters). Submit queries and manuscripts to Jennifer Klein *with an SASE.* Finished manuscripts should be 45,000 words. All submissions should be typed and double spaced.

Submission guidelines: Write with an SASE for guidelines.

Tips and comments: The heroines of love stories are between the ages of 14 and 15, and they are having their first real encounters with romance. This means they have moved beyond the "first kiss" stage and are now involved with actual relationships. Through their eyes the reader experiences the once-in-a-lifetime thrill and intensity of being part of a couple—the high points and the low. There are no restrictions on settings, but plots must be accessible to the average American teenage girl.

David R. Godine, Publisher

9 Hamilton Place
Boston, MA 02108-4715
(617) 451-9600
(617) 350-0250 (fax)
E-mail: info@godine.com
Web site: www.godine.com

Description: Book publisher.

Established: 1970, started publishing children's books in 1980.

Seeks: The list is deliberately eclectic and features works that many other publishers can't or won't support, books that won't necessarily become bestsellers but that still deserve publication.

Accepts unsolicited/unagented: No. Godine does not accept unsolicited manuscripts or proposals. Due to the large number of submissions, Godine will not be able to return any materials not accompanied by a self-addressed stamped envelope. *Authors are advised to have their agent contact Godine if they would like the company to consider a project.*

Recent fiction titles:

The Man Who Lived Alone by Donald Hall; illustrated by Mary Azarian
The Secret Garden by Frances Hodgson Burnett

A Little Princess by Frances Hodgson Burnett

The Christmas Junk Box & the Very Best Christmas Tree by Tony King; illustrated by Michael McCurdy

Preferred form of submission/contact: Write with an SASE, e-mail a request, or go to the Web site.

Prefer manuscript/illustration packages, or separate: No.

Include with illustrator query: Strongly advises against sending original artwork or irreplaceable documents; while all reasonable care will be taken with such materials, Godine cannot be held responsible in the event of damage or loss.

Tips and comments: For catalog requests, please contact Customer Service Department. All Godine hardcover and softcover books are printed on acid-free paper. Many hardcovers are still bound in full cloth.

Dawn Publications

14618 Tyler Foote Road
Nevada City, CA 95959
(800) 545-7475
(530) 478-7541 (fax)
E-mail: Dawnpub@oro.net
Web site: www.dawnpub.com

Seeks: Dawn is primarily an inspiration and nature awareness publisher for adults and children. In part the company grew out of the enthusiastic public response to the now-classic *Sharing Nature with Children* by Joseph Cornell, the eminent naturalist and nature educator. Increasingly the company's goal is to teach children the wonders of nature and of themselves through high-quality picture books, including trade books suitable for use in the classroom. Nature is a great teacher. We learn not only respect for nature but for ourselves. As we learn the values of nature, we become aware of the values of human life as well. Nature affirms in young people their natural inclination toward beauty, truth, and a sense of unity and harmony with all life. At the same time, the work must be engaging to young minds.

Accepts unsolicited/unagented: Yes. Some publications come from unsolicited submissions and first-time authors. Please be aware, however, that Dawn is a small company and receives *thousands* of queries or manuscripts annually and accepts only half a dozen or fewer for publication. Please observe directions for submissions. Please enclose a cover letter with the manuscript describing your work, the intended age of the audience, your other publications if any, your motivation for writing, and relevant background.

Description of nonfiction titles: The best way to get a sense of Dawn's publishing mission is to examine some of the company's books (see below for a selection of titles).

Recent nonfiction titles:

Sharing Nature with Children by Joseph Cornell

The Tree in the Ancient Forest by Carol Reed-Jones (Jones uses the literary technique of repetitive, cumulative verse to portray with scientific accuracy the remarkable web of plants and animals living around a single old tree. It reminds us of the ecological interdependence of life.)

A Dandelion Seed by Joseph Anthony (Anthony uses the realistic science of a seed's development as a metaphor for our journey through life.)

Preferred nonfiction titles: Dawn generally does not publish material that is a fictional story; includes chapters; contains animal dialogue that presents animals in a highly anthropomorphic light; merely explains nature; is a fantasy; is a retelling of a legend (as most legends have a strong element of the supernatural); is centered primarily on human situations or foibles; is pure science.

Preferred form of submission/contact: Query or manuscript is fine. Be aware that most picture books are 32 pages. Indicate where you want your page breaks to be—don't send 32 separate sheets. (However, if you have a mockup that meaningfully enhances appreciation of the work, send it. Be sure to enclose an SASE if you want it returned.)

Time to reply: Please allow at least two months for a response.

Desired illustrator qualifications: The company likes to retain the option of selecting the artist. If you are presenting artwork, please indicate whether the art and text are a package.

Prefer manuscript/illustration packages, or separate: Either way is fine.

Include with illustrator query: Samples or portfolio are best. Those that meet the company's artistic style will be kept on file for possible future projects. No cartoon or computer art. If you wish to have your portfolio returned to you, please send a large SASE with enough postage to have your work returned.

Submission guidelines: Write with an SASE for guidelines.

Tips and comments: Dawn is a nature education publisher of nonfiction picture books, teachers guides, nature activity books, and biographies. Please take these guidelines to heart as they are meant to assist you in submitting manuscripts that are likely to be of interest. Always enclose an SASE! It is often very helpful for authors to review the current catalog. Please enclose a large $0.99 SASE to receive the catalog. Or review it on the Web at www.DawnPub.com.

Dial Books for Young Readers

345 Hudson Street, 3rd Floor
New York, NY 10014-3657
(212) 366-2800

Corporate structure/parent: Penguin Putnam Books.

Description: Publisher.

Seeks: Publishes books in the following categories: picture books, easy-to-read, and middle-grade and YA novels.

Accepts unsolicited/unagented: No manuscripts. Queries accepted. See below for guidelines.

Preferred form of submission/contact: Query. No unsolicited manuscripts. A query letter should briefly describe your manuscript's plot, genre (i.e., picture book, easy-to-read, or middle-grade or YA novel), the intended age group, and your publishing credits, if any. If you like, you may send no more than one page of the manuscript of shorter works (i.e., picture books) and a maximum of 10 pages of longer works (novels, easy-to-reads). Do not send more than the specified amount; any excess will not be read. Never send cassettes, original artwork, marketing plans, or faxes. Manuscript pages sent will not be returned. In response, you will receive a form letter either requesting the manuscript or letting you know that the manuscript isn't right for Dial.

Time to reply: Never call or fax to inquire about the status of an unsolicited submission; instead write a letter only if the reply time has exceeded four months.

Include with illustrator query: Samples. Never send original art. Please do not phone to inquire about your submission. Art samples should be sent to Ms. Toby Sherry (samples will not be returned without a self-addressed stamped envelope).

Submission guidelines: No specific guidelines, but you can request a recent catalog if you send a 9 by 12-inch envelope with four 34-cent stamps attached. Please do not send cash or checks. This is one way to become informed as to the style, subject matter, and format of the company's books, as is a trip to your local library or bookshop.

Tips and comments: Read, read, read! And familiarize yourself with the company's books. Full manuscripts sent without a prior query will be returned unread. If you do not live in the United States, you must send an international reply coupon.

DK INK

Web site: www.dk.com

Description: In May 2000, DK was acquired by Pearson plc, an international media company with market-leading businesses in education, strategic commercial development, international television production, and consumer publishing. This acquisition saw DK join the Penguin Group, as Peter Kindersley stepped down from his executive role at DK and Anthony Forbes Watson became chief executive of both DK and Penguin UK.

Dog-Eared Publications

Box 620863
Middleton, WI 53562-0863
Web site: www.dog-eared.com

Description: Book publisher.

Key people:

Publisher: Nancy Field

Seeks: Aim is to turn young readers into environmentally aware earth citizens and to foster a love of science and nature in the new generation. How? By capturing first their interest and then their hearts and minds with interactive games, mysteries, puzzles, and stories.

Recent nonfiction titles:

Leapfrogging Through Wetlands by Margaret Anderson, Nancy Field, and Karen Stephenson; illustrated by Michael Maydak (Children investigate the world of sedges, rushes, ducks, and frogs in this beautifully illustrated, action-packed book. Youngsters come to understand the importance and diversity of wetlands by becoming wetland detectives, traveling through a wetland maze or with migrating waterfowl.) 1999 Ben Franklin award winner in category of science/environment

Discovering Wolves by Nancy Field and Corliss Karasov; illustrated by Cary Hunkel (*Discovering Wolves* investigates current research and wolf-human conflicts in addition to the natural history of wolves. It helps dispel myths about wolves as predators, while making clear their plight as threatened or endangered species).

Discovering Earthquakes by Nancy Field and Adele Schepige; illustrated by Nancy Lynch; winner of 1996 Parents' Choice Approval.

Down East Books

PO Box 679
Camden, ME 04843
(207) 594-9544
(207) 594-7215 (fax)
Web site: www.downeastbooks.com

Description: Regional Maine publisher

Books per year and description: 2 or 3 per year, with regional setting (Maine or New England themes only).

Seeks: Regional stories with true-to-life adventure or well-founded natural history receive our most serious attention.

Accepts unsolicited/unagented: Yes.

Preferred form of submission/contact: Query.

Time to reply: Two to eight weeks.

Prefers manuscript/illustration packages, or separate: Prefers separate—do not illustrate your work unless you are a professional artist. Prefers to select illustrators and photographers ourselves.

Include with illustrator query: Use ink, not pencil; send originals, not copies (include SASE).

Preferred photography: Prefer black and white to color. Send glossy prints, not negatives.

Submission guidelines: Please write with an SASE.

Tips and comments: Avoid the temptation to moralize—themes and/or "lessons" may be *subtly* suggested but not explicitly stated. The idea is to entertain (reading is fun), not to lecture. Present text and illustrations separately—no dummies. Indicate the age level the story is designed to reach.

Dutton Children's Books

345 Hudson Street
New York, NY 10014
(212) 414-3397 (fax)
Web site: www.penguinputnam.com

Corporate structure/parent: Penguin Putnam Inc.

Description: Children's book company that publishes books for babies through young adults for the trade and institutional markets.

Established: 1852.

Key people:

Publisher: Stephanie Owens Lurie

Associate publisher and editor in chief: Lucia Monfried

Editorial director: Donna Brooks

Executive editor: Tamar Mays

Art director: Sara Reynolds

Editors: Susan Van Metre, senior editor; Meredith Mundy Wasinger, editor; Sarah Ketchersid, editor

Books per year and description: Approximately 110: board books, picture books, easy to reads, chapter books, middle-grade and young adult fiction, nonfiction for all ages, and novelty books.

Percentage by first-time authors: 10 percent.

Seeks: Fresh ideas and voices with immediate kid appeal and heart.

Accepts unsolicited/unagented: Prefers to receive query letters first.

Description of fiction titles: Highly imaginative, fully realized, and expertly written books that ring true as they transport young readers.

Recent fiction titles:

Fire Bringer by David Clement-Davies (a classic hero tale set in Scotland about a young stag who defeats a tyrannical new Lord of the Herd; ages 12 and up)

Shakespeare's Scribe by Gary Blackwood (historical novel wherein a boy named Wedge apprentices with Shakespeare's traveling company and meets a man who claims to be Wedge's father; ages 10–14)

Website of the Warped Wizard by Eric Kimmel (a hilarious parody of computer games and medieval legends; ages 7–11)

Preferred fiction titles: Looking for novels with unusual, high-concept plots and an authentic narrative voice. Not looking for novels whose main purpose is to profile a teenage problem or issue.

Description of nonfiction titles: For younger readers: narrative; for middle-grade readers: quirky, often interactive; for older readers: comprehensive and thought-provoking.

Recent nonfiction titles:

Rimshots by Charles Smith Jr. (an exciting look at many different aspects of basketball through dynamic poems and photographs; ages 8 and up).

365 Adventures of Discovery (Discovery Kids) (a year's supply of ideas about how to experiment with and be thrilled by the real world; ages 7 to 11).

Food Rules: The Stuff You Munch, Its Crunch, Its Punch, and Why You Sometimes Lose Your Lunch by Bill Haduch; illustrated by Rick Stromoski (comprehensive book on food and nutrition for kids offers hundreds of mouth-watering stories, jokes, recipes, rumors, and facts)

Preferred nonfiction titles: Looking for subjects with immediate kid appeal and curricular value. Not looking for standard photoessays.

Preferred form of submission/contact: Prefers to receive one-page query letters with a self-addressed stamped envelope for reply.

Time to reply: Aims to reply to query letters within a month of receipt and requested manuscripts within three months of receipt.

Time to publish: Within approximately 12 months for books without illustrations. Usually publishes full-color books within 18 months of delivery of final, acceptable artwork.

Accepts simultaneous submissions: Yes, but please notify in cover letter.

Number of illustrators used annually: 100 or more.

Desired illustrator qualifications: Previous training in illustration, professionalism, creativity, outstanding draftsmanship, knowledge of the picture book format, and ability to tell a story in artwork.

Prefer manuscript/illustration packages, or separate: Prefer to review them separately. Writers who are not trained in illustration do not need to supply artwork or find an illustrator.

Include with illustrator query: A query letter with samples or tear sheets is sufficient. Appointments for portfolio review can be arranged with the art director.

Time to reply: If an illustrator is only sending samples, they will be kept on file until an appropriate project is found. If an illustrator is submitting a book idea, then the company prefers to receive a query letter with sample, and a response will be sent within one month of receipt.

Purchases freelance photography: Sometimes, for nonfiction books.

Preferred photography: Previous training in photography, professionalism, creativity, outstanding talent, and a unique perspective.

Terms for writers: Terms are based on our sales projections for each book. Typically there is a total 10 percent royalty for hardcovers and 6 percent for paperbacks, which is split between author and illustrator.

Terms for illustrators: Same.

Submission guidelines: Write to Susan Finch, editorial assistant, Dutton Children's Books.

Tips and comments: Become familiar with the Dutton list through library and bookstore research. Ask your local bookseller or librarian to show you a recent Penguin Putnam catalog. Write about what is important to you, hone your craft, know your audience, familiarize yourself with children's book formats, and identify where your work would fit in. Strive to be unique and make a statement. Remember, your book has to compete with "louder" media, such as TV, the Internet, video games, movies, and music. This is not the time to be quiet or to stick with the tried and true.

Eakin Press

PO Box 90159
Austin, TX 78709-0159

Description: Book publisher.

Established: 1978.

Key people:

Acquisitions/submissions editors: Ed Eakin and Virginia Messer

Books per year: 25 or more.

Percentage by first-time authors: 50 percent.

Seeks: Books on Texas and the southwestern United States.

Accepts unsolicited/unagented: Yes.

Description of fiction titles: Southwest historic or culture.

Recent fiction titles:

Angora Kidd by CeCe Benningfield; illustrated by Dan Arnold

Coyote Tales: How Coyote Brought Color to the Desert by Frances Agnes Johnson; illustrated by Jackie Gulledge Zweiger

Abuelito Eats with His Fingers by Janice Levy; illustrated by Layne Johnson

Description of nonfiction titles: History, culture

Recent nonfiction titles:

Texans Behind the News by Dede Casad

Today's Tejano Heros by Sammye Munson

The Buffalo Train Ride by Desiree Webber

Preferred nonfiction titles: History and culture relating to Texas and the southwestern United States.

Preferred form of submission/contact: Query.

Time to reply: Six weeks.

Time to publish: 12 to 18 months.

Accepts simultaneous submissions: Yes.

Number of illustrators used annually: Approximately five.

Desired illustrator qualifications: The ability to illustrate *for* children.

Prefer manuscript/illustration packages, or separate: Accepts manuscript/illustration packets for review.

Include with illustrator query: Samples.

Time to reply: One to three months.

Educators Publishing Service, Inc.

31 Smith Place
Cambridge, MA 02138-1089
(617) 547-6706
(617) 547-0412 (fax)
Web site: www.epsbooks.com

Description: Educational publisher. EPS publications teach reading, vocabulary, spelling, English, handwriting and typing, and elementary math and are used by students from kindergarten through high school. EPS also publishes materials for assessment and for students with learning differences.

Key people:

Publisher: John Hall

Acquisitions/submissions editor: Address correspondence to Acquisitions Editor

Seeks: Looking for supplementary materials for the regular K to 12 classroom that teach reading, vocabulary, spelling, grammar, comprehension, and elementary math. Particularly interested in workbook series, but will gladly consider any proposals for high-quality material that is useful to teachers and students.

Recent nonfiction titles:

Wordly Wise 3000 by Kenneth Hodkinson and Sandra Adams

Explode The Code: A Supplementary Program for Beginning Readers by Nancy M. Hall and Rena Price

Clues to Meaning by Ann L. Staman

Preferred form of submission/contact: Send an outline, a sample chapter, or a complete manuscript.

Time to reply: Eight to 10 weeks. EPS will notify you with a postcard on receipt of your submission.

Terms for writers: Variable contract with royalties.

Submission guidelines: Include a brief cover letter describing the unique features of your manuscript; make sure the letter contains your complete address and a daytime telephone number. Include a resume or brief description of your background and experience.

Tips and comments: *All authors must be teachers or educators.*

Eerdmans Books for Young Readers

255 Jefferson Avenue SE
Grand Rapids, MI 49503
(616) 459-4591
(616) 459-6540 (fax)

Description: Publisher.

Key people:

Editor in chief: Judy Zylstra (also acts as acquisitions/submissions editor)

Books per year and description: Currently publishes 12 to 15 books a year. Eerdmans Books for Young Readers publishes picture books and middle reader and young adult fiction and nonfiction.

Seeks: Manuscripts that nurture children's faith in God and that help children and young people understand and explore life in God's world—its wonder and joy, but also its challenges.

Accepts unsolicited/unagented: Yes.

Recent titles:

Silent Night: The Song and Its Story by Margaret Hodges and illustrated by Tim Ladwig

Psalm Twenty-Three illustrated by Tim Ladwig

Sing a New Song written and illustrated by Bijou Le Tord

Joseph written and illustrated by Brian Wildsmith

Preferred form of submission/contact: Complete manuscripts for picture books and middle readers under 200 pages. For longer books, send a query letter and three or four sample chapters. Any manuscript submitted should be typed, double spaced. Please keep a copy of your submission. While every effort will be made to safeguard your manuscript, the company cannot be held responsible if it is lost. Please include a cover letter telling something about yourself, your writing credentials, and your manuscript. Be sure to write your name and address on the manuscript itself, as well as on the cover letter. Include an appropriately sized and stamped envelope for a response and the return of your manuscript.

Time to reply: Please understand that the company receives at least 3,000 submissions a year. It may take us two to three months to respond to your manuscript submission.

Desired illustrator qualifications: Professionals.

Prefer manuscript/illustration packages, or separate: Please do not send illustrations with picture book manuscripts *unless you are a professional illustrator*. If you do submit artwork, send color photocopies rather than original art. Please include SASE for return of anything submitted for consideration.

Include with illustrator query: Send color photocopies rather than original art. Please include SASE for return of anything submitted for consideration.

Tips and comments: Request a recent catalog by sending an 8 by 10-inch envelope with postage for four ounces. You may find it helpful to review titles at your local library or bookstore to see whether your manuscript is appropriate.

E.M. Press, Inc.

PO Box 336
Warrenton, VA 20188
(540) 349-9958 (phone/fax; call first to fax)
E-mail: empress2@erols.com
Web site: www.empressinc.com

Description: A traditional small publishing company. Has published 30 titles over the course of its 10-year history. Also offers editorial services such as editing and book packaging. Publishes children's books, young readers, and adult nonfiction. As a small press, E.M. is proud of having survived—E.M. believes in publishing only the best works. E.M. learns more about production and marketing with each title and loves working closely with its authors and illustrators.

Established: 1991,

Key people:

Publisher: Beth A. Miller

Acquisitions/submissions editor: Montana Umbel

Books per year and description: Two titles per year. Young reader books.

Percentage by first-time authors: 75 percent.

Seeks: Quality and innovation.

Accepts unsolicited/unagented: Absolutely.

Description of fiction titles: Innovative and spirited.

Recent fiction titles:

Sassparilla's New Shoes by Ming and Wah Chen (A young Asian girl must make do with her sister's hand-me-down shoes—a lesson in making lemonade from lemons. It is a flight of imagination and is beautifully illustrated.)

Preferred fiction titles: Not looking for the same old themes.

Description of nonfiction titles: Stories that teach us lessons—covertly.

Recent nonfiction titles:

Looking for Pa by Geraldine Susi (a Civil War story about a young boy and his family's hardships here in Virginia)

Preferred nonfiction titles: Not looking for the same old stories retold.

Preferred form of submission/contact: By query letter and a brief manuscript. Please include an SASE.

Time to reply: Two months.

Time to publish: 18 months to two years.

Accepts simultaneous submissions: Yes.

Number of illustrators used annually: Two.

Desired illustrator qualifications: The ability to use their hands, not just the computer.

Prefer manuscript/illustration packages, or separate: Either.

Include with illustrator query: Samples.

Time to reply: Two months.

Purchases freelance photography: No.

Terms for writers: Royalties, which vary by the project.

Terms for illustrators: Royalties, which vary by the project.

Submission guidelines: Write and request guidelines—please include an SASE.

Enslow Publishers Inc.

40 Industrial Road, Box 39
Berkeley Heights, NJ 07922
(201) 379-8890
Web site: www.enslow.com

Description: Book publisher.

Seeks: Areas of particular interest are biographies (multicultural, contemporary, sports, etc.); social issues books; high-interest topics for reluctant readers; self-help books for young people on their personal problems; science books (experiments, environments, animals).

Accepts unsolicited/unagented: Query first, please. See below.

Description of fiction titles: Enslow publishes only nonfiction titles.

Description of nonfiction titles: Enslow Publishers, Inc. publishes nonfiction works suitable for students in grades 2 to 4, 4 to 6, 7 to 9, or 10 to 12.

Preferred nonfiction titles: If you have some special knowledge of or are an expert on the subject you wish to propose, terrific. Don't be reluctant to explain why you are especially qualified to write this book. Also be sure to tell about other works, if any, that you have published. It can't be emphasized enough that the text needs to be written in a simple manner. Stylistically, the most important part of the book is that it addresses young people in a clear and interesting way without patronizing them. Each chapter should be broken up by descriptive heading that outlines the text. The back matter of the book should include suggestions for further reading (a bibliography), chapter notes, an index, and perhaps a glossary of terms and chronology. Enslow books usually contain black-and-white illustrations (photos, pen-and-ink drawings, or both.) It is the author's responsibility to provide finished illustrations. If you intend to submit artwork, Enslow prefers to see samples of it before receiving the finished version, as the company or its advisers may want to make some suggestions.

Preferred form of submission/contact: Query. To submit your proposal, it is best to start with a brief query letter. A short letter allows the quickest reply. However, you may want to include a table of contents, outline, and sample chapter with your proposal if you feel that these materials are necessary to better explain and define your idea. If you would like your materials returned, please enclose a self-addressed and stamped envelope (SASE) with sufficient postage. Please do not fax any proposals or queries. In your letter, please tell why the book you are proposing is necessary. Does it fill a gap? What are the intended length and grade level of your work? How would this book fit into a school curriculum? What other books are there on the subject, and what are their strengths and weaknesses? How do these books compare to your project in terms of their approach to the subject and grade level? If you have any thoughts about the marketing for this book, please provide those as well.

Include with illustrator query: Art is the responsibility of the author.

Tips and comments: Before sending your proposal, check the shelves of your library and bookstore, as well as book review sources, for competing titles. If you have some special knowledge of, or are an expert on the subject you wish to propose, terrific. Don't be reluctant to explain why you are especially qualified to write this book. Also be sure to tell about other works, if any, that you have published. Request the latest book catalog (which is a wise way to educate yourself *before* making any submissions or proposals) by sending an 8 1/2 by 11-inch SASE with postage of $1.67, along with a check for $2.

Erica House LLC & AmErica House LLC

PO Box 1109
Frederick, MD 21702
E-mail: eribooks@ericahouse.com
E-mail: americahouse@ericahouse.com
Web site: www.ericahouse.com

Description: Erica House LLC and AmErica House LLC are twin international book and music publishing companies, headquartered in Maryland. Both Houses specialize in fiction and nonfiction about/for people who face a major challenge in life and who are determined to overcome their obstacle by turning stumbling blocks into stepping stones.

Key people:

Publisher: Willem Meiners

Accepts unsolicited/unagented: Erica House invites and encourages new talent to submit their work for consideration to be published.

Preferred form of submission/contact: Erica House encourages new talent to query the company. The fact that you have not been previously published does by no means indicate that you have not got what it takes to become a successful author. Every famous writer once began as an anonymous unknown. *Query by e-mail or by snail mail (with an SASE!).*

Submission guidelines: Write with an SASE or visit the Web site. Only provide a brief outline and some bio information. If Erica House considers your manuscript interesting, it will then invite you to submit the entire work.

FACTS ON FILE

11 Penn Plaza
New York, NY 10001
(212) 967-8800
Web site: www.factsonfile.com

Description: Book publisher producing high-quality reference materials for the school library market and nonfiction trade.

FAIRVIEW PRESS

2450 Riverside Avenue S.
Minneapolis, MN 55454
(800) 544-8207
(612) 672-4980 (fax)
Web site: www.press.fairview.org

Description: Book publisher.

Key people:

Editors: Lane Stiles and Jessica Thoreson

Description of titles: Fairview Press publishes books related to family issues; however, it does tend to have a wide definition of family issues: relationships, social issues, community issues, women's and men's issues, aging, grief and loss, parenting, growing-up issues, early childhood, and some physical health and workplace issues. Fairview is also getting into children's picture books on family issues, values and virtues, problem-solving and coping skills, relationships, personal growth, cultural diversity, and special needs.

Preferred form of submission/contact: Submissions should include a cover letter, outline of book, marketing plan for the book, and self-addressed stamped envelope.

FARRAR, STRAUS AND GIROUX BOOKS FOR YOUNG READERS

19 Union Square West
New York, NY 10003
(212) 741-6900

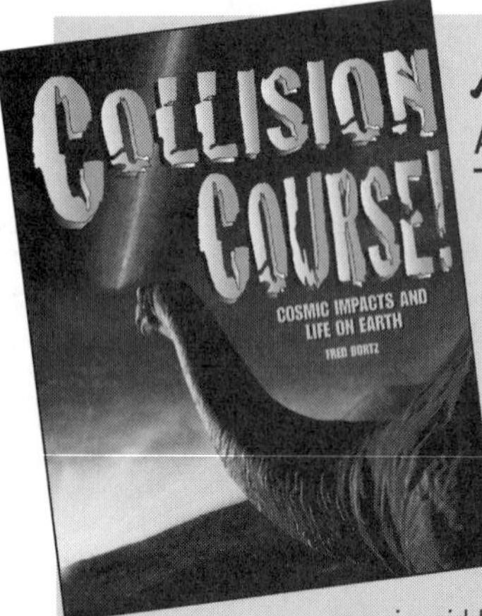

Meet Dr. Fred

Author

Dr. Fred is the author of eight books. The first one was published in 1990. Titles include *Superstuff!* (Franklin Watts, 1990); *Catastrophe! Great Engineering Failure—and Success* (Scientific American Books for Young Readers, W. H. Freeman, 1995); *To the Young Scientist: Reflections on Doing and Living Science* (Franklin Watts, 1997); *Martian Fossils on Earth? The Story of Meteorite ALH84001* (Millbrook Press, 1997); *Techno-Matter* (Twenty-First Century Books, 2001); *Collision Course! Cosmic Impacts and Life on Earth* (Millbrook Press, 2001). His core audience is middle school and junior high, though he has a picture book under contract. He was born in Pittsburgh, Pennsylvania, on November 20, 1944. He has a B.S., M.S., and Ph.D. in physics from Carnegie-Mellon University and a diploma in writing for children and teenagers from the Institute of Children's Literature.

Before Dr. Fred became a full-time children's book author, he worked for four universities and two corporations. He taught physics and mathematics at the college level, doing research in many areas (including nuclear reactors, automotive pollution control systems, computer engineering, magnetic information storage, and science education). Currently, besides writing children's science, he also teaches writing for the Institute of Children's Literature and Chatham College, writes newspaper reviews of popular science books for adults, and teaches a physics lab at Chatham—just because he likes to. He has been married for nearly 34 years, and his wife is a part-time teacher, part-time consultant to congregations, and a community leader. He is the father of two grown children, one (a son) an elementary school science teacher and the other (a daughter) a librarian. Both are married, and his son is the father of twins, a boy and a girl born just after Thanksgiving 1998.

How did you get your first book published?

My first contracted book was never published. In the early 1980s, I had been circulating a proposal called "Real Robots," which got favorable rejections but was never accepted. My writing credits included a children's article based on my work at the time called "Inside the Disk Drive." Seeing that title, an editor at a major publishing house invited me to submit a proposal for a book he had in mind, "Anatomy of a Computer." When I delivered an outline and summary that he liked, he offered me a contract and an advance (half payable on signing and half on acceptance). Unfortunately, the market was soon awash in children's computer books, and most were bad—with reviews to match. By the time I submitted my first draft, the outlook for the project was less encouraging. Still, the editor asked me to press on with a revision, while at the same time pushing back the projected publication date. When he asked for a second revision, I requested and got an additional quarter of the advance when I turned it in. The editor then requested a few more changes, which I agreed to work on after I got written confirmation of his intent to publish the work.

Not long after I submitted those changes, the editor left the company, and the project was canceled. I wrote to request the balance of my advance and, predictably, got no results. Finally, I sent a polite but firm note to the president of the company with a copy of the editor's letter confirming his intent to publish. Much to my surprise, the president apologized and sent a check, assuring me that they would be glad to consider future proposals. At the same time, I was building up a consulting sideline, reviewing science and technology manuscripts for publishers, especially Franklin Watts (part of Grolier). That work gave me excellent insights into what they published and the process of publication. I also wrote children's science book reviews for a quarterly publication, and I followed those with a commentary article. My reviews had caught the attention of Jean Reynolds, now editorial director at the Millbrook Press but then editor in chief of the New Book of Knowledge encyclopedia (NBK), also part of Grolier. My commentary inspired Jean to write me a letter inviting me to consult on NBK. One of my first suggestions was to add an article on materials science, a topic that was not even in the index. Jean allowed me to select an expert author and to transform that expert's work into child-friendly language.

When we finished, I recognized that there was a book crying to be written on the subject. The result was a successful proposal for my first book, *Superstuff! Materials That Have Changed Our Lives*. It sold almost 7,000 library copies over a six-year lifetime. Most recently, Superstuff! provided the basis of a reorganized and updated treatment of the same topic, *Techno-Matter: The Materials Behind the Marvels.* TFCB is a Millbrook imprint, and Jean Reynolds applied the final editing touches to that book, my third for Millbrook and my eighth overall.

Did you have an agent when you published your first book?

The difficulties with *Anatomy of a Computer*, though resolved in a comfortable way, persuaded me to look for an agent. I found a good one in a market guidebook, and she agreed to take me on. She sent the *Superstuff!* proposal to Franklin Watts, knowing that I had already sent the same thing by way of NBK with a good word from Jean Reynolds. Two editors brought it up at the same editorial meeting! That almost killed it, but the agent knew the circumstances and assured them that I wasn't trying to market it behind her back. Over the years, the agent and I developed different views of the way to develop my career. We parted amicably, and she is earning commissions on all my current books.

Since then, I've sold one more and have several proposals under consideration, with others in development. The message is that you don't necessarily need an agent, but you should carefully consider what an agent can offer you. For the first several years, I definitely benefited by having an agent to act as a sounding board and to help with negotiating. In retrospect, I think I stuck with my agent longer than I should have. Editors tell me that I am an excellent advocate for my own work. They are willing to put up with my occasional overzealousness and lack of diplomacy in negotiation because they know that I will listen to their side of the issue.

Do you have any advice, in terms of finding an agent, for a writer starting out?

Don't let the search for an agent take priority over your learning the market and where your work might fit. The good agents expect you to have some battle scars as well as talent, because they won't want you to give up on a manuscript rather than revise it after several rejections. It's nearly as difficult for your work to be accepted by an agent as it is to be accepted by an editor. Most important, having the wrong agent for you is worse than having no agent.

Are your books illustrated?

Millbrook's nonfiction books are very visual. I had some strong ideas about what photos and images would work best with *Martian Fossils* and *Collision Course!* so I negotiated a photo research

continues

fee and located every image in both books. My under-development picture book hasn't reached the point of selecting the illustrator.

Do you have any advice, in terms of finding an illustrator, for a writer starting out?

Generally, let the publisher do that. It's hard enough to be a good writer. Often the illustrator will see something wonderful in your words that you never could have envisioned, and publishers usually know much better than you do which illustrators are most likely to "click" with your work.

What procedures do you follow when you write?

I need to jump from one project to another. I tend to be very intense, but not for long stretches—say more than two hours. Then I need something else to do. I usually just squeak in under the deadline because I'm not disciplined enough to break down the work into neat pieces laid out along a time line. I drive myself crazy with that sometimes, and I don't ask my editors what they think!

Where do you get your ideas?

Ideas are everywhere. The trick is recognizing them. I know I have something good when I see it through the eyes of my audience and get excited. Two examples: For a long time, colleagues had been asking me to write about engineering for middle-graders and teens. I agreed it was an admirable thought, but I couldn't figure out an appealing angle. Then I was fortunate enough to hear a lecture by Henry Petrosky, speaking about his wonderful book for adults, *To Engineer Is Human: The Role of Failure in Successful Design.* That angle was too good not to steal—I mean, adapt. The result was *Catastrophe! Great Engineering Failure—and Success.*

The second idea is one that I always say "dropped out of the sky." Five weeks after I quit my day job, I heard NASA's announcement of possible fossil evidence of ancient life on Mars. Questions bubbled in my head, and I wrote them down. I soon realized I had a book in the story of a potato-shaped meteorite from Mars. Science thrives on questions, so I put a question mark in the title and in each chapter heading. My proposal for *Martian Fossils on Earth? The Story of Meteorite ALH84001* reached Jean Reynolds's desk the day before an editorial meeting, and I had good news before the week was out.

What do you think are the key differences between writing for children and writing for adults?

Kids are harder to fool. Adults like to think they're reading "important" books by important authors. Kids read good books, and they usually don't care who wrote them—although they tend to be loyal to authors whose work has captured their interest in the past.

How did you learn to write?

I have a natural talent and a lot of formal education, but I had to learn how to apply and connect my knowledge and talent to my audience's needs. Writing is much more craft than art, and you don't become a craftsperson without lots of practice. If you develop some artistry, that's "gravy."

Anything you really wish somebody had told you when you started out?

Love and respect both your audience and your subject. Work hard and expect to succeed, but be prepared to face disappointment. The disappointments—and I still have many—make the successes ever so sweet!

Corporate structure/parent: Imprints include Sunburst Paperbacks, Aerial Fiction, Mirasol/libros juveniles, and R & S Books.

Description: Book publisher.

Established: 1945.

Key people:

Editorial director: Margaret Ferguson

Executive editor: Beverly Reingold

Editor: Robert Mayes

Other editors: Wesley Adams, senior editor; Janine O'Malley, assistant editor

Books per year: 60 to 80.

Percentage by first-time authors: 5 percent.

Seeks: Quality literary works of fiction and some nonfiction (picture book age through young adults).

Accepts unsolicited/unagented: Yes.

Description of fiction titles: Of particular literary merit.

Recent fiction titles:

Joey Pigza Loses Control by Jack Gantos

Memories of Summer by Ruth White

Lizzie at Last by Claudia Mills

The Boxer by Kathleen Karr

At the Sign of the Star by Katherine Sturtevant

Preferred fiction titles: Quality but no formulaic work or didactic stories.

Description of nonfiction titles: Of literary merit rather than textbook approach (though the company does *not* publish many nonfiction titles).

Recent nonfiction titles:

The Longitude Prize by Joan Dash

Invisible Enemies by Jeanette Farrell

Preferred nonfiction titles: Material not often written about for children.

Preferred form of submission/contact: Query and sample chapters, or full manuscript if under 100 pages. All contact should be through the mail—not by fax or e-mail.

Time to reply: One to three months.

Time to publish: Two years or more.

Accepts simultaneous submissions: Yes, but it should be stated in the cover letter.

Number of illustrators used annually: Numerous.

Desired illustrator qualifications: Talent, the ability to envision a text as a finished product—as a book.

Prefer manuscript/illustration packages, or separate: Accepts together, but prefers to review them separately.

Include with illustrator query: Resume and samples.

Time to reply: One to three months.

Purchases freelance photography: Very rarely.

Terms for writers: Advance against royalty, usually 7 to 10 percent for hardcover fiction, 4 to 5 percent for picture book text only.

Terms for illustrators: Advance against royalty, 8 to 10 percent for text and art; 4 to 5 percent for art only; 2 to 3 percent for interior and black-and-white; flat fee for cover art only.

Submission guidelines: Send SASE with $0.34 stamp.

Tips and comments: If you're interested in doing picture books and have not yet published one, it is useful to have a dummy to present so the editors can see how you envision a book.

FEMINIST PRESS

365 Fifth Avenue, 5th Floor
New York, NY 10016
(212) 817-7915
(212) 817-1593 (fax)
Editorial inquiries: (212) 817-7918
E-mail: hmcmaster@gc.cuny.edu
Web site: www.feministpress.org

Description: The Feminist Press at The City University of New York offers alternatives in education and in literature. The Feminist Press is a nonprofit, tax-exempt educational and publishing organization that works to eliminate gender stereotypes in books and schools and to provide literature with a broad vision of human potential.

Books per year and description: List includes one or two books each year for children and young adults, *very few of which are drawn from unsolicited manuscripts.*

Seeks: The Feminist Press is, in general, interested in primary texts that will have broad, long-term sales in bookstores, as well as the possibility of use in primary or secondary school classrooms. Through publications and projects, The Feminist Press attempts to contribute to the rediscovery of the history of women in the United States and internationally and the emergence of a more humane society. For the children's book program, The Feminist Press is currently considering original manuscripts only for chapter books for readers ages 8 and up, but will also consider reprints or imports of already existing children's books.

Preferred fiction titles: The qualities The Feminist Press looks for are multicultural/international settings, strong central female characters of all ages, important and challenging themes, and, of course, charm, humor, and excellent writing. Please do not send original picture books (books with prominent illustration on every page, and only brief text, intended for young children). Manuscripts of this kind will be returned unread.

Preferred form of submission/contact: To submit a project, please send a proposal that includes a cover letter outlining the nature, scope, and intended audience of your work; the table of contents and up to 30 sample pages (typed double spaced); and your resume. For previously published books, please include sales figures if available, and emphasize why you feel that the book merits republication. Please also indicate how you heard about The Feminist Press.

Time to reply: The Feminist Press is a nonprofit publisher with a small staff. Please be patient and allow a generous amount of time to reply.

Submission guidelines: Write, e-mail, or check the Web site for guidelines.

Tips and comments: Look at the catalog carefully before you submit to get a sense of whether your project is appropriate for The Feminist Press. Submissions will not be discussed on the phone; if you have questions about the publication policy, write with specific inquiries.

FENN PUBLISHING COMPANY

34 Nixon Road
Bolton, Ontario L7E 1W2
Canada
Web site: www.hbfenn.com

Description: Book publisher.

Established: 1982.

Seeks: Canadian Fiction, nonfiction, picture books.

Accepts unsolicited/unagented: Yes.

Description of fiction titles: Canadian fiction.

Preferred fiction titles: Looking for juvenile titles that pertain to Canada.

Description of nonfiction titles: Canadian nonfiction.

Preferred nonfiction titles: Canadian content.

Preferred form of submission/contact: A writer should contact Fenn in one of the following ways: Submit a completed manuscript; submit a letter of inquiry and detailed premise synopsis; submit a table of contents and chapter summary.

Time to reply: Two to three months.

Prefer manuscript/illustration packages, or separate: Either.

Include with illustrator query: Samples; resume with an SASE.

Time to reply: Two to three months.

Purchases freelance photography: Yes.

Submission guidelines: Write with an SASE for guidelines. Submissions are accepted on PC-formatted disk or hard copy; submissions should be accompanied by concise author biography, reviews, and marketing plan; submissions should not contain original illustrations or photography.

Tips and comments: Please adhere to our guidelines.

FITZHENRY & WHITESIDE LIMITED

195 Allstate Parkway
Markham, Ontario L3R 4T8
Canada
(905) 477-9700
(905) 477-9179 (fax)
Web site: www.fitzhenry.ca

Established: April 1966.

Recent fiction titles:

Next Stop! Written by Sarah Ellis; illustrated by Ruth Ohi (On Saturday, Claire rides the bus and sits right up front so she can help the driver. At the front of the bus Claire can see all of the chaos as people rush to and from their transit rides. Claire helps the bus driver announce the various stops on the route so everyone can get to their destinations. Before long a very special surprise passenger joins Claire and the driver for the final leg of the happy bus ride home.)

A River Apart by Robert Sutherland (An action-packed depiction of the War of 1812. Set along a border area near Ogdensburg, New York, and Prescott, Ontario, *A River Apart* follows the adventures of young Jamie Shaw, a reluctant participant in a war that pits friend against friend.)

Lost in Spain by John Wilson (Ted and his parents are very exited about their European summer vacation. Unfortunately, their longed-for trip leads them directly into the dangers and intrigues of the burgeoning Spanish Civil War of 1936.)

Forest House

PO Box 738
Lake Forest, IL 60045-0738
(847) 295-8287
(847) 295-8201
E-mail: info@forest-house.com
Web site: www.forest-house.com

Description: Forest House Publishing Co., Inc., is a family-owned and -operated publishing company, which provides unique, high-quality educational books to teachers, librarians, and parents who care about what children read.

Franklin Watts

Grolier Publishing
90 Sherman Turnpike
Danbury, CT 06816
(203) 796-2605
(203) 797-3899 (fax)
Web site: www.publishing.grolier.com

Corporate structure/parent: Grolier Publishing, a leading publisher of reference, educational, and children's books. Imprints are Children's Press, Franklin Watts, Orchard Books, and Grolier Educational.

Description: Provides parents, teachers, and librarians with the tools they need to enlighten children to the pleasure of learning and prepare them for the road ahead.

Books per year and description: Almost 200 titles per year in nonfiction, particularly for middle-level and teenage readers.

Description of nonfiction titles: The Watts list boasts a fascinating array of biographies, social studies, history and science books. From *First Books*, Franklin Watts' longest-running series, to the range of titles published for the secondary school level,

Watts books provide a broad cultural and historical overview, stimulate curiosity, and encourage in-depth research and lively debate.

Recent nonfiction titles:

The African Slave Trade by Shirlee P. Newman
Egyptian Mummies by Henrietta McCall
African-Americans and the Presidency by Christopher B. Booker
Rain Forest by Fiona Macdonald
Ancient Times by Guy Austrian

Preferred nonfiction titles: Watts books are designed to inform, educate, and entertain children and young adults.

Include with illustrator query: Samples. *Please, no original art.*

Submission guidelines: Write with an SASE.

Frederick Warne Books

Penguin Putnam BFYR
345 Hudson Street
New York, NY 10014

Corporate structure/parent: Penguin Putnam Inc.

Description: Publisher.

Established: 1865.

Accepts unsolicited/unagented: At this time, most Penguin Putnam Inc. imprints do not accept unsolicited manuscripts. If you would like your work to be considered for publication by a major publisher, Penguin Putnam Inc. recommends that you work with an established literary agent.

Tips and comments: Among other classics, Warne published *The Tale of Peter Rabbit* by Beatrix Potter (which by the way was originally turned down by Warne and the five other publishers to whom Potter submitted).

Free Spirit Publishing

400 First Avenue N., Suite 616
Minneapolis, MN 55401-1724
(800) 735-7323
(612) 337-5050
E-mail: help4kids@freespirit.com
Web site: www.freespirit.com

Description: Publisher of high-quality nonfiction books for children and teens, parents, teachers, counselors, and others who live with or work with young people.

Established: Founded in 1983 by author and educator Judy Galbraith, Free Spirit was the first publisher to offer self-help materials for young people. Today it is the only publisher specializing in Self-Help for Kids and Self-Help for Teens.

Books per year: Plans to publish 20 new titles per year.

Seeks: Titles in three main areas: (1) self-help books for children and teens, (2) enrichment activities for classroom teachers and youth workers, and (3) books on successful parenting and teaching strategies. Award-winning books are recognized and respected for providing creative, practical resources. Ongoing needs include nonfiction books in these topic areas: mental and emotional health issues (early childhood through adolescence), social skills, school success, creative teaching and learning, gifted and talented youth, learning differences, family issues, social action, violence prevention, and healthy youth development.

Accepts unsolicited/unagented: Query only please. See below for details.

Description of fiction titles: Nonfiction books only.

Recent nonfiction titles:

What Kids Need to Succeed (510,000 in print)

The Gifted Kids' Survival Guides (260,000 in print)

Fighting Invisible Tigers: A Stress Management Guide for Teens (170,000 in print)

Preferred nonfiction titles: Does not publish the following: fiction or storybooks, books with animal characters, books with religious or new age content, single biographies or autobiographies, and memoirs.

Preferred form of submission/contact: Query before sending full manuscripts. If you want assurance that your submission reached the publisher, please enclose a self-addressed stamped reply postcard. If you want your materials returned to you in the event that they don't meet current needs, include a self-addressed return envelope with sufficient postage. Proposals should include the following information: Who wrote the book? Tell about yourself and your relevant background. What's the book about? Include a brief overview, an outline or table of contents, and two sample chapters. Who will read the book? Include age ranges and audience description. What other books are available on your topic? How is your book different? Send your submissions to Attention: Acquisitions.

Time to reply: Please be patient! Reply time is one to four months. Your idea might be precisely what Free Spirit is looking for. Or Free Spirit might request revisions to your proposal. If you're a subject-matter expert in need of a writer, Free Spirit can suggest a good match for you and can also put professional writers together with credentialed coauthors.

Terms for writers: Advance plus royalties. You can expect a high level of personal attention from the editors and the promotions and sales departments. The strong backlist ensures that your book will have a long life in print.

Tips and comments: Look through the company's books and study the latest catalog. You'll find Free Spirit books at your local bookstore, library, or schools. To request a copy of the Parent's Choice Approved catalog, write, call, or see the online catalog at www.freespirit.com. Free Spirit cares about young people and the issues and challenges they face every day. The company's mission is to provide children and teens with the tools they need to succeed in life and to make a difference in the world. Free Spirit publishes high-quality nonfiction books for children and teens, parents, teachers, counselors, and others who live with or work with young people.

Front Street Books, Inc.

20 Battery Park Avenue
Asheville, NC 28801
(828) 236-3097
(828) 236-3098
E-mail: contactus@frontstreetbooks.com
Web site: www.frontstreetbooks.com

Description: Book publisher

Established: Front Street is an independent press incorporated on April 1, 1994.

Key people:

Publisher: Stephen Roxburgh, president and publisher

Editor: Joy Neaves (also acts as acquisitions/submissions editor)

Associate publisher: Nancy Hogan Zimmerman

Art director: Helen Robinson

Books per year: Six.

Percentage by first-time authors: Believes in new voices; half of authors are previously unpublished.

Accepts unsolicited/unagented: Front Street is willing to consider unsolicited manuscripts.

Description of fiction titles: Front Street's picture books reflect the joy, spontaneity, and energy of infants and toddlers. Middle-grade chapter books address the various settings and activities of school-age children. Young adult fiction often deals with children in crisis, children at risk, and offers hope and succor, however difficult the subject.

Recent fiction titles:

Robert and the Robot by Eva Schwab

Beaver's Lodge by Ingrid and Dieter Schubert

The School Trip by Tjibbe Veldkamp; illustrated by Philip Hopman

Preferred fiction titles: Front Street believes in and is committed to publishing and exposing young readers to the best literature available in other countries, cultures, and languages. Front Street also believes that books should be beautiful to look at and to hold.

Preferred form of submission/contact: Please enclose a dated cover letter so that Front Street has your name and return address. Front Street regrets that its unable to return materials unless you provide a self-addressed stamped envelope. If there is no SASE included, it will be assumed the materials can be discarded. Front Street is unable to return manuscripts to destinations outside the United States. Do not send submissions as e-mail attachments. Submissions sent in this manner will be automatically deleted. *Fiction:* If under 100 pages, submit the complete manuscript. If over 100 pages, submit one or two sample chapters and a plot summary. Front Street will request the balance of the manuscript if interested. *Poetry:* Please send a selection of no more than 25 poems that are representative of your work. Front Street will request more if we are interested. *Anthologies:* Front Street will only consider anthologies of work by various authors if accompanied by a detailed proposal and permissions budget. *Nonfiction:* A detailed proposal and sample chapter will suffice. *Other:* Whatever it takes to give a sense of the project.

Time to reply: All submissions considered in the order they are received. This is a time-consuming practice, so please be patient in awaiting a response.

Accepts simultaneous submissions: Accepted but discouraged.

Prefer manuscript/illustration packages, or separate: *Picture books:* Not currently accepting texts only for picture book manuscripts. Will accept picture book texts accompanied by artwork. If you are the artist or are working with an artist, please include the manuscript, a dummy, and a sample reproduction of artwork rendered in the manner and style representative of the final artwork. Do not send original art. Cannot be held responsible for damaged or lost materials.

Tips and comments: Current catalog is available online at www.frontstreetbooks.com; familiarize yourself with the list before making submissions. It is important for you to know in advance that if Front Street's decision is negative, you will receive a form rejection letter. This procedure enables Front Street to reduce the time it takes to respond to submissions, time it can devote to reviewing more submissions.

Fulcrum Resources

Fulcrum Publishing
16100 Table Mountain Parkway, Suite 300
Golden, CO 80403
Web site: www.fulcrum-books.com

Description: Fulcrum Publishing is a Colorado-based publishing company that produces and sells quality full-color and black-and-white books to an international market.

Established: Founded in 1984.

Key people:

Acquisitions/submissions editor: Please send submissions to T. J. Baker, Fulcrum Books editor.

Seeks: Fulcrum Resources publishes books and support materials for teachers, librarians, parents, and elementary through middle school children in the subjects of science and nature, literature and storytelling, history, multicultural studies, and Native American and Hispanic cultures. Authors hail from 45 states, Canada, England, Australia, and Africa.

Accepts unsolicited/unagented: Always eager to hear about a manuscript or work-in-progress in the areas in which the company publishes. Accepts unsolicited manuscripts from authors and from literary agents, *but please familiarize yourself with the company's books.*

Recent fiction titles:

The Eagle and the Rainbow

Earth Tales from Around the World

Recent nonfiction titles:

Do Bees Sneeze? Questions Kids Ask about Insects

Preferred form of submission/contact: Please send typed manuscripts and proposals, including an author biography, by regular mail. Will not accept submissions via e-mail. If you are creating a longer work, please send a proposal instead of a full manuscript. In the proposal include a table of contents, one or two sample chapters, and a market analysis of your book that compares your book with competing books.

Time to reply: It will take up to four weeks to evaluate your book proposal and respond. Please do not call about your submission; you will be informed of the decision by mail.

Prefer manuscript/illustration packages, or separate: If your work is illustrated, include two or four sample illustrations (size 8 1/2 by 11). Please do not send originals. However, illustrations are not necessary. If you would like a response and the return of your materials, be sure to include a self-addressed stamped envelope.

Include with illustrator query: If you are an illustrator, feel free to send in two to four sample copies of your work (no larger than 8 1/2 by 11). They will be kept on file for the possibility of future book projects. You will be contacted if an appropriate project arises. Also, if you feel your work has changed or improved over time, please send in additional sample copies. Please do not send originals.

Time to reply: You will be contacted if an appropriate project arises.

Submission guidelines: Write with an SASE or go to the Web site.

Gibbs Smith, Publisher

PO Box 667
Layton, Utah 84041
Web site: www.gibbs-smith.com

Description: Publisher.

Established: 1969.

Key people:

Vice president: Madge Baird

Senior editor: Suzanne Taylor

Editors: Gail Yngve, Linda Nimori, Monica Weeks, and Glenn Law

Seeks: Children's outdoor activity books and children's picture books.

Accepts unsolicited/unagented: Gibbs Smith, publisher, is pleased to receive unsolicited submissions by mail.

Description of fiction titles: Publishes very little in the way of fiction.

Recent fiction titles:

Bullfrog Pops! by Rick Walton
Phantom of the Prairie: Year of the Black-Footed Ferret by Jonathan London

Preferred fiction titles: Novels, short story collections, and essay collections will be returned without being read.

Description of nonfiction titles: Nonfiction titles are mostly nature-oriented picture books.

Recent nonfiction titles:

"Galapagos" Means "Tortoises" by Ruth Heller
Ancient Ones: The World of the Old-Growth Douglas Fir by Barbara Bash
Animals You Never Even Heard Of by Patricia Curtis
Bears by Ian Sterling

Preferred form of submission/contact: Start with a query letter accompanied by an SASE, an outline, a comparative market evaluation, and 10 sample pages of manuscript. If photographs will be part of your project, please submit 12 to 15 sample photographs as duplicate transparencies or color copies; though the publisher will make every effort to return the photographs, Gibbs Smith, publisher, does not take responsibility for lost or damaged photographs received as part of a query or submissions process.

Time to reply: Please allow six to 12 weeks for response.

Include with illustrator query: Samples and resume—do not send originals, please.

Time to reply: Artists' and designers' samples will be filed for editorial reference.

Tips and comments: Novels, short story collections, and essay collections will be returned without being read.

Gifted Education Press

10201 Yuma Court
PO Box 1586
Manassas, VA 20108
(703) 369-5017
E-mail: mdfish@cais.com
Web site: www.cais.com/gep

Description: Publisher of books and periodicals on educating gifted students materials for teachers, parents, and gifted students.

Description of nonfiction titles: During the past two decades, Gifted Education Press has been publishing books on teaching gifted students. These books concentrate on the following areas: teaching philosophy and logic—middle and high school (3 books); teaching social studies and humanities—upper elementary, middle, and high school (10 books); background for teaching gifted students—kindergarten through high school (9 books); parenting gifted children—all ages (2 books); science and technology—upper elementary through high school (3 books).

G. P. Putnam's Sons, BFYR

Penguin Putnam BFYR
345 Hudson Street, 14th Floor
New York, NY 10014
Web site: www.penguinputnam.com/about/children/puffin.htm

Corporate structure/parent: Penguin Putnam Inc.

Description: Publisher.

Established: 1872, though the first children's book wasn't published until a number of years later. One of the first children's titles published by G. P. Putnam's Sons was the 1925 Newbery Honor book *Nicholas* by Anne Carrol Moore.

Key people:

Publisher and president: Nancy Paulsen

Books per year and description: Publishes about 50 trade hardcover books a year for children, including lively, accessible picture books and some of today's strongest voices in fiction.

Accepts unsolicited/unagented: Accepts full picture book manuscripts for review. Please see below for further submission specifics.

Description of fiction titles: Middle grade; chapter books; young adult.

Preferred form of submission/contact: *Picture books:* Accepts full picture book manuscripts for review. Art should not be sent until specifically requested. *Fiction* (middle grade, chapter books, and young adult): Please send a query letter before submitting fiction. Please include a synopsis and one to three sample chapters. Your query letter and sample chapters will be circulated among the editors, and the entire work will be requested on interest. *Nonfiction:* Please send a query letter before submitting nonfiction. Please include a synopsis and one or two sample chapters, as well as a table of contents. Your query letter and sample chapters will be circulated among the editors, and the entire work will be requested on interest. Submissions must include an SASE (self-addressed stamped envelope) for a reply.

Submission guidelines: Please send all submissions to Putnam Children's Editorial, Manuscript Editor, 14th floor. If you wish to have your materials returned, your SASE must have the correct postage.

Tips and comments: If you would like to receive a catalog, you must send a 9 by 12-inch envelope with the appropriate postage.

Greene Bark Press, Inc.

PO Box 1108
Bridgeport, CT 06601-1108
(203) 372-4861
(203) 371-5856 (fax)
E-mail: greenebark@aol.com
Web site: www.greenebarkpress.com

Description: Book publisher of hardcover books for children.

Established: 1981.

Key people:

Publisher: Thomas J. Greene.

Acquisitions/submissions editor: Michele Hofbauer.

Books per year and description: 4 to 6 hardcover fiction picture books.

Percentage by first-time authors: 25 to 50 percent.

Seeks: Original stories with a lot of imagery that lend themselves well to colorful illustrations.

Accepts unsolicited/unagented: Yes, but only with an SASE.

Description of fiction titles: Does not publish either novels or chapter books. Picture books are original, colorful and incorporate a moral or some value added.

Recent fiction titles:

To Know the Sea by Frances Gilbert (A young princess from a mountain village longs for the sea. It takes the lore of the sea, the history and experience of an old sea captain to give the princess the will and desire to venture from the mountain and sail on a ship of her own.)

Preferred fiction titles: Originality, imagery, color, good reading material.

Time to reply: Six to eight weeks, sometimes longer.

Time to publish: 12 to 18 months.

Accepts simultaneous submissions: Yes, in fact, it is encouraged.

Number of illustrators used annually: One or two.

Desired illustrator qualifications: Originality, creativity, imagination, and flexibility.

Prefer manuscript/illustration packages, or separate: Prefer to view them together. Ordinarily does not select the illustrator to work with the writer, but rather keeps a file of samples from illustrators whose work the company has liked. Gives that file to the writer to let the author select the illustrator with whom he or she would like to work. Between them they collaborate and work out the details.

Include with illustrator query: Samples.

Time to reply: Four to six weeks.

Purchases freelance photography: No.

Terms for writers: No advances. Royalties between 10 and 15 percent of the wholesale price of the book. All other rights are shared 50/50.

Terms for illustrators: No advances. Either straight work for hire or 5 percent royalty based on the wholesale price of the book.

Submission guidelines: Send an SASE addressed to Guidelines c/o Greene Bark Press.

Tips and comments: No modern versions of old themes, animal stories (e.g., cats, dogs, etc.), baby themes, and advocacy (e.g. divorce, disability, death, etc.).

Grolier Educational Publishing

90 Sherman Turnpike
Danbury, CT 06816
(203) 796-2605
(203) 797-3899 (fax)
Web site: www.publishing.grolier.com

Corporate structure/parent: Grolier Publishing.

Description: Grolier Educational is a publisher of high-quality reference materials, in print and electronic form, including general encyclopedias, online services, and a line of multivolume, specialty reference sets, aimed at elementary, junior high, and senior high school students. Grolier Educational offers students at all grade levels new ideas and outstanding research sources.

Accepts unsolicited/unagented: No.

Recent nonfiction titles:

American Scene: Lives (grades K–12)

Animal Families (grades 3–8, full-color photographs and illustrations)

Meet Vivian Vande Velde

Author

Vivian Vande Velde has published 19 books, including: *Troll Teacher* (Holiday House; illustrated by Mary Jane Auch, ages 4–8), *Ghost of a Hanged Man* (Marshall Cavendish, ages 8–12), *A Hidden Magic* (Harcourt; illustrated by Trina Schart Hyman, ages 8–12), *The Rumpelstiltskin Problem* (Houghton Mifflin, ages 12 and up), and *The Changeling Prince* (HarperPrism, adult). She was born in New York on June 18, 1951. She took all the interesting literature courses and then dropped out. Before she became a children's book author, she mostly did secretarial work. She's done books ranging from a picture book (4–8) to two marketed for adults, but most of her books are for young adults and for middle-grade students.

How did you get your first book published?

My first book was *A Hidden Magic,* originally published by Crown in 1984, now reissued by Harcourt. I knew I wanted to write a fairy tale kind of story because I've always enjoyed fairy tales myself. Growing up, I loved the Disney movies *Snow White, Cinderella,* and *Sleeping Beauty.* But I always wondered why the princess in those stories was always perfect. Except for the color of their hair, you could use the same words to describe each of them: beautiful, kind, always knew what to say, knew how to sing and dance, was a friend to the forest creatures, and then she got into some trouble and needed a brave and handsome prince to come along and rescue her. (How come they never had a bad hair day? Why didn't any of them wear glasses like I have to? And didn't they ever move their hands a lot while they were talking—the way I do—and knock over a glass of water onto the lap of somebody important?) And the prince in those stories never had any personality except being handsome and brave. Except for the style of the drawing, you wouldn't be able to tell which prince went with which princess.

So I decided I wanted to write a book where I would have a lot of the fairy tale conventions (princes and princesses, castles, magical creatures), but the characters would be different from what people might normally expect. But writing was harder work than I had anticipated: What should I have happen next that would be logical but that nobody would expect? How do I make readers like the characters I'm writing about? How much description is enough so that people can imagine what is happening, but not too much because I don't want to bore anyone? It took me two years to write *A Hidden Magic* (obviously, I took a lot of breaks); then once I did finish, I sent the manuscript out 32 times before number 33, Crown, said yes. I was very fortunate to have Trina Schart Hyman selected to do the illustrations. But—because she was committed to other projects first—we had to wait for her. So: Two years to write the book, two years to find a publisher, two years for the illustrations—this book took a total of six years from that first glimmer of "I think I know what I'll write about" till the book was available on bookstore and library shelves.

continues

Did you have an agent when you published your first book?
No, and still no.

Are you still with your first publisher?
I've worked with several publishers from the very beginning. While I was busy with that long, hard work of gathering those 32 rejections for my first book, I went ahead and wrote a second book and was sending that out, too. I ended up getting the manuscripts accepted, one at one publishing company, the other at a different house, within a month of each other. When I wrote my first young adult book, the people at Crown said they were more interested in books for younger audiences. For all I know, they may have hated the book and were just being polite, but at that time I learned that Jane Yolen was getting her own imprint at Harcourt and that she was interested in young adult fantasy and science fiction, so I sent her a query. She was my editor for several books before she stopped working for Harcourt, and since then I've worked with Michael Stearns for several more books. But when a book doesn't seem right for Harcourt (sometimes I realize this right away, and sometimes they have to tell me so), I will send the manuscript where it seems more appropriate.

Do you have any advice, in terms of finding a publisher, for a writer starting out?
As long as you believe in a project, keep sending it out. Again, my first book was rejected 32 times and then accepted with only copyediting changes. It was a matter of finding the right editor working for the right publishing company at the right time. Thirty-two remains my own personal record, but I have had stories accepted after multiple rejections. I do have to say, however, that I'm not always that persistent with a project. Sometimes, after a few rejections, I'll reread the story and tell myself, "You know, the editors may be right about this one." I don't throw it away (ha—anyone who's ever visited my house could tell you I never throw anything away!), but I'll put the manuscript in a drawer. Maybe in a year or so I'll look at it again and suddenly realize how to fix it. Or I might say, "No, the story doesn't work, but this character is interesting. Maybe if I put him in a different story. . . ." Or I'll use the setting of an old story. Persistence/luck/talent—I've been on panels that have discussed the ratio of how important those qualities are, and almost always that's the order they're given in.

What procedures do you follow when you write?
After diddling around for two years writing my first book—writing one day, knitting a sweater for two weeks, going on vacation, writing another day—I've found that if I work a little bit every day, things go much more smoothly. Not that I truly work every day, but that at least is my intention. I've frequently found that if I set myself down to work, the ideas come much more easily than if I'm just kind of vaguely waiting for those ideas.

Where do you get your ideas?
With *Dragon's Bait,* I wanted to write a story about revenge and how sometimes trying to get revenge just makes the situation worse than it was to begin with. I decided to write about someone accused of doing something she hadn't really done—because I figured that's something that has happened to everyone.

I had been doing some research on medieval times for another book I was writing when I came across a footnote about the Templar knights being disbanded in disgrace over trumped-up charges. This sounded so tantalizing that I looked further into the matter, and I thought it was such an interesting story that it needed to be told. At the same time, and having nothing to do with any of that, I knew that my mother, who lived in France during World War II, had a friend who had a house in the country and took in children. I'd read books about English kids leaving London but not French kids leaving Paris, which was a slightly different situation since London was being bombed, but the Germans were actually in France. Anyway, despite several centuries being between them, the two stories came together in my head in *A Coming Evil,* a story about a French girl during World War II who meets a ghost of a Templar knight.

At the risk of alarming those who are unaware that many of my books have ghosts, vampires, and characters who spend part of their lives as various animals, I do have to say that often the germ of the story is something that really happened, expanded through many steps of "what if," disguised, and then sent through the agitate/spin/rinse cycle.

What do you think are the key differences between writing for children and writing for adults?

I don't see my two adult novels as being that different from my young adult fantasies. But here's a thought on the subject: While adults (at least those adults who like to read) will read many books in a lifetime, any children's book is best read by any one particular child for only a three- to four-year span; so any book that a child reads is going to have a much greater impact than most books that an adult will read. Also, children are at a stage in their lives where they are learning, forming opinions, having their personalities shaped, and what they read will influence that. Not many books meant for adults will change someone's life. What a responsibility!

Dress through the Ages (grades 3–8, full-color illustrations)
Include with illustrator query: Samples. *No original art, please.*
Submission guidelines: Write with an SASE for guidelines.

GREENWILLOW BOOKS

1350 Avenue of the Americas
New York, NY 10019
Web site: www.harpercollins.com/hc/aboutus/imprints/willow.asp

GP mailed 7/19

Corporate structure/parent: HarperCollins.
Description: Book publisher.
Established: 1974. Since its inception in 1974, Greenwillow Books has been publishing books for children of every age. Greenwillow Books hopes that at the heart of each book there is honesty, emotion, and depth—conveyed by an author or an artist who has something that is worth saying to children and who says it in a way that is worth reading.

Books per year and description: Greenwillow Books publishes picture books, fiction for young readers of all ages, and nonfiction primarily for children under seven years of age

Seeks: Greenwillow Books publishes picture books, fiction for young readers of all ages, and nonfiction primarily for children under seven years of age.

Accepts unsolicited/unagented: Yes.

Preferred titles: Read many children's books (especially those on the Greenwillow list), decide what you like or don't like about them, then write the story you want to tell (not what you think Greenwillow wants to read), and send it!

Preferred form of submission/contact: Manuscript.

Time to reply: Tries to respond within 10 weeks' time.

Accepts simultaneous submissions: Accepts—and encourages—simultaneous submissions to other publishers and ask only that you so inform Greenwillow Books.

Prefer manuscript/illustration packages, or separate: Accepts packages. If your work is illustrated, Greenwillow asks to see a typed text, rough dummy, and a copy of a finished picture. *Please do not send original artwork* with your submission. Greenwillow asks that you *please include a self-addressed stamped envelope* large enough to accommodate your material so that, if necessary, it may be returned to you.

Submission guidelines: No special guidelines. Please read through the profile and note the suggestions.

Tips and comments: Greenwillow asks that completed manuscripts be typed and double spaced. Because one person opens all submissions and directs them to the proper editors, please address your manuscript simply to "Editorial Department, Greenwillow Books." All submissions should be no larger than 9 by 12.

GROSSET & DUNLAP

345 Hudson Street
New York, NY 10014
Web site: www.penguinputnam.com/about/children/puffin.htm

Corporate structure/parent: Penguin Putnam. In 1982, Grosset & Dunlap was bought by G. P. Putnam's Sons (later known as The Putnam Berkley Group), which merged with Penguin USA in 1996 to become Penguin Putnam. One of several imprints among the Books for Young Readers division, Grosset remains a mass-market publisher of children's books.

Description: Known for originality, quality, and value, Grosset & Dunlap currently publishes many well-known book lines, including the All Aboard series of paperback picture books and All Aboard Reading, a paperback program for newly independent readers with more than 60 titles in print. Other Grosset series include THE ZACK FILES, a chapter-book series by humorist Dan Greenburg, and the innovative Planet Dexter science books.

Established: 1898.

Key people:

Publisher and president: Vivian Antonangeli

Books per year: 100 to 125 new titles a year.

Accepts unsolicited/unagented: At this time most Penguin Putnam Inc. imprints do not accept unsolicited manuscripts. If you would like your work to be considered for publication by a major publisher, Penguin Putnam Inc. recommends that you work with an established literary agent.

GROUP PUBLISHING, INC.

PO Box 481
Loveland, CO 80539
(970) 669-3836
Web site: www.grouppublishing.com

Description: Publisher, Christian.

Terms for writers: Both single-author royalty books and multiple-author compilations assigned on a works-for-hire basis.

Submission guidelines: Write with an SASE or visit the Web site for guidelines. If you have a manuscript that meets the criteria listed under "Tips," Group Publishing would like to know about it. Submissions should include a cover letter briefly summarizing your book and your background; an outline (book structure); an introduction detailing how your book fits into a ministry setting and why people need or want your book (write this as if the buyer were reading it while he or she browses in a bookstore); two sample chapters (written and formatted in such a way that any average church leader could read, understand, and implement your ideas with his or her group) or two sample lessons (if it's a book full of meeting ideas) or about a dozen sample ideas (if it's a book of short ideas, devotions, skits, or the like); if you would like your submission returned, please include SASE.

Seeks: *Writing Group Curriculum*—always looking for good writers who know kids, understand active learning, and have the ability to write lessons that help kids apply the Bible to their lives. Group Publishing's editors have set up a trial assignment system to allow potential writers to try their hand at writing curriculum. Check out the various curriculum lines at your local Christian bookstore. Then write and request a trial assignment specifying the age level and curriculum line that interests you. For quick processing, write "Trial Assignment Request" on the outside of the envelope and include a stamped self-addressed envelope. Group Publishing will try to respond to your trial assignment as quickly as possible (based on current project deadlines).

Tips and comments: Group Publishing's mission is to encourage Christian growth in children, youth, and adults. To that end, Group publishes more than 30 titles each year under the following imprints: Group Publishing, Inc.—resources for Christian education in local churches, including youth and children's ministry; Vital Ministry Books—resources for Christian pastors and leaders, including family ministry; Vacation Bible School—five-day courses for preschool through fifth grade. Each course includes games, crafts, snacks, music, video, Bible adventures, and more. New course each year. All courses incorporate active- and interactive-learning techniques.

GRYPHON HOUSE BOOKS, INC.

PO Box 207
Beltsville, MD 20704-0207

Description: Gryphon House publishes books of active educational experiences for young children (ages 1 to 8).

Seeks: Looking for books of creative, participatory learning experiences that have a common conceptual theme to tie them together. The books should be on subjects that teachers want to do on a daily basis in the classroom. If a book caters to a particular market in addition to teachers, that would be a plus.

Accepts unsolicited/unagented: No manuscripts.

Preferred form of submission/contact: Prefers to receive a letter of inquiry rather than a manuscript. Include the proposed title, the purpose of the book, table of contents, introductory material, and a dozen or so pages of the actual activities.

Submission guidelines: Please write a letter answering these questions: Research your competition. Find and review books similar to yours. You can find books in the library, *Books in Print,* retail bookstores, and teacher and school supply stores. How are they selling? Identify your market. Is there a need for another book on your topic? Why? Describe specifically what your book does that others do not. What makes your book unique? Why is this a book that teachers want to own? Is it one they will use every day? Who has reviewed or tested your book? What classes or workshops have you led? Expert in the field? Gryphon is not terribly interested in knowing how your children, or teachers with whom you work have liked the material. Gryphon would, however, be most interested in knowing how the material was received by teachers with whom you had no direct contact. What is your background? Why did you write this book? How are you qualified to write this book? Any previous publications? How will you be able to promote your book? Workshops at professional meetings? Active demonstrations at bookstores and school supply stores? What else? Also include a copy of the table of contents and a dozen or so pages of activities.

GULLIVER BOOKS

15 E. 26th Street
New York, NY 10010
(212) 592-1000

Corporate structure/parent: Harcourt Trade Publishers (which is a division of Harcourt, Inc.).

Description: Book publisher.

Key people:

Editorial director: Elizabeth Van Doren

Editor: Garen Eileen Thomas

Books per year and description: Gulliver publishes 25 to 30 new titles per year, primarily picture books but also select chapter books, novels, and nonfiction titles.

Accepts unsolicited/unagented: Only agented, previously published, or members of SCBWI (Society or Children's Book Writers and Illustrators).

Description of fiction titles: Limited number of contemporary chapter books; also some historical fiction.

Recent fiction titles:

School Trouble for Andy Russell by David Adler

Preferred form of submission/contact: For picture books: send the manuscript; for fiction: send a query letter.

Time to reply: Six to eight weeks.

Time to publish: Picture book schedules are dependent on the illustrator's schedule; fiction titles take approximately two years.

Accepts simultaneous submissions: Prefers not to.

Prefer manuscript/illustration packages, or separate: Either.

Include with illustrator query: Tear sheets; postcards.

Time to reply: Samples are kept on file. and if the company is interested, you'll be contacted.

Purchases freelance photography: No.

Terms for writers: Advance and royalties.

Terms for illustrators: Advance and royalties.

HACHAI PUBLISHING

156 Chester Avenue
Brooklyn, NY 11218
(718) 633-0100
(718) 633-0103 (fax)
E-mail: info@hachai.com
Web site: www.hachai.com

Description: Book Publisher specializing in Jewish books for children.

Established: 1989.

Key people:

Acquisitions/submissions editor: Dina Rosenfeld

Books per year and description: Judaica picture books; 4 to 6 per year.

Percentage by first-time authors: 75 percent.

Seeks: Judaica; morals and values.

Accepts unsolicited/unagented: Yes.

Description of fiction titles: Jewish subject matter and day-to-day life events and activities explained.

Recent fiction titles:

The Bravest Fireman by Leah Zytman; illustrated by Leah Malka Diskind
My Jewish Days of the Week, by Dvora Waysman; illustrated by Melanie Schmidt
Shimmy the Youngest by Miriam Elias; illustrated by Aidel Backman

Preferred fiction titles: Books about Jewish subject matter; morals and values.

Description of nonfiction titles: None.

Preferred form of submission/contact: Send manuscript with an SASE for return and/or response.

Time to reply: Six weeks.

Time to publish: Depends on the scheduling with the artist—usually one to two years.

Accepts simultaneous submissions: Yes.

Number of illustrators used annually: Four to six.

Desired illustrator qualifications: Primary color artwork.

Prefer manuscript/illustration packages, or separate: Separately.

Include with illustrator query: Samples, color copies. *Please do not send originals.*

Time to reply: Six weeks.

Purchases freelance photography: No.

Terms for writers: Flat fee.

Terms for illustrators: Flat fee.

Submission guidelines: Send an SASE for guidelines or go to the Web site.

HARCOURT, INC.

525 B Street, Suite 1900
San Diego, CA 92101
(619) 699-6810
(619) 699-6777 (fax)
Web site: www.harcourtbooks.com

Corporate structure/parent: Harcourt, Inc., is the parent company to Harcourt Trade Publishers, which includes the following imprints for children's books: Green Light Readers, Gulliver Books, Harcourt Paperbacks, Harcourt Young Classics, Odyssey Classics, Red Wagon Books, Silver Whistle, and Voyager Books/Libros Viajeros.

Description: Book publisher.

Established: 1920.

Key people:

Publisher: Louise Pelan

Acquisitions/submissions editors: Allyn Johnston, Michael Stearns, and Jeannette Larson

Books per year and description: Approximately 160 to 180 books in the following categories: picture books, teen fiction, books for babies, and a selection of nonfiction.

Percentage by first-time authors: Approximately 20 percent.

Seeks: Picture books, teen fiction, books for babies, and a selection of nonfiction.

Accepts unsolicited/unagented: No manuscripts.

Description of fiction titles: Must have high literary quality.

Recent fiction titles:

Counterfeit Son by Elaine Alphin
Dream Freedom by Sonia Levitin
The Body of Christopher Creed by Carol Plum-Ucci

Meet Janet Wong

Author

Janet Wong has written nine books (five poetry collections and four picture books) for all ages, pre-K through university—for instance, *Good Luck Gold* (McElderry/Simon & Schuster, 1994); *Behind the Wheel: Poems about Driving* (McElderry/Simon & Schuster, 1999); *Grump* (McElderry/Simon & Schuster, 2001); *This Next New Year* (Foster/FSG, 2000); *The Trip Back Home* (Harcourt, 2000). She was born in Los Angeles on September 30, 1962. She has a B.A. in history from the University of California–Los Angeles and a law degree from Yale Law School. Before she became a children's book author, she was a corporate and labor/employment lawyer for GTE and director of labor relations for Universal Studios Hollywood. Visit her Web site at www.janetwong.com

How did you get your first book published?

I owe the publication of my first book to Myra Cohn Livingston, my poetry teacher. When I quit my law job in September 1991, I planned to write for a year and see whether I could sell a book. I thought I'd write picture books or middle-grade novels, never poetry! I hated poetry. But I heard Myra speak at a one-day seminar at UCLA Extension, and I knew I could learn something from her. I didn't want to learn poetry, though, so it wasn't until 26 rejections later (rejections for picture book manuscripts) that I decided that I needed to learn to write for children—and decided to study with her. I thought that studying rhyme and rhythm would help me write a better picture book. The next thing I knew, the only thing I wanted to write was poetry. Myra sold my first book for me by showing it to her longtime editor, Margaret McElderry. I was very lucky. I got my "yes" call from Margaret in March 1993.

Did you have an agent when you published your first book?

I don't have an agent.

Do you have any advice, in terms of finding an agent, for a writer starting out?

I don't think that a brand new writer for children needs to have an agent. I think it's better just to write as many good books as you can and send them out to editors you meet at conferences or hear about from published friends.

Are you still with your first publisher?

Yes, I am fortunate that Margaret McElderry still works with me. We have a couple of forthcoming picture books due to be published in the next few years, including *You Have to Write* (spring 2002) and *Homegrown House* (spring 2003). Margaret and Simon & Schuster have treated me very well, and I love working with them. They regularly send me to reading conferences as a speaker—and even trust me with their credit card to order room service! But I also work with editors at two additional publishers, FSG and Harcourt, which have been equally wonderful. So many people say it, and it's true: It would be unrealistic to expect one publisher to publish all my work, especially because I tend to write in spurts and like to sell my manuscripts right away!

continues

Do you have any advice, in terms of finding a publisher, for a writer starting out?

Look at the very newest books, in an independent children's bookstore—if you can—since the selection will be more diverse than what you'll typically find in a chain store. Find the books you love. Do several of them happen to be published by the same publisher? Go to conferences and listen closely to the editors, and if you like what you hear, invite yourself to send them your manuscripts!

What do you think are the key differences between writing for children and writing for adults?

Writing for children, I feel I have a greater responsibility to the reader. A responsibility not to be preachy, but not to be overly negative, either.

How did you learn to write?

Almost everything I know about poetry I learned from Myra Cohn Livingston. Her book *Poem-Making* (HarperCollins) is written for children but a great book for adults, too.

Anything you really wish somebody had told you when you started out?

Once your first book is published, your new mission begins: to keep your book alive! Great books go out of print each year, some just two or three years after publication. Give children's books as presents whenever you need to buy a gift, and encourage your friends to share your books with their families and friends, too. Children's books are not just for children. Don't be shy about keeping your "babies" alive and well. Remember the wonderful words—first penned by David McCord, I think—"A book is a present you can give again and again"!

Fiona's Private Pages by Robin Cruise

Pharoah's Daughter by Julius Lester

Preferred fiction titles: Good character development and plot. Not looking for fluffy romance. Historical fiction and fantasy are strong on the list.

Description of nonfiction titles: Very little nonfiction. The text must be fresh and innovative and very trade oriented.

Recent nonfiction titles:

Girl Stuff: A Survival Guide to Growing Up by Margaret Blackstone and Elissa Guest

Preferred form of submission/contact: Query.

Time to reply: Six to eight weeks.

Time to publish: Depends on status of the art. Can be up to two or three years for a picture book.

Accepts simultaneous submissions: No.

Number of illustrators used annually: Most likely working with 100 illustrators at any given time, in various stages of development.

Desired illustrator qualifications: High-quality draftsmanship; ability to render characters with consistency; fresh, innovative style. *Not* cartoony or down-market styles.

Prefer manuscript/illustration packages, or separate: Either, but not unsolicited.

Include with illustrator query: Resume and copies of samples. But please, *no originals.*
Time to reply: Six to eight weeks.
Purchases freelance photography: Yes, occasionally.
Terms for writers: 10 percent for all text or text and art together .
Terms for illustrators: 5 percent for an illustrated book.
Submission guidelines: Write to Manuscript Submissions, Harcourt Children's Books (see address given earlier).
Tips and comments: Work with an agent who knows the company's list!

HarperCollins Children's Books

1350 Avenue of the Americas
New York, NY 10019
(212) 261-6500
Web site: www.harperchildrens.com

Description: One of the oldest and largest children's book publishers, publishing for ages newborn through young adult in hardcover, paperback, and novelty formats. Imprints include Joanna Cotler Books, Laura Geringer Books, Greenwillow Books, Avon, Harper-Festival, HarperTrophy, and HarperTempest.
Established: 1876.
Key people:
Publisher: Susan Katz
Editor in chief: Kate Morgan Jackson
Acquisitions/submissions editors:
Elise Howard, director of paperback publishing
Emily Brenner, director of novelty publishing
Robert Warren, hardcover editorial director
Alix Reid, hardcover editorial director
Phoebe Yeh, hardcover editorial director
Barbara Lalicki, hardcover editorial director
Katherine Brown Tegen, editorial director at large
Joanna Cotler, publisher, Joanna Cotler Books
Laura Geringer, publisher, Laura Geringer Books
Susan Hirschman, publisher, Greenwillow Books
Books per year and description: 525 titles per year, hardcover and paperback novelty.
Percentage by first-time authors: About 10 percent.
Seeks: Middle-grade novels; holiday picture books; holiday novelty.
Accepts unsolicited/unagented: Only agented manuscripts.
Description of fiction titles: Very wide-ranging, from literary to licensed-based commercial.
Recent fiction titles:
The Wander by Sharon Creech

A Series of Unfortunate Events by Lemony Snicket
Where Do Balloons Go by Jamie Lee Curtis

Preferred fiction titles: Looking for holiday picture books in particular; looking for middle-grade fantasy.

Description of nonfiction titles: Primarily confined to the *Let's Read and Find Out Science Book* series and poetry.

Recent nonfiction titles:
It's Raining Pigs and Noodles by Jack Prelutsky
How to Talk to Your Dog by Jean Craighead George

Preferred nonfiction titles: New titles for the science series.

Preferred form of submission/contact: Proposal, manuscript, or query *sent via agent.*

Time to reply: Two to four weeks.

Time to publish: 18 months.

Accepts simultaneous submissions: Yes.

Number of illustrators used annually: About 250.

Desired illustrator qualifications: Range of styles; ability to work fast; picture book experience.

Prefer manuscript/illustration packages, or separate: Prefer separately.

Include with illustrator query: Portfolio or tear sheets.

Time to reply: Two to four weeks.

Purchases freelance photography: No.

Terms for writers: 5 to 10 percent list in cloth; 3 to 6 percent list in paper.

Terms for illustrators: Same as above.

Submission guidelines: Doesn't distribute guidelines.

Tips and comments: Authors need to come to us through an agent—the major agencies know the company's needs.

HarperTrophy

HarperCollins
1350 Avenue of the Americas
New York, New York 10019
(212) 261-6500
Web site: www.harperchildrens.com/hch

Corporate structure/parent: HarperCollins (HC also includes the following imprints for young readers: Avon, Joanna Cotler Books, Laura Geringer Books, Greenwillow Books, HarperFestival, and HarperTempest).

Description: Publisher.

Accepts unsolicited/unagented: No.

Recent fiction titles:
Always Wear Clean Underwear! by Marc Gellman
"Could Be Worse!" by James Stevenson

Hello, I Lied by M. E. Kerr
. . . *And Now Miguel* by Joseph Krumgold

Submission guidelines: Unfortunately, the volume of submissions HarperTrophy receives prevents the company from reading unsolicited manuscripts or proposals.

HEALTH COMMUNICATIONS, INC.

3201 S.W. 15th Street
Deerfield Beach, Florida 33442
(800) 851-9100
Web site: www.hcibooks.com

Description: Publisher.

Seeks: Teens and children, young adult fiction and children's illustrated books.

Accepts unsolicited/unagented: Proposals only—please follow guidelines as specified here.

Preferred form of submission/contact: The publishing process at HCI begins with a book proposal, which is evaluated by the editorial department. To ensure that book proposals are evaluated on an equal basis and that all necessary information is provided, HCI requires prospective authors to follow the submission guidelines in preparing their proposals. *Do not send a complete manuscript unless asked to do so.* All submissions are evaluated on the basis of content, author credentials, and marketability. Submissions that do not conform to these guidelines are rejected. No online submissions will be accepted.

Time to reply: 1 to 10 weeks but sometimes, depending on volume, up to three times as long.

Submission guidelines: Include a cover letter containing your name, return address, and daytime phone number with your proposal. The cover letter is for HCI's records and will not be returned to you. Proposal must include the following: *Author information:* Send your bio or curriculum vitae. Include information on professional credentials, current occupation, previously published works, any public speaking or promotional experience you have, and any television or radio appearances you have made. *Marketing data:* Supply detailed information on the marketability of your book, including target audience (Who is it? How big is it? How do you know it exists?); competing titles (What other books on the same or a similar topic have already been published? How popular are they?); uniqueness value (What makes your book interesting and different from others already on the market? Why would readers choose your book over others currently available?); marketing plan (How do you intend to promote the book? What marketing channels can you propose? Do you have access to any special avenues for marketing the book?). *Manuscript sample:* Please *do not* submit bound or two-sided copies of your manuscript. Please send no more or less than the following: (1) detailed outline of the book (please do not send spiral-bound manuscripts); (2) table of contents; (3) introduction; (4) two sample chapters. *Spelling:* Use the first spelling listed in the most recent edition of *Webster's New International Dictionary* or *Webster's Collegiate Dictionary.*

Punctuation and style: Do not use the serial comma. Refer to the most recent edition of *The Chicago Manual of Style* regarding numbers and any other points of style.

Health Press

PO Box 1388
Santa Fe, NM, 87504
(505) 474-0303
E-mail: goodbooks@healthpress.com
Web site: www.healthpress.com

Description: Health Press presents an award-winning line of books for children and adults on a wide variety of medical conditions to meet the need for easy access to responsible, accurate patient education materials. Written and reviewed by medical professionals, these easy-to-understand books focus on providing explanation, reassurance, and answers to questions patients ask.

Recent nonfiction titles:

The Book of You: The Science and Fun! of Why You Look, Feel, and Act the Way You Do by Sylvia Funston

How the Body Works by Steve Parker

Private and Personal: Questions and Answers for Girls Only by Carol Weston

Hendrick-Long Publishing Co., Inc.

PO Box 25123
Dallas, TX 75225-1123
(214) 358-4677
(214) 352-4768 (fax)
E-mail: hendrick-long@worldnet.att.net

Description: Book publisher focusing on material relating to the history, geography, animals, folklore, or natural setting of Texas and the Southwest.

Established: The company was established in 1969.

Key people:

Acquisitions/submissions editor: Joann Long

Seeks: Material submitted should relate to the company's primary focus—nonfiction or historical fiction about Texas or the Southwest—and should be suitable for young readers. Audiences range from kindergarten through young adult.

Accepts unsolicited/unagented: Yes.

Preferred titles: Age-appropriate manuscripts dealing with Texas and the Southwest. No poetry.

Preferred form of submission/contact: Please send a query letter, a synopsis or outline, one or two chapters, and a table of contents. A brief resume is often useful, but it is not required. Please designate whether the work is a multiple submission.

Time to reply: Tries to respond to query letters and submissions in one to two months.

Accepts simultaneous submissions: In most cases, not interested in multiple submissions. Please designate whether the work is a multiple submission.

Prefer manuscript/illustration packages, or separate: Packages are accepted. All material should be book length. Text/picture books should be at least 32 pages. If art is included with the proposal, please send a copy of at least one illustration; *please, no originals!*

Include with illustrator query: Samples.

Time to reply: Tries to respond in one to two months.

Tips and comments: Please enclose a self-addressed stamped envelope to answer your query or return your manuscript, if necessary. If you do not send an envelope, the manuscript will be kept on file for one month after a response to your proposal has been sent. After one month, manuscripts whose authors have not asked for their return are discarded.

HENRY HOLT BOOKS FOR YOUNG READERS

115 W. 18th Street
New York, NY 10011
Web site: www.henryholt.com/byr
Guidelines: www.henryholt.com/byr/authorsubmit.htm

Description: Henry Holt and Company publishes a wide variety of books for children of all ages including picture books, fiction, and nonfiction.

Key people:

Art director: Martha Rago

Accepts unsolicited/unagented: The Books for Young Readers department accepts solicited as well as unsolicited submissions.

Recent fiction titles:

Blue Avenger Cracks the Code by Norma Howe (Blue's new challenge is tackling the greatest mystery in all literature: Who wrote Shakespeare's plays?)

Attack of the Fifty-Foot Teacher by Lisa Passen (Watch out for Miss Irma Birmbaum—the meanest teacher in town!)

Recent nonfiction titles:

Learning to Graph from a Baby Tiger by Anne Whitehead Nagda and Cindy Bickel (The innovative book uses graphs to tell the story of T. J., a Siberian tiger cub born at the Denver Zoo. T. J. is orphaned when he is just a few weeks old.)

Preferred form of submission/contact: The department prefers to see complete manuscripts. Authors may submit photocopies. Include a brief cover letter with your manuscript that contains your current address and a description of your manuscript. You may want to include other pertinent information such as a list of previously published works. All submissions must be accompanied by a self-addressed stamped envelope for the return of your material if it cannot be used. Do not overpackage. A simple manila envelope will protect your manuscript sufficiently. *Do not send more than one manuscript at a time.*

Time to reply: Expect a reply within three to four months.

Prefer manuscript/illustration packages, or separate: You should not submit illustrations with picture book texts unless you are, yourself, the illustrator.

Include with illustrator query: Color or black-and-white photocopies, prints of original illustrations, or slides should be sent.

Time to reply: *The art director reviews all materials sent to her attention.* A reply can be expected only if samples are accompanied by a self-addressed stamped envelope. Please do not send original art or any materials that you would not want damaged, as that is always a risk. *By drop-off:* Portfolios are reviewed on Mondays without an appointment. Portfolios should be left in the morning with the receptionist, for pickup at 5:00 or the following morning. Please specify whether there is a time you need to have your materials returned. Label portfolios clearly with your name and who you are dropping off for. *By appointment:* Appointments for an in-person portfolio review can be made for alternating Tuesday mornings, between 10:00 and 12 noon. Please call Nicole Stanco at (212) 886-9297 to schedule about three weeks in advance of desired date.

Tips and comments: Although the company would like to be able to comment specifically on each manuscript, the large volume of submissions received precludes this. The company is unable to acknowledge receipt of manuscripts unless a self-addressed stamped postcard is fastened to the cover letter of the submission.

HIGHSMITH PRESS

PO Box 800
Fort Atkinson, WI 53538-0800
(920) 563-9571
(920) 563-4801 (fax)
E-mail: hpress@highsmith.com
Web site: www.hpress.highsmith.com

Key people:

Publisher: Donald L. Sager (also acts as acquisitions/submissions editor)

Books per year: Publishes approximately 20 new titles a year (the press has more than 100 titles currently in print).

Seeks: Highsmith Press is interested in proposals or manuscripts on the following subjects: guides to library-related resources on the Internet for youth; concise handbooks written for young people that creatively develop library and research skills; reference books for middle school and senior high school students; creative reading activity books that can be used by children's and school librarians and teachers to stimulate reading among youth; practical handbooks for librarians addressing common problems or new trends; basic handbooks for teachers and librarians that offer instructional activities, lesson plans and resources that develop information seeking and computer skills among children and young people; storytelling resources for children's librarians, teachers, and professional storytellers that feature interesting and easy-to-learn stories and storytelling techniques, with a special emphasis on multicultural themes.

Accepts unsolicited/unagented: Highsmith Press accepts unsolicited proposals and manuscripts from prospective authors and welcomes your inquiries.

Description of fiction titles: None.

Description of nonfiction titles: Resource books.

Preferred form of submission/contact: For manuscripts less than 100 pages, Highsmith Press would like to receive the entire work for review, including illustrations. For longer manuscripts, please send selected sections and illustrations that best describe the project, including the introduction. Highsmith Press also welcomes outlines of prospective projects, particularly if they are reference books. Please include a cover letter summarizing the purpose of the work and its potential market. Identify any other recent books that have been published on a similar topic, and describe how your book differs. In your letter state which computer software you used (or plan to use) to develop your manuscript. Attach a current resume listing your qualifications. Include a self-addressed stamped envelope so Highsmith Press may return your material. Or submit by e-mail (*four pages or less*) to hpress@highsmith.com

Time to reply: Highsmith Press seeks to reach a decision on each submission or proposal within 60 days, but to achieve this goal you must cooperate in following submission guidelines (please read our profile in its entirety).

Accepts simultaneous submissions: Highsmith Press is not troubled by manuscripts that are being simultaneously submitted to other publishers.

Purchases freelance photography: Will consider photos submitted with manuscripts.

Preferred photography: No guidelines, but will consider photos submitted with manuscripts.

Terms for writers: The specific terms for authors and illustrators will vary with the nature of each project. However, Highsmith Press does provide very competitive royalties and advances, and emphasizes quality design and high production standards.

Terms for illustrators: See above.

Tips and comments: Highsmith Press recommends that you review its online catalog to see the types of materials it publishes. Essentially, Highsmith Press's primary interests are concise and practical professional handbooks for librarians, library reference books, and resources that aid librarians and teachers to develop and stimulate reading interests and to facilitate library and information skills among youth (preschool through high school).

Hodder Children's Books

338 Euston Road
London NW1 3BH
United Kingdom
(44) 207 873 6000
(44) 207 873 6024 (fax)
Web site: www.madaboutbooks.com

Corporate structure/parent: Hodder Headline.

Description: Children's book publisher.

Established: 1868.

Key people:

Publisher: Margaret Conroy

Acquisitions/submissions editors: Kate Burns (picture books); Anne Clark (nonfiction); Chris Kloet (fiction)

Books per year and description: 400 or more books in the following categories: picture books, young fiction, young adult, nonfiction, home learning, audio, and poetry.

Percentage by first-time authors: 1 percent.

Seeks: Highly original stories that really stand out from the rest.

Accepts unsolicited/unagented: Yes, but *no* poetry, rhyming picture book texts, ABCs, or counting books.

Description of fiction titles: Two sorts: mass-market series books and literary fiction.

Recent fiction titles:

Animal Ark series (mass market; *Kittens in the Kitchen, Pony in the Porch*, etc.) by Lucy Daniels ("where animals come first")

Skellig by David Almond (literary fiction; winner of the Carnegie Medal and the Whitbread Award)

Preferred fiction titles: Quality, originality, and a good plot! Not looking for gentle stories about bears or talking inanimate objects.

Description of nonfiction titles: Hodder Wayland titles are aimed at schools and libraries. Hodder children's nonfiction is mostly home-learning, teen self-help, or humorous looks at historical topics.

Recent nonfiction titles:

Traditions from Africa (also China, India, the Caribbean)

The History of the Asian Community in Britain by Rozzina Visram (also *The History of African and Caribbean Communities in Britain*)

Hidden under the Ground, written and illustrated by Peter Kent

Preferred nonfiction titles: Not actively seeking unsolicited nonfiction.

Preferred form of submission/contact: Please send a synopsis and sample chapter to The Reader, Hodder Children's Books, 338 Euston Road, London, England NW1 3BH.

Time to reply: Four to six weeks.

Time to publish: One year.

Accepts simultaneous submissions: Yes.

Number of illustrators used annually: Hundreds.

Desired illustrator qualifications: Exceptional artists; high-quality work.

Prefer manuscript/illustration packages, or separate: Prefers separate illustration submissions.

Include with illustrator query: Samples will not be returned, so it is important not to send original artwork. Color copies and black-and-white copies will do.

Time to reply: Four to six weeks with an SASE for reply.

Purchases freelance photography: Occasionally.

Preferred photography: Depends on the project requirement.

Terms for writers: Completely variable.

Terms for illustrators: Mostly flat fees for covers. Royalty deals may be negotiated for inside illustrations.

Submission guidelines: Call, fax, or write to Hodder Children's Books Editorial Department.

Tips and comments: Know the list and review the writer's guidelines and catalogs before you consider submitting a manuscript. It's clear from looking at the books what types of illustrations are desired. The company receives more than 100 unsolicited manuscripts each week, most of which are terrible or completely unsuitable for the list. The children's book market is highly competitive, and a book needs to be exceptional to succeed.

Hohm Press

PO Box 31
Prescott, AZ 86302
Web site: www.hohmpress.com

Description: Publisher.

Established: 1975.

Accepts unsolicited/unagented: No.

Submission guidelines: At present Hohm is not accepting any children's books.

Holiday House

425 Madison Avenue
New York, NY 10017
Web site: www.holidayhouse.com

Description: Holiday House is a small independent trade publisher of children's books only. Specializes in quality hardcovers from the picture book level to young adult, both fiction and nonfiction.

Key people:

Art director: Claire Counihan

Seeks: While Holiday House publishes books for grades kindergarten and up, it is now especially interested in acquiring literary middle-grade novels.

Accepts unsolicited/unagented: Queries only, please.

Description of fiction titles: Holiday House specializes in quality hardcovers from the picture book level to young adult.

Recent fiction titles:

That Apple Is Mine! retold and illustrated by Katya Arnold

Mailbox Magic written and illustrated by Nancy Poydar

Preferred fiction titles: Holiday House does not publish mass-market books, including, but not limited to, board books, pop-ups, activity books, sticker books, coloring books, series books, or paperback originals.

Description of nonfiction titles: Holiday House specializes in quality hardcovers from the picture book level to young adult.

Recent nonfiction titles:

Drip! Drop! How Water Gets to Your Tap by Barbara Seuling; illustrated by Nancy Tobin

Apples, written and illustrated by Gail Gibbons

Preferred form of submission/contact: Please send a query letter only, describing what the manuscript is about, for picture books as well as books for older readers. *A self-addressed stamped envelope or postcard must be included for a reply.*

Time to reply: Please allow two months for a response. A proposal under serious consideration may require more time. If you have any questions about a submission, please send a self-addressed stamped postcard. No phone calls, please.

Accepts simultaneous submissions: No.

Desired illustrator qualifications: Holiday House specifically looks for work that is highly original and geared to the trade market; humor, multicultural work, historical work, fantasy and folklore, jacket art; illustrators who are professional and competent and have a strong understanding of the process involved in illustrating a children's book. Holiday House is not interested in work that is geared to the mass market.

Include with illustrator query: If you wish to submit, please send photocopies of full-color samples and of black-and-white line work. Never send original artwork. Holiday House does not accept certified or registered mail.

Time to reply: Holiday House does not comment individually on artwork submissions. If the company wishes to schedule a portfolio review based on your submitted work, you will be contacted. Holiday House does not have a drop-off policy and does not schedule portfolio reviews without first receiving samples.

HOUGHTON MIFFLIN COMPANY

222 Berkeley Street
Boston, MA 02116
(617) 351-5000
(617) 351-1111 (fax)
E-mail: childrens_books@hmco.com
Web site: www.houghtonmifflinbooks.com
Children's Books information can be heard at (617) 351-5959

Description: Book publisher.

Established: 1832.

Key people:

Publisher: Anita Silvey

Submissions coordinator: Hannah Rodgers

Books per year and description: 90 to 100, including picture books, novels, board books, and paperbacks.

Percentage by first-time authors: 10 percent,

Accepts unsolicited/unagented: Yes. The Children's Book Division will read unsolicited manuscripts. *Please send them by conventional mail only. No e-mailed or faxed manuscripts.*

Recent fiction titles:
Henry Hikes to Fitchburg by D. B. Johnson
Whiteblack the Penguin Sees the World by H. A. and Margret Rey
Gathering Blue by Lois Lowry (Walter Lorraine Books)
Recent nonfiction titles:
Girls Think of Everything by Catherine Thimmesh
Kids on Strike by Sue Campbell Bartoletti
The Top of the World: Climbing Mount Everest by Steve Jenkins

Preferred form of submission/contact: *Fiction:* manuscript; *Nonfiction:* synopsis and sample chapters.

Time to reply: Eight to 12 weeks.

Time to publish: Two years.

Accepts simultaneous submissions: Yes.

Number of illustrators used annually: 40 to 60.

Prefer manuscript/illustration packages, or separate: Illustration samples should be submitted to the art department, but if the package is an illustrated manuscript, it can be submitted to the editorial department. *You do not have to furnish illustrations*, but if you wish, a few comprehensive sketches or duplicate copies of original art will suffice.

Include with illustrator query: Queries to the art department should include samples and a cover letter. Please do not send slides. Do not send original artwork. Please *do* send color photocopies, tear sheets, or photos. Please send an SASE if you would like your samples returned to you.

Time to reply: 12 to 16 weeks.

Terms for writers: 5 to 10 percent royalties on retail price.

Terms for illustrators: Even split with the author.

Submission guidelines: Request by mail with an SASE; call (617) 351-5959 for recorded guidelines; or view online at www.hmco.com/trade/faq.html#manuscript

Tips and comments: No manuscripts that are handwritten or submitted on computer disk. When submitting to any publishing house, it is always a good idea to check your local bookstore or library to get a sense of what kinds of books they publish. *You do not have to furnish illustrations with your submission*, but if you wish, a few comprehensive sketches or duplicate copies of original art will suffice. Please send only your strongest work.

Hyperion Books for Children

114 Fifth Avenue
New York, NY 10011
(212) 633-4400

Corporate structure/parent: Disney Publishing Worldwide, Inc.

Description: Book publisher.

Established: 1990.

Key people:

Publisher: Lisa Holton

Books per year and description: Approximately 150 titles in picture books, series, young adult fiction, middle-grade fiction, and some nonfiction.

Percentage by first-time authors: 5 percent.

Seeks: Strong, character-driven picture books and innovative young adult fiction.

Accepts unsolicited/unagented: No.

Description of fiction titles: Innovative new voices and classic stories.

Recent fiction titles:

The Doll People by Ann M. Martin and Laura Godwin

The Windsinger by William Nicholson

No More Dead Dogs by Gordon Kerman

Preferred fiction titles: Innovative and character-driven.

Recent nonfiction titles:

Tiger Time for Stanley by Griff

When John & Caroline Lived in the White House by Laurie Coulter

In the Time of the Knights by Shelley Tanaka

Preferred form of submission/contact: Through a literary agent.

Time to reply: Within four to six weeks.

Time to publish: Within 18 months of acceptance of text or 18 months after acceptance of approved art (if applicable).

Accepts simultaneous submissions: Yes.

Number of illustrators used annually: Approximately 80.

Desired illustrator qualifications: Broad-general.

Prefer manuscript/illustration packages, or separate: Prefer to review separately.

Include with illustrator query: Query through an agent.

Terms for writers: Variable by title.

Terms for illustrators: Variable by title.

Submission guidelines: Through a literary agent.

Tips and comments: It is the policy of the publishing house to work only with agented authors. If a writer would like to work with Hyperion Books for Children, they will have a greater chance of success if they submit their work through a literary agent. Present portfolio through an agent.

Ideals Children's Books

1501 County Hospital Road
Nashville, TN 37218

Corporate structure/parent: An Imprint of Hambleton-Hill Publishing, Inc.

Description: Publisher.

Seeks: Fiction and nonfiction picture books for preschool and beginning readers. Book lengths generally are 24, 32, or 48 pages and vary from 600 to 2,000 words.

Accepts unsolicited/unagented: Ideals Children's Books accepts submissions only from agented authors and members of the Society of Children's Book Writers and Illustrators (SCBWI). Authors who have previously published books may also submit with a list of writing credits. Please become familiar with our publications and the children's market before you submit material.

Description of fiction titles: Picture books for preschool and beginning readers.

Description of nonfiction titles: Nonfiction picture books for preschool and beginning readers. Book lengths generally are 24, 32, or 48 pages, and vary from 600 to 2,000 words.

Preferred nonfiction titles: Document all quotes, statistical information, and unusual facts. Provide photocopies of sources if possible.

Preferred form of submission/contact: Prefers to see the entire manuscript rather than a query letter.

Time to reply: Reply time is three to six months. Please include a self-addressed stamped envelope (SASE) for a response.

Accepts simultaneous submissions: Simultaneous submissions of book-length manuscripts are acceptable, but please identify them as such in your cover letter.

Tips and comments: Include a self-addressed envelope stamped with appropriate postage for the return of your manuscript in case it does not suit the company's editorial needs. Manuscripts that are not accompanied by the appropriate SASE will not be returned. If you desire only a reply, just include a standard SASE. If no SASE is included, no response will be sent.

Illumination Arts Publishing Co., Inc.

PO Box 1865
Bellevue, WA 98009
(888) 210-8216
(425) 644-7185
(425) 644-9274 (fax)
E-mail: liteinfo@illumin.com
Web site: www.illumin.com

Description: Illumination Arts publishes high-quality, enlightening children's picture books with enduring, inspirational, and spiritual values. The company's aim is to touch peoples' lives with inspiration and transformation. Illumination Arts is currently seeking fiction and nonfiction stories of 500 to 2,000 words.

Established: 1987.

Key people:

Publisher: John Thompson

Editorial director: Ruth Thompson (receives all submissions)

Acquisitions and development: Andrea Hurst

Art director and advertising: Cheryl Kerry

Books per year: Three to five.

Percentage by first-time authors: 70 percent.

Seeks: Inspirational; humorous in fiction or nonfiction categories.

Accepts unsolicited/unagented: Yes.

Description of fiction titles: Designed to inspire children (and adults) and enrich their lives.

Recent fiction titles:

The Little Wizard written and illustrated by Jody Bergsma (A beautifully illustrated inspirational story tells of a boy on a challenging journey to secure a magical potion to cure his dying mother.)

To Sleep with the Angels by H. Elizabeth Collins; illustrated by Judy Kuusisto (A sleepy-time story reassures children and encourages them to seek their own angels.)

The Bonsai Bear by Bernard Libster; illustrated by Aries Cheung (A Bonsai master uses techniques to keep his pet bear small.)

Wings of Change by Franklin Hill; illustrated by Aries Cheung (A happy little caterpillar resists life's evolution and the inevitable change into a butterfly.)

Preferred fiction titles: Spiritual nonreligious books; fun and cheerful subject matter, inspirational stories.

Description of nonfiction titles: Currently has a limited nonfiction list. Welcomes other nonfiction titles.

Recent nonfiction titles:

The Right Touch (helps children avoid sexual abuse).

Preferred nonfiction titles: Good stories that satisfy our guidelines

Preferred form of submission/contact: Send submission to Ruth Thompson. If the author would like a response (and a return of the manuscript), he or she *must* include an SASE with sufficient return postage.

Time to reply: Makes every effort to reply within four weeks; however, due to high volume, it may take as long as eight weeks.

Time to publish: One and a half to two years, occasionally longer.

Accepts simultaneous submissions: Yes.

Number of illustrators used annually: Usually three.

Desired illustrator qualifications: Looking for a variety of artistic styles and media. The work should be appealing to both children and adults and the illustrator must be suited to the specific project.

Prefer manuscript/illustration packages, or separate: Prefers to review manuscripts and art separately, though does have one author–illustrator combination. Each of the works—manuscript and art—must be good enough to stand on its own. Illumination Arts will not discriminate, but it is rare to hit on exactly what the company is after in both instances.

Include with illustrator query: Samples; resumes; personal portfolios.

Time to reply: Illumination Arts collects art samples and replies when it selects an artist for a particular book.

Purchases freelance photography: No.

Terms for writers: Royalties and generous book discounts.

Terms for illustrators: Same.

Submission guidelines: Guidelines are by request (with an SASE) from Illumination Arts or can be found on the Web site.

Tips and comments: Be patient. Illumination Arts strives for perfection, and therefore it may take a while to get back to you. Keep in mind that Illumination Arts isn't working against you but with you (and for your best interest). Be willing to participate very actively in the marketing of your book. Be willing to follow the story line of the book being illustrated; be willing to submit sketches, then rough copies and further development before final art. Submit artwork on schedule and according to the agreement. Please understand that Illumination Arts must reject many good stories for a variety of reasons: The company may have a similar story, the story doesn't fit into the company's time schedule, or it just doesn't "grab" anybody. Illumination Arts does not have time to edit submissions.

Incentive Publications, Inc.

3835 Cleghorn Avenue
Nashville, TN 37215
(615) 385-2934
(615) 385-2967 (fax)
E-mail: info@incentivepublications.com
Web site: www.incentivepublications.com

Description: Book publisher of supplementary education materials. *No fiction.*

Established: 1969.

Key people:

Acquisitions/submissions editor: Angela Reiner

Books per year: 25 to 30.

Percentage by first-time authors: 20 percent.

Seeks: Supplementary education materials—*not* textbooks.

Accepts unsolicited/unagented: Yes.

Description of fiction titles: Does not publish any fiction works.

Description of nonfiction titles: Educational, K–12.

Preferred nonfiction titles: Research-based and engaging text for students.

Preferred form of submission/contact: Query letter or sample/selection of the manuscript.

Time to reply: Six to eight weeks.

Time to publish: One to two years.

Accepts simultaneous submissions: Yes.

Number of illustrators used annually: Five to 10.

Desired illustrator qualifications: Student- and teacher-friendly; warm and open style.

Prefer manuscript/illustration packages, or separate: Either.

Include with illustrator query: Samples.

Time to reply: Four weeks.

Purchases freelance photography: Rarely.

Terms for writers: Variable by project.

Terms for illustrators: Variable by project.

Submission guidelines: Request by mail with an SASE or via phone.

Jalmar Press/Innerchoice Publishing

PO Box 1185
Torrance, CA 90505
Web site: www.jalmarpress.com

Jalmar Press/Innerchoice Publishing is, at the present time, not publishing stories for children. Our books, for the most part, address children's problems for a parent, teacher, counselor, or caregiver.

Jewish Lights Publishing

A Division of LongHill Partners, Inc.
PO Box 237
Sunset Farm Offices, Rt. 4
Woodstock, VT 05091
(802) 457-4000
(802) 457-4004 (fax)
Web site: www.jewishlights.com

Corporate structure/parent: LongHill Partners, Inc.

Description: Publishes books that reflect the Jewish wisdom tradition for people of all faiths, all backgrounds. Books focus on the quest for self and seeking meaning in life. They deal with issues of personal growth, of religious inspiration.

Recent fiction titles:

For Heaven's Sake by Sandy Eisenberg Sasso; illustrated by Kathryn Kunz Finney

In God's Name by Sandy Eisenberg Sasso (Multicultural, nonsectarian, nondenominational—like an ancient myth in its poetic text and vibrant illustrations, this modern fable about the search for God's name celebrates the diversity and, at the same time, the unity of all the people of the world.)

Recent nonfiction titles:

The Book of Miracles: A Young Person's Guide to Jewish Spiritual Awareness by Lawrence Kushner

The 11th Commandment: Wisdom from Our Children by the children of America (multicultural, nonsectarian, nondenominational)

Jewish Publication Society

2100 Arch Street, 2nd Floor
Philadelphia, PA 19103
(215) 832-0600
(215) 568-2017 (fax)
Web site: www.jewishpub.org/Store
Guidelines: www.jewishpub.org/writers/index.htm
About: www.jewishpub.org/whoweare/index.htm

Description: Jewish Publication Society has several children's book manuscripts under contract—enough to fill its publication needs for the next several seasons. Therefore, it is not currently accepting children's book submissions.

John Milton Society for the Blind

475 Riverside Dr., Rm. 455
New York, NY 10115
(212) 870-3335
(212) 870-3229 (fax)
E-mail: order@jmsblind.org
Web site: www.jmsblind.org

Journey Books

1700 Wade Hampton Boulevard
Greenville, SC 29614
(800) 845-5731
(800) 525-8398 (fax)
Web site: www.bjup.com

Description: Publisher.

Key people:

Acquisitions/submissions editor: Gloria Repp

Seeks: Christian fiction, biography, and nonfiction for children and teens. Looking for manuscripts that reflect the highest Christian standards of thought, feeling, and action.

Accepts unsolicited/unagented: Yes.

Preferred fiction titles: Main characters should be fully developed. Plots should have plenty of action. Do not send short stories, picture books, rhyming text, poetry, drama, or romance; do not send proposals for tracts, craft books, curriculum aids, or study guides; do not send stories that involve magic, witchcraft, or time travel; do not send stories that include profanity or minced oaths or that portray main characters who engage in unscriptural activities such as drinking, dancing, and smoking.

Preferred nonfiction titles: Do not send stories that include profanity or minced oaths or that portray main characters who engage in unscriptural activities such as drinking, dancing, and smoking.

Preferred form of submission/contact: Include five chapters and a brief synopsis of the rest of the book. *Lengths:* ages 6 to 8: 3,000 to 9,000 words; ages 9 to 12: 10,000 to 40,000 words; ages 12 and up: 40,000 to 60,000 words.

Time to reply: Allow three months for a response to your submission.

Submission guidelines: Include a cover letter stating your target audience and your professional background; include five chapters and a brief synopsis of the rest of the book; send a typed or computer-printed submission. Double-space and number your pages consecutively throughout; do not send an audiocassette or computer disk in lieu of a manuscript. If you want your manuscript to be returned, please enclose a self-addressed stamped envelope with correct postage. Please do not submit by phone, fax, or e-mail. Please note that extensive evaluation and editing of your work is impossible.

Just Us Books

356 Glenwood Avenue
East Orange, NJ 07017
(973) 672-7701
(973) 677-7570 (fax)
Web site: www.justusbooks.com

Description: Just Us Books, Inc. is an independent publishing company specializing in books and learning materials for children and young people.

Established: 1988.

Seeks: Books that focus on black history, culture and experiences.

Accepts unsolicited/unagented: Yes.

Description of fiction titles: Books that focus on the experiences of black children, ages 2 to 12.

Recent fiction titles:

Annie's Gifts by Angela Medearis; illustrated by Anna Rich

Bright Eyes, Brown Skin by Cheryl Willis Hudson and Bernette Ford; illustrated by George Ford

Description of nonfiction titles: Books that focus on the experiences of black children, ages 2 to 12.

Recent nonfiction titles:

Afro-Bets First Book about Africa, by Veronica Freeman Ellis; illustrated by George Ford

Afro-Bets Book of Black Heroes from A to Z, vol. 1 by Wade Hudson and Valerie Wilson Wesley

Susie King Taylor: Destined to Be Free, by Denise Jordan; illustrated by Higgins Bond

---

Kamehameha Schools Press

1887 Makuakāne Street
Honolulu, HI 96817
(808) 842-8876
(808) 842-8875 (fax)
Web site: www.ksbe.edu/pubs/KSPress/catalog.html

Recent nonfiction titles:

From the Mountains to the Sea: Early Hawaiian Life by Julie Stewart Williams; illustrated by Robin Yoko Racoma (Descriptions of life, activities, and the natural environment in the Hawaiian Islands before Western contact. Accessible to students yet informative for adults. Winner 1997 Ka Palapala Po`okela Award for Excellence in Children's Books.)

Hawaiian Canoe-Building Traditions (rev. ed.), developed by Naomi N.Y. Chun; illustrated by Robin Y. Burningham (Heavily illustrated text describes the steps in building, the various types and the sailing of ancient Hawaiian canoes, from the selection and felling of logs through the navigation of an ocean-crossing voyage. Updated to include notes on the voyages of the Hökūle`a and the construction of the Hawai`iloa and the Mauloa.)

Kamehameha the Great (rev. ed.) by Julie Stewart Williams; illustrated by Robin Yoko Burningham (The first ali`i nui to unite and rule all of the islands of Hawai`i and founder of the kingdom's principal ruling dynasty. *Kamehameha the Great* is available in a Hawaiian-language edition as *`O Kamehameha Nui*, translated by Hana Pau and edited by Ipo Wong.)

Kar-Ben Copies, Inc.

6800 Tildenwood Lane
Rockville, MD
(800) 452-7236
(301) 881-9195
E-mail: karben@aol.com
Web site: www.karben.com

Description: Publishes Jewish books for young children and families. Also Jewish calendars.

Established: 1975.

Key people:

Publishers: Judye Croner and Madeline Wikler

Acquisitions/submissions editors: Judye Croner and Madeline Wikler

Books per year and description: Five to six picture books.

Percentage by first-time authors: 10 percent.

Seeks: Jewish themes only—holiday, life cycle, activity.

Accepts unsolicited/unagented: Yes.

Description of fiction titles: All related to Jewish themes.

Recent fiction titles:

Sammy Spider's First Purim by Sylvia Rouss

Hannukkah Fun by Judye Groner and Madeline Wikler

A Costume for Noah: A Purim Story by Susan Remick Topek

Fins and Scales: A Kosher Tale by Deborah Miller and Karen Ostrove

Preferred fiction titles: Stories related to Jewish holidays, day-to-day life, games, and activities.

Description of nonfiction titles: See above.

Recent nonfiction titles

Shabbat Fun for Little Hands by Katherine Janus Kahn (simple activities centered around charity, candles, and blessings over the bread and wine with a board game)

Thank You God! A Jewish Child's Book of Prayers by Judyth Groner and Madeline Wikler (a first prayer book for young children)

Preferred nonfiction titles: Jewish themes and context.

Preferred form of submission/contact: Manuscript with an SASE.

Time to reply: Four to six weeks.

Time to publish: Within one year.

Accepts simultaneous submissions: Yes, as long as notice is given.

Number of illustrators used annually: Six to eight.

Desired illustrator qualifications: Art appropriate to the story.

Prefer manuscript/illustration packages, or separate: Prefers to review the work separately but will consider a package. It is, however, much less likely that it will be accepted in that format.

Include with illustrator query: Samples and tear sheets—*not* originals!

Time to reply: Four to six weeks.

Purchases freelance photography: No.

Terms for writers: Small advance with a 6 to 8 percent royalty rate.

Terms for illustrators: Same.

Submission guidelines: Send SASE.

Tips and comments: Read some of the company's books first, and browse the bookstores to check out the competition—see what else is available on the topic to avoid duplication.

Key Porter Kids

Key Porter Books
70 The Esplanade
Toronto, Ontario M5E 1R2
Canada
(416) 862-7777
(416) 862-2304 (fax)
Web site: www.keyporter.com

Description: Under the Key Porter Kids (KPK) imprint, the list includes high-quality nonfiction, young adult fiction, and picture books by authors such as Margaret Atwood, Tom King, Laszlo, Gal, Tim Wynne Jones, Hanet Lunn, Carol, Matas, Henry Kim, and Mathew Fernandes.

Kids Can Press

29 Birch Avenue
Toronto, Ontario M4V 1E2
Canada
E-mail: info@kidscan.com

KidsRights

8902 Otis Avenue
Indianapolis, IN 46216
(800) 892-KIDS (5437)
(877) 543-7001 (fax)
E-mail: kidsrights@jist.com
Web site: www.kidsrights.com

Description: KidsRights is committed to helping individuals and families heal. KidsRights publishes and distributes books, videos, games, pamphlets, and play therapy materials.

Recent nonfiction titles:

When Mommy Got Hurt: A Story for Young Children about Domestic Violence by Ilene Lee and Kathy Sylwester

Struggle to Be Strong: True Stories about Teens Overcoming Tough Times, edited by Al Desetta, M.A., of Youth Communication, and Sybil Wolin, Ph.D., of Project Resilience

Tips and comments: KidsRights' goal is to help counselors, teachers, medical personnel, corrections caseworkers, and police officers get practical, helpful, and encouraging materials into the hands of those who need them.

Kingfisher

Editorial Department
New Penderel House
283-288 High Holborn
London, WC1V 7 HZ
United Kingdom
(01144) 207-242-4979 (fax)

Description: Unfortunately Kingfisher is not accepting unsolicited submissions at our U.S. office. Authors' agents are invited to send inquiries to the editorial department in London—Kingfisher does not accept unsolicited manuscripts or proposals. All submissions must come through an agent.

Laura Geringer Books

10 E. 53rd Street
New York, NY 10022-5299
(212) 207-7000
Web site: www.harperchildrens.com

Corporate structure/parent: HarperCollins

Description: Book publisher.

Key people:

Editorial director: Laura Geringer

Seeks: Laura Geringer Books publishes picture books, illustrated chapter books, and fiction for the middle grades and young adults.

Accepts unsolicited/unagented: It is not necessary to have an agent. Laura Geringer Books treats unsolicited and agented manuscripts with equal care and concern.

Description of titles: Picture books, illustrated chapter books, and fiction for the middle grades and young adults.

Preferred titles: Laura Geringer Books has no rules for subject matter, length, or vocabulary but looks instead for ideas that are fresh and imaginative. Good writing that involves the reader in a story or subject that has appeal for children is also essential.

Preferred form of submission/contact: Because of the tremendous amount of manuscripts Laura Geringer Books receives daily, *the company is no longer accepting unsolicited picture book manuscripts*; should you wish to submit a picture book manuscript, please send a detailed letter of query first. Laura Geringer Books is still accepting unsolicited middle-grade and young adult novels.

Time to reply: Manuscripts are read in the order in which they are received. Laura Geringer Books tries to reach a decision within two to three months, but occasionally it may take longer. All submitted manuscripts will receive a response. If you do not hear from the company, it is because your work is still under consideration, and it is not necessary to call. Manuscripts may be delivered in person to the receptionist on the 16th floor, but it is unfair to both the author and the editor to expect an on-the-spot decision. Each manuscript is given careful consideration, and the company allows time to evaluate its reactions.

Prefer manuscript/illustration packages, or separate: Accepts manuscript and illustrations packages, however, illustrations are not necessary. In the case of picture books, the company is always glad to see sample sketches, a few finished illustrations, or a rough dummy. However, in the early stages of consideration, *it is the text that is most important.*

Include with illustrator query: If you are submitting your artwork for consideration, please do not send original art. Slides, reproductions, postcards, color copies, and black-and-white copies are acceptable. Please indicate which items you wish to have returned and which the company may keep. For the safe return of your work, please read the instructions for manuscripts.

Submission guidelines: Write with an SASE for guidelines, but mostly, read this profile and check out the Web site for more insight into the kinds of books published, which in turn will help you determine what Laura Geringer Books is looking for.

Tips and comments: Read as many children's books as you can get your hands on. You'll see some things you like and others you don't, and the more you read, the more you'll begin to figure out what you want to write about, what style you want to take, and to what age group you'd like to appeal. Also study Laura Geringer's titles to give you more of a specific idea of the kinds of books the company likes to publish. Unless Laura Geringer Books feels a manuscript has potential for its list, it is not possible to give specific criticisms. Editorial criteria vary from publisher to publisher, and another house may be eager to publish a manuscript that does not meet Laura Geringer's needs. The company is usually not able to make a commitment for publication until the editors have carefully considered an entire manuscript or, in the case of a novel, at least a number of chapters and a detailed outline.

Lee & Low Books

95 Madison Avenue
New York, NY 10016
(212) 779-4400
(212) 683-1894 (fax)
Web site: www.leeandlow.com

Description: Book publisher specializing in multicultural themes. Lee & Low Books, an award-winning children's book publisher that specializes in multicultural themes, considers unsolicited manuscripts from writers at all levels of experience.

Key people:

Editor in chief: Elizabeth Szabla

Percentage by first-time authors: The company makes a special effort to work with writers and artists of color and encourages new voices.

Seeks: Lee & Low Books is dedicated to publishing culturally authentic literature. The company is interested in both fiction and nonfiction picture books for children ages 2 to 10.

Accepts unsolicited/unagented: Yes. Lee & Low Books, an award-winning children's book publisher that specializes in multicultural themes, considers unsolicited manuscripts from writers at all levels of experience.

Description of fiction titles: The company's goals are to meet a growing need for books that address children of color—who make up more than half of the urban school population—by providing stories on subjects that they can identify with and relate to. It is also our goal to present literature that all children can enjoy and that promotes a greater understanding of one another.

Preferred fiction titles: Manuscripts should be no longer than five typed, double-spaced pages (approximately 1,000 words). Lee & Low Books provides literature that is relevant and realistic to young readers. Of special interest are stories set in contemporary America. Please note: At this time, Lee & Low Books is not considering folktales and animal stories. *Stories in these genres, as well as manuscripts for middle-grade and young adult fiction and nonfiction, will be returned unread.*

Preferred nonfiction titles: Manuscripts should be no longer than five typed, double-spaced pages (approximately 1,000 words). Lee & Low Books provides literature that is relevant and realistic to young readers. Of special interest are stories set in contemporary America. *Manuscripts for middle-grade and young adult nonfiction will be returned unread.*

Preferred form of submission/contact: Manuscript submissions should include a cover letter and self-addressed stamped envelope. (No international postal coupons, please.) Queries and/or proposals are discouraged; Lee & Low Books prefers to read complete manuscripts. Lee & Low Books does not accept submissions via electronic mail.

Time to reply: Reporting time is four to 12 weeks. Questions regarding the status of a submission after 12 weeks must be made in writing to the address above; please do not call.

Accepts simultaneous submissions: Multiple submissions will be considered; please indicate in cover letter.

Include with illustrator query: Artists should send tear sheets, nonreturnable slides, or illustration samples (color photocopies are fine). Please do not send original artwork.

Tips and comments: The company is interested in both fiction and nonfiction picture books. Lee & Low Books is dedicated to publishing culturally authentic literature. The company makes a special effort to work with writers and artists of color and encourages new voices.

LERNER PUBLISHING COMPANY

241 First Avenue N.
Minneapolis, MN 55401
(612) 332-3344
(612) 332-7615 (fax)
Web site: www.lernerbooks.com

Corporate structure/parent: Lerner Publishing Group.

Description: Book publisher.

Established: Lerner Publications Company was established more than 40 years ago and has maintained its commitment to publishing noteworthy books.

Key people:

Acquisitions/submissions editor: Jennifer Zim

Seeks: Primarily publishing nonfiction for children in grades 4 through 12, this imprint features titles with beautiful photography and compelling text that inspire, educate, and entertain on a great variety of subjects.

Accepts unsolicited/unagented: Yes.

Description of fiction titles: Primarily publishes nonfiction.

Preferred fiction titles: Likes to see unique, honest stories that stay away from unoriginal plots, moralizing, religious themes, and anthropomorphic protagonists. Does not publish alphabet books, textbooks, workbooks, songbooks, puzzles, plays, or religious material.

Preferred nonfiction titles: Especially interested in new ideas and fresh topics. Likes to see multicultural themes. Make sure your writing avoids racial and sexual stereotypes. Does not publish alphabet books, textbooks, workbooks, songbooks, puzzles, plays, or religious material.

Preferred form of submission/contact: Prefers to see a completed manuscript, but will accept an outline and sample chapters for longer biographies or fiction. An SASE is required for all submissions.

Time to reply: Allow two to six months for a response (response time is generally three to four months). You will be notified of any decision regarding your manuscript at the earliest possible time. Please do not expect a personal response from an editor, as time does not permit this. If you would like confirmation that your manuscript has been received, please send a self-addressed stamped postcard.

Prefer manuscript/illustration packages, or separate: You do not need to send art with your submission as the company generally commissions its own artists, but if you are sending art samples, do not send originals.

Include with illustrator query: Samples.

Submission guidelines: Submissions to Lerner Publications Company, a division of Lerner Publishing Group, are accepted in the months of March and October *only*. Submissions received in any month other than March or October will be returned *unopened* to the sender. Accepts requests for guidelines and catalogs year-round. Please address requests to Guideline Request, and send a business-sized SASE. To receive both a catalog and guidelines, write to Catalog Request and send a 9 by 12-inch SASE with $3.20 postage.

Tips and comments: The best way to familiarize yourself with the list is to study the catalog or find the company's books in the library. For a catalog, send a self-addressed 9 by 12-inch envelope with $3.20 in postage.

LIGHTWAVE PUBLISHING

PO Box
160 Maple Ridge
British Columbia V3X 7G1
Canada
Web site: www.lightwavepublishing.com

Recent titles:

I Want to Know About . . . (a series: the Bible, God, Jesus, The Ten Commandments, church) (These fun and informative hardback books are a great way to learn about the basics of Christianity. They are full of fascinating facts, articles, and puzzles. They are packed with full-color photos, cartoons, and graphics.)

What If I Owned Everything? by Larry Burkett (Twins Jeremy and Jenny embark on an adventure of the imagination as they learn about how God wants them to handle their money.)

SMOKY MOUNTAIN SERIES by Larry Burkett, includes *A Home for the Hamsters* (Life in the Smoky Mountains is full of fun and adventure! Sarah, Joshua, and baby sister Carey live in a Smoky Mountain state park with their parents, who are forest rangers. Surrounded by natural beauty and built-in adventure, there is always fun stuff to do, and important lessons to learn.); *Last Chance for Camp*; and others.

LINNET BOOKS

PO Box 657
2 Linsley Street
North Haven, CT 06473
(203) 239-2702
(203) 239-2558 (fax)
E-mail: books@shoestringpress.com
Web site: www.shoestringpress.com

Corporate structure/parent: The Shoe String Press, Inc.

Description: Publisher.

Meet Julie Anne Peters

Author

Julie Anne Peters has 9 books published, with the 10th under contract. Her most recent releases are *Define "Normal"* (Little, Brown, 2000; ages 10 and up); the *Snob Squad* series (Little, Brown, ages 9–12); *Love Me, Love My Broccoli* (Avon/HarperCollins, 1999, ages 10 and up); and *How Do You Spell G-E-E-K?* (Little, Brown, 1996, ages 9–12). *Define "Normal"* was an American Library Association (ALA) Best Book for Young Adults 2001 and an ALA Best Book for Reluctant Young Adult Readers 2001.

Julie Anne was born in Jamestown, New York, on January 16, 1952. Her books are geared for young adult and middle-grade readers. She has two early chapter books for six- to nine-year-old readers as well. She has a master's in business and computer information systems from the University of Colorado at Denver; a bachelor of science degree in computer and management systems from the Metropolitan State College of Denver, and a bachelor of arts in elementary education from the Colorado Women's College. She has worked as a computer systems engineer, computer programmer, research assistant, fifth-grade teacher, secretary, file clerk, office grunt, and concessionaire at the zoo. Against all advice, she quit her day job to become a writer. It's a drag to be indigent, she discovered, but a powerful motivator to achieving success!

How did you get your first book published?

The manuscript for my first book, *The Stinky Sneakers Contest,* had been making the rounds for a year, collecting dust in slush piles at every major publishing house. One day I received a call from this editor at Little, Brown in Boston. Her name was Megan Tingley, which was about all I heard because I'd fainted. (I still faint every time she calls, but that's another story.) She said, "Julie, we like your style; we think it has lots of kid appeal, and we'd be interested in this book if you'd be willing to cut it." Cut? I thought. I can cut. I can add. I can divide and conquer if you'll publish this manuscript. I held my desperation in check and replied, "Sure, no problem."

"Okay," Megan said. "Then we'd need you to cut the manuscript in half to fit into our Springboard Series format." Cutting in half meant reducing a 60-page manuscript to 32-pages—exactly 32 pages. No sweat, I figured, until I actually tried to do it. You try eliminating half your story and see how easy it is. I'd been living on Cream of Wheat for six months, though, so the motivation was there. I revised the manuscript and sent it back. Megan phoned a few weeks later. "Well, the length is right," she told me, "but the story still needs some work." She offered suggestions—several hundred suggestions. We went through this process of recommendations and revisions over the course of a year until I was finally offered a contract. Oh, happy day. Of course, this is where the real work on a book begins. Two and a half years later *The Stinky Sneakers Contest* was published.

Did you have an agent when you published your first book?

I didn't have an agent for my first book, or my second or third. After the third, I realized I wasn't going to be making a living anytime soon publishing one book a year, and my creditors were lining up at the door. The children's market had taken one of its cyclical dives, and I wasn't even getting nibbles on any of my other manuscripts, so I knew it was time to find an agent. Why? Because an agent would be able to sell everything I couldn't. Yes, my well of naiveté ran deep!

I asked my editor, Megan Tingley, which agents she'd recommend—who she liked working with, who she thought could put up with my paranoid/schizophrenic personality, and so forth. She gave me four names, and I sent out query letters. Each of the agents called me, and I interviewed them. The only one who asked me, "What are your expectations of an agent?" was Wendy Schmalz at Harold, Ober Associates. When I told her I wanted her to get me into the movies, she laughed. That did it for me. All the other agents, besides having no sense of humor, were too money grubbing for my taste. Not that I don't relish money (and vast quantities of it coming my way), but Wendy was the only one who talked about developing a long-term career plan. I made the right choice. She still laughs at my jokes.

Do you have any advice, in terms of finding an agent, for a writer starting out?

Don't be so desperate that you'll let anyone represent you. Your agent is your strongest advocate, your ally, and your champion. He or she can make or break your career (not to mention your spirits). And if you expect your agent to sell everything you write, your well of naiveté runs deep, too.

Are you still with your first publisher?

Yes, I'm still with Megan Tingley, who now has her own imprint at Little, Brown. We have a solid relationship built on years of working together, overcoming challenges, and trusting each other as writer and editor.

What procedures do you follow when you write?

My writing process varies with each book. Sometimes I'll start with a story idea; other times a character, or even a title. That's what happened with *Revenge of the Snob Squad.* I had no story, no characters—just this great title. The process of backing a story into a title causes severe butt burn—it's not recommended. I don't usually begin writing until I've worked the whole book out in my head. Even then the characters must be screaming to be let out of my brain before I'll put pen to paper. I'm sadistic that way.

Typically I'm at different stages in three or four books in progress. For example, I might have one book to review in galley; another manuscript completed and waiting on editorial comments; a third being plotted or first drafted; and a fourth rattling around in my skull, collecting bone fragments. If I am working on a first draft, I commit three or four hours every morning to dedicated, uninterrupted writing time. The one ritual I'll admit to is that I write my first drafts in longhand on Big Chief tablets. I think it's something about getting in touch with my inner penmanship teacher.

Where do you get your ideas?

From boxes of Cracker Jacks! Who knows where ideas come from? What I tell kids (who seem to think ideas are the magic they're missing in order to be a writer) is, "It's not the idea that counts. It's what you bring to it—your unique perspective, your experiences, your imagination. Each of you

continues

has an idea-generating machine right above your eyeballs. All you need to do is turn it on and let it go to work."

What do you think are the key differences between writing for children and writing for adults?

There aren't any. Whether you're writing for the 6-year-old in you, or the 12-year-old, or the teen or 40-something, writing is connecting with other people. I do believe that writing for young people is harder, but only because it's a more sophisticated art. It takes longer to learn to do well.

How did you learn to write?

I never wrote a word of fiction until I was 38 years old. With kids I add, "Now I'm 39." (It gets a bigger laugh with adults.) I never had any formal training; never wrote in school or attended writing workshops. Everything I learned, I learned in books. How-to books and children's books; young adult novels and teen 'zines. I studied technique and style and the fundamentals of storytelling. Then I practiced and practiced and practiced, and produced pages and pages of trash. But the quality of the trash improved with each attempt. I still practice, and I still produce work less than worthy of my readers. My trash stash continues to accumulate, but hopefully at a slower rate. Practice, patience, and perseverance pay dividends. But the desire to learn, to learn how to do it better, and to grow as a writer is what carried me through. Still does.

Anything you really wish somebody had told you when you started out?

Read. Read children's literature. Read young adult literature. Stay current on what's being published, on what young people are reading, the things they care about. Study the masters, old and new. Seek out the work that moves you, excites you, and analyze it. Aspire to more than publication. If you get discouraged, go read a stack of children's books. They'll have the same effect on you as they do on young readers. They'll lift your spirits; take you on journeys; challenge you to think and question and explore. Read until you fall in love with children's literature all over again. Until you're reminded why you want to do this.

Seeks: Current focus is on quality nonfiction for children and young adults.

Accepts unsolicited/unagented: Yes.

Description of fiction titles: Focusing on nonfiction titles.

Description of nonfiction titles: Quality nonfiction for children and young adults.

Preferred nonfiction titles: Does not publish poetry, picture books, or fiction.

Preferred form of submission/contact: Send synopsis of your book and a few sample chapters (no more than 20 pages). Please do not send original artwork.

Time to reply: Tries to reply in a timely manner, but due to the number of submissions received on a daily basis, it could take several months.

Accepts simultaneous submissions: Does not like to consider manuscripts that are being simultaneously submitted to other publishers.

Submission guidelines: Please write with an SASE or send an e-mail for guidelines.

Tips and comments: If you wish to have your manuscript returned, please include SASE with ample postage. Manuscripts submitted without SASE (or ample postage) will not be returned to the author.

Little, Brown and Company Children's Books

Three Center Plaza
Boston, MA 02108
(617) 227-0730
(617) 063-2864 (fax)

Corporate structure/parent: Time Warner is the parent company. Little, Brown and Company Children's Books (including the former Joy Street Books imprint) also has the imprint Megan Tingley Books.

Description: Children's book publisher.

Established: 1847.

Key people:

Publisher and vice president: John Keller

Acquisitions/submissions editors: Maria Modugno, Cindy Eagan, and John Keller

Books per year and description: 69 picture books; 32 middle-grade fiction; 2 YA.

Percentage by first-time authors: 5 percent.

Seeks: Picture books—mostly fiction; young adult novels.

Accepts unsolicited/unagented: No.

Description of fiction titles: Picture books; board books; pop-up and lift-the-flap editions; chapter books and general fiction for middle and young adult readers.

Recent fiction titles:

I Love You Like Crazy Cakes by Rose A. Lewis; illustrated by Jane Dyer

Underwear Do's and Don'ts written and illustrated by Todd Parr

The Serpent Slayer and Other Stories of Strong Women retold by Katrin Tchana; illustrated by Trina Schart Hyman

Saint George and the Dragon illustrated by Trina Schart Hyman (Caldecott winner)

Maniac Magee by Jerry Spinelli (Newbery winner)

Preferred fiction titles: Little, Brown publishes children's books in three general categories of fiction based on the age range of the prospective audience: picture books (ages 2–8), middle grade (ages 8–12), and young adult (age 12 and up). Picture book texts run approximately 1,000 words or less in length. Middle-grade texts average 15,000 to 25,000 words, and young adult texts range from 25,000 to 35,000 words. For fiction, the company's preference is to see the complete manuscript. In addition to the categories mentioned, Little, Brown is also looking for multicultural titles.

Description of nonfiction titles: Books for middle and young adult readers. Must appeal to book buyers as well as librarians.

Recent nonfiction titles:

Inside the Hindenburg by Mireille Majoor; illustrated by Ken Marschall (a giant cutaway book)

Life: Our Century in Pictures for Young People edited by Richard B. Stolley, photographs from *Life* (with narratives from nine notable children's authors)

Into a New Country, Eight Remarkable Women of the West by Liza Ketchum

In the Goal with . . . Briana Scurry by Matt Christopher

Preferred nonfiction titles: Middle grade (ages 8–12), and young adult (age 12 and up). Middle-grade texts average 15,000 to 25,000 words, and young adult texts range from 25,000 to 35,000 words. For nonfiction works, a proposal, outline, and three sample chapters are acceptable for a submission (but please remember that Little, Brown does *not* accept unsolicited manuscripts)

Preferred form of submission/contact: Through a literary agent or at the direct solicitation of one of our editors—unsolicited manuscripts will not be reviewed.

Time to reply: Query: one month; manuscript: three months

Time to publish: One to two years.

Accepts simultaneous submissions: Yes.

Number of illustrators used annually: 55.

Desired illustrator qualifications: Unique style and how well an illustrator can match their art with a specific manuscript.

Prefer manuscript/illustration packages, or separate: Little, Brown accepts both.

Include with illustrator query: Tear sheets and samples are easiest to circulate to all members of editorial.

Time to reply: Circulates samples internally and only replies to an artist if interested in seeing more work.

Purchases freelance photography: Not frequently. May use photographs for sports bios or young adult cover designs.

Preferred photography: Usually has a specific image in mind depending on the project. Therefore, needs vary from one project to the next.

Terms for writers: Advance against royalties. The specific terms vary for each project.

Terms for illustrators: Advance against royalties. The specific terms vary for each project.

Submission guidelines: Send letter and SASE to Little, Brown's editorial department with request for guidelines

Tips and comments: *Writers:* Submit one manuscript at a time; currently seeking multicultural titles. *Illustrators:* Submit a variety of samples that display different subject matter and styles. Please don't attempt to pitch ideas on the telephone.

Lobster Press

1250 René-Lévesque Boulevard West, Suite 2200
Montreal, Quebec H3B 4W8
Canada
Web site: www.lobsterpress.com

Description: Lobster Press presently publishes books for ages 12 and under. Its publishing program includes picture books, chapter books, and nonfiction books.

Established: June 1997.

Accepts unsolicited/unagented: See below for submission specifics.

Preferred fiction titles: For youth fiction, looking for manuscripts in three categories: Early chapter books for readers who are 6 to 8 years old (6,000–12,000 words), junior fiction for 8- to 12-year-olds (14,000–22,000 words), and young adult fiction for children over 12 (25,000–60,000 words). Particularly interested in early chapter books that form a series and that have a character or characters children will want to follow. All stories must be well paced with a compelling plot line.

Preferred nonfiction titles: For nonfiction books, Lobster Press is looking for well-written and engaging manuscripts that will inform readers about a range of subjects, including career paths, health and coping, sports, science, and business and finance. How-to manuscripts are also welcome as are travel books for families. Nonfiction books target children ages 6 to 9, youth ages 9 to 12, teens, and parents, depending on the topic. Books that can grow into series are of particular interest. Will consider queries, completed manuscripts, and the first three chapters of a manuscript if accompanied by an outline.

Preferred form of submission/contact: *For fiction:* If a story is strong and the writing is good, will consider the first three chapters of a manuscript if accompanied by an outline. *For nonfiction:* Will consider queries, completed manuscripts, and the first three chapters of a manuscript if accompanied by an outline. Multiple submissions of up to five manuscripts are welcome.

Time to reply: It may take up to six months for a response. No editorial comment will be forthcoming unless Lobster Press feels that a manuscript is publishable.

Accepts simultaneous submissions: Will not accept a simultaneous submission unless you have clearly stated in the covering letter that another publisher is considering your work.

Desired illustrator qualifications: Because most books have children as their main characters, Lobster Press needs to see how you portray children in different attitudes. Also interested in seeing illustrations of animals or expressive animals' characters.

Include with illustrator query: Samples and resume. Please do not send originals.

Time to reply: If Lobster Press feels it can use your work in the future, it will keep your samples on file. If Lobster Press does not think it can use your work, it will return it if you provide a self-addressed envelope with sufficient Canadian postage.

Submission guidelines: Write with an SASE or go to the Web site for guidelines. All work should be typewritten, double spaced, and have a 1 1/2-inch left- and right-hand margin. Write your name, return address, and telephone number on the title page, and give the word count. Also, print your name on every page of the manuscript. *Stories sent by e-mail will not be considered.* If you choose to submit your work to Lobster Press, please remember to include a covering letter. Please stamp or write your name and return address on the back of each sample illustration for identification purposes.

LONGMAN

1185 Avenue of the Americas
New York, NY 10036
Web site: www.ablongman.com

Corporate structure/parent: Addison-Wesley.

Description: Educational publisher; textbooks.

Accepts unsolicited/unagented: Yes.

Preferred form of submission/contact: Always interested in hearing about new ideas for textbooks. Please see guidelines for detailed submission requirements.

Submission guidelines: Write with an SASE or see Web site for exhaustive guidelines on preparing for manuscript submission.

Loyola Press

3441 N. Ashland Avenue
Chicago, IL 60657
(800) 621-1008
(773) 281-0555 (fax)
E-mail: editorial@loyolapress.com
Web site: www.loyolapress.com

Description: Publisher.

Seeks: Elementary textbooks. Largest department focuses on educational books. As the publishers of the newly revised *Christ Our Life* and *Voyages in English* series, Loyola provides textbooks for nearly a third of the children in Catholic schools. Also publishes supplementary books and materials for classroom use.

Description of nonfiction titles: Loyola Press has published *Voyages in English* since 1943. The new 1999 edition remains a writing and grammar series that builds skills now for future success. Also publishes *Phonics in Action*, *Writing in Action*, *Vocabulary in Action*, *Exercises in English*, and a helpful, affordable grammar skills handbook and practice book series. Although Loyola Press does not have a reading series, its *Voyages in English* writing and grammar series offers a literature model for teachers to follow using their own choice of literature. *Exercises in English* is a workbook with plenty of practice in grammar and may be used with any language arts textbook.

Accepts unsolicited/unagented: No. See below for submission guidelines.

Description of fiction titles: Does not consider fiction, poetry, drama, music, or manuscripts with no spiritual applications.

Preferred form of submission/contact: Send a copy of your proposal, not your entire manuscript, to the editorial department. Your proposal should include the following: a one-paragraph description of the book's themes; description of the book's intended audience. Be specific. For example: "young Catholics (aged 18–35) seeking an understanding of Catholic traditions of prayer and devotional practices" instead of "everyone who is interested in prayer." Also include a summary of your book's unique features. In other words, explain what your book offers that other books do not. What does it give a reader that he or she cannot get anywhere else? Enclose an extended outline or chapter summary showing how you develop the theme; one or two sample chapters; a summary of your qualifications for writing this book; a stamped self-addressed mailer if you wish your materials returned.

Time to reply: Proposals are often read by several people, any of whom may be facing deadline pressure or a heavy travel schedule. Thus, it can take anywhere from two weeks to three months to respond to your proposal. If you wish verification that your proposal was received, please include a stamped self-addressed postcard, which an editorial assistant will return to you without comment.

Submission guidelines: Write with an SASE, send an e-mail, or check the Web site.

Tips and comments: In most cases, Loyola turns down manuscripts because they are unsuitable for the list. Loyola Press serves its mission, its readers, and its authors by concentrating on those books that it knows it can publish successfully. Loyola turns down many proposals not because they are unsound but because it does not think it could publish them well.

LUTTERWORTH PRESS

PO Box 60
Cambridge, CB1 2NT
England
(44) 122 335 0865
(44) 122 336 6951 (fax)
E-mail: publishing@lutterworth.com
Web site: www.lutterworth.com

Description: Publisher

Books per year and description: Publishes up to 50 books a year, but for each one that it publishes, the company is offered a great many that it cannot take on.

Accepts unsolicited/unagented: No. Please send synopsis and sample chapters only. Please see below for details.

Description of fiction titles: Interesting stories with some adventure and each with a Christian theme.

Recent fiction titles:

Probable Sons by Amy Le Feuvre (a Victorian tale of conversion)

Teddy's Button by Amy Le Feuvre (a moving story from the Victorian era)

Jamaican Schoolgirl by Elizabeth Batt

Preferred fiction titles: For nonfiction, looks for books that are authoritative, and needs to be told of any special qualifications that the author has for writing the book.

Description of nonfiction titles: Many fiction books tell the stories of men and women and their Christian faith (i.e., our Faith and Fame series tell the stories of men and women who went all over the world with their Christian faith).

Recent nonfiction titles:

Friends of the Chiefs: The Story of Robert Moffat by Iris Clinton

Horseman of the King: The Story of John Wesley by Cyril Davey

Lady with a Lamp: The Story of Florence Nightingale by Cyril Davey

Preferred form of submission/contact: Rather than sending your complete typescript in the first instance, it is usually better to send a synopsis of the book, with a detailed contents list and a sample chapter or two. This will save you money and may well save both you and the company time, whether the book is one that the company can publish or not. The company often has to reject books that might otherwise be suitable because they are presented in a form that makes reading them too difficult. If you are in any doubt about how to present a typescript, you should look in an author's guide for suggestions on how to do so. Lutterworth cannot, for example, consider handwritten books, books presented on disk without a printout, or books printed out on continuous stationery. And furthermore, *please do not submit typescripts by e-mail*, although Lutterworth does welcome e-mail inquiries.

Submission guidelines: Write with an SASE, send an e-mail, or check the Web site.

Tips and comments: Lutterworth is a commercial publishing house and has to make a profit from the books that it publishes. However good your book is, Lutterworth will be unable to publish it unless the company can see how it will be able to sell it, so it is important that Lutterworth should be able to see what the potential market for the book will be and how it may be reached. The more that you can tell about this, the easier it will be to consider your book favorably.

MAGINATION PRESS

750 First Street, NE
Washington, D.C. 20002
Web site: www.maginationpress.com

Corporate structure/parent: American Psychological Association.

Description: Book publisher.

Established: 1987.

Key people:

Managing editor: Darcie Conner Johnston

Books per year and description: Up to 12 picture books and young reader titles per year.

Percentage by first-time authors: 50 percent.

Seeks: Publishes books dealing with the psychotherapeutic treatment or resolution of children's serious problems and psychological issues, which is why so many are written by mental health professionals.

Accepts unsolicited/unagented: Yes.

Description of fiction titles: See above.

Recent fiction titles:

The Very Lonely Bathtub by Ann Rasmussen, Psy.D., and Marc Nemiroff, Ph.D.; illustrated by Kate Flanagan (About a child who suddenly turns obstinate—Claudia used to love her bathtub, now she won't go near it.)

Sparky's Excellent Misadventures: My A.D.D. Journal, by Me (Sparky) by Phyllis Carpenter and Marti Ford; illustrated by Peter Horjus (ADD books are a specialty of Magination Press. This book is a fictional week-in-the-life account of a funny, lovable boy with ADD.)

Preferred fiction titles: Magination Press publishes illustrated storybooks of a clearly psychological nature for children. Magination is looking for a good story with a plot young children can follow. In illustrations Magination is after well-drawn characters. In Magination books, there must be an internal, psychological process taking place throughout the book. This means that the child's feelings at the beginning of the book must be shown to change throughout and then conclude in a different place than they began.

Description of nonfiction titles: Topics covered include learning disabilities, divorce, and asthma. Informative and engaging.

Recent nonfiction titles: See the Web site.

Preferred nonfiction titles: Informative books about topics that are of a clearly psychological nature.

Preferred form of submission/contact: Submit a query.

Time to reply: Three to five months.

Time to publish: 12 to 18 months after acceptance.

Accepts simultaneous submissions: Yes.

Number of illustrators used annually: 10 to 15.

Desired illustrator qualifications: Professionals whose artwork will complement the book in question. Each book is unique—Magination doesn't have a specific "look" that it is seeking. What is most important is that the illustrations work with the text to make a winning combination.

Prefer manuscript/illustration packages, or separate: Everything is evaluated on its own merit; therefore, it is fine to send a manuscript in conjunction with illustrations, but each part of the package must be worthy in its own right.

Include with illustrator query: Query with samples and SASE (if the illustrator wants the samples returned). No electronic submissions, *please*.

Time to reply: Samples of an illustrator's work are kept on file and as projects come up, illustrators with whom Magination wishes to work are contacted

Purchases freelance photography: No.

Terms for writers: 5 to 15 percent in royalties.

Terms for illustrators: Variable and paid by the project.

Submission guidelines: On request with an SASE or visit the Web site (only writers' guidelines are available).

Tips and comments: Study the submissions guidelines carefully, and take a look at Magination's books *prior* to making a submission. It is also advisable that the author take the time to research the existing book market and be able to explain how his or her book would fit into the existing market given its unique strengths.

MARGARET K. MCELDERRY BOOKS

1230 Avenue of the Americas
New York, NY 10020
(212) 698-2761
(212) 698-2796 (fax)
Web site: www.SimonSaysKids.com

Corporate structure/parent: Simon & Schuster Children's Publishing.

Description: Book publisher.

Key people:

Publisher: Brenda Bowen

Executive editor: Emma D. Dryden

Assistant editor: Kristen McCurry

Editor at large: Margaret K. McElderry

Books per year and description: Between 25 and 30 books per year, in subcategories picture books, middle-grade fiction, young adult fiction, poetry, and fantasy.

Percentage by first-time authors: 50 percent.

Seeks: Humorous middle-grade fiction; interesting middle-grade historical fiction; young picture books; edgy young adult.

Accepts unsolicited/unagented: Accepts query letters for all formats.

Description of fiction titles: A variety: humorous, contemporary, historical, thoughtful, and so on.

Recent fiction titles:

24 Hours by Margaret Mahy (a thought-provoking YA novel set during a period of 24 hours in which a teenage boy has life-changing adventures)

Understanding Buddy by Marc Kornblatt (contemporary middle-grade fiction in which two fifth-grade boys come to understand each other and in the process come to understand a little bit more about life and death and everything in between)

River Boy by Tim Bowler (a beautifully lyrical novel about a girl's relationship with her dying grandfather)

The Year of Miss Agnes by Kirkpatrick Hill (middle-grade fiction set in Alaska after World War II in which a special teacher arrives in a one-room Athabascan Indian schoolhouse and changes the lives of the students forever)

Preferred fiction titles: Looking for: humorous middle-grade fiction; interesting historical fiction; edgy young adult fiction. Not looking for Harry Potter knockoffs.

Description of nonfiction titles: Doesn't publish much nonfiction, but if so, looks for interesting or obscure subjects or people that would be of interest to a wide range of readers.

Recent nonfiction titles:

The Planet Hinters by Dennis Brindell Fradin (an accessible and fascinating account of how the planets were discovered, illustrated with photos and prints)

Never Were Men So Brave by Susan Provost Beller (a graphic portrayal of the men who fought bravely in the Irish Brigade during the Civil War, illustrated with photos and prints)

Preferred nonfiction titles: Interesting or obscure history/biography made accessible for young readers.

Preferred form of submission/contact: Please send a query letter for any format, including picture book.

Time to reply: Will reply to queries within two weeks; we will reply to manuscripts within three to four months.

Time to publish: Anywhere from 18 months to three years, depending on the format and circumstances.

Accepts simultaneous submissions: If the company responds positively to a query letter and asks to see your manuscript, be sure to notify that your submission is a multiple submission in your cover letter.

Number of illustrators used annually: Too many to count!

Desired illustrator qualifications: Illustrators who are comfortable with character development, landscapes, animals, and children.

Prefer manuscript/illustration packages, or separate: Prefer to review manuscripts without illustrations.

Include with illustrator query: Resume, color samples, and tear sheets.

Time to reply: Within a month.

Purchases freelance photography: Yes, but not often.

Preferred photography: A photographer's comfort with form and composition.

Terms for writers: Advance and a royalty.

Terms for illustrators: Advance and a royalty, or flat fee, depending on the project.

Submission guidelines: Send a #10 SASE to McElderry Books.

Tips and comments: *Authors:* Do not send anything that you don't love; read a lot of children's books to see what's being published and what's been published; read your work out loud—whether it's a picture book or a novel—to be sure the text flows smoothly and you don't stumble over the language or structure. Familiarize yourself with the picture the company publishes. *Illustrators:* Prepare samples of the kind of work you love to do and that you are most comfortable doing. The art department would rather see excellent samples of one style of work than mediocre samples of four different styles of work. Be sure to write to us for our guidelines before you submit your work. And again, read books!

May Davenport Publishers

26313 Purissima Road
Los Altos Hills, CA 94022
(650) 948-6499
(650) 947-1373 (fax)
Web site: www.maydavenportpublishers.com

Description: Publisher.

Seeks: Now interested in fictional novels (50,000–70,000 words) for the TV-oriented teenagers—the 15- to 18-year-olds.

Accepts unsolicited/unagented: Currently only accepting manuscripts for older teens.

Recent fiction titles:

A Fine Line by Constance D. Casserly (Sixteen-year-old girl dumps 17-year-old boyfriend and he stalks her. Fortunately, the girl's caring peers lightened the text in this love–hate traumatic novel. A teacher's guide is available.)

The Newman Assignment by Kurt Haberl (A developmentally disabled, educable janitor and a rambunctious high school boy went on a "quest" together and faced the world differently thereafter. A Teacher's Guide is available.)

Drivers' Ed Is Dead by Pat Delgado (Drivers' ed is dropped from the school curriculum, so two teens surreptitiously opened a driving school business. A Teacher's Guide is available.)

When the Dancing Ends by Judy L. Hairfield (Greek American teens had problems with Greek family values vs. American family values and said so dramatically in their journals. A Teacher's Guide is available).

Preferred fiction titles: There is a need for teenagers to know how to write effectively before they graduate from high schools in the United States. Reading contemporary fictional literature of their own generation may motivate them to value descriptive adjectives, similes, and intriguing plots with admirable youthful characters. Novels should be entertaining and suitable as supplementary readings to the famous novels (Melville's *Billy Budd* or *Moby Dick*, or Hawthorne's *Scarlet Letter*, or Hemingway's war stories, etc.) that teachers in English courses prefer to expose their students to in middle and high schools. Just show your own writing talent. Being humorous is a plus. For example, *Magda Rose* by Paul Luria, published in the spring 1999 (a sixth-grade teacher tells his students about his first love, Magda Rose, and about her parents, who are Holocaust survivors)—this author wrote a serious story not devoid of humor—about a pervasive issue. Story is informative and not pedantic.

Preferred form of submission/contact: Has enough preschool to third grade (500 words) read-and-color manuscripts on file and out-of-print books to be reprinted. *Not accepting anymore.* Try magazines (children's, pets', environment, etc.)—magazines use fillers; or try newspapers. Also has enough (30,000–40,000 words) juvenile novels on file for grades 3 to 6. *Can't accept another juvenile story right now.*

Tips and comments: Try it. Write fictional novels for older teens so they can empathize with your characters' conflicts and solutions. The author of *Tug of War* was challenged with a historical theme and wrote her novel humorously, too. Try it with contemporary teens.

Meadowbrook Press

5451 Smetana Drive
Minnetonka, MN 55343
(952) 930-1100
(800) 338-2232
(952) 930-1940 (fax)
E-mail: awiechmann@meadowbrookpress.com
Web site: www.meadowbrookpress.com

Description: Book publisher.

Established: 1975.

Key people:

Publisher: Bruce Lansky

Acquisitions/submissions editor: Bruce Lansky

Books per year and description: Approximately eight. Categories include poetry, short story, fiction, and nonfiction.

Percentage by first-time authors: 25 percent.

Seeks: Currently, looking for short stories for the Newfangled Fairy Tales series (A Newfangled Fairy Tale takes a known fairy tale or a traditional fairy tale theme and switches some of the main elements around in a way that is surprising, witty, amusing, humorous, and makes a point.) Looking for your funniest poems for inclusion in future children's poetry anthologies. And looking for stories for the Girls to the Rescue collection, which encourages self-esteem in girls by portraying high-spirited heroines and emphasizing a "you can do it" attitude. See writers' guidelines for more details.

Accepts unsolicited/unagented: Yes.

Description of fiction titles: Anthologies, short stories, and poems.

Recent fiction titles:

Girls to the Rescue, Book #7, edited by Bruce Lansky (encourages self-esteem in girls by portraying high-spirited heroines and emphasizing a "you can do it" attitude)

Preferred fiction titles: Novels of any kind; poetry.

Description of nonfiction titles: Party planning; how-to; activity titles.

Preferred form of submission/contact: Query.

Time to reply: Four months.

Time to publish: 12 to 18 months.

Accepts simultaneous submissions: Yes.

Desired illustrator qualifications: Liveliness of characters.

Prefer manuscript/illustration packages, or separate: Separately.

Include with illustrator query: Resume and samples.

Time to reply: Four months.

Submission guidelines: Mail request with an SASE or visit the Web site for detailed guidelines.

Tips and comments: *Please* review guidelines before submitting any works. Please familiarize yourself with the company's titles and illustrations before submitting anything.

MEGAN TINGLEY BOOKS

Three Center Plaza
Boston, MA 02108
(617) 227-0730
(617) 063-2864 (fax)

Corporate structure/parent: Little, Brown and Company Children's Books (including the former Joy Street Books imprint).

Description: Children's book publisher.

Established: 2000.

Key people:

Publisher and vice president: John Keller

Acquisitions/submissions editor: Megan Tingley

Books per year and description: *Megan Tingley Books* is a new imprint of Little, Brown; therefore, no pattern has been established yet. Books include fiction/nonfiction, in the following categories: picture books (ages 2–8), middle grade (ages 8–12), and young adult (age 12 and up).

Seeks: Primarily picture books.

Accepts unsolicited/unagented: No. But authors may submit a one-page query letter for fiction and nonfiction manuscripts. Please mark the envelope "Query" and address to Alvina Ling, editorial assistant, Megan Tingley Books (see prior address).

Description of fiction titles: Picture books with some fiction for middle-grade and young adult readers.

Recent fiction titles:

Underwear Do's and Don'ts written and illustrated by Todd Parr

Look-Alikes by Joan Steiner

Just Like a Baby by Rebecca Bond

Preferred fiction titles: Primarily picture books. This imprint does *not* consider "genre" novels for publication (including mystery, romance, and science fiction).

Description of nonfiction titles: Publishes a limited number of nonfiction titles for middle and young adult readers

Recent nonfiction titles:

The Girls' Guide to Life by Catherine Dee

The Book of Bad Ideas, written and illustrated by Laura Huliska-Beith

Preferred nonfiction titles: Middle grade (ages 8–12), and young adult (age 12 and up). Middle grade texts average 15,000 to 25,000 words, and young adult texts range 25,000 to 35,000 words. For nonfiction works a proposal, outline, and three sample chapters are acceptable for a submission (but please remember that Megan Tingley Books does *not* accept unsolicited manuscripts).

Preferred form of submission/contact: Authors may submit a one-page query letter for fiction and nonfiction manuscripts. Please mark the envelope "Query" and address to: Alvina Ling, editorial assistant, Megan Tingley Books (see prior address). Manuscripts are reviewed only through literary agents or at the direct solicitation of one of our editors—unsolicited manuscripts will not be reviewed.

Time to reply: Query: one month; manuscript: three months.

Time to publish: One to two years.

Accepts simultaneous submissions: Yes.

Number of illustrators used annually: Variable.

Desired illustrator qualifications: Unique style and how well an illustrator can match their art with a specific manuscript.

Prefer manuscript/illustration packages, or separate: Megan Tingley Books accepts manuscript/illustration packages.

Include with illustrator query: Tear sheets and samples are easiest to circulate to all editorial staff.

Time to reply: Circulates samples and only replies to an artist if interested in seeing more work.

Preferred photography: Usually has a specific image in mind depending on the project. Therefore, needs vary from one project to the next.

Terms for writers: Advance against royalties. The specific terms vary for each project.

Terms for illustrators: Advance against royalties. The specific terms vary for each project.

Submission guidelines: Send a letter and an SASE to Little, Brown's editorial department with request for guidelines.

Tips and comments: Submit one manuscript at a time; seeking multicultural titles. Submit a variety of samples that display different subject matter and styles. Please *don't* attempt to pitch ideas on the telephone. With queries, it is advisable to include information about the author's qualifications—including previous publications. Please also include a brief description of the project, why you think there is a market for the project, a list of the competition (if any), and whether the manuscript is being submitted to other publishers simultaneously. Please also enclose an SASE for return of all materials and/or confirmation of receipt.

Meriwether Publishing Ltd./Contemporary Drama Service

885 Elkton Drive
Colorado Springs, CO 80919
(719) 594-4422
(719) 594-9916 (fax)
E-mail: merpcds@aol.com
Web site: www.meriwetherpublishing.com
Web site: contemporarydrama.com

Description: Book (theater-related) and play publisher.

Established: 1970.

Key people:

President: A. Mark Zapel

Vice president: Theodore Zapel

Executive editor: Arthur Zapel

Christian submissions: Rhonda Wray

School submissions: Ted Zapel

Percentage by first-time authors: 50 percent.

Seeks: Books on theatrical arts subjects and/or books of monologues, duologues, or short plays—preferably for high-school-aged children. Collections of scripts/plays for school and church.

Accepts unsolicited/unagented: Yes.

Description of fiction titles: Publishes only fiction plays.

Preferred fiction titles: Looking for one-act plays, for school and church (Easter and Christmas, especially).

Description of nonfiction titles: Theatrical arts—acting.

Preferred form of submission/contact: Query letter with a selection from the manuscript attached—be sure to include an SASE.

Time to reply: Four to six weeks.

Time to publish: One year or the following season.

Accepts simultaneous submissions: Yes.

Purchases freelance photography: No.

Terms for writers: 10 percent royalty to a maximum amount or 10 percent royalty for the life of the publication (indefinitely). Terms are negotiable.

Meet David Adler

Author

David Adler has had 155 books published, mostly for elementary school–age children, including THE CAM JANSEN MYSTERY series (1980–present, Viking Press); the PICTURE BOOK BIOGRAPHY series (1989–present, Holiday House); the Andy Russell books (1998–present, Harcourt); *We Remember the Holocaust* (1989, Holt); *Lou Gehrig: The Luckiest Man* (1997, Harcourt). He was born in New York City on April 10, 1947. He has a B.A. in economics from Queens College and an M.B.A. in marketing from New York University. Before he became a children's book author, he was a math teacher and an editor.

How did you get your first book published?

My first book was *A Little at a Time.* I was fortunate. It was accepted by the first publisher I sent it to, Random House.

Did you have an agent when you published your first book?

I did not have an agent for my first book, but I have one now. I knew this agent from my work as an editor.

Do you have any advice, in terms of finding an agent, for a writer starting out?

Before a writer looks for an agent, he or she should have a publishable manuscript to show the agent. Then, speak with someone knowledgeable in publishing circles and ask for recommendations.

Are you still with your first publisher?

I am no longer with my first publisher. My editor there has moved on, so I did, too.

Submission guidelines: By mail with an SASE (for catalogs, include $1 on SASE for postage) or go to the Web site.

Tips and comments: Study the catalog; send an SASE and send a *hard copy* of the manuscript. Always on the lookout for creative nonfiction on theatrical arts subjects.

MILKWEEDS FOR YOUNG READERS

430 First Avenue N., Suite 400
Minneapolis, MN 55401-1743
(612) 332-3192
(612) 332-6248 (fax)
Web site: www.milkweed.org

Description: Book publisher.

Seeks: Milkweed Editions publishes with the intention of making a humane impact on society, in the belief that literature is a transformative art uniquely able to convey the es-

Do you have any advice, in terms of finding a publisher, for a writer starting out?
Check the lists of publishers, and find one who does books like the ones you hope to do.

Are your books illustrated?
My books are illustrated, but my editors find the illustrators.

What procedures do you follow when you write?
I work every day writing. I set a definite schedule and keep to it. My work day is 8:30 A.M. until about 5:30 P.M.

Where do you get your ideas?
My fiction is all character based. My characters are based mostly on people I know or have met in my travels. I then imagine my characters in specific settings.

What do you think are the key differences between writing for children and writing for adults?
When someone writes for children, he or she cannot assume the reader has any knowledge of the subject.

How did you learn to write?
I have always loved to write and then learned from my work as an editor and from editors of my books.

Anything you really wish somebody had told you when you started out?
Write the kinds of books you like to read, and love the book you write before you send it to a publisher.

sential experiences of the human heart and spirit. To that end, Milkweed Editions publishes distinctive voices of literary merit in handsomely designed, visually dynamic books, exploring the ethical, cultural, and esthetic issues that free societies need continually to address. Milkweed Editions is looking for high-quality novels for readers aged 8–13 for its children's book publishing program, Milkweeds for Young Readers. Milkweed is especially interested in fiction set in the contemporary world and in fiction that explores our relationship to the natural world.

Accepts unsolicited/unagented: Yes. Milkweed welcomes submissions from writers who have previously published a book of fiction or nonfiction for children or adults, or a minimum of three short stories or pieces of nonfiction in nationally distributed commercial or literary journals. Translations are welcome.

Recent fiction titles:
The Monkey Thief by Aileen Kilgore Henderson
The Gumma Wars and *Business as Usual* by David Haynes
Behind the Bedroom Wall by Laura E. Williams
The Boy with Paper Wings by Susan Lowell

Summer of the Bonepile Monster by Aileen Kilgore Henderson

Preferred fiction titles: At this age, readers are ready for well-written books that range widely in subject matter, from fantasy to fiction grounded in history to books about everyday life. Manuscripts should be of high literary quality, embody humane values, and contribute to cultural understanding. Please note that Milkweed does not publish children's picture books, poetry, or collections of stories.

Preferred form of submission/contact: Manuscript.

Time to reply: Review process can take from one to six months.

Submission guidelines: Your children's manuscript must be 90–200 pages; typed or computer printed on good-quality white paper; double-spaced; submitted with a stamped self-addressed, return book-mailer large enough to accommodate the manuscript (or the manuscript cannot be returned). Please indicate whether you want Milkweed simply to recycle the manuscript—in this event, submit your manuscript with a self-addressed stamped envelope for a reply. You can write to receive a catalog; enclose $1.50 for postage. Thank you for your interest in Milkweed Editions, and good luck in your writing endeavors.

Tips and comments: Milkweed Prize for Children's Literature: Milkweed Editions is pleased to announce its writing competition for quality children's novels intended for readers in the 8–13 age group. This competition is part of Milkweed's children's book publishing program for middle graders. The prize: Milkweed has restructured the prize beginning with the 1996 competition: in the past Milkweed has solicited manuscripts specifically for the contest, but for the 1996 and subsequent contests, Milkweed Editions will award the Milkweed Prize for Children's Literature to the best manuscript for children ages 8–13 that Milkweed accepts for publication during the calendar year by a writer not previously published by Milkweed. Submission directly to the contest is no longer necessary. Since Milkweed will now be choosing the winner from the manuscripts it accepts for publication during a given year, all manuscripts submitted to Milkweed will automatically be considered for the prize. Judging will be by Milkweed Editions, and the winner of the prize will receive a $2,000 cash advance as part of any royalties agreed upon in the contractual arrangement negotiated at the time of acceptance. Laura E. Williams won the 1996 prize for her novel *Behind the Bedroom Wall.* Aileen Kilgore Henderson won the 1995 prize for her novel *The Summer of the Bonepile Monster,* and the winner of the 1994 prize was Isabel Marvin for her novel *A Bride for Anna's Papa.*

MILLBROOK PRESS, INC.

PO Box 335
2 Old New Milford Road
Brookfield, CT 06804
(203) 740-2220
(203) 775-5643 (fax)
Web site: www.millbrookpress.com

Corporate structure/parent: The Millbrook Press has the following imprints: Twenty-first Century Books and Copper Beech. The Millbrook Press is also in the process of creating a third imprint, which is still unnamed at this time.

Description: The Millbrook Press is a midsized publishing firm with a list of approximately 130 titles per year. Millbrook prides itself on its quality nonfiction geared to a school and library curriculum. The list also incorporates trade novelty texts and historical-based fiction.

Established: 1990.

Key people:

Publisher: Jean E. Reynolds

Trade publisher: Judy Korman

Books per year and description: Specifically a children's book publisher. Concentrations are on school subjects: science, social studies, math, biographies, history, and so forth. Additionally, the company's divisions include a picture book line, arts and crafts, hobbies, careers and sports, and historical fiction books.

Seeks: Millbrook is always looking for new and interesting nonfiction ideas that can be used in a classroom setting (if not educational titles, then titles that can be used for book reports or research, etc.). *Does not accept unsolicited picture book or fiction manuscripts.*

Accepts unsolicited/unagented: Yes; however, it is *crucial* that authors obtain the guidelines *before* submitting. Guidelines may be obtained by sending an SASE to the Millbrook offices with a request or from the Web site (click on the "editorial guidelines" icon). *Do not* send anything that does not correspond with the guidelines. *No unsolicited picture book or fiction manuscripts.*

Description of fiction titles: Literary fiction and picture books.

Description of nonfiction titles: School and library oriented, for all age groups, with just about any topic.

Recent nonfiction titles:

A series on the Holocaust by Ted Gottfried

A science series with experiments for kids to try at home or school by Vicki Cobb

Meet My Grandmother: She's a —— by Lisa Tucker McElroy (a careers series that follows a day in the life of grandmothers such as Sandra Day O'Connor and Senator Dianne Feinstein)

A series on sports teams and stadiums/arenas by Tom Owens

Preferred nonfiction titles: Accepts nonfiction manuscripts so long as they are appropriate for school and library use (for varying grade levels).

Preferred form of submission/contact: *Obtain guidelines first* (to be certain that your manuscript is appropriate). Send a brief cover letter and the first few chapters of your manuscript. *Always* include an SASE if you want a reply.

Time to reply: One month.

Time to publish: One to two years.

Accepts simultaneous submissions: Yes.

Number of illustrators used annually: Approximately 24.

Desired illustrator qualifications: The art department does not encourage unsolicited samples. However, specific guidelines are available. Send an SASE to the editorial assistant with a request for illustrator's guidelines.

Prefer manuscript/illustration packages, or separate: No, separately only.

Include with illustrator query: *Again, the art department does not encourage submissions.* But resumes, clips, samples, and so forth, may be sent to the associate art director. *If you are determined to make a submission, please review the company's books and only submit what will work with the collections.*

Time to reply: The art department will not reply unless they are interested in the artist's work. *Nothing will be returned to the artist, even if an SASE is enclosed.*

Purchases freelance photography: No.

Terms for writers: Royalties, advance, flat fees—it is variable by the project.

Terms for illustrators: Same.

Submission guidelines: Send a request with an SASE to Manuscript Guidelines (at the address listed earlier), or get them on the Web site. No e-mail submissions are accepted.

Tips and comments: Do your homework! Know the market and what the company is likely to publish. Check out the Web site and catalogs to see the types of books published. Most of all, the company loves creativity and new ideas—but again, only when they fit into the Millbrook mold. Above all: *Get the guidelines and stick to them!* If you'd like to make a submission, it's in everyone's best interest for you to follow the guidelines and make your submission in the correct format. Remember: No picture books and no fiction. The Web site will address virtually all of your questions so spend some time there, do some research, and learn about who Millbrook is and what it publishes—*before you send a manuscript.*

Mitchell Lane Publishers, Inc.

34 Decidedly Lane
Bear, DE 19701
(302) 834-9646
(302) 834-4164 (fax)

Description: Book publisher.

Established: 1993.

Key people:

Publisher: Barbara J. Mitchell

Acquisitions/submissions editor: Barbara J. Mitchell

Books per year and description: 30 in children's biography.

Seeks: Hires writers on a work-for-hire basis. Determines the assignments and selects the authors.

Accepts unsolicited/unagented: No.

Description of fiction titles: No fiction.

Description of nonfiction titles: Multicultural biography.

Recent nonfiction titles:

Julia Roberts (a Real-Life Reader biography)
Legends of Health & Fitness
Famous People of Hispanic Heritage
Christina Aguilera (a Real-Life Reader biography)

Preferred form of submission/contact: Send resume and writing samples.

Time to reply: When there is an assignment for the writer.

Time to publish: One year.

Accepts simultaneous submissions: No.
Number of illustrators used annually: One to three.
Desired illustrator qualifications: Realistic portraiture.
Include with illustrator query: Resume and samples to be kept on file.
Time to reply: When there is a project assignment.
Purchases freelance photography: Occasionally.
Terms for writers: Outright purchase for a fee, which is variable.
Terms for illustrators: Outright purchase of all rights for a fee, which is variable.
Tips and comments: Offers writing assignments to experienced nonfiction writers *after* reviewing resumes and writing samples. *Send samples that do not need to be returned.*

MONDO PUBLISHING

980 Avenue of the Americas, 2d Floor
New York, NY 10018
(212) 268-3560
(212) 268-3561 (fax)
Web site: www.mondopub.com

Description: Children's educational and trade book publisher.
Established: As a professional development organization in 1986; as a book publisher in 1992.
Key people:
Publisher: Mark Viners
Acquisitions/submissions editors: Leslie Bockol, Susan Der Kazarian, Elizabeth Jaffe, and Janice Leotri
Books per year and description: Children's fantasy, animal, realistic fiction, nonfiction; 15 trade titles and 150 educational titles. ✓
Percentage by first-time authors: 2 percent.
Seeks: Books that are playful, informative, and poignant, with characters children can relate to. Range is from kindergarten though fourth grade.
Accepts unsolicited/unagented: No.
Description of fiction titles: Written in a style and point of view that is accessible to children. The characters are lively and fun, getting themselves into and out of situations—some familiar, some not so familiar—but all solvable by kids themselves.
Recent fiction titles:
Deadbolts and Dinkles by Kathy Kennedy Tapp
Tuttle's Shell by Salvatore Mordocca
My Lucky Hat by Kevin O'Malley
The Twiddle Twins by Howard Goldsmith (series, Chapter Books, Mystery)
Winky Bille by Pamela Jane (series, Chapter Books)
Preferred fiction titles: There is no subject matter—except potty books—that won't be considered, as long as it is well written and appropriate for the age group. No religious material.
Description of nonfiction titles: Kid-friendly; well written; clearly illustrated.

Recent nonfiction titles:
Pro Sports—How Did They Begin? by Don Wulffson
Journey to a New Land: An Oral History by Kimberly A. Weinberger
Songs of Myself: An Anthology of Poems and Art compiled by Georgia Heard
Forest Fires by Josephine Nobisso

Preferred nonfiction titles: No ABC or counting books. No religious subjects.

Preferred form of submission/contact: If you are a previously published writer (or if you have an agent), please send entire manuscript. Queries are accepted, however, if you are previously published or agented, you may contact directly or through your agent with a complete manuscript.

Time to reply: Queries: two weeks; manuscripts: four months

Time to publish: Six months to one year.

Accepts simultaneous submissions: Yes.

Number of illustrators used annually: 15.

Desired illustrator qualifications: Work that is unique and high quality. Illustrators must be able to meet tight deadlines.

Prefer manuscript/illustration packages, or separate: Either way.

Include with illustrator query: Prefers to be contacted with samples (10 color copies or tear sheets, cover letter, and resume).

Time to reply: Will only call if we are interested in working with the illustrator.

Purchases freelance photography: Yes.

Preferred photography: High-quality photos that can be used for fiction as well as nonfiction, although photography is used mostly for nonfiction titles.

Terms for writers: Competitive terms for writers.

Terms for illustrators: Competitive terms for illustrators.

Submission guidelines: Send an SASE with appropriate postage. If you are interested in seeing catalogs, send $3.20 in postage (for priority mail).

Tips and comments: Know your craft. Send your best, and be patient during the review process. Be able to work within tight deadlines. The company needs to work with illustrators who can meet our demanding schedules. Know the company's books before you submit. The trade line is small and most books fold into the educational program too. Therefore, the subject matter and language on all submissions must be appropriate for the educational as well as trade markets.

MOON MOUNTAIN PUBLISHING, INC.

80 Peachtree Road
North Kingstown, RI 02852 USA
(401) 884-6703
(401) 884-7076 (fax)
E-mail: hello@moonmountainpub.com
Web site: www.moonmountainpub.com

Description: Publisher of children's picture books.

Books per year and description: Less than 3 percent of the manuscripts reviewed.

Seeks: Fiction only, including fantasy, folktale, contemporary, and bedtime for any age group up to about 12 years.

Accepts unsolicited/unagented: Yes.

Description of fiction titles: Picture books in either prose or verse.

Recent fiction titles:

Hello Willow by Kimberly Poulton; illustrated by Jennifer O'Keefe

Petronella by Jay Williams; illustrated by Margaret Organ-Kean

Hamlet and the Magnificent Sandcastle by Brian Lies

Preferred form of submission/contact: Manuscript or query.

Time to reply: Approximately three months. Please do not call.

Prefers manuscript/illustration packages, or separate: Together, but please don't submit your own art if you are not a professional artist.

Submission guidelines: Please include an SASE. No electronic manuscript submissions, though electronic queries are welcome.

Tips and comments: Manuscripts should be no longer than 2,000 words, and most should be shorter. Avoid holiday stories; explicit religious content; straightforward counting and alphabet books (although might consider a counting or alphabet book with an original, story-telling approach).

Morehouse Publishing

4475 Linglestown Road
Harrisburg, PA 17112
(717) 541-8130
(717) 541-8136
E- mail: morehouse@morehouse.com
Web site: www.morehousegroup.com

Description: Hardcover and paperback publisher. Morehouse Publishing has traditionally published for the Episcopal Church and the Anglican Communion.

Key people:

Editorial director: Debra K. Farrington

Acquisitions/submissions editor: Submissions should be sent to the attention of Debra K. Farrington.

Books per year and description: 35 per year—not all children's titles.

Percentage by first-time authors: Many are by new authors.

Seeks: Morehouse Publishing endeavors to provide books and materials that give expression to the diverse biblical and theological views, opinions and understandings that characterize today's Church.

Accepts unsolicited/unagented: Queries only, please.

Preferred form of submission/contact: Submit query with one-page synopsis of the book, an annotated table of contents, one page comparing the book to others like it on the market, a resume, an introduction to the book, and one sample chapter to Debra K. Farrington. Include a self-addressed manila mailer with adequate postage so the proposal can be returned at a later date.

Time to reply: Six weeks to two months.

Accepts simultaneous submissions: Simultaneous submissions should be identified.

Terms for writers: Advances on royalties are negotiable and paid on signing of contract and final ms submission.

Tips and comments: Call (800) 877-0012 for a free copy of the book catalog.

MORGAN REYNOLDS

620 S. Elm Street, Suite 223
Greensboro, NC 27406
Web site: www.morganreynolds.com

Description: Morgan Reynolds publishes serious-minded nonfiction books for juvenile and young adult readers. Titles complement elementary and secondary school curriculums for young readers ages 10 to 18.

Seeks: Well-crafted biographies that present the subject's personality and development as a human being.

Submission guidelines: Send an SASE.

Tips and comments: The narrative voice should never be patronizing. Avoid speaking directly to the reader. Language should be kept precise and to the point. Strive to create reader interest by presenting the story in an exciting manner. Do not try to generate interest with an elaborate or cute writing style.

NATIONAL GEOGRAPHIC SOCIETY

1145 17th Street NW
Washington, DC 20036
(202) 828-5492
(202) 429-5727 (fax)
E-mail: jtunstal@ngs.org
Web site: www.nationalgeographic.com

Description: Book publishing arm of the National Geographic Society, specializing in nonfiction books with a multicultural orientation.

NBM

Terry Nantier
555 8th Avenue, Suite 1202
New York, NY 10018
E-mail: terry@nbmpub.com
Web site: www.nbmpub.com

Seeks: Please familiarize yourself with the company through the Web site or by getting our catalog (there is nothing in the catalog that isn't on the Web site). Interested in most everything from fantasy to humor, including mystery, general fiction, and so forth. Not interested in superheroes.

Accepts unsolicited/unagented: Please submit samples only. See below for details.

Description of fiction titles: Fantasy, science fiction, fairy tales, spy tales—all in comic format.

Recent fiction titles:

The Last Knight: An introduction to Don Quixote by Will Eisner and Miguel de Cervantes

The Princess and the Frog by Will Eisner

The Wind in the Willows: Vol. 1. The Wild Wood by Kenneth Grahame, adapted by Michel Plessix

Max Friedman: No Pasaran by Vittorio Giardino (Max Friedman series of spy graphic novels [*Orient Gateway, Hungarian Rhapsody*] with a suspenseful tale set in the Spanish Civil War)

Preferred form of submission/contact: To submit: please send a one-page synopsis of your story that includes any pertinent background and some character development. Please do not at first send a complete finished story as that will only delay an answer greatly. To submit electronically: Send no more than 3 to 4 jpegs at no more than 300K size each, uncompressed. Best yet: send us a link to your site with samples.

Number of illustrators used annually: No need for illustrations alone, including covers.

Desired illustrator qualifications: Not set up to create teams (i.e., match a writer with an artist or vice versa).

Prefer manuscript/illustration packages, or separate: Yes, accepts them.

Include with illustrator query: For the art, please send copies of a few finished pages or pencils for the project or at least of previous work in the same style you plan on using.

Submission guidelines: Check out the Web site, send an e-mail, or write with an SASE.

Tips and comments: If you want anything back, including an answer (unless positive), please include a self-addressed stamped envelope.

New Canaan Publishing Company Inc.

PO Box 752
New Canaan, CT 06840
Web site: www.newcanaanpublishing.com

Description: Publisher.

Seeks: Primary areas of interest are educational works and stories for children aged from 6 to 14 years (grades 1–9). Very interested in works in the areas of the sciences and history. Interested in promoting traditional themes which are supportive of conventional families and of Christian morality.

Accepts unsolicited/unagented: Yes.

Recent fiction titles:

Olive, the Orphan Reindeer by Michael Christie

Journey to the Edge of Nowhere by Janet Baird

Indian Gold by Steve Givens

Preferred form of submission/contact: Manuscripts, synopses, and/or chapter samples are acceptable via mail (no e-mail, please).

Time to reply: 10 to 12 weeks.

Submission guidelines: Please write with an SASE or visit the Web site. Fiction stories should be exciting to read and should not contain themes incompatible with Christian morality. Ideal word length would be between 10,000 and 20,000 words for fiction stories (with educational materials, much will depend on the subject matter involved). Please, no short stories designed as picture books.

Tips and comments: New Canaan are dismayed to find that a staggering proportion of fiction manuscripts that we receive deal with dysfunctional or single-parent family situations. We would welcome stories built around traditional two-parent families. Divorce themes, humanistic themes, talking inanimate objects, and fairy tale fantasy themes are unlikely to be accepted. Particularly welcome are works that encapsulate a specific Christian-compatible moral principle, packaged into a story able to be enjoyed by a wider audience. For example, the first fiction title in the Triangle Club series, *Indian Gold*, teaches kids the value of wisdom, strength, and integrity through the vehicle of a nonreligious adventure story. The next story in the series, *Tornado Warning*, carries the message that it is wrong to judge merely by appearances.

New Hope Publishers

PO Box 12065
Birmingham, AL 35202-2065
E-mail: new_hope@wmu.org
Web site: www.newhopepubl.com

Corporate structure/parent: Woman's Missionary Unit.

Description: Christian publisher.

Seeks: Children's leadership books, multicultural books, and books that teach children about their purpose in God's plan.

Accepts unsolicited/unagented: Yes.

Recent fiction titles:

Joy's Discovery by Jane Chu
God's World and Me from A to Z by Judy Langley
Best Friends Forever? by Renee Holmes Kent
Shoes On, Shoes Off by Catherine Compher

Preferred fiction titles: Books that show characters with leadership qualities, tell stories of missionaries, include bible lessons, are about friendship, biographies, or youth ministry.

Preferred form of submission/contact: Complete manuscript is preferred but detailed proposals with chapter summaries and writing samples are also accepted.

Terms for writers: Royalty or flat fee.

Submission guidelines: Write with an SASE or visit the Web site. Authors must supply sources of quotations and documentation of all facts cited in the work. Always include a cover letter with a synopsis of the book, purpose statement, intended audience, projected length of the book, and author bio. The bio should include other published works by the author.

North-South Books

1123 Broadway, Suite 800
New York, NY 10010
(212) 463-9736
(212) 633-1004 (fax)

Description: North-South Books is a small, fiercely independent publisher of children's books. Its roots are in Europe, where its sister company, Nord-Süd Verlag, was founded more than thirty years ago. The aim of the founders was to build bridges—bridges between authors and artists from different countries and between readers of all ages around the world. The company name expresses this idea, and so does its logo: An Inuit child eating a banana.

Tips and comments: North-South believes that children should be exposed to as wide a range of artistic styles as possible, so the company never shies away from work that's unusual. But whether an author or artist is from France or Russia, Poland or the United States, North-South books always have universal themes that children everywhere can respond to.

NorthWord Press

5900 Green Oak Drive
Minnetonka, MN 55343
(952) 936-4700

Corporate structure/parent: Creative Publishing International, Inc.
Description: Book publisher.
Established: 1984.
Books per year and description: 8 to 10 nature and wildlife titles (nonfiction).
Percentage by first-time authors: 40 percent.
Seeks: Nature and wildlife.
Accepts unsolicited/unagented: Yes.
Description of fiction titles: Nonfiction only.
Description of nonfiction titles: Nature and wildlife.
Recent nonfiction titles:
We Are Bears by Molly Grooms
Whitetail Deer by Laura Evert
Ferocious Fangs, by Sally Fleming
Preferred nonfiction titles: No poetry.
Preferred form of submission/contact: Query or manuscript.
Time to reply: Four to six weeks.

Time to publish: 12 to 18 months.
Accepts simultaneous submissions: Yes.
Number of illustrators used annually: Two to four.
Prefer manuscript/illustration packages, or separate: Either.
Include with illustrator query: Resume and samples.
Time to reply: Four to six weeks.
Purchases freelance photography: Yes.
Terms for writers: Flat fee/work for hire.
Terms for illustrators: Flat fee/work for hire.
Submission guidelines: Send an SASE with request.

Oliver Press

Charlotte Square
5707 West 36th Street
Minneapolis, MN 55416-2510
(952) 926-8981
(952) 926-8965 (fax)
Web site: www.mindspring.com/~theoliverpress/

Description: Publisher.
Recent nonfiction titles:
Amazing Archaeologists and Their Finds by William Scheller
You Are the Juror by Nathan Aaseng
Soldiers, Cavaliers, and Planters: Settlers of the Southeastern Colonies by Kieran Doherty

Tips and comments: Oliver Press's history titles focus on people, on the individuals whose thoughts and actions influenced the lives we lead today. Oliver Press offers six curriculum-based series: *Profiles*: collective biographies of men and women whose lives are woven together by common historical threads; *Great Decisions*: discussions that put students in the shoes of leaders; *Innovators*: advances in technology told through the stories of the people who made them; *Shaping America*: collective biographies that chronicle the early settlement of our country; *Business Builders*: stories of enterprising individuals who built businesses in new fields; *In the Cabinet*: examinations of the successes and failures of notable presidential advisers.

Orca Book Publishers

PO Box 5626, Station B
Victoria, British Columbia V8R 654
Canada
(250) 380-1229
(250) 380-1892 (fax)
Web site: www.orcabook.com

Meet Verla Kay

Author

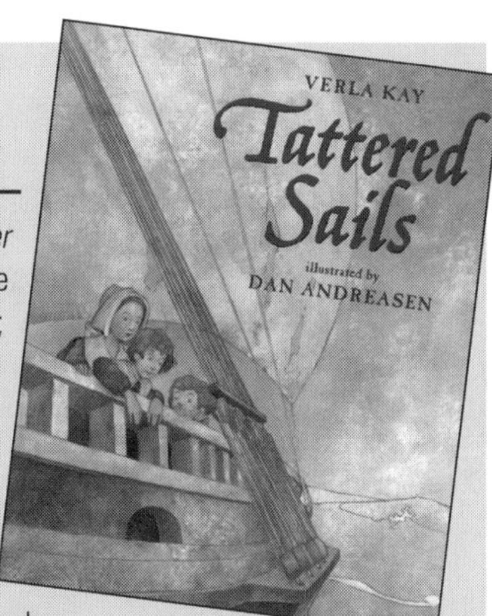

Verla Kay is the author of many books, including *Gold Fever* (Putnam's, 1999; historical fiction picture book about the 1849 California gold rush story); *Iron Horses* (Putnam's, 1999; nonfiction picture book about the building of the transcontinental railroad); *Tattered Sails* (Putnam's, 2001; historical fiction picture book about a family sailing to America in the 1600's); and the forthcoming *Homespun Sarah* (Putnam's Sons, 2002; historical fiction picture book about a 1700s colonial girl). She was born in California on October 25, 1946, and graduated from Watsonville High School. She also has Institute of Children's Literature diplomas (regular and advanced courses) and a Writer's Digest Novel-Writing diploma. She has worked cutting chives in the fields and in the lab of a strawberry processing plant (she counted the bacteria in the strawberries to make sure they were safe for human consumption). She was a teacher's aide in the classroom, the summer school secretary for a grammar school, and the wedding coordinator at her church. She's been a desk clerk and night auditor for motels; worked in the accounts receivable and payable departments of a huge food company; was the traffic director of two different radio stations, a real estate salesperson, a supervisor and district manager of a home party toy company; owned and managed a laundromat; managed a condominium complex; and ran a licensed daycare in her home.

Verla writes picture books for children of all ages. Two-year-olds love them, and so do adults and all the ages in between. She writes for the child in her that she used to be. Since she hated history when she was growing up, she wanted to show the fun side of history to young children, so when they had to learn it, they would find it interesting and not boring. She always hated to write when she was a child and even as an adult. It wasn't until she was a grandmother that she realized she wasn't the world's worst writer just because she had to write things over and over again to get them right. The moment of truth came when she realized that good writers are good writers because they write things over and over until they are just right.

How did you get your first book published?

I still remember the day I got the phone call: December 10, 1994. But I'm getting ahead of myself. Before I could get that call, I needed to write the book and get it into the hands of a publisher that wanted to buy it. The first book I sold was *Covered Wagons, Bumpy Trails*. Only it wasn't called that when I was sending it out. My working title for that book was "Finding a Place." (And no, I never really liked that title, but I couldn't think of anything better.)

I got a lot of flack about that book when I wrote it. I wrote it in a new style of writing that I'd come up with, a style I call "cryptic rhyme." It's bits and pieces of words that paint a vivid picture for the reader, leaving the reader to fill in the blanks in the story. Most of it isn't even in full sentences. The entire book is only around 180 words long, yet because of the brevity of cryptic rhyme, it tells a full story of a family moving to California in a wagon train.

continues

People told me I'd made a big mistake, targeting the book for younger readers, because schools (at least the ones out here in California) teach American history in the fourth through sixth grades. I looked at those people and said, "Yes, that's true. But don't you think the younger children would like to learn about this subject, too?" They just shook their heads, knowing I was making a grave marketing/writing mistake. I believed my gut feelings were right and ignored the nay-sayers and continued to write my book.

It took me two years to complete those little 180 words. Writing is difficult if you're going to have your story rhyme and still make every word make sense and be pertinent to the story. It's even more difficult when you have to also make sure it is true to history. But eventually, I got the story written in a form that I was happy with.

And then, I started marketing it. Over and over I sent it out. It made the rounds of publishing houses for three and a half years. Two of the houses kept it for 10 months each before rejecting it! It went to a total of 12 different publishers before it was pulled from the slush pile at G. P. Putnam's Sons. The day I got that phone call was one of the most exciting days of my life! Those words, "We love your story and want to publish it," were absolute music to my ears.

Six months later, I sold a second book to Putnam, and six months after that, a third one. The funny thing is, we had some delays on the first book due to a change of illustrators, and it wasn't published until October 2000, six years after it sold! My second and third books were both published in 1999—so my first book sold is my third book published, and my third book sold was my second book published, and my second book sold was my first book published. Are you confused? So was I! The publishing business is a crazy, topsy-turvy world, but I wouldn't change it for anything. It might not always make a lot of sense, but it's never dull!

The trail of that first book of mine started with an idea about 11 years before I finally saw it on the shelf of a bookstore. If you want to write children's books, I'd say the first thing you should learn is to never hold your breath waiting for anything to happen, and the second thing is to never give up. It may take a long time, but you can get there.

Did you have an agent when you published your first book?

No, I sold my first two books on my own and had an offer pending on my third book when I finally got my present, wonderful agent. I'd had one agent before, but that relationship was a disaster for me, and I felt very fortunate to have gotten out of that agreement before any of my books sold. Believe me when I say it's much better to have no agent at all than to have an agent that isn't a good match for you. Pick your agent as carefully as you would a lifetime mate. Do not take "any" agent, just because he or she will take you.

You will laugh when you find out how I found my perfect agent. It was a total accident on my part. I wasn't even looking for one. I was the desk clerk in a little motel in my little way-off-in-the-sticks town and was checking in a couple one night. As I usually did, I was chattering away with them as I checked them in. Something came up, and I mentioned I was a writer. The man immediately said, "Oh? What do you write?"

So I told him, "Historical picture books."

"Have you published any?" he asked.

"I have two under contract with Putnam," I said, standing a little taller than my normal 5' 2".

"Oh," he said. "Who's your agent?"

"I don't have one," I said.

"You don't?" He looked at me in amazement. Turns out he was the father-in-law of the chairman of the board of one of the most prestigious literary agencies in New York and his son-in-law's sister, whom he regularly played golf with, was a children's book agent there. The end result? He looked at my stories the next day and gave me her phone number, telling me to tell her he'd said to call her. I did, and after looking at my work, she took me on as a client.

I honestly feel that it was meant to be. But, it would never have happened if I hadn't talked about my writing. So my advice to people wanting to make a contact is to tell everyone that you are a writer. You never know who will be related to or know someone that might be able to help you along your way.

Do you have any advice, in terms of finding an agent, for a writer starting out?

Make sure, before you take on an agent, that the agent will be a good match for you. Talk to the agent on the phone, and make it a long phone call. Find out whether the agent wants the same things for you that you do.

If you want to write lots of picture books, and your agent only wants to sell middle-grade novels, you are not going to be happy with this agent. If the agent wants authors that produce two or three books a year and you only want to write one every two or three years, again, you are not going to be a good match for each other. Just because an agent is wonderful with one author, doesn't mean you will be happy with this agent. Does this agent edit and request revisions before sending manuscripts out? Some do, some don't. Is the agent forceful and "high powered"? If you are a laid-back, easygoing person, you might not be happy with that agent. Do you have an overactive sense of humor? Don't pick a totally serious, someone-who-rarely-smiles agent! Do you want an agent to "direct" your career? Or just someone to market stories for you?

These are all very important things to know about a potential agent. Picking the right agent will make your life very much easier. Picking the wrong one will plunge you into a pit of frustration that might turn into a complete nightmare for both of you.

One very important thing, that often a new writer doesn't realize, is that when you have an agent, you do not get any money from your publisher. Your agent will get all of it, take out his or her share, and then forward the remaining balance to you. Make sure you are very comfortable with this person and that you can trust them implicitly, as they will be handling all the money for the lifetime of any books they sell!

Where do you get your ideas?

Everywhere! Newspapers, history books—all around me. I have so many ideas, I won't be able to write them all if I never got another one. And I get more ideas all the time. Getting an idea is easy for me; but turning the idea into a strong story line, with problems and solutions and still staying true to history, while making it rhyme—that's where the big challenge is for me.

continues

What do you think are the key differences between writing for children and writing for adults?

The age of the main character is one very important thing in most children's books. Children are much more likely to be interested in a child character than an adult, and they will put the book down very fast unless the main character has a situation that is something they are interested in. Toddlers aren't going to be interested in reading a story about the stock market or getting a date for a prom, and teenagers won't be much interested in a story about an old folks' home—unless there are teenagers in the story with a problem the teens reading the book can identify with.

When you write for children, you need to be very careful what you say. Children, especially young ones, will pretty much believe anything they see in print, while adults know better. Also, when writing for children, you don't have the luxury of starting at the beginning and slowly building a story. With children today, you need to bang! right into the thick of the problem with the first line if you are going to get and keep their attention. In today's fast-paced world, a world of instant information on the Internet and fast-paced video games, you need to grab their attention fast and keep the pace moving to keep them reading.

How did you learn to write?

I always got good grades in school in English (even though I hated writing!), but it wasn't until I took the Institute of Children's Literature's basic writing correspondence course that I feel I really learned how to write. They not only taught me how to write for kids but also how to market what I wrote. If not for that course, I honestly think I'd still be struggling to sell my first book, instead of having eight books sold right now. I highly recommend their course to every serious aspiring children's writer. I don't think the course would be very good for someone who just wants to write as a hobby. But it is wonderful for serious writers who want to pursue the dream of getting a children's story published some day.

Anything you really wish somebody had told you when you started out?

Read children's books! Read current, new children's books. Lots of them. As many as you can possibly get your hands on. Learn your craft as well as you possibly can. Write. You will learn more by writing than from anything else. Get into or start a critique group. Even a "group" of two will help you. Submit, and as long as you believe what you are writing is good, don't give up!

Description: Publisher of quality books for young readers by Canadian authors.

Established: 1984.

Key people:

Publisher: Robert Tyrrell

Acquisitions/submissions editors: R. Tyrrell (young adult fiction); M. de Vries (children's picture books and juvenile books)

Books per year: 20.

Percentage by first-time authors: 20 percent.

Seeks: Fiction. Strong story dealing with both historical and contemporary issues.

Accepts unsolicited/unagented: Yes, query first with outline and three to four sample chapters.

Description of fiction titles: Novels dealing with contemporary issues, strong character development.

Recent fiction titles:

Before Wings by Beth Goobie

Caged Eagles by Eric Walters

Alone at Ninety Foot by Katherine Holubitsby

Description of nonfiction titles: Fiction only.

Preferred form of submission/contact: Query with outline and sample chapters (three to four).

Time to reply: Six to eight weeks.

Time to publish: 12 to 18 months.

Accepts simultaneous submissions: No.

Number of illustrators used annually: 10 to 12.

Desired illustrator qualifications: High-quality art by Canadian illustrators.

Prefer manuscript/illustration packages, or separate: Occasionally accept them together.

Include with illustrator query: Send resume and any of the above, especially samples.

Time to reply: Six to eight weeks.

Purchases freelance photography: Yes.

Terms for writers: 10 percent of retail for novels; 5 percent of retail for picture books.

Terms for illustrators: 5 percent of retail.

Submission guidelines: Send SASE with request.

Orchard Books

Grolier Publishing
90 Sherman Turnpike
Danbury, CT 06816
(203) 796-2605
(203) 797-3899 (fax)
Web site: www.publishing.grolier.com

Corporate structure/parent: Grolier Publishing.

Description: Orchard Books is one of America's most distinguished publishers of literature for children and young adults.

Key people:

Acquisitions/submissions editors: Please submit your queries to the editors based on the following guidelines: Sarah Caguiat: select nonfiction, middle-grade fiction of all kinds, and fun and quirky picture books. Ana Cerro: humorous picture books, historical and contemporary fiction, and poetry—no sci-fi or fantasy. Rebecca Davis:

imaginative, playful picture books, middle-grade and young adult fiction, humorous tales, and poetry for all ages.

Seeks: Publishes picture books, fiction, and nonfiction for readers aged 2 to 16.

Accepts unsolicited/unagented: Orchard does not accept unsolicited manuscripts.

Recent fiction titles:

City Pig by Karen Wallace; illustrated by Lydia Monks

Day with the Bellyflops by Francine Bassède; illustrated by Francine Bassède

Dog's Day by Jane Cabrera; illustrated by Jane Cabrera

Don't Do That, Kitty Kilroy! written and illustrated by Cressida Cowell

Dr. Duck by H. M. Ehrlich; illustrated by Laura Rader

Preferred form of submission/contact: Does not accept query letters. Be sure to include a self-addressed stamped envelope for a response. Do not expect the editor to give you comments. Far too many queries are received for this to be possible.

Prefer manuscript/illustration packages, or separate: Illustrations are not necessary. Publishers often prefer to accept stories without them and find their own artists. Often a story will be accepted and the accompanying illustrations rejected. If you have illustrations, do not send original art. Send only one or two photocopied samples.

Include with illustrator query: Illustrators may send their samples to the art director. *Do not send original art.*

Submission guidelines: Write with an SASE or go to the Web site.

Tips and comments: Illustrations are not necessary. Publishers often prefer to accept stories without them and find their own artists. Often a story will be accepted and the accompanying illustrations rejected. Orchard Books publishes hardcover children's books for preschoolers through young adults—primarily picture books and novels, and a limited amount of nonfiction. Orchard does not publish books for parents or teachers, paperback originals, activity books, or books packaged with cassette tapes, games, stuffed animals, elastic green slime, or other merchandise.

Our Sunday Visitor

200 Noll Plaza
Huntington, IN 46750
(219) 356-8400
E-mail: booked@osv.com
Web site: www.osv.com

Description: Catholic publishing company founded to serve the needs of the church.

Established: 1912.

Key people:

Editor in chief: Greg Erlandson

Acquisitions/submissions editors: Jacquelyn Lindsey; Michael Dubruiel; Beth McNamara

Books per year: Varies each year, though usually four or five.

Percentage by first-time authors: 5 percent.

Seeks: Apologetics and catechetics; reference, prayer; heritage and saints; family; parish.

Accepts unsolicited/unagented: Yes.

Description of fiction titles: Does not publish fiction titles.

Description of nonfiction titles: Books to encourage, inspire and strengthen the faith of average Catholics.

Preferred nonfiction titles: Sacramental preparation; prayer books; books on saints.

Preferred form of submission/contact: Cover letter with name, address and telephone number; manuscript working title, anticipated length and completion date; comparison to other books on the same or similar subject (i.e. the competition); unique quality of your book; chapter outline; author qualifications and sample chapters.

Time to reply: Two months.

Time to publish: One to three years.

Accepts simultaneous submissions: Yes.

Number of illustrators used annually: 11.

Desired illustrator qualifications: Styles needed for particular project.

Prefer manuscript/illustration packages, or separate: Yes.

Include with illustrator query: Resume and samples.

Time to reply: Two months.

Purchases freelance photography: Rarely.

Preferred photography: Quality, creativity, and cost.

Terms for writers: Varies: 10 to 12 percent of net royalties; average advance.

Terms for illustrators: Varies: Most illustration payment is based on predetermined fee, rather than royalty rate.

Submission guidelines: Send an SASE.

Tips and comments: Check what books the company has already published. Refer to author guidelines.

Overmountain Press

PO Box 1261
Johnson City, TN 37605
(423) 926-2691
(423) 929-2464 (fax)
E-mail: bethw@overmtn.com
Web site: www.overmtn.com

Corporate structure/parent: Silver Dagger Mysteries is an imprint of Overmountain Press. Same address and telephone numbers. Web site: www.silverdaggermysteries.com

Description: Book publisher.

Established: 1970.

Key people:

Publisher: Archer Blevins

Acquisitions/submissions editor: Beth Wright

Books per year and description: Three regional (southern Appalachian) picture books; four southern mystery (young adult).

Percentage by first-time authors: 50 percent.

Seeks: Regional (southern Appalachian).

Accepts unsolicited/unagented: No. Call first.

Description of fiction titles: Picture books; mystery.

Recent fiction titles:

You Don't Pat a Bee by Thelma Kerns

The Green Star of Oz by Roger S. Baum

Bloody Mary by Patrick Bone

Dead Ball Foul by Kayla McGrady

Preferred fiction titles: Mystery set in the southeastern United States; picture books set in southern Appalachia.

Description of nonfiction titles: None.

Preferred form of submission/contact: Query by mail (see the Web site for mystery guidelines).

Time to reply: Two months.

Time to publish: One to two years.

Accepts simultaneous submissions: Yes.

Number of illustrators used annually: Three.

Desired illustrator qualifications: Illustrators who are talented and have a stylistic approach that works with the company's look.

Prefer manuscript/illustration packages, or separate: Prefers manuscript/illustration packages.

Include with illustrator query: Samples and resume.

Time to reply: No reply. Samples kept on file and reviewed when looking for an artist to work on a project. Only contacts the artist if a project arises.

Purchases freelance photography: No.

Terms for writers: 7.5 to 15 percent of the realized price.

Terms for illustrators: 7.5 percent of the realized price.

Submission guidelines: *Overmountain:* call or write with an SASE for guidelines; *Silver Dagger:* on the Web site.

Tips and comments: Call first to see whether your project will fit with the list. *Do not* e-mail queries. Call (Beth Wright) to see whether Overmountain is interested.

PACIFIC PRESS PUBLISHING ASSOCIATION

PO Box 5353
Nampa, ID 83653-5353
Web site: www.pacificpress.com

Corporate structure/parent: Seventh-day Adventist Church.

Description: Publisher.

Established: 1874.

Key people:

Acquisitions/submissions editors: Book acquisitions editor, for queries (if you're sending a query), or book acquisitions proposals, for proposals.

Books per year: Approximately 5 to 10.

Accepts unsolicited/unagented: Yes.

Description of fiction titles: Early Reader series—storybooks for 7- to 9-year-olds. They are usually 96 pages, about 11,000 words, or 50 manuscript pages. Sunshine books are Pacific Press's line of picture books for preschoolers. Starburst series (storybooks for 9- to 12-year-olds—typically running 128 pages, about 15,000–20,000 words, or 90–120 manuscript pages).

Recent fiction titles:

Sunshine series

The Shoebox Kids series

Detective Zack series

Preferred form of submission/contact: Query letter is preferred (and will get preferential treatment), proposal, or manuscript (discouraged and will likely languish for many moons before it is reviewed—best not to submit).

Time to reply: Queries, two to three weeks (with an SASE). Or include an e-mail address and Pacific might even reply sooner. Proposals up to three months; manuscripts, perhaps 6 months or more.

Accepts simultaneous submissions: Yes.

Terms for writers: Pacific Press pays royalty on the wholesale price of books: 12 percent royalty on regular paperback books, up to 15,000 copies; 16 percent royalty after 15,000; 14 percent royalty on hardcover books up to 15,000 copies, 16 percent royalty after 15,000; 8 percent royalty on paperbacks of 64 pages or less; 6 percent royalty on children's picture books (6 percent goes to illustrator), 8 percent royalty after 15,000.

Terms for illustrators: 6 percent royalty on children's picture books, 8 percent royalty after 15,000.

Submission guidelines: Write with an SASE or visit the Web site. *Queries*: No more than two pages. In it you should, first, get the editors' attention. Tell, in a compelling way, what you'd like to write about; tell a little about yourself. If you are a Seventh-day Adventist, be sure to say so. Tell why you want to write this book. Tell why you are particularly qualified to do so. If you are a published writer, tell where the editors can see your work or include tear sheets from one or two published articles. *Book proposals* must include a cover letter with a one-paragraph description of what you are proposing: what your book is about; who your book is written for; why it is unique; introduce yourself (your background—particularly anything relevant to your subject and writing); proposed length of the manuscript; whether you are submitting elsewhere simultaneously; an overview of the book; the market and the competition; for topical or inspirational books, include a two-to-four-page chapter outline, summarizing in one paragraph the content of each chapter and its relation to the book as a whole. For story books, give a plot synopsis that gives more detail than the overview, showing how the plot develops. Please include an SASE.

Parenting Press, Inc.

PO Box 75267
Seattle, WA 98125
(206) 364-2900
(206) 364-0702
Web site: www.parentingpress.com

Description: Publisher.

Established: 1979.

Books per year: 4 to 6.

Seeks: Children need tools for problem solving, conflict resolution, and acknowledging and dealing with feelings. Parenting Press offers books that teach these skills to children and adults. Parenting Press books help build a solid foundation of mutual respect, self-esteem, and communication.

Recent fiction titles:

The Way I Feel by Janan Cain (a book to encourage children to understand emotions, how they change, and develop a vocabulary to express themselves).

Preferred fiction titles: Rarely publishes "children's stories" or "activities" books unless they have some other strong component.

Preferred form of submission/contact: Please send a letter of inquiry including the following information: Research your competition. Find and review similar books to yours. You can find books in independent bookstores, children's bookstores, libraries, and *Books in Print*. How are they selling? Talk to booksellers and librarians. Identify your market. Is there a need for another book on your topic? Why? Describe specifically what your book does that other books do not. Describe your book: What is special about your book? Why will people who already own many children's and parenting books wish to buy your book? Who has reviewed your book? Children or adults? Classes or workshops you lead? Expert in the field? We are primarily interested in feedback from people who do not have direct contact with you (your children, friends, and students are less likely to be objective). A suggestion: Have a friend give a copy to someone who doesn't know you. Describe yourself: What is your background? Why did you write the book? How are you qualified to write this book? Any previous publications? How are you able to promote your book? What sort of promotion does your experience or interest equip you for? Workshops at professional meetings? Programs for children? What else? If you want your material returned, please include a self-addressed stamped envelope big enough to hold it all.

Time to publish: 12 to 18 months after acceptance.

Desired illustrator qualifications: Looks for illustrations that show children as alive. Likes to see children with emotions and personality. Most illustrations are black and white, occasionally color.

Include with illustrator query: Invites illustrators to submit an illustration on speculation. These illustrations are then field tested with potential customers. Parenting Press then evaluates the responses and chooses an illustrator. If you wish to be considered, send a couple of sample illustrations of children.

Terms for writers: Parenting Press pays a royalty on each book sold. For picture books, the royalty is split between the author and illustrator.

Submission guidelines: Write with an SASE or check the Web site.

Tips and comments: The more your book extends the company's current line of books, the better its chances are.

PAULIST PRESS

997 Macarthur Boulevard
Mahwah, NJ 07430
Web site: www.paulistpress.com

Description: The goal of our Paulist Press is to publish quality books on Christian and Catholic themes. All book ideas should be religious in nature, written for the Christian and/or Catholic market.

Books per year and description: Approximately 12 children's titles a year. Children's books published by Paulist Press fall into one of the following Categories (please keep these categories in mind when you submit ideas): *Preschool picture books* (ages 2–5), introducing Christian and Catholic themes to the very young: These books hold a few words on each page. The illustrations are just as or more important than the text. Be sure to include suggestions for illustrations; however, Paulist Press reserves the right for final decisions on all illustrations. *Books of blessings and prayer books* (ages 5–8): These books include family blessings and traditional Catholic prayers. *Chapter books* (ages 8–12): Paulist Press is looking for more titles like those in "The Emerald Bible Collection"—imaginative fiction or nonfiction chapter books for the middle reader on Christian themes. *Young adult biographies* (ages 9–14): We are always looking for biographies on the saints and modern heroes. Refer to our two titles *Mother Teresa* and *Maximilian Kolbe*. *Catholic Guidebooks* (ages 5 and up): These books explain some component of our Catholic tradition to the young. Refer to our title *A Walk through Our Church*. *Gift Books* (all ages): These titles are hardcover books for the family on classic topics such as the saints, favorite Bible stories, holidays, and more.

Accepts unsolicited/unagented: Does accept unsolicited manuscripts; however, most titles have been commissioned. Tries to work with familiar authors.

Preferred form of submission/contact: Include a cover letter with your manuscript that summarizes your story and describes which category (listed below) and age group you have in mind. Include a resume of your education, work experience, and published works. Your manuscript should be typed, double-spaced, on an 8½ by 11-inch sheet of white paper. Always send a copy of your work (keep your original). Include a self-addressed stamped envelope (SASE) with your manuscript if you would like Paulist Press to return it to you.

Submission guidelines: All children's manuscripts should be directed to Susan O'Keefe.

Tips and comments: Familiarize yourself with Paulist Press publications—for a recent catalog of publications, please call (800) 218-1903.

Peachtree Publishers Ltd.

1700 Chattahoochee Avenue
Atlanta, GA 30318
(404) 876-8761
(404) 875-2578 (fax)
Web site: www.peachtree-online.com

Description: Book publisher.

Established: 1978.

Key people:

Publisher: Margaret Quinlin

Acquisitions/submissions editor: Helen Harriss

Books per year and description: 10 to 15 titles in picture books, middle readers, and young adult categories.

Percentage by first-time authors: 0 to 20 percent per year.

Seeks: Children's, middle readers, young adult, nonfiction, and regional books.

Accepts unsolicited/unagented: Yes.

Description of fiction titles: Fiction books fall into the children and young adult categories

Preferred fiction titles: Not interested in science fiction, romance, fantasy, or poetry.

Description of nonfiction titles: Health, regional, and parenting.

Preferred form of submission/contact: Query or manuscript.

Time to reply: Allow four months for a reply.

Time to publish: Varies by book.

Accepts simultaneous submissions: Yes.

Number of illustrators used annually: 10 to 20.

Prefer manuscript/illustration packages, or separate: Packages okay, but not necessary to have illustrations for a manuscript submission—won't be held against you.

Include with illustrator query: Send portfolio or samples of artwork but please, *no originals*.

Time to reply: Varies—holds materials on file and reviews for appropriateness of each project.

Purchases freelance photography: No.

Terms for writers: Variable.

Terms for illustrators: Variable.

Submission guidelines: Write for guidelines and include an SASE.

Tips and comments: Get the guidelines; submit your query or manuscript *by mail*—not fax or e-mail; read the kinds of books the company has published in the past; review your material with experts/appropriate audience before submitting.

Pelican Publishing Company, Inc.

PO Box 3110
Gretna, LA 70054-3110
Web site: www.pelicanpub.com

Description: Book publisher.

Established: 1926.

Books per year and description: 15 titles per year; picture books (ages 5–8) in fiction and nonfiction and some middle reader titles (ages 8–12) in fiction.

Percentage by first-time authors: 15 percent are by first-time *children's* authors.

Seeks: Books with holiday, ethnic, and regional content.

Accepts unsolicited/unagented: Yes.

Description of fiction titles: Addressing a specific niche—regional or holiday subjects and often educational without being overtly so.

Recent fiction titles:

Pennsylvania Dutch Night Before Christmas by Chet Williamson

Cajun Night after Christmas by Jenny Jackson Moss and Amy Dixon

Why Cowgirls Are Such Sweet Talkers by Laurie Lazzaro Knowlton

Preferred fiction titles: Not looking for general topics, self-esteem, talking animals, and science fiction or fantasy.

Description of nonfiction titles: Targeted subject matter—history, regional, and holiday themes; educational without being overt.

Recent nonfiction titles:

Historic Baton Rouge Coloring Book by Joseph A. Arrigo

Tiger Woods, Golf Superstar by David R. Collins (children's biography)

Preferred nonfiction titles: Will consider biographies, light historical subjects, and holiday themes. No young adult (teen) or middle readers (unless it's Louisiana related).

Preferred form of submission/contact: Query.

Time to reply: Minimum of one month.

Time to publish: Nine to 18 months.

Accepts simultaneous submissions: No.

Number of illustrators used annually: 10 to 15.

Desired illustrator qualifications: Professional looking art. Fully developed illustrations including backgrounds. No cartooning. Illustrators must be strong in the area of illustrating people.

Prefer manuscript/illustration packages, or separate: Yes, accepts manuscripts in conjunction with illustrations.

Include with illustrator query: Resumes, samples, and tear sheets—portfolio *to be kept on file*.

Time to reply: Replies only if a suitable assignment arises.

Purchases freelance photography: No.

Terms for writers: Negotiable.

Terms for illustrators: Royalties or a flat payment. Negotiable.

Submission guidelines: Send SASE (with $0.34 in return postage) or go to the Web site, where guidelines are posted.

Tips and comments: Study the catalog (which is available online) and follow the submission guidelines. Get at least one writing credit (magazine, newspaper, placing in a contest) before submitting and include with your credentials (listed in cover letter).

Meet Peter Sis

Illustrator and Author

Peter Sis is the illustrator and sometimes author of numerous children's books for ages 1 to 100, including *Hansel & Gretel by the Brothers Grimm* (Prague, 1975), illustrations; *The Bean Boy* by George Shannon, (1984), illustrations; and *Tibet: Through the Red Box* (1998), text and illustrations. He was born in Brno, Czechoslovakia, on May 11, 1929. He attended various art schools, the Academy of Applied Arts in Prague, and the Royal College of Art. Before he became a children's book illustrator, he was a radio show host.

How did you get your first book published?

I wrote a story about a Rainbow Rhino, and nobody wanted to touch it. But it gave me a chance to make the rounds and meet all of the children's book publishers of that time. That paid dividends later on. What was essential in getting my first illustrator's deal was that a friend of mine sent my work to Maurice Sendak, who in turn introduced me to the publishing industry and Greenwillow Books in particular.

Did you have an agent when you published your first book?

I did not have an agent when I started out as an illustrator, though I do have one now—we sort of found one another. At this point, I could not possibly handle everything myself, which is why I have the agent.

Do you have any advice, in terms of finding an agent, for a writer starting out?

I do not think you need an agent to find work. I think everyone is his or her own best agent. Go to New York or Boston for a week and introduce yourself. You only need an agent or producer/manager when you have too much to handle by yourself. How can someone who represents 27 people represent someone so special like you?

Are you still with your first publisher?

Yes. Because it's my first publisher.

Do you have any advice, in terms of finding a publisher, for a writer starting out?

Take your time and find the right one. It might be forever or, rather, a very long-term relationship.

Are your books illustrated?

I illustrate my own books. I always work with myself—actually, at the moment, I'm thinking of using someone else!

Do you have any advice, in terms of finding an illustrator, for a writer starting out?

Check out the School of Visual Arts in New York City—it's a pool of talent.

What procedures do you follow when you write?

I do not consider myself a writer. I have to write to explain the things I've drawn.

Where do you get your ideas?

From every aspect of life.

What do you think are the key differences between writing for children and writing for adults?

I think the key differences are to read as a child and to read as an adult. That is to say, you as the author of children's books must look at what you write both through the eyes of a child (your audience) and through the eyes of an adult (that you are).

How did you learn to write?

I do not think I can write, so for me it's just a question of envy.

Anything you really wish somebody had told you when you started out?

Trust in yourselves. I would like to say to everybody, Make very, very sure in the beginning that all sails and instruments and captain and waves are right, because once it takes off, it just might get very fast and very hard to control!

Perfection Learning Corporation

1000 North Second Avenue
PO Box 500
Logan, Iowa 51546-0500

Corporate structure/parent: Perfection Learning Corporation's imprints are Cover-to-Cover, Summit Books, Retold Classics.

Description: Book and curriculum publishers, prebinder, and distributor of trade books.

Established: 1926.

Key people:

CEO: Steven Keay

Acquisitions/submissions editors: Sue Thies, books; Julie Schumacher, curriculum

Books per year and description: Around 100 books a year—chapter books, retold anthologies, novels, and informational books.

Percentage by first-time authors: 50 percent.

Seeks: Hi/lo (high-interest topics for reluctant readers) manuscripts for students in grades 2 to 6, 4 to 8, or 6 to 12. More specific manuscript and submission guidelines are available on the Web site: www.perfectionlearning.com

Accepts unsolicited/unagented: Yes.

Description of fiction titles: All genres; need high-interest boy stories.

Recent fiction titles:

The Message, the Promise, and How Pigs Figure In by M. J. Cosson (On a scuba-diving vacation in Maui, 14-year-old Jon Olivera encounters a pearl-colored fish with an important message about protecting ocean environments.)

River of Ice by Linda Baxter (As Stalin's grip tightens on Russia, Sasha and his mother try to escape from their home in Moscow to join the rest of their family in Latvia.)

Description of nonfiction titles: High-interest, low-reading-level titles.

Recent nonfiction titles:

Tarnished Legacy: The Story of the Comstock Lode by Ellen Hopkins (Virginia City, once the richest little city in the west, is now a ghost town. Follow the rise and fall of this silver-mining town and its inhabitants, and find out the legacy Virginia City left.)

Animal Geography-Africa by Joanne Mattern (Visit the deserts, savannas, rain forests, and rivers of Africa and learn what animals inhabit these various regions. Then go to Madagascar and meet some animals that can only be found on this island.)

Preferred nonfiction titles: Looking for sports-related titles. Also looking for "wheels" books (racing, hot cars, etc.).

Preferred form of submission/contact: Query with synopsis and a few sample chapters.

Time to reply: Can be a year or more.

Time to publish: Within 12 months.

Accepts simultaneous submissions: Yes.

Number of illustrators used annually: 50.

Prefer manuscript/illustration packages, or separate: Either is fine.

Include with illustrator query: Samples and resume.

Purchases freelance photography: Yes.

Preferred photography: Search photography by subject.

Terms for writers: Varies by project.

Terms for illustrators: Varies by project.

Submission guidelines: Go to Web site: www.perfectionlearning.com

Tips and comments: Please do not send picture book manuscripts. Please do your homework before you send unsolicited manuscript; 90 percent of what is received doesn't fit the guidelines.

PHILOMEL BOOKS

345 Hudson Street
New York, NY 10014
(212) 414-3610
(212) 414-3395 (fax)
Web site: www.penguinputnam.com

Corporate structure/parent: Penguin Putnam Inc.

Description: Children's trade book publisher.

Established: 1980.

Key people:

Publisher: Patricia Lee Gauch

Books per year and description: 25; picture books and young adult novels.

Seeks: Historical fiction, multicultural or cross-cultural picture books, fantasy, and very young fiction. Mostly looking for a story idea that attempts the new, that sees a situation in a different way, or takes a step beyond the boundaries of what has been done before. Literary fiction for young adults.

Accepts unsolicited/unagented: Yes.

Description of fiction titles: Highly literary fiction, historical fiction, science fiction, sports fiction, and fantasy.

Recent fiction titles:

Queen's Own Fool by Jane Yolen
Over the Wall by John Ritter
Lord Brocktree by Brian Jacques
I am Morgan LeFay by Nancy Springer
The Wings of Merlin by T. A. Barron

Preferred fiction titles: Not looking for mass-market and highly mainstream.

Preferred nonfiction titles: Doesn't usually publish nonfiction.

Preferred form of submission/contact: Query first; will request first three chapters if interested.

Time to reply: Three to six months.

Time to publish: Two to three years.

Accepts simultaneous submissions: Yes.

Number of illustrators used annually: 15.

Desired illustrator qualifications: Wacky, distinctive, fun art; cultural or stylized art; colorful, bright illustrations; collage; and so forth.

Prefer manuscript/illustration packages, or separate: Either way.

Include with illustrator query: Relevant publishing history, resume if applicable, and samples.

Time to reply: Three to six months.

Purchases freelance photography: No.

Preferred photography: None.

Submission guidelines: Send an SASE and request for writer's guidelines.

Tips and comments: Query first.

Phyllis Fogelman Books

Penguin Putnam BFYR
345 Hudson Street
New York, NY 10014
Web site: www.penguinputnam.com/about/children/puffin.htm

Corporate structure/parent: Penguin Putnam.

Description: Publisher.

Established: 1999.

Key people:

Publisher and vice president: Phyllis Fogelman

Books per year: 15 to 20.

Accepts unsolicited/unagented: At this time most Penguin Putnam Inc. imprints do not accept unsolicited manuscripts. If you would like your work to be considered for publication by a major publisher, Penguin Putnam Inc. recommends that you work with an established literary agent.

PLACE IN THE WOODS

Different Books
3900 Glenwood Avenue
Golden Valley, MN 55422

Corporate structure/parent: Different Books is an imprint of The Place in the Woods publisher.

Description: Book publisher.

Established: 1980.

Key people:

Publisher: Rogor Hammer

Acquisitions/submissions editor: Rogor Hammer

Books per year and description: Two; multicultural, diversity, especially stories in which heroes/heroines have a disability and overcome adversity.

Percentage by first-time authors: 100 percent.

Seeks: Manuscripts with multicultural characters and appeal and diversity. Especially interested in stories in which heroes/heroines have a disability and overcome adversity.

Accepts unsolicited/unagented: Yes. Actually *prefers* them.

Description of fiction titles: Multicultural characters and diversity play a primary role in the company's selections, especially stories in which heroes/heroines have a disability and overcome adversity.

Recent fiction titles:

Little Horse by Frank Minogue

The Flying Frog Circus by Dawn Rosewitz

Simon the Daredevil Centipede by Phil Siegel

Preferred fiction titles: Multicultural characters and diversity play a primary role in our selections, especially stories in which heroes/heroines have a disability and overcome adversity.

Description of nonfiction titles: Historical essays on American minorities.

Recent nonfiction titles:

American Woman

Hispanic America

Preferred nonfiction titles: Looking for essays/stories on Asian Americans.

Preferred form of submission/contact: Either is fine.

Time to reply: Two to four weeks, though occasionally longer. If a quick reply is needed, please request an answer by a specific date.

Time to publish: One to two years.

Accepts simultaneous submissions: No.

Number of illustrators used annually: Two.

Desired illustrator qualifications: Realistic situations; no fantasy or star wars; nothing that will scare children.

Prefer manuscript/illustration packages, or separate: Yes, accepts them together; however, it is rare that both are accepted. Usually, the manuscript is stronger.

Include with illustrator query: Samples and portfolio review.

Time to reply: Samples are filed. No reply is given unless the artist's work fits with the publisher's needs. The artist is contacted when an appropriate project is up for illustration.

Purchases freelance photography: Rarely.

Terms for writers: $250 per story, which is repaid with each reprint. If the book sells well, everyone wins.

Terms for illustrators: $250 for cover art; $10 for interior.

Submission guidelines: Send an SASE with request for guidelines.

Tips and comments: Be honest and direct. Be open and share your thinking. The company uses a collaborative approach. If the company commits to you, you (the author or artist) are expected to commit to and give your all on the project.

Pleasant Company Publications

8400 Fairway Pl.
Middleton, WI 53562
(608) 836-4848
(608) 828-4768 (fax)
Web site: www.americangirl.com

Established: 1986.

Key people:

Acquisitions/submissions editor: Erin Falligant

Art director: Jane Varda

Books per year and description: 30 fiction titles; 10 nonfiction.

Percentage by first-time authors: 5 to 10 percent.

Seeks: Stand-alone historical fiction, historical mysteries, contemporary fiction, and advice and activity books (nonfiction). Target audience is girls ages 8 to 13.

Accepts unsolicited/unagented: Yes.

Description of fiction titles: *Historical fiction* (for girls 8–12): High-quality stories that illuminate life in a significant time and place in American history and show how American girls were touched by events/concerns that shaped the United States. *Historical mysteries* (for girls 10 and up): Mysteries that are set against a rich historical and geographical backdrop that is integral to the plot, with a 10- to 12-year-old female protagonist who has a strong emotional stake in solving a mystery that significantly affects her life or the lives of those she loves. *Contemporary fiction* (for girls 10 and up): Novels that capture the spirit of contemporary American girls and feature an 11- to 13-year-old protagonist who demonstrates the hopes, thoughts, and emotions unique to that precarious age between childhood and teenhood. In addition to thoughtfully developed characters and plots, stories should incorporate a discernible sense of place.

Recent fiction titles:
Historical mysteries:
The Night Flyers by Elizabeth McDavid Jones
Contemporary fiction:
Smoke Screen by Amy Goldman Koss

Preferred fiction titles: *Historical mysteries:* Main characters of diverse cultures and distant time periods (17th/18th century). Main characters should be multidimensional, courageous, and resourceful—not merely "clever young sleuths." *Contemporary fiction:* Offer an alternative to the graphic content found in much of today's young adult literature. Not seeking manuscripts that delve into mature themes such as sexuality or deviant behavior. No science fiction or first-romance stories.

Description of nonfiction titles: Advice and activity books on subjects of interest or concern to girls aged 8 to 12. Books should encourage girls to dream and should reinforce their self-confidence and curiosity as they prepare to navigate adolescence.

Recent nonfiction titles:
Paper Clip Jewelry by Kelli Peduzzi
Help! A Girl's Guide to Divorce and Stepfamilies by Nancy Holyoke

Preferred nonfiction titles: Looking for nonfiction specifically targeted to girls, not for concepts that would appeal to both boys and girls.

Preferred form of submission/contact: *Historical fiction:* Send queries or complete manuscripts. *Historical mysteries:* Send queries only. *Contemporary fiction:* Send complete manuscript—no queries. Nonfiction: Send queries or complete manuscripts.

Time to reply: One to three months.

Time to publish: One to two years.

Accepts simultaneous submissions: Yes.

Number of illustrators used annually: Approximately 50 to 60; fiction uses about 25 to 30; magazine, about 20; activity books, 8 to 10.

Desired illustrator qualifications: Excellent rendering skills, figurative compositions, and mastery of medium; references (proven ability to hold schedule); good communication skills; patience (some projects may take two and a half years to complete); strong visual match to support and enhance brand; and a willingness to revise, particularly at sketch stage but also at final if art direction has not been fully realized.

Prefer manuscript/illustration packages, or separate: Rarely do they arrive together. Would not exclude, but illustration is usually sought independently.

Include with illustrator query: Research products to decide whether your style could be a match, and then send samples, brief resume, and contact information.

Time to reply: Try to respond promptly. If the style sample is not at all close to the company's work, it will be discarded. Stamped, addressed, multiple-choice postcards are helpful. All illustrator resumes are filed, so keep the file updated.

Purchases freelance photography: Rarely. Mostly sets up our own shoots.

Preferred photography: Same competencies as illustrators, plus photographers need to work especially well with children and art directors.

Terms for writers: Pays authors royalties or purchases work outright.

Terms for illustrators: All work is purchased outright. No royalties.

Submission guidelines: Writers may send a request for guidelines, along with an SASE, to Submissions Editor, Pleasant Company Publications, 8400 Fairway Place, Middleton, WI 53562.

Tips and comments: *Writers:* Before submitting manuscripts, request and review complete writers' guidelines, and read existing publications to get a feel for voice and target audience. *Illustrators:* Study books in depth and know the level of your creative development. Everything the company publishes features girls and ranges from classic, narrative, painterly illustration to contemporary, mixed-media styles. Everything has to be of the highest standard—nothing mass market. Get a good rep and get into the annuals. That's where the company sources most of the illustrators that it uses.

Polar Bear & Company

PO Box 311
Solon, ME 04979
(207) 643-2795
E-mail: polarbear@skow.net
Web site: www.polarbearandco.com

Description: Book publisher and art distributor.

Established: 1991.

Key people:

Publisher: Ramona du Houx

Acquisitions/submissions editor: Alex du Houx

Books per year: Two.

Percentage by first-time authors: 90 percent.

Seeks: Motto: "Mythology for modern democracy brings variety to everyday life." Seeks books that enhance our cultural diversity, highlighting important social, environmental, and political issues.

Accepts unsolicited/unagented: Yes.

Description of fiction titles: Intriguing, lively titles that convey the importance of liberty and justice for all by means of plot and characters that are dynamic. Likes mythological characters that are made current in history by relating to modern themes.

Recent fiction titles:

Manitiou: A Mythological Journey in Time by Ramona du Houx (a tale of self-discovery involving Greek gods and goddesses)

Preferred fiction titles: Original works, good dialogue, and *no* violence like that in the movies.

Description of nonfiction titles: Philosophy and poetry.

Preferred nonfiction titles: Exploring mysteries.

Preferred form of submission/contact: Query or manuscript with an SASE if the author would like a response.

Time to reply: Three to six months.

Time to publish: Six months.

Accepts simultaneous submissions: Yes.

Number of illustrators used annually: Three.

Desired illustrator qualifications: See the Web site for insight into our style.

Prefer manuscript/illustration packages, or separate: *Separately.*

Include with illustrator query: Resume and samples.

Time to reply: Six months.

Purchases freelance photography: No, but does put photos on Web site.

Preferred photography: Classic photography by photographers who are clearly "concerned." Have a look at the photo gallery on the Web site to get a better idea of what the company is after.

Terms for writers: Terms are variable. Writers who have invested in their books can receive between 45 and 50 percent, others receive a standard 10 percent of royalties.

Terms for illustrators: The terms are, again, variable. Those who have invested in their book would receive terms as indicated above, whereas standard for illustrators is 10 to 15 percent.

Submission guidelines: Works individually with prospective writers and artists (as opposed to having guidelines). It is best to study the Web site for style and objective before putting pen to paper or submitting a query or manuscript. Also offers consultancy for writers, authors, and illustrators.

Tips and comments: An author must have a clear reason of why he or she wants to write. It is critical for the author to be focused on what it is that he or she wants to convey through the story. There must also be an inherent belief that cultural diversity is good for the country and that everyone can make a difference. Looking for clearly defined characters who are lively. If you have written something that you think is important to highlight, something that you think makes a difference in our society, the company will look at your work. *Please* keep away from fast, violent action.

PRICE STERN SLOAN

Penguin Putnam BFYR
345 Hudson Street
New York, NY 10014
Web site: www.penguinputnam.com/about/children/puffin.htm

Corporate structure/parent: Penguin Putnam Inc.

Description: Price Stern Sloan titles that fall into the preschool children's mass-merchandise categories. Price Stern Sloan is best known for a number of their proprietary brands, some of which include Mad Libs, Wee Sing, Mr. Men & Little Miss, Serendipity, Crazy Games, and Doodle Art.

Established: Early 1960s.

Key people:

Publisher: Jon Anderson

Books per year: Approximately 75.

Meet Fred Bowen

Kids' Sports Author and Columnist

Fred Bowen had a very sports-happy childhood. He was a passionate Little Leaguer who loved to read about sports in newspapers, magazines, and books. Now he's a coach. He's been coaching kids' basketball and baseball teams for the past 12 years. He has written five baseball books and four basketball books, for kids ages 7 to 12. His books combine sports fiction with a little real sports history, and he always includes a bonus history chapter at the end. His latest book is *Winners Take All* (September 2000). It's the ninth book in his AllStar SportStory Series (Peachtree Publishers, Atlanta). *Winners Take All* is a baseball story about a good kid who makes a bad decision to cheat in a crucial game. His cheating clinches the win, but his life starts to unravel when another kid discovers the cheating and threatens to tell. Though many of his books are oriented towards boys, *Off the Rim* most easily crosses the gender line—it has a girl on the cover. All his books, however, include girl characters.

Fred was born in Marblehead, Massachusetts, on August 3, 1953. He has a B.A. in history and political science from the University of Pennsylvania and a law degree from George Washington University National Law Center. He has been a practicing attorney since 1978 and is currently a full-time attorney for the federal government, in Washington, D.C. In April 2000, he started writing a weekly sports column for kids in the *Washington Post.* The books were his springboard to the column. Take a look at Fred Bowen's Web site: www.fredbowen.com.

How did you get your first book published?

In my late 20s and early 30s, I wrote movie and video reviews for local newspapers in the Washington, D.C., area. The experience served two purposes: I became addicted to publication, and I learned to write for a general audience. When my children were born, I gave up my movie and video writing. But I still wanted to write. So when I started reading sports books to my son, I thought (as I am sure many parents have thought), "I could write a better book than this." Having had some writing experience, I decided to give it a try.

First, I wrote a young adult novel with a sports theme. It did not really work. During a break from that book, I wrote a much shorter book for younger readers, *T. J.'s Secret Pitch.* I thought that book was pretty good, and so I sent it to about 12 publishers over the course of a year and a half. I got a few "good" rejections. An editor at one publishing house made a big difference. She rejected the manuscript but sent along the comments from three of her readers. They thought the story had a lot of promise and gave me tips to improve it. I also gave the book to my 8-year-old son, Liam. He gave me great advice too. Liam said, "Dad, you need more games in this book. Kids like to read about games." A short while later, when spring was in full bloom, I took a week off from my job as a lawyer and sat on my back porch and rewrote *T. J.'s Secret Pitch.* I incorporated the suggestions of the three readers and my son. Yes, I included more games in the book. I sent the book back to the encouraging editor, but by that time she had left and I got a form rejection letter back. That was very discouraging.

continues

But by this time my wife Peggy had spotted a notice in a newsletter for children's writers. The notice was about an upcoming librarians' conference that included a breakfast talk by author Bruce Brooks on the subject of "Baseball, Boys, Books, and Big Ideas." My wife called the librarian who was organizing it and asked if we could attend. She said, "Sure." After the talk, Peggy and I roamed around the publishers' trade show at the conference. We started talking to a woman at the Peachtree booth, who said she was filling in for her sister. I told her about my manuscript (which I didn't have with me). She encouraged me to send it to her sister at Peachtree. Her sister, Margaret Quinlin, happened to be the president of the company.

I sent my manuscript to Peachtree and didn't hear anything for months. Finally, Margaret wrote me a note saying that she loved the manuscript and that she was going to show it to some other people at Peachtree. Some weeks after that, I received a call at work from Stephanie Thomas, an editor at Peachtree and the editor of my first four books.

I answered the phone: "Hello, Fred Bowen." I was expecting a lawyer on the other end.

"Hello, Fred, this is Stephanie Thomas from Peachtree Publishers and I just love T. J."

Peachtree published *T. J.'s Secret Pitch* about 18 months later.

T. J.'s Secret Pitch had a little sports history weaved into the story and my wife got the idea to have a special section at the back that talked a little more about the history. Then I got the idea of doing a series of books that combined sports fiction with a little real sports history. Peachtree said, "Go for it." So I did.

Did you have an agent when you published your first book?

I do not have an agent. My wife, Peggy Jackson, who is very active in the editing and marketing of the books, also acts as my agent.

Do you have any advice, in terms of finding a publisher, for a writer starting out?

First, you must have a manuscript that is as close to finished (in other words, ready to be published) as you can make it. Publishers do not have the time and resources to do a lot of heavy editing, especially with new writers. Second, be ready to explain who the audience for your book is and how the publisher will be able to reach that audience. If there are books like yours in the market, be ready to explain why your book is different. If there are no books like yours, be ready to explain why you believe there is a need for the book. Third, listen to any constructive suggestions you receive from anyone who reads your manuscript. If you know any librarians or booksellers, show it to them. Also, show your manuscript to kids! Finally, don't give up. But keep writing or working on other ideas while you are looking for a publisher. You will be more attractive to a publisher if you can say that you have other ideas for books.

What procedures do you follow when you write?

As a full-time attorney, I can only work about an hour or two a day on my writing, and so I must work very efficiently. I usually write on my lunch hour and on the subway back and forth to my office. First, I develop a rough outline of each chapter. Then I outline in detail. This outline does not have to be perfect by any means, but it must be detailed enough so that I know precisely where the story is going at all times. My readers (ages 7–12) do not like loose ends to their stories or long, slow passages. So the outline (and the story that follows) must be carefully plotted and briskly paced. I cannot stress strongly enough to new writers that they should not fall into the trap of writing "when they are in the mood." In my opinion, if a writer is going to be productive, the writer must have a schedule and write even when he or she does not feel like writing.

Where do you get your ideas?

My books are the interplay of plot, an overall theme, and a historical backdrop. My ideas have different starting points. Sometimes they start with the story; other times they start with the theme or the history. Most of my stories are drawn from my experiences as a kid and as a coach. The coaching has not only been great fun; it has been valuable research for my books.

What do you think are the key differences between writing for children and writing for adults?

I think that children's fiction must be much faster paced and more carefully plotted than adult fiction. Young readers want a good story that answers their constant question of "what happens next?"

How did you learn to write?

I have mostly learned to write by writing. As I said, I wrote movie and video reviews. These were good experiences in writing on deadline and for a general audience. Although some people find them helpful, I have never had a course in creative writing or been part of a writers group. I did, however, have one academic experience that was helpful. At the University of Pennsylvania, I took a seminar in Russian history. The professor broke the seminar into smaller groups. My group of three met for an hour or so every week. Each member had to produce a three- to six-page essay every two weeks on some subject in Russian history. And (this is the most important point) the members of the seminar had to read the essay out loud in class and defend it in front of the other members of the seminar.

I found that reading out loud is a wonderful way to sharpen your writing. Whenever my voice stopped or stumbled, it was usually a good indication that the passage needed to be rewritten. After several humiliating experiences stumbling my way through my seminar readings, I presented an essay during one of the final meetings of the class. I read the essay smoothly, without a single stumble. When I was finished, the room was silent. The professor removed his cigarette (I am old enough to remember when smoking was allowed in classes) from his mouth and said, "That, Mr. Bowen, is how you should write."

Anything you really wish somebody had told you when you started out?

I wish somebody had told me about the importance of networking. I was already published before I discovered the Society of Children's Book Writers and Illustrators, which has local chapters all over the country. I wish I had known about SCBWI's writers conferences where editors will read your manuscript for a small fee. I also wished I had read more "insider" books (like this one), magazines, and newsletters. Initially, I concentrated too much on just sending my manuscript "over the transom" to publishers. I should have been doing more person-to-person networking and reading about the business.

Finally, let me say that writing for children is the most rewarding experience that I have had in my life outside of my relationships with my family. And the most fun. I have received letters from kids who proclaim that I am the greatest author ever! Sometimes the kids misspell author. Still this is high praise. Even better are the letters from teachers and parents who tell me that certain kids did not like to read until they read my books. That is the highest praise of all.

Accepts unsolicited/unagented: At this time most Penguin Putnam Inc. imprints do not accept unsolicited manuscripts. If you would like your work to be considered for publication by a major publisher, Penguin Putnam Inc. recommends that you work with an established literary agent.

PRO LINGUA ASSOCIATES

20 Elm Street
Brattleboro, VT 05301
Web site: www.prolinguaassociates.com

Description: Publisher.

Key people:

Senior editor: Ray Clark

Seeks: Particular focus at present is on English as a second or foreign language, although open to considering materials for teaching language and culture in general or other languages or cultures specifically.

Accepts unsolicited/unagented: Pro Lingua is always interested in considering new, original texts and teacher resources for publication.

Description of fiction titles: See recent titles for a sampling of titles for children and ESL readers.

Recent fiction titles:

Grandparents Are Special: A Reader for Upper Elementary and Middle School Students by Allyson Rothburd

Aesop's Fables compiled by Raymond C. Clark; illustrated by Hanna Bonner (Story Cards; advanced beginner to advanced, primary school to adult)

North American Indian Tales compiled by Susanna J. Clark; illustrated by Ken Rainbow Cougar (These 48 animal stories were collected from American Indian tribes across North America. Many of the tales explain how the world came to be as it is: "How Chipmunk Got Her Stripes"; "Why Dogs Don't Talk"; "Wind"; Bluebird and Coyote"; "How Fire Came to the Sierras"; "Butterflies." The illustrations by a popular Native American artist and storyteller, draw on symbols and motifs from the many cultures represented to reflect the wisdom and mystery of the great oral tradition of the "animal people" tales.)

Time to reply: It usually takes us several weeks to review materials. We do not mind if you call or write to ask how our review is going. We sometimes have several proposals to consider at once and very little time to review them, particularly at busy times of the year.

Submission guidelines: Write with an SASE or check our Web site. Pro Lingua will work with you in developing your material if the company feels that it will promote effective language learning, if it feels that there would be a market for it that we could reach, and if it fits into the publishing schedule. If you are not sure yet of any of the following information, guess as well as you can. It will help Pro Lingua understand your idea. In submitting your proposal, please provide the following information: author's name, address, home and work phone numbers, fax number, and e-mail address; proposed title. Also: Who will use the book? Describe the book briefly in a sentence or two. Why is this book needed? How does it differ from other books now available? How is it better?

Briefly describe how you have developed and tested the material. Include a tentative table of contents; as many units, lessons, or chapters as you feel are needed to show the presentation of the material effectively; and curriculum vitae.

Tips and comments: If you would like your proposal returned in the event that Pro Lingua cannot accept your work for publication, please send a stamped self-addressed envelope.

PROMETHEUS BOOKS

59 John Glenn Drive
Amherst, NY 14228
(716) 564-2711 (fax)
E-mail: slmitchell@prometheusbooks.com
Web site: www.prometheusbooks.com

Description: Nonfiction publisher focusing on alternative viewpoints.

PUFFIN BOOKS

Penguin Putnam BFYR
345 Hudson Street
New York, NY 10014
Web site: www.penguinputnam.com/about/children/puffin.htm

Corporate structure/parent: Penguin Putnam Inc.

Description: Publishing approximately 225 titles a year, Puffin is able to deliver the finest in every age group: lift-the-flaps and picture books for young children, Puffin Easy-to-Reads for first-time readers, Puffin Chapters and fun original fiction for middle graders, and unforgettable critically acclaimed teen fiction for older readers. Where else can a reader find A. A. Milne's classic *Winnie-the-Pooh* books next to the weird and wacky tales of Jon Scieszka and Lane Smith? Or the best-selling Spot lift-the-flap books by Eric Hill beside the moving novels of S. E. Hinton?

Established: 1941.

Key people:

Publisher: Tracy Tang

Books per year: Approximately 225.

Accepts unsolicited/unagented: At this time most Penguin Putnam Inc. imprints do not accept unsolicited manuscripts. If you would like your work to be considered for publication by a major publisher, Penguin Putnam Inc. recommends that you work with an established literary agent.

Description of fiction titles: Noted Puffin picture book authors and illustrators include Ludwig Bemelmans, Jan Brett, Eric Carle, Tomie dePaola, Ezra Jack Keats, Robert McCloskey, Rosemary Wells, and Caldecott Medal and Honor winner Paul O. Zelinsky. Middle graders and teen readers devour books by Puffin's fiction authors, who include

Lloyd Alexander, Betsy Byars, Barbara Cooney, Roald Dahl, Jean Fritz, Jean Craighead George, S. E. Hinton, Astrid Lindgren, Katherine Paterson, and Mildred D. Taylor.

Ragweed Press

Box 2023
Charlottetown, PEI C1A 7N7
Canada
(902) 566-5750
(902) 566-4473 (fax)
E-mail: books@ragweed.com
Web site: www.ragweed.com

Description: Book publisher specializing in women's interest.

Established: 1980.

Books per year and description: 6 to 10 titles in total—including adult titles.

Seeks: Ragweed Press publishes children's literature for ages 4 to 8 and 9 to 14 (especially ones with girl heroes). Aims to portray the lives of women and men, girls and boys, with integrity—without the language of sexism, racism, homophobia, and other forms of discrimination.

Accepts unsolicited/unagented: Yes, but only from Canadian writers.

Include with illustrator query: Illustration submissions should be copies, ideally ones that can be kept on file for future reference.

Tips and comments: If you are considering submitting a manuscript, familiarize yourself with the kind of books Ragweed publishes. Submissions sent from outside Canada that use non-Canadian stamps on the SASE will be neither considered nor returned. Ragweed accepts multiple submissions (for manuscripts, please indicate whether it is a multiple submission; for illustrations, Ragweed will assume that it is a multiple submission). Please note that Ragweed does not accept electronic submissions. Ragweed Press is committed to publishing works that contribute to the cultural and social identity of Canada. Therefore, Ragweed only publishes single-authored works by Canadians and only uses works by Canadian illustrators.

Rainbow Publishers

PO Box 261129
San Diego, CA 92196
(858) 271-7600

Corporate structure/parent: Two imprints: Rainbow Books and Legacy Press.

Description: Book publisher.

Established: 1979.

Key people:

Publisher: Dan Miley

Acquisitions/submissions editor: Christy Allen

Books per year and description: All in religion; Rainbow Books are Christian education materials for kids' teachers. Legacy Press books are nonfiction for kids.

Percentage by first-time authors: About 50 percent.

Seeks: *Rainbow Books:* Reproducible activity and curriculum for kids' teachers in an evangelical Christian setting (church, home school, Bible clubs); *Legacy Press:* Nonfiction for kids 2 to 12, especially preteens.

Accepts unsolicited/unagented: Yes, both.

Description of fiction titles: No fiction.

Recent nonfiction titles:

Rainbow Books:

Favorite Bible Children (a reproducible activity and curricula series for teachers of kids ages 2 to grade 4; books)

Legacy Press:

God's Girls (1 and 2) by Karen Whiting (a set of devotional activity books for preteen girls that includes ideas for crafts and parties)

Preferred nonfiction titles: Must be able to write from an evangelical Christian perspective. No poetry.

Preferred form of submission/contact: Send an SASE for writers guidelines. Proposals only. *No e-mail proposals.*

Time to reply: Six weeks to three months.

Time to publish: One to three years.

Accepts simultaneous submissions: Yes.

Number of illustrators used annually: Five to 10.

Desired illustrator qualifications: Interiors: black and white, preferably on disk; covers: four-color, preferably on disk.

Prefer manuscript/illustration packages, or separate: Separate.

Include with illustrator query: Resume and samples.

Time to reply: Six weeks.

Purchases freelance photography: No.

Terms for writers: Rainbow Books: flat fee; Legacy Press: royalties and advance dependent on project.

Terms for illustrators: Rainbow Books: flat fee per project; Legacy Press: paid per illustration.

Submission guidelines: Send an SASE to the prior address.

Tips and comments: Know the Christian book market, what's hot and what's not. Be able to work quickly to make the project more lucrative to you.

RAINTREE STECK-VAUGHN

466 Southern Boulevard
Chatham, NJ 07928
(201) 514-1525
(201) 514-1612

Description: Book publisher.

Seeks: Publishes nonfiction books for all children from kindergarten to young adult for the school and library market. Does not consider any historical fiction.

Accepts unsolicited/unagented: Queries first, please. Accepts solicited and unsolicited material. Each receives equal treatment, so please do not feel that it is necessary to have an agent.

Preferred form of submission/contact: Prefers a query letter before submitting anything. The proposal should include information about any similar texts already available in the market. It should also include the length and reading level of the proposed manuscript.

Time to reply: Tries to read proposals and manuscripts in the order they are received. You may expect a decision within three months, but in certain cases it may be longer.

Terms for writers: Contract details will be worked out only after a proposal is accepted for publication since the terms vary with the nature of each project.

Submission guidelines: Read profile and for further information write with an SASE for a copy of current catalog and guidelines (which are essentially the same as the profile here).

Tips and comments: A self-addressed stamped envelope should be included with your submission if you wish it to be returned. Your SASE should be the correct size with the proper postage. The company is sometimes inundated with material and therefore cannot always take the time to give specific criticisms when rejecting a manuscript. What may not fit the company's needs may be exactly what another publisher is looking for. If you would like a catalog (it is advisable and helpful to see the kinds of publications that the company publishes), please send a self-addressed stamped envelope for the amount of $3. Please do not expect a commitment for publication until the company has carefully considered an entire manuscript or in some cases, a detailed outline, and a number of chapters.

Random House Books for Young Readers

Teens Web site: www.randomhouse.com/teens
Kids Web site: www.randomhouse.com/kids/books

Corporate structure/parent: Random House Children's Book imprints include Alfred A. Knopf Books for Young Readers; Bantam Books for Young Readers; Crown Books for Young Readers; Delacorte Press Books for Young Readers; Disney Books for Young Readers; Doubleday Books for Young Readers; Dragonfly Books; Laurel-Leaf Books; Lucas Books; Random House Books for Young Readers; Sesame Workshop (formerly Children's Television Workshop); Wendy Lamb Books; Yearling Books.

Tips and comments: Because of the volume of materials that are received, *Random House now only accepts unsolicited manuscripts only if submitted to one of two contests*: The Marguerite de Angeli Contest for a first middle-grade novel, written for children 7 to 10 years old (guidelines can be found at www.randomhouse.com/kids/games/marguerite.html), and the Delacorte Press Contest for a first young adult novel, written for readers 12 to 18 years old (guidelines can be found at www.randomhouse.com/kids/games/delacorte.html). If your work meets the criteria for one of the contests, please submit your text manuscript. You can also make a written request for rules and guidelines;

please include a self-addressed stamped envelope. *All other types of manuscripts must be submitted through an agent or at the request of an editor.* Staff members of Random House Children's Books cannot recommend particular agents.

Reader's Digest Children's Publishing, Inc.

Reader's Digest Road
Pleasantville, NY 10570-7000
Web site: www.readersdigestkids.com

Corporate structure/parent: Reader's Digest Association (distributed by Simon & Schuster)

Description: Publisher.

Tips and comments: Children mean the world to Reader's Digest, and each book published must meet the following criteria: It must educate, entertain, enrich, and inspire its young readers. Although the company is only nine years old (just like many of its readers!), it has published over 500 books and sold some 15 million copies in the United States alone. Readers Digest titles are also sold around the world and have been translated into 28 different languages. From evergreen licenses such as Barbie to innovative novelty books to high-quality reference titles, you'll find Reader's Digest Children's Books inspire kids to use their creativity and imagination.

Red Deer Press

Mackimmie Library Tower, Room 816
2500 University Drive, NW
Calgary, Alberta T2N 1N4
Canada
(403) 220-2351
(403) 210-8191 (fax)
E-mail: khanson@ucalgary.ca
Web site: www.reddeerpress.com

Description: Book publisher. For 25 years, Red Deer Press has been an institutionally affiliated publisher of literary fiction, nonfiction, drama, poetry, children's illustrated books, young adult fiction, teen fiction, and adult trade titles. The press's mandate is to develop books by, about, or of interest to North Americans with special emphasis on the west.

Established: Incorporated in 1975,

Key people:

Editor: Peter Carver, children's editor

Books per year and description: Two to three children's picture books; two to three early reader books; two to three young adult titles.

Percentage by first-time authors: 30 to 40 percent.

Seeks: Red Deer Press is looking for books of exceptional quality that have a unique story to tell.

Accepts unsolicited/unagented: Yes, accepts unsolicited manuscripts, although only manuscripts written by Canadians.

Description of fiction titles: Hard-hitting, gutsy realistic fiction and compellingly realized fantasy fiction.

Recent fiction titles:

Lean Mean Machines by Michele Marineau, translated by Susan Ouriou

Graveyard Girl: Stories by Wendy Lewis

Close-Ups: Best Stories for Teens edited by Peter Carver

Description of nonfiction titles: To date has only published one nonfiction title.

Recent nonfiction titles:

Let's Get Going: A Step-by-Step Guide to Successful Outings with Children by Candace Weisner

Preferred form of submission/contact: Query and sample to Peter Carver, children's editor.

Time to reply: Four to six months.

Time to publish: Six months to one year.

Accepts simultaneous submissions: Yes.

Number of illustrators used annually: Three to four.

Desired illustrator qualifications: Quality work in a style that suits the particular story.

Prefer manuscript/illustration packages, or separate: Prefers to review separately.

Include with illustrator query: Resume and samples.

Time to reply: Doesn't reply unless there is a book project for the artist. Files the samples and keeps them on file for six months.

Purchases freelance photography: Occasionally, but only for book jackets.

Preferred photography: An image that suits the book.

Terms for writers: A standard percentage of royalties.

Terms for illustrators: A standard percentage of royalties.

Submission guidelines: From the Red Deer Web site.

Red Wheelbarrow Press

E-mail: publisher@rwpress.com
Web site: www.rwpress.com

Established: 1997.

Books per year: A new press, with only one published title thus far.

Accepts unsolicited/unagented: At the present time, *not accepting unsolicited manuscripts or queries.*

Recent fiction titles:

The Ambitious Baker's Batter written and illustrated by Wendy Seese (Poetry and prose tell the tale of a doughnut maker who sets out to create something "more important" than doughnuts. The whimsical main character engages the reader in his experiments, employing all five senses and the color spectrum.)

Reidmore Books

c/o Nelson Thomson Learning
1120 Birchmount Road
Toronto, Ontario M1K 5G4
Canada
(416) 752-9100
(800) 430-4445 (fax)
E-mail: customerservice
Web site: www.nelson.com

Corporate structure/parent: Nelson Thomson Learning.

Description: Publisher specializing in K to 12 social studies materials.

Description of nonfiction titles: Coursework materials.

Recent nonfiction titles:

Beginnings: From the First Nations to the Great Migration by Jamieson (grades 4–7)

Finding Your Voice: You and Your Government by Flaig and Galvin (grades 5–7)

Digital Images of Japan by Gambier (photo CD; grades 7–9)

Digital Images of the Northern Circumpolar World by Zoltai and Gambier (photo CD; grades 6–8)

Japan: Its People and Culture, 2nd edition by Parsons, Salyzyn, and Smith (grades 7–9)

Preferred nonfiction titles: Social studies texts.

Richard C. Owen Publishers, Inc.

PO Box 585
Katonah, NY 10536
(914) 232-3903
(914) 232-3977
Web site: www.rcowen.com

Description: Children's book publisher.

Established: 1986.

Key people:

Publisher: Richard C. Owen

Acquisitions/submissions editor: Janice Bolamo, children's books

Books per year and description: 15 story books (K–second grade); 3 author autobiographies (ages 7–11).

Percentage by first-time authors: 90 percent.

Seeks: Good literature story books for K to second grade; short snappy articles for second grade level; fiction and nonfiction.

Accepts unsolicited/unagented: Yes.

Description of fiction titles: Interesting, quick, engaging, easy reading.

Recent fiction titles:

I Meowed (a little cat's voice brings a nice surprise)

And Then There Were Birds (how birds came to fill the treks with color and song)

Wolf Song (two wolves mature)

Diving for Treasure (the search for treasure along the coast of Florida)

Preferred fiction titles: Wants original, realistic, contemporary stories as well as tall tales, folktales, legends and myths of all cultures. Does not want nostalgia, sweet, cute or talking animals; no holiday or religious themes, lessons, morals, vocabulary lists or language skills; no manuscripts that demean individuals or groups or present violence as acceptable behavior.

Description of nonfiction titles: Short, fascinating, vivid nonfiction; informational but with a story line that appeals to children.

Recent nonfiction titles:

The Little Book of Street Rods

Armadillo

Preferred nonfiction titles: Rich yet simple, informational stories; accurately researched; a good, engaging read.

Preferred form of submission/contact: Write (or go to the Web site) for guidelines; send manuscript with an SASE.

Time to reply: One to three months.

Time to publish: One to three years.

Accepts simultaneous submissions: Yes.

Number of illustrators used annually: 15 to 20.

Desired illustrator qualifications: Bright, child-appeal illustrations; not bizarre or cartoony.

Prefer manuscript/illustration packages, or separate: Separately.

Include with illustrator query: Samples.

Time to reply: Retains the samples and does not reply unless rejecting.

Purchases freelance photography: Yes.

Preferred photography: Child appeal; natural, candid, vivid.

Terms for writers: 5 percent.

Terms for illustrators: Flat fee—$100 to $150 per piece.

Submission guidelines: Send an SASE or go to the Web site.

Tips and comments: *Writers:* Be patient and cooperative; know your craft, your audience, and your objective. Manuscripts should be typewritten and double-spaced with your name, phone number, and the page number on every page. Include a short cover letter with your name, address, telephone number, and manuscript title as well as an SASE with sufficient return postage. *Illustrators:* Send samples and updates. Looking for natural and candid art—unspoiled pictures. Most of the characters are 5-, 6-, and 7-year-old, human, contemporary children. The artist must be able to sustain the appearance of a character or characters and spirit of the story from page to page throughout the book. Seeking to avoid preconceived, stereotyped images. You must enclose a cover letter with your name, address, and the types of samples you are submitting along with an SASE with sufficient postage for return of art samples (prefers to return an artist's work rather than destroy it). Aims to publish good books with appealing language, characters, and action that children can read in one sitting. Please write clearly and simply, yet with style, richness, and voice. Familiarize yourself with the company's style before submitting.

Rising Moon

PO Box 1389
Flagstaff, AZ 86002-1389
(520) 774-5251
(520) 774-0592
Web site: www.northlandpub.com

Corporate structure/parent: Northland Publishing (established 1989).

Description: Trade book publisher.

Established: 1997.

Key people:

Publisher and president: David Jenney

Editor: Aimee Jackson

Books per year and description: 12 picture books (trade) for ages 3 to 8.

Percentage by first-time authors: Of the 12 books per year published, one or two of them is written by a first-time author.

Seeks: Traditional story picture books with national appeal (universal themes) for ages 3–5 and 5–8.

Accepts unsolicited/unagented: No.

Description of fiction titles: Picture books.

Recent fiction titles:

Jane vs. the Tooth Fairy by Betsy Jay; illustrated by Lori Osiecki

Chewy Louie by Howie Schneider

Clarence Goes Out West and Meets a Purple Horse by Jean Ekman Adams

Preferred fiction titles: Books for children of preschooler age through age 8; broad subject with wide appeal and universal themes; wry and humorous story elements; exceptional Spanish/English stories.

Description of nonfiction titles: None.

Preferred form of submission/contact: Through his or her agent.

Time to reply: *No longer replies to unsolicited manuscripts.* The usual response time to an agent is approximately two weeks.

Time to publish: Two to three years.

Accepts simultaneous submissions: Yes, but please notify.

Number of illustrators used annually: 12.

Desired illustrator qualifications: Highly creative individuals with ideas of their own. At the same time illustrators need to follow "the vision" of the author and the publisher. Professional in meeting deadlines and fulfilling commitments.

Prefer manuscript/illustration packages, or separate: Yes.

Include with illustrator query: Samples and tear sheets followed by telephone review.

Time to reply: Immediately.

Terms for writers: Advance against royalty (net or list).

Terms for illustrators: Same.

Submission guidelines: Call (800) 346-3257 or visit the Web site. Submissions (via agents) should include entire picture book manuscripts in the range of 300 to 1,000 words in length.

Tips and comments: Be persistent. Do *not* try to illustrate what is outside your capabilities or style. Get feedback from others before making submissions. Do not send original artwork—quality color copies (with an SASE for return) work very well. Query by mail only. Will not respond to queries via phone, fax, or e-mail. Address all art submissions to the art director, and include a cover letter with information regarding your publishing history. Please get involved with SCBWI (local chapters and national). It is the *best* resource for children's writers and illustrators of all backgrounds and levels of experience.

RONSDALE PRESS

3350 West 21st Avenue
Vancouver, British Columbia
Canada V6S 1G7
(604) 738-4688
(604) 731-4548 (fax)
E-mail: ronhatch@pinc.com
Web site: www.ronsdalepress.com

Description: Publisher.

Established: 1988.

Seeks: Publishes a small number of books for children in the age 8 to 15 range. Especially interested in YA historical novels. No longer publishes 32-page picture books.

Accepts unsolicited/unagented: Yes.

Recent fiction titles:

The Ghouls' Night Out by Janice MacDonald; illustrated by Pamela Breeze Currie
Terra Incognita by Anne Metikosh
Cuthbert and the Merpeople by Kathy Mezei; illustrated by Anne Stratford
Vanilla Gorilla by Bill New; illustrated by Vivan Bevis

Preferred fiction titles: YA historical novels.

Preferred form of submission/contact: Query letter with a sample, or if you are sure Ronsdale is a good match for you, you can send the entire manuscript. Otherwise send a substantial section from the first part of the manuscript. Include also a brief bio (half a page will do), and list your previous publications, if you have any.

Time to reply: Within one month.

Submission guidelines: Please include a self-addressed, stamped envelope (or international coupons) for the return of the manuscript—in case Ronsdale does not accept it.

Even if you do not want the manuscript returned, enclose an SASE for the reply. You do want a reply, don't you? If you would like the receipt of your manuscript acknowledged, please provide an extra SAS postcard for that purpose.

Tips and comments: Browse the catalog to see the sorts of books Ronsdale has published in the past. It would also be wise to look at some of Ronsdale's books in libraries or bookstores. Better still, buy a volume or two, and read them to see what Ronsdale likes to publish, what the company finds important. Remember that Ronsdale is a literary publisher, which means that it scouts for thoughtful work that extends the way we perceive the world. Ronsdale also looks for writing that shows the author has read widely in contemporary and earlier literature. Ronsdale, like other literary presses, is not interested in mass-market or pulp materials. Mystery stories or fiction that is entirely plot-driven should be sent to the publishers who specialize in these forms.

Rosen Publishing Group

29 E. 21st Street
New York, NY 10010
(212) 777-3017
(212) 253-6915
E-mail: rosened@erols.com

Description: Book publisher

Seeks: The Rosen Publishing Group publishes young adult and middle school nonfiction titles for sale to school and public libraries. Each book is aimed at pre-teen or teenage readers and addresses them directly. Interested in material that is supplementary to the curriculum, scholastic in nature, and covers subject matter of particular interest to the young adult or middle school reader. Publishes young adult books at two different reading levels. Some young adult books are written at the seventh- to ninth- grade reading level. Manuscripts at this reading level run approximately 30,000 words in length. Other young adult books are called "high/low books." These books for teenagers present topics of high-interest level but are written at the lower fourth- to sixth-grade reading level. Manuscripts at this reading level run approximately 8,000 words in length. Books for middle school readers are written at a fifth- to eighth- grade reading level. Manuscripts at this reading level run approximately 5,000 words in length.

Accepts unsolicited/unagented: Yes.

Preferred nonfiction titles: Areas of particular interest include careers, current trends, coping with social and personal problems, character-building behavior, drug abuse prevention, multicultural topics, science, and sports.

Preferred form of submission/contact: If you are interested in writing, please send a resume, cover letter, and sample writings to the prior address, attention: Acquisitions. If you would like to propose a new title or series idea, please submit a query letter. Please do not submit unsolicited manuscripts for review, because the company cannot take responsibility for returning them. Please include a self-addressed stamped envelope with your submission.

Time to reply: An acquisitions editor will contact any potential authors.

Tips and comments: Please highlight any experience you have in working with or writing for a preteen or teen audience. Ideally, we would like to see a writing sample that addresses the audience for which you are interested in writing, Also, please provide a list of topics about which you would like to write. An acquisitions editor will contact any potential authors.

St. Anthony Messenger Press

1615 Republic Street
Cincinnati, OH 45210
(513) 241-5615
(800) 488-0488
(513) 241-0399 (fax)
E-mail: stanthony@americancatholic.org
Web site: www.AmericanCatholic.org

Description: Catholic Christian book publisher.

Established: 1970.

Key people:

Publisher: Jeremy Harrington, OFM

Acquisitions/submissions editor: Lisa Biedenbach, managing editor

Books per year: Fewer than five.

Seeks: Books that educate and inspire Catholic Christians. Looking for universal applicability.

Accepts unsolicited/unagented: Yes.

Description of fiction titles: Does not publish fiction.

Description of nonfiction titles: Books that educate and inspire Catholic Christians.

Recent nonfiction titles:

Can You Find Jesus? Introducing Your Child to the Gospel
Jesus Grows Up
One-of-a-Kind Friends
Saints and Heroes for Kids
Can You Find Bible Heroes?
Introducing Your Child to the Old Testament

Preferred nonfiction titles: Does not publish fiction, poetry, autobiography, personal reflections, and art books.

Preferred form of submission/contact: Address your description (brief—less than 500 words) and an outline of the book to Lisa Biedenbach. Tell about your subject, the approximate length of the book, and the intended audience.

Time to reply: Six to eight weeks.

Time to publish: One to two years.

Accepts simultaneous submissions: No.

Number of illustrators used annually: Approximately 12.

Desired illustrator qualifications: Professional quality; good concepts; familiarity with Catholic symbols.

Prefer manuscript/illustration packages, or separate: Separately.

Include with illustrator query: Samples, tear sheets, or personal portfolio review.

Time to reply: Within a few weeks.

Purchases freelance photography: Yes.

Preferred photography: Professional quality; good concepts; familiarity with Catholicism.

Terms for writers: Usually pays an advance on royalty of $1,000. Usually pays 10 to 12 percent royalty on net receipts.

Terms for illustrators: Varies.

Submission guidelines: Write or call to request them.

Tips and comments: Know the market—the company is targeting people seeking inspiration for their spiritual life or help with special problems and is providing materials and tools for parents, teachers, and religious educators. Submit a letter with resume and samples. Company mission is "to spread the Word that is Jesus Christ in the style of Saints Francis and Anthony. Through print marketed in North America and worldwide, we endeavor to evangelize, inspire, and inform those who search for God and seek a richer Catholic, Christian, human life. Our efforts help support the life, ministry, and charities of the Franciscan Friars of Saint John the Baptist Province, who sponsor our work."

Saint Mary's Press

702 Terrace Heights
Winona, MN 55987-1320
(800) 533-8095
Web site: www.smp.org

Description: Book publisher for youth, ages 10 to 19, and for adults as they minister to youth in schools, parishes, and homes—employing all appropriate settings, means, and media.

Accepts unsolicited/unagented: Yes.

Recent nonfiction titles:

Better Than Natural and Other Stories by Lisa-Marie Calderone-Stewart (The characters in this collection of stories experience wonder and struggle, hurt and forgiveness, failure and success, and tears and laughter. You will enjoy them as wonderful stories about the joys and struggles of growing. And if you wish, they can serve as a starting point for searching out your own answers about life, God, and faith.)

Good News, Day by Day, Bible Reflections for Teens by Dee Bernhardt

Preferred form of submission/contact: In your proposal, which should be less than 10 pages, please include a cover letter with a personal introduction describing your background and experience. (Please prepare this carefully. First impressions are important.) Also include brief statement about your manuscript, its purpose, audience(s), uses; a tentative title for your manuscript an annotated table of contents; a date of availability for a completed manuscript; an estimated word count; your address, phone numbers, and e-mail address.

Submission guidelines: If you send a manuscript or sample of your work, please include a stamped self-addressed envelope large enough to hold and protect it or a check for an amount sufficient to cover return postage and packaging. Be sure to keep a copy of the manuscript for yourself. Saint Mary's Press cannot be responsible for returning manuscripts at our cost or for loss or damage. Please do not send an electronic file as your initial submission.

Tips and comments: To learn more about Saint Mary's Press browse the Web catalog or call 800-533-8095 and ask for a free catalog. Before submitting to Saint Mary's Press, please consider the following: Am I clearly in touch with the needs of Saint Mary's audiences? Which audience? Is my material written to satisfy that audience's needs?

Does my work offer something new, significant, or unique? Am I qualified to create a work on this subject? Of this type? Will my work be fresh in the eyes of its audience at the time it is published (generally a year after manuscripts are accepted)? Has my work been critiqued by those who are qualified to do so?

SANDCASTLE

226-2040 W. 12th Avenue
Vancouver, British Columbia V6J 2G2
Canada
(604) 733-4868
(604) 733-4860 (fax)
E-mail: bhp@beachholme.bc.ca
Web site: www.beachholme.bc.ca/index.html

Corporate structure/parent: Beach Holme Publishing.

Description: Book publisher.

Seeks: Beach Holme's Sandcastle imprint adorns an award-winning line of young adult novels for readers aged 8 to 12. Particularly interested in works that have a historical or regional basis and are set in Canada. When submitting this type of manuscript, include ideas for teachers guides or educational resources and appropriate topics for a classroom situation if applicable.

Accepts unsolicited/unagented: Yes, from Canadian authors only.

Description of fiction titles: Young adult novels for readers aged 8 to 12.

Preferred fiction titles: Beach Holme no longer publishes illustrated children's books.

Preferred form of submission/contact: Manuscript. When submitting, include ideas for teachers guides or educational resources and appropriate topics for a classroom situation if applicable. Please submit your manuscript with a cover letter (clearly stating if this is an exclusive or multiple submission); a brief author biography (information regarding previously published material, education, interests, relevant contacts); first three chapters (maximum 30 pages) of the work and a brief synopsis of the plot development, key events, central characters, setting/locale, and format. Please send full stories when submitting a collection. Do not submit original art or text. Please note that the company will not proceed to the next step, acceptance for publication, until receiving the full manuscript, an approximate page count of the finished manuscript, the word processing program used (we will require manuscripts on disk if accepted in DOS, Windows, or ASCII text only as we use IBM computers), a self-addressed stamped envelope with sufficient Canadian postage for return of submission or correspondence if desired. Proofread your submission for spelling and grammatical errors that divert attention from the story. Send clean, double-spaced typed copy. Your full address and telephone number should be on the cover, and your name should be on the top right-hand corner of every page.

Time to reply: All unsolicited submissions are processed by date of arrival and will be dealt with in that order. Up to three editors in-house will assess your manuscript should this prove necessary. Goal is to reply to all submissions within four or five months. Please remember that this is a small publisher with limited personnel that receives more than 200 queries or manuscripts a month. If it takes longer than four months to respond to your submission, write and your manuscript will be appraised post haste.

Accepts simultaneous submissions: Yes, but must notify.

Tips and comments: Beach Holme is a long-standing and reputable literary press that has expanded into a number of specific genres due to an evolution of tastes, market needs, and personnel. For an overview of the press's history, visit the Beach Holme Web site. When assessing material, the company considers the following: originality and quality of the prose; intriguing plot development; credible dialogue and consistent narrative voice; innovations in genre technique; thematic cohesion; topical and contemporary content; previous publishing credits (i.e., published stories, poems, or excerpts); market niche potential; appeal to a definable audience and compatibility with other titles on the list. *No electronic submissions of any kind.* The company does not have the staff or the time to give you extensive reasons for rejection. *Canadian authors only.*

Sasquatch Books

615 Second Avenue, Suite 260
Seattle, WA 98104
(206) 467-4300
(206) 467-4301 (fax)
E-mail: books@sasquatchbooks.com
Web site: www.sasquatchbooks.com

Description: Sasquatch Books publishes works whose stories, content, or themes are directly related to the Pacific Northwest and the West in general. At this time, Sasquatch is not considering new children's book proposals.

Scholastic

555 Broadway
New York, NY 10012
(212) 343-6100
Web site: www.scholastic.com

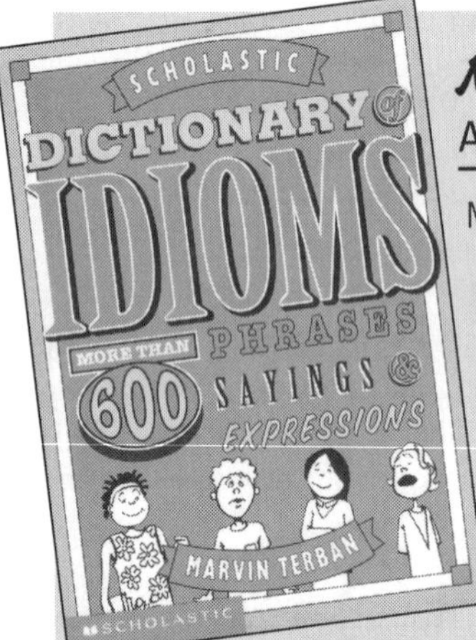

Meet Marvin Terban

Author

Marvin Terban, the "master of word play," is the author of *Checking Your Grammar* (1993); *Dictionary of Idioms* (1996); *The Scholastic Dictionary of Spelling* (1998); *Punctuation Power* (2000); *Building Your Vocabulary* (2002) (all with Scholastic); *Eight Ate: A Feast of Homonym Riddles* (1982); *In a Pickle: And Other Funny Idioms* (1983); the forthcoming *Guide to the English Language* (Children's Book-of-the-Month Club, 2002), and many others. And he's also been a full-time teacher of English, Latin, drama, and public speaking for 38 years!

Mr. Terban, as his students call him, was born in Chelsea, Massachusetts, April 28, 1940. He holds a B.A. from Tufts and an M.F.A. from Columbia University. He teaches at the Columbia Grammar and Preparatory School in New York City. His books focus on the English language and are primarily for grades 1 to 8 with an emphasis on grades 3 to 6. He has made visits to hundreds of schools across the United States, South America, Europe, and Japan. His lively presentations include "Who Says English Can't Be Fun?" and "How a Book Is Born."

How did you get your first book published?

I'd always wanted to write a children's book that got published, ever since I was writing for my high school paper. In my mid-30s, I decided to put my efforts toward that goal full-time. I read books on writing books, joined an organization of children's writers, took courses at two New York City colleges, and so forth. I sent out a few manuscripts and got them rejected. One day at my school's book fair, I saw a small storybook written and illustrated by one of the third-grade mothers who was working the cash register that day. I told her that I had written some homonym riddles that I had used in my English class, and I wanted to see whether I could get them published. She asked to see them, illustrated three, and sent my manuscript to her editor. A month later her editor called me and told me that she wanted to publish my text but not the third-grade mother's pictures. What a dilemma. I called the illustrator and told her what her editor had said. She said that she knew it was wrong to send in a text with pictures, to cut me loose, and she would pick up her career elsewhere. (She was right. She is now a very successful author with a series of her own.) I sold my text (it was *Eight Ate,* published about 18 months later in 1982 and still in print) to the editor who moved on to another publishing house, and I published one book a year with that house for the next 12 years. (One year I published two books with them.)

Did you have an agent when you published your first book?

I have never had an agent except for one brief period. I have sold 25 books (23 published; 2 due out in 2002) without an agent. Once an agent saw me speak at a children's book writers conference, approached me, asked if I had an agent, and when I told her no, asked if she could be my agent. I told her that I was doing fine selling my books on my own. She asked whether I had any manuscripts that I hadn't been able to sell. I told her that I had four picture books that I hadn't had any luck with, and she offered to try to sell them for me. I sent her the manuscripts and didn't hear from her for three years except for a few vague postcards. She once introduced herself to my wife at a conference as my agent, and that surprised my wife since she didn't know I had one. Years passed, and I got a postcard notifying me that my "agent" had gone out of the business and moved away. So much for having an agent.

Do you have any advice, in terms of finding an agent, for a writer starting out?

My experience has been that you don't need an agent. You need a really good manuscript, the names and addresses of appropriate editors (at publishing houses that publish your kind of book), envelopes, stamps, a postal scale, and a good, brief cover letter. If an author can sell a book on his or her own, the author can keep all the advances and royalties. However, from what my friends tell me, a good agent—one that works hard for you, supports you, encourages you, holds your hand, gives you good advice, can negotiate the best contract for you, and answers and returns your phone calls—is a treasure. How to find one if you really want one? Ask your friends who are published authors to recommend one. But most editors will tell you that they are looking for good manuscripts. Period. And they don't much care where they came from. Many, many unagented books are published every year.

Do you have any advice, in terms of finding a publisher, for a writer starting out?

Go to a children's bookstore or a chain bookstore with a good children's department and spend hours and hours looking at all the books. Find books that you really like and check who published them. Those are the publishers you'd like to be published by. Get addresses and phone numbers from the phone book. Call. Speak to the editors who answer. Find out what their submission policies are, what kind of books they're looking for, and so forth. Make copies of your best manuscript, write a brief cover letter, and send it out. Keep your fingers crossed and wait. You might also want to send the same manuscript to more than one publisher. Publishers may frown on this practice, but it takes so long to get a rejection letter back that a whole year may go by, two publishers may have rejected your book, and you're still stuck nowhere. But before you do anything, learn how to write a good, publishable book.

Are your books illustrated?

I have had several different illustrators. Some have been well known (like Giulio Maestro and John O'Brien), and others have been in-house illustrators who got paid up front and whose names are not on the covers. I have never chosen my own illustrator. The publisher wants to do that. But I have often been given the privilege of seeing the rough drawings and being asked to comment on them. Often my suggestions have been taken into account, resulting in what I thought were better illustrations. For instance, in one of my books, of 20 original illustrations using human figures, 17 were of men and boys. When I pointed out how one-sided that was, the editor asked the illustrator to redraw some illustrations using females. That made for a much better book, I thought. Editors and art directors usually like authors who don't meddle or mess with the illustrator. However, if you have an excellent working relationship with your editor, you might gingerly ask to see some of the work of a prospective illustrator. If you are invited by the publisher, you might offer your suggestions, comments, and criticisms. But most first-time authors don't get to have much influence on the artwork.

continues

Do you have any advice, in terms of finding an illustrator, for a writer starting out?

Don't try to find an illustrator. Unless you are the illustrator or married to the illustrator or aren't willing to sell your book without a specific illustrator's work, leave the choice of the illustrator up to the editor and the art director. Do the best job you can on the words, and let the publisher worry about the pictures.

Where do you get your ideas?

I got my first ideas from teaching English. I tried to develop fun activities, homework assignments, and tests for my students. I was able to rework this material into publishable form. Now editors suggest projects for me.

How did you learn to write?

I was a good English student in grade school, high school, and college. I was editor of the school newspaper and literary magazine throughout junior and senior high school. As a teenager, I also wrote a weekly column for my local, hometown newspaper. In my late 30s, when I decided that I wanted to try to become a published children's book author, I knew that I didn't really know much about it, so I began to read all I could. I got books from the library or bookstores on the subject of how to write and publish a children's book. Many of the authors of those books (Barbara Seuling, James Cross Giblin, Frieda Gates, Connie Epstein, among others) later became my friends. Then I took two very good courses on writing children's books. One was at the New School and one was at Bank Street College on West 112th [in New York City]. The latter was a monthly workshop for unpublished writers. I also joined the Society of Children's Book Writers and Illustrators and began attending their annual conference in New York. (Later I began helping run those conferences myself.) Sometimes friends of friends send me manuscripts to read and ask me to comment on them. I agree to do it only if they agree in advance to accept whatever I might say, no matter how direct and honest. Most manuscripts are terrible because people mistakenly think that writing for children has to be an easy thing to do. It isn't. You have to prepare yourself—read books about writing, read children's books by the dozen, take courses, join with a group of other aspiring au-

Description: The Scholastic Trade Book division is an award-winning publisher of original children's books under various hardcover and paperback imprints. Scholastic publishes 500 books per year, including *Harry Potter, Animorphs, The Baby-sitters Club, The Magic School Bus, Dear America, Captain Underpants,* and *Clifford the Big Red Dog* as well as licenses such as Pokémon and Scooby Doo, which are distributed to stores and schools. Scholastic Press, Cartwheel Books, Scholastic Paperbacks, Arthur A. Levine Books, Scholastic Reference and The Blue Sky Press are the Scholastic Trade Book imprints. Scholastic's ten school-based Book Fairs, used by nearly half of all teachers in the United States and nearly 40 million families, help children build their own libraries of high-quality books at affordable prices. Scholastic Book Clubs give children and parents the opportunity to review and purchase hundreds of high-quality, age-appropriate titles from Scholastic and other publishers as well as support their local school.

Accepts unsolicited/unagented: No.

thors and meet frequently to critique each other's manuscripts, commiserate about rejection letters, and celebrate each other's successes.

Anything you really wish somebody had told you when you started out?

Writing can be a very solitary, sometimes lonely, activity. It has to be. But a writer must not get isolated. I kept my day job, and though I'll soon have 25 books published, I don't intend to give it up. I love going into work every day, schmoozing with my fellow teachers, talking to my students, having lunch in the lunchroom, and so forth. I even like the faculty meetings. I also was very happy that I joined the Society of Children's Book Writers and Illustrators many years ago. I read their Bulletin, chock full of news and tidbits about the publishing field. I go to meetings and conferences at which children's book authors gather. I even speak at some of them. I formed a monthly authors group that meets the second Tuesday of the month at my house. It's a self-help, therapy, professional, gossip, help-one-another, pass the cookies kind of group, and it's been enormously supportive throughout the years.

I read children's books and books about children's books. I never make the mistake of thinking that writing a book for children is easy. Some people say it's harder than writing for adults, but I wouldn't know since I've never written for adults. Its rewards are enormous, and I don't mean financial. Seeing a book you wrote displayed in the window of a bookstore is a great thrill. Having children ask for your autograph and teachers eager to meet you because you wrote a book that got published is an ego boost like no other. There are plenty of downsides, of course, especially the vault full of rejection letters that the average author collects. But about 5,000 new children's books are published in this country every year—5,000!—and somebody has to write them.

I wish I could remember who said that success happens when opportunity meets preparedness. That person was a genius. If an aspiring author prepares him- or herself—reading books, going to talks, joining groups, taking classes, and so forth—and constantly strives to improve the quality of his or her writing and, when ready, begins to submit manuscripts to logical publishers, it can happen. The opportunity will present itself if you're prepared enough. Be thick skinned, and remember that the rewards are worth the struggles. Good luck!

Seedling Publications, Inc.

4079 Overlook Drive E.
Columbus, OH 43214-2931
(614) 451-2412
(614) 451-2412 (fax)
E-mail: sales@seedlingpub.com
Web site: www.seedlingpub.com

Description: Book publisher.

Established: 1991.

Seeks: Natural language and predictable text are requisite to Seedling's publications. Patterned text acceptable, but must have a unique story line. Seedling Publications, Inc., accepts manuscripts for beginning reader texts in an 8-, 12-, or 16-page format (including the title page). Average word length not over 150 to 200 words.

Accepts unsolicited/unagented: Yes.

Description of fiction titles: Titles are for beginning readers. Please see below for examples.

Recent fiction titles:

My Class (A counting book from one to six for the youngest of readers. The boys and girls add up to 21 children ready for picture day. 8 pages/14 words.)

The Royal Family (The royal family's portrait day turns into a disaster as the royal dog and cat create chaos. Practice of basic vocabulary. 8 pages/17 words.)

The Puppet Show (One basic vocabulary word [*the*] introduces all the materials and children involved in the production of "The Gingerbread Man." Child-centered in every way. 8 pages/15 words.)

Magnets (This very simple photographic book invites the reader to predict and test theories of magnetic forces on common objects. Very interactive. 8 pages/28 words.)

Two Points (A girl tries to shoot the basket until she finally succeeds with loads of support from her friends. Great self-concept builder. 8 pages/40 words.)

I Can Write. Can You? (All those first words children write—*Mom, Dad, zoo*—are in print and in Nick's handwriting. Photographs capture functional settings for beginning writers. 8 pages/30 words.)

Here's Skipper (An energetic dog emerges from a tent to play with his owner, a young girl. Bright illustrations and bold, clear print support the youngest of readers. 8 pages/28 words.)

Runaway Monkey (This runaway monkey can be found in the most unusual places. Limited vocabulary and very supportive illustrations make this a perfect book for the very beginner. 8 pages/39 words.)

I Am (An ideal book for self-concept building within the classroom community. Ideal for a social studies unit. 8 pages/32 words.)

Jump, Frog (A frog follows a boy home after a romp around the pond. An easy read using very basic vocabulary. Clear illustrations convey the story. 8 pages/33 words.)

Squeaky Clean (Unusual vehicles went through the car wash before they entered a parade, led by a "squeaky clean" drum major. 8 pages/29 words.)

My Giraffe (A girl takes her pet giraffe on a romp through the city. So many common activities take on a new perspective! Beginning readers will romp through this easy-to-read too! 8 pages/35 words.)

Preferred titles: Poetry, books in rhyme. Full-length picture books or chapter books are not being accepted at this time.

Preferred form of submission/contact: Manuscript. Please thoroughly review the profile before making any submissions.

Prefer manuscript/illustration packages, or separate: Either. Illustrations are not necessary when making submissions.

Include with illustrator query: Resume and samples.

Tips and comments: Intent is to provide a child-sized book for a child-sized task; one in which success is guaranteed. Dedicated to the creation of high-quality early literacy books that truly support the beginning reader.

17TH STREET PRODUCTIONS

33 W. 17th Street, 11th Floor
New York, NY 10011
(212) 645-3865
(212) 633-1236 (fax)

Corporate structure/parent: Alloy Online, Inc.
Description: Packager.
Established: 1987.
Key people:
Publisher: Leslie N. Morgenstein
Acquisitions/submissions editor: Jennifer Klein
Director of development: Josh Bank
Books per year and description: 150 per year; young adult, middle grade, and early readers.
Percentage by first-time authors: 25 percent.
Seeks: Middle grade and young adult.
Accepts unsolicited/unagented: Yes.
Description of fiction titles: Series fiction for middle-grade and young adult readers.
Recent fiction titles:
Love Stories:
Sweet Valley High Senior Year
Sweet Valley University
Thoroughbred
Thoroughbred: Ashleigh
Sweet Valley Junior High
Fearless
Preferred fiction titles: Series fiction for young adult and middle-grade readers.
Description of nonfiction titles: For the teen and middle-grade market.
Preferred nonfiction titles: Original titles for young adult and middle-grade readers.
Preferred form of submission: Query.
Time to reply: Six to eight weeks.
Time to publish: Four to six months.
Accepts simultaneous submissions: Yes.
Number of illustrators used annually: Dozens.
Prefers manuscript/illustration packages, or separate: Either.
Include with illustrator query: Resumes, samples, tear sheets, and portfolio review are all acceptable.
Time to reply: Variable.
Purchases freelance photography: Yes.
Terms for writers: Variable.
Terms for illustrators: Variable.
Submission guidelines: Send an SASE with request.

Shoe String Press, Inc.

PO Box 657
2 Linsley Street
North Haven, CT 06473
(203) 239-2702
(203) 239-2558 (fax)
E-mail: books@shoestringpress.com
Web site: www.shoestringpress.com

Description: Publisher.

Seeks: Current focus is on quality nonfiction for children and young adults.

Accepts unsolicited/unagented: Yes.

Description of fiction titles: Focusing attention on nonfiction titles.

Preferred fiction titles: No poetry, picture books, or fiction.

Description of nonfiction titles: Quality nonfiction for children and young adults.

Preferred form of submission/contact: Send synopsis of your book and a few sample chapters (no more than 20 pages). Please do not send original artwork.

Time to reply: Tries to reply in a timely manner, but due to the number of submissions received on a daily basis, it could take several months.

Accepts simultaneous submissions: Does not like to consider manuscripts that are being simultaneously submitted to other publishers.

Submission guidelines: Please write with an SASE or e-mail for guidelines.

Tips and comments: If you wish to have your manuscript returned, please include SASE with ample postage. Manuscripts submitted without SASE (or ample postage) will not be returned to the author.

Sierra Club Books

85 Second Street, 2d Floor
San Francisco CA 94105-3441
(415) 977-5500
(415) 977-5799 (fax)
Web site: www.sierraclub.org

Recent nonfiction titles:

Animals You Never Even Heard Of by Patricia Curtis
Blue Potatoes, Orange Tomatoes by Rosalind Creasy
Buffalo Sunrise: The Story of a North American Giant by Diane Swanson

Preferred nonfiction titles: Sierra Club Books is seeking nonfiction projects intended for the general reader. Interested in great nature writing, first-person narratives, and all subjects relating to ecology and the environment.

Preferred form of submission/contact: Outline and sample chapter of proposed book.

Submission guidelines: Please send to Editorial Department, Sierra Club Books. Include an SASE if you would like your manuscript returned.

Meet Gary Raham

Illustrator and Author

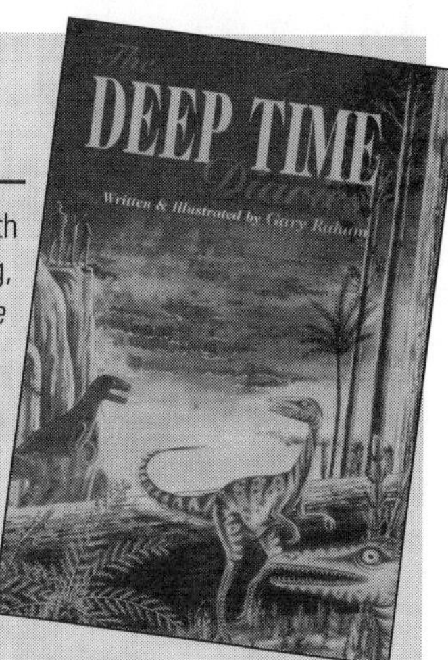

Gary Raham is the author of several books for fourth through sixth grade and above: *The Deep Time Diaries* (Fulcrum Publishing, 2000), *Explorations in Backyard Biology: Drawing on Nature in the Classroom* (Teacher Ideas Press, Libraries Unlimited, 1996), *Sillysaurs: The Dinosaurs That Could Have Been* (coloring book, Biostration, 1990), and *Dinosaurs in the Garden* (Plexus Publications, 1988). He has also written many video scripts, filmstrip scripts, articles for children's magazines, articles for adult audiences, and short stories. He was the editor of two volumes of the SCBWI Author/Illustrator Directory. He has three other book-length projects under negotiation.

Gary was born on November 12, 1946, and has B.S. and M.S. degrees in biology from the University of Michigan. After college, he taught high school and junior high science for two years at Akron, Colorado. He then worked as an illustrator and graphic designer for 27 years for a commercial printer while freelancing artwork and writing part-time. He currently operates his own business, Biostration, and divides his time between biomedical illustration, design, and book writing. He has taught courses in writing and illustrating through Colorado State University and the Colorado School of Mines. He does volunteer work with the Master Naturalist Program of the City of Fort Collins and has edited newsletters for the Guild of Natural Science Illustrators and the Fort Collins Rockhounds.

How did you get your first book published?

The book was much easier to write than to get published. The initial idea was circulated by an agent for Bess Wallace Agency for a year. She got some nibbles, but nothing firm. She contacted at least nine or 10 publishers. After this time, the agent left to go back into teaching and the manuscript reverted to me. I submitted the idea to a publisher in Florida (Flora and Fauna Publications) who liked the concept immediately. The lead came through a Writer's Digest market listing. The publisher wanted a completed manuscript within a year. I needed longer, writing and illustrating part-time. I worked on the project six months, submitted what I had, and said I could now complete the rest within a year. He offered a contract and $500 advance with the completed manuscript. I completed the manuscript on schedule, but by that time the editor had a chance to sell the publishing part of his business overseas. He contracted to have Plexus Publishing do the prepress work and publishing. They were supposed to complete this in one year, but it took closer to two and a half years. The advance was nearly a year late as well. The good news: *Dinosaurs in the Garden* is a quality hardback book that was well reviewed and is still in print. Total income has been no more than $6,000 with over half that coming the first year after publication. This would not be considered a typical children's book but is more a book for the young naturalist of about junior high age or older.

continues

Do you have any advice, in terms of finding a publisher, for a writer starting out?

Find out who publishes books that you admire and that fit with your interests by visiting bookstores and libraries. Look them up in references like *Writer's Market* and *Children's Writers and Illustrator's Market* to find the names of editors and addresses for Web sites. Watch for writer's conferences that may be featuring editors from houses you admire. The Society of Children's Book Writers and Illustrators (SCBWI) has a national Web site at www.scbwi.org that lists events nationwide. Regional SCBWI chapters like mine—the Rocky Mountain Region—also have Web sites (www.rmcscbwi.org). Join a writers group and/or a writer's e-mail mailing list on an Internet provider, and network on the information superhighway.

Are your books illustrated?

Being an illustrator, too, I have always illustrated my own work with both art and photos. But usually the choice of illustrator is best left to the art director at your publishing house. They know who does the right work in a professional manner. Educational publishers, however, may require that you find (and pay for) your own illustrations.

Do you have any advice, in terms of finding an illustrator, for a writer starting out?

The same networking techniques apply as for finding a publisher. Many areas are developing organizations for self-publishers, however, and these organizations may have members who are illustrators. CIPA (Colorado Independent Publishers Association) operates out of Denver and CPP (Centennial Pens and Publishers) operates in northern Colorado. You can sometimes find hungry, young artists in local universities through their art departments. Artist organizations include the Graphic Artist's Guild, the Guild of Natural Science Illustrators, and the Society of Illustrators. Well-known illustrators may be booked a year or more ahead.

What procedures do you follow when you write?

It's important to write regularly, even if it's only for a short time each day. Set a time to write and make that a priority in your day. Keep a small notebook handy to jot down those sudden inspirations, though.

Where do you get your ideas?

I read constantly in many areas and jot down ideas on scraps of paper. If an idea seems really promising, I give it a manila folder and start collecting related information. The more you "ideate," the easier it gets. Before long you find that you always have your "antennas" out and wiggling for interesting concepts.

What do you think are the key differences between writing for children and writing for adults?

Writing for children is condensed, tightly focused writing. Adults might give you several paragraphs to "hook" them, but you must catch children's attention immediately with an exciting lead. Adults will read longer pieces while children's articles are typically 500 to 1,000 words long. You can take pride if you can explain how an insect eye works, for example, in just a few, nontechnical words. Good picture books may take many revisions to make every word work just so. Like poetry, they are condensed language with several levels of meaning woven together. The great thing about writing for kids is that their curiosity about many subjects is high.

How did you learn to write?

I had a natural aptitude for writing and did well in creative writing exercises in school. I had no other formal training, but when I decided to pursue writing seriously I joined a science fiction writers group in Denver. Everyone was talented, and many had published works. Once you survive the first few self-image-denting critiques, you learn a lot very quickly about effective writing—as long as you continue writing on a regular basis. For commercial science writing, I had to unlearn some of the techniques used to write formal, scientific papers—things like using active rather than passive verbs and using language accessible to everyone, not just the scientifically literate.

Anything you really wish somebody had told you when you started out?

Decide whether writing is really important to you. If it is, make time for it. Don't expect to make a lot of money doing it—especially in the short run. It's all right to fit writing in around child raising or another job. It may help if the other job is either related to what you write about, pertains to some other aspect of publishing, and does not consume huge hunks of your discretionary time. Read tons of good books to plant a template of quality writing in your brain. Network. Prime yourself with writing skills and place yourself in the path of success, and opportunity will eventually run into you.

Silver Moon Press

160 Fifth Avenue
New York, NY 10010
(800) 874-3320
(212) 242-6799 (fax)
Web site: www.silvermoonpress.com

Books per year and description: In just a few years Silver Moon has created nearly 50 titles in such areas as science, multiculture, and biographies. Silver Moon's biggest and most exciting area of study, however, is historical fiction. Silver Moon publishes American historical fiction and has a particular interest in New York State history and the Revolutionary War.

Recent fiction titles:

Stories of the States series (10 titles; exciting historical novels that show the diversity and strength of our American culture. Each volume concludes with a short "Historical Postscript" that tells more about the real people depicted in the story, and provides valuable background information on the era described.)

Recent nonfiction titles:

GET INSIDE GUIDES series (two titles; focuses on familiar topics and shows us that there's much more to them than meets the eye. What really happens behind the scenes at a ranch? What do insiders and experts know about baseball?)

SCIENCE LAB series (four titles; shows youngsters the relationship between science in the classroom and science in the real world)

Number of illustrators used annually: Five or six.

Desired illustrator qualifications: Silver Moon prefers realistic style. Silver Moon uses its illustrators to create 10 black-and-white interior illustrations for our historical adventures.

Include with illustrator query: Illustrators should send their samples or postcards to Karin Lillebo. None of the artwork will be returned, so they should not send portfolios of original artwork.

SILVER WHISTLE

15 E. 26th Street
New York, NY 10010
(212) 592-1005
(212) 592-1010 (fax)

Corporate structure/parent: Silver Whistle is an imprint of Harcourt Trade Publishers (which is a division of Harcourt, Inc.).

Description: Children's book publisher.

Key people:

Editorial director: Paula Wiseman

Acquisitions/submissions editor: Tamson Weston, associate editor

Books per year and description: 16 to 20 board books, picture books, and novels.

Percentage by first-time authors: 10 percent.

Seeks: Original and exciting manuscripts with a strong voice, in both picture books and novels.

Accepts unsolicited/unagented: Yes.

Description of fiction titles: Literary fiction with a strong voice and a timeless quality.

Recent fiction titles:

Auntie Claus by Elise Primavera

Hoops by Robert Burleigh; illustrated by Stephen Johnson

My Little Red Toolbox by Stephen Johnson

Description of nonfiction titles: A varied list of biography and general nonfiction.

Preferred nonfiction titles: All types for all ages.

Preferred form of submission/contact: Query for novels; complete manuscript for picture books.

Time to reply: Two months.

Time to publish: One year in fiction; varies for picture books for when the author can deliver.

Accepts simultaneous submissions: Yes.

Prefer manuscript/illustration packages, or separate? Accepts packages.

Include with illustrator query: Samples.

Time to reply: Views portfolios in the office on Tuesdays, when authors bring them in. They can pick them up the same day. When samples are mailed, they are kept on file but the company generally does not respond.

Purchases freelance photography: No.

Submission guidelines: Send an SASE.

Simon & Schuster Books for Young Readers

Simon & Schuster
1230 Avenue of the Americas
New York, NY 10020
Web site: www.simonsays.com

Corporate structure/parent: Simon & Schuster.

Description: Simon & Schuster Children's Publishing, one of the leading children's book publishers in the world, is composed of the following imprints: Aladdin Paperbacks, Atheneum Books for Young Readers, Little Simon, Margaret K. McElderry Books, Rabbit Ears Audio Books, Simon & Schuster Books for Young Readers, and Simon Spotlight. While maintaining an extensive award-winning backlist, the division continues to publish acclaimed and best-selling books for children of all ages—including such high-profile characters as Eloise, Raggedy Ann & Andy, Henry & Mudge, and Shiloh. Simon Spotlight, an imprint wholly devoted to media tie-ins, has become one of the fastest-growing imprints in the children's book industry, with bestselling series based on Nickelodeon's Rugrats, Blue's Clues, CatDog, The Wild Thornberrys, and Jim Henson's Bear in the Big Blue House properties.

Seeks: Publishes books in all categories—fiction, nonfiction, YA, picture books, board books, and so forth.

Accepts unsolicited/unagented: Unfortunately, due to the workload of the editorial staff, S&S cannot accept unsolicited manuscripts. If you are seeking publication, S&S recommends you have an agent represent you and your work. S&S regrets that it isn't able to recommend a specific agent but wishes you success in finding a home for your manuscript.

Soundprints

353 Main Avenue
Norwalk, CT 06851
(203) 846-2274
(203) 846-1776 (fax)
E-mail: sndprnts@ix.netcom.com
Web site: www.soundprints.com

Corporate structure/parent: Trudy Corporation.

Description: Book publisher; children's books.

Established: 1987.

Key people:

Associate publisher: Ashley Anderson

President: Bill Burnham

Editorial assistant: Chelsea Shriver

Books per year and description: 16.

Percentage by first-time authors: 0 percent.

Seeks: Fact-based fiction. Nature, multiculturalism, and history. No anthropomorphic animals.

Accepts unsolicited/unagented: No.

Description of fiction titles: All fact-based and stemming from true events or facts.

Recent fiction titles:

Bumblebee at Apple Tree Road by Laura Galvin (A bumblebee queen prepares her hive for spring.)

Sori's Harvest Moon Day (A young Korean girl prepares for the Korean festival of Chu-Suk.)

Preferred titles: No anthropomorphism of animals; well-researched subject matter.

Preferred form of submission/contact: Query.

Time to reply: Six weeks.

Number of illustrators used annually: 12.

Desired illustrator qualifications: Realism.

Prefer manuscript/illustration packages, or separate: Separately.

Purchases freelance photography: No.

Terms for writers: Work for hire; no royalties.

Terms for illustrators: 5 percent royalties.

Submission guidelines: Send an SASE with request for guidelines or request via e-mail.

STEMMER HOUSE PUBLISHERS, INC.

2627 Caves Road
Owings Mills, MD 21117
(410) 363-3690
(410) 363-8459 (fax)
E-mail: stemmerhouse@home.com
Web site: www.stemmer.com

Description: Book publisher.

Established: 1975.

Key people:

Publisher: Barbara Holdridge

Acquisitions/submissions editor: Barbara Holdridge

Books per year and description: One or two picture books.

Percentage by first-time authors: 50 percent.

Seeks: Nonfiction primarily (e.g., natural history).
Accepts unsolicited/unagented: Yes.
Description of fiction titles: Folktales primarily or fact-based fiction.
Recent fiction titles:
My Ocean Liner: Across the North Atlantic on the Great Ship Normandie by Peter Mandel
Description of nonfiction titles: Mostly natural history.
Recent nonfiction titles:
Ask Me If I'm a Frog by Ann Milton (questions and answers about frogs)
Preferred form of submission/contact: Query or manuscript.
Time to reply: One to two weeks.
Time to publish: Two to three years.
Accepts simultaneous submissions: Yes.
Number of illustrators used annually: Two or three.
Desired illustrator qualifications: Realism
Prefers manuscript/illustration packages, or separate: No preference; does accept packages.
Include with illustrator query: Samples.
Time to reply: One to two weeks.
Purchases freelance photography: No, only if the author supplies it with the text.
Terms for writers: Royalties.
Terms for illustrators: Same.
Tips and comments: Send an SASE for catalog to familiarize yourself with the kind of things Stemmer publishes. *For authors:* no rhymed stories. *For illustrators:* no anthropomorphism.

Story Place

1735 Brantley Road, #1611
Fort Meyers, FL 33902
(775) 206-7437 (fax)
E-mail: tsp@thestoryplace.com
Web site: www.thestoryplace.com

Description: Publisher focusing on new and different ideas.

Teacher Created Materials

PO Box 1040
Huntington Beach, CA 92647
Web site: www.teachercreated.com

Description: Educational publisher.
Key people:
Editor in Chief

Seeks: Educational books successfully tested in the classroom, written by credentialed professionals.

Accepts unsolicited/unagented: Yes.

Description of nonfiction titles: Educational materials for classroom use.

Recent nonfiction titles:

1000 Instant Words by Dr. Fry

Five Senses Thematic Unit

Baseball Easy Reader

Submission guidelines: Send an SASE or check Web site; mail submissions to the editor in chief. Please submit 10 to 12 sample pages (minimum requirement); a tentative outline or table of contents; a one-page summary describing the intended audience, content, and objectives of your manuscript; a self-addressed envelope with sufficient postage if you would like your material returned. No electronic submissions.

Through the Bible Publishers

1133 Riverside Avenue
Fort Collins, CO 80524
(970) 484-8483
(970) 495-6700 (fax)
E-mail: discipleland@throughthebible.com
Web site: www.throughthebible.com

Description: Through the Bible Publishers exists to help the Church of Jesus Christ fulfill the Great Commission. Through the Bible creates and distributes Christian education resources that feature excellence in biblical content, educational methodology and product presentation. Through the Bible's primary responsibility is to serve the local and international Church.

Established: 1935.

Seeks: Seeking freelance writers of Bible curriculum for elementary-level children who are willing to generate alternative activities and questions, along with rewriting and fine-tuning existing text. Looks for the following qualities: a knowledge of and love for the Word of God; creativity and originality; ability to produce material appropriate to grade level; willingness to carefully follow directions and rewrite, if necessary; ability and determination to meet deadlines; capability of submitting both hard and soft copy.

Accepts unsolicited/unagented: Yes.

Preferred form of submission/contact: If you believe you can help Through the Bible, please submit a resume along with samples of your materials written for children to Guidelines@ThroughTheBible.com or fax to (970) 495-6700.

Submission guidelines: Send to Andrea Taylor, project director at DiscipleLand.

Tips and comments: DiscipleLand is a new Bible curriculum designed to help children ages 2 to 14 reach their fullest potential in Christ. It challenges kids to go deeper into the Bible and equips them to be disciples of Jesus.

Tilbury House, Publishers

2 Mechanic Street
Gardiner, ME 04345
(800) 582-1899
(207) 582-8227 (fax)
E-mail: tilbury@tilburyhouse.com
Web site: www.tilburyhouse.com

Description: Book publisher.

Established: The original company, Harpswell Press, is approximately 30 years old. Harpswell merged with Dog Ear Press in 1990 and took the name Tilbury House.

Key people:

Publisher: Jennifer Elliott

Acquisitions/submissions editor: Jennifer Elliott

Books per year: Two.

Percentage by first-time authors: 20 percent.

Seeks: Books that explore cultural diversity, nature, and the environment.

Accepts unsolicited/unagented: Yes.

Recent fiction titles:

Shy Mama's Halloween by Anne Broyles; illustrated by Leane Morin

Lights for Gita by Rachna Gilmore; illustrated by Alice Priestley

Preferred fiction titles: Looking for original content that crosses borders—real and imaginary.

Description of nonfiction titles: Science, history, and regional (Maine).

Recent nonfiction titles:

Sea Soup: Phytoplankton by Mary M. Cerullo, photography by Bill Curtsinger (children's science; grades 3–7)

Project Puffin: How We Brought Puffins Back to Egg Rock by Stephen W. Kress, as told to Pete Salmansohn

Preferred nonfiction titles: Engaging text related to science, history, and regional (Maine) subjects.

Preferred form of submission/contact: Query or manuscript.

Time to reply: One month or sooner.

Time to publish: One to two years.

Accepts simultaneous submissions: Yes, if notified on submission.

Number of illustrators used annually: Two to three per year.

Desired illustrator qualifications: Realism; *no* cartoons.

Prefer manuscript/illustration packages, or separate: Either way.

Include with illustrator query: Samples, postcards, and color photocopies.

Time to reply: If an SASE is enclosed, will acknowledge receipt of the artist's materials (which will be kept on file).

Purchases freelance photography: Rarely.

Terms for writers: Standard royalty contract.

Terms for illustrators: Standard royalty contract.

Submission guidelines: Request via mail with an SASE or on Web site.

Tips and comments: Look at catalog and guidelines on the Web site. Realize that this is a small publisher with a specific niche. To improve your chances, try to fit the company's focus.

TIME WARNER BOOKS

1271 Avenue of the Americas
New York, NY 10020
Web site: www.twbookmark.com

Accepts unsolicited/unagented: No. Unfortunately, Time Warner Trade Publishing is not able to consider unsolicited manuscript submissions at this time (the same applies to unsolicited jacket art submissions), nor can Time Warner recommend any literary agents. Many major publishers have a similar policy. If you are interested in having a manuscript considered for publication by a major book publisher, Time Warner recommends that you first enlist the services of an established literary agent.

TOMMY NELSON

404 BNA Drive, Building 200, Suite 508
Nashville, TN 37217
(615) 902-2415 (fax)
Web site: www.tommynelson.com

Corporate structure/parent: Tommy Nelson, the children's company of NelsonWord Publishing Group, publishes original, children's material that is well written and/or illustrated and that has spiritual value for girls and boys from birth through age 14.

Accepts unsolicited/unagented: Yes.

Preferred fiction titles: Stories that demonstrate values in general, rather than Christian values, usually aren't as specific as the Christian Booksellers Association (CBA) market demands.

Preferred nonfiction titles: Same.

Preferred form of submission/contact: For picture books, please send a complete manuscript. For juvenile fiction, send a synopsis and a sample chapter. All manuscripts must be typed, double-spaced, with page number and title at the top of every page. Please include your name and address on the cover/title page of the manuscript. Enclose a self-addressed postage-paid mailer for your manuscript to be returned. Otherwise, your materials will not be returned. *All proposals must have a spiritual takeaway but must not be authoritarian or preachy.*

Time to reply: Please allow 10 to 12 weeks for response, due to the length of the review process.

Meet Virginia Allyn

Illustrator

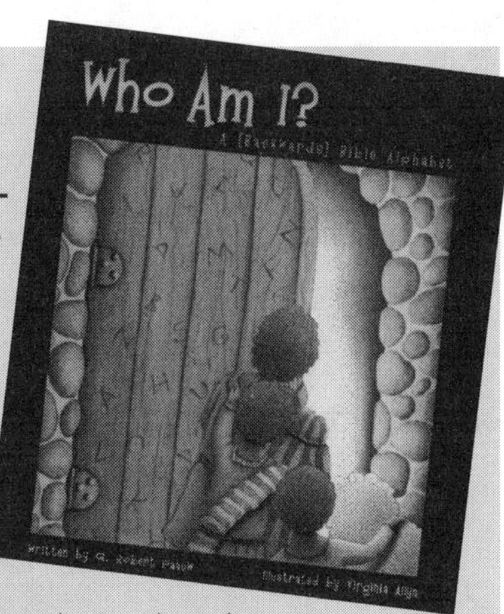

Virginia Allyn is the illustrator of *Who Am I? A Backwards Bible Alphabet* by G. Robert Paauw (IBS Publishing, March 2001). She was born in Americus, Georgia, in 1962, and graduated in 1980 from Manatee High School in Bradenton, Florida. She was and is a Federal Express dispatcher. She does her illustration work at night and on weekends. She's a single mom with a 19-year-old daughter, Megan, who is getting the formal art training she never had (she is a freshman at The Ringling School of Art in Sarasota, Florida). She likes to illustrate for the five-and-over group, so she can throw in a lot of little silly, funny things, and the kids will be old enough to catch them.

How did you get your first book published?

I have always wanted to be an artist. When I was in grade school, my favorite time was when the teacher gave us sheets of manila paper and told us to get out our crayons. I loved everything about art: The smell of the paper, the names of the crayons—bittersweet, goldenrod, midnight blue (still my favorite color)—and having your picture put up on the blackboard.

One day a man from the newspaper came to kindergarten class to take photos of our artwork. Well, let me tell you, I colored my little heart out and sure enough that weekend there was my picture in full color in the Sunday paper—my first published work! My mom still has that picture and the Sunday paper! After graduating from high school, I spent the next 20 years raising my daughter as a single parent. I couldn't afford to go to art school, and I didn't know any other way of "becoming" an artist so I let that dream go for a while. I had a secure job, a comfortable house, a great daughter, and life was good. I still loved to draw and color. I illustrated letters and packages to my family, and birthday cards, but I never thought I could do anything professionally with it without the proper schooling.

Then, the dreaded day came when my daughter started talking about going off to college. Yikes! She was leaving and I was going to be sitting home alone eating TV dinners and doodling on the *People* magazine. The next day I went to the art store and bought some oil paints and watercolors and brought them home. I practiced painting every night after work and every weekend and through trial and error, I taught myself how to use the different brushes, mediums, canvas, and paper. I studied other artists and tried to develop a style of my own. I decided I would try to be a greeting card illustrator because I had long admired Mary Engelbreit and Susan Branch's artwork.

But one day, in the children's section of a bookstore, I had the "lightning bolt" moment. On one of the shelves standing face out was a copy of William Joyce's *Santa Calls*. I had never seen artwork like that in a children's book, and I decided right then and there that I was going to be a

continues

children's book illustrator no matter what it took. I bought the book and hurried home. I started drawing illustrations for the classic fairy tales and nursery rhymes. I did a lot of Humpty Dumpty because I like to paint eggs. I also went on the Internet and searched for other children's book illustrators, and eventually I found the Children's Writers and Illustrator's message board (www.write4kids.com). I started reading the postings everyday, and I learned a lot about starting out in the publishing world. I also met someone there who changed my life. She was a wonderful writer with five books under contract. One day she posted a beautiful poem on the board, and I thought it would be good practice for me to do an illustration for it. So I worked on it that night, and the next day I scanned it in and sent it to her via e-mail. She immediately wrote me back and asked to see more examples of my artwork. Well, this was the first time anyone outside my family had shown interest in my artwork, and I was over the moon! I sent her the best pieces I had and she wrote back and told me how to put a professional portfolio together and how to submit it to publishers. I was still working on the portfolio when she e-mailed excitedly one day to tell me she had shown my original samples to an agent friend of hers and that the agent was interested in representing me. Wheee!

Two days later, I signed on with the Melanie Colbert Agency and that was in December of 1999. Also, during that Christmas vacation, my daughter put together a Web site to showcase my portfolio. Everything was falling into place, and I couldn't believe my good luck but incredibly, it was about to get better. In July, I got an e-mail from the associate editor at IBS Publishing saying she had seen my Web site and loved the illustrations. She went on to describe a children's alphabet book they were publishing based on Bible verse, and she asked me whether I would be interested in illustrating it. The book would be 64 pages long and require 26 full-color illustrations and each letter of the alphabet illustrated.

Woo-hoo!

I e-mailed her back to say I was very interested and gave her my agent's name to contact. In the meantime, I worked up three sample illustrations (one rough sketch, one pen and ink, and one with oil glaze added over the pen and ink) and e-mailed them to the associate editor. I suggested that the pen-and-ink stage could be scanned and used as a companion coloring book before the oil glaze was added. They liked the idea and the samples, and they called my agent and she negotiated the contract. (This is one of the many reasons I am so thankful to have an agent. She understands all the complicated nuances of a publishing contract that I don't have the time or desire to learn.) Soon, the book designer was sending me the complete manuscript with illustration notes included, and I started working on the rough sketches. Sometimes if I had a question I would scan in the sketch and e-mail it to the designer, and she could give me immediate feedback. After the roughs were approved, I started the pen-and-ink drawings. When they were finished, I sent them off to the publisher to be scanned for the coloring book. After the scanning, they were sent back to me for application of the oil glazes. The final artwork was finished on time in December 2000 and the book, *Who Am I? A Backwards Bible Alphabet,* came out in March 2001.

I could not have had a better experience with a publisher. The editor and book designer were a dream to work with. I had never considered that my first book would be for the religious market, but now I'm very thankful I got to work with such wonderful professionals.

Do you have any advice, in terms of finding an agent, for an illustrator starting out?

Network. Join an illustrating message board and make connections. Having a Web site can only help you, and it's great to be able to say, "You can see samples of my artwork at www.virginiaallyn.com"

Are you still with your first publisher?

I would happily work with IBS again because it was such a great experience. I'm also looking forward to working with more mainstream publishers.

Do you have any advice, in terms of finding a publisher, for an illustrator starting out?

Try to get an agent. But while you are looking for an agent, read about the different publisher's requirements, and make sure you are submitting appropriate material. Put together as professional a portfolio as you can. If your artwork is great, you'll get noticed through the slush.

Do you write the text for the books you illustrate?

I did not write the first book I illustrated; G. Robert Paauw did. But I do love to write and work at night in bed on my laptop computer. My portfolio includes illustrated rhymes and stories.

What procedures do you follow when you work?

I still work a full-time job, so I have to do my artwork at night and on the weekends. I turned my daughter's bedroom into a studio after she left for college. It made me feel a little better about her leaving—well, actually, a lot better. It's a big room, and I like having my drawing table and the computer, printer, and scanner all in the same room. While I was working on the book, I would come home from work at 5:30 every night, eat dinner, and then go straight to work on the illustrations. Sometimes I wouldn't quit until one or two in the morning. When you start painting and everything is flowing right, the time just flies by.

Where do you get your ideas?

I keep a sketchbook journal and floppy disks with me at all times, and I fill them with little scraps of ideas that pop into my head. I also keep a yellow pad by the bed because my best ideas come at four in the morning. I've learned to sketch in the dark! For some reason, food inspires many of my rhymes. I just finished one called "Blue Cheese Moon." I also have rhymes about peas, onions, marmalade, sea grape jelly—whatever I was craving on a particular day, I suppose.

Anything you really wish somebody had told you when you started out?

Stop dilly-dallying! You certainly won't get published if you don't submit anything. Get online and start up a critique group; then keep practicing and learning until you feel you're ready. I have a little sign on my desk that I live by; it says, "Tomorrow's just an excuse away." Don't put off your dream for another day. You can do it.

Submission guidelines: With your submission, please include the following: a little about yourself (background, experience, publishing history); a short summary of your proposal; why your idea is different from other Christian books/products already on the market; the target market of your product idea.

Tips and comments: Because the company sells primarily to the CBA market, writers and illustrators who would like to publish with Tommy Nelson should become familiar with children's book in CBA stores. *We cannot respond to phone or fax inquiries.*

TOR/FORGE BOOKS

175 Fifth Avenue
New York, NY 10010
(212) 388-0100
(212) 388-0191(fax)
Web site: www.tor.com

Corporate structure/parent: Tom Doherty Associates, LLC.

Description: Publisher of trade books. Full-category, hardcover and mass-market books.

Established: 1980.

Key people:

Publisher and president: Thomas Doherty
Publisher, children's and YA division: Kathleen Doherty
Associate publisher and vice president, marketing: Linda Quinton
Acquisitions/submissions editor: Jonathan Schmidt

Books per year and description: 15 to 25 books; all categories.

Percentage by first-time authors: 0 to 2 percent.

Seeks: Middle grade through YA; all categories.

Accepts unsolicited/unagented: Yes.

Description of fiction titles: Diverse.

Recent fiction titles:

Hidden Talents by David Lubar (fiction, YA)
Jumping Off the Planet by David Gerrold (scientific, YA)
Not with our Blood by Elizabeth Masse (historical fiction, YA)

Preferred fiction titles: Always in search of a good, strong story.

Description of nonfiction titles: Accurate, fun-fact, popular offbeat subjects.

Recent nonfiction titles:

Encyclopedia Weird by Sheila De LaRosa
How to Get Straight A's by Gordon W. Green
Face to Face with the Unknown by Sherri Stieger

Preferred nonfiction titles: Looking for unique concepts, popular subjects.

Preferred form of submission/contact: Send manuscript, query if below middle-grade readership.

Time to reply: Three months.

Time to publish: 18 to 24 months.

Accepts simultaneous submissions: No.
Number of illustrators used annually: 10 or more.
Purchases freelance photography: Yes.
Terms for writers: Advance against royalties.
Submission guidelines: Send letter of request with an SASE.
Tips and comments: Become familiar with what the company is publishing and submit appropriately.

TRADEWIND BOOKS, LTD.

2216 Stephens Street
Vancouver, British Columbia V6K 3W6
Canada
E-mail: tradewindbooks@eudoramail.com
Web site: ww.tradewindbooks.com/tradewindbooks/index.html

Description: Publisher.
Accepts unsolicited/unagented: Yes.
Recent fiction titles:

The Girl Who Lost Her Smile by Karim Alrawi; illustrated by Stefan Czernecki (In the wondrous city of Baghdad lives a young girl called Jehan. One morning, Jehan wakes and sees that her smile is lost. She looks everywhere. Jugglers and fire-eaters come to help her find it. Artists paint murals on the walls of her room. They all try their hardest to entertain Jehan, but still, she cannot find her smile. Published in the United States by Winslow Press.)

Wherever Bears Be by Sue Ann Alderson; illustrated by Arden Johnson (published in the United States by Tricycle Books, Berkeley, California; in Canada and the United Kingdom by Tradewind Books)

Mr. Belinsky's Bagels by Ellen Schwartz; illustrated by Stefan Czernecki (Mr. Belinsky's bagel shop, frequented by a colorful group of loyal neighborhood customers, is threatened with competition.)

Where Are My Onions? by Paulette Sarmonpol; illustrated by Silvia Vignale

Preferred form of submission/contact: All submissions must include an indication that writers have actually seen at least three of the publisher's books. *No unsolicited manuscripts will be accepted without this proviso.* Picture book manuscripts are accepted with an SASE. Sample chapters only of novels for young readers, accompanied by an outline of the text.

TRANSWORLD CHILDREN'S BOOKS

61–63 Uxbridge Road
Ealing, London W5 5SA
United Kingdom
(02) 0 8579 2652
(02) 0 8579 5479

Description: Book publisher.

Established: 1950.

Key people:

Publisher: Philippa Dickinson

Books per year: 60 to 80.

Percentage by first-time authors: 10 percent.

Seeks: Original and innovative stories—from picture books to complex novels for older children. Strong and imaginative titles.

Accepts unsolicited/unagented: Yes.

Description of fiction titles: They have a broad appeal; high-quality writing for children of all ages.

Recent fiction titles:

Bad Dreams by Anne Fine

Midnight over Sanctaphrax by Paul Stewart and Chris Riddell

Billy the Bird by Dick King-Smith

Preferred form of submission/contact: Manuscript, cover letter, and an SASE.

Time to reply: One month.

Time to publish: One year.

Accepts simultaneous submissions: Yes.

Prefer manuscript/illustration packages, or separate: Fine together.

Include with illustrator query: Resume and samples.

Time to reply: One month.

Terms for writers: Variable by project.

Terms for illustrators: Variable by project.

Submission guidelines: By writing to the editorial department with a request or phoning.

Tips and comments: Create your own style; the company does not encourage/endorse stylistic copies of other author's work.

Trellis Publishing

PO Box 16141
Duluth, MN 55816
(715) 399-0780
(715) 399-0781 (fax)
E-mail: trellis@trellispublishing.com
Web site: www.trellispublishing.com

Description: Publisher. Trellis was an idea in 1996—could a publishing company be formed to concentrate only on one character, and then develop that character into more than one book or product? Trellis is the answer!

Established: 1996.

Key people:

Author: Mary Koski

Director of publicity and promotion: Angel Carlson

Recent fiction titles:

Impatient Pamela Calls 9-1-1 by Mary Koski; illustrated by Dan Brown

Impatient Pamela Says: "Learn How to Call 9-1-1!" by Mary Koski and Lori Collins

Impatient Pamela Asks: "Why Are My Feet So Huge?" by Mary Koski

Tips and comments: Trellis's first book, *Impatient Pamela Calls 9-1-1,* was two years in the making, since all facets of the publishing business had to be learned—art direction, production and printing, transportation, distribution, marketing, and promotion. Each stage has its own challenges and rewards, but nothing was as exciting as having the first book roll off the press in June 1998.

TRICYCLE PRESS

PO Box 7123
Berkeley, CA 94707
(510) 559-1600
(510) 559-1626
Web site: www.tenspeed.com

Corporate structure/parent: Ten Speed Press.

Description: Children's book publisher.

Established: 1993.

Key people:

Publisher: Nicole Geiger

Acquisitions/submissions editors: Nicole Geiger, Summer Laurie, and Abigail Samoun

Books per year and description: 20 to 25 books; cookbooks, picture books, fiction, activity, learning and young adult chapter books.

Percentage by first-time authors: 60 percent.

Accepts unsolicited/unagented: Yes.

Description of fiction titles: Stories that are different from the average—humor, highlighting different cultures, and lyrical illustrations and text.

Recent fiction titles:

The Pumpkin Blanket by Deborah Twiney Zagwÿn (This tells a story about Clee, her blanket, autumn, and loss.)

Storm Boy by Paul Owen Lewis (A young Native American prince finds himself in the land of the whale people—illustrated with Northwest motifs.)

The Diary of Chickabiddy Baby by Emma Kallok (This reads like a private summer journal. The author was 10 when she wrote this.)

Preferred fiction titles: Fresh ideas, original stories, characters that will touch the readers—nontraditional stories. Not after stories that more conventional publishing houses might publish.

Recent nonfiction titles:

G Is for Google by David Schwartz (teaches math in a fun, light-hearted manner for children 8 and up)

Tractor-Trailer-Trucker: All about Trucking by Joyce Slayton Mitchell (full-color photos for children ages 7 and up)

Preferred form of submission/contact: Would prefer that nonagented authors send a complete manuscript for picture books or a first chapter and outline for longer works. Please, *no* query letters.

Time to reply: Eight to 16 weeks.

Time to publish: Variable, though most often a book will be published between six months and two years after acceptance.

Accepts simultaneous submissions: Yes.

Desired illustrator qualifications: An original style that communicates emotion—characters that readers can seize on.

Prefer manuscript/illustration packages, or separate: Unless the author can also illustrate at a *professional* level, separate submissions are preferred.

Include with illustrator query: Samples with a variety of subjects and situations.

Time to reply: Keeps illustrators' samples on file and reviews them when a project arises that needs illustrating.

Purchases freelance photography: Yes.

Preferred photography: Professional-quality work and a really good eye.

Terms for writers: Negotiable based on contract.

Terms for illustrators: Same.

Submission guidelines: Send an SASE with a request for guidelines, or go to the Ten Speed Web site.

Tips and comments: Please review guidelines *before* submitting a manuscript. Looking for an original style but also characters with whom children will feel an emotional connection.

TROLL BOOK CLUBS/PUBLISHING

100 Corporate Drive
Mahwah, NJ 07430-9986
Web site: www.troll.com

Description: Troll releases entertaining, inspiring, and informative children's books for the retail market, ages 4 to 12.

Seeks: Troll publishes outstanding books for children from the age of 4 to 14 that entertain, inspire, or inform.

Accepts unsolicited/unagented: No.

Submission guidelines: Troll considers only agented manuscripts.

Tips and comments: Many Troll books have won prestigious literary awards, including the coveted Coretta Scott King Honor Award, the American Bookseller Pick of the Lists, the Bologna Book Award, and the Parents' Choice Award. Recent successes have included the critically acclaimed *I Love You Stinky Face* and the best-selling Grumpy Bunny series. For more than 40 years, Troll Book Clubs have helped America's educators encourage a life-long love of learning and reading in their students. Every month, Troll

Meet Kersten Hamilton

Author

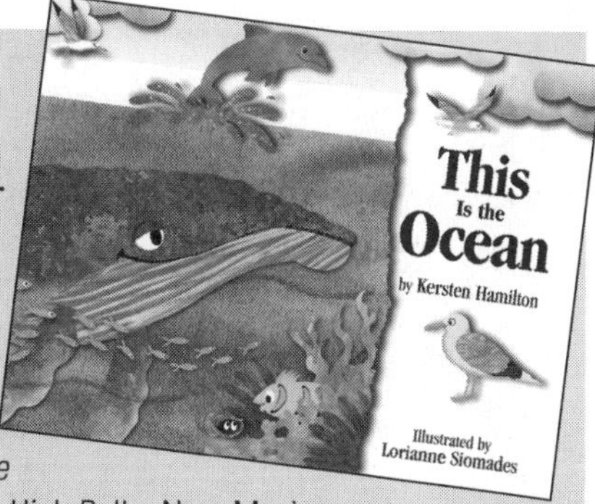

Kersten Hamilton is the author of *Natalie Jean and the Haints Parade* (Tyndale, 1991); *Rockabye Rabbit* (Cool Kids Press, 1995); *The Butterfly Book: A Kid's Guide to Attracting, Raising and Keeping Butterflies* (John Muir Publications, 1997); *This Is the Ocean* (Boyds Mills Press, 2001); and *Firefighters to the Rescue* (Viking, forthcoming). She was born in a trailer park in High Rolls, New Mexico, on October 19, 1958 . . . or maybe it was 1959. Her parents, who were not very practical people, neglected to inform anyone of her arrival. After their divorce when she was six, she filled out the paperwork herself whenever she moved from school to school (and they moved a lot), so the dates never matched. So she had no birth certificate, no social security card, and no reliable paper records. This eventually added a great deal of trauma to her life. Which is a good thing, if you want to be a writer. It is always helpful to start early and have an interesting life!

Kersten decided to become a writer when she was six years old. "That has always been my focus," she says, "but I don't seem to be able to get there the same way other people do. I did finish the ninth grade before I dropped out of high school. I loved learning, but the things I knew I needed to become a writer were hard for me. I could not spell. I would study every day for a week, only to bring home another F in spelling. Reading came slowly. The words on the page didn't make sense to me phonetically. I did know that I needed to learn to type. It took me a couple of semesters in middle school to manage a D+, as I recall. My real education—the one that matters most—came through living. As a child, I tracked caribou and arctic wolves in Alaska, caught tiny tree frogs in the swamps and rain forests of the Pacific Northwest, and chased dust devils and rattlesnakes across the high desert of New Mexico. I explored every piece of the world I could touch, taste, smell, or throw a rock at."

Before she became a children's book author, she worked as a ranch hand, a wood cutter, a lumberjack, a census taker, a wrangler for wilderness guides, and an archaeological surveyor. She fried donuts for a while, worked as a nanny, and was a personal companion to an elderly lady. After she married, she trained as an EMT and ran a day care for medically fragile children to help support the family while her husband finished school.

How did you get your first book published?

I started working on becoming a writer at six; I wrote my first novel at 19; I submitted my first book at 21; I sold my first books at 28. Sometime between 21 and 28, I gave up counting my rejection slips. I simply made bonfires of them every few months. I had spent my whole life learning about story, how to move the reader, how to make them laugh and cry, but I had no respect for rules. I didn't understand that writing well is not enough. For instance, there are reasons that picture book text, chapter books, or novels should be a certain length. Editors live inside a world governed by rules, and the rules are enforced by budget constraints. No matter how brilliant the

continues

writing is, the chances of an editor getting a picture book that has 10 pages of text past the acquisitions committee is very small, because it will cost more to produce. Learn everything you can about the business of book selling! My first book sales were a direct result of understanding that editors have specific needs. If you write well and can meet those needs, your books will sell.

In my case, I had started attending a writers critique group. One of the ladies in the group brought back notes from a writers conference. She said that Julie Smith of David C. Cook publishers needed picture books for a new line similar to Little Golden books. They should be 250 words long, and she had a list of themes. I chose two themes, went home, and wrote two picture books that day. I put them both in an envelope and sent them away the next morning. I heard back in less than a month—Julie wanted to buy both books!

Did you have an agent when you published your first book?

I did not have an agent for my first five books. I do have one now: Etta Wilson, of March Media, who has become a good friend. I met Etta while I was working at a writers conference in Florida.

Do you have any advice, in terms of finding an agent, for a writer starting out?

Don't get discouraged. No agent can make your dreams come true. Only you can do that. Believe in yourself, but be tough on yourself. If your writing isn't selling, there is a reason. Figure out what it is and fix it. Set short-term, achievable goals, and follow through on them. "I will sell my book" is not an achievable goal, because you are not in control of the market. "I will finish my novel and mail it to a publisher" is achievable.

Are you still with your first publisher?

No. I write too many different types of material to stay with one publisher.

Do you have any advice, in terms of finding a publisher, for a writer starting out?

Network. Go to conferences and meet editors. Never stop learning.

Are your books illustrated?

Some of my books are illustrated. I have had the same illustrator for one four-book series, and two chapter books. I have never had the opportunity to choose my illustrator, so sometimes their vision of the book has been a surprise.

Do you have any advice, in terms of finding an illustrator, for a writer starting out?

The publishers you dream about working with—the big ones in New York—have their own stable of illustrators. When they buy your first picture book, they will choose an illustrator who has had good reviews to pair with their brilliant new writer—you. So don't worry about it. Work on being a wordsmith; work on learning about the trade.

What procedures do you follow when you write?

Deadlines are helpful to me. If I don't have a real deadline looming, I give myself one. If I must finish a novel in two months, creative tension builds. I am sure to produce three picture books in that time. No novel, just picture books, like tornadoes spawned by a hurricane. And then the big storm breaks, and the novel rages through me.

Where do you get your ideas?

I have more ideas in a day than I could write about in a year! But not all of them are good ideas. In fact, some of them are lousy, and I don't know it until after I have written the whole book. I try to let a book sit for a few months (yes, months!) before I send it out. About half of the time, when I read it again, I say, "What was I thinking?" and bury it under my mulch pile of manuscripts to cook some more.

What do you think are the key differences between writing for children and writing for adults?

A book is always a collaboration between the author and the reader. Your story is not complete until it springs to life inside your reader. To make it come alive, you must know what your reader knows—how deep is their pool of knowledge? What do they understand about life? Pain? Love? Loss? How can you touch those emotions and that understanding? The only difference between writing for an adult and writing for the youngest child is the depth of the knowledge pool you have to work with. Their hearts are the same, and their needs for an exciting, satisfying story are just the same.

I know some writers look down on "children's authors." But if we don't draw them into our books—if we don't capture their imaginations, teach them to love stories—then there will be no bestselling adult novels. Because there will be no readers.

How did you learn to write?

I learned writing from the very best teachers I could find, and you should, too. My teachers were George McDonald, Katherine Paterson, Rudyard Kipling, C. S. Lewis, L. M. Montgomery, Ellis Peters, Robert Heinlein, Louis L'Amour—the list goes on and on and on. Of course, I have never met any of them personally. But every time I hold one of their books in my hands, I hold their skill and their knowledge. As a writer, you should never read a book without learning about pacing, style, character, setting. In fact, I take books apart. Literally. I will take the cover off and get a good set of markers. I go through the text marking parts that affect me. I write notes in the margins. I study books to understand how the author made me laugh or cry. Design your own writing course by choosing the authors you love best! One word of caution: if you want to be published, read books that are being published today. Styles in storytelling change, even if the stories don't!

Anything you really wish somebody had told you when you started out?

If you live only to write, you won't have much to say. Get out and live. Taste and touch and feel the world. Love people and learn about them. And most important of all, for those of you who are lucky enough to be moms or dads, it takes the same creative energy to raise a child as it does to write a book. You are creating with your whole life, writing on a living heart. You simply use actions and emotions and voice and hugs to create, instead of a pencil or computer. Books will some day turn to dust. Your children never will. I could have lots more books than I do now if I had spent less time with my children—but I wouldn't trade the time I have spent with my children for all the books in the world!

Book Clubs offer a wide variety of affordable children's literature to educators, parents, and the children they love. The Troll School & Library Division provides educators with innovative instructional programs and quality books for schools and libraries. Troll's Reading is Fundamental, Inc. (RIF) is the nation's oldest and largest not-for-profit children's literacy organization.

Turtle Press

403 Silas Deane Highway
PO Box 290206
Wethersfield, CT 06129-0206
Web site: www.turtlepress.com

Description: The turtle, traditionally, has been the symbol of longevity and reliability in Eastern thought. This theme of longevity has been a guiding principle for Turtle Press. Turtle Press prides itself on producing products that are timeless additions to the martial arts world, a unique blend of tradition and innovation that is the company's hallmark.

Established: 1989.

Description of fiction titles: Adventure with martial arts tie-in.

Recent fiction titles:

A Part of the Ribbon People by Ruth Hunter and Debra Fritsch

Description of nonfiction titles: Practical martial arts.

Recent nonfiction titles:

Martial Arts Training Diary for Kids by Dr. Art Brisacher

UAHC Press

633 Third Avenue
New York, NY 10017
(212) 650-4120
(888) 489-UAHC
(212) 650-4119 (fax)
E-mail: press@uahc.org
Web site: www.uahcpress.com

Description: Book publisher.

Established: 1873.

Key people:

Publisher: Ken Gesser

Acquisitions/submissions editor: Rabbi Hara Person

Books per year: Five

Percentage by first-time authors: 40 percent

Seeks: Publish books intended primarily for Reform Jewish readers. Looking for picture books for children.

Accepts unsolicited/unagented: Yes.

Description of fiction titles: Currently UAHC is looking strictly for children's fiction—picture books with Jewish themes.

Recent fiction titles:

The Chanukah Blessing by Peninnah Schram (learning to welcome the stranger and the true meaning of giving presents on Hanukkah)

Come, Let Us Be Joyful! The Story of Hava Nagila by Fran Manushkin (about the creation of the song "Hava Nagila")

Preferred fiction titles: Fictional picture books with Jewish themes.

Description of nonfiction titles: Most of UAHC's nonfiction titles are Jewish textbooks.

Recent nonfiction titles:

To Learn Is to Do: A Tikkun Olam Road Map by Sharon Halper (A textbook for children, grades 3–5; using texts from the Torah [Old Testament], children are taught about the importance of helping to heal the world.)

Preferred nonfiction titles: Jewish textbooks for children and young adults.

Preferred form of submission/contact: For picture books, the entire manuscript should be submitted (with an SASE); for textbooks, submit an outline for the project, an annotated table of contents, and a sample chapter (with an SASE).

Time to reply: Four to eight weeks.

Time to publish: One to two years.

Accepts simultaneous submissions: Yes.

Number of illustrators used annually: Five.

Desired illustrator qualifications: Variable, depending on the project.

Prefer manuscript/illustration packages, or separate: Prefer to view separately.

Include with illustrator query: Samples and tear sheets.

Time to reply: Four to eight weeks.

Purchases freelance photography: Yes.

Preferred photography: Variable, depending on the project.

Terms for writers: Depends on the project.

Terms for illustrators: Depends on the project.

Submission guidelines: Write (with an SASE), call, fax, or e-mail a request.

Tips/comments: UAHC is a publisher that specializes in Jewish books that are geared toward the Reform Jewish movement. Most, but not all, texts are written for a Reform Jewish audience, though all publications are intended for Jewish (or those interested in the Jewish faith and traditions) readers.

Unity House

1901 NW Blue Parkway
Unity Village MO 64065
(816) 524-3550
(816) 251-3552
Web site: www.unityworldhq.org

Corporate structure/parent: Unity School of Christianity.

Description: Publisher of "spiritual resources for daily living"; books and multimedia.

Established: 1889.

Key people:

Senior director: Allen Liles, Outreach Department

Editor: Michael Maday

Associate editor: Raymond Teague (in charge of acquisitions)

Books per year and description: One a year. Alternates years with a children's picture book and a young adult novel.

Percentage by first-time authors: 25 percent.

Seeks: Those that reflect the Unity spiritual philosophy (nondogmatic, positive, practical Christianity that encourages people to turn within for guidance and discover spiritual truths for themselves; affirms the goodness in all life, and endorses affirmative prayer and meditation).

Accepts unsolicited/unagented: Yes.

Description of fiction titles: Spiritual, high-quality works that help young people discover their inner goodness and God connection (the Christ within). Titles reflect Unity philosophy—not mainstream Christian, not dogmatic.

Recent fiction titles:

Picture books:

Adventures of the Little Green Dragon by Mari Privette Ulmer; illustrated by Mary Maass (10 delightfully original tales about the adventures and misadventures of a most appealing and likeable little green dragon; winner of the 2000 Benjamin Franklin Award for best children's picture book)

The Sunbeam and the Wave by Harriet Hamilton; illustrated by Connie Bowen, (teaches that children are loved as part of the wonderful world around them)

Young adult novels:

Marni's Mirror by Cheryl Silva (tells about a teenager who discovers how to use positive thoughts and emotions to improve self-worth and relationships)

Shadow's Stand by Raymond Teague (featuring a dog and two teens in a story of humane awareness and compassion)

Preferred fiction titles: Looking for stories consistent with Unity's spirituality and teachings.

Description of nonfiction titles: In line with Unity principles and teachings.

Preferred nonfiction titles: Looking for metaphysical Christian books based on Unity principles, as well as inspirational and self-help books based on metaphysics and practical spirituality.

Preferred form of submission/contact: Prefer query letter or query with proposal and two or three sample chapters.

Time to reply: Within eight weeks.

Time to publish: Once a book goes into production after acceptance, the production time is generally seven to nine months.

Accepts simultaneous submissions: Yes.

Number of illustrators used annually: One.

Desired illustrator qualifications: Quality.
Prefer manuscript/illustration packages, or separate: Either.
Include with illustrator query: Resume and samples.
Time to reply: No reply but query and samples kept on file for consideration for future projects.
Purchases freelance photography: Not usually.
Preferred photography: Quality.
Terms for writers: Royalty of 10 percent of net receipts; cash advance of $1,500 against royalties.
Terms for illustrators: Varies: (1) percentage split between author and illustrator; each receives $1,500 advance, or (2) set fee for job.
Submission guidelines: Write or call for a copy.
Tips and comments: Get guidelines. Be familiar with Unity.

Urban Ministries, Inc.

1551 Regency Court
Calumet City, IL 60409
(708) 868-7100

Description: Publisher.
Established: 1970.

Viking Books

Penguin Putnam BFYR
345 Hudson Street
New York, NY 10014
Web site: www.penguinputnam.com/about/children/puffin.htm

Corporate structure/parent: Penguin Putnam Inc.
Description: Publisher.
Established: 1933.
Key people:
Publisher: Regina Hayes
Books per year: Approximately 60 titles.
Accepts unsolicited/unagented: At this time most Penguin Putnam Inc. imprints do not accept unsolicited manuscripts. If you would like your work to be considered for publication by a major publisher, Penguin Putnam Inc. recommends that you work with an established literary agent.
Tips and comments: The current Viking list is known for such classic characters as Madeline, Corduroy, Pippi Longstocking, Roald Dahl's Matilda, Rosemary Wells's Max & Ruby, The Stinky Cheese Man, Cam Jansen, and Froggy. Viking publishes the entire

works of Ezra Jack Keats, including *The Snowy Day,* winner of the Caldecott Medal, and Robert McCloskey, author of *Make Way for Ducklings,* a Caldecott winner, and Homer Price. Viking publishes approximately 60 titles per year, ranging from books for very young children such as board and lift-the-flap books to sophisticated fiction and nonfiction for teenagers.

Volcano Press

PO Box 270
Volcano, CA 95689-0270
(800) 879-9636
(209) 296-4995 (fax)
Web sites: www.volcanopress.com
E-mail: sales@volcanopress.com

Description: Volcano Press has been publishing books on domestic violence for 30 years. *Battered Wives*, published in 1976, contains the powerful "Letter from a Battered Wife," which readers still request permission to copy so they can use the letter to carry on their valuable work.

VSP Books

PO Box 17011
Alexandria, VA 22302
Web site: www.vspbooks.com

Accepts unsolicited/unagented: No.
Submission guidelines: Does not accept unsolicited manuscripts or queries.
Tips and comments: VSP is a small publisher with a limited list and works with a select group of authors and illustrators.

Walker and Company Books for Young Readers

435 Hudson Street
New York, NY 10014
(212) 727-8300

Description: Book publisher.
Established: 1961.
Key people:
Publisher: Emily Easton
Editor: Timothy Travaglini
Books per year and description: 20 books; picture books, middle grade, and young adult.

Percentage by first-time authors: 10 percent.

Seeks: Middle-grade and young adult novels; innovative, nonfiction in all age groups; historical fiction; poetry.

Accepts unsolicited/unagented: Yes. Dedicated to working with new talent and accepts unagented and unsolicited manuscripts, but please follow guidelines (available by request with an SASE) to improve your chances and enable your manuscript or art to receive the consideration it deserves.

Description of fiction titles: Most are modern-day settings, some are humorous, and others are poignant and edgy.

Recent fiction titles:

Dear Mrs. Ryan, You're Ruining My Life by Jennifer B. Jones

My Life, Take Two by Paul Many

The Baboon King by Anton Quintana

Preferred fiction titles: Looking for a compelling voice, original settings (whether it be everyday America or something unique), and a fresh story line. Not looking for science fiction, fantasy, "problem" novels, or any manuscript that emphasizes its message over and above its story line.

Description of nonfiction titles: History; science (some); nature (particularly animals and environments).

Recent nonfiction titles:

Slinky, Scaly Slithery Snakes by Dorothy Hinshaw Patent

Girl Thoughts by Judith Harlan

A North American Rain Forest Scrapbook by Virginia Wright-Frierson

Preferred nonfiction titles: Topics with mass appeal as well as an element that ties in with curriculum.

Preferred form of submission/contact: Full manuscript for picture books; query plus synopsis and first three chapters on works for older children.

Time to reply: Two to three months.

Time to publish: One to two years.

Accepts simultaneous submissions: Yes, but please advise in the cover letter that you've submitted your manuscript to other publishers; and if another publisher makes an offer while the manuscript is still at Walker, please inform immediately.

Number of illustrators used annually: Approximately 16.

Desired illustrator qualifications: Each project is different. Keeps postcards and similar samples on file for reference and reviews the files when looking for a new artist

Prefer manuscript/illustration packages, or separate: Accepts them together, but there is no need to send illustrations if you are *not* an illustrator. Submitting only a manuscript or artwork will not hinder your chances of acceptance.

Include with illustrator query: Samples and/or tear sheets.

Time to reply: Two to three months.

Purchases freelance photography: Very infrequently.

Preferred photography: Same as rules for illustrators—it varies by the project.

Terms for writers: Standard.

Terms for illustrators: Standard.

Submission guidelines: Write with a business-sized SASE for guidelines or 9 by 12-inch SASE for a catalog. All manuscripts should be typed and double-spaced. Single-spaced or handwritten manuscripts are difficult to read and may result in a return of your work without consideration. Include a cover letter that includes your current address, telephone number, and a brief description of your manuscript. You may also want to include other pertinent information such as a list of previously published works. Because cover letters and manuscripts often become separated, please also include your name, address, and telephone number on the front page of the manuscript, too. All submissions must be accompanied by an SASE for a reply. Do *not,* under any circumstances, send original art.

Tips and comments: Read children's books; familiarize yourself with the publishing programs of *any* publishing house to which you plan to submit. Feel free to submit samples and tear sheets.

WHITECAP BOOKS

351 Lynn Avenue
North Vancouver, British Columbia V7J 2C4
Canada
(604) 980-9852
(604) 980-8197 (fax)
Web site: www.whitecap.ca

Description: Publisher.

Key people:

Editorial director: Robin Rivers

Seeks: Juvenile nonfiction.

Accepts unsolicited/unagented: Yes.

Description of nonfiction titles: Natural history; nature.

Recent nonfiction titles:

A World of Difference by Dianne Young (explores the similarities and differences between animals from around the world)

Welcome to the World of Porcupines by Diane Swanson

Whose House is This? by Wayne Lynch (Who lives in this forest cave? Who nests in this tiny hole in the tree trunk? See a picture of the animal who lives there and a collection of amazing facts about it.)

Time to reply: Two to three months for the initial review. Whitecap will then contact you, either to ask for the complete manuscript for more serious consideration or to return the sample material in the SASE provided.

Submission guidelines: Please adhere to the following submission guidelines: Include a synopsis. Depending on the type of manuscript, the synopsis should include information about the main characters and events, the setting and time period, the approach (narrative, humorous, first-person account), and the theme or range of topics. A table of contents listing the chapters or stories and their length. Information about proposed illustrations or photographs (number planned, black and white, or color). One sample chapter that is representative of the total manuscript. If you are uncertain as to whether your idea is appropriate for Whitecap Books, please send a short (half to one page) query letter to the editorial director, Robin Rivers.

White Mane Kids

63 W. Burd Street
PO Box 152
Shippensburg, PA 17257
(717) 532-2237
(717) 532-6110 (fax)
E-mail: marketing@whitemane.com

Corporate structure/parent: White Mane Publishing Co., Inc.

Description: Book publisher.

Established: 1987

Key people:

Acquisitions/submissions editor: Harold Collier

Books per year: 12 to 18.

Percentage by first-time authors: 50 percent.

Seeks: Historical fiction novels for middle-grade readers.

Accepts unsolicited/unagented: Yes.

Description of fiction titles: Historical; suitable for grades 5 and up.

Recent fiction titles:

Retreat from Gettysburg by Kathleen Ernst

Freedom Calls by Kem Knapp Sawyer

Young Heroes of Gettysburg by William Thomas Vennec

Preferred fiction titles: Looking for titles with accurate historical information.

Preferred form of submission/contact: Query letter (proposal guidelines are available and should be consulted prior to submitting).

Time to reply: 30 days.

Time to publish: One year.

Accepts simultaneous submissions: Yes.

Number of illustrators used annually: Two to three (for book covers only).

Desired illustrator qualifications: Historical illustrations.

Prefer manuscript/illustration packages, or separate: Either.

Time to reply: Respond only if interested in working with the illustrator.

Purchases freelance photography: No.

Terms for writers: Negotiable and variable.

Terms for illustrators: Same.

Submission guidelines: Call, write (include SASE), or e-mail your request. Guidelines are only available for writers.

Tips and comments: At this time, does not publish picture books.

Wiley Children's Books

605 Third Avenue
New York, NY 10158
(212) 850-6206
(212) 850-6095 (fax)
Web site: www.wiley.com

Corporate structure/parent: John Wiley & Sons.
Description: Educational, nonfiction book publisher.
Seeks: Primarily history, science, and other activities.
Preferred form of contact/submission: Query.

Williamson Publishing

Box 185
Charlotte, VT 05445
Web site: www.williamsonbooks.com

Description: Publisher.
Recent fiction titles:
Tales of the Shimmering Sky: Ten Global Folktales with Activities
Tales Alive! Ten Multicultural Folktales with Activities
Recent nonfiction titles:
Alphabet Art: With A–Z Animal Art & Fingerplays
The Little Hands Nature Book: Earth, Sky, Critters & More
Math Play! 80 Ways to Count & Learn
Stop, Look, & Listen: Using Your Senses from Head to Toe
Rainy Day Play: Explore, Create, Discover, Pretend
Big Fun Craft Book: Creative Fun for 2- to 6-Year-Olds
Shapes, Sizes & More Surprises! A Little Hands Early Learning Book
Boredom Busters!: The Curious Kids' Activity Book
Adventures In Art: Art & Craft Experiences for 8- to 13-Year-Olds
Hand-Print Animal Art

Winslow Press

115 E. 23d Street, 10th Floor
New York, NY 10010
(212) 254-2025
(212) 254-1595 (Fax)
E-mail: winslow@winslowpress.com
Web site: www.winslowpress.com

Description: Children's book publisher.

Established: 1997.

Key people:

Publisher: Diane Kessenich

Books per year and description: Publishes 20 books per year: approximately 2 young adult novels, 12 picture books, and 6 middle-grade novels (usually connected to a series).

Percentage by first-time authors: Approximately 25 percent.

Seeks: Open to all genres.

Accepts unsolicited/unagented: Yes.

Recent fiction titles:

Apples, Apples, Apples by Nancy Elizabeth Wallace (picture book for ages pre-K–grade 3)

The Runaway Tortilla by Eric A. Kimmel (picture book for ages pre-K–grade 1)

Aria of the Sea by Dia Calhoun (young adult novel)

Preferred fiction titles: Open to all subject areas.

Description of nonfiction titles: The program that is evolving will consist of books that meet the highest standards of design and production and can segue nicely into an informational/educational enhancement program on the company's Web site.

Preferred nonfiction titles: Not interested in formulaic nonfiction series.

Time to reply: Approximately three to four months, but trying to improve.

Time to publish: Varies.

Accepts simultaneous submissions: Yes.

Number of illustrators used annually: Approximately 20.

Desired illustrator qualifications: Professionalism that's compatible with high industry standards.

Prefer manuscript/illustration packages, or separate: Will review them together if the author/illustrator prefer this. *Do not send original art.* Submit color copies or tear sheets. Include tear sheets or color copies with illustrator query; *do not send original art.* Samples that appeal to the designers get filed.

Purchases freelance photography: No.

Terms for writers: Varies.

Terms for illustrators: Varies.

Submission guidelines: Via e-mail or send an SASE with request.

Tips and comments: Visit the Web site (www.winslowpress.com); each title has its own home page and that will help writers and illustrators get a good idea of what it is that the company is looking for stylistically.

Woman's Missionary Union, SBC

PO Box 830010
Birmingham, AL 35283
(205) 991-8100
(205) 991-4990 (fax)

Corporate structure/parent: Auxiliary to the Southern Baptist Convention.

Description: Publisher.

Key people:

Acquisitions/submissions editor: Editorial Department

Seeks: Resources related to prayer, ministry, Bible study, spiritual development, social issues, cultural diversity and cooperation, leadership and missionary biographies, and stories.

Accepts unsolicited/unagented: Yes.

Preferred form of submission/contact: Complete manuscript.

Terms for writers: Variable—flat fee purchase for works for hire or royalty based on sales.

Submission guidelines: Write with an SASE for guidelines. Submissions should include query/cover letter with synopsis, purpose statement, target audience, projected length, and completion date; author's biographical information—other published works and credentials; manuscript outline and three chapters or complete manuscript; working title and three alternatives; market and competitive titles (list some).

World Book, Inc. (Headquarters)

233 N. Michigan Avenue, Suite 2000
Chicago, IL 60601
(312) 729-5800
(312) 729-5600 (fax)
Web site: www.worldbook.com

Description: Publisher, educational.

Recent nonfiction titles:

Animals of the World (This series appeals to a young child's curiosity about animals and is a quick source of answers to commonly asked questions.)

Christmas Around the World (Explore holiday and cultural traditions from around the world in a 19-volume set.)

Ecology (Travel through rain forests, deserts, polar lands, and across oceans with this beautiful and informative series.)

Encyclopedia of People and Places (This lavishly illustrated set builds on children's natural curiosity about the world around them while answering a wide range of questions about people and places.)

Preferred nonfiction titles: Early childhood, art and activities, general reference, geography, mathematics, personal development, study skills, social studies, and science.

Young Spirit

1125 Stoney Ridge Road
Charlottesville, VA 22902
E-mail: editorial@hrpub.com
Web site: www.hrpub.com

Corporate structure/parent: Hampton Roads Publishing Company.

Description: Publisher.

Seeks: Young Spirit books that will stimulate the intellect, teach valuable lessons in a metaphysical context, and allow children's spirits to grow.

Accepts unsolicited/unagented: Yes.

Description of nonfiction titles: Books aim to stimulate children's growth, both intellectually and spiritually.

Preferred form of submission/contact: Proposals only. Please include a synopsis, a chapter-by-chapter outline, and one or two sample chapters. Please, typed or computer-printed, only; no handwritten manuscripts, electronic, Web-based, or e-mail submissions. *Shorter titles* for Young Spirit may be sent whole, with artwork included.

Time to reply: Up to several months.

Accepts simultaneous submissions: Yes.

Number of illustrators used annually: Variable.

Prefer manuscript/illustration packages, or separate: Accept them together.

Include with illustrator query: Send a small sample of your work—send copies, as artwork may be kept indefinitely if you do not specifically ask for its return.

Time to reply: Will contact the illustrator if an assignment arises.

Tips and comments: Please enclose SASE if you would like your manuscript returned to you. Be sure that your cover letter contains your complete address (including phone number).

Zino Press

PO Box 52
Madison, WI 53701
(800) 356-2303
Web site: www.zinopress.com

Description: Publisher.

Key people:

Acquisitions/submissions editor: Dave Schreiner

Seeks: Nonfiction or fiction multicultural literature that covers a topic not yet explored by others.

Accepts unsolicited/unagented: Yes.

Description of fiction titles: Original fiction that tells an unusual story and composed in rhyme.

Recent fiction titles:

Fall Is Not Easy written and illustrated by Marty Kelley
What's Up with You Taquandra Fu? by Matt Cibula; illustrated by Brian Strassburg

Preferred fiction titles: Rhyme and original multicultural stories.

Recent nonfiction titles:

How to Be the Greatest Writer in the World by Matt Cibula; illustrated by Brian Strassburg
One Nation, Many Peoples: Immigration in the United States by Julia Pferdehirt

"That Grand, Noble Work" : Exploring the Constitution by Colleen O. Murray

A Drawing in the Sand: The Story of African American Art written and illustrated by Jerry Butler

Sweet Words So Brave: The Story of African American Literature by Barbara K. Curry and James Michael Brodie; illustrated by Jerry Butler

Preferred nonfiction titles: Original multicultural stories.

Time to reply: One month.

Submission guidelines: Write with an SASE or visit our Web site. Please send completed manuscripts only with an SASE. Submissions should express values that lead to tolerance, greater awareness of self and others, understanding, kindness, and compassion; be accurate and verifiable when the material is nonfiction; not present stereotypes and should, in fact, seek to challenge racist and sexist stereotypes; be relevant to contemporary issues and experiences; not be a retold fairy tale; be written clearly and with children in mind; lend itself to lively illustrations.

Tips and comments: Any story submitted to Zino Press should also teach the positive values of kindness and tolerance. Project positive images that leave a lasting impression.

ZONDERVAN PUBLISHING HOUSE

5300 Patterson Avenue SE
Grand Rapids, MI 49530-0002
(616) 698-6900
E-mail: zpub@zph.com
Web site: www.zondervan.com

Corporate structure/parent: HarperCollins Publishers.

Description: Book publisher.

Seeks: Unless you have had direct and personal contact with a Zondervan Publishing House acquisitions editor about your manuscript or book proposal, *Zondervan prefers that new authors submit their book ideas to "First Edition," located on the Web site of the Evangelical Christian Publishers Association* (http://www.ecpa.org/FE/index.html). Follow the directions given for posting your book proposal. Zondervan regularly reviews proposals posted there. Thank you for your understanding about these necessary policies in regard to the thousands of proposals Zondervan receives each year.

Accepts unsolicited/unagented: Please see above. The Zondervan Publishing House Book Group editorial staff is unable to take query calls or answer query letters from authors and agents. To be considered by the review editors, both previously published books and manuscript proposals must be submitted by mail to Zondervan. Although every proposal is reviewed, Zondervan cannot acknowledge any submission or return any material that does not include an appropriately sized, self-addressed stamped envelope. If you do not send return postage, your material will be discarded and you will not receive a response to your submission. Zondervan is unable to acknowledge receipt of your submission or give status reports.

Description of titles: Zondervan Publishing House publishes evangelical and nondenominational trade, academic, and professional books primarily for Christian readers.

While Zondervan publishes books within the historic evangelical mainstream of Christian faith and practice, it does not hesitate to publish books that represent the various currents within that mainstream.

Recent fiction titles:

Mud Pie Annie: God's Recipe for Doing Your Best by Sue Buchanan and Dana Shafer (Mud Pie Annie uses her God-given creativity to make mud pies and other treats.)

Peter's First Easter by Walter Wangerin Jr.; illustrated by Timothy Ladwig

Recent nonfiction titles:

Prayer Partners Prayer Book: Prayers to Pray Each and Every Day by Alice Joyce Davidson

Picture That! Bible Storybook by Tracy Harrast

Preferred form of submission/contact: Cover letter and sample chapters. Your cover letter should address the following questions: What is the book's subject matter and approach? Specifically for whom is the book written? Be precise. What distinguishes your book from others on the subject? What need or purpose does your book fulfill that the others do not? What are your qualifications for writing this book? Why is your book appropriate for Zondervan Publishing House? Include a sample chapter or two; a brief, one-paragraph synopsis of each of the other chapters; an appropriately sized, self-addressed stamped envelope for the return of your proposal of you want it returned). If you are submitting a previously published book, please send a copy of the book in lieu of a manuscript

Time to reply: Three months.

Submission guidelines: Your cover letter, sample chapters, and one-paragraph synopsis must all be typed with a clean typewriter ribbon or printed from a computer using Times New Roman 12-point type or similar serif font. Do not hand-write or hand-print your submission. Double-space your material, retaining ample margins. Use only one side of quality 8 1/2 by 11-inch white bond paper (not onion skin or any other thin paper). Bind your material only with rubber bands or an oversized binder clip. Do not staple, paste up, or attach anything that will interfere with photocopying should multiple copies be necessary for committee review. Consecutively number your pages throughout. Type your name and address on each document you submit. Submit only clean and easily readable photocopies. Mail your material flat in an envelope with adequate postage. Do not fold your submission.

Tips and comments: What *not* to submit: Do not send audiocassettes, computer disks, or videotapes in lieu of typed manuscripts. Although Zondervan Publishing House does extensive editing on manuscripts, it does not have the staff for re-writing, "ghost-writing," or to serve as coauthors. You may want to contact local universities or colleges, writers guilds, or editorial services for such assistance. Zondervan does not review proposals for tracts; booklets; sermons; dissertations; four-color children's storybooks; coloring books; game, puzzle, or craft books (except for children); books of quotations or poetry; short story collections; plays; romances; Sunday school curriculum; high school textbooks; or books on tape.

SECTION TWO

Children's Magazine Publishers

ADVOCATE

301A Rolling Hills Park
Prattsville, NY 12468
(518) 299-3103

Corporate structure/parent: PKA Publication.
Description: Bimonthly tabloid.
Established: 1987.
Key people:
Publisher: Patricia Keller
Seeks: Publishes photos, poetry, art, and fiction.
Preferred form of contact/submission: Complete manuscript.
Time to reply: Two months.

AIM

PO Box 1174
Maywood, IL 60153
(708) 344-4414
Web site: www.aimmagazine.org

Description: AIM is an acronym for America's Intercultural Magazine.
Established: 1975.
Key people:
Editor: Myron Apilado, Ed.D.
Associate editor: Ruth Apilado
Fiction editor: Mark Boone
Photo editor: Betty Lewis
Articles per year and description: 12; why racism is wrong.
Percentage by first-time authors: 60 percent.
Seeks: Short stories, essays, articles showing that people from different racial/ethnic backgrounds are more alike than they are different.

Accepts unsolicited/unagented: Yes.
Preferred articles: Not interested in articles that moralize.
Preferred form of submission/contact: Send manuscript.
Time to reply: Two months.
Time to publish: Two months.
Accepts simultaneous submissions: Yes, but please specify if your submission has been sent elsewhere simultaneously.
Number of illustrators used annually: Eight.
Desired illustrator qualifications: Looks for good artists.
Prefer manuscript/illustration packages, or separate: Together is fine.
Include with illustrator query: Samples are best.
Time to reply: One month.
Purchases freelance photography: Occasionally.
Preferred photography: Clarity and crispness.
Terms for writers: $15 to $25 per article or story.
Terms for illustrators: $25.
Submission guidelines: Send check for $5 with request.
Tips and comments: Submission must deal with racial problems. Do not submit sloppy work. *Aim*'s focus is on racial issues and problems. Please bear that in mind when writing and submitting to the magazine.

ALL ABOUT YOU

6420 Wilshire Boulevard
Los Angles, CA 90048
E-mail: fortj@emapusa.com

Key people:
Editor: Jane Fort

AMERICAN CAREERS

6701 W. 64th Street
Overland Park, KS 66202
(913) 362-7788
(913) 362-4864 (fax)

Corporate structure/parent: Career Communications, Inc.
Description: Quarterly career magazine for middle and high school students.
Established: 1990.
Key people:
Articles editor: Mary Pitchford
Art director: Jerry Kanabel
Preferred form of contact/submission: Query (include clips).

American Cheerleader

250 W. 57th Street, Suite 420
New York, NY 10107
(212) 265-8890
(212) 265-8908 (fax)
Web site: www.americancheerleader.com

Corporate structure/parent: Lifestyle Ventures LLC, which also publishes *Dance Spirit*, *Dance Teacher*, *Pointe*, *In Motion*, and *Stage Directions* magazines.

Description: The only national magazine written for the more than 3.3 million young people involved in cheerleading throughout the United States. Bimonthly.

Established: 1995.

Key people:

Editorial director: Julie Davis

Managing editor: Meredith Cristiano

American Girl

8400 Fairway Place
Middleton, WI 53562
Web site: www.americangirl.com

Corporate structure/parent: Pleasant Company Publications is the parent company to *American Girl*; Pleasant Company is a subsidiary of Mattel.

Description: *American Girl* is a bimonthly four-color magazine for girls ages 8 and up. The purpose of the publication is to celebrate girls, yesterday and today. *American Girl* readers are girls in the formative years, girls who dream big dreams. *American Girl* hopes to encourage that dreaming and to reinforce each reader's self-confidence, curiosity, and self-esteem as she prepares to navigate adolescence in the years ahead.

Established: 1992.

Key people:

Editor in chief: Kristi Thom

Managing editor: Barbara Stretchberry

Articles per year and description: Fiction, 6; nonfiction, 20.

Percentage by first-time authors: Approximately 10 percent.

Seeks: See the category "Girls Express" in the writers' guidelines for extensive insight, but in general, the "Girls Express" section offers the most opportunities for freelance writers. Looking for short profiles of girls who are into sports, the arts, interesting hobbies, cultural activities, and other areas. A key: The *girl* must be the star, and the story must be from her point of view. Be sure to include the age of the girls you're pitching. Also interested in how-to stories—how to send away for free things; hot ideas for a cool day; how to write the president and get a response. "Girls Express" stories have to be told in 175 words or less. The magazine staff is looking for contemporary and historical fiction up to 2,300 words. The protagonist should be a girl between 8 and 12. No science fiction, fantasy, or first-romance stories. The staff is looking for good children's literature with thoughtfully developed characters and plots. The staff is looking for visual puzzles, mazes, math puzzles, word games, simple crosswords, cartoons, and other ideas. Seasonal ideas are especially welcome at least six months before publication.

Accepts unsolicited/unagented: Yes.

Preferred form of submission/contact: The staff prefers to receive ideas in query form rather than finished manuscripts.

Time to reply: At least three months.

Time to publish: About six months.

Accepts simultaneous submissions: Yes.

Number of illustrators used annually: 30.

Desired illustrator qualifications: Ability to convey emotions; ability to illustrate children—specifically girls.

Prefers manuscript/illustration packages, or separate: Yes, can review simultaneously but prefers queries to manuscripts.

Include with illustrator query: Samples and a resume.

Purchases freelance photography: No.

Terms for writers: Negotiable terms. Typically $1 per word.

Terms for illustrators: Variable.

Submission guidelines: Send an SASE, attention of the magazine department assistant. All submissions must be sent to the attention of the magazine department assistant.

Tips and comments: To get the best idea of what the magazine is looking for, refer to the "Writers' Guidelines"—that is the most comprehensive explanation and will be most helpful. But in general, familiarize yourself with the publication before you send *anything*. Many nonfiction pieces pick up on themes from the fiction, but if your idea really grabs the staff, they'll find a way to use it. Famous adult women in history have their place in *American Girl*, but better are the little-known stories about girls in history. Past historical nonfiction pieces have featured girls and dancing lessons, girls affected by the blizzard of 1888, and beloved dolls owned by girls through history. The format of most historical pieces is not running text but copy blocks that work with photos. As such, any photo research leads you offer when you query will give the staff a better idea of the feasibility of the story. A key: Think visually when you propose your historical piece. Some of the most successful contemporary nonfiction pieces have been sports related, but that doesn't mean other contemporary topics or profiles are out of the question. A key: Look for new twists on familiar topics. The staff prefers to receive contemporary nonfiction ideas in query form rather than finished manuscripts.

ANIMALAND (ASPCA)

No longer being published.

Meet Marianne Olson Mitchell

Author

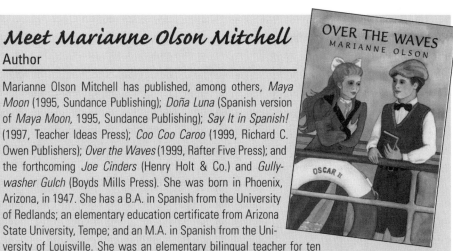

Marianne Olson Mitchell has published, among others, *Maya Moon* (1995, Sundance Publishing); *Doña Luna* (Spanish version of *Maya Moon,* 1995, Sundance Publishing); *Say It in Spanish!* (1997, Teacher Ideas Press); *Coo Coo Caroo* (1999, Richard C. Owen Publishers); *Over the Waves* (1999, Rafter Five Press); and the forthcoming *Joe Cinders* (Henry Holt & Co.) and *Gullywasher Gulch* (Boyds Mills Press). She was born in Phoenix, Arizona, in 1947. She has a B.A. in Spanish from the University of Redlands; an elementary education certificate from Arizona State University, Tempe; and an M.A. in Spanish from the University of Louisville. She was an elementary bilingual teacher for ten years in California and Arizona. Later she was an adjunct Spanish teacher at the University of Louisville for three years. She has written for all ages, from early readers to adults (teachers). But her main interest is writing for the 8 to 12 group. She is married and has no children and two dogs.

How did you get your first book published?

When I was a teacher in California, I heard a folktale called "The Legend of the Mayan Moon." Over the years, I had tried to find that story in a book or anthology. I asked teachers, librarians, and professors of Mexican culture whether they knew this tale. None did. Finally, I found it in an old folktale collection from the 1930s. This was a story that was about to die if it didn't get republished. I couldn't let that happen. So I rewrote it (dozens of times, in two languages!) and started sending it out. Since I wanted the story published both in Spanish and English, I only targeted publishers that did multicultural or bilingual stories. The third house I sent it to, Sundance Publishing, finally took it. I say "finally" because the manuscript languished there for a year or so with no response. I was about to pull the submission and send it somewhere else when I went to the Highlights Writers Workshop at Chautauqua, New York. There, I met editor Pat Broderick of Teaching PreK–8 magazine. I told her my situation, and she said, "I know those folks at Sundance. I'll call them for you!" She did, and after that they got in touch with me. That was in 1992. The book, now titled *Maya Moon* in English and *Doña Luna* in Spanish, came out the spring of 1995.

Sundance did a nice job with the book, and the illustrations are fantastic. However, I wish I had worked harder at finding a trade publisher. Since Sundance is an education publisher, *Maya Moon* is not available at bookstores. It is sold through their catalog, which is marketed to schools. I sell it myself through school book fairs and at writing conferences.

Did you have an agent when you published your first book?

No, I didn't have an agent when I published my first book, but I did have one for a year—until she decided to stop being an agent. It's actually a really flukey story how we found each other. When we connected, I wasn't even looking for an agent. I read on a message board for children's writers that

continues

someone had an Internet site called "Writer's Island," where authors and illustrators could post a snippet of their work. The site manager then invited agents and editors to drop by and see what was there. It was a bargain to get my work listed, so I gave it a go. I posted a partial of a picture book story I had tried to submit on my own with no luck. In a few weeks, I was notified that agent Pesha Rubenstein was interested and wanted to get in touch with me. We e-mailed each other, I sent her the whole story, and she took me on. She sent my story to eight houses. On the sixth try, Henry Holt bought it (*Joe Cinders*). It is now being illustrated, and I hope it will be out by fall 2002.

Do you have any advice, in terms of finding a publisher, for a writer starting out?

As you read, notice who published the book and when. Sometimes you can even find an editor's name in the acknowledgments. Send for catalogs and guidelines. Get a market guide and read it in detail, noting who might be a good market for what you write, who takes unsolicited, and what they want and don't want. If a publisher says "no unsolicited," you can still write them a query letter and pitch your project. It takes some study to understand the unique slants of different publishers, but it's well worth the effort. You will save yourself (and them) lots of wasted time if you stick to their needs. If they only publish nonfiction, don't send them fiction, poetry, or drama. Go to conferences if you can and meet editors there.

Are your books illustrated?

Most of my books are illustrated—all by different illustrators. My *Say It in Spanish* book for teachers has only black-and-white line art; some of it is mine and some done by a graphic artist. But when you work with different publishers, as I have, you'll find that the publishers want to choose the artist, so you may find that every book you publish is illustrated by a different person.

Do you have any advice, in terms of finding an illustrator, for a writer starting out?

Most of the time the author will not have a say in choosing the illustrator. That's the job of the publisher and the art director. However, they may ask you for suggestions. The editors at Boyds Mills Press asked me to suggest some illustrators for my story *Gullywasher Gulch*. But in the end, they made the choice. It helps if you get to know the different styles of art found in picture books and the names of the illustrators. Some styles are cartoony, some realistic, and some could hang side by side with the great art found in museums. What style best suits the kind of story you've written? Realize, too, that the top, award-winning artists are going to be booked up for many years with projects. The publisher may want the book out sooner. Top illustrators are also expensive. Your publisher may not want to spend so much on a new, untested author.

What procedures do you follow when you write?

I try to write every day. Sometimes it's only prewriting in my head, trying out plot lines and dialogues. It's important for me to think through the whole story all the way to the end before I begin writing. Otherwise, I get lost. It's like planning a car trip, studying the map and knowing where you will stop, where you will get gas, and what your exit is.

The time spent on writing varies with my schedule and the type of story. If I get caught up in a story, I'll write until my dogs start begging for a walk. A short rebus story for a magazine can be written (and rewritten several times!) in a day. But a longer work, like my historical fiction, took four years to complete. There was a ton of research to do, including a trip to Sweden. The story structure began with a list of chapter headings. I added a few notes about what would happen in each chapter, who would be in each scene, and what the point of each chapter was. That gave me a rough outline, or "map," to follow.

Where do you get your ideas?

When I first started out, there were a couple of old folktales I wanted to retell. I worried that after I did them, I'd run out of ideas. Fortunately, that didn't happen. When you start thinking like a writer, ideas will jump out at you everywhere. I have found ideas in family stories, in looking at nature as I walked my dogs, and in the anecdotes friends told me. Some came from my childhood memories, some were in dreams, and one I found in my front yard. A couple of years ago I was cleaning out pack rat nests from the cactus around my house. I wondered whether I'd find some valuable trinket a pack rat had stashed there. What I found was a story idea about a boy doing the same chore and finding a lost charm bracelet. That story, "Pack Rat Puzzle," appeared in the December 2000 issue of *Highlights for Children*. The real problem with ideas is finding the time to get them all down. I keep an "idea file," a notebook where I jot down the spark, or the title, or the bare bones of the story before it slips away.

What do you think are the key differences between writing for children and writing for adults?

With children's stories you have to jump into the story problem right away. You have to hook the reader on the first page, or the first paragraph if it's a magazine story. Children's authors are competing for readers' attention with television, movies, video, and computer games. If you don't hook the reader right away, he's gone. I haven't written adult novels, but I read them often. I get impatient, even bored, with adult books that wander around or take too long to get to the point.

Another difference is keeping in mind the age of your intended reader. When writing for adults, that isn't a concern. But the subject matter, point of view, story length, word choice, sentence structure, tone, and types of predicaments your characters get into all vary with different age levels. Most magazine stories, for example, can't have characters doing something too dangerous or foolish. When you write for young adults, however, you have more freedom to let your characters get into all kinds of trouble. You can tell the story from different points of view and be creative with style and structure.

Anything you really wish somebody had told you when you started out?

To aspiring authors and illustrators I would say "Never give up!" This business is hard and very competitive, so you want to send out your best, most polished work. Every day more opportunities are opening up with e-books and interactive material. Don't overlook the education publishers, either. They don't just publish textbooks. Many need fiction and nonfiction for picture books, early readers, and chapter books. If you have a teaching background, they need activities, lesson plans, and supplementary material. For both illustrators and authors, there is less competition with education publishers than with trade publishers.

continues

And of course, read, read, read. Know what's being published today. A lot has changed since the books of your childhood came out. Learn as much about the business as possible, not just the writing part. Be willing to hustle and promote your work when it's published. Be willing to work with editors if your art or manuscript needs changes. What you both want is the best book possible.

Most of all, enjoy the process. Publishing is an up-and-down experience, and you can't let the disappointments get you down. Keep in mind that a rejection does not mean that you personally are being rejected. There are many reasons for a rejection even though editors may not have the time to explain them to you. Always have a backup market in mind, and get that work out there again. Celebrate every big and small victory along the way.

Believe in your role as artist and/or author. If anyone shoots a putdown your way, just smile and tell them that this is what you love to do. Who can argue with that?

APPLESEEDS

99 Perkins Point Road
Newcastle, ME 04553
(207) 563-6997 (fax)
E-mail: barbara_burt@post.harvard.edu
Web site: www.cobblestonepub.com/pages/appmain.htm

Key people:

Editors in chief: Susan Buckley and Barbara Burt
Managing editor: Lou Waryncia
Marketing manager: Manuela Meier
Publisher: Jack Olbrych
Art director: Ann Dillon

Articles per year and description: Approximately 125 to 135 articles per year. Illustrations vary by issue topic. Some issues are heavily illustrated; others rely more on photos.

Percent by first-time authors: Approximately 25 percent.

Seeks: Looking for articles that relate to the magazine's specific themes that fall within the following formats: *feature articles*: one to four pages (the issue estimates about six of these types of articles)—includes nonfiction, interviews, and how-to; *departments*: Fun Stuff (games or activities relating to the theme, two pages); Reading Corner (literature piece, two to four pages); By the Numbers (math activities relating to the theme, one page); Where in the World (map activities, two pages); Your Turn (theme-related opportunities for children to take action, one page); Experts in Action (short profile of professional in field related to theme, one page); The Artist's Eye (fine or folk art relating to theme, one page). Assume 100 to 150 words per page.

Accepts unsolicited/unagented: No. Query only, please.

Recent articles: Recent themes have included Statue of Liberty; Paul Revere; Food: From Field to Table; Children of the Middle Ages; Growing Up on the Erie Canal; The U.S. Capitol; Sacred Places; Exploring the Sahara; Becoming an Artist.

Preferred articles: *Appleseeds* is a multidisciplinary social studies magazine for children ages 7 to 10 (primarily in grades 3 and 4). *Appleseeds* is looking for articles that are lively and age-appropriate and exhibit an original approach to the theme. Scientific and historical accuracy is extremely important. Authors are urged to use primary sources and up-to-date resources for their research. And remember, your article must stimulate the curiosity of a child.

Preferred form of submission/contact: Query. Write a brief description of your idea, including a list of sources you plan to use, your intended word length, and any unique angle or hook you think will make your piece irresistible to its intended audience (7- to 10-year-olds and their teachers and parents).

Time to reply: Queries may be submitted at any time before the deadline, but queries sent well in advance of deadline may not be answered for several months.

Number of illustrators used annually: Varies. Could be one per issue to eight per issue.

Desired illustrator qualifications: The ability to capture the spirit of an article, either in feeling or in presentation of individuals or action. Illustrators must realize that the magazine's primary audience is children.

Prefer manuscript/illustration packages, or separate: Does not accept unsolicited material, but does encourage authors to suggest illustrations/photos in their queries.

Include with illustrator query: Illustrators may send resumes, samples, tear sheets, and so forth.

Time to reply: Generally does not respond to illustrator queries. Files all material and chooses illustrators on an article-by-article basis.

Purchases freelance photography: Yes.

Preferred photography: Images must relate to the theme of an issue.

Terms for writers: Approximately $50 per page; *Appleseeds* purchases all rights to material.

Submission guidelines: Go to the Web site or write with an SASE.

Tips and comments: Writers may propose an article for any issue. The article idea must be closely related to the theme of the issue. Please include a completed query. Each query must be written separately; however, you may mail them together. Feel free to include copies of published writing samples with your query if you have not yet written for *Appleseeds*. After the deadline for query proposals has passed, the editors will review the suggestions and assign articles. This may take several months—don't despair! *Appleseeds* may suggest modifications to your original proposal or assign an entirely new idea. Please do not begin work until you've received a detailed assignment sheet!

Archaeology's Dig Magazine

135 William Street, 8th Floor
New York, NY 10038
(212) 732-5154
(212) 732-5707 (fax)
E-mail: editor@dig.archaeology.org
Web site: www.dig.archaeology.org

Corporate structure/parent: Archaeological Institute of America.

Established: January 1999.

Key people:

Editor in chief: Stephen Hanks

Art director: Ken Feisel

Associate/photo editor: Jarrett Lobell

Articles per year and description: Approximately 60 features and departments per year (six issues) and accompanying illustrations/photo on archaeology and paleontology subjects.

Percentage by first-time authors: Almost none.

Seeks: Queries on stories about archaeology-related subjects that haven't been covered in the magazine before.

Accepts unsolicited/unagented: No manuscripts

Recent articles:

"Who Were the Vikings?"

"Greece's Glorious Games: The Ancient Olympics"

"Games People Played: Ancient Board Games"

"Project Pompeii: Excavations at the Famous Site"

"Who Built the Pyramids?"

"Saving a Civil War Submarine: Excavation of the Hunley"

"What is Underwater Archaeology?"

Preferred articles: Looking for stories about archaeology, mainly with a historical hook that are written in a kid-friendly, conversational tone.

Preferred form of submission/contact: Query with previous writing samples.

Time to reply: Within two weeks.

Time to publish: Two to four months.

Accepts simultaneous submissions: No.

Number of illustrators used annually: About 6 to 10.

Desired illustrator qualifications: Illustrations are assigned by the art director, depending on the story.

Prefer manuscript/illustration packages, or separate: Separately.

Include with illustrator query: Samples and tear sheets.

Time to reply: One to two months.

Purchases freelance photography: Yes.

Preferred photography? The magazine asks photographers for specific types of shots. Does not accept random photos.

Terms for writers: $0.50 cents per word.

Terms for illustrators: Negotiated individually with the illustrator.

Submission guidelines: Write or send an e-mail with a request and self-addressed stamped envelope.

Babybug

PO Box 300

Peru, IL 61354

Web site: www.cricketmag.com (click on Babybug)

Corporate structure/parent: Cricket Publishing. *Babybug* is a publication of the Cricket Publishing Group (which is also the parent company of Cobblestone Publishing). Cricket Publishing also publishes *Ladybug*, *Spider*, *Cricket*, *Click*, *Cicada*, and *Muse* magazines.

Key people:

Editor in chief: Marianne Carus

Editor: Paula Morrow

Senior art director: Ron McCutchan

Art director: Suzanne Beck

Assistant to editor: Julie Peterson

Editorial submissions: Submissions editor

Seeks: *Babybug* features simple stories and poems, words and concepts, illustrated in full color by the best children's artists from around the world.

Accepts unsolicited/unagented: Yes.

Preferred articles: *Stories:* very simple and concrete; 4 to 6 short sentences maximum. *Poems:* rhythmic, rhyming; 8 lines maximum. *Nonfiction:* very basic words and concepts; 10 words maximum. *Activities:* parent–child interaction; 8 lines maximum.

Preferred form of submission/contact: Manuscript. *Babybug* will consider any manuscripts or art samples sent on speculation and accompanied by a self-addressed stamped envelope. Submissions without an SASE will be discarded.

Time to reply: Please allow six to eight weeks' response time for manuscripts.

Prefers manuscript/illustration packages, or separate: Yes, accepts them together. Authors/illustrators may submit a complete manuscript with art samples. The manuscript will be evaluated for quality of concept and text before the art is considered.

Include with illustrator query: Artists should submit review samples of artwork to be kept in *Babybug*'s illustrator files. *Babybug* prefers to see tear sheets or photoprints/ photocopies of art. If you wish to send an original art portfolio for review, package it carefully, insure the package, and be sure to include return packing materials and postage.

Time to reply: Please allow 12 weeks for art samples.

Terms for writers: Rates vary: $25 minimum; payment on publication. *Babybug* purchases first publication rights with reprint option; in some cases all rights. Payment within 45 days of acceptance.

Terms for illustrators: Rate: $500/spread ($250/page). Physical art remains the property of the illustrator.

Submission guidelines: Write for guidelines and include SASE or go to the Web site. For a sample issue of *Babybug*, please send $5 to *Babybug* Sample Copy, PO Box 300, Peru, IL 61354. *Note:* Sample copy requests from foreign countries must be accompanied by International Postal Reply Coupons (IRCs) valued at U.S. $5. Please do not send a check or money order. Direct art samples to Suzanne Beck, art director. Direct questions about rights to Mary Ann Hocking, rights and permissions manager

Tips and comments: *Babybug* would like to reach as many children's authors and artists as possible for original contributions, but standards are very high, and *Babybug* will accept only top-quality material. *Before* attempting to write or illustrate for *Babybug*, be sure to *familiarize yourself with the publication and the targeted age group.*

Blabber Mouth

PO Box 417
Mendon, MA 01756
(508) 529-6630
(508) 529-6039 (fax)
E-mail: submit@blabbermouthonline.com
Web site: www.blabbermouthonline.com

Description: Bimonthly magazine focusing on teen interests and issues.

Key people:

Articles editor: Amy Saunders

Black Belt for Kids

(Santa Clarita, CA)

No longer being published.

Boys' Life

PO Box 152079
1325 W. Walnut Hill Lane
Irving, TX 75038

Corporate structure/parent: Boy Scouts of America.

Description: *Boys' Life* is a general interest, four-color monthly with a circulation of 1.3 million.

Established: 1911, and published continuously ever since.

Key people:

Editor in chief: J. D. Owen
Managing editor: W. E. Butterworth IV
Articles editor: Michael Goldman
Fiction editor: Rich Haddaway
Director of design: Joseph P. Connolly
Art director: Eric Ottinger

Articles per year and description: All articles and illustrations are for children in all categories of interest.

Percentage by first-time authors: Publishes first-time writers, but it is variable.

Seeks: Anything that is family-appropriate and would interest an 11- to 12-year-old boy. All articles for *Boys' Life* must interest and entertain boys ages 8 to 18. Write for a boy you know who is 12. The readers demand crisp, punchy writing in relatively short, straightforward sentences. Editors demand well-reported articles that demonstrate high standards of journalism.

Accepts unsolicited/unagented: Yes, with an SASE for response.

Recent articles:

"Prairie Sailors" (A dammed river turns ranchland into waterfront for landlocked Scouts—A Scout Program.)

"Sun Racers" (High school engineers test solar-powered cars on a 1,600-mile, cross-country trek.)

"Hot Diggity Dog!" (Yum! Here's everything you ever wanted to know about an all-American food.)

Preferred articles: No adult reminiscences. Boy-centered stories and features. No guns; no hunting.

Preferred form of submission/contact: Query for nonfiction (enclose an SASE); manuscript for fiction (enclose an SASE).

Time to reply: Six to eight weeks.

Time to publish: Six months to two years.

Accepts simultaneous submissions: Yes.

Number of illustrators used annually: 50 or more.

Desired illustrator qualifications: Creativity; craftsmanship; appropriateness for assignment; ability to conceive ideas.

Prefer manuscript/illustration packages, or separate: Separately.

Include with illustrator query: Samples and tear sheets.

Time to reply: Six to eight weeks. Return postage/packaging must be included with the query for a return of materials and reply.

Purchases freelance photography: By assignment only; some stock photos are used.

Preferred photography: Sharp, clear action shots that enhance the subject of the feature.

Terms for writers: Columns, $150 to $400; features, $400 to $1,500; fiction, $750 and up. Buys first-time rights for original unpublished material.

Terms for illustrators: $250 to $2,500.

Submission guidelines: Send SASE (#10 envelope) to the magazine with a request for guidelines.

Tips and comments: Read at least one full year of magazine issues so that you are familiar with what and how the magazine does things. Then submit. If you have them, it helps the editors to see clips and samples. As with writers, illustrators should also study back issues of the publication to familiarize themselves with its style, image, and content. The magazine assigns work for specific features. Follows the *New York Times Manual of Style and Usage.*

Boys' Quest

103 N. Main
PO Box 227
Bluffton, OH 45817-0227
(419) 358-4610

Corporate structure/parent: Bluffton News Publishing & Printing Co.

Description: *Boys' Quest* is a magazine created for boys from 6 to 13 years, with youngsters 8, 9, and 10 the specific target age.

Key people:

Articles editor: Marilyn Edwards

Art editor: Diane Winebar

Established: 1995

Seeks: *Boys' Quest*'s point of view is that every young boy deserves the right to be a young boy for a number of years before he becomes a young adult. As a result, *Boys' Quest* looks for articles, fiction, nonfiction, and poetry that deal with timeless topics, such as pets, nature, hobbies, science, games, sports, careers, simple cooking, and anything else likely to interest a young boy. The ideal length of a *Boys' Quest* piece—nonfiction or fiction—is 500 words.

Accepts unsolicited/unagented: Yes.

Preferred articles: Looking for lively writing, most of it from a young boy's point of view—with the boy or boys directly involved in an activity that is both wholesome and unusual. Needs nonfiction with photos and fiction stories—around 500 words—puzzle, poems, cooking, carpentry prospects, jokes, and riddles.

Preferred form of submission/contact: *Boys' Quest* prefers to receive complete manuscripts with cover letters, although it does not rule out query letters. *Boys' Quest* does not answer submissions sent by fax. All submissions must be accompanied by a self-addressed stamped envelope, with sufficient postage.

Time to reply: *Boys' Quest* attempts to make quick decisions on all submissions.

Accepts simultaneous submissions: Will entertain simultaneous submissions as long as that fact is noted on the manuscript.

Desired illustrator qualifications: Most art will be by assignment, in support of features used. The magazine is anxious to find artists capable of illustrating stories and features and welcomes copies of sample work, which will remain on file. Work inside is pen and ink.

Include with illustrator query: The magazine welcomes copies of sample work, which will remain on file.

Time to reply: *Boys' Quest* attempts to make quick decisions on all submissions.

Purchases freelance photography: Yes.

Preferred photography: Uses a number of black-and-white photos inside the magazine, most in support of articles used. Payment is $5 to 10 per photo used, depending on the quality and $5 for color slides.

Terms for writers: *Boys' Quest*, as a new publication, is aware that its rates of payment are modest at this time. But the magazine pledges to increase those rewards in direct proportion to its success. Meanwhile, *Boys' Quest* will strive to treat its contributors and their work with respect and fairness. That treatment, incidentally, will include quick decisions on all submissions. *Boys' Quest* will pay a minimum of $0.05 a word for both fiction and nonfiction, with additional payment given if the piece is accompanied by appropriate photos or art. *Boys' Quest* will pay a minimum of $10 per poem or puzzle, with variable rates offered for games, carpentry projects, and so on. A complimentary copy of the magazine will be sent to each writer who has contributed to a given issue. *Boys' Quest* buys first American serial rights and pays on publication. It welcomes the contributions of both published and unpublished writers.

Terms for illustrators: $35 for a full page and $25 for a partial page.

Submission guidelines: Write with an SASE for guidelines. Submissions should be sent to the attention of the editor.

Tips and comments: Nonfiction pieces that are accompanied by black-and-white photos are far more likely to be accepted than those that need illustrations. The magazine is anxious to find artists capable of illustrating stories and features and welcomes copies of sample work, which will remain on file. Every contributor must remember *Boys' Quest* publishes only six issues a year, which means the magazine's editorial needs are extremely limited. It is obvious that *Boys' Quest* must reject far more contributions that it accepts, no matter how outstanding they may seem.

BREAD FOR GOD'S CHILDREN

PO Box 1018
Arcadia, FL 34265
(863) 494-6214
(863) 993-0154 (fax)
E-mail: bread@desoto.net

Description: Bimonthly magazine designed as a teaching tool for Christian families.

Key people:

Editor: Judith M. Gibbs

CALIFORNIA CHRONICLES

California Chronicles, a publication of the Cobblestone Publishing Group, ceased publication following the May 2000 issue.

CALLIOPE

30 Grove Street, Suite C
Peterborough, NH 03458
Web site: www.cobblestonepub.com/pages/callmain.htm

Corporate structure/parent: Cobblestone Publishing (which is a subsidiary of Cricket Publishing Group).

Description: Magazine devoted to world history.

Established: In 1981, it was originally named *Classical Calliope*. It was renamed *Calliope* in 1990.

Key people:

Editors in chief: Rosalie Baker and Charles Baker

Managing editor: Lou Waryncia

Art director: Ann Dillon

Marketing manager: Manuela Meier

Publisher: Jack Olbrych

Articles per year: Approximately 130 to 150.

Percentage by first-time authors: Approximately 20 percent.

Seeks: *Calliope* covers world history (East/West) and is looking for lively, original approaches to the subject.

Accepts unsolicited/unagented: Query only.

Preferred articles: *Feature articles:* 700 to 800 words. Includes in-depth nonfiction, plays, and biographies. *Supplemental nonfiction:* 300 to 600 words. Includes subjects directly and indirectly related to the theme. Editors like little-known information but encourage writers not to overlook the obvious. *Fiction:* Up to 800 words. Includes authentic historical and biographical fiction, adventure, and retold legends, relating to the theme. *Activities*: Up to 700 words. Includes crafts, recipes, woodworking, or any other interesting projects that can be done either by children alone or with adult supervision. Sketches and description of how activity relates to theme should accompany queries. *Poetry*: Up to 100 lines. Clear, objective imagery. Serious and light verse considered. Must relate to theme. *Puzzles and games* (please, no word finds): Crosswords and other word puzzles using the vocabulary of the issue's theme. Mazes and picture puzzles that relate to the theme.

Preferred form of submission/contact: Query. For your idea to be considered, a query must accompany each individual idea (however, you can mail them all together) and must include the following: a brief cover letter stating the subject and word length of the proposed article, a detailed one-page outline explaining the information to be presented in the article, an extensive bibliography of materials the author intends to use in preparing the article, and a self-addressed stamped envelope.

Time to reply: Queries may be submitted at any time, but queries sent well in advance of deadline may not be answered for several months. Go-aheads requesting material proposed in queries are usually sent five months prior to publication date. Unused queries will be returned approximately three to four months prior to publication date.

Number of illustrators used annually: Varies. Could be one per issue to five or more per issue.

Desired illustrator qualifications: Artists who can capture the essence of an article.

Accepts manuscript/illustration packages, or prefers separate: Queries from author/illustrators may be submitted at the same time. Authors are encouraged to submit art suggestions.

Purchases freelance photography: Yes.

Preferred photography: To be considered for publication, photographs must relate to a specific theme. Writers are encouraged to submit available photos with their query or article. If you have photographs pertaining to any upcoming theme, please contact the editor by mail or fax, or send them with your query. You may also send images on speculation. Recent themes have included Pyramids and Tombs at Giza, Alexandria under the Ptolemies, Ancient Celts (100 B.C. to A.D. 100), Dead Sea Scrolls, Ancient Khmer Empire, Silk Road, Leonardo da Vinci, Louis XIV, and Voyages of Captain Cook.

Terms for writers: Stories and articles pay $0.20 to $0.25 per printed word; games, puzzles, and poetry pay on an individual basis. *Calliope* purchases all rights to material.

Submission guidelines: Go to the Web site or write with an SASE.

Tips and comments: Keep in mind that *Calliope* is aimed at youths from ages 8 to 14. Writers are encouraged to study recent back issues for content and style. (Sample issues are available at $4.95. Send 7 1/2 by 10 1/2-inch self-addressed, $2 stamped envelope.) All material must relate to the theme of a specific upcoming issue to be considered. Authors are urged to use primary resources and up-to-date scholarly resources in their bibliography. Writers new to *Calliope* should send a writing sample with the query. If you would like to know whether your query has been received, please also include a stamped postcard that requests acknowledgment of receipt. In all correspondence, please include your complete address as well as a telephone number where you can be reached. A writer may send as many queries for one issue as he or she wishes, but each query must have a separate cover letter, outline, bibliography, and self-addressed stamped envelope. All queries must be typed.

Campus Life

465 Gundersen Drive
Carol Stream, IL 60188
(630) 260-0114 (fax)
E-mail: clmag@campuslife.net
Web site: www.christianitytoday.com

Corporate structure/parent: *Campus Life* is published bimonthly by Christianity Today International.

Description: *Campus Life*'s contemporary and relevant editorial deals with the real life issues of high school and college students, including sex, spiritual concerns, friendships, school, and music.

Key people:

Editor: Christopher Lutes
Managing editor: Mark Moring
Assistant editor: Amber Penney
Design director: Doug Johnson

Seeks: First-person stories that capture experiences from the lives of teenagers are readers' favorites. These can be dramatic narratives or stories that highlight a "life lesson" learned through common everyday adolescent experiences. A first-person story must be highly descriptive and incorporate fictional technique. While avoiding simplistic religious answers, the story should demonstrate that Christian values or beliefs brought about a change in the young person's life. Since this is the magazine's editorial bread and butter, experienced freelancers should consider writing "as told to" first-person stories based on an experience from an interviewee's life. Guidelines for writing first-person stories are available on request.

Accepts unsolicited/unagented: No. Queries only. Don't query until you've studied at least one issue of *Campus Life* (sample copy available for $2).

Preferred articles: In addition to the first-person stories already mentioned, *Campus Life* also looks for humor, fiction, and information for teens considering a Christian college. All such writings must be tied to the teenager's life experience. *Campus Life* also

Meet Rich Davis

Illustrator

Rich Davis has illustrated many children's books, including *Tiny's Bath* (Viking/Puffin/Scholastic, 1999); *When Tiny Was Tiny* (Viking/Puffin/Scholastic/Houghton Mifflin, 1999); *101 Ways to Spoil Your Parents* (Garborgs 1998); *Tiny the SnowDog* (Viking/Puffin 2002); and the forthcoming *Firefighters to the Rescue* (Viking, 2003). He was born in Houston, Texas, in 1958, and grew up in Memphis, Tennessee. He moved to Siloam Springs, Arkansas; shortly afterward he married. He's thoroughly southern! His early art education as a boy was on any open space in the middle of a room where he could spread out. His college art education started in his fourth year, and then he went three more at Belhaven College and Memphis State University, graduating with a B.F.A. in graphic design. He was a cartoonist—both gag and editorial—at the university's magazine. His first job as a teenager was in a print shop where he became well familiar with the sound of presses running and the smell of oily ink. Later he worked at an advertising agency and a corporate advertising department. And currently, he's at a greeting card company called Dayspring (owned by Hallmark) by which he's still employed some 14 years later. He loves to write for the toddlers through first grade age group.

How did you get your first book published?

I came into the publishing world through the back door walking backward! It was not a burning desire to be published that brought me in; rather, I loved how children's books made me feel as an artist and their potential for good. I am a young man yet at 32 had a stroke. And a couple of years after that had a very serious internal injury that led to fibromyalgia, a chronic pain and exhaustion disease. Pain led me into children's books. I found that when I went to the children's section in bookstores that I would sit down on the floor and enter into a world I loved by opening the books there. It was a magical world that would somehow make the pain bearable. I began drawing the art I saw, and I studied visually what I was enjoying—every day and night. Slowly I began to draw my own characters and make my own scenes. I had a full-time job doing greeting cards for Dayspring (still do) during the day, but still after creating all day, I was strongly compelled to do my children's book art. Finally after collecting all this art that I was doing for fun, I began to wonder, "what am I supposed to do with all this?"

I heard about a workshop for children's books in Memphis, where I grew up and still had family there. This was in June of 1996. It was for "writing" books, but I was curious enough to want to find out for myself whether there was anything in books for me. So, I showed up. I had written a story called *One Night on the Ark* (which still is unpublished) and painted a few of the pictures for it as well as drawn many sketches for it. I decided to throw my portfolio in the trunk of the car just in case I had an opportunity to show someone there—but this was a writer's conference!

Entering that conference was my first step into the industry without me knowing it. There I met a wonderful writer/illustrator named Bobette McCarthy who had at that time already done 10 books. I also met another key person, Elizabeth Law, senior editor for Viking Penguin.

From that conference I took away the resolve to enter the speeding freeway of sending work by mail into the seemingly endless slush piles of the publishing houses. I sent out six mailings simultaneously and waited. Within three months I had heard back from four houses, with one rejecting the work and three writing letters requesting to see more. I busily jumped in and put together more work and stories—that in itself was a huge job!

I picked up the phone in October 1997 to hear the chipper voice of Denise Cronin at Viking Penguin asking me if I wanted to accept a two-book contract on a manuscript written by Cari Meister about a young boy and a humongous dog named Tiny. And Tiny was born!

Did you have an agent when you published your first book?

I did not and I do not. I have been approached by an agent who wanted to represent me, but I have not felt that I was ready for that relationship yet. Maybe in time if my need is high enough because of the time I need to be painting instead of rustling up work.

Do you have any advice, in terms of finding an agent, for an illustrator starting out?

I would advise starting out without one. This will put you in the place of learning how things work in the industry and cause you to research, call people, and pursue answers to important issues. I think that is important. And when contracts began to come in, I called my regional adviser for SCBWI, Sandy Fox, and asked how to find answers to the very legalistic language of contracts. She referred me to a literary lawyer named Mary Flower in New York who is very reasonable and very enjoyable to work with. She helped me a lot, and still does! The e-groups for writers and illustrators online are another wonderful outlet for finding accurate information from seasoned veterans and from others who love this field like I do. They love to chat about the struggles and are quick to lend encouragement and help.

Are you still with your first publisher?

Yes! I started with Viking Penguin, and I've worked for them as they have offered books. One factor is that my work with them began with the Tiny the big dog series, and it has continued to grow from its success. These being easy-to-read category books, it is a good place to have a series that kids can relate to and enjoy. Another factor is the excellent editor that I have worked with on these, Judy Carey. She has made my experience in the publishing world a very enjoyable one. She's a great communicator, prompt with her communication, very professional but has made me "feel at home" in the publishing world. I think that when a person does several jobs for someone, it is saying a lot of positive things on both sides of the fence. Because I have a regular in-house art job doing greeting cards each day, I do not have the pressure of having to rustle up as many jobs as I can get. I am much more leisurely about it, and that has afforded me the way to have a good working relationship with Viking—they really are great people!

Do your write the text for the books you illustrate?

All of the times that I have tried to sell my stories, they have been warmly greeted with encouragement that the idea was great, but I needed work on how to write it. I worked very hard for a period of time trying to get my stuff published but in the end felt I was being divided in my energies and goals. I felt my greatest encouragement and chance was with my pictures, and so I tucked the stories into bed, kissed their forehead, and said, "See you in the morning."

continues

What procedures do you follow when you work?

I believe with all my heart that art is built step by step on "confidence." If you don't have the confidence, you're probably not even going to try. So whenever I sit down to do art, I always ask myself what the easiest place on the art is and begin there—maybe it's that the grass is going to be green and the sky blue! I'm confident of that, and so I get those colors out, mix them with a lot of raw abandon, and go for it. Usually when I've put down what I know, something else pops out as the next step. And the next.

As far as carrying a book through from start to finish, yes, I have a method. I get a calendar and start at the deadline and subtract a week so that when I finish I will be a week ahead. Then I figure out how many paintings I can do in a month and divide the total number into it. I figure an amount of time for the quick sketches for a small dummy, time for it to be evaluated by the art director/editor, and time to take that feedback and integrate it into tight drawings at 100 percent that I will transfer down on illustration board.

I live by the creed "Plan your work, then work your plan." Leave room in your schedule for unexpected mishaps or delays, and leave time in your schedule to be with your family!

Where do you get your ideas?

Everywhere. Being creative is something practiced across the board of life, not just in art. I try and keep a sharp edge on creativity because there is nothing worse than to feel burned out and used up with everything feeling the same. Most of my ideas come from places or people or circumstances where I am caught in my emotions. Things I feel strongly about. You certainly can't force them to come—that makes it worse—but you can put some bird feed in the feeder that will attract the birds! I play a lot of "what if?" What if there was a manhole cover right there on the floor and it started to slide back and a big nose stuck out?! Or, two birds are side by side on a power line—what if they could talk? What would they be saying? "Hey, Fred, let's go dive-bomb that guy before he gets to his car!"

I have found that creativity is birthed out of need. There is a need that comes up—it needs a solution—brainstorming and writing things down off the top of my head (whether they make sense or not!), one thing leading to another. And I try to sketch sometimes instead of write words, just as fast as I can. It is fun. I'm much more relaxed about finding ideas now. I actually look forward to it for the most part.

Anything you really wish somebody had told you when you started out?

Enjoy what you do! Really explode into the enjoyment—let it take you away into its own world. Pray about all your decisions that come your way at the drawing board. After all, the greatest creator is God, and he definitely wants to help you with your work!

Take time each day to draw anything you like as a warmup for the day. Understand that taking on any book project is signing up for a whole lot of work! A lot! Don't be fooled into believing you'll make a lot of money doing books. It probably won't happen for a lot of us. Have a reason that will carry you through the discouraging low times and keep you going for the duration.

Accept criticism on your work as something to be considered—sometimes it will be just what you need, and other times you will throw it out with the trash. But try to welcome it if you really want to improve. Be sure your "details" are carefully looked after in your art. Each piece is a series of little details.

Make it your aim to serve your "customer"—the kids who will buy it; the editor at the publishing house; the publishing house that contracted you. If you have to have your artwork your way every time, you probably won't get a lot of calls. Save that kind of art work for your own art that you do for yourself on the side. Be cheerful and interested when you make communication to your customers. It goes a long way!

offers several regular departments that are largely staff written. Specific writer's guidelines for fiction, first-person, and humor pieces are available on request. Essays and how-to articles are not wanted. There are a few exceptions, yet even exceptions must be highly anecdotal and demonstrate a clear understanding of the magazine's style and editorial philosophy. Manuscripts are rejected if they become moralistic or preachy; offer simplistic solutions; take an adult tone; use religious clichés and overuse/misuse religious language; lack respect and empathy for teenagers.

Preferred form of submission/contact: Query. No manuscript solicitations.

Time to reply: Expect a response in three to six weeks.

Accepts simultaneous submissions: Yes, but simultaneous submissions must be indicated on the first page.

Terms for writers: Based on difficulty and length, $0.15 to $0.20 per word.

Tips and comments: The first-person or "as told to" first-person story is the best way for a new writer to break into the magazine's freelance pool (1,200–2,500 words). It is also the best way for a seasoned writer to remain there. It's no overstatement to say that the personal narrative is the magazine's editorial "mainstay." Follow these guidelines and your manuscript will receive serious consideration. Study first-person stories. *Guideposts* and *Reader's Digest* are excellent resources. Most of all, study the first-person stories that appear in *Campus Life* before submitting anything.

CAREER WORLD

900 Skokie Boulevard, Suite 200
Northbrook, IL 60062-4028

Description: *Career World* magazine highlights careers, vocational type jobs, and pre-college articles for students 12 to 18.

Key people:

Articles editor: Carole Rubenstein

Accepts unsolicited/unagented: No unsolicited manuscripts.

Terms for writers: Pay is $100 to $400 for all rights.

Careers & Colleges

989 Avenue of the Americas
New York, NY 10018
(212) 563-4688
Web site: www.careersandcolleges.com

Description: Career magazine for high school juniors and seniors.

Key people:

Editorial director: Don Rauf

Cat Fancy

PO Box 6050
Mission Viejo, CA 92690
Web site: www.animalnetwork.com/cats

Description: *Cat Fancy* is a consumer magazine directed to the general cat-owning population and dedicated to improve the lives of cats worldwide.

Percentage by first-time authors: While 80 percent of the feature articles that appear in *Cat Fancy* are assigned to writers we work with regularly, the magazine does occasionally accept a feature or feature sidebar from a new contributor.

Seeks: Short stories, how-to pieces, word puzzles, quizzes, and craft projects in Kids for Cats, a section aimed at readers between 8 and 15 years old. Good-quality photographs are essential to craft projects.

Accepts unsolicited/unagented: *Cat Fancy* does not read or accept unsolicited manuscripts; however, the editors are happy to consider article queries. Unsolicited manuscripts sent with a self-addressed stamped envelope are returned unread. Those without an SASE are discarded.

Preferred form of submission/contact: Please send a written query with an SASE if you have an article idea.

Tips and comments: Before you send anything, read past issues of the magazine to acquaint yourself with the type of material used. Past issues are available at many public libraries, pet stores, bookstores, or newsstands.

Catholic Faith & Family

33 Rossotto Drive
Hamden, CT 06514
(203) 288-5600
(203) 288-5157 (fax)
E-mail: editor@twincircle.com

Description: Biweekly mostly aimed at adults but with some children's content.

Key people:

Articles editor: Loretta G. Seyer

Art director: Tom Brophy

CHICKADEE

370 King Street W., Suite 300
Toronto, Ontario M5V 1J8
Canada
(416) 971-5275
(416) 971-5294 (fax)
E-mail: owl@owlkids.com
Web site: www.owl.on.ca

Corporate structure/parent: Owl Communications.

Key people:

Managing editor: Angela Keenlyside

Seeks: *Chickadee* is intended for children aged 3 to 9. The magazine publishes fiction and nonfiction that meets the objectives and philosophy of Owl Communications. *Chickadee* contains a high proportion of stories, puzzles, activities, and observation games that young readers can enjoy on their own. Each issue also contains a longer story or poem that may be read aloud to children, or shared with an older reader.

Accepts unsolicited/unagented: Yes.

Preferred articles: *Chickadee* seeks articles that inform and stimulate children and are also enjoyable to read. Avoid sexist and ethnic stereotypes and do not give animals human characteristics. Keep the age range of the readers in mind, but do not talk down to them. An easy, lively style and a clear logical presentation of ideas are more important than limiting vocabulary for young readers. Accuracy is of utmost importance. A bibliography and a list of research references for scientific data are required.

Preferred form of submission/contact: *Chickadee* prefers to read completed manuscripts of stories and articles, accompanied by photographs or suggestions of visual references where they are appropriate. Do not send queries. *Chickadee* also likes to know something about the writer's credentials. If possible, first-time submissions should be accompanied by examples of previously published work.

Time to reply: Six to eight weeks are required to properly review submissions.

Desired illustrator qualifications: Great attention is paid to the quality of photographs and illustrations used in *Chickadee*. Most illustrations are commissioned.

Prefer manuscript/illustration packages, or separate: Art and photographs may accompany written submissions, but *Chickadee* usually contracts art and photography separately.

Time to reply: Six to eight weeks are required to review submissions properly.

Purchases freelance photography: Yes.

Preferred photography: Unsolicited photographs are seldom used unless they accompany an article. Photographers' stock lists are welcome. Photographs should be high-quality color transparencies. Duplicates may be submitted, but the originals will be required for reproduction. Photographs must be well packaged and are best sent by registered mail. For photo information, write and request a photo package.

Terms for writers: Fees range from $100 to $250 for longer features and $10 to $100 for shorter features, depending on the scope of the material. Owl Communications requires extensive rights to material to accommodate both its needs and those of its affiliated foreign-language magazines. Sample contracts outlining the basic requirements are available on request.

Submission guidelines: For the section of the magazine intended to be read aloud by an adult, stories should be 300 to 800 words. Material for the sections that children can read or explore by themselves is always highly visual, and the copy usually runs from 10 to 100 words. *Chickadee* welcomes new ideas for puzzles and simple activities with clear instructions. Craft ideas should be based on materials found around the average household.

Tips and comments: *Chickadee* urges authors, illustrators, and photographers to become familiar with *Chickadee* before submitting material. Magazines may be purchased directly from Owl Communications, found on newsstands, or borrowed from the library. Sample copies: $4.28 (includes all taxes); please send $1.50 money order (no stamps—includes GST) for a reply to manuscripts. *Chickadee* is published by Owl Communications, a registered, nonprofit charitable organization with the following aims: To encourage children to read for enjoyment and discovery, to help children learn more about the world around them, to stimulate children to enjoy, respect, and conserve their natural environment, and to give children a wealth of ideas to use constructively.

Child Life

PO Box 567
Indianapolis, IN 46206-0567
(317) 636-8881
Web site: www.cbhi.org

Corporate structure/parent: Children's Better Health Institute.

Accepts unsolicited/unagented: No. *Child Life* is not accepting manuscripts for publication at this time. After reprinting nostalgic stories during the 75th anniversary, the publishers have decided to make nostalgia the permanent format. Health articles will be handled in-house or assigned. All unsolicited material will be returned.

Children's Digest

PO Box 567
Indianapolis, IN 46206-0567
(317) 636-8881
Web site: www.cbhi.org

Corporate structure/parent: Children's Better Health Institute.

Key people:

Editor: Lise Hoffman

Art director: Phyllis Lybarger

Seeks: *Children's Digest* has a constant need for high-quality stories, articles, and activities with health-related themes. "Health" is a broad topic that includes exercise, nutrition, safety, hygiene, and drug education. *Children's Digest* is especially interested in material concerning sports and fitness, including profiles of famous amateur and professional athletes; "average" athletes (especially children) who have overcome obstacles to excel in their areas; and new or unusual sports, particularly those in which children can participate. Although the magazine's emphasis is on health, *Children's Digest* certainly uses material with more general themes. *Children's Digest* would especially like to see more holiday stories, articles, and activities. Please send seasonal material at least eight months in advance. *Children's Digest* also welcomes recipes that children can make on their own with minimal adult supervision. Ingredients should be healthful, so avoid using fats, sugar, salt, chocolate, and red meat. In all material submitted, please avoid reference to eating sugary foods, such as candy, cakes, cookies, and soft drinks.

Accepts unsolicited/unagented: Yes.

Preferred articles: Health information can be presented in a variety of formats: fiction, nonfiction, poems, and puzzles. Fiction stories with a health message need not have health as the primary subject, but they should include it in some way in the course of events. Characters in fiction should adhere to good health practices, unless failure to do so is necessary to a story's plot. Nonfiction articles dealing with health subjects should be fresh and creative. Avoid an encyclopedic or "preachy" approach. *Children's Digest* tries to present our health material in a positive manner, incorporating humor and a light approach wherever possible without minimizing the seriousness of what the magazine is saying. *Children's Digest* readers want stories that are a little longer and "meatier" than others (fiction: 500–1,500 words; nonfiction: 500–1,000 words). Fiction is especially needed: adventure, mystery, science fiction, and humorous stories. Some fiction may have a subtle health message, but this magazine, too, uses factual features to educate about good health. Games, puzzles, crafts, and hobbies are also welcome, as are nonfiction articles about sports, nature, and the environment.

Preferred form of submission/contact: Completed manuscript only.

Time to reply: About three months are required to review manuscripts properly. Please wait three months before sending status inquiries.

Accepts simultaneous submissions: Simultaneous submissions are discouraged.

Desired illustrator qualifications: Please do not send drawings or other artwork. Children's Digest *prefers to work with professional illustrators of its own choosing.*

Prefer manuscript/illustration packages, or separate: Manuscript only.

Purchases freelance photography: Yes.

Preferred photography: *Children's Digest* does not purchase single photographs. *Children's Digest* purchases short photo features (up to six or eight pictures or photos that accompany articles and help illustrate editorial material. (Please include captions and model releases.) *Children's Digest* buys one-time rights to photos.

Terms for writers: Minimum $0.12 a word. Fiction, 500 to 1,500 words; nonfiction, 500 to 1,000 words; poetry, $15 minimum; photos, $15 minimum; puzzles and games, no fixed rates (send an SASE to receive separate guidelines for activities). Payment is made on publication. Each author receives 10 complimentary copies of the issue in which his or her material is published. *Children's Digest* purchases all rights to manuscripts.

Terms for illustrators: *Children's Digest* buys one-time rights to photos.

Submission guidelines: Write with an SASE for guidelines. Please send the entire manuscript. All work is on speculation only; queries are not accepted, nor are stories assigned.

Tips and comments: Readers are preteens; please bear that in mind as you write your story. Remember that characters in realistic stories should be up-to-date. Many of the magazine's readers have working mothers and/or come from single-parent homes. *Children's Digest* needs more stories that reflect these changing times but at the same time communicate good, wholesome values. Reading the *Children's Digest* editorial guidelines is not enough! Careful study of current issues will acquaint writers with each title's "personality," various departments, and regular features, nearly all of which are open to freelancers. Sample copies are $1.25 each (U.S. currency) from the Children's Better Health Institute, PO Box 567, Indianapolis, IN 46206.

Children's Playmate

PO Box 567
Indianapolis, IN 46206-0567
(317) 636-8881
Web site: www.cbhi.org

Corporate structure/parent: Children's Better Health Institute.

Key people:

Editor: Terry Harshman

Art director: Chuck Horsman

Seeks: *Children's Playmate* uses easy-to-read fiction for beginning readers, as well as poems, rhyming stories, and nonfiction. *Children's Playmate* has a constant need for high-quality stories, articles, and activities with health-related themes. "Health" is a broad topic that includes exercise, nutrition, safety, hygiene, and drug education. *Children's Playmate* is especially interested in material concerning sports and fitness, including profiles of famous amateur and professional athletes; "average" athletes (especially children) who have overcome obstacles to excel in their areas; and new or unusual sports, particularly those in which children can participate. Although the magazine's emphasis is on health, *Children's Playmate* certainly uses material with more general themes. *Children's Playmate* would especially like to see more holiday stories, articles, and activities. Please send seasonal material at least eight months in advance. *Children's Playmate* also welcomes recipes that children can make on their own with minimal adult supervision. Ingredients should be healthful, so avoid using fats, sugar, salt, chocolate, and red meat. In all material submitted, please avoid reference to eating sugary foods, such as candy, cakes, cookies, and soft drinks.

Accepts unsolicited/unagented: Yes.

Preferred articles: Health information can be presented in a variety of formats: fiction, nonfiction, poems, and puzzles. Fiction stories with a health message need not have health as the primary subject, but they should include it in some way in the course of events. Characters in fiction should adhere to good health practices, unless failure to do so is necessary to a story's plot. Nonfiction articles dealing with health subjects should be fresh and creative. Avoid an encyclopedic or "preachy" approach. *Children's Playmate* tries to present health material in a positive manner, incorporating humor and a light approach wherever possible without minimizing the seriousness of what is being said.

Preferred form of submission/contact: Completed manuscript only.

Time to reply: About three months are required to review manuscripts properly. Please wait three months before sending status inquiries.

Accepts simultaneous submissions: Simultaneous submissions are discouraged.

Desired illustrator qualifications: Please do not send drawings or other artwork. *Children's Playmate* prefers to work with professional illustrators of our own choosing.

Prefer manuscript/illustration packages, or separate: Manuscript only.

Purchases freelance photography: Yes.

Preferred photography: *Children's Playmate* does not purchase single photographs. *Children's Playmate* purchases short photo features (up to six or eight pictures or photos that accompany articles and help illustrate editorial material. (Please include captions and model releases.) *Children's Playmate* buys one-time rights to photos.

Terms for writers: Up to $0.17 a word (fiction/nonfiction: 300–600 words); poetry, $15 minimum; photos, $15 minimum; puzzles and games, no fixed rates (send an SASE to receive separate guidelines for activities). Payment is made on publication. Each author receives 10 complimentary copies of the issue in which his or her material is published. *Children's Playmate* purchases all rights to manuscripts.

Terms for illustrators: *Children's Playmate* buys one-time rights to photos.

Submission guidelines: Write with an SASE for guidelines. See entry on *Children's Digest* for more information.

Tips and comments: Readers are children ages 6 to 8 years old; please bear that in mind as you write your story. See *Children's Digest* entry for more information.

CHIRP

370 King Street W., Suite 300
Toronto, Ontario M5V 1J8
Canada
(416) 971-5275
(416) 971-5294 (fax)
E-mail: owl@owlkids.com
Web site: www.owl.on.ca

Corporate structure/parent: Owl Communications.

Description: Discovery magazine for ages 3 to 6.

Key people:
Editor in chief: Marybeth Leatherdale
Creative director: Tim Davin
Note: See *Chickadee* and *Owl* for submission information.

Cicada

PO Box 300
315 Fifth Street
Peru, IL 61354
(312) 939-1500
(815) 224-6615 (fax)

Corporate structure/parent: Carus Publishing Company.

Description: *Cicada* is a literary magazine for teenagers and young adults. *Cicada*, for ages 14 and up, publishes original short stories, poems, and first-person essays written for teens and young adults.

Established: 1998.

Key people:
Editor in chief: Marianne Carus
Acquisitions/submissions editors: Debby Vetter and John D. Allen
Senior art director: Ron McCutchan

Articles per year and Description: Fiction, 60–70; poetry, 25–30; essay, 6.

Percentage by first-time authors: 25–30 percent.

Seeks: Fiction and poetry, chiefly in the genres of humor, fantasy, science fiction, mystery, and romance. Fiction/articles: up to 5,000 words. Novellas: up to 15,000 words (one novella per issue). Poems: up to 25 lines. Book reviews: 300 to 700 words.

Accepts unsolicited/unagented: Yes.

Preferred articles: Primarily judges manuscripts on literary merit. Looking for originality of style, depth of thought, and emotional engagement. *Fiction:* Looking for realistic, contemporary, historical fiction, adventure, humor, fantasy, and science fiction; main protagonist should be 14 or older; stories should have a genuine teen sensibility and be aimed at readers in high school or college. *Nonfiction:* First-person experiences that are relevant and interesting to teenagers. *Poetry:* Serious or humorous; rhymed or free verse. *Other:* Book reviews providing in-depth, thoughtful commentary.

Preferred form of submission/contact: Complete manuscript is preferable.

Time to reply: Within three months.

Time to publish: Within one year.

Accepts simultaneous submissions: Yes.

Number of illustrators used annually: 36 to 46.

Desired illustrator qualifications: Unusual style and strong characterization

Prefer manuscript/illustration packages, or separate: Prefers to review them separately.

Include with illustrator query: Color samples or tear sheets are required. *Please address all art samples to* Ron McCutchan, senior art director (same address as above).

Time to reply: Within eight to 10 weeks.

Purchases freelance photography: Yes, but only occasionally.

Preferred photography: The same elements that are sought in artwork.

Terms for writers: $0.25 per word for first serial rights for fiction and nonfiction and up to $3 per line for poetry. Payment on publication.

Submission guidelines: Guidelines are available at www.cicadamag.com. *Please address all manuscripts to* submissions editor. An exact word count should be noted on each manuscript submitted. For poetry, indicate number of lines instead. Word count includes every word but does not include the title of the manuscript or the author's name.

Tips and comments: Read several back issues of *Cicada* before submitting a story or poem. The best (and *only*) way to learn *Cicada* style is by reading the publication.

CLASS ACT

PO Box 802
Henderson, KY 42419-0802
(270) 826-1085
Web site: www.henderson.net/~classact

Description: *Class Act* is published monthly September through May and is primarily for teachers of English in grades 6 through 12.

Key people:

Editor: Susan Thurman

Seeks: Looking for practical teacher tips, classroom games, composition ideas, literature activities, and study sheets appropriate for students in middle school, junior high, or senior high school. Writing in a style suitable for students is most important. Looking for ideas from one paragraph to five typewritten pages long. Please double-space. The audience may be either the classroom teacher or the students. Issues include articles, tips and ideas for teachers, and ready-to-use activities designed for teachers to photocopy and pass out to their students.

Accepts unsolicited/unagented: Yes.

Preferred articles: *Class Act* likes to use material that is clever, requiring thought and creativity from students. *Class Act* does not like mindless busy work. *Class Act* loves material with a humorous, light-hearted, offbeat, or down-to-earth approach—the kind real teachers use with real students. Remember, *Class Act* is interested in ideas that have practicality. Please don't send your master's thesis!

Preferred form of submission/contact: Manuscript.

Time to reply: *Class Act* tries to get a response to an author within four weeks after receiving a manuscript.

Terms for writers: Payment ranges from $10 to $40. Payment is for all rights and is made on acceptance and return of signed form stating the work is your own and has not been published elsewhere. An author's copy is sent on publication.

Submission guidelines: Send submissions to Susan Thurman, editor. Please enclose an SASE with your submission; otherwise, *Class Act* will assume you don't want the manuscript returned if it is not used. E-mail submissions are encouraged, as long as they are not attachments.

Tips and comments: Sample copies are $3 each.

Click

332 S. Michigan Avenue
Suite 1100
Chicago, IL 60604
Web site: www.cobblestonepub.com/pages/clickmain.html

Corporate structure/parent: Cobblestone Publishing (which is a subsidiary of the Cricket Publishing Group).

Description: The goal of *Click* is to allow young children access to the world of ideas and knowledge in an age-appropriate yet challenging way. It is often assumed that many areas of human endeavor and knowledge are uninteresting and beyond the understanding of young children. However, *Click* assumes otherwise and attempts to provide children with a clear and inviting introduction to many of the same phenomena and questions about the world that intrigue their adult counterparts. *Click* also attempts to introduce children to the processes of investigation and observation and encourages children to be active participants in the search for knowledge and understanding of their world.

Established: October 1997.

Articles per year and description: *Click* is published 10 times a year, contains 36 pages, and each issue includes an 8-page "Parent's Companion." Each issue of *Click* is built around a central theme. Articles and photo essays are usually between 200 and 400 words; stories are usually between 600 and 1,000 words.

Accepts unsolicited/unagented: Yes, but please familiarize yourself with *Click* (by reading multiple back issues) before you even consider submitting a manuscript.

Preferred articles: Each issue of *Click* is built around a central theme. *Click* themes introduce children to ideas and concepts within the natural, physical, or social sciences; the arts; technology; math; and history. *Click* presents nonfiction concepts to young children through a variety of formats: articles, photo essays, and stories. *Click* is looking for articles and photo essays that explain the how and why of something in a friendly, engaging, perhaps humorous way. *Click* therefore prefers a more informal, conversational style (as opposed to a formal, textbook style). The best articles tackle one idea or concept in depth rather than several ideas superficially. *Click* also publishes stories that contain and explain nonfiction concepts within them. Since it is part of Click's mission to encourage children to question, observe, and explore, successful stories often show children engaged in finding out about their universe—with the help of supportive, but not all-knowing, adults.

Preferred form of submission/contact: Manuscript. *Click* would like to publish articles and stories from as many authors as possible. However, *Click* will accept only material of the highest quality. Please do not query first.

Time to reply: Allow 12 to 16 weeks to receive a reply.

Prefer manuscript/illustration packages, or separate: Articles and artwork will be considered for publication separately.

Include with illustrator query: Send samples. Most artwork for *Click* is commissioned by the art director. If you are sending original artwork to be considered with your article, package it carefully and insure the package. Be sure to include packing materials and postage for the return of unused artwork.

Submission guidelines: Go to the Web site or write for guidelines (include an SASE). Please address all manuscript submissions to *Click* Magazine 332 S. Michigan Avenue, Suite 1100, Chicago, IL 60604. Please include an exact word count on each manuscript submitted. Count all words except the title and author's name. Authors submitting manuscripts for consideration are required to provide a bibliography that lists all resource materials and complete notes as to the sources of facts and information given.

Tips and comments: Familiarize yourself with *Click.*

CLUBHOUSE & *CLUBHOUSE JR.* (aka *Focus on the Family Clubhouse* & *Focus on the Family Clubhouse Jr.*)

8605 Explorer Drive
Colorado Springs, CO 80920
(719) 531-3400
(719) 531-3499 (fax)
Web site: www.clubhousemagazine.com

Description: Focus on the Family has two publications: *Focus on the Family Clubhouse* (which is for 8- to 12-year-old boys and girls) and *Focus on the Family Clubhouse Jr.* (which is for 4- to 8-year-olds). The purpose of the magazines is to entertain, inspire, and teach Christian values and concepts.

Established: *Clubhouse* was established in February 1987; *Clubhouse Jr.* in January 1988.

Key people:

Editor in chief: Chuck Johnson
***Clubhouse* editor:** Jesse Florea
***Clubhouse Jr.* editor:** Annette Bourland
Acquisitions/submissions editor: Suzanne Hadley

Articles per year and description: *Articles:* 36, fiction, craft, Bible stories, and nonfiction. *Illustrations:* 96 realistic, cartoon, wacky, and color only.

Percentage by first-time authors: 10 percent.

Seeks: Fresh, exciting literature that promotes biblical thinking, values, and behavior. This could include young and middle reader fiction (adventure, choose-your-own-adventure, historical, multicultural, sports, or sci-fi). Word length for middle fiction ranges between 1,200 and 1,700 words. Young fiction: 500 to 1,000. Nonfiction needs include arts, crafts, cooking, games/puzzles, how-to, science, animal. Word length: 500 to 1,000.

Accepts unsolicited/unagented: Yes.

Recent articles: Sigmund Brouwer wrote the lead fiction piece in one issue, about a boy in a Kentucky coal-mine town during the Depression. After doing work for the mine boss, the mine boss decides not to pay the boy what they'd agreed. The boy goes to the local store and tells the owner he won't be able to buy the dress for his mom as planned. Although the boy doesn't say what happened, the store owner figures it out, rallies the town and is able to surprise the boy's mother with the dress on Christmas morning. The message of the story is dealing with people who treat you unfairly. The readers also see God's love shown in practical ways as the town folks come together to support the hard-working boy.

Preferred articles: See above. Not looking for preachy or moralizing fiction. Looking for realistic dialogue. Grown-ups shouldn't always come to the rescue or have all the answers. Endings of stories shouldn't tie up in a neat little bow. Looking for real life.

Preferred form of submission/contact: Entire manuscript.

Time to reply: Four to six weeks.

Time to publish: Articles: Within a year. Illustrations are by assignment only and are printed two months after an assignment is received.

Accepts simultaneous submissions: No.

Number of illustrators used annually: 30.

Desired illustrator qualifications: Age-appropriate style. Attention to details within the stories they're illustrating. Putting themselves into illustrations.

Prefer manuscript/illustration packages, or separate: On rare occasion. The magazine has one writer-illustrator whom it has worked with for years. But that's it.

Include with illustrator query: Samples and tear sheets. Mail to Tim Jones, art director. Reports in two to three months. Samples returned with an SASE; samples kept on file.

Purchases freelance photography: Yes.

Preferred photography: 35mm transparencies. Assignment based. Very few stock photos used.

Terms for writers: Pays on acceptance. Buys first North American serial rights for mss. Buys first rights or reprint rights for artwork and photographs. Original artwork returned at job's completion. Pays $150 to $300 for stories; $100 to $150 for articles. Illustrators paid $300 to $700 for color cover; $200 to $700 for color inside. Pays photographers by the project or per photo.

Terms for illustrators: See above.

Submission guidelines: Writers/illustrators/photographers guidelines for SASE. Sample magazines 9 by 12-inch SASE and three first-class stamps.

Tips and comments: Think outside the box. The magazines receive more than 150 manuscripts a month—90 percent of which are contemporary fiction set in North America. Give the readers a global and historical perspective. Take the readers to different times or places. Share in the adventure as you bring characters to life. Don't think that the stories have to be explicitly Christian, but they should be built on a Christian foundation and not contradict biblical teaching and values. Test your writing on children. You're competing against 200 cable TV channels and high-tech video games, so your writing must be fun, fast-paced, and exciting.

Meet Lou Waryncia

Magazine Managing Editor

Lou Waryncia is managing editor of Cobblestone Publishing Company's six magazines for children ages 7 to 16: *Cobblestone, Faces, Calliope, Odyssey, Appleseeds,* and *Footsteps* (since 1998). Cobblestone publishes 50 magazines a year. Cobblestone also publishes occasional books that he also oversees. The two latest are *Readings and Activities for Character Education* by Diane L. Brooks (a resource guide for teachers and students), and *Erie Canal: New York's Gift to the Nation.* He has also written educational social studies workbooks for Silver Burdett & Ginn and served as a staff writer for *Big Blue Dot*—a kid's trend magazine.

Lou was born in Troy, New York, in 1959, and grew up in Halfmoon, New York. He has a B.A. in journalism/mass communication from Street Bonaventure University. He has been editing publications since high school. He spent 11 years at *CD Review* magazine moving from assistant editor to managing editor to editor in chief. He also worked at Photographic Book Company in New York City as an assistant editor and as a financial editor for the Ayco Corp. Plus he spent three years helping in prepress at Dartmouth Printing Co. His affiliation with Cobblestone goes back to 1984, when he began freelancing for the company as a copyeditor and proofreader.

As an editor, what do you look for in a children's article and in a potential author?

Since our magazines deal with history and science, we look for stories that accurately present the details of our theme. We then like to take this further to present the stories behind the main story. We look for details about daily life and work that don't make it into the history books. As for authors, we always try to work with known authorities on a special topic. We then extend our search to other writers who have a unique angle on the subject.

Do you have any advice for an author starting out in the children's writing field, in terms of how to get a published?

I believe the best way to get started as a writer is to write. Practice the craft as much as possible. Building a portfolio of work also can lead to bigger assignments, and maybe that book. Editors are always looking for new and interesting ideas. For our magazines, your query will get noticed if it's original, has a unique angle, has good sources, is presented well, and, most of all, is written well. Also, do your research. Don't waste an editor's time by sending him or her a story/book idea that doesn't match the company's mission.

Do you prefer that authors have agents when they come to you with an idea?

We do not work with agents, and I have no experience working with them. For my company, however, it would be a negative if we had to work with them. We prefer to deal with people directly. I would never assume someone is a better writer because they have an agent.

continues

Do you work with illustrators?

We work with authors and illustrators separately. We create magazine articles based on our themes and choose an artist who we feel can capture that theme.

What in your opinion makes an author easy to work with?

First, a good writer makes everything better. With our magazines, someone who can write appropriately for children also helps. Someone who is able to take suggestions and editing also makes the creative process go that much easier. Having work show up on time, with the correct word count, and in a readable electronic format also helps.

What do you think are the key differences between writing for children and writing for adults?

You need to understand that children don't understand things the same way as adults do. Their vocabulary is different. They don't have the same life experiences. You need to simplify but not dumb down. Most of all you need to be as honest as possible.

Do you recommend formal training for children's writers, or do you think it's a question of practice or of natural ability?

A bit of both. As someone who has studied journalism, I believe that formal training can help a lot. But I also believe there are a lot of creative people out there who have a natural ability to write or can become better writers the more they write.

COBBLESTONE

Cobblestone Publishing
30 Grove Street
Peterborough, NH 03458
(603) 924-7209, ext. 22
(603) 924-7380 (fax)
Web site: www.cobblestonepub.com

Corporate structure/parent: Cobblestone Publishing is a division of the Cricket Publishing Group. Cobblestone Publishing publishes the following six magazines for young people ages 8 to 15: *Cobblestone* (U.S. history), *Calliope* (world history), *Faces* (cultural anthropology), *Footsteps* (African American history), and *Odyssey* (science/space), and *Appleseeds* (theme-based social studies for ages 7 to 9). *California Chronicles* ceased publication as of May 2000.

Description: "*Cobblestone*, the magazine that makes American history come alive" for readers ages 9 to 14.

Established: 1980.

Key people:

Editor: Meg Chorlian

Managing editor: Lou Waryncia

Art director: Ann Dillon

Marketing manager: Manuela Meier

Publisher: Jack Olbrych

Articles per year and description: American history: Eight to 10 articles; four to five illustrations.

Percentage by first-time authors: 20 percent.

Seeks: Primarily nonfiction American history (feature length) but also accepts 700- to 800-word *feature articles* that include plays, first-person accounts, and biographies; 300- to 600-word *supplemental nonfiction* directly and indirectly related to the issue's theme; up to 800 words in *fiction*; *poetry* up to 100 lines; and *activities* up to 700 words on crafts, recipes, woodworking projects, and so forth.

Accepts unsolicited/unagented: No

Recent articles:

"The House Becomes a Home" by William B. Bushong (John and Abigail Adams move into the [unfinished] White House in November 1800.)

"'I Can Be Useful': First Ladies and Their Causes" by Ruth Tenzer Feldman

"Geographically Speaking" by Dennis O'Brian (Departments)

Cartoon Connection (Departments)

Brain Ticklers (Departments)

Preferred articles: Those that make American history "come alive."

Preferred form of submission/contact: Query.

Time to reply: Up to six months.

Time to publish: Three to four months.

Accepts simultaneous submissions: No, *Cobblestone* buys all rights.

Number of illustrators used annually: Approximately 40 per year.

Desired illustrator qualifications: Historically accurate representations.

Prefer manuscript/illustration packages, or separate: Review separately.

Include with illustrator query: Samples.

Time to reply: Two months.

Purchases freelance photography: Yes.

Preferred photography: Photos related to the theme—see the theme list (which you can obtain by sending for Writers' Guidelines).

Terms for writers: $0.20 to $0.25 per word on publication; *Cobblestone* buys all rights.

Terms for illustrators: On a piece-by-piece basis; approximately $200 for a full page of art and adjusted accordingly depending on the configuration.

Submission guidelines: Send an SASE to the address noted earlier.

Tips and comments: *Cobblestone* wants its readers' reaction to be "Wow! I didn't know that!" That's why each full-color, 52-page themed issue of *Cobblestone* is packed with lively and compelling articles and sidebars. Historic photographs, original illustrations, primary documents, maps, activities, and contests complement the text and appeal to young readers. To ensure historical accuracy and interesting reading, *Cobblestone* works closely with historians, leading children's writers, and museum personnel.

College Bound

2071 Clove Road, Suite 206
Staten Island, NY 10304-1643
(718) 273-5700
(718) 273-2539 (fax)
E-mail: editorial@collegebound.net
Web site: www.collegebound.net

Description: *College Bound* is designed to provide high school students with a view of college life from the inside.

Key people:

Editor in chief: Gina LaGuardia

Art director: Giulio Rammairone

Articles per year and description: *College Bound* is published six times throughout the academic year, with a national edition published in January.

Seeks: *College Bound* is composed of both regular departments and full feature articles. Departments run approximately 500 to 1,000 words in length. Features are usually 1,200 to 1,500 words. *College Bound* looks for original thought-provoking ideas—be creative! Or, give your "spin" on some topics *College Bound* is interested in covering in future issues (see below for *College Bound* features). Departments: *Clip Notes:* Includes informative college admissions facts and advice as well as interesting tidbits on teenage "happenings" related to junior and senior students' lifestyles. *Books:* In every issue, *College Bound* reviews books and guides that make college life and preparation easy. If reviewing is your thing and you can be objective and add style and flair, this may be the department for you! *Traditions:* In an effort to give *College Bound*'s high school readership an inside look at college life, this department offers you the opportunity to write about events on your campus that are timeless and entertaining. Some examples: "Mini Lollapalooza" at the University of Maryland; an annual Casino Night at Bay Path College, Massachusetts. *Focus:* This department provides an in-depth profile of a community organization, student-founded group, or other college- and high school–related group of interest. *Techie Trends:* Presents exciting news about happenings in the techno-world and cyberspace, including software reviews, cool "Web Sightings," and more. *Applause!:* All about academic accolades, schools that have won awards, big scholarship winners, and the like. *That's Life:* Covers a variety of topics ranging from Money Tips, Current Events, Social Commentaries, and so forth; previous topics include "Dealing with Parental Alcoholism," "Yoga Soothes School Stress," and "Roomie Disputes." *Class Cut-Up:* Make the readers laugh! This department features reader-submitted comics, jokes, one-liners, and so on. *Interview:* Gives readers an inside look at the college application process, presenting a profile of various college administrators, deans, teachers, career advisers, and others.

Accepts unsolicited/unagented: Yes.

Recent articles:

Features:

"Your Social Life (as You Know It) Is about to Change: How You Can Make a Smooth Transition!"

Overview of interesting and wacky college course offerings

Profiles of teens who go "above and beyond"

"Electronic Classrooms: Learning in Cyberspace"

"I Can Get Credit for That?!" (weird and wacky course offerings)

How to impress your professors

Preferred articles: Keep in mind that the tone of *College Bound*'s articles is very light-hearted and informative. Imagine you're relating your experiences to a younger sibling or friend. You want to tell them "how it really is" and give them helpful pointers to make the transition between high school and college easier to handle. College students from around the country (and those young at heart!) are welcome to serve as correspondents to provide *College Bound*'s teen readership with personal accounts on all aspects of college. Share your expertise on everything from living with a roommate, choosing a major, and joining a fraternity or sorority, to college dating, interesting course offerings on your campus, how to beat the financial aid headache, and other college application nightmares.

Preferred form of submission/contact: Query. *College Bound* would also like to get an idea of how well you report, write, and interpret stories. With your query, enclose two or three samples of your writing from your college newspaper, composition class, or other sources. Photocopies are a good idea, as *College Bound* cannot guarantee the safe return of all clips. All queries should be accompanied by an SASE.

Time to reply: Five weeks.

Time to publish: Normal editorial lead time is four months.

Terms for writers: *College Bound* typically pays $15 to $50 for department inclusions and $50 to $75 for feature articles: rates depend on length of story, topic, and research involved. *College Bound* usually buys all rights. *College Bound* will consider buying second rights if your published piece has not appeared in a national magazine, high school–oriented publication, or any other magazine written primarily for college-bound teenagers. For all departments and features, you will receive payment on publication.

Submission guidelines: Write with an SASE, fax, or e-mail your request. Please send all submissions to Gina LaGuardia, editor in chief, or by e-mail.

Tips and comments: Structure your query/article proposal in the following manner: Begin with the lead you expect to put on the article. Make it catchy—grab the editors' attention! Write a summary of your intended areas of coverage. Give specifics about who you plan to interview, what types of real-life anecdotes you'll include, which resource you plan to utilize, and what conclusion the story might reach. Familiarize yourself with *College Bound* before you submit ideas. Get to know the magazine's style and what kinds of articles the editors love. *College Bound* is also online with a World Wide Web site. In cyberspace, the writing opportunities are endless!

Conqueror

8855 Dunn Road
Hazelwood, MO 63042-2299
E-mail: gyouth8855@aol.com
Web site: www.upci.org/youth

Description: Religious publication for United Pentecostal teens.
Key people:
Editor: Travis Miller
Seeks: Articles and fiction of 600 to 800 words
Terms for writers: $20 to $30 for first or second rights on publication.

CosmoGirl!

1790 Broadway, 11th Floor
New York, NY 10019
(212) 841-8473
(212) 582-7067 (fax)
E-mail: inbox@cosmogirl.com
Web site: www.cosmogirl.com

Corporate structure/parent: Hearst Corporation.
Description: Monthly teen beauty magazine.
Key people:
Articles editor: Lauren Smith
Art director: Lisa Shapiro
Photo editor: Georgia Paralemos

Counselor

4050 Lee Vance View
Cold Springs, CO 80918
(719) 536-0100
(719) 536-3045 (fax)

Description: *Counselor* is the weekly take-home paper for the middle-grade to junior levels of the Scripture Press Sunday School curriculum. Its purpose is to reflect the life-changing power of the Gospel in the lives of boys and girls. *Counselor* is for readers ages 8 through 11.

Seeks: Lively, interesting, true stories that show children how biblical principles can be applied to their everyday lives; stories that are Christ centered, not merely moral. Kids in action stories that show children involved in Christian activity at home or abroad. True-to-life fiction with lots of action and dialogue that shows the Holy Spirit at work in the lives of children. Stories that reveal inner attitudes, spiritual conflicts, good decision-making, effects of prayer, issues of Christian character, salvation. Short, nonfiction articles about subjects of interest to children, written in an easy-to-read format (300–400 words). True stories of historical and contemporary Christian "heroes," written with lots of child appeal. Puzzles and varied activities with a Christian focus.

Accepts unsolicited/unagented: Yes.

Preferred articles: What to avoid: minisermons and tacked-on morals. Christian jargon—won't be understood by non-Christians. Adult-sounding dialogue.

Preferred form of submission/contact: Complete manuscripts with photos if available; SASE if you wish the manuscript returned; stamped postcard if not.

Purchases freelance photography: Yes.

Preferred photography: Purchases photographs in conjunction with story submissions.

Terms for writers: $0.07 to $0.10 cents per word for all rights or first or reprint rights with pickup rights on acceptance. Authors are sent complimentary copies of their published material.

Submission guidelines: Write or fax for guidelines. What to send: Complete manuscripts with photos if available; SASE if you wish manuscript returned; stamped postcard if not. Stories should be 900 to 1,000 words, double-spaced, computer-generated or typed on 8½ by 11-inch manuscript. On page 1: name, address, telephone, social security number, word count, and rights offered. If nonfiction, story subject's current address; note from subject (or parents if story subject is under 16) stating that subject is willing to have story published; letter from story subject's pastor confirming subject's commitment to Christ.

Crayola Kids

1716 Locust Street
Des Moines, IA 50309-3023
(515) 284-2390
(515) 284-2064 (fax)
E-mail: bpalar@mdp.com

Corporate structure/parent: *Crayola Kids* is published by Meredith Publishing Services and Binney & Smith (the makers of Crayola crayons).

Description: *Crayola Kids* is a brightly colored, fun-filled magazine that presents top-quality children's literature and related coloring, drawing, crafting, and fact-based activities as a creative and intellectual springboard for prereaders and early readers. The magazine is for 3- to 8-year-olds. The mission of *Crayola Kids* magazine is to excite young children about the magic of reading and the joy of creativity—and, in so doing, help parents encourage successful learning.

Established: April 1994.

Seeks: Interested in highly creative multicultural, nonsexist activities, visual puzzles, games, and craft ideas. Also publishes brief interviews with children's book authors and illustrators. Tell your story or activity idea and what's unique and fun about it. Convince the editors that kids will love reading it, doing it, or making it. Features: 150 to 250 words. Crafts/activities: one to four pages.

Accepts unsolicited/unagented: Yes.

Preferred articles: Each bimonthly issue focuses on a single theme and features a full-length reprint of a previously published picture book (trade book) and related puzzles, crafts, and activities. Issue themes are carefully selected for how vitally linked they are to the needs and interests of all children in the audience. Activities must be fresh, exciting, and challenging to children in the magazine's target age range 3 to 8 years). In addition to the material aimed directly at young children, *Crayola Kids* offers a Family section with activities that involve a small degree of parental involvement, such as food preparation or a craft requiring minimal adult assistance. The family section also will occasionally feature material that is better suited for small groups than for an individual reader.

Preferred form of submission/contact: Please include a resume and sample copies of your work and a self-addressed stamped envelope. At this time *Crayola Kids* does not accept original, unpublished fiction or poetry (unless you are between the ages of 3 and 8).

Time to reply: Please allow four weeks to receive a reply.

Terms for writers: Rates: $50 to $250 (may vary). For stories and activities previously unpublished, Meredith Corporation purchases the material outright. The work becomes the property of Meredith Corporation, and it is copyrighted in the name of Meredith Corporation. Payment is made on acceptance. For material previously published, Meredith Corporation purchases nonexclusive, second-serial publication rights. Fees vary. Payment is made on acceptance.

Submission guidelines: Write with an SASE or fax for guidelines. Please address all editorial submissions to Editor, Crayola Kids, Meredith Publishing Services, or fax your submission.

Tips and comments: Please be accurate. Double-check all of your facts, and send photocopies of documentary source material you might have used. Please provide the names, addresses, and phone numbers of sources you talked to or used. If you are providing an activity or craft idea, please kid-test the project with a child in the magazine's target age range and share his or her comments. Include clear step-by-step directions for every craft activity. Provide simple sketches or Polaroid shots (not to be used for publication but to assist the editors in understanding the steps involved). *Crayola Kids* is on a Macintosh system that uses WordPerfect. You can send your story on a disk. If you use other software on your Macintosh or if you use an IBM computer, you can also send your material by disk, and it can be converted. Of course, *Crayola Kids* will take your work the old-fashioned way—printed on paper, too! Use double-spacing, please. For a sample copy, please send $2.95, attention: *Crayola Kids* Sample Copy.

CRICKET

PO Box 300
Peru, IL 61354
Web site: www.cricketmag.com

Corporate structure/parent: *Cricket* magazine is published by the Carus Publishing Company.

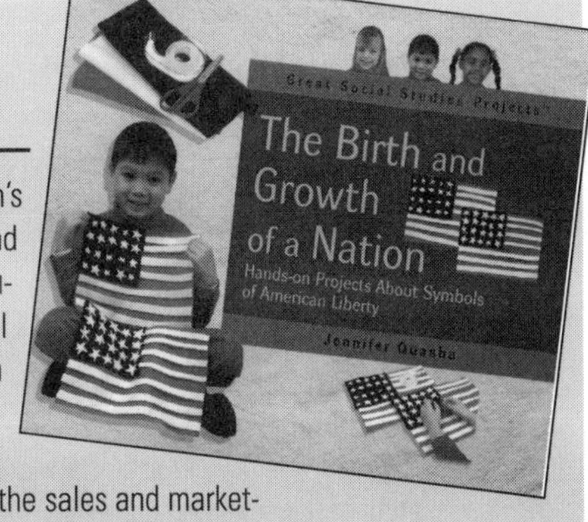

Meet Jennifer Quasha

Author

Jennifer Quasha has written a range of children's books for the third through seventh grade school and library market, including for ROSEN PUBLISHING'S AMERICAN LIBRARY OF LIVES AND TIMES series and Great Social Studies Projects x6 books. She was born in Boston on December 3, 1971. She has a B.S. from the Boston University College of Communication. Before she became a children's book author, she worked in the sales and marketing departments of two book publishing companies for a total of five years.

How did you get your first book published?

I write mainly for the school and library market, which is very different from the trade market. I got my first book published there through a contact made at one of the publishing houses I worked at. Most, if not all, books published by the school and library market are nonfiction and therefore research based. If I have ideas, I can pitch the publishing house although they stick to a curriculum-based publishing schedule. My books appear nine months to a year after I hand them in! I don't handle any of the illustrations—the publishing house does that.

Did you have an agent when you published your first book?

I do have an agent for the adult books that I write, and I got her through a friend of a friend of a friend. I can't stress enough: Networking and contacts will get your stuff—whatever that may be—in front of someone who will actually read it, not ignore it. Blind-sending is good and necessary, but not one-tenth as fruitful as knowing somebody.

Are you still with your first publisher?

Yes, because I keep getting work from them—a lot of work!

Do you have any advice, in terms of finding a publisher, for a writer starting out?

Ask questions; read books; check into associations; send your work. Try to get access any way you can.

Are your books illustrated?

Yes. My publisher handles all the illustrations for my kids' books.

Do you have any advice, in terms of finding an illustrator, for a writer starting out?

When I have had to find an illustrator for my other books (for adult trade) I asked people and found one. Surprise—through networking!

continues

What procedures do you follow when you write?

I love to write, and therefore most days I don't have to make myself write. I really honestly love it. If anything, I want more work—I want to write more. However, I also write nonfiction. I don't have to have an inspiration like fiction writers may have. If I am ever not in-the-mood to write, I work, but I do something else—that is, I research more; I send out invoices; I keep my files up-to-date; I keep track of income versus "out"-come. There's much more to the business of writing than just writing.

Where do you get your ideas?

From things I love to do. I love crafts and pets, so I write about crafts and pets. If you love gardening, skateboarding, painting toenails—write about what you love.

What do you think are the key differences between writing for children and writing for adults?

Writing for children helps your writing for adults. Paring down, cleaning up, simplifying, it's all part of writing for kids. It's harder because once you are an adult you make things more complicated in general, including your writing. Keep it simple.

How did you learn to write?

I knew I wanted to write, so I went to college and got a communication degree rather than a straightforward liberal arts education. I didn't really like school so much, so every time I have considered going back for a higher degree, I can never seem to get myself there.

Description: *Cricket*, for ages 9 to 14, publishes original stories, poems, and articles written by the world's best authors for children and young adults.

Established: In September 1973, the Open Court Publishing Company started publication of *Cricket*, a literary magazine for young people. *Cricket* is now published by Carus Publishing Company.

Key people:

Editor in chief: Marianne Carus
Senior art director: Ron McCutchan
Editor: Deborah Vetter
Senior editor: John D. Allen
Associate editor: Julia M. Messina

Seeks: *Fiction:* Realistic, contemporary, historical, humor, mysteries, fantasy, science fiction, folktales, fairy tales, legends, and myths. *Nonfiction:* Biography, history, science, technology, natural history, social science, archaeology, architecture, geography, foreign culture, travel, adventure, and sports (a bibliography is required for all nonfiction articles). *Poetry:* Serious, humorous, and nonsense rhymes. *Other:* Crossword puzzles, logic puzzles, math puzzles, crafts, recipes, science experiments, games and activities from other countries, plays, music, and art. *Length:* Stories: 200 to 2,000 words (two to eight pages). Articles: 200 to 1,500 words (two to six pages). Poems: Not longer than 50 lines (one page, two pages maximum). An exact word count should be noted on each manuscript submitted. For poetry, indicate number of lines instead. Word count includes every word, but does not include the title of the manuscript or the author's name.

Accepts unsolicited/unagented: Yes, manuscripts.

Preferred articles: See above.

Preferred form of submission/contact: Manuscript only. Please do not query first.

Desired illustrator qualifications: Always looking for strong realism. Many assignments will require artist's research into a particular scientific field, world culture, or historical period. *Cricket* accepts work in a number of different styles and media, including pencil, pen and ink, watercolor, acrylic, oil, pastels, scratchboard, and woodcut. While *Cricket* needs humorous illustration, it cannot use work that is overly caricatured or "cartoony."

Prefer manuscript/illustration packages, or separate: Separately.

Include with illustrator query: Send tear sheets or photoprints/photocopies. Please do not send original artwork. Be sure that each sample is marked with your name, address, and phone number. Any review samples of artwork will be considered. Samples of both color and black-and-white work (where applicable) are appreciated. *Please address all art samples to* Ron McCutchan, senior art director (same address as above).

Time to reply: Allow 12 weeks.

Terms for writers: Stories and articles: Up to $0.25 per word. Poems: Up to $3 per line; payment on publication. *Cricket* normally purchases the following rights for works appearing in the magazine: For stories and poems previously unpublished, *Cricket* purchases first publication rights in the English language. *Cricket* also requests the right to reprint the work in any volume or anthology published by Carus Publishing Company on payment of half the original fee.

Terms for illustrators: A flat fee per feature is usually negotiated. Payment is made on publication. For commissioned artwork, first publication rights plus promotional rights (promotions, advertising, or any other form not offered for sale) are subject to the following terms: Physical art remains the property of the illustrator. Payment is made within 45 days of acceptance. *Cricket* retains the additional, nonexclusive right to reprint the work in any volume or anthology published by *Cricket* subject to pro-rata share of 7 percent royalty of net sales.

Submission guidelines: Go to the Web site or write for guidelines. *Please address all manuscript submissions to the* submissions editor.

Tips and comments: *Cricket* publishes articles for children ages 9 to 14. *Writers:* Write for them and to them but not down to them. Please review back issues of the publication before submitting any manuscripts. *Cricket* does not publish an advance list of themes. Submissions on all appropriate topics will be considered at any time during the year. *Illustrators:* It is especially helpful to see pieces showing young people, animals, action scenes, and several scenes from a narrative (i.e., story) showing a character in different situations and emotional states.

Crusader

1333 Alger SE
Grand Rapids, MI 49507
(616) 241-5616
(616) 241-5558
Web site: www.gospelcom.net/cadets

Corporate structure/parent: Calvinist Cadet Corps.

Established: 1958.

Key people:

Editor: G. Richard Broene

Art director: Robert DeJonge

Articles per year and description: Articles (500–1,000 words): approximately 7 per year. Fiction (900–1,500 words): approximately 14 per year. Illustrations: 10 to 12 per year.

Percentage by first-time authors: 5 percent.

Seeks: Adventure, comics, inspirational, sports. All fiction should be about boy's interests—sports, outdoor activities, problems with an emphasis on a Christian perspective. No simple moralisms. Avoid simplistic answers to complicated problems. Length: 800 to 1,500 words.

Accepts unsolicited/unagented: Yes, with an SASE.

Recent articles: Magazine samples are available with a 9 by 12-inch SASE.

Preferred articles: No fiction articles or fantasy, science fiction, fashion, horror, or erotica.

Preferred form of submission/contact: Send complete manuscript with cover letter including theme of story.

Time to reply: One to three months.

Time to publish: Usually publishes manuscripts four to 11 months after acceptance.

Accepts simultaneous submissions: Yes.

Number of illustrators used annually: Two to three.

Prefer manuscript/illustration packages, or separate: Yes.

Include with illustrator query: Samples.

Time to reply: One to three months.

Purchases freelance photography: Yes.

Preferred photography: Nature photos and photos for boys ages 9 to 14.

Terms for writers: $0.04 to $0.06 per word and one contributor's copy.

Terms for illustrators: Varies.

Submission guidelines: 9 by 12-inch SASE (with four first-class stamps) for sample magazine, guidelines, and themes.

Tips and comments: Keep in mind that the magazine is dedicated to reaching and discipling boys for Christ. Any submissions should bear that in mind.

Crystal Ball

PO Box 98
Ripley, OH 45167
(937) 392-4549

Corporate structure/parent: Starwind Press publications.

Description: *Crystal Ball* is a publication for young adults who enjoy reading science fiction and fantasy. It features writing by both adults and kids.

Key people:

Editor: Marlene Powell

Assistant editor: Susannah C. West

Seeks: Science fiction and fantasy. Articles of scientific and technological interest. Profiles of and interviews with scientists and technologists, both well known and unsung. Trend pieces on developments in science and technology. How-to pieces on creating neat technological gadgets. Reviews of neat science and technology places to visit, such as museums, universities, or NASA installations. Reviews of science fiction and fantasy books that would intrigue our readers. (Reviews of both newly published books and old standards are equally welcome—they could run the gamut from Jules Verne and Conan Doyle to Jane Yolen and Cynthia Voight). Profiles of or interviews with sci-fi or fantasy authors. Word length: 1,000 to 5,000 words.

Accepts unsolicited/unagented: Yes.

Preferred articles: Please don't "write down" to your audience just because they're kids.

Preferred form of submission/contact: Manuscript.

Time to reply: The magazine is rather short-staffed, so please allow eight to 12 weeks for a response. If you haven't received a communication within 16 weeks, please feel free to withdraw the manuscript from consideration.

Accepts simultaneous submissions: Appreciates nonsimultaneous submissions, with one manuscript per mailing.

Desired illustrator qualifications: Story illustrations (full, half, and quarter page), cartoons, fillers and illustrations for nonfiction articles. Art should be camera-ready.

Include with illustrator query: Samples.

Time to reply: Please allow eight to 12 weeks for a response, if you've requested one.

Terms for writers: Payment rates currently \$0.01 to \$0.04/word. Pays on acceptance. Retains the right to reprint stories in other Starwind Press publications (reprint rights 30 percent of current first rights). After publication in *Crystal Ball*, you are free to market the story elsewhere, provided the magazine is credited as the magazine of first publication.

Terms for illustrators: Pays on acceptance. Retains the right to reprint illustrations in other Starwind Press publications (reprint rights 30 percent of current first rights). \$10 for full-page and half-page illustrations; \$5 for quarter-page illustrations; \$5 for cartoons and fillers. Work for illustrations is on assignment.

Submission guidelines: Write for guidelines with an SASE.

Tips and comments: Please include your name, address, story title, and word count on the story's first page. Include title and your last name on inside pages as well. Please don't "write down" to your audience just because they're kids.

Dance Spirit

250 W. 57th Street, Suite 420
New York, NY 10107
(212) 265-8890
(212) 265-8908 (fax)
Web site: www.americancheerleader.com

Corporate structure/parent: Lifestyle Ventures LLC, which also publishes *American Cheerleader*, *Dance Teacher*, *Pointe*, *In Motion*, and *Stage Directions* magazines.

Description: *Dance Spirit* magazine is read by more young dancers and their teachers than any other dance publication.

Devo'Zine

1908 Grand Avenue
PO Box 340004
Nashville, TN 37203-0004
(615) 340-7200
Web site: www.upperroom.org

Corporate structure/parent: The Upper Room.

Description: Written by youth and adults who care about them, *Devo'Zine* helps youth (aged approximately 12–18) to develop a lifetime pattern of prayer and spiritual reflection. The magazine is designed to help readers grow in their faith and explore the relevancy of the Christian faith for the issues they face. Ideas may be expressed through Scripture, prose, poetry, prayers, stories, songs, art, or photographs. Readers and writers include persons of many different denominations and cultures.

Discoveries

6401 The Paseo
Kansas City, MO 64131-1213
(816) 333-7000, ext. 2728
(816) 333-4439 (fax)
E-mail: kneal@nazarene.org, vfolsom@nazarene.org

Corporate structure/parent: *Discoveries* is published by WordAction Publishing.

Description: *Discoveries* is a full-color weekly story paper for third and fourth graders. It is published by WordAction Publishing Company and correlates directly with the WordAction Sunday School curriculum. It is designed to connect Sunday school learning with the daily growth of a middle-grade child. Please follow the guidelines here when submitting materials to *Discoveries.*

Key people:

Editor: Virginia Folsom

Executive editor: Randy Cloud

Assistant editor: Emily Freeburg

Articles per year: 52 issues of *Discoveries* come out in a year.

Percentage by first-time authors: About 50 percent.

Seeks: *Stories:* Submit contemporary, true-to-life portrayals of 8- to 10-year-olds. Write on third- and fourth-grade reading level. The maximum is 500 words. Show character building and scriptural application without authorial intrusion. Let the story teach the moral. A trite, overly didactic summing up of the theme is not acceptable. Use the active rather than passive voice, and write in the third person. *Discoveries* needs middle-grade characters who don't live in an ideal world, or do and say ideal things, but ones who live in a *real* world, who do and say real things. Dialogues should be written exactly as children would say them. If adults talk, the words should be written exactly as adults would say them. *Discoveries* will not publish stories with contrived endings. Avoid fantasy, science fiction, abnormally mature or precocious children, personification of animals, and so forth. Do not use extensive cultural or holiday references, especially distinctly American ones. *Discoveries* has an international audience. Themes and outcomes should conform to the theology and practices of the Church of the Nazarene, Evangelical Friends, Free Methodist, Wesleyan, and other Bible-believing Evangelical churches. *Puzzles:* Use the theme list as a guide. The puzzles have to correlate with the Middler Sunday School lesson of the week. Puzzle instructions should be concise, and a separate answer sheet must be included with the submission. Give clever ideas. *Discoveries* generally does not publish word finds unless they are unique. *Discoveries* needs fresh, innovative approaches to puzzles. Most of all, readers should not feel like they are doing homework. The puzzles should be fun. *Cartoons:* Submit spot cartoons only. *Discoveries* does not publish a continuing strip. Humor should be directed toward children and should involve children. Avoid adult viewpoints. *Bible trivia:* Write on a third- to fourth-grade reading level. Trivia should be 100 to 200 words. Write on topics such as life in Bible times or unique Bible characters or stories. Everything must be factual, and please document your sources.

Accepts unsolicited/unagented: Yes.

Preferred articles: Looking for age-appropriate, exciting pieces that adhere to *Discoveries'* guidelines.

Preferred form of submission/contact: Writers are welcome to send their material to *Discoveries* with an SASE, which will be returned if the material does not conform to *Discoveries* needs.

Time to reply: Six to eight weeks. Allow six to eight weeks or more for a response to your submission.

Time to publish: Because the paper is published as part of a curriculum, *Discoveries* publishes one to two years after acceptance.

Accepts simultaneous submissions: Yes.

Number of illustrators used annually: *Discoveries* does not accept illustrations.

Purchases freelance photography: No.

Terms for writers: *Stories: Discoveries* pays $0.05 per word for multiuse rights. *Discoveries* reserves the right to reprint these manuscripts in *Discoveries* with no additional compensation. Authors may sell reprint rights to other publications with audiences that do not overlap with *Discoveries*' audience. Only occasionally does *Discoveries* make exceptions to this guideline. *Puzzles:* Payment is $15 per puzzle. *Cartoons:* Payment is $15 per cartoon. *Bible trivia:* Payment is $0.05 per word. Contributors will receive four complimentary issues of *Discoveries* on publication. *Discoveries* may select manuscripts a couple of years before publication. *Discoveries* will inform you of the projected publication date. *Discoveries* pays approximately one year before the date of issue

Submission guidelines: Write or send an e-mail and request them. Include an SASE if you ask by regular mail.

Tips and comments: Stories must be compact, simple, and well written, preferably with an element of surprise or suspense. Puzzles must be creative and original. Cartoons must contain material third and fourth graders would find funny. Trivia must be exciting and something unusual.

DISCOVERY

475 Riverside Drive, Room 455
New York, NY 10115
(212) 870-3335
(212) 870-3229 (fax)
E-mail: order@jmsblind.org
Web site: www.jmsblind.org

Corporate structure/parent: John Milton Society for the Blind.

Description: *Discovery* is a Christian Braille magazine printed four times each year by the John Milton Society for the Blind in New York City. *Discovery* is a quarterly religious digest for youth, ages 8 to 18. It contains short stories, poems, quizzes, inspirational, historical, and other educational articles on a thematic basis, with an occasional pen pal column. It is 44 pages long and contains materials reprinted from over 20 magazines.

Established: 1935 (*Discovery* was first published in Braille in 1935). Since 1935, *Discovery* has been sent free to libraries, schools, and individuals anywhere in the world who can't see to read regular print.

Key people:

Executive director and editor: Darcy Quigley

Acquisitions/submissions editors: Ingrid Peck, Assistant Editor

Articles per year and description: Articles: approximately 40 *reprinted articles* and poems *from other magazines*. Five to seven of these are original works—not reprints. Illustrations: none.

Percentage by first-time authors: 5 percent.

Seeks: Ready to print with little to no editing involved—*most of what* Discovery *publishes is reprinted from other publications*. Each issue contains poems, short stories, inspirational articles, quizzes, humorous pieces, recipes, and a pen pals section. Articles and fictional pieces range from 500 to 1,500 words, fillers range from 10 to 150 words, and poetry and prayers range from 5 to 30 lines. Magazines focus on different themes each quarter. May use poems, prayers, quizzes, short stories, and articles that have a religious focus, that deal with seasonal events (Christmas, Lent, Easter, etc.), or that pertain to issues that would be of interest to blind or visually impaired persons, both youth and adult. A list of sources *Discovery* typically reprints material from is available on request.

Accepts unsolicited/unagented: Yes.

Recent articles: Recent themes include families; overcoming fear; using your gifts/talents; creativity/imagination. Ongoing themes: Christian holidays (Christmas and Easter).

Preferred articles: Encouraging, inspirational, Christian themes; timeless pieces, not dated materials; virtually perfect, ready-to-print articles (needing little to no editing). *Discovery* cannot work extensively with writers.

Preferred form of submission/contact: Send complete manuscript with an SASE. Please see guidelines before submitting articles and review word length requirements.

Time to reply: Six to 12 months.

Time to publish: Six to 12 months.

Accepts simultaneous submissions: Yes.

Number of illustrators used annually: No illustrations.

Purchases freelance photography: No.

Terms for writers: Will send credit copy in Braille (if requested) and a record of publication letter. Does not purchase copyright (obtains permission to reprint only). No fees are paid to writers.

Submission guidelines: Write with an SASE or review on Web site.

Tips and comments: Review the list of magazines *Discovery* typically reprints from (which is included with the guidelines) and familiarize yourself with the style.

DISCOVERY TRAILS

1445 Boonville Avenue
Springfield, MO 65802-1894
(417) 862-2781
(417) 862-6059 (fax)
E-mail: UElemCurr@ag.org
Web site: www.radiantlife.org

Corporate structure/parent: Gospel Publishing House.

Description: *Discovery Trails* is for boys and girls 10 to 12 (slanted toward older group). *Discovery Trails*'s mission is "To provide appropriate age-level fiction stories that promote Christian living through application of biblical principles. To promote awe of our almighty God through interesting bytes of information about His creation. To develop interest in the product through exciting, kid-centered search for Bible truth via the Discovery Kids. To provide fun Bible-related/reinforcing activities and puzzles that help kids learn more about God's Word."

Key people:

Articles editor: Sinda S. Zinn

Art director: Dale Gehris

Established: *Discovery Trails* is a replacement for *Junior* as of April 1999.

Seeks: Fictional mysteries, serials, humorous, adventure, and ethnic stories that present realistic characters working out their problems according to Bible principles: strong story line, presenting Christianity in action without being preachy. Historical, scientific, or natural material with a spiritual lesson. Poetry expressing feelings or reactions with which children will identify. Bits & Bytes of quirky facts, puzzles, interactive activities, quizzes, word games, and fun activities that address social skills on a focused topic with accurate research, vivid writing, and spiritual emphasis. Crafts, how-to articles, and recipes should be age-appropriate, safe, and cheap; express newness/originality and accuracy; have a clear focus and an opening that makes kids want to read and do it. Length: fiction, 800 to 1,000 words; nonfiction, 300 to 500 words; fillers: up to 300 words.

Accepts unsolicited/unagented: Yes.

Preferred articles: Articles with reader appeal, emphasizing some phase of Christian living. Avoid the encyclopedia repeat. *Fiction:* The plot must be logical, natural, and forceful. Avoid coincidences. It should flow naturally from the setting and personalities of the main characters. The plot should have a distinct conflict that builds to a climax. The characters should be interesting, believable, and realistic. Avoid types. They should be active, not just pawns to move the plot along. They should grow and change in believable ways—not too much, too little, or too soon. Describe a character's looks and reveal his personality through his actions. The style: Use precise, active, vivid words. Avoid hackneyed phrases. Keep a consistent perspective on both the time tense (past or present) and the point of view (first person, second person, omniscient, or particularly of character). The conclusion must flow naturally from the plot, and characters don't force the conclusion to make a point the story didn't. Open-ended stories are acceptable. *Nonfiction:* Structure your article. You should be able to state the purpose of the article in one sentence and be able to outline the article's major points and conclusion. Then write smooth transitions. The conclusion should tie the parts of the article together and stress its purpose. Include a bibliography of facts with every nonfiction submission.

Preferred form of submission/contact: Manuscript.

Terms for writers: Payment of $0.07 to $0.10 per word is made on acceptance.

Submission guidelines: Write or e-mail for guidelines. Address manuscripts to *Discovery Trails* editor. Manuscript should be double-spaced. Your name, address, number of words, and first or second (reprint) rights or simultaneous submission should appear at the top of page 1. Include a self-addressed stamped envelope for return of manuscript.

Tips and comments: Keep in mind the Christian nature of *Discovery Trails*. The first paragraph should begin with action, at the critical moment, the core of the problem. Use precise, colorful words. Avoid clichés and overused phrases. Be brief. If you can use fewer words, do so. Avoid "preachiness."

Dolphin Log

870 Greenbrier Circle, Suite 402
Chesapeake, VA 23320
E-mail: cousteau@cousteausociety.org
Web site: www.dolphinlog.org

Corporate structure/parent: The Cousteau Society.

Key people:

Editor: Lisa Rao

Dramatics

2343 Auburn Avenue
Cincinnati, OH 45219-2819
(513) 421-3900
(513) 421-7077 (fax)
Web site: www.etassoc.org

Corporate structure/parent: The Educational Theatre Association.

Description: *Dramatics* is an educational theater magazine published since 1929 by the International Thespian Society, a nonprofit honorary organization dedicated to the advancement of secondary school theater. (In the 1980s, the Educational Theatre Association was formed to oversee the society as well as a distinct professional association for teachers.) *Dramatics* is published nine times a year, September through May. It has a circulation of about 35,000. Approximately 80 percent of its readers are high school theater students; about 10 percent are high school theater teachers. Other subscribers include libraries, college theater students and teachers, and others interested in educational theater.

Key people:

Editor: Don Corathers

Art director: William Johnston

Seeks: Buys four to eight articles for each issue; general length 800 to 4,000 words. Articles are accepted on any area of the performing arts, including film and dance. A typical issue might include an interview with someone who has made a significant contribution to the theater; an article describing some innovative approach to blocking, costume design, or set construction; a survey of leading theater schools describing what they look for in students; and a photo spread, with copy, on some groundbreaking performer or theater group. Short news items, book reviews, and humor pieces (if they're funny) are also part of the mix.

Accepts unsolicited/unagented: Yes.

Preferred articles: The primary editorial objectives of the magazine are to provide serious, committed young theater students and their teachers with the skills and knowledge they need to make better theater; to be a resource that will help high school juniors and seniors make an informed decision about whether to pursue a career in theatre and about how to prepare for a theater career; and to prepare high school students to be knowledgeable, appreciative audience members for the rest of their lives.

Preferred form of submission/contact: Prefers to see a finished manuscript but will respond to query letters. Phone and e-mail queries are discouraged. Sample copies of the magazine cost $2.50. Subscriptions cost $18 a year.

Terms for writers: Honorariums of $25 to $400 are paid for accepted work. Payment is based on quality of work, amount of editing or rewriting needed, length of work, and inclusion of photos or graphics. Contributors also receive five free copies of the issue in which their piece appears and may obtain additional copies at a minimal charge.

Tips and comments: What makes *Dramatics* editors cranky: Writers who are too lazy or careless to do basic reporting and research. Very few articles are complete with only one quoted source. Writers who misrepresent themselves as experts or are not up-front about whether and where a piece has been previously published. Submissions that ignore or misunderstand *Dramatics'* audience; articles that either talk down to *Dramatics'* readers or are way over their heads. (If a piece has footnotes, it's probably too academic for *Dramatics*.) Contributors who create an impression of conflict of interest by writing about an organization in which they themselves are involved—although *Dramatics* does sometimes publish first-person accounts. Would-be playwrights who do not understand the basic conventions of play script format or even the basic conventions of the stage. Writers who are impossible to get a hold of, or who do not return messages. What makes *Dramatics* happy: Writers who really understand *Dramatics'* audience. Writers who bring lots of strong, specific article ideas to the table, and keep abreast of topics recently covered by the magazine. Contributors who submit written queries or complete articles, rather than interrupting the editors' work to make a sales pitch by phone. Writers who understand the need for editorial input and can make and/or accept necessary changes gracefully. Writers who can provide publishable photography to go along with their pieces (snapshots are not publishable). Illustration ideas are also appreciated. Writers who include student voices in their pieces when appropriate, as well as a variety of other sources. Writers whose work is well organized, factual, and clean. And if nothing else, writers willing to work for what *Dramatics* can afford to pay.

Elle Girl

1633 Broadway
New York, NY 10019

Description: Girl's edition of *Elle* magazine. Four issues scheduled for 2002. For girls age 12 to 17.

Established: August 2001.

Key people:

Editor: Brandon Holly

Encounter

8121 Hamilton Avenue
Cincinnati, OH 45231-2323
(513) 931-4050
(513) 931-0950 (fax)

Corporate structure/parent: Standard Publishing Company

Description: *Encounter* (formerly *Straight*) is a weekly magazine for Christian teenagers, published quarterly by the Standard Publishing Company. *Encounter* is distributed through churches in the United States and other English-speaking countries. It's designed to correlate with Standard Publishing's Young Teen and High School curriculum.

Seeks: Fiction must appeal to teenagers and have an interesting, well-constructed plot. The main characters should be contemporary teens who cope with modern-day problems using Christian principles. Stories should be uplifting, positive, and character building, but not preachy. Conflicts must be resolved realistically, with thought-provoking and honest endings. Accepted length is 1,100 to 1,500 words. Nonfiction is accepted. *Straight* uses articles on current issues from a Christian point of view, teen profiles, and humor. Nonfiction pieces should concern topics of interest to teens, including school, family life, recreation, friends, part-time jobs, dating, and music. Devotions are done by assignment only. If you'd like to be considered for an assignment, please let *Encounter* know. Poetry is accepted from teens only. The author's birth date must accompany all poetry submitted.

Preferred form of submission/contact: Manuscript. *Send seasonal material 9 to 12 months in advance.* All submissions must be accompanied by a self-addressed stamped envelope, or your submission will not be returned. Manuscripts are submitted on speculation.

Time to reply: Expect to wait six to eight weeks.

Desired illustrator qualifications: Art is done by assignment only. If you'd like to be considered for an assignment, please let *Encounter* know.

Prefer manuscript/illustration packages, or separate: *Encounter* uses photos of teens and teen activities and those that accompany or illustrate articles.

Purchases freelance photography: Yes.

Preferred photography: Photos of professional quality are appreciated. Submit high-contrast, black-and-white glossy and color transparencies. *Encounter* uses photos of teens and teen activities and those that accompany or illustrate articles. All photos should feature teens who are conservative in appearance, with no revealing clothing or outrageous hairstyles. Teens should have a natural, expressive appearance, not an artificial, posed, "too perfect" look. Package photos carefully and enclose a self-addressed mailing label, postage, and return packing.

Terms for writers: Payment is on acceptance. *Encounter* pays $0.03 to $0.07 per word. *Encounter* purchases first rights and reprint rights. Rates for teen submissions vary.

Terms for illustrators: Art rates are negotiable. Photos bring $50 to $75 for inside use. Color shots for cover use are $125. Rates for teen submissions vary.

Submission guidelines: Manuscripts are submitted on speculation. Please type on 8 1/2 by 11-inch, nonerasable paper, one side of the sheet only. Double-space and leave generous margins. Type your name, address, and Social Security number on the first sheet, as well as the approximate word count. Due to the various types of software, *Encounter* requests that you contact the magazine before submitting disks. *Encounter does not accept submissions by fax.*

Tips and comments: Teenagers today are different from the way they were when you were a teen, even if you are a young person. Get to know teens before you begin to write for them. Many manuscripts are rejected simply because the plot or vocabulary is outdated for modern teens. Some teenagers read no higher than sixth-grade level. Don't write down to kids, but keep this in mind as you write. Words should be simple. Stories should be short and direct. A tacked-on moral does not make a religious story. Make your characters Christian, and the religious slant will take care of itself. *Encounter* looks for material to correlate with Bible school lessons, so each quarter the magazine is considering specific topics. If you request it, *Encounter* will put you on its mailing list to receive quarterly themes. *Encounter* is produced long before its publication date. Send seasonal material nine to 12 months in advance. Please get to know the magazine. Sample issues are available on request (enclose an SASE, please).

FACES

Cobblestone Publishing
30 Grove Street, Suite C
Peterborough, NH 03458
E-mail: facesmag@yahoo.com
Web site: www.cobblestonepub.com/pages/facemain.htm

Corporate structure/parent: Cobblestone Publishing (which is a subsidiary of the Cricket Publishing Group).

Key people:

Editor: Elizabeth Crooker Carpentiere
Managing editor: Lou Waryncia
Art director: Ann Dillon
Marketing manager: Manuela Meier
Publisher: Jack Olbrych

Seeks: All material must relate to the theme of a specific upcoming issue in order to be considered. *Feature articles*: about 800 words; includes in-depth nonfiction highlighting an aspect of the featured culture, interviews, and personal accounts. *Supplemental nonfiction*: 300 to 600 words; includes subjects directly and indirectly related to the theme. Editors like little-known information but encourage writers not to overlook the obvious. *Fiction*: up to 800 words; includes retold legends, folktales, stories, and original plays from around the world, and so forth, relating to the theme. *Activities*: up to 700 words; includes crafts, games, recipes, projects, and so forth, which children can do either alone or with adult supervision. Should be accompanied by sketches and description of how activity relates to theme. *Poetry*: up to 100 lines; clear, objective imagery; serious and light verse considered; must relate to theme. *Puzzles and games*: crossword and other word puzzles using the vocabulary of the issue's theme; mazes and picture puzzles that relate to the theme.

Accepts unsolicited/unagented: No. Queries only, please.

Preferred articles: Lively, original approaches to the subject are the primary concerns of the editors in choosing material. All material must relate to the theme of a specific upcoming issue to be considered.

Preferred form of submission/contact: Query only.

Time to reply: Queries may be submitted at any time before the deadline, but queries sent well in advance of deadline may not be answered for several months.

Purchases freelance photography: Yes.

Preferred photography: To be considered for publication, photographs must relate to a specific theme. Writers are encouraged to submit available photos with their query or article. Buys one-time use. If you have photographs pertaining to any upcoming theme, please contact the editor by mail or fax, or send them with your query. You may also send images on speculation. Some recent themes include the United Nations, Bahamas, Saudi Arabia, Vatican City, Finland, South Africa, Ukraine, British Columbia, Canada, and Samoans.

Terms for writers: $0.20 to $0.25 per printed word; puzzles, games, and poetry pay on an individual basis. *Faces* purchases all rights to material.

Terms for illustrators: Suggested fee range for professional quality photographs: quarter page to full page, color, $25 to $100. Please note that fees for nonprofessional quality photographs are negotiated.

Submission guidelines: Go to the Web site or write with an SASE. A query must consist of all of the following information to be considered (please use nonerasable paper): a brief cover letter stating the subject and word length of the proposed article, a detailed one-page outline explaining the information to be presented in the article, an extensive bibliography of materials the author intends to use in preparing the article (if appropriate), and a self-addressed stamped envelope. Writers new to *Faces* should send a writing sample with the query. If you would like to know whether your query has been received, please also include a stamped postcard requesting acknowledgment of receipt. In all correspondence, please include your complete address as well as a telephone number where you can be reached.

Tips and comments: Lively, original approaches to the subject are the primary concerns of the editors in choosing material. Writers are encouraged to study recent back issues for content and style. (Sample issues available at $4.95. Send 7 1/2 by 10 1/2-inch or larger self-addressed stamped $2 envelope.) All material must relate to the theme of a specific upcoming issue to be considered.

FLICKER

PO Box 660544
Birmingham, AL 35266-0544
Web site: www.members.aol.com/yellowhamr

Preferred form of submission/contact: Manuscript.

Terms for writers: $0.10 per word on acceptance for fiction and nonfiction; $25 for poems; $30 for puzzles; $10 for jokes. Author receives three complimentary copies of the magazine in which the work appears. *Flicker* reserves the right to edit purchased manuscripts. *Flicker* buys all rights to submissions.

Submission guidelines: To be read and considered for publication, submissions must be typed or computer-generated, be double-spaced, have the author's name, Social Security number, address, phone number, and word count at the top of the first page of the manuscript; and have a self-addressed stamped envelope with sufficient postage to be returned.

Tips and comments: Following editorial suggestions for manuscript improvements may increase the likelihood of acceptance but will not guarantee acceptance. Even though *Flicker* gives special care to each submission, the magazine cannot assume responsibility for lost material, so *be sure to keep a copy of your manuscript.*

FLORIDA LEADER

PO Box 14081
Gainesville, FL 32604
(352) 373-6907
(352) 373-8120 (fax)
E-mail: oxendine@compuserve.com
Web site: www.floridaleader.com

Corporate structure/parent: Oxendine Publishing, Inc., which produces four publications for high school and college students, three of which are distributed in Florida and one nationally. The Florida publications are read by students at 70 colleges and more than 343 public high schools. In October 1993, Oxendine Publishing launched a national leadership magazine called *Student Leader,* which is read by the top 5 percent of active students at more than 890 colleges and universities nationwide.

Description: *Florida Leader* magazine features academic-major and career articles, current financial aid and admissions information, and stories on other aspects of college life for current or prospective college students. The high school edition of *Florida Leader* is published in January, June, and August with a circulation of 25,000.

Key people:

Publisher and editor in chief: W. H. "Butch" Oxendine Jr.
Managing editor: Kay Quinn King
Assistant editor: Teresa L. Beard
Art director: Jeffrey L. Riemersma

Seeks: Full-length articles (about 1,000 words) should include 7 to 12 sources, quoting student and collegiate leaders, as well as appropriate sources. Primary sources, for the most part, should be from colleges, high schools, and businesses within the state. College and corporate sources should be varied geographically and demographically.

Accepts unsolicited/unagented: Yes. Please include an SASE for return of manuscript.

Preferred form of submission/contact: Query or manuscript. Include an SASE. Writers may query ideas for articles or discuss possible assignments already on the calendar. If possible, state availability of photos with query.

Number of illustrators used annually: Mostly uses photographs.

Prefer manuscript/illustration packages, or separate: Either.

Purchases freelance photography: Yes.

Preferred photography: Mostly as an accompaniment to submitted articles—from the author or the sources.

Terms for writers: Articles by first-time writers may be used, but only experienced writers will receive payment, which varies from $35 to $75 per piece. All writers will receive at least one full-color copy of their article.

Submission guidelines: Send an SASE to receive writer's guidelines, an editorial calendar, or $3.50 for guidelines and a sample issue. Copy should be double-spaced and follow Associated Press style. When students are mentioned by name, first reference should include year in school, institution they attend, and, if relevant, their major. The full names, titles, addresses, and daytime phones of all interview subjects should be included separately with each submission. Articles may be edited for space and content. Writers are responsible for the accuracy of all information in the article.

Tips and comments: On-site or "remote" internships for students are available for one or more semesters.

FOOTSTEPS

Cobblestone Publishing
30 Grove Street, Suite C
Peterborough, NH 03458
(603) 924-7209
(603) 924-7380 (fax)
Web site: www.footstepsmagazine.com
Illustrator's guidelines: www.cobblestonepub.com/pages/illustratorsguidelines

Corporate structure/parent: Cricket Magazine Group.

Established: June 1999.

Key people:

- **Associate editor:** Rosalie F. Baker
- **Managing editor:** Lou Waryncia
- **Art director:** Ann Dillon
- **Acquisitions/submissions editor:** Charles F. Baker
- **Marketing manager:** Manuela Meier
- **Publisher:** Jack Olbrych

Articles per year and description: *Footsteps* focuses on African American history and heritage for students in grades 4 through 8.

Percentage by first-time authors: Variable.

Seeks: Theme related. Writers may propose an article for any issue, so long as it is closely related to the theme. *Feature articles*: 600 to 750 words; includes in-depth nonfiction, plays, interviews, and biographies. *Supplemental nonfiction*: 300 to 600 words; includes in-depth subjects related to the theme. Editors like little-known or offbeat information but encourage writers not to overlook the obvious. Especially interested in the "stories behind the stories." *Fiction*: up to 700 words; includes authentic retellings of historical and biographical fiction, adventure, and legends related to the theme. *Activities*: up to 600 words includes crafts, recipes, puzzles, games, and other creative projects that children can do alone or with adult supervision. Query should be accompanied by sketches and detailed descriptions of how activity works and relates to the theme.

Accepts unsolicited/unagented: Yes.

Recent articles:

"The Making of a General" by Frances Maclean (September 2000; meet Toussaint Louverture and find out how he came to lead a slave revolt that resulted in a declaration of freedom and independence for Haiti.)

"An Open Letter to the Girls Killed in the Church Bombing" by Dianne Swann-Wright (May 2000; on September 15, 1963, opponents of the civil rights movement in Birmingham, Alabama, placed 19 sticks of dynamite beneath the steps of the Sixteenth Street Baptist Church. The explosion that followed killed four young girls. Dianne Swann-Wright was a girl of 13 growing up in Baltimore, Maryland, when this took place. As a young black girl, she identified with these girls because they were about her age. Here she writes a symbolic letter to them, relating what their deaths meant to the civil rights movement and to her.)

"The 'Greats' of the Early Years" by Donn Rogosin (March 2000; read about some of the many outstanding black baseball players during the early days of baseball history. Also, see a list of former Negro Leagues players who have been inducted into the Baseball Hall of Fame.)

"Black Dream Builders" by Devorah Major (January 2000; many blacks made names for themselves in California during the Gold Rush; read about some of them.)

Preferred articles: Well- and accurately researched stories. *Footsteps* focuses on African American history and culture for young people ages 8 to 14. *Footsteps* is looking for articles that are lively and age-appropriate and exhibit an original approach to the theme of the issue. Cultural sensitivity and historical accuracy are extremely important. Authors are urged to use primary sources and up-to-date scholarly resources for their research. And don't forget to make it interesting!

Preferred form of submission/contact: Query with manuscript sample.

Time to reply: One to three months.

Time to publish: Approximately six months.

Accepts simultaneous submissions: No.

Number of illustrators used annually: Variable.

Desired illustrator qualifications: Familiarity with the magazine's themes.

Prefer manuscript/illustration packages, or separate: No preference; will review submissions together or separately.

Include with illustrator query: Resume and samples.

Time to reply: Most illustration is done in house by the design team at Cobblestone.

Purchases freelance photography: Yes.

Preferred photography: Theme-related shots.

Terms for writers: $0.20 to $0.25 per word.

Terms for illustrators: Spots, $10 to $40; quarter page, $30 to $60; half page, $50 to $115; three-quarters page, $80 to $150; full page, $100 to $210. Covers are assigned and paid on an individual basis.

Submission guidelines: Send SASE to Cobblestone for guidelines and also request theme list. Write a brief description of your idea, including unusual sources you plan to use, your intended word length, and any unique angle or hook you think will make your article irresistible to the magazine's audience (children 8 to 14 years old and their parents and teachers). Queries may be submitted at any time before the deadline, but queries sent well in advance of deadline may not be answered for several months. Go-aheads requesting material proposed in queries are usually sent at least several months before publication date. Unused queries will be returned with an SASE. When making submissions, please include a completed query and an SASE. Each query must be written separately. Feel free to include published writing samples with your query. Do not begin writing your proposed article until you have heard from the editor. *Mail queries to* Charles F. Baker, editor.

Tips and comments: Do thorough research before querying and know the themes for the upcoming year. There is no point submitting pieces that don't fit within the guidelines and theme framework, so do your homework—it'll save you lots of time in the end. Some previous themes include American Negro Theater (1930s–1950s); Cape Verde Islands; Early Life of Martin Luther King Jr.; Railroads; Early Music; Colonial Slavery.

For Seniors Only

339 N. Main Street
New York, NY 10956
(914) 638-0333

Description: Career, college, and travel articles for high school students.

Key people:

Publisher: Darryl Elberg
Articles/fiction editor: Judi Oliff
Art director: David Miller

Fox Kids

4219 W. Burbank Boulevard
Burbank, CA 91505
(818) 953-2210
(818) 953-2220 (fax)
E-mail: bananadog@aol.com
Web site: www.foxkids.com

Description: Quarterly for Fox Kids Club members (as in Fox TV network).
Key people:
Articles editor: Scott Russell
Art director: Tim Sims

FRIEND

50 E. North Temple
Salt Lake City, UT 84150-3226
Web site: www.lds.org

Corporate structure/parent: The *Friend* is published by the Church of Jesus Christ of Latter-day Saints (a.k.a. the Mormon Church).

Description: Mormon children's magazine for 3- to 11-year-olds.

Key people:

Editor: Vivian Paulsen

Art director: Mark Robison

Seeks: Short stories, nonfiction articles, poetry, and activities. In addition to short stories, nonfiction articles, poetry, and activities the *Friend* also uses picture, holiday and sports stories, rebus, and manuscripts that portray different cultures. The *Friend* also publishes some handicraft, science, and homemaking projects. Cartoons, games, and puzzles about pets, nature, history, religion, and simple recipes of appealing foods (to children) are also welcome.

Accepts unsolicited/unagented: Yes.

Preferred articles: Stories should be uplifting and full of substance without preaching and moralizing. Content should focus on character-building qualities with wholesome characters. Because the *Friend* is circulated worldwide, the editors are especially interested in stories with universal settings, conflicts, and characters—particularly based on true experiences. Biographies of living people are not accepted. *Friend* does not need science and nature articles (currently overstocked) and *rarely* accepts serial articles.

Preferred form of submission/contact: Manuscript; query letters are not suggested.

Time to reply: Within two months when an SASE is enclosed. If there is no SASE provided, the manuscript will not be returned, nor will a response be provided.

Time to publish: It is variable and not uncommon for an article to appear in publication a year or more after acceptance.

Accepts simultaneous submissions: No.

Number of illustrators used annually: Artwork is not accepted through freelance submissions. Art assignments are made by staff art department.

Purchases freelance photography: No.

Terms for writers: Stories and articles: $0.10 per word and up. Poems: $25 minimum. Recipes: $12. Activities and games: $12 and up. Additional payment may be made for outstanding manuscripts. The *Friend* does not pay for children's contributions.

Submission guidelines: Write to the *Friend* and include an SASE for return postage.

Tips and comments: The targeted group is boys and girls up to 12 years old. Write with appropriateness but do not talk down or condescend. Appropriate humor is a constant need. Stories and articles should be no longer than 1,000 words in length, and very short stories (up to 250 words) and nonfiction are needed for younger readers and preschool children. All nonfiction articles should be accompanied by source references.

Girls' Life

4517 Harford Road
Baltimore, MD 21214
(410) 426-9600
(410) 254-0991 (fax)
Web site: www.girlslife.com

Description: Bimonthly general interest magazine for girls age 9 to 15.

Established: August 1994.

Key people:

Editor in chief: Karen Bokram

Acquisitions/submissions editor: Kelly White

Creative director: Chun Kim

Articles per year: 10 to 15 articles per issue.

Percentage by first-time authors: 15 percent.

Seeks: *Girls' Life* is a service-oriented magazine for 10- to 14-year-old girls. *Girls' Life* features articles on beauty, body, relationships, siblings, friends, first crush (and related articles), as well as craft and party ideas. Feature articles cover puberty, depression, drug use relationships, and other relevant "big issue" subjects that preteen and young teen girls would likely be facing in their day-to-day lives.

Accepts unsolicited/unagented: Yes.

Recent articles: Please see a current copy of the magazine for the most up-to-date articles.

Tips and comments: Writers who have thoroughly familiarized themselves with *Girls' Life*'s fun, light-hearted yet informal and informative magazine. No features on subjects like bird watching, pine cone collecting, and so on.

Preferred form of submission/contact: Query letter.

Time to reply: Six to eight weeks.

Time to publish: All illustrations are specifically assigned by the creative director. The scheduling depends on the article and into what issue it is slated. If it is selected for the next forthcoming issue, with obvious time variables, it will be published within one to two months.

Accepts simultaneous submissions: Yes.

Number of illustrators used annually: 15 to 20 illustrators.

Desired illustrator qualifications: Conceptual; colorful; bright; trendy; creative.

Prefer manuscript/illustration packages, or separate: Usually separately.

Include with illustrator query: Pitch with letter, resume, and samples, and tear sheets if available.

Time to reply: Tries to turn it around in two to four weeks.

Purchases freelance photography: Yes.

Preferred photography: Composition, color, feelings, and creativity.
Terms for writers: Payment on publication.
Terms for illustrators: Payment on publication.
Submission guidelines: E-mail *Girls' Life* for guidelines at editorial@girlslife.com or download from "Contact Us" at www.girlslife.com.
Tips and comments: Read the magazine! And more than one issue, too, to get an idea of the style, what it is the editors are looking for, and the *Girls' Life* voice.

The Goldfinch

State Historical Society of Iowa
402 Iowa Avenue
Iowa City, 52240
(319) 335-3916
Web site: www.iowahistory.org/publications/goldfinch/goldfinch.html

After over two years of discussion and analysis, both internally and with interested outside parties, the State Historical Society of Iowa has determined to discontinue publication of *The Goldfinch* magazine, effective with the Spring 2000 issue (vol. 21, no. 3).

GrandStories

471 Arsenal St, #14
Watertown, MA 02472
Web site: www.grandstories.com

Corporate structure/parent: Max Media, Inc.
Description: New publication that will include stories for children ages 3 to 10.
Key people:
Editor and publisher: Maxim Antinori
Seeks: Book-length and short stories.
Terms for writers: On royalty basis of copies sold.
Submission guidelines: Go to Web site or send an SASE.

Group Magazine

PO Box 481
Loveland, CO 80539
(970) 669-3836
Web site: www.grouppublishing.com

Corporate structure/parent: Group Publishing, Inc.
Seeks: *Group* needs articles on successful youth ministry strategies, including youth-led ministry ideas, understanding kids and youth culture, recruiting/training/keeping adult

leaders, family ministry, staff issues, serving and training parents, professionalism, and self-nurture. How-to articles on personal spiritual growth, time management, issues vital to working with young people, leadership skills (listening, discussion leading), worship ideas, handling specific group problems, fun and experiential programming ideas, and active-learning meeting plans and retreats. "Try This One" section needs short ideas for group use. These include games, fund-raisers, crowd breakers, Bible studies, helpful hints, and discussion starters. "Hands-on Help" section needs miniarticles (up to 150 words) that feature tips for youth leaders on outreach ideas, managing their personal lives, and working with youth, adult leaders, and parents. "Strange but True!" is a regular one-page feature (up to 500 words) that profiles a strange, funny, or remarkable youth ministry experience.

Terms for writers: Word length and payment: *Group* articles: 500 to 700 words, $125; 800 to 1,100 words, $150; 1,200 to 1,700 words, $175; 2,000 and up words, $225. Departments: "Try This One" (up to 300 words), $35; "Hands-on Help" (up to 175 words), $35; "Strange but True!" (up to 500 words), $40.

Submission guidelines: Manuscripts should be typewritten or printed from a computer, double-spaced, on one side of the paper. Please include a brief cover letter with information about the author and article. Your name, address, phone number, and Social Security number should appear on the cover letter and the upper-right corner of first page. Each page should be numbered and include title or your name. Include a stamped self-addressed envelope for return of unaccepted manuscript. *Group* is working nine to 10 months ahead of distribution. Please keep that in mind if you are submitting dated or seasonal material. No fiction, prose, or poetry. Payment is on acceptance. *Group* buys all rights.

Time to reply: Normal response time to manuscript submissions is eight to 10 weeks.

Tips and comments: *Group* believes that young people learn best by doing. The key to spiritual growth is biblical truth learned and applied in real-life situations. Relationships form the best context for kids' growth. Young people can do the work of ministry—they can think, lead, and handle significant responsibilities. Effective youth leaders are well-trained coaches, teachers, and spiritual mentors who are passionate advocates of young people. Parents and other faithful adults are crucial to kids' spiritual growth. Youth ministry is a high calling, worthy of a life commitment.

GUIDE

55 West Oak Ridge Drive
Hagerstown, MD 21740
E-mail: guide@rhpa.org
Web site: www.guidemagazine.org

Description: *Guide* is made with 10- to 14-year-old kids in mind. Each week the full-color magazine features stories and puzzles to show how Jesus can make a positive difference in their lives. There's also a weekly Bible study that will help them understand in simple terms how God works in our world. The editors are members of the Seventh-day Adventist church.

Key people:

Editor: Randy Fishell

Designer: Brandon Reese

GUIDEPOSTS FOR KIDS

PO Box 638
Chesterton, IN 46304
(219) 929-4429
(219) 926-3839 (fax)
E-mail: gp4k@guideposts.org
Web site: www.gp4k.com

Corporate structure/parent: Guideposts.

Established: Following the May/June 2001 issue *Guideposts for Kids* will transition into an e-zine. The magazine will exist entirely on the Web. The Web site was created in May 1999.

Key people:

Editor in chief: Mary Lou Carney

Acquisitions/submissions editor: Rosanne Tolin (on the Web site)

Articles per year and description: Will buy numerous children's articles so the content of the Web site remains fresh.

Percentage by first-time authors: 5 percent or less.

Seeks: A variety of kid-friendly topics: school, friends, how-tos, trivia, animals, science, historical events, fiction, sports, and music.

Accepts unsolicited/unagented: Yes.

Recent articles:

"Dip, Dip, Goose" (on the history of pens, with a sidebar on gel pens and a recipe for invisible ink)

"Are You on Homework Overload?" (empowering tips and a list of homework help Web sites)

Preferred articles: Good, clean, punchy writing. Not encyclopedic entries.

Preferred form of submission/contact: Query or manuscript.

Time to reply: Six weeks.

Time to publish: This tends to be variable depending on the article and the scheduling.

Accepts simultaneous submissions: Yes.

Terms for writers: $100 to $500 for all rights. For short, 50-word kid profiles, $50.

Submission guidelines: Write for writers' guidelines (enclose an SASE), or go to the Web site (look in the "Parents Place" under Guidelines Requests).

Tips and comments: Don't preach. And *please*, *please* study the Web site before sending your submission! Keep in mind that interactivity on the Web is important. Providing links, sidebars, or other tie-ins with your article is a definite plus.

GUIDEPOSTS FOR TEENS

16 E. 34th Street
New York, NY 10016
Web site: www.gp4teens.com/home.asp

Description: *Guideposts* magazine is a monthly inspirational, interfaith, nonprofit publication written by people from all walks of life. Its articles present tested methods for developing courage, strength and positive attitudes through faith in God. *Guideposts*' writers express viewpoints from a variety of Protestant, Catholic, and Jewish faith experiences.

Seeks: Writing a short feature is often the easiest way of making a sale to *Guideposts*. Study the magazine to get an idea of the desired style and tone.

Accepts unsolicited/unagented: Yes.

Recent articles:

Regular columns:
"His Mysterious Ways"
"What Prayer Can Do"
"Angels Among Us"
"The Divine Touch"

Additionally, features full-length manuscripts and shorter-length pieces.

Preferred articles: No fiction, essays, or sermons, and *Guideposts* rarely presents stories about deceased or professional religious people. No book-length material.

Preferred form of submission/contact: Manuscript.

Time to reply: Allow two months for a reply.

Terms for writers: Full-length manuscripts (750–1,500 words): $250 to $500, occasionally higher. Shorter manuscripts (250–750 words): $100 to $250. Short features and fillers (under 250 words): $25 to $100.

Submission guidelines: On Web site or by mail with an SASE. Don't try to tell an entire life story in a few pages. Focus on one specific happening in a person's life. The emphasis should be on one individual. Bring in as few people as possible so that the reader's interest stays with the dominant character. Decide what your spiritual point, or "take-away," will be. Everything in the story should be tied in with this specific theme. Don't leave unanswered questions. Give enough facts so that the reader will know what happened. Use description and dialogue to let the reader feel as if he or she were there, seeing the characters, hearing them talk. Dramatize the situation, conflicts, and struggle, and then tell how the person was changed for the better or the problem was solved. Manuscripts must be typed, double-spaced, and accompanied by a self-addressed stamped envelope.

Tips and comments: Most important: study the magazine. A typical *Guideposts* story is a first-person narrative written in simple, dramatic, anecdotal style with a spiritual point that the reader can "take away" and apply to his or her own life. The story may be the writer's own or one written in the first person for someone else. Even short features, such as "His Mysterious Ways," "What Prayer Can Do," "Angels Among Us," and "The Divine Touch" use this format. Writing a short feature is often the easiest way of making a sale to *Guideposts*.

HIGH ADVENTURE

1445 Boonville Avenue
Springfield, MO 65802
(417) 862-2781, extension 4177
E-mail: royalrangers@ag.org
Web site: www.ag.org.royalrangers/highadventure

Corporate structure/parent: The General Council of the Assemblies of God, Royal Rangers Department. Sister publication of *High Adventure Leader* (adult).

Description: Ministers to tens of thousands of young boys in the Assemblies of God international boys program (Royal Rangers) and to their leaders, who are called commanders. Strives to use qualitative and substantive material that would encourage the boys toward physical, mental, spiritual, and social development and to assist the commanders to develop and maintain a consistent Christian lifestyle to model before the boys.

Established: August 1971.

Key people:

Editor in chief: Rev. Gerald W. Parks

Articles per year and description: 70 to 90 articles and 30 to 35 illustrations.

Percentage by first-time authors: Approximately 60 percent.

Seeks: *Articles:* adventure, inspirational, Christian living, Holy Spirit, salvation, self-helps, youth issues with Christian emphasis, and indoor and outdoor activities and events. *Other:* biographies, cartoons, features, fillers, crafts, missionary stories, news items, photographs (color), puzzles, and testimonies.

Accepts unsolicited/unagented: Yes.

Recent articles:

"Snowshoeing in the Colorado Rockies" by Mike Laliberty (personal experience of a local outpost of boys hiking in the mountains of Colorado)

"A Story about Michael Gurian: How Society Fails Boys and What We Can Do About It" by Janis Dworkis (how the church needs strong, godly male role models to mentor young boys in the faith and help them to develop a Christlike character)

"The Young Boy and John 3:16," author unknown (story of a young boy and how the Scriptures came to life and gave the boy a new perspective and love for God)

Preferred articles: Looking for manuscripts that utilize positive and uplifting personal testimonies or stories that relate to boys ages 5 to 17 and adult leaders 18 years and older. (Sixteen pages of the publication are directed at the boys' interests, and a 16-page middle insert is geared to train and encourage the adult leaders.)

Preferred form of submission/contact: Writers can contact by query or with a manuscript submission. Also, one can access the Web site at ag.org.royal-rangers/highadventure and check out the *High Adventure* page.

Time to reply: If a manuscript is unacceptable, it would be returned to the author in a timely fashion. If it is under consideration, *High Adventure* would request of the author to allow it to hold the manuscript for a period of six to 12 months with the author's permission. *High Adventure* would then determine at that predetermined time where the manuscript would best fit the needs of the publication.

Time to publish: Articles are published generally within a six- to 12-month period. The publications are all issued quarterly.

Accepts simultaneous submissions: Yes.

Number of illustrators used annually: Generally three to four.

Desired illustrator qualifications: Expects illustrators and/or writers to exemplify a Christlike lifestyle that would be reflected in their work.

Prefers manuscript/illustration packages, or separate: Generally manuscripts are submitted and reviewed separately.

Include with illustrator query: Recent work samples only.

Time to reply: Replies to illustrators are handled in three to six months.

Purchases freelance photography: No.

Terms for authors: Terms and fees for submissions depend on specific word count, content, and so forth.

Terms for illustrators: Same.

Submission guidelines: Writer's and illustrators guidelines, accompanied by a recent sample of the magazine publication, are available by written request and a 9 by 12-inch SASE. The manuscript should be typed (letter-quality typewriter or printer), double-spaced, with ample margins, and on one side of the paper. Submissions should be on one of the following media: a 3 1/2-inch floppy, zip, or jaz disk and a hard copy of the manuscript. Keep a photocopy of your manuscript(s). The editor cannot be responsible for loss of manuscripts in mail or otherwise. Do not submit photocopies. Accompany manuscript(s) with a self-addressed stamped return envelope. Return envelope must have sufficient postage to ensure the return of your manuscript in the event it does not meet the magazine's need. *New writers:* If a writer is unknown to the editor, a letter of introduction is appreciated. Give personal background, church affiliation, whether layman or minister, and so on. Submit seasonal material at least eight months in advance. You are welcome to submit photographs of the event/season you are writing about along with a picture of yourself. The magazine will insert photos, space permitting.

Tips and comments: Be informative, use good taste, make stories uplifting and encouraging, and be persistent!

HIGHLIGHTS FOR CHILDREN

Editorial Department
803 Church Street
Honesdale, PA 18431
(570) 253-1080
Web site: www.highlights.com

Corporate structure/parent: Highlights.

Description: Monthly with motto "fun with a purpose."

Established: *Highlights for Children* was established in Honesdale, Pennsylvania, in 1946.

Key people:
Manuscript coordinator: Beth Troop
Art director: Janet Moir McCaffrey

Seeks: Frequent needs include humor, mystery, sports, and adventure stories; retellings of traditional tales; stories in urban settings; and stories that feature world cultures. Nonfiction articles geared to younger readers (ages 3–7) are especially welcome. These articles should not exceed 400 words. References or sources of information must be included with submissions.

Accepts unsolicited/unagented: Yes.

Preferred articles: *Fiction:* Should have an engaging plot, strong characterization, and lively language. Stories for younger readers (ages 3–7) should be 400 words or less. Stories for older readers (8–12) should be 900 words or less, and should be appealing to younger readers if read aloud. Stories that teach by positive example, rather than preach, are preferred. Suggestions of crime and violence are taboo. Rhyming stories are seldom purchased.

Preferred form of submission/contact: Prefers to see a manuscript rather than a query.

Terms for writers: Buys all rights, including copyright, and does not consider material previously published. All material is paid for on acceptance. *Fiction stories:* Payment $100 and up. *Rebus stories:* Payment $75 and up. *Nonfiction:* $100 and up. *Crafts:* $25 and up. *Finger plays/action rhymes:* $25 and up. *Party plans:* $50 and up. *Verse:* $25 and up.

Submission guidelines: Accepts material, including seasonal material, year-round. Submissions must include a self-addressed stamped envelope for possible return. Color 35mm slides, photos, or art reference materials are helpful and sometimes crucial in evaluating submissions. Prefers not to receive submissions electronically. Will not pay persons under age 15 for contributions.

Tips and comments: *Fiction:* Should have an engaging plot, strong characterization, and lively language. *Nonfiction:* Focused articles are more successful than broad factual surveys. Firsthand experience or research based on consultation with experts is preferred.

Holidays & Seasonal Celebrations

1204 Buchanan
PO Box 10
Carthage, IL 62321
(217) 357-2591
(217) 357-6789 (fax)

Description: Quarterly entirely devoted to holiday topics for pre-K through 3.

Hopscotch

PO Box 164
Bluffton, OH 45817-0164
(419) 358-4610

Description: *Hopscotch* is a magazine created for girls from 6 to 12 years, with youngsters 8, 9, and 10 the specific target age. The magazine's point of view is that every young girl deserves the right to be a young girl for a number of years before she becomes a young adult.

Key people:

Editor: Marilyn Edwards

Editorial assistant: Diane Winebar

Seeks: *Hopscotch* looks for articles, fiction, nonfiction, and poetry that deal with timeless topics, such as pets, nature, hobbies, science, games, sports, careers, simple cooking, and anything else likely to interest a young girl. *Hopscotch* leaves dating, romance, human sexuality, cosmetics, fashion, and the like to other publications. The ideal length of a *Hopscotch* nonfiction piece is 500 words or less, although *Hopscotch* is not about to turn down a truly exceptional piece if it is slightly longer than the ideal. *Hopscotch* prefers fiction to not run over 1,000 words. *Hopscotch* is always in need of cute and clever recipes, well-written and illustrated crafts, riddles, and jokes.

Accepts unsolicited/unagented: Yes. All submissions must be accompanied by a self-addressed stamped envelope, with sufficient postage.

Recent articles: See below for some examples of recent article subjects.

Preferred articles: Looking for lively writing, most of it from a young girl's point of view—with the girl or girls directly involved in an activity that is both wholesome and unusual. Examples have included girls in a sheep to shawl contest, girls raising puppies that are destined to guide the blind, and girls who take summer ballet lessons from members of the New York City Ballet.

Preferred form of submission/contact: *Hopscotch* prefers to receive complete manuscripts with cover letters, although it will not rule out query letters. *Hopscotch* does not answer submissions sent in by fax.

Accepts simultaneous submissions: *Hopscotch* will entertain simultaneous submissions as long as that fact is noted on the manuscript.

Desired illustrator qualifications: Most art will be by assignment, in support of features used. The magazine is anxious to find artists capable of illustrating stories and features and welcomes copies of sample work, which will remain on file.

Prefer manuscript/illustration packages, or separate: Accept them together; see writer's tips later.

Include with illustrator query: The magazine welcomes copies of sample work, which will remain on file.

Purchases freelance photography: Yes, in fact, it increases the author's chances of being published if the story is accompanied by photographs.

Preferred photography: *Hopscotch* uses a number of black-and-white photos inside the magazine, most in support of articles.

Terms for writers: *Hopscotch* will pay a minimum of $0.05 a word for both fiction and nonfiction, with additional payment given if the piece is accompanied by appropriate photos or art. *Hopscotch* will pay a minimum of $10 per poem or puzzle, with variable rates offered for games, crafts, cartoons, and the like. *Hopscotch* buys first American serial rights and pays on publication. *Hopscotch welcomes the contributions of both published*

Meet Kevin O'Malley

Illustrator

Kevin O'Malley has illustrated *Humpty Dumpty Egg-Splodes; Bud; Leo Cockroach, Toy Tester; Who Killed Cock Robin;* and *Testing Miss Malarkey.* He makes children's books for the times when a parent is reading to their children/child on the couch in the living room. He was born in Philadelphia in 1961 and raised in a little town called Lansdale, Pennsylvania. He graduated high school with a self-proclaimed 867 combined score on the SAT—721 English and the remainder in math. He graduated from the Maryland Institute, College of Art, in Baltimore, Maryland. Before Kevin became a children's book illustrator, he was a dishwasher, slide show producer, seasonal display director, and made Santa houses for malls. He is the second of six kids. None of his siblings are artistically inclined. His mother is a creative soul and his father a fine doctor.

How did you get your first book published?

Fate. I was rejected about 100 times. I was working as a display designer and had had enough. A salesman at the company had had enough as well. We quit the same day. He suggested I come to his deck-building party the following weekend. At the party I was introduced to a fellow who made mass-market books for kids. We had lunch the following week. He suggested I visit the Sesame Street Publishing folks. The women there suggested I contact three agents. Two of the agents turned me down. The third told me she would take me on because an artist she represented had been visiting the day my portfolio was reviewed and insisted that I be represented. We took an idea I had for a revised *Froggy Went A-Courtin'* to Stewart, Tabori and Chang. Andy Stewart told me he used to sing the old folksong when he was in college and because of that, he published my fist book in 1989.

Did you have an agent when you published your first book?

I have been represented by the same agent since 1989.

Do you have any advice, in terms of finding an agent, for an illustrator starting out?

An agent sure made it easier. I believe enough in my work to still think I could have gotten my work published without her. On the other hand, I'm not as gray up top thanks to her fine work.

Are you still with your first publisher?

My first publisher is no longer doing original kids' books. I'd like to think I had nothing to do with their change in business planning.

Do you have any advice, in terms of finding a publisher, for an illustrator starting out?

Keep it simple, direct, and by all means original. That's easy enough, huh?

Do your write the text for the books you illustrate?

An editor sends me the work of an author, and I decide whether I'd like to draw the pictures. When I write and illustrate my own work, I prepare a "dummy book" with text and illustrations in place. This work is copied by my rep and sent to interested parties.

What procedures do you follow when you work?

I work very quickly and rarely take lunch. I start at 8:30 and work until about 3 o'clock. In the summertime my attic heats up to about 10,000 degrees. On those days I decide to quit when I start sweating on the artwork. I try to write for at least an hour a day. Most of the time I do the writing in longhand.

Where do you get your ideas?

This gets to the nature of creativity. I have no idea what compels me to create stories. It can be a word, phrase, or scene from a movie. I once built a story up from a single event in a scene from the movie *Godzilla vs. Mothra.* I think it's true that everybody has one story to tell and that's enough. But storytellers just can't seem to stop (even when we're told to).

Anything you really wish somebody had told you when you started out?

As painful as it is for folks to hear, practice is the only way to improve. I was never the best artist in my class, and I will never be the best artist of my generation. I never cared. It's the personal development that's fun. Opening up your eyes and taking a look at everything. Try new stuff. Make mistakes. The world is full of really cool stuff. I just wish there was more time to learn.

and unpublished writers. A complimentary copy of *Hopscotch* will be sent to each writer who has contributed to a given issue.

Terms for illustrators: Payment for art is $25 for partial illustrations and $35 for full-page illustrations. For photography, payment is $5 to $10 per photo, depending on the quality and $5 for color slides.

Submission guidelines: Write with an SASE for guidelines. Sample copies are available for $3 within the United States and $4 outside the United States. All payment must be in U.S. funds.

Tips and comments: For aspiring contributors, it's important to remember that *Hopscotch* uses nonfiction 3 to 1 over fiction. And, *those pieces that are accompanied by black-and-white photos are far more likely to be accepted that those that need illustrations*. Every *Hopscotch* contributor must remember *Hopscotch* publishes only six issues a year, which means the magazine's editorial needs are extremely limited. An annual total, for instance, will include some 30 to 36 nonfiction pieces, 9 or 10 short stories, 18 or so poems, 6 cover illustrations, and a smattering of puzzles, crafts, and the like. It is obvious that *Hopscotch* must reject far more contributions than it accepts, no matter how outstanding they may seem.

HUMPTY DUMPTY'S

PO Box 567
Indianapolis, IN 46206-0567
(317) 636-8881
Web site: www.cbhi.org/magazines/humptydumpty/

Corporate structure/parent: Children's Better Health Institute.

Key people:

Editor: Sheila Rogers

Art director: Rebecca Ray

Seeks: *Humpty Dumpty's* has a constant need for high-quality stories, articles, and activities with health-related themes. "Health" is a broad topic that includes exercise, nutrition, safety, hygiene, and drug education. *Humpty Dumpty's* is especially interested in material concerning sports and fitness, including profiles of famous amateur and professional athletes; "average" athletes (especially children) who have overcome obstacles to excel in their areas; and new or unusual sports, particularly those in which children can participate. Although *Humpty Dumpty's* emphasis is on health, the magazine certainly uses material with more general themes. *Humpty Dumpty's* would especially like to see more holiday stories, articles, and activities. Please send seasonal material at least eight months in advance.

Accepts unsolicited/unagented: Yes.

Recent articles:

"Vegetable Soup"

"In the Snow"

"The Little Red Mitten"

Preferred articles: Health information can be presented in a variety of formats: fiction, nonfiction, poems, and puzzles. Fiction stories with a health message need not have health as the primary subject, but they should include it in some way in the course of events. Characters in fiction should adhere to good health practices, unless failure to do so is necessary to a story's plot. Because *Humpty Dumpty's* is designed to be read to children who are not yet reading independently, the editors look for submissions with a good "read-aloud" quality. In all material submitted, please avoid reference to eating sugary foods, such as candy, cakes, cookies, and soft drinks.

Preferred form of submission/contact: Completed manuscript only.

Time to reply: About three months are required to review manuscripts properly. Please wait three months before sending status inquiries.

Accepts simultaneous submissions: Simultaneous submissions are discouraged.

Desired illustrator qualifications: Please do not send drawings or other artwork. *Humpty Dumpty's prefers to work with professional illustrators of its own choosing.*

Prefer manuscript/illustration packages, or separate: Manuscript only.

Purchases freelance photography: Yes.

Preferred photography: *Humpty Dumpty's* does not purchase single photographs. *Humpty Dumpty's* purchases short photo features (up to six or eight pictures or photos that accompany articles and help illustrate editorial material). Please include captions and model releases.

Terms for writers: Up to $0.22 a word (fiction/nonfiction—up to 500 words). *Poetry:* $15 minimum. *Photos:* $15 minimum. *Puzzles and games:* No fixed rates (send SASE to receive separate guidelines for activities). Payment is made on publication. Each author receives 10 complimentary copies of the issue in which his or her material is published. *Humpty Dumpty's* purchases all rights to manuscripts.

Terms for illustrators: *Humpty Dumpty's* buys one-time rights to photos.

Submission guidelines: Write with an SASE for guidelines. Manuscripts must be typewritten and double- or triple-spaced. The author's name, address, telephone number, date of submission, and the approximate word count of the material should appear on the first page of the manuscript. Title pages are not necessary. Keep a copy of your work. *Humpty Dumpty's* will handle your manuscript with care but cannot assume responsibility for its return. Please send the entire manuscript. All work is on speculation only; queries are not accepted, nor are stories assigned. The editors cannot criticize, offer suggestions, or enter into correspondence with an author concerning manuscripts that are not accepted nor can they suggest other markets for material that is not published. Material cannot be returned unless it is accompanied by a self-addressed stamped envelope and sufficient return postage.

Tips and comments: *Humpty Dumpty's* is for children ages 4 to 6; please bear that in mind as you write your story. Because *Humpty Dumpty's* is designed to be read to children who are not yet reading independently, the editors look for submissions with a good "read-aloud" quality. Remember that characters in realistic stories should be up-to-date. Many of *Humpty Dumpty's* readers have working mothers and/or come from single-parent homes. *Humpty Dumpty's* needs more stories that reflect these changing times but at the same time communicate good, wholesome values. Reading *Humpty Dumpty's* editorial guidelines is not enough! Careful study of current issues will acquaint writers with each title's "personality," various departments, and regular features, nearly all of which are open to freelancers. Sample copies are $1.25 each (U.S. currency) from the Children's Better Health Institute, PO Box 567, Indianapolis, IN 46206.

I.D.

4050 Lee Vance View
Colorado Springs, CO 80918
(719) 536-3296 (fax)
E-mail: northamg@cookministries.org
Web site: www.cookministries.org

Description: Weekly Bible study paper for Sunday high school students.

Key people:

Editor: Glynese Northam
Senior designer: Jeffrey P. Barnes
Designer: Joe Matisek

INSIGHT

55 W. Oak Ridge Drive
Hagerstown, MD 21740
(301) 791-7000
E-mail: lpeckham@rhpa.org or insight@rhpa.org
Web site: www.rhpa.org

Description: *Insight* is a weekly Christian magazine for teenagers.

Key people:

Articles editor: Lauri Peckham

Art director: Doug Bendall

Seeks: *On the Edge:* true "drama in real life" stories. Can be written in third person (someone else's story) or first person (your own); 800 to 1,500 words. Please include real photos of the people and incident if possible. *It Happened to Me:* personal experience stories written in first person. Should tell about an unusual experience that taught a lesson or had a lasting impact. Please include a photo of the author if possible. Word count: 600 to 900 words. *So I Said:* true short stories or opinion pieces written in first person. Focuses on common, everyday events and experiences that taught the writer something edifying. If it's a story, it must include dialogue, in which the writer states what he/she has learned. This is an opinion piece, preferably communicated through narrative. Word count: 300 to 500 words.

Accepts unsolicited/unagented: Yes.

Preferred form of submission/contact: Manuscript.

Purchases freelance photography: With stories only.

Preferred photography: Real-life pictures and author pictures to accompany stories

Terms for writers: On the Edge, $50 to $100; It Happened to Me, $50 to $75; So I Said, $25 to $50.

Submission guidelines: Please include your name, address, phone number, and Social Security number (necessary for payment) with all submissions. Send an SASE to have your manuscript returned. Submission to *Insight* constitutes permission to edit as necessary.

Tips and comments: *Insight* prints mostly true stories with a teen's point of view; *Insight* looks for good storytelling elements such as a dramatic beginning, realistic dialogue, and believable, alive characters; *Insight* prefers stories that take a Christ-centered, positive approach to topics of teen interest in simple, current language.

INTEEN

1551 Regency Court
Calumet City, IL 60409
(708) 868-7100
(708) 868-7105 (fax)
E-mail: unil551@aol.com

Description: Quarterly magazine publishing Sunday school lessons and features for urban teens.

Key people:

Editor: Katara A. Washington

Art editor: Larry Taylor

Jack and Jill

PO Box 567
Indianapolis, IN 46206-0567
(317) 636-8881
Web site: www.cbhi.org

Description: Magazine for young and middle readers

Corporate structure/parent: Children's Better Health Institute.

Key people:

Editor: Daniel Lee

Art director: Emilie Frazier

Seeks: *Jack and Jill* has a constant need for high-quality stories, articles, and activities with health-related themes. "Health" is a broad topic that includes exercise, nutrition, safety, hygiene, and drug education. *Jack and Jill* is especially interested in material concerning sports and fitness, including profiles of famous amateur and professional athletes; "average" athletes (especially children) who have overcome obstacles to excel in their areas; and new or unusual sports, particularly those in which children can participate. Humorous stories are especially needed. Nonfiction material may deal with sports, science, nature—even historical and biographical articles. Most nonfiction features touch in some way on health and fitness. Although the magazine's emphasis is on health, *Jack and Jill* certainly uses material with more general themes. *Jack and Jill* would especially like to see more holiday stories, articles, and activities. Please send seasonal material at least eight months in advance.

Accepts unsolicited/unagented: Yes.

Preferred articles: Health information can be presented in a variety of formats: fiction, nonfiction, poems, and puzzles. Fiction stories with a health message need not have health as the primary subject, but they should include it in some way in the course of events. Characters in fiction should adhere to good health practices, unless failure to do so is necessary to a story's plot. Nonfiction articles dealing with health subjects should be fresh and creative. Avoid an encyclopedic or "preachy" approach. *Jack and Jill* tries to present its health material in a positive manner, incorporating humor and a light approach wherever possible without minimizing the seriousness of what it is saying. In all material submitted, please avoid reference to eating sugary foods, such as candy, cakes, cookies, and soft drinks.

Preferred form of submission/contact: Completed manuscript only.

Time to reply: About three months are required to review manuscripts properly. Please wait three months before sending status inquiries.

Accepts simultaneous submissions: Simultaneous submissions are discouraged.

Desired illustrator qualifications: Please do not send drawings or other artwork. *Jack and Jill prefers to work with professional illustrators of its own choosing.*

Prefer manuscript/illustration packages, or separate: Manuscript only.

Purchases freelance photography: Yes.

Preferred photography: Does not purchase single photographs. Purchases short photo features (up to six or eight pictures or photos that accompany articles and help illustrate editorial material). Please include captions and model releases. Buys one-time rights to photos.

Terms for writers: Up to $0.17 per word (fiction/nonfiction—500 to 800 words); poetry—$15 minimum; photos—$15 minimum; puzzles and games—no fixed rates. (Send SASE to receive separate guidelines for activities.) Payment is made on publication. Each author receives 10 complimentary copies of the issue in which his or her material is published. *Jack and Jill* purchases all rights to manuscripts.

Terms for illustrators: *Jack and Jill* buys one-time rights to photos.

Submission guidelines: Write with an SASE for guidelines. Manuscripts must be typewritten and double- or triple-spaced. The author's name, address, telephone number, date of submission, and the approximate word count of the material should appear on the first page of the manuscript. Title pages are not necessary. Keep a copy of your work. *Jack and Jill* will handle your manuscript with care but cannot assume responsibility for its return. Please send the entire manuscript. All work is on speculation only; queries are not accepted, nor are stories assigned. The editors cannot criticize, offer suggestions, or enter into correspondence with an author concerning manuscripts that are not accepted, nor can they suggest other markets for material that is not published. Material cannot be returned unless it is accompanied by a self-addressed stamped envelope and sufficient return postage.

Tips and comments: *Jack and Jill* stories and articles are written at about a second- or third-grade reading level. Content is heavy on fiction, using realistic, adventure, mystery, and fantasy. Readers range in age from 7 to 10; please bear that in mind as you write your story. Remember that characters in realistic stories should be up-to-date. Many of *Jack and Jill*'s readers have working mothers and/or come from single-parent homes. *Jack and Jill* needs more stories that reflect these changing times but at the same time communicate good, wholesome values. Reading the editorial guidelines is not enough! Careful study of current issues will acquaint writers with each title's "personality," various departments, and regular features, nearly all of which are open to freelancers. Sample copies are $1.25 each (U.S. currency) from the Children's Better Health Institute, PO Box 567, Indianapolis, IN 46206.

JUMP

21100 Erwin Street
Woodland Hills, CA 91367
(818) 594-0972 (fax)
E-mail: letters@jumponline.com
Web site: www.jumponline.com

Corporate structure/parent: Weider

Description: Monthly magazine for female teens "who dare to be real."

Key people:

Editor: Lori Berger
Managing editor: Maureen Meyers
Editorial assistant: Elizabeth Sosa

Junior Baseball

PO Box 9099
Canoga Park, CA 91039
E-mail: dave@juniorbaseball.com
Web site: www.juniorbaseball.com

Description: Bimonthly magazine for youth baseball players, 7 to 17, their parents, coaches and associate organizations.

Seeks: Nonfiction of 1,000 to 15,000 words: how-to, interview/profiles with major league players, leagues and tournaments, industry, and parents.

Terms for writers: $50 to $100 on publication for all rights.

Keynoter

3636 Woodview Trace
Indianapolis, IN 46268
Web site: www.Keyclub.org

Key people:

Executive editor: Amy L. Wiser

Kids' Wall Street News

PO Box 1207
Rancho Santa Fe, CA 92067
(760) 591-7681
(760) 591-3731 (fax)
E-mail: info@KwsNews.com
Web site: www.kidswallstreetnews.com

Description: *Kids' Wall Street News* magazine was the first publication created especially for youth about finance and economics. Its goal is to provide information and facts that will empower and educate youth so they can make positive choices for today and tomorrow.

Key people:

Editor in chief: Kate Allen

Note: With continued growth of the Internet, *Kids' Wall Street News* has decided to publish exclusively online going forward.

Kidz Ch@t

8121 Hamilton Avenue
Cincinnati, OH 45231
(513) 931-4050
(513) 931-0950 (fax)

Description: *Kidz Ch@t* (formerly *RADAR*) is a weekly Sunday school publication for children in grades 3 and 4. The purpose of *Kidz Ch@t* is to help third and fourth graders make God's Word their guide for daily living. Circulation 55,000.

Corporate structure/parent: Standard publishing.

Key people:

Editor: Gary Thacker

Seeks: *Fiction:* The main character of the story should be a 9- or 10-year-old in a situation involving one or more of the following: mystery, animals, sports, adventure, school, travel, and relationships (with parents, friends, and others). *Nonfiction:* Purchases articles of 200 to 225 words dealing with the world: animals, nature, geography, cultures, and the environment. Articles should have a religious emphasis. Document your articles with the sources that you have used. *Puzzles and activities:* Puzzles correlate with the quarterly theme list or with holidays and special occasions. Some types of puzzles used are word searches, acrostics, crosswords, fill-in-the-blanks, and matching. Use the Holy Bible, New International Version, for puzzles unless otherwise noted on the theme list. Answers to all puzzles should be given. Puzzles should be short and challenging, but not too difficult. Purchases activity and craft ideas that correlate with the theme list or with holidays and special occasions. These should be fun and easy enough to do in a few steps.

Accepts unsolicited/*unagented:* *Yes.*

Preferred articles: *Fiction*: Stories should have believable plots. They should be wholesome and teach Christian values. Make prayer, church attendance, and Bible reading a natural part of the story. Brief references to such actions throughout the story will do more than tacking a moral onto the end of the story. Fiction is to be written with a particular theme in mind. Refer to the theme list for issues to be addressed. Consider the time of year when writing and what middle-grade children are doing at home and school. The word length is 475 words maximum. No biblical fiction. No stories with talking or personified animals or objects. *Nonfiction:* Articles should have a religious emphasis. Document your articles with the sources that you have used. The word length should be 200 to 225 maximum.

Preferred form of submission/contact: Manuscript.

Time to reply: Allow three to four weeks after the due date for consideration of materials submitted for a specific theme. (The due date is on the quarterly theme list.)

Terms for writers: *Fiction/nonfiction:* \$0.03 to \$0.07 per word. *Puzzles:* \$15 to \$17.50. Payment is on acceptance. Contributors receive four copies of the issue in which their work appears. The magazine purchases full rights, first rights, and reprint rights.

Submission guidelines: Place your name, address, Social Security number, and approximate number of words in your manuscript on the first page. Enclose an SASE with all submissions. The paper's features correlate with Standard Publishing's new Middler Sunday school curriculum. Submissions purchased fit in with specific themes. A quarterly theme list is available on request. You may also request that your name be placed on the mailing list to receive the most current theme list four times a year. Sample issues of *Kidz Ch@t* are available. Please enclose one SASE when requesting a theme list and/or sample copy. A #10 business envelope is large enough to hold these materials.

Tips and comments: Keep in mind that children today are different from the way they were when you were a child. Get to know children before you begin writing. Writing should be simple in construction and incorporate age-appropriate language.

Pamela Duncan Edwards

Author

Pamela Duncan Edwards is the author of 15 books for children ages 3 to 9, including *Livingstone Mouse, Four Famished Foxes and Fosdyke, Some Smug Slug, Barefoot—Escape on the Underground Railroad* (all with HarperCollins between 1995 and 1997); *Honk! The Story of a Prima Swanerina*, and *Warthogs in the Kitchen* (both with Hyperion 1998). She was born in England on June 17, 1940. In 1977, she left England with her husband. He is a publisher of a newspaper in Washington, D.C. She owned a preschool in England and later became a children's librarian when she moved to the United States. She has two grown-up sons, Robert and Alistair, both of whom were educated in the United States, and both have become lawyers. She also has one grandchild, Jackson.

How did you get your first book published?

My first book was *Some Smug Slug,* which I took in dummy book form, along with some illustrations by Henry Cole, to four publishers. Three accepted it. I had the idea of writing it in alliteration, using the letter S. If I remember correctly, this was a new idea at the time, and perhaps this helped to catch the publishers' interest. Once I had it in my head, I wrote it quickly, but I mulled that idea over for some time before I put pen to paper. It usually takes about 18 months from writing the manuscript to the book being published. Six weeks later, I took a second book to HarperCollins (the same publisher). Katherine Tegen, the editor, accepted this one, too, and decided that this one—*Four Famished Foxes*—should come out first (fall 1995) because it was more of a fall book. Therefore, my second submitted book came out before my first (spring 1996).

Did you have an agent when you published your first book?

No, I do not use an agent.

Are you still with your first publisher?

I publish with HarperCollins, Hyperion Disney, and Putnam. My editor, Katherine Tegen, moved from HarperCollins to Disney and kindly asked me to continue doing books with her there, which I was more than happy to agree to, but I also continued to work with Harper. Katherine has now moved back to Harper, and I will work with her there but will continue to work with Hyperion (in a way, it's a very small industry). In addition, I also have a series of American history books with Putnam, the first of which, *The Boston Tea Party,* will be out in summer 2001.

Do you have any advice, in terms of finding a publisher, for a writer starting out?

Look at lots of books in the library and bookstores. Find out who publishes the type of books you have written. Call that publishing house, and ask for the name of an editor who might be interested in that type of manuscript. Write to that editor explaining in a very short way the theme of the story and ask whether you might submit the manuscript. When you get a reply, you will then have a

continues

contact to work with. I don't think it's worth sending unsolicited manuscripts. Most publishers don't want them.

Are your books illustrated?

All of my books are illustrated. I work mostly with Henry Cole but also with other illustrators. Henry and I submitted *Some Smug Slug* together, but that is not the usual procedure. Most publishers prefer to find an illustrator for you because they know the best ones to handle the particular type of manuscript. It is certainly not necessary to submit illustrated manuscripts. Fortunately, editors are experienced in knowing what is good without the benefit of illustrations.

Do you have any advice, in terms of finding an illustrator, for a writer starting out?

Don't try to find your own illustrator. It might even prove to be a deterrent to having the manuscript accepted.

What procedures do you follow when you write?

I write as it comes to me, and I mull my ideas over and over in my head—mostly in the middle of the night—before I put anything down on paper. In this way, I have the structure of the story planned before I start to use pencil and paper. I never write first on my computer—I have to use paper and pencil to get my ideas down.

Where do you get your ideas?

I am a keen observer and a keen listener because I am always looking for the next story. *Livingstone Mouse* came about because I found that a mouse mom had torn my mail into shreds in my mailbox and had made herself a tiny nest for her babies. After putting her into the wood pile, we began to think how funny it would be if she had five baby mice all trying to grow up in that paper

LADYBUG

PO Box 300
Peru, IL 61354
Web site: www.cricket.com

Description: *Ladybug*, a magazine for young children ages 2 to 6, is published by the Cricket Magazine Group. *Ladybug* features original stories and poems written by the world's best children's authors.

Key people:

Editor in chief: Marianne Carus
Editor: Paula Morrow
Senior art director: Ron McCutchan
Art director: Suzanne Beck

Accepts unsolicited/unagented: Will consider any manuscripts or art samples sent on speculation and accompanied by a self-addressed stamped envelope. Submissions without an SASE will be discarded.

nest. She would have to throw them out to find places to build nests of their own. Livingstone became one of those baby mice who decided that he would try to find China—as his place to live.

What do you think are the key differences between writing for children and writing for adults?

Children are very literal and take everything you say seriously. Therefore, you have to know how to joke and, more important, how to get that joke over on paper.

How did you learn to write?

I did not have formal training as a writer. I think the best writers are those to whom writing is a passion and who do it because they can't help it. I have always written, even if it were only long letters home, observing funny or poignant things happening around me. However, I had to read armfuls of children's books to realize how to write for children. Children like lots of dialogue and not so much description. The best advice I was given was "Show, don't tell," which means don't forget you have illustrations to rely on, and you don't have to explain every gesture that is taking place.

Anything you really wish somebody had told you when you started out?

The best advice I could possibly give is, Don't give up. Remember how many times most people have to submit manuscripts before they have one taken. If a publisher rejects it and says, "This doesn't fit in with our plans," that's probably true. It doesn't mean your manuscript is bad; it just means it's not what that particular publisher is looking for at that moment. Perhaps your book is great, but it's about dogs and the publisher already has a dog book in the works. If that's so, they don't want another dog book. Keep trying. It's well worth it for the joy you will feel when your first book is accepted.

Preferred articles: *Fiction*: read-aloud stories, picture stories, original retellings of folk and fairy tales, and multicultural stories. Length: up to 850 words. *Rebuses*: focus on concrete nouns. Length: up to 250 words. *Nonfiction*: concepts, vocabulary, and simple explanations of things in a young child's world. Length: up to 300 words. *Poetry*: rhythmic, rhyming; serious, humorous, and active. Length: up to 20 lines. *Other*: learning activities, games, crafts, songs, and finger games. See back issues for types, formats, and length. An exact word count should be noted on each manuscript submitted. Word count includes every word but does not include the title of the manuscript or the author's name.

Time to reply: Please allow six to eight weeks response time for manuscripts.

Prefer manuscript/illustration packages, or separate: Authors/illustrators may submit a complete manuscript with art samples. The manuscript will be evaluated for quality of concept and text before the art is considered.

Include with illustrator query: Artists should submit review samples of artwork to be kept in illustrator files. Prefers to see tear sheets or photoprints/photocopies of art. *Direct art samples to* Suzanne Beck, art director.

Time to reply: 12 weeks for art samples.

Terms for writers: Stories and articles, up to $0.25 per word, $25 minimum; poems, up to $3 per line, $25 minimum. Payment on publication.

Terms for illustrators: Full-color, $500/spread ($250/page); black and white, $50/spot. Payment within 45 days of acceptance. Purchases first publication rights with reprint option; physical art remains the property of the illustrator.

Submission guidelines: Guidelines are available on the Web site or by mail with an SASE. *Please address all manuscript submissions to* submissions editor

Tips and comments: Study up. *Ladybug* would like to reach as many children's authors and artists as possible for original contributions, but the magazine's standards are very high, and *Ladybug* will accept only top-quality material. Before attempting to write for *Ladybug*, be sure to familiarize yourself with this age child.

LISTEN

55 W. Oak Ridge Drive
Hagerstown, MD 21740
(301) 393-4010
(301) 393-4055 (fax)
E-mail: listen@healthconnection.org
Web site: www.rhpa.org

Corporate structure/parent: The Health Connection.

Established: 1948.

Key people:

Editor in chief: Larry Becker

Acquisitions/submissions editor: Anita Jacobs

Articles per year and description: Approximately 60 articles and 50 illustrations. Categories: stories; testimonials; personality; factuals; self-help; activity.

Percentage by first-time authors: 15 to 20 percent.

Seeks: *Listen*'s subject is positive lifestyle for teens. It includes a well-known personality each month, having a tobacco-, alcohol-, and drug-free lifestyle. *Listen* includes self-help articles, current events relating to teen experiences, activities (e.g., biking, hiking, etc.), puzzles.

Accepts unsolicited/unagented: Yes.

Recent articles: The April 2000 issue focused on violence. One highlight was the inclusion of material that offered alternatives to violence and ways of learning to get along with each other.

Preferred articles: Stories that are true to life illustrating how teens made good choices.

Preferred form of submission/contact: Preferably a query letter or by e-mail (to listen@healthconnection.org).

Time to reply: Four to six weeks.

Time to publish: Nine to 12 months.

Accepts simultaneous submissions: Yes.

Number of illustrators used annually: One primary illustrator who contracts out assignments.

Include with illustrator query: Tear sheets.

Terms for writers: Approximately $0.07 to $0.15 per word. Articles should be from 1,000 to 1,200 words in length.

Submission guidelines: By writing, e-mailing, or calling us.

Tips and comments: Approach your topic in a fresh way that will catch the attention of a teenager. Remember to keep it positive as much as possible. Life is complex enough—offer ways to make it better.

LIVE

1445 Boonville Avenue
Springfield, MO 65802
E-mail: rl-live@gph.org
Web site: www.radiantlife.org

Key people:

Adult curriculum editor: Paul R. Smith

LIVE WIRE

8121 Hamilton Avenue
Cincinnati, OH 45231
(513) 931-4050
(513) 931-0950 (fax)
E-mail: standardpub@attmail.com
Web site: www.standardpub.com

Description: Weekly for 10- to 12-year-olds who "want to connect with Christ."

Key people:

Articles editor: Margie Redford

Art director: Sandy Wimmer

MH-18

400 S. 10th Street
Emmaus, PA 18098
Web site: www.hm-18.com

Description: Men's-type magazine for 13- to 18-year-old boys. Men's health, sports, fitness, girls, gear, and life.

Corporate structure/parent: Rodale Press.

Key people:

Editorial assistant: Jenny Everett

Seeks: Nonfiction only to 2,000 words; also fillers and short material.

Terms for writers: $1 per word for all rights on acceptance.

MUSE

PO Box 300
Peru, IL 61354
Web site: www.musemag.com

Corporate structure/parent: Cricket Magazine Group.

Description: *Muse* is a nonfiction magazine for children ages 8 to 14. The goal of *Muse* is to give as many children as possible access to the most important ideas and concepts underlying the principal areas of human knowledge. It takes children seriously as developing intellects by assuming that, if explained clearly, the ideas and concepts of an article will be of interest to them.

Established: In October 1996, the Cricket Magazine Group, in conjunction with *Smithsonian* Magazine, launched *Muse*.

Key people:

Editor: Diana Lutz

Art director: John Grandits

Photo editor: Carol Parden

Seeks: Each article must be about a topic that children can understand. The topic must be a large one that somehow connects with a fundamental tenet of some discipline or area of practical knowledge. The treatment of the topic must be of the competence one would expect of an expert in the field. On the other hand, *Muse* does not want articles that could be mistaken for chapters in a textbook. Instead, *Muse* prefers the author visit the scientist or research site and report on what he or she sees or hears there. An article must be interesting to children, who are under no obligation to read it.

Accepts unsolicited/unagented: *Muse* prefers queries to unsolicited manuscripts. However, manuscripts may be submitted to the Cricket Magazine Group for review, and any that are considered suitable for *Muse* will be forwarded. Such manuscripts will also be considered for publication in *Cricket*, *Spider,* or *Ladybug*.

Preferred form of submission/contact: Articles for *Muse* are commissioned. Authors interested in being considered for commissioned work should send a query including a resume, writing samples, and detailed story ideas. *Muse* cannot respond to a query that doesn't include story ideas. It is also important to describe any relevant areas of expertise. Once commissioned, authors are required to submit as many drafts as are necessary. Articles will be assigned at between 1,000 and 1,500 words, and drafts should be sent by e-mail. Authors are also required to provide *Muse* with a bibliography that lists all resource material (including names, addresses, and telephone numbers of key persons interviewed for an article). Please note that because of the unique mission of *Muse*, extensive rewrites are often necessary.

Time to reply: Please allow 16 weeks for a reply.

Terms for writers: Payment for unsolicited manuscripts is $0.25 a word. Higher rates are negotiated on the basis of experience. Payment is made within 60 days of acceptance. *Muse* retains the option to buy nonexclusive reprint and reproduction rights at half the original fee. Authors will receive three complimentary copies of the issue in which their article appears.

Submission guidelines: To receive writers guidelines please go to the Web site or send SASE to Writers Guidelines, PO Box 300, Peru, IL 61354.

Tips and comments: Articles should meet the highest possible standard of clarity and transparency aided, wherever possible, by a tone of skepticism and humor.

My Friend

50 Street Paul's Avenue
Boston, MA 02130
(617) 522-8911
(617) 541-9805 (fax)
E-mail: pauline.org
Web site: www.myfriend@pauline.org

Corporate structure/parent: Pauline Books & Media.

Description: "My Friend, the Catholic magazine for Jesus' favorite friends."

Established: 1979.

Key people:

Editor in chief: Sr. Donna William Giaimo

Acquisitions/submissions editors: Sr. Kathryn James Hermes

Articles per year and description: 50 articles in both fiction and nonfiction categories. Inspirational and teaching stories are the categories in which *My Friend* accepts unsolicited articles; all other categories are by commission only.

Percentage by first-time authors: 20 percent.

Seeks: Fiction stories that have different twists and reflect the toys, games, and issues of kids today but also entwine Christian values.

Accepts unsolicited/unagented: Yes.

Recent articles:

"Feels Like Tug of War and I'm the Rope" by Mary Bahr Fritts (friendship and religious difference)

"That Forever Grin" by May Ovington (fashion and popularity)

"Just One Little Goal" by Marian Luctkar-Flude (teamwork)

Preferred articles: Excellent writing; "gripping" plots; meaning and relevance for today's kids; tight writing; original slant with an element of the unexpected.

Preferred form of submission/contact: Manuscript.

Time to reply: Two months.

Time to publish: Six months to a year.

Accepts simultaneous submissions: No.

Number of illustrators used annually: 15.

Prefer manuscript/illustration packages, or separate: Separately.

Include with illustrator query: Resume and samples. Prefers to work with artists who use computer transmissions.

Time to reply: Four weeks.

Purchases freelance photography: Infrequently.

Terms for writers: Fiction: $85 to $150.

Terms for illustrators: $75 to $250.

Submission guidelines: Write to *My Friend* for a copy of the guidelines.

Tips and comments: Works mainly with submissions of substance that require very little editing. Needs lively, fun, provocative, realistic fiction pieces.

NATURE FRIEND

2727 Press Run Road
Sugarcreek, OH 44681
(330) 852-1900
(330) 852-3285 (fax)

Description: Monthly nature magazine.

Key people:

Editor: Marvin Wengerd

NEW MOON

PO Box 3620
Duluth, MN 55803-3620
(218) 728-5507
(218) 728-0314 (fax)
Web site: www.newmoon.org

Corporate structure/parent: New Moon Publishing.

Description: "New Moon: the magazine for girls and their dreams."

Established: 1993.

Key people:

Managing editors: Deb Mylin and Bridget Grosser. Send submissions to Deb Mylin's attention.

Articles per year and description: 30 per year; 18 or more illustrations; 12 pieces written by freelance writers. Note: 70 to 75 percent of each issue is written by girls ages 8 to 14 so there is not a lot of content written by adults.

Percentage by first-time authors: 50 percent.

Seeks: Submissions to regular feature departments: Women's Work (profiling a woman and her job); Her Story (profiling a woman from the past and her contribution to the world); Body Language (articles for girls about their bodies and development—menstruation, acne, depression, body image, yoga); and Fiction (with girls as the main character). All articles relate to each issue's overall theme.

Accepts unsolicited/unagented: Yes.

Recent articles:

"Herbal Heritage" by Constance García-Barrio (Her Story article about African American herbal remedies and how they're passed on from generation to generation)

"Ommm. . . ." by Ellen Williams (Body Language article about how yoga can help you relax)

"Bombs Away!" by Lisa Vihos (Woman's Work article about a bomb technician)

Preferred articles: *New Moon* only accepts writing by girls and women. Looking for pieces aimed at the magazine's audience (8- to 14-year-old girls) that specifically fit with each issue's theme. The Girls Editorial Board picks all the pieces that will appear in the magazine, and there is obvious opposition to articles that are overtly didactic in nature.

Preferred form of submission/contact: Queries or manuscripts are welcome by electronic or regular mail.

Time to reply: Two to four months.

Time to publish: Four months following acceptance.

Accepts simultaneous submissions: Yes.

Number of illustrators used annually: Roughly 20.

Desired illustrator qualifications: Variety of styles that is appropriate for adolescent girls. Artist's samples whose style fits with the magazine are kept on file. When assigning a job, someone goes through the samples on file to match the job with the illustrator.

Prefer manuscript/illustration packages, or separate: The preference is to review manuscripts and illustrations separately, but will look at a full packet if it is sent. The reason for this being that illustration assignments come much later in the process.

Include with illustrator query: Nothing specifically is required but samples work well.

Time to reply: No reply. Will file the work for future reference.

Purchases freelance photography: Infrequently.

Preferred photography: It's a stylistic issue. Looking for something that matches with the tone and style of the article.

Terms for writers: $0.06 to $0.12 per word. *New Moon* buys all rights.

Terms for illustrators: $150 to $300 depending on the job. That is for first-time North American rights.

Submission guidelines: Send an SASE to *New Moon* at Adult Writer's Guidelines, New Moon, or visit the Web site at www.newmoon.org/nmg/adult_guidelines.htm

Tips and comments: Above all else, do your homework. Know *New Moon*'s style and subject matter before sending your work. *Writers:* Get familiar with the magazine by reading *a year's worth* of back issues. The editors get lots of inappropriate submissions, and that's just a waste of time for the author and the publisher—pay attention to the list of upcoming themes and deadlines. *Illustrators:* Send a packet of black-and-white and color work for us to keep on file for future reference and possible assignments.

NICK JR.

1515 Broadway, 40th Floor
New York, NY 10036
(212) 258-7500
(212) 846-1752 (fax)
Web site: www.nickjr.com

Description: Monthly learning magazine for kids and parents.

Key people:

Articles editor: Wendy Smolen
Art director: Don Morris

ODYSSEY

30 Grove Street, Suite C
Peterborough, NH 03458
Web site: www.odysseymagazine.com
Illustrator's guidelines: www.cobblestonepub.com/pages/illustratorsguidelines

Corporate structure/parent: *Odyssey* is a subsidiary of Cobblestone Publishing (which is a subsidiary of the Cricket Publishing Group.

Key people:

Editor: Elizabeth Lindstrom
Managing editor: Lou Waryncia
Art director: Ann Dillon

Seeks: *Odyssey* is interested in articles rich in scientific accuracy and lively approaches to the subject at hand. The inclusion of primary research (interviews with scientists focusing on current research) are of primary interest to the magazine. Keep in mind that this magazine is essentially written for 10- to 16-year-old children. *Feature articles:* 750 to 950 words. Includes in-depth nonfiction articles (an interactive approach is a definite plus!); Q & A interviews, plays, and biographies are of interest as well. *Supplemental nonfiction:* 200 to 500 words. Includes subjects directly and indirectly related to the theme. Editors like little-known information but encourage writers not to overlook the obvious. *Fiction*: up to 1,000 words. Includes science-related stories, poems, science fiction, retold legends, and so forth, relating to the theme. *Department features*: 400 to 650 words. Includes Far Out; Places, Media, People to Discover, and Fantastic Journeys. Not a bad idea to consult back issues for direction of these departments that are also theme related. *Activities*: up to 750 words. Includes critical thinking activities, experiments, models, science fair projects, astrophotography projects, and any other science projects that can be done by children alone, with adult supervision, or in a classroom setting. Query should be accompanied by sketches and description of how activity relates to theme.

Accepts unsolicited/unagented: Please query first.

Preferred articles: Submitted manuscripts must be directly related to the theme of the issue. Be sure to study the theme list and guidelines before proceeding. *Odyssey* is interested in articles rich in scientific accuracy and lively approaches to the subject at hand. Keep in mind that this magazine is essentially written for 10- to 16-year-old children.

Preferred form of submission/contact: Query. Writers new to *Odyssey* should send a writing sample with the query. If you would like to know if your query has been received, please also include a stamped postcard that requests acknowledgment of receipt. In all correspondence, please include your complete address as well as a telephone number and/or e-mail address where you can be reached.

Time to reply: Queries may be submitted at any time, but queries sent well in advance of deadline may not be answered for several months. Go-aheads requesting material proposed in queries are usually sent four months prior to publication date. Unused queries will be returned approximately three to four months prior to publication date.

Include with illustrator query: If you would like to be considered for *illustration assignments* for Cobblestone's magazines, please send photocopies, tear sheets, or other nonreturnable samples of your work to Ann Dillon, Art Director, Cobblestone Publishing, 30 Grove Street, Suite C, Peterborough, NH 03458; (603) 924-7209, ext. 18. Please keep your file updated by sending samples of your latest work periodically.

Purchases freelance photography: Yes.

Preferred photography: To be considered for publication, photographs must relate to a specific theme. Writers are encouraged to submit available photos with their query or article. *Odyssey* buys one-time use only. Suggested fee range for professional-quality photographs: quarter to full page, black and white, $15 to $100; color, $25 to $100. Please note that fees for nonprofessional-quality photographs are negotiated. Cover fees are set on an individual basis for one-third use, plus promotional use. All cover images are color. Text images are primarily color. Color transparencies, slides, and color prints can be submitted for inside black/white use since they can be scanned at the printer. Prices set by museums, societies, stock photography houses, and so forth, are paid or negotiated. If you have photographs pertaining to any upcoming theme, please contact the editor by mail or fax, or send them with your query. You may also send images on speculation.

Terms for writers: $0.20 to $0.25 per printed word; activities are paid on a case-by-case basis.

Terms for illustrators: Spots, $10 to $40; quarter page, $30 to $60; half page, $50 to $115; three-quarter page, $80 to $150; full page, $100-$210. Covers are assigned and paid on an individual basis.

Submission guidelines: Go to the Web site or write with an SASE for guidelines. A query must consist of all of the following information to be considered: A brief cover letter stating the subject and word length of the proposed article, a detailed one-page outline explaining the information to be presented in the article, a bibliography of sources (including interviews) the author intends to use in preparing the article, and a self-addressed stamped envelope. A writer may send as many queries for one issue as he or she wishes, but each query must have a separate outline, bibliography, and self-addressed stamped envelope. Telephone queries are not accepted unless the material is extremely time-sensitive to a specific issue. Please type all queries. *Mail queries to* Editorial Department, or send them via e-mail them to bethlindstrom2000@hotmail.com

Tips and comments: Writers are encouraged to study recent back issues for content and style. (Sample issues are available at $4.95. Send 10 by 13-inch self-addressed $2

stamped envelope.) All material must relate to the theme of a specific upcoming issue in order to be considered.

On Course

1445 Boonville Avenue
Springfield, MO 65802-1894
(417) 862-2781
(417) 866-1146 (fax)
E-mail: oncourse@ag.org

Description: Magazine for Christian students.

Key people:

Editor: Melinda Booze

Art director: David Danielson

On the Line

616 Walnut Avenue
Scottdale, PA 15683-1999
(724) 887-8500
(724) 887-3111 (fax)
E-mail: info@mph.org or mary@mph.org
Web: www.mph.org/cp

Corporate structure/parent: *On the Line* is a subsidiary of Faith and Life Resources Division (which is a division of Mennonite Publishing House, Inc.).

Description: *On the Line* is a monthly magazine for children ages 9 to 14 that reinforces Christian values.

Key people:

Editor: Mary Clemens Meyer

Seeks: *On the Line* needs articles (300–500 words) and stories (1,000–1,800 words), puzzles, quizzes, appropriate light verse, and cartoons. Please see below for content objectives.

Accepts unsolicited/unagented: Yes.

Preferred articles: *On the Line* uses materials that do the following: Help readers feel they are persons of worth. Help handle problems. Encourage readers to live up to their potential. Introduce the wonders of God's world—nature, art, music, poetry, and human relationships. Help children accept other races and cultures as their equals. Nurture a desire for world peace and provide tools for peaceful living. Make the message of the Bible attractive. Help children grow toward commitment to Christ and the Church. Help Mennonite readers appreciate their Christian heritage and learn about current activities of their church.

Preferred form of submission/contact: Manuscript.

Tips and comments: *On the Line* helps upper elementary and junior high school children understand and appreciate God, the created world, themselves, and others. Please bear this in mind when writing for your audience. Reading several back issues of the magazine will give you a better idea of *On the Line*'s style and objective.

OWL

370 King Street W., Suite 300
Toronto, Ontario M5V 1J8
Canada
(416) 971-5275
(416) 971-5294 (fax)
E-mail: owl@owlkids.com
Web site: www.owl.on.ca

Corporate structure/parent: *Owl* is published by Owl Communications, a registered, nonprofit charitable organization with the following aims: To encourage children to read for enjoyment and discovery, to help children learn more about the world around them, to stimulate children to enjoy, respect, and conserve their natural environment, and to give children a wealth of ideas to use constructively.

Description: *Owl*, the discovery magazine for kids, is aimed at children over eight.

Seeks: *Owl* includes a wide range of material. Feature articles are about animals, nature phenomena, science, people, experiments, technology—in fact, anything in the world that is of interest to this age group and is in keeping with the objectives and philosophy of Owl Communications. *Owl* is informative and intellectually challenging in a lively, fun way, but it is never preachy. As well as articles and stories, innovative puzzles and imaginative activities play an important role in this "hands-on" magazine.

Accepts unsolicited/unagented: Yes.

Preferred articles: *Owl* seeks articles that inform and stimulate children and are also enjoyable to read. Avoid sexist and ethnic stereotypes, and do not give animals human characteristics. Keep the age range of the readers in mind, but do not talk down to them. An easy, lively style and a clear logical presentation of ideas are more important than limiting vocabulary for young readers. Accuracy is of utmost importance. A bibliography and a list of research references for scientific data is required.

Preferred form of submission/contact: *Owl* prefers to receive detailed outlines of suggested articles, rather than brief queries. *Owl* also likes to know something about the writer's credentials. If possible, first-time submissions should be accompanied by examples of previously published work.

Time to reply: Six to eight weeks are required to review submissions properly.

Desired illustrator qualifications: Great attention is paid to the quality of photographs and illustrations used in *Owl*. Most illustrations are commissioned.

Prefer manuscript/illustration packages, or separate: Art may accompany written submissions, but *Owl* usually commissions art and photography separately.

Time to reply: Six to eight weeks are required to properly review submissions.

Purchases freelance photography: Yes.

Preferred photography: Unsolicited photographs are seldom used unless they accompany an article. Photographers' stock lists are welcome. Photographs should be high-quality color transparencies. Duplicates may be submitted, but the originals will be required for reproduction. Photographs must be well packaged and are best sent by registered mail. For photo information, write and request a photo package.

Terms for writers: Fees range from $200 to $500 for features depending on the scope and research involved. There is no fixed rate for puzzles, games, activities, and other material. Owl Communications requires extensive rights to material to accommodate both its needs and those of its affiliated foreign-language magazines. Sample contracts outlining the basic requirements are available on request.

Submission guidelines: Stories or articles run 500 to 1,000 words: activities (which should require minimum adult supervision and be based on easy-to-find items) are 500 words or less. Puzzles and game ideas should be accompanied by suggestions for visuals. Please send a $1.50 money order (no stamps—includes all taxes) for a reply to manuscripts.

Tips and comments: Authors, illustrators, and photographers are urged to become familiar with *Owl* before submitting material. Magazines may be purchased directly from Owl Communications, found on newsstands, or borrowed from the library. Sample copies: $4.28 (includes all taxes). Please send a $1.50 money order (no stamps—includes all taxes) for a reply to manuscripts.

POCKETS

1908 Grand Avenue
PO Box 340004
Nashville, TN 37203-0004
(615) 340-7333
E-mail: pockets@upperroom.org

Corporate structure/parent: Upper Room.

Description: *Pockets* is for children ages 6 through 11 with a target reading age of 8 through 11. Though some children may share the publication with their families, it is primarily designed for personal enjoyment.

Established: 1981.

Key people:

Editor in chief: Janet R. Knight

Acquisitions/submissions editor: Lynn W. Gilliam

Art director: Chris Schechner

Articles per year and description: *Pockets* publishes one story for younger children in each issue. Written for 5- to 7-year-olds, these stories should be no more than 600 words. Pockets is a 48-page magazine with illustrations on each page; 45 fiction stories; 4 to 6 Scripture stories; 10 nonfiction articles; 30 poems.

Percentage by first-time authors: 70 percent.

Seeks: Submissions do not have to be overtly religious but should reflect daily living, lifestyles, and problem solving based on living as faithful disciples. They should help children know that the Christian life is not always a neatly wrapped moral package but is open to the continuing revelation of God's will in their lives. *Pockets* uses seasonal material, both secular and liturgical. The magazine is primarily written by adults. *Pockets* welcomes submissions from children, too. *Pockets* is nondenominational. Readers include children of many cultures and ethnic backgrounds. These differences should be reflected in the lifestyles, living environments (suburban, urban, rural, reservation) families (extended families, single-parent families), and peoples' names. Stories should show appreciation of cultural differences, not that one is better than another.

Accepts unsolicited/unagented: Yes—but each issue has a theme so it's best to request a list of the themes by sending an SASE. New themes are available each year in late December. Previously published authors automatically receive themes at that time. Others request themes by sending an SASE.

Recent articles: Please see recent issues of the magazine.

Preferred articles: Fiction and Scripture stories should be 600 to 1,400 words. Primary interest is in stories that can help children deal with everyday life. *Pockets* prefers real-life settings but occasionally uses fables. *Pockets* does not accept stories about talking animals or inanimate objects. Fictional characters and some elaboration may be included in scripture stories, but the writer must remain faithful to the story. Stories should contain lots of action, use believable dialogue, be simply written, and be relevant to the situations faced by this age group in everyday life. Children need to be able to see themselves in the pages of the magazine. The tone should not be preachy or didactic. Use short sentences and paragraphs. When possible, use concrete words instead of abstractions. However, do not write down to children. Use terms that are inclusive (e.g., *humankind, persons, human beings, everyone*). Poems should be short, not more than 24 lines. *Pockets* continues to need articles involved in environmental, community, and peace/justice issues.

Preferred form of submission/contact: No queries.

Time to reply: Within six to eight weeks.

Time to publish: Articles are often slotted for a specific issue, so, depending on the subject matter, it could be published within eight weeks, or it could be on "long-term hold" for eight to 18 months.

Accepts simultaneous submissions: No.

Number of illustrators used annually: The number of illustrators is variable. There are illustrations with every story, and there are 23 to 30 articles per issue.

Desired illustrator qualifications: Someone who *hears* what the magazine needs and works to interpret the story or poem appropriately and accurately. It is also crucial that illustrators (and writers) submit work in a timely manner.

Prefer manuscript/illustration packages, or separate: To date, there has not been a writer who has also illustrated his or her own story. The art designer selects the artists and the art that will accompany each story.

Include with illustrator query: Send samples and tear sheets. Responses are made only to those who supply an SASE.

Time to reply: Not too quickly—twice per year—and only if the submission is accompanied by an SASE.

Purchases freelance photography: Primarily in connection with nonfiction articles.

Preferred photography: Shots that clearly illustrate and relate to the nonfiction article in question. Action shots and faces (not backs of heads) are especially useful.

Terms for writers: Stories pay $0.14 per word; poetry puzzles and games pay $25 and up per piece.

Terms for illustrators: $650 for the cover; up to $300 (depending on the size and color—four color/two color) for inside art.

Submission guidelines: "Writers' Guidelines and Themes" is sent free of charge on receipt of an SASE. A sample copy of the magazine requires a 7 1/2 by 10 1/2-inch (or larger) SASE with $1.10 postage.

Tips and comments: Send for themes, guidelines, and sample issues. Read, read, read and study the materials for useful insights. Realize also that *Pockets* receives more than 200 manuscripts per month; obviously, the magazine utilizes what will work best for the publication. Make sure the art is appropriate (send for a copy of the magazine). Do not send original art, and include an SASE for a response.

POINTE

250 W. 57th Street, Suite 420
New York, NY 10107
(212) 265-8890
(212) 265-8908 (fax)
Web site: www.americancheerleader.com

Corporate structure/parent: Lifestyle Ventures LLC, which also publishes *American Cheerleader*, *Dance Teacher*, *Dance Spirit*, *In Motion*, and *Stage Directions* magazines.

Description: *Pointe* magazine is an international ballet magazine for ballet dancers and serious ballet students.

POJO'S WORLD

2121 Waukegan Road, Suite 120
Bannockburn, IL 60015
Web site: www.hsmedia.com

Corporate structure/parent: H&S Media.

Description: Bimonthly for teens interested in collectible card games, video games, comic books, and action figures.

Key people:

Editor: Nancy Davies

Preferred form of submission/contact: Query.

Terms for writers: Varies for first North American serial rights, all rights or reprint rights.

PRIMEDIA

850 Third Avenue
New York, NY 10022
(212) 407-9700
(212) 935-4237 (fax)
Web site: www.primedia.com

Description: Primedia is a major magazine publisher with many titles of interest to youth. They include *16 Magazine*, *16's Superstars*, *Seventeen*, *SuperTeen*, *Teen Beat*, *Teen Beat AllStars*, *Teen Machine*, and *Tiger Beat*.

PURPOSE

Mennonite Publishing House, Inc.
616 Walnut Avenue
Scottdale PA 15683-1999
(724) 887-8500
(724) 887-3111 (fax)
E-mail: info@mph.org and horsch@mph.org
Web: www.mph.org/cp

Corporate structure/parent: *Purpose* is a subsidiary of Faith and Life Resources Division (which is a division of Mennonite Publishing House, Inc.).

Description: *Purpose* is a monthly in weekly parts targeted at older youth and adults of all ages. Focus on action oriented, discipleship living.

Key people:

Editor: James E. Horsch

Acquisitions/submissions editor: James E. Horsch

Seeks: *Purpose* needs short anecdotal stories and features (up to 750 words) and verse (up to 12 lines). See below for more details.

Accepts unsolicited/unagented: Yes.

Preferred articles: *Purpose* prefers terse, fast-moving writing style in first person. Purpose is interested in articles and stories that do the following: Illustrate Christians applying their faith to daily life. Strengthen the Christian faith of readers. Empower readers in decision-making. Stress loyalty to the church and its ministries. Support Christians who participate in the secular community. Inspire interest in the culture and history of other peoples. Highlight biographical and historical stories of Christian leaders, places, and events. Emphasize hobbies, nature, travel, art, science, and seasonal topics from a Christian perspective.

Purchases freelance photography: Yes.

Preferred photography: Clarity and quality.

Terms for illustrators: Rates on art and photographs vary according to quality.

Tips and comments: Readers of *Purpose* are committed Christians who want to apply their faith in daily life. Articles in *Purpose* suggest ways to resolve issues consistent with biblical principles. Such situations may arise in a variety of settings such as among the family, on the job, in the church as well as the community. It helps to keep these basic (but very important) ideas in mind when writing articles for submission to *Purpose.*

POWER AND LIGHT

6401 The Paseo
Kansas City, MO 64131-1284
(816) 333-7000
(816) 333-4439 (fax)
E-mail: mprice@Nazarene.org
Web site: www.Nazarene.org

Description: Weekly story paper for fifth and sixth graders published by Church of the Nazarene.

Key people:

Editor: Matt Price

RANGER RICK

8925 Leesburg Pike
Vienna, VA 22184
(703) 790-4000
Web site: www.nwf.org/rrick

Corporate structure/parent: National Wildlife Federation.

Description: Wildlife/nature magazine for ages 7 to 12.

Key people:

Editor: Gerald Bishop

Design director: Donna Miller

REACT

711 Third Avenue
New York, NY 10017
(212) 450-0900
E-mail: srgarvey@react.com
Web site: www.react.com

Seeks: Before you write, keep in mind: Young Americans in the first throes of teenhood want you to write with clarity and come to them free of any preconceived ideas of who and what they are.

Accepts unsolicited/unagented: Query first.

Preferred articles: Report long but write short. Write with style. To put readers at ease, be personal in your writing tone. When writing for *React,* you'll have a lot more success if you consider these tips: Walk their walk. See events through their eyes. Let their world be your world. Let their questions be your questions. Don't talk down. Do not preach. Be as professional and rigorous in reporting as you would be writing for adults. Be honest.

Preferred form of submission/contact: Assignments are based on query letters of one page—three or four paragraphs should be enough. Propose only one topic per query. Your query should include the following: Your central theme or point in more than a few sentences. Your sources on all sides of the issues. Whom will you interview? The story's general direction. Briefly tell how you'll organize it. A summary of your most important writing credits. Attach one or two writing samples and a self-addressed stamped envelope and send to Articles Editor, *React* Magazine, 711 Third Avenue, New York, NY 10017.

READ

Weekly Reader
200 First Stamford Place
PO Box 120023
Stamford, CT 06912-0023
(203) 705-3500
(203) 705-1661 (fax)
Web site: www.weeklyreader.com

Corporate structure/parent: Ripplewood.

Established: 1950.

Key people:

Editor in chief: Rosanna Hansen

Acquisitions/submissions editor: Suzanne I. Barchers

Articles per year and description: 18 issues per year contain approximately three stories and articles plus one play per month. Each story, play, or article has one to three illustrations.

Seeks: Short stories of high student interest for middle and high school students. Plays (readers theater style) of 3,000 to 4,000 words are also of interest.

Accepts unsolicited/unagented: Yes.

Recent articles:

Adaptation of Joseph Bruchac's novel *The Heart of a Chief* into a play about the use of American Indian terms for school mascots

Article by Carlos Morton about the Day of the Dead

"Faith" by Sherwood Smith (a short story about a girl who believes in magic)

Preferred articles: Strong, carefully crafted short stories, 2,000 to 3,000 words long, that appeal to teens. No sex or explicit language. Stories must compete with previously published works drawn from established writers the magazine has published, such as Jane Yolen, Will Hobbs, and T. A. Barron.

Preferred form of submission/contact: Send a manuscript with an SASE. *Read* appreciates those manuscripts that can be discarded if not used. For a quicker response, include your e-mail address.

Time to reply: Two to three weeks. For a quicker response, include your e-mail address.

Time to publish: Varies—six to 12 months. *Read* has a long lead time. If, for example, you have a manuscript for a winter theme, send it at least nine months ahead.

Accepts simultaneous submissions: Yes, but please inform. *Read* prefers a single submission with a limited time frame, such as "This is an exclusive submission for your consideration for three weeks."

Number of illustrators used annually: 15 or more.

Desired illustrator qualifications: Ability to work with tight deadlines; flexibility. We use a variety of styles.

Prefer manuscript/illustration packages, or separate: No packages.

Include with illustrator query: Samples and resume are standard.

Time to reply: Illustrators are contacted when a project comes up that fits their style.

Purchases freelance photography: Yes, though rarely. *Read* uses photo researchers.

Terms for writers: Varies.

Terms for illustrators: Varies.

Submission guidelines: Send a request with a 6 by 8-inch envelope, two stamps.

Tips and comments: Review sample issues carefully. Check out the Web site for related materials. Understand the audience of middle and high school students. For a quicker response, include your e-mail address.

Scholastic

555 Broadway
New York, NY 10012
(212) 343-6100
Web site: www.scholastic.com

Description: Scholastic's 35 classroom magazines include *The New York Times Upfront*, *Scholastic News*, *Junior Scholastic*, *Scholastic Scope*, *Science World*, *Literary Cavalcade*, and *Let's Find Out*. Each classroom magazine is grade-specific, with content appropriate to student abilities and school curriculum requirements representing grades pre-K through high school.

School Mates

3054 Route 9W
New Windsor, NY 12553
(914) 562-8350
(914) 561-CHES (fax)

Description: Bimonthly magazine for young chess players from United States Chess Federation.

Key people:

Editor: Peter Kurzdorfen
Art editor: Jami Anson

Science Weekly

2141 Industrial Parkway, Suite 202
Silver Spring, MD 20904
(301) 680-8804
(301) 680-9240 (fax)

Corporate structure/parent: *Science Weekly* has an association with Steck-Vaughn Co. (a Harcourt Classroom Education Company). It is distributed exclusively by Steck-Vaughn Company.

Description: *Science Weekly* is published 16 times per year on seven different grade levels. There is also an eight-page "Teaching Notes" section for parents and educators. Each writer is assigned a single topic, which they develop on all of these levels—including labs, writing, math, language arts, and critical thinking activities.

Established: 1983.

Key people:

Editor in chief: Deborah Lazar

Publisher: Dr. Claude Mayberry Jr.

Assistant editor: Emily Schuster

Articles per year and description: None. The format of *Science Weekly* is non-freelance oriented. Each issue is written by a single writer. *Science Weekly* doesn't use freelance submissions.

Accepts unsolicited/unagented: No.

Seeks: Writers who can challenge students with solid science concepts with an entertaining and educational focus.

Recent articles: Each issue covers a single science topic. The text and activities are coordinated to apply to several different grade levels. Recent issue topics have included chocolate, secret codes, crystals, and the stomach.

Preferred form of submission/contact: *Science Weekly* only works with writers in the Washington, D.C., metropolitan Area (including Maryland and Virginia) who are able to be part of the in-house editorial process. *Science Weekly* accepts resumes *only*. Writers should be able to write about science for all different grade levels and be able to develop activities on the specified topic. An educational background and children's writing experience are pluses.

Time to reply: Promptly.

Number of illustrators used annually: One.

Prefer manuscript/illustration packages, or separate: *Science Weekly* does not accept submissions—only resumes.

Terms for writers: Writers are paid on a per-issue basis.

Submission guidelines: If, after review of a resume, an editor determines the appropriateness of the candidate, the writer will be contacted for writing a sample issue. The writer will be assigned a topic and provided with full guidelines and materials. General guidelines are *not* provided on inquiry (because unsolicited submissions are *not* accepted).

Tips and comments: Please contact *Science Weekly* with your resume only—and only if you live in the D.C. metro area. If the staff thinks that you will be an appropriate match for the publication, you will be contacted.

SCOUTING

1325 W. Walnut Hill Lane
PO Box 152079
Irving, TX 75015-2079
(972) 580-2367
(972) 580-2079 (fax)
Web site: www.scouting.org.mags/scouting

Corporate structure/parent: Boy Scouts of America.

Description: The magazine is published by the Boy Scouts of America six times a year. Issues are January–February, March–April, May–June, September, October, and November–December. It is mailed to about one million adult volunteer and professional Scout leaders (Scouters). Subscription is included as part of each Scouter's annual registration fee.

Seeks: *Scouting* magazine articles are mainly about successful program activities conducted by or for Cub Scout packs, Boy Scout troops, and Venturing crews. *Scouting* also includes features on winning leadership techniques and styles, profiles of outstanding individual leaders, and inspirational accounts (usually first person) of scouting's impact on an individual, either as a youth or while serving as a volunteer adult leader.

Preferred form of submission/contact: A query with a synopsis or outline of a proposed story is essential. Include a stamped self-addressed envelope to ensure a reply.

Time to reply: Within three weeks.

Number of illustrators used annually: Uses about four to six cartoons in each issue. They are normally one panel, although occasionally a one-column, vertical three panel.

Terms for writers: Pays on acceptance. Purchases first rights unless otherwise specified (purchase does not necessarily guarantee publication). Photos, if of acceptable quality, are usually included in payment for certain assignments. Payment rates depend on the professional quality of an article. Payment is from \$300 to \$500 for a short feature, \$650 to \$800 for a major article, and more for quality articles by frequent contributors.

Tips and comments: Writers or photographers should be familiar with the scouting program and *Scouting* magazine. A sample copy will be sent if you provide a stamped, self-addressed 9 by 12-inch envelope and \$2.50.

SEVENTEEN

850 Third Avenue
New York, NY 10022
(212) 407-9700
(212) 407-9899 (fax)
Web site: www.seventeen.com

Description: Young women's monthly fashion and beauty magazine.

Key people:

Editor in chief: Patrice G. Adcroft
Executive editor: Roberta Caploe
Deputy editor: Tamara Glenny
Art director: Carol Pagliuco

Sharing the Victory

8701 Leeds
Kansas City, MO 64129
(816) 921-0909
(816) 921-8755 (fax)
Web site: www.fca.org

Description: Christian athletics magazine.

Key people:

Editors: David Smale and Allen Palmeri
Art director: Frank Grey

Skipping Stones

PO Box 3939
Eugene, OR 97403
(541) 342-4956
E-mail: skipping@efn.org
Web site: www.efn.org/skipping

Description: *Skipping Stones* is for ages 8 to 17. It's a forum for communication and learning from each other. *Skipping Stones* is sensitive to diversity and respectful of all values, opinions, and perspectives. *Skipping Stones* prefers to publish material that encourages multicultural and nature awareness.

Established: 1988

Key people:

Editor in chief: Arun N. Toké

Articles per year and description: All of the numbers are variable and approximate: 50 poems (by youth under 19 years of age); 10 stories; 20 articles; 6 to 8 photoessays.

Percentage by first-time authors: 60 percent.

Seeks: Short pieces under 750 words. Nonfiction, fiction, and poetry pieces (*see guidelines for details*). Multicultural and international awareness stories as well as travelogues, nature appreciation, personal reflections, and journal entries.

Accepts unsolicited/unagented: Yes.

Recent articles:

Photoessay on Taiwan by Henry Westheim,
"Returning Home to Mexico" by David Lipp

"The Legacy: Thoughts of an Adopted Youth" by Melanie Spillane
"The Peanut: An Experience on a Train Journey in India" by Alpana Das
"Prayers and Other Nonsense" by Kathleen Ahrens (story set in Taiwan)

Preferred articles: Authenticity, originality, creativity, passion, simplicity, and beauty. Leave out the "preachiness."

Preferred form of submission/contact: Query or manuscript is fine but include an SASE if you want a response.

Time to reply: Three months.

Time to publish: Three to six months.

Accepts simultaneous submissions: Yes.

Number of illustrators used annually: Four or five adults but more youth.

Desired illustrator qualifications: A fresh look, a creative person, and cultural sensitivity.

Prefer manuscript/illustration packages, or separate: Accepted together.

Include with illustrator query: Samples, tear sheets, and a personal portfolio—with an SASE, of course.

Time to reply: If interested, the reply is very fast.

Purchases freelance photography: Yes.

Preferred photography: Crisp, beautiful images; unposed; illustrative of culture, celebrations, daily life, living conditions and lifestyles. Must be appealing to young people. Good contrast for black-and-white image reproduction.

Terms for writers: The magazine is a labor of love. As a general rule, writers are offered complimentary copies of the publication.

Terms for illustrators: The same applies—will send extra copies of the issue if needed.

Submission guidelines: With an SASE or from the Web site.

Tips and comments: Be original; be creative and be open to criticism from the editors. *Skipping Stones* tries to utilize illustrators of the same cultural background as the culture that is featured in any given story or article.

SOCCER JR.

27 Unquowa Road
Fairfield, CT 06430-5015
(203) 259-5766
(203) 256-1119 (fax)
E-mail: e-mailsoccerjr@soccerjr.com
Web site: www.soccerjr.com

Corporate structure/parent: Scholastic.

Description: *Soccer Jr.* is the premier publication for youth players between the ages of 8 and 16. It was founded in 1992 and since then has grown to be the largest paid circulation soccer magazine in the United States. *Soccer Jr.* also publishes two special editions, *Soccer for Parents* and *Coaches Edition*. *Soccer Jr.*'s editorial mission is to be the primary source of information and entertainment for youth soccer players, as well as their parents and coaches.

Established: 1992.

Key people:

Managing editor: Owen Lockwood

Editor: Jill Schoff

Percentage by first-time authors: The magazine mostly works with regular contributors but is open to new writers.

Seeks: "Great Goals" (reruns of important goals using still images from video footage); "Half Time" (a spread hosted by our mascots Junior and Barbara that's loaded with interactive puzzles, jokes and games); "You Make the Call" (a series of features that challenge readers' knowledge of the laws of the game. In each feature, several scenarios are illustrated with drawings and words. The readers are asked to "make the call" and can then read why their answer was right or wrong). Other regular features include biographies of great players in comic book format, short soccer fiction, and star interviews.

Recent articles:

"Tour de France" (a kid's-eye view of what the World Cup is all about)

"April Heinrichs" (a picture story biography of the first woman inducted into the National Soccer Hall of Fame)

"Mia Hamm" (the darling of American soccer answers questions submitted by *Soccer Jr.* readers)

Preferred articles: *Soccer Jr.* editorial falls into two basic categories: that which helps players improve their performance and that which is simply enjoyable to read. In the first category, features and departments provide instruction in skills, rules, training, nutrition, injury recovery and prevention, and advice about making soccer-related decisions. In the second category are features and departments about major soccer events, interviews, profiles of stars, picture stories, fiction, inspirational essays, puzzles, posters, and games.

Preferred form of submission/contact: *Soccer Jr.* requests a query for any feature ideas, but any fiction pieces can be sent complete. Please send any fiction articles to the attention of Jill Schoff, associate editor. All submissions, unless specifically requested, are on a speculative basis. Please provide a brief personal bio, including your involvement in soccer, if any, and a listing of any work you've had published.

Accepts simultaneous submissions: Please indicate whether a manuscript has been submitted elsewhere or previously published.

Terms for authors: Payment is on acceptance of first rights and ranges from $50 to $600, depending on the complexity and length of the story. Most fiction stories range from 1,000 to 1,500 words.

Time to reply: Four to six weeks. Please do not call during this time.

Submission guidelines: No guidelines. *Soccer Jr.* asks all potential writers to understand the magazine's voice. *Soccer Jr.* writes to kids, not to adults. To request a sample copy, send $4, which includes postage. Non-U.S. residents, please send $8. *Soccer Jr.* prefer to receive a computer file along with the hard copy of a manuscript. Please save the file as "text only" and mail it on disk or send it via e-mail as an attached file.

Tips and comments: *Soccer Jr.* is written for boys and girls ages 8 to 14 who play soccer. It is published in March, May, July, September, October, and December by Scholastic, Inc. The editorial focus is on the fun and challenge of the sport. Every issue contains star interviews, moves and skills, coverage of major soccer events (with a focus on U.S. teams), lively graphics, action photos, posters, games, puzzles and contests. Fair play and teamwork are emphasized.

SPELLBOUND

PO Box 2248
Schiller Park, IL 60176
Web site: www.eggplant-productions.com/spellbound

Corporate structure/parent: Eggplant Literary Productions, Inc.

Description: *Spellbound* is a quarterly publication of fantasy short stories and poems aimed at 9- to 13-year-olds. Each issue will have a creature of the issue and a short seasonal theme.

Preferred form of submission/contact: Only accepts e-mail submissions. Snail mail submissions will be returned to the author/poet/artist without consideration.

Submission guidelines: Poetry submissions should be sent to Marcie Lynn Tentchoff: poembound@eggplant-productions.com; fiction submissions and artwork should be sent to Raechel Henderson Moon: spellbound@eggplant-productions.com

Tips and comments: Please remember that the magazine's readers are children aged 9 to 14. Gore and adult situations are simply not a good idea. Humor, mild chills and thrills, gross stuff, and thoughtful insights into supernatural creatures are more in line with what the magazine is seeking. All submissions must fit one of the upcoming themes to be considered. You can find out upcoming themes online at www.eggplant-productions.com /spellbound/

SPIDER

PO Box 300
Peru, IL 61354
Web site: www.cricket.com

Established: In January 1994, Cricket Magazine Group of Carus Publishing Company launched *Spider*, a magazine for children ages 6 to 9.

Key people:

Editor in chief: Marianne Carus
Editor: Laura Tillotson
Art director: Tony Jacobson

Seeks: *Fiction*: realistic, easy-to-read stories, fantasy, folk- and fairy tales, science fiction, fables, and myths. *Nonfiction*: nature, animals, science, technology, environment, foreign culture, and history (a short bibliography is required for all nonfiction articles, and copies of research material will be required for all accepted articles). *Poetry*: serious, humorous, and nonsense rhymes. *Other*: recipes, crafts, puzzles, games, brain teasers, and math and word activities. *Length:* stories: 300 to 1,000 words; poems, not longer than 20 lines; articles: 300 to 800 words; puzzles/activities/games, 1 to 4 pages. An exact word count should be noted on each manuscript submitted. Word count includes every word but does not include the title of the manuscript.

Accepts unsolicited/unagented: Yes, manuscripts only.

Preferred articles: There is no theme list for upcoming issues. Submissions on all appropriate topics will be considered at any time during the year.

Preferred form of submission/contact: Manuscript only. Please do not query first. *Spider* will consider any manuscripts or art samples sent on speculation and accompanied by an SASE.

Time to reply: Please allow 12 weeks to receive a reply to submissions.

Include with illustrator query: *Spider* prefers to see tear sheets or photoprints/photocopies of art. If you must send original art as part of a portfolio, package it carefully and insure the package. *Please address all art samples to* Tony Jacobson, art director.

Time to reply: Please allow 12 weeks to receive a reply to submissions.

Purchases freelance photography: Yes.

Preferred photography: *Spider* will also consider submissions of photography, either in the form of photoessays or as illustrations for specific nonfiction articles. Photographs should accompany the manuscript. Color photography is preferred, but black-and-white submissions will be considered depending on subject matter. Photocopies or prints may be submitted with the manuscript, but original transparencies for color or good-quality black-and-white prints (preferably glossy finish) must be available on acceptance.

Terms for writers: *Stories and articles:* up to $0.25 per word (1,000 words maximum). *Poems:* up to $3 per line. Payment on publication. For stories and poems previously published, *Spider* purchases second North American publication rights. Fees vary, but are generally less than fees for first serial rights. Payment is made on publication. Same applies to accompanying art.

Terms for illustrators: A flat fee is usually negotiated. First publication rights plus promotional rights (promotions, advertising, or in any other form not offered for sale to the general public without payment of an additional fee) for commissioned artwork are subject to these terms: Physical art remains the property of the illustrator. Payment is made within 45 days of acceptance. *Spider* retains the additional, nonexclusive right to reprint the work in any volume or anthology published by *Spider* subject to pro-rata share of 7 percent royalty of net sales.

Submission guidelines: Guidelines are available online or via mail with an SASE. *Please submit all manuscripts to* submissions editor.

Tips and comments: Spend time reviewing *Spider*—review back issues of the magazine before you make any submissions. For art samples, it is especially helpful to see pieces showing children, animals, action scenes, and several scenes from a narrative showing a character in different situations. *Spider* would like to reach as many children's authors and artists as possible for original contributions, but its standards are very high, and the magazine will accept only top-quality material.

Meet Wendy Wax

Author

Wendy Wax is the author of *Inside the Aquarium* (Contemporary Books, 1989), *Ten Things I Know about Kangaroos* (Contemporary Books, 1989), *Say No and Know Why* (Walker Publishing, 1991), *Do You See What I See?* (HarperCollins, 1998), and *Empire Dreams* (Silver Moon Press, 2000). She was born in Detroit on October 9, 1963, and has a B.F.A. from the University of Michigan. Before she became a children's book author, she was managing editor for a children's book packager, production associate for a design studio specializing in magazines, and creative associate for a medical ad agency. She writes for preschool through sixth grade. She also works as a collage artist, creating collage illustrations for magazine articles, advertisements, and children's textbooks.

How did you get your first book published?

I got my first children's book published when I was managing editor at the Kipling Press. My job was to create book lists, and so I did—then I wrote one of the books myself. It was called *Where Does Bubble Come From?* and was part of a series under a pseudonym. Since it was my first children's book, I didn't realize how simple the text needed to be. At first I wrote something long enough to be a dissertation! Then I narrowed it down. Since then I find it easy to write for younger levels. Our books were mostly published by Contemporary Books in Chicago, so they approved my list and then the manuscript. It was pretty easy, and I felt very lucky.

Did you have an agent when you published your first book?

No, and I still don't.

Do you have any advice, in terms of finding an editor, for a writer starting out?

Just go for it. Editors all have such different opinions, so I'd show it to as many as possible—even if two are at the same publishing company. And when you get responses, take the suggestions, criticisms, and so forth, seriously! You don't have to believe it, but pay attention. It may be helpful. Also, if you want to get a children's book published, read as many children's books as possible—especially the ones on display at the bookstores. Not that yours should be like others, but just to see what's being bought. Also, if it's for children, humor is always good no matter what the subject.

Are you still with your first publisher?

No. Just because I've met so many others since then.

Do you have any advice, in terms of finding a publisher, for a writer starting out?

Look at books that are similar to yours (in subject matter or style) in the bookstore, and go to those publishers. By the same token though, you might want to try other publishers too—they might want a book like yours because they don't have one yet.

Are your books illustrated?

Yes, all of my books are illustrated, and I've worked with many different artists. Most often, it's the publisher who chooses the illustrator, so depending on the editor, the publishing house and any number of other factors, each of an author's books may be illustrated by a different artist.

Do you have any advice, in terms of finding an illustrator, for a writer starting out?

As the author, you don't really need to worry about finding an illustrator (nor, in most cases, will you even have a say). The publisher will probably know what he or she wants. But, if you want to do some research, for your own piece of mind, look at illustrator source books. I take out a page every year in the Directory of Illustration, and they have lots of good illustrators. Look at other children's books for illustration ideas or at least style ideas. Usually there are illustration style trends going on.

What procedures do you follow when you write?

No schedule. I just get excited over ideas and can't wait to write them down. I keep a notebook with me for jotting down and then elaborate when I get to the computer.

Where do you get your ideas?

Everywhere—dreams, conversations, things I see, things I hear, subjects I'm interested in.

What do you think are the key differences between writing for children and writing for adults?

Less text for children, and the humor is sillier.

How did you learn to write? Did you pursue any formal training, or was it just a question of practice, or something else?

I've kept journals all my life and have just always enjoyed writing. Mostly stream of consciousness—which definitely helps me write for a child's level.

Anything you really wish somebody had told you when you started out?

Be sure about what age your target audience is. Give specifics when you submit your manuscript to a publisher (i.e., 24 or 32 pages for picture books is usually the standard). The publisher will ultimately decide how long the book should be, but the more specifics you have down, the easier it will be for the editor to see what you see.

Sports Illustrated for Kids

Time & Life Building
Rockefeller Center
New York, NY 10020
Web site: www.sikids.com

Description: Sports magazine aimed at children 8 to 13, from *Sports Illustrated.*

Key people:

Managing editor: Neil Cohen

Seeks: Nonfiction of 100 to 1,500 words, especially for 16-page bimonthly section, "Girls and Sports Extra."

Terms for writers: Pays $75 to $1,000 on acceptance for all rights.

Story Friends

616 Walnut Avenue
Scottdale, PA 15683-1999
(724) 887-8500
(724) 887-3111 (fax)
E-mail: info@mph.org
E-mail: rstutz@mph.org
Web: www.mph.org/cp

Corporate structure/parent: *Story Friends* is a subsidiary of Faith & Life Resources Division (which is a division of Mennonite Publishing House, Inc.).

Description: *Story Friends* is a monthly magazine for children ages 4 to 9 that reinforces Christian values.

Key people:

Editor: Rose Mary Stutzman

Acquisitions/submissions editor: Rose Mary Stutzman

Seeks: *Story Friends* needs stories (300–800 words), poems (6–20 lines), and activities that speak to the needs of all children.

Accepts unsolicited/unagented: Yes.

Preferred articles: Stories should do the following: Provide positive ways to express love and caring. Introduce readers to children from many cultures. Reinforce the values taught by the church family. Focus on God's creation and how to care for it. Acquaint children with a wide age range of friends. Portray Jesus as a friend who cares about their happy and sad experiences. Mirror the joys, fears, temptations, and success of the readers in the story characters. Emphasize that each one is unique and important.

Preferred form of submission/contact: Manuscript.

Submission guidelines: Write with an SASE or send an e-mail to request guidelines.

Tips and comments: *Story Friends* has a young audience, and it is important to write to children's level but not talk down to them. Familiarize yourself with *Story Friends* publication before making any submissions.

SuperOnda

425 Pine Avenue
Santa Barbara, CA 93117
Web site: www.superonda.com

Description: Quarterly for Hispanic students 18 to 24.

Key people:

Deputy managing editor: Jim Medina

Seeks: Looking for writers with expertise on the Internet and advice for college students.

Preferred form of submission/contact: Query by mail or e-mail to jmedina@hbinc.com

Terms for writers: Pay and rights vary.

TEEN LIFE

No longer being published.

TEEN VOGUE

4 Times Square
New York NY 10036

Description: New girls' edition of *Vogue* magazine.

Key people:

Editor: Amy Astley

Seeks: Beauty and fashion articles for brand-savvy teens 12 to 16.

Submission guidelines: SASE or e-mail to: aastley@vogue.com

TODAY'S CHRISTIAN TEEN

PO Box 100
Morgantown, PA 19543
(610) 913-0796
(610) 913-0797 (fax)
E-mail: tcpubs@mkpt.com

Corporate structure/parent: Marketing Partners, Inc.

Established: 1990.

Key people:

Editor in chief: Jerry Thacker

Acquisitions/submissions editor: Elaine Williams

Articles per year and description: 15 to 18 articles focusing on practical issues teens face from a conservative, biblical perspective (e.g., prayer, worship, friends, family, using what God has given them, and time and money management).

Percentage by first-time authors: Approximately 5 to 10 percent.

Seeks: Practical advice for Christian teens—helping them in their everyday life.

Accepts unsolicited/unagented: Willing to review any submissions.

Recent articles:

"A Cry for Help" by Gail Gaymer Martin (Many consider suicide a cry for help. But, if the cry is not heard, if the signs are not noticed, tragedy occurs. Recognizing the signs and responding in appropriate ways can make all the difference. It can save a life.)

"Comfort Zone" by Rebecca Lyles (All around us are people we don't see. Lost, homeless, needy people who are easy to overlook. Sometimes, even when we notice them, we miss the opportunity to extend the love of Christ. It's time to reach out beyond our comfort zones.)

"Getting Along with Them" by Alan Cliburn (There is a secret to surviving through those struggles with parents. The secret is found in the strength Christ gives us to obey and to restrain ourselves when angry. Even you can get along with your parents!)

Preferred articles: Interesting, practical articles for teens. Not looking for fiction.

Preferred form of submission/contact: May send a manuscript via e-mail or regular mail.

Time to reply: *Today's Christian Teen* reviews articles in January/February for the next school year, so it depends when an author makes a submission.

Time to publish: Usually about a year.

Accepts simultaneous submissions: Yes, but tries not to publish the same article at the same time another magazine may be publishing.

Number of illustrators used annually: None.

Terms for writers: $150 per article of 800 to 1,000 words (less for shorter articles).

Submission guidelines: Send #10 SASE for guidelines. Send 9 by 12-inch SASE with $0.99 postage for sample of magazine.

Tips and comments: Keep it interesting and practical.

TOGETHER TIME

6401 The Paseo
Kansas City, MO 64131

Description: *Together Time* is a full-color weekly story paper for 3- and 4-year-olds that correlates directly with the WordAction Sunday School curriculum. It is designed to connect Sunday school learning with the daily living experiences and growth of the child. We depend on freelance contributors for our supply of poems and activities.

Key people:

Editor: Melissa Hammer

Assistant editor: Kathleen M. Johnson

Seeks: *Poems:* Write on a 3- and 4-year-old level of understanding. Prefer rhythmic, pattern poems, but will accept free verse if thought and "read aloud" effect flow smoothly. Include word pictures of subject matter relating to everyday experiences. Submit four to eight lines. *Crafts and activities:* Write on a 3- and 4-year-old level of understanding. They should be simple and within the child's ability when aided by the parent. *Finger plays:* Write on a 3- and 4-year-old level of understanding. Show character building or scriptural application. Submit contemporary, true-to-life portrayals of 3- to 4-year-old children. Avoid portrayals of extremely precocious, abnormally mature children. Themes and outcomes should conform to the theology and practices of most Bible-believing Evangelical churches.

Accepts unsolicited/unagented: Yes.

Preferred articles: Avoid extensive cultural and holiday references. *Together Time* has an international audience.

Time to reply: Please allow eight to 10 weeks or more for a response to your submission.

Desired illustrator qualifications: All artwork is assigned on a work-for-hire basis. *Together Time* publishes a wide variety of artistic styles that appeals to and adequately represents 3- and 4-year-olds.

Prefer manuscript/illustration packages, or separate: Either is fine.

Include with illustrator query: *Together Time* welcomes portfolio submissions for future assignment consideration.

Time to reply: Please allow eight to 10 weeks or more for a response to your submission.

Terms for writers: For poems, $0.25 cents per line ($2 minimum) for all rights; crafts and activities, $15; finger plays: *Together Time* pays $0.25 cents per line. *Together Time* reserves the right to reprint these manuscripts in *Together Time* with no additional compensation. Authors may sell reprint rights to other publications with audiences that do not overlap *Together Time*. Contributors receive complimentary contributor copies of *Together Time* on publication. *Together Time* reserves the right to edit purchased manuscripts to fit current editorial needs.

Terms for illustrators: Payment is $40 for black-and-white line art and $75 for full-color art.

Submission guidelines: Write with an SASE for guidelines.

Tips and comments: Include an SASE with each submission. Rejected manuscript and editorial comments will be returned. Manuscripts are accepted several months prior to publication. *Together Time* will inform you of the projected publication date and date of issue.

TOUCH

PO Box 7259
Grand Rapids, MI 49510
(616) 241-5558 (fax)

Key people:

Editor: Sara Lynne Hilton

Seeks: Columns that appear on a regular basis: "Praline and Cousin Clyde's Funny Tales." Readers send in jokes to our jokester cats. Still looking for a variety of puzzles and activities. Word searches have been overdone, so try a new format for your puzzles. "Quizzes:" Looking for interesting and unique quizzes or interactive articles to which the girls can respond. Topics should be of interest to girls, ages 9 to 14. "How-to articles:" Occasionally will publish a short how-to column to give girls tips on doing things they would like to do or a better way of doing what they do. This could include tips on baby-sitting, studying, sports, exercise, games, getting along with people, hang gliding, in-line skating, horseback riding, waterskiing, taking photos, etiquette, safety, baking, hiking, money, makeup, giving a party, and so forth. Prayerfully consider the ideas. Manuscripts should be between 500 and 900 words. Please indicate for which month you would like your manuscript considered.

Accepts unsolicited/unagented: Yes.

Preferred articles: Likes to see articles that relate to girls who are between the ages of 9 and 14. Topics of the manuscripts should build girls up in Christian character, but they should not be preachy. Prefers realistic stories and not always happy-ever-after endings. Readers appreciate a sense of humor, so your manuscripts should be fun to read as well as educational and inspirational. Readers can be stretched, so feel free to challenge them as well. Standing columns for which freelance material is not needed are the following: "God-sightings:" a column provided by our readers to tell about times in their lives or in someone else's when they knew they saw God being God; "Dear Faith:" Faith is the girl with all the answers and replies to the letters written by our readers; "Stories about Real Heroes:" *Touch* features a real person and tells his or her life story; "Discovery Bible Lessons:" three Bible lessons are based on the annual theme, and these are used in GEMS Girls' Club Bible studies and encouraged to be used as personal devotions by those who do not attend GEMS.

Preferred form of submission/contact: Manuscript.

Time to reply: You can expect to hear within four weeks if your manuscript has been rejected. The magazine holds stories that have potential until there are a variety to consider for an issue. The editors read final copy by April 1. If the editors plan to hold your manuscript, they will notify you via a postcard, and you can expect a final decision by April. If you prefer not to tie up your manuscript for this waiting period, please let the magazine know and your manuscript will be returned.

Submission guidelines: Write for guidelines and a list of upcoming themes. If you would like a copy of *Touch* (please familiarize yourself with the publication before submitting), please send an 8 1/2 by 11-inch SASE and include $1 for postage and handling.

Tips and comments: *Touch* fills up quickly so get your manuscripts in early. Each year, along with badge work, activities, and service projects, the magazine focuses a Bible study around a theme. Each issue of *Touch* has its own unique theme. You are encouraged to keep the annual theme in the back of your mind as you write, even though you do not need to make this the theme of your articles. Choose topics from the theme list or pick one of your own. Feel free to contribute to any of the columns as well. Stories and articles are to be short and to the point. If you are a writer familiar with *Touch*, you may or may not recognize the name GEMS Girls' Clubs. You may remember the ministry as Calvinettes. The name has been changed to GEMS Girls' Clubs to be a more viable name with which the girls can identify. GEMS stands for Girls Everywhere Meeting the Savior. The ministry, however, remains the same.

TURTLE

PO Box 567
Indianapolis, IN 46206-0567
(317) 636-8881
Web site: www.cbhi.org

Corporate structure/parent: Children's Better Health Institute.

Description: Magazine for preschool kids.

Seeks: *Turtle* has a constant need for high-quality stories, articles, and activities with health-related themes. "Health" is a broad topic that includes exercise, nutrition, safety, hygiene, and drug education. *Turtle* is especially interested in material concerning sports and fitness, including profiles of famous amateur and professional athletes; "average" athletes (especially children) who have overcome obstacles to excel in their areas; and new or unusual sports, particularly those in which children can participate. Although *Tur-*

tle's emphasis is on health, the magazine certainly uses material with more general themes. *Turtle* would especially like to see more holiday stories, articles, and activities. Please send seasonal material at least eight months in advance.

Accepts unsolicited/unagented: Yes.

Preferred articles: Health information can be presented in a variety of formats: fiction, nonfiction, poems, and puzzles. Fiction stories with a health message need not have health as the primary subject, but they should include it in some way in the course of events. Characters in fiction should adhere to good health practices, unless failure to do so is necessary to a story's plot. Because *Turtle Magazine* is designed to be read to children who are not yet reading independently, the editors look for submissions with a good "read-aloud" quality. In all material submitted, please avoid reference to eating sugary foods, such as candy, cakes, cookies, and soft drinks.

Preferred form of submission/contact: Completed manuscript only.

Time to reply: About three months are required to review manuscripts properly. Please wait three months before sending status inquiries.

Accepts simultaneous submissions: Simultaneous submissions are discouraged.

Desired illustrator qualifications: Please do not send drawings or other artwork. Turtle *prefers to work with professional illustrators of its own choosing.*

Prefer manuscript/illustration packages, or separate: Manuscript only.

Purchases freelance photography: Yes.

Preferred photography: No single photographs. *Turtle* purchases short photo features (up to six or eight pictures or photos that accompany articles and help illustrate editorial material). Please include captions and model releases.

Terms for writers: Up to $0.22 a word (fiction/nonfiction—up to 500 words); poetry, $15 minimum; photos, $15 minimum; puzzles and games, no fixed rates. Send an SASE to receive separate guidelines for activities. Payment is made on publication. Each author receives 10 complimentary copies of the issue in which his or her material is published. *Turtle* purchases all rights to manuscripts.

Terms for illustrators: *Turtle* buys one-time rights to photos.

Submission guidelines: Write with an SASE for guidelines. Manuscripts must be typewritten and double- or triple-spaced. The author's name, address, telephone number, date of submission, and the approximate word count of the material should appear on the first page of the manuscript. Title pages are not necessary. Keep a copy of your work. *Turtle* will handle your manuscript with care, but cannot assume responsibility for its return. Please send the entire manuscript. All work is on speculation only; queries are not accepted, nor are stories assigned. The editors cannot criticize, offer suggestions, or enter into correspondence with an author concerning manuscripts that are not accepted nor can they suggest other markets for material that is not published. Material cannot be returned unless it is accompanied by a self-addressed stamped envelope and sufficient return postage.

Tips and comments: *Turtle Magazine* is for preschool children ages 2 to 5; please bear that in mind as you write your story. Because *Turtle Magazine* is designed to be read to children who are not yet reading independently, the editors look for submissions with a good "read-aloud" quality. Remember that characters in realistic stories should be up-to-date. Many of *Turtle*'s readers have working mothers and/or come from single-parent homes. *Turtle* needs more stories that reflect these changing times but at the same time communicate good, wholesome values. Reading *Turtle*'s editorial guidelines is not enough! Careful study of current issues will acquaint writers with each title's "personality," various departments, and regular features, nearly all of which are open to freelancers. Sample copies are $1.25 each (U.S. currency) from the Children's Better Health Institute, PO Box 567, Indianapolis, IN 46206.

TWIST

270 Sylvan Avenue
Edgewood Cliffs, NJ 07632

Corporate structure/parent: Bauer Publishing.

Description: *Twist*, a new teen magazine published by Bauer Publishing, captures the energy, attitude, and interests of young women. The magazine stresses reality over fantasy, and serves as a forum for the concerns and passions of its 14- to 19-year-old readers.

Seeks: All features should include the voices and input of real teenagers wherever possible, either in an as-told-to format or through direct quotation. Real-life stories will deal with school, friends, romance, and a broad selection of relevant current issues. Other articles will also cover beauty, college and careers, entertainment, health and fitness, self-improvement, and other related subjects. Teenage writers are encouraged to submit work.

Accepts unsolicited/unagented: Query letters are preferred to manuscript submissions.

Preferred articles: Submissions should capture the energy, attitude, and interests of young women. Articles stress reality over fantasy—*Twist* serves as a forum for the concerns and passions of its 14- to 19-year-old readers.

Preferred form of submission/contact: Query letters are preferred to manuscript submissions. If possible, queries should include a selection of clips of previously published work. Unpublished writers may be asked to submit articles on speculation.

Submission guidelines: Write for guidelines with an SASE. Inquiries and submissions may be sent to the prior address; do not phone or fax. Please include a self-addressed envelope for reply.

Tips and comments: To write for *Twist*, the best way to break in is to study the magazine—available on newsstands nationwide. Do not phone or fax. Please include a self-addressed envelope for reply.

U.S. KIDS

PO Box 567
Indianapolis, IN 46206-0567
(317) 636-8881
Web site: www.cbhi.org

Corporate structure/parent: Children's Better Health Institute.

Description: *U.S. Kids* features a variety of reading and interactive opportunities for children ages 5 to 10. The magazine is designed to help children understand the world around them, to excite interest in learning, to develop imagination and creativity, and to develop reading and thinking skills as well as good health habits.

Seeks: Real Kids: focusing on kids doing something a bit out of the ordinary that other kids would like to read about. This category is also for kids who have done something heroic or exemplary—true-life adventure (e.g., hobbies, music, science and math, art and entertainment, kids in sports, etc.). Real World: featuring articles that explore the wonders of the world (e.g., animals, nature, space, technology, other cultures, communications, safety, careers, hobbies, current affairs, etc.). How It Works: seeking articles that explain how things work, from the familiar to the unusual; past examples include how popcorn pops, how a blimp floats, and how a piano makes music. Fit Kids: exploring health and fitness through articles on exercise, nutrition, sports, latest medical information, and so forth. Poster Pages: featuring a poster of a different animal each issue. *This is done in-house or assigned to a specific writer or artist.* Activities: including "Adventures of the Puzzle Squad" and the game on the back page, which are assigned or done in-house. Puzzles, games, and crafts are always welcome. Activities may stand alone or be story related. All interactives should reinforce in a fun way skills that children learn in school. Byline is given for activity. *Word length:* rebus, 200 words; poem, maximum 32 lines; nonfiction, 500 words; short story, 400 to 600 words.

Accepts unsolicited/unagented: Yes, but only send complete manuscript for fiction or poetry. For nonfiction, send query or complete manuscript.

Preferred articles: Material submitted will be judged on the author's ability to appeal to and write for children. Any subject of interest to children will be considered. However, *U.S. Kids* does have a need for high-quality stories, articles, and activities with health-related themes. For fiction *U.S. Kids* is interested in compelling stories with good plots and well-developed characters.

Preferred form of submission/contact: Send a complete manuscript for fiction or poetry. For nonfiction, send query or complete manuscript.

Time to reply: Please allow eight to 10 weeks for consideration of the manuscript.

Accepts simultaneous submissions: Simultaneous submissions are discouraged.

Number of illustrators used annually: Please do not send drawings or other artwork. *U.S. Kids* prefers to work with professional artists of its own choosing.

Prefer manuscript/illustration packages, or separate: *U.S. Kids* accepts manuscripts with accompanying photographs but not drawings or artwork.

Purchases freelance photography: Yes.

Preferred photography: All photographs accompanying manuscripts must be full color. If possible, please include photo sources. Photos should include children as often as possible and be clear and reproducible. Include captions and model releases. *U.S. Kids* prefers slides or transparencies. Manuscripts submitted without photos should include suggestions for photos or illustrations.

Terms for writers: Fiction/nonfiction, up to \$0.20/word; poetry, minimum \$15; activities, payment varies; photographs, fees negotiated separately. Payment is made on publication. Each author is sent two complimentary copies of the issue in which his or her material is published. Additional copies may be purchased. *U.S. Kids* purchases all rights to manuscripts.

Terms for illustrators: *U.S. Kids* buys one-time rights to photos.

Submission guidelines: Manuscripts should be typewritten and double-spaced. The following should appear on the first page of all material: author's name, address, telephone number, Social Security number, and an approximate word count of the material. Sample copies are available for $2.50 (U.S. currency). Make check payable to CBHI and send to *U.S. Kids*.

URBAN MINISTRIES, INC.

1551 Regency Court
Calumet City, IL 60409
(708) 868-7100

Description: Publisher of multiple magazines: *Preschool Playhouse*, *Primary Street*, *Juniorway*, *J.A.M.*, and *Inteen*.

Established: 1970.

Key people:

Editor in chief: A. Ogbonnaya, Ph.D.

Acquisitions/submissions editors:

Preschool Playhouse editor: Katherine Steward
Primary Street editor: Judy Hull
Juniorway editor: Delores Bell
J.A.M. editor: Connie Taylor
Inteen and young adult editor: Katara Washington

Articles per year and description: Each publication listed publishes 13 assigned Bible lessons for ages pre-K through 25 years old.

Percentage by first-time authors: 50 percent.

Seeks: Other than a few poems, short essays, or stories, assignments are made based on Bible Scriptures.

Prefer manuscript/illustration packages, or separate: Prefers to make assignments.

Include with illustrator query: Resume and samples.

Time to reply: One to three months.

Purchases freelance photography: Very rarely.

Terms for writers: Usually $150 per assignment.

Terms for illustrators: Varies, depending on the assignment.

Submission guidelines: Writers should make a written request with an SASE to the editorial department and illustrators should direct their requests to the vice president of creative services (with an SASE). Please do not send manuscripts; assignments are made based on resumes, writing, and art samples.

Tips and comments: Review the publications and send your resume and samples of your writing.

Weekly Reader

200 First Stamford Place
PO Box 120023
Stamford, CT 06912
(203) 705-3500
E-mail: galaxy@weeklyreader.com
Web site: www.weeklyreader.com

Description: Weekly Reader Corporation, a unit of WRC Media, Inc., is a publisher of materials for elementary and secondary schools, with over 90 percent of the school districts in the United States using its materials. The best known of Weekly Reader's publications is *My Weekly Reader*, a newspaper for children in the elementary grades. Weekly Reader also publishes *Career World; Current Events*; *Current Health 1; Current Health 2; Current Science; Human Sexuality Supplement*; *Know Your World Extra; My Weekly Reader, Edition 1; My Weekly Reader, Edition 2; My Weekly Reader, Edition K; My Weekly Reader, Pre-K Edition*; *Read Magazine*; *Teen Newsweek*; *Weekly Reader, Edition 3; Weekly Reader, Edition 4*; *Weekly Reader, Senior Edition*; and *Writing* (Middletown).

What! A Magazine

108-93 Lombard Avenue
Winnipeg, Manitoba R3B 3B1
Canada
(204) 985-8173
(204) 943-8991 (fax)
E-mail: what@fox.nstn.ca

Description: *What! A Magazine* is a national publication targeted to Canadian teenagers. The magazine is distributed six times a year, free of charge, to 1,000 high schools from coast to coast. The current circulation is 200,000. *What! A Magazine* endeavors to provide an editorial and design mix that is empowering, interactive, and entertaining.

Key people:

Editors: Leslie Malkin and Stu Slayen

Seeks: Freelance writers are invited to submit queries to the editor of *What! A Magazine*. No fiction or poetry submissions from professional writers will be accepted.

Accepts unsolicited/unagented: No. Query only, please.

Preferred articles: For more information, study the publication.

Preferred form of submission/contact: Query.

Terms for writers: *What! A Magazine* will only consider first rights.

Submission guidelines: Write for guidelines (with an SASE) or call for more information. A query or pitch to *What! A Magazine* should include the following: a working story title, a one-sentence explanation of the angle, a justification and proposed treatment, potential contacts, and proposed length. Freelance writers are encouraged to send published writing samples along with their query.

Tips and comments: Please include SASE with your query.

Wild Animal Baby

8925 Leesburg Pike
Vienna, VA 22184
(703) 790-4000
Web site: www.nwf.org/wildanimalbaby

Corporate structure/parent: National Wildlife Federation.

With

PO Box 347
Newton KS 67114
(316) 283-0454 (fax)
E-mail: deliag@gcmc.org

Corporate structure/parent: *With* is a subsidiary of Faith and Life Resources Division (which is a division of Mennonite Publishing House, Inc.).

Description: *With* seeks to empower youth to be radically committed to a personal relationship with Jesus Christ, to peace and justice, and to sharing God's good news through word and action. Frequency: six times a year. Audience: youth ages 12 to 18.

Established: 1968.

Key people:

Editor: Carol Duerksen

Acquisitions/submissions editor: Carol Duerksen

Articles per year and description: Teen audience; 30 articles per year each with one to three illustrations on Christian themes.

Percentage by first-time authors: 5 percent.

Seeks: True teen stories and illustrations to enhance those stories. *With* features a different theme in each issue, such as peer pressure, faith, sex and dating, prayer, service and mission, and relationships. *With* uses first-person and fiction pieces ranging from 800 to 1,800 words. *With* also needs how-to articles, poetry, and meditations. Stories are to be told from the perspective of a teenager so that they ring "authentic" even if written by an adult.

Accepts unsolicited/unagented: Yes.

Preferred articles: Looking for true teen stories. Stories are to be told from the perspective of a teenager so that they ring "authentic" even if written by an adult.

Preferred form of submission/contact: Manuscript.

Time to reply: One month.

Time to publish: Six to 12 months.

Accepts simultaneous submissions: Yes.

Number of illustrators used annually: Approximately six.

Desired illustrator qualifications: Appealing to teens.

Prefer manuscript/illustration packages, or separate: Packages are fine. Either way.

Include with illustrator query: Samples and resume.

Time to reply: One month.

Meet Rukhsana Kahn

Author

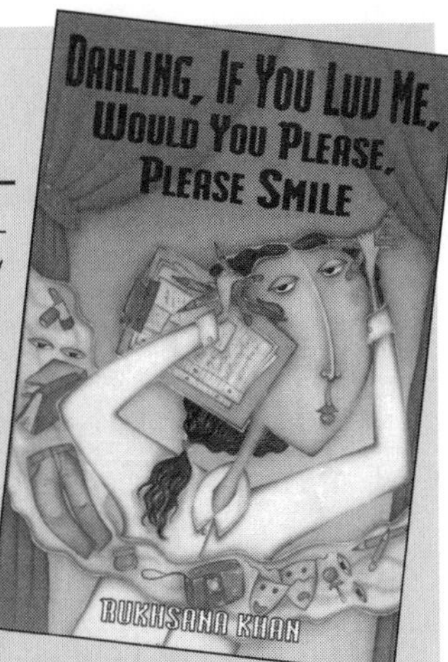

Rukhsana Kahn has written five books, including *Bedtime Ba-a-a-lk* (Stoddart Kids, 1998); *The Roses in My Carpets* (Holiday House/ Stoddart Kids, 1998); *Dahling, If You Luv Me, Would You Please, Please Smile* (young adult novel, Stoddart Kids, 1999); *Muslim Child* (short story collection, Albert Whitman/Napoleon Publishing, 1999); and the forthcoming *The Kite Thief* (to be published by Scholastic Canada, fall 2001). She was born in Lahore, Pakistan, on March 13, 1962. She trained as a biochemical technician and worked as a quality control technician in a pharmaceutical firm. She writes for a range of children, from picture books to young adult. She's a storyteller and has been to numerous storytelling festivals and enjoys telling stories, particularly from Middle Eastern cultures.

How did you get your first book published?

The first book that I sold never did go on to get published. In 1992 I went to Pakistan, my place of birth, and while visiting the lovely Shalimar gardens, built in circa 1642, I got a story idea. When I got back, I wrote T*he Shade of Shalimar,* and it was accepted in 1995 by a small Canadian publisher. But within six months my editor left and moved to another publisher. With her gone, my picture book was in limbo. The rights to it were eventually purchased by one of my current publishers, Stoddart Kids, but I didn't like the idea of them publishing it because my publisher at Stoddart had rejected Shalimar before. She'd liked it but thought it too esoteric for a picture book. So I tried to take it back to my former editor, the one at the new house, who'd liked it enough to buy it in the first place, but things didn't work out there. In the end, I'm glad it wasn't published. It was too esoteric for a picture book. And what I realized a long time after is that it wasn't a complete story. What I'd actually written was the climax of a novel. There was too much backstory that the reader wasn't in on. So I filed Shalimar away to be a future novel.

In the meantime I wrote another story that was set during that 1992 visit to Pakistan. During that visit, I took a side trip up to Peshawar Pakistan to visit my Afghani refugee foster child. At that time the war with Russia was still going on. Based on that meeting, I wrote *The Roses in My Carpets,* a serious story about the experiences of a refugee boy. In the same few months, I wrote a humorous little story called *Bedtime Ba-a-a-lk,* about a girl who tries to count sheep but the sheep rebel and give her a hard time. I also wrote a story about a crippled boy in Pakistan who's great at flying kites (that story also grew from my trip to Pakistan). In the summer of 1996, all three were accepted for publication. *Roses* and *Bedtime Ba-a-a-lk* were accepted by Stoddart Kids, and *Kite Thief* was accepted by Scholastic Canada.

I had no idea which would be my first book. Due to illustration challenges, *Bedtime Ba-a-a-alk* became my first book—the illustrator just happened to be quicker. It took a whole year for the publishers (Holiday House and Stoddart) to agree on an illustrator for *Roses.* At the time I thought

continues

that was a long time. An illustrator was chosen rather quickly for *Kite Thief,* but what with one thing and another, that didn't work out, and *Kite Thief* languished. It will finally be published this year, five years after it was originally accepted.

Do you have any advice, in terms of finding an agent, for a writer starting out?

I suggest you work on honing your craft before you attempt getting an agent. Too many beginning writers focus on the agent aspect, thinking that it's some kind of lottery, that if they just get an agent on board, somehow their genius will be noticed by the masses. It doesn't work that way. First and foremost, you need to polish your craft as a writer. This is a very competitive field. Yes, there are flukes, but for the most part, those who succeed do so through hard work and determination, and more perspiration than inspiration.

Are your books illustrated?

I have different illustrators for each of my books. I had no say in the matter. The publisher always chose the illustrators. That said, I'm pleased with the way the artists have rendered my stories.

Do you have any advice, in terms of finding an illustrator, for a writer starting out?

Don't bother. That's the publisher's realm of expertise. To second-guess them is not wise. One friend of mine said that once the story's out of her hands, she refuses to imagine what the artist will do with the story. She just lets herself be pleasantly surprised.

What procedures do you follow when you write?

I tend to write when it comes to me, though I do try to write whether I feel like it or not. Sometimes it just won't come. And I know it's useless that day. Other times, I might begin writing without feeling like it, but within moments, the scene takes hold and I'm transported into the story. Then I usually end up writing more than I expected to.

Where do you get your ideas?

From things that bug me. Some of the stories I've written are in response to things I didn't do that I wish I had done. For example, the climactic scene of my novel was the stimulus in writing it and was based on an incident when I, like the protagonist, was in eighth grade. When kids in the class were making fun of a girl who'd attempted suicide, I said nothing to stand up for her. The neat thing about writing is that you can go back and change that. In the novel, the main character has the guts I didn't have and stands up for the other girl. I even created a whole friendship between the maligned girl and the main character. You can set things right in stories. That's one thing I love about them.

What do you think are the key differences between writing for children and writing for adults?

I'd say the complexity of the language is the main difference. You need to show more and tell less with children. And you need to address issues that are of concern to children, not adults. But for the most part, I don't really change my approach. I actually write to please myself. If I can make myself laugh, or cry, or feel the way the story needs to go, I consider that I've done my job.

How did you learn to write?

I read a lot of how-to books because I needed to understand structure. But I learned to write mainly by reading. Reading voraciously. And then getting frustrated because I couldn't find books that conveyed some of the things I wrestled with. The things that I wanted to read about. So I thought perhaps I'd have to write them myself.

Anything you really wish somebody had told you when you started out?

The one piece of advice I wish I'd had was that perseverance counts for a lot more than talent in this business. But in the end, talent is what sets you apart, so don't neglect it.

Purchases freelance photography: Yes.

Preferred photography: Teens in natural settings, not posed and not glamour shots.

Terms for writers: $0.06 $0.10 cents per word.

Terms for illustrators: $50 to $60 per illustration.

Submission guidelines: Guidelines, themes, and sample copy available for SASE. (Send a $1.20 SASE for sample copy.)

Tips and comments: Send *With* something that stands out above the other things that cross the desk. Obtain the guidelines and sample copies of the magazine before making any submissions. Show *With* that teens will like your work.

Wild Outdoor World (W.O.W.)

PO Box 1329
Helena, MT 59624
(406) 449-1335
(406) 449-9197 (fax)
E-mail: wowgirl@uswest.net

Corporate structure/parent: *W.O.W.* is published by the Rocky Mountain Elk Foundation, an international nonprofit wildlife and habitat conservation organization.

Description: *Wild Outdoor World (W.O.W.)* was founded on the belief that too many children today lack connection to the natural world, a connection essential to the development of well-grounded adults who can make informed decisions about North America's natural resource treasures. *W.O.W.* goes to classrooms across the United States and Canada. The goal is to increase children's appreciation and respect for the wild world. With classroom use in mind, *W.O.W.* looks for realistic, unbiased, ecologically sound reading material. *W.O.W.* promotes ethical behavior in the outdoors and respect for wild animals and the land.

Established: Premiered in 1993 as *Falcon for Kids*, published by Falcon Press. Purchased by the Rocky Mountain Elk Foundation in 1996, which changed the name to *Wild Outdoor World (W.O.W.)*.

Key people:

Executive editor: Kay Morton Ellerhoff

Editorial director: Carolyn Zieg Cunningham (direct story submissions/proposals to editorial director)

Art director: Bryan Knaff

Production director: Theresa Morrow Rush

Percentage by first-time authors: Can't say. Buys stories it likes, whether first-time writer or experienced. Tends to get comfortable with certain writers and reuse them. Especially encourages submissions from those with science/wildlife/education background.

Seeks: "Making a Difference" material—school, home, or community projects in which kids are making a difference for wildlife/habitat.

Accepts unsolicited/unagented: Yes.

Recent articles:

"A Winter's Tale" by Alan Belford (A circle-of-life story; liked its message: Two cross-country skiers on a day's outing stumble across the thoroughly picked-over remains of a deer. With a little detective work, they discover the many different kinds of wild animals that have been feeding on the deer, depending on it for survival.)

"Lion Kings" by John Becker (A heartening story of how wildlife managers and other concerned citizens are making a difference to benefit a troubled species. Florida panthers are among the world's most endangered animals. The Florida Fish and Wildlife Conservation Commission is working to expand and protect habitat, build safe passages across highways, reintroduce panthers into appropriate areas. Article includes interviews with experts involved in the project—this approach works well for the magazine.)

Preferred articles: Features North American settings/animals almost exclusively. Scientific accuracy is a must. Big-picture conservation, wildlife management, career stories (wildlife biologist, fisheries expert, game warden, wildlife photographer, etc.) No pet stories or "soft, fuzzy" animal stories. Overloaded with bug stories.

Preferred form of submission/contact: Query preferred.

Time to reply: Three to four months (that will improve—the magazine has hired an administrative assistant!).

Time to publish: May hold articles for a couple of years, sometimes longer (alas). Editorial plans can shift unexpectedly depending on needs of state wildlife agency partners.

Accepts simultaneous submissions: Yes.

Number of illustrators used annually: Three to four.

Desired illustrator qualifications: Kid-friendly; accepts direction from art director; ability to meet tight deadlines.

Prefers manuscript/illustration packages, or separate: Review separately.

Include with illustrator query: All materials are helpful. Perhaps best to start with samples and brief introduction that includes publication credits.

Time to reply: Six months, but trying to improve this record.

Purchases freelance photography: Yes (however, mostly works with stock agencies).

Preferred photography: Clarity, good color saturation, and sensitivity to wild animals' well-being.

Terms for writers: Pay on acceptance $200 for average feature-length (800 words); $50 to $100 for short items (300 words or less).

Terms for illustrators: Varies; payment agreed on in advance.

Submission guidelines: Download from Web site (www.wildoutdoorworld.org), or write to request (include an SASE).

Tips and comments: *Writers:* Looking for solid, informative, accurate articles imaginatively presented, with a gentle conservation message that emphasizes the importance of habitat to the survival of wildlife. Avoid anthropomorphism. *Illustrators:* Looking for imaginative, hope-filled, light-hearted—yet essentially accurate—depictions of wildlife. Avoid anthropomorphism.

Wonder Time

6401 The Paseo
Kansas City, MO 64131
E-mail: dfillmore@nazarene.org or pcraft@nazarene.org

Key people:

Associate editor: Patty Craft

Word Aflame Publications

8855 Dunn Road
Hazlewood, MO 63042
E-mail: WAPeditor@aol.com
Web site: www.wap@upci.org

Description: Publisher of several Sunday school periodicals. Word Aflame Publications is the creator of Sunday school literature for all ages. Word Aflame produces literature for children as young as 2 years of age and continues through adult levels. Primary objective: Inspiration—to portray happy, victorious living through faith in Jesus Christ.

Established: 1969.

Key people:

Editor in chief: Richard M. Davis

Children's editor: Barbara Westberg

Acquisitions/submissions editor: Lisa Henson

Articles per year and description: Teen and youth levels; 110 to 120 of each level.

Percentage by first-time authors: 25 percent. Accepts freelance manuscripts for Teens on Target and Youth Challenge.

Seeks: Fiction or nonfiction manuscripts (less than 1,500 words in length) that are spiritually inspiring or biblically based. Also 400-word Devotions, puzzles, practical life items, short free verse, and so forth, for take-home papers.

Accepts unsolicited/unagented: Yes. Word Aflame *does not solicit freelance manuscripts for any levels except the teen, youth, and adult levels. Word Aflame* does accept freelance manuscripts for Teens on Target, Youth Challenge, and the adult-level paper The Vision.

Preferred articles: Write to and for young people, but do not belittle or write down to them. Especially, do not make the mistake of categorizing or of thinking "youth" is a particular state of immature existence. Choose subjects relevant to this age group. Most subjects are relevant if properly handled, and today's youth are interested in more than clothes, fashion, career, and dating.

Preferred form of submission/contact: For information and guidelines, go to the Web site; to submit manuscripts, mail to the address as specified.

Time to reply: Four to six weeks.

Time to publish: Teen and youth publications are currently in "recycle" until 2002. Nothing new will be published until that time, but manuscripts will be put on file for future use.

Accepts simultaneous submissions: Yes.

Number of illustrators used annually: Approximately five.

Desired illustrator qualifications: Those who can follow the guidelines.

Prefer manuscript/illustration packages, or separate: Illustrations are by assignment only.

Include with illustrator query: Samples and/or portfolio.

Time to reply: Will reply *only* if interested in the illustrator's work, and even then, it may be a while until an appropriate assignment becomes available.

Purchases freelance photography: No.

Terms for writers: Poetry, $8 to $12; manuscripts, $10 to $30; Devotions, $8 to $15.

Terms for illustrators: Varies based on the assignment.

Submission guidelines: By request—via either mail or e-mail.

Tips and comments: Because of its wide readership, *Word Aflame* stays *very* conservative in all of its literature—everything should have an inspiring message or biblical application. Please study carefully the nature and content of the publication for which you desire to write. (Free sample available on request. If you are corresponding via e-mail and would like printed samples, you must send an SASE and request samples.) Read widely . Before writing, make sure you have a good story item. Know where you are taking your reader. Write with a positive outlook. Use active verbs and modern language, but do not use slang. Select picturesque names for people, places, and things. Do not generalize—be specific! Write tight and to the point. Use anecdotes and illustrations. Show what you mean rather than telling it. Be consistent in style. Be sensitive and creative. Avoid preachiness. A good story must have conflict—deal with it in a realistic manner. Stories must be original—no copied work or copyright infringements! However, other publications may give you ideas. Be creative! If anything is desired "as is" from another source, be sure to indicate this to the editor so permission may be requested for usage. Use the King James Version when quoting Scriptures. Double-check all scriptural quotations and references. Use the Cambridge Bible as a guide for punctuation and capitalization of Scriptures. Do not abbreviate. (This includes scriptural references.) Send the original manuscript to Word Aflame Publications. Please make a copy to keep in your files. This is vital as manuscripts sometimes are lost in the mail.

WORLD (NATIONAL GEOGRAPHIC WORLD)

1145 17th Street, NW
Washington, D.C. 20036-4688
Web site: www.nationalgeographic.com/world/index.html

Corporate structure/parent: National Geographic Society.

Key people:

Executive editor: Julie Agnone

Seeks: *World* accepts writing samples (published clips from other publications). *World*'s articles are conceived by the staff and assigned accordingly.

Accepts unsolicited/unagented: No. Please see below.

Preferred form of submission/contact: Please submit a brief cover letter and clips from other publications.

Time to reply: *World* assigns stories based on experience and expertise. *World* keeps clips and makes assignments as they come up.

Tips and comments: *World*'s use of writers is different from that of many magazines. Most story ideas come from staff editors. *World* conceives photographs, plans layouts, and researches the article before a writing assignment is made. Writers are chosen based on their demonstrated ability to write for children. *World* also tries to match subjects with writers who have relevant experience. *World* hears from far more prospective contributors than it could possibly use. Most that get utilized are writers with clips from other national consumer magazines for children. If you wish to be considered for future assignments, please send a cover letter and published writing samples to the address specified earlier.

YES

3968 Long Gun Place
Victoria, British Columbia V8N 3A9
Canada
(250) 477-5543
(250) 477-5390
E-mail: info@yesmag.bc.ca
Web site: www.yesmag.bc.ca

Corporate structure/parent: Peter Piper Publishing, Inc.

Established: 1996.

Key people:

Managing editor: Shannon Hunt

Articles per year and description: Approximately 100 articles and 14 illustrations; categories include nature, science, technology, environment, math, and so on—all nonfiction targeted to *Yes*'s readership age group of 8 to 14 years old.

Percentage by first-time authors: 20 percent.

Seeks: Nonfiction articles in science, technology, math, engineering geared toward 8- to 14-year-olds.

Accepts unsolicited/unagented: Yes, but a query is recommended as the first step.

Recent articles:

"Tracking the Untrackable" by Megan Kopp (how wildlife researchers track chipmunks, fish and butterflies)

"Welcome to Nano Land" by Emily Chung (introduction to nanotechnology)

"Saving Seahorses" by Kathiann M. Kowalski (highlighting these unusual and threatened fish and Project Seahorse, the people who are trying to save them)

Preferred articles: *No* science fiction, puzzles, or crosswords. What *Yes* does look for is interesting and educational pieces that introduce young readers to the world of science.

Preferred form of submission/contact: Query via e-mail (Shannon@yesmag.bc.ca) or via mail (include an SASE).

Time to reply: Approximately three weeks.

Time to publish: From three to six months.

Accepts simultaneous submissions: Yes.

Number of illustrators used annually: Approximately five, but these are assignments *only.*

Desired illustrator qualifications: It is variable—depending on the article that *Yes* is trying to illustrate.

Prefer manuscript/illustration packages, or separate: *Yes* will accept them as a package, but the preference of the editors leans *very strongly* to receiving a *query first.*

Include with illustrator query: Because *Yes* keeps everything on file, the art department likes to receive samples—and *nothing* should be submitted that the artist wants returned (because *Yes* keeps them for deciding on future assignments).

Time to reply: Approximately three weeks for a query; for illustrations, they will be kept on file (i.e., if *Yes* is interested in contracting the artist for work, the staff will contact the artist. Could be a month could be a year or not at all).

Purchases freelance photography: Yes.

Preferred photography: It varies, but most often looking to publish nature shots.

Terms for writers: $0.15 per word (Canadian) for one-time print rights.

Terms for illustrators: Variable.

Submission guidelines: Visit the Web site (www.yesmag.bc.ca), or send an SASE via mail.

Tips and comments: Visit the Web site to read sample articles and obtain the writers' guidelines; consider buying a back issue of the magazine (available on the Web site); include a sample of your writing with your query. Send samples of your work to give *Yes* an idea of your style (but *only send material that doesn't have to be returned*), and *Yes* will contact you if the magazine is able to utilize your particular skills.

YM

685 Third Avenue
New York, NY 10017
(212) 499-2000
(212) 499-1698 (fax)
E-mail: annemarie@ym.com
Web site: www.ym.com

Description: *YM* (young and modern) is a national magazine for girls and young women ages 12 to 24.

Key people:

Editor: Annemarie Iverson

Executive editor: Ellen Seidman

Young Salvationist

PO Box 269
Alexandria, VA 22313-0269
(703) 684-5500
(703) 684-5539 (fax)
E-mail: uswarcry@aol.com and ys@usn.salvationarmy.org

Corporate structure/parent: The Salvation Army.

Description: *Young Salvationist* is published 10 times yearly by The Salvation Army in the United States. Its purpose is to help young Salvationists develop a mature Christian faith and personal ministry.

Seeks: Looking for writers who can present material relevant to contemporary Christian teens. *Young Salvationist* readers are high school/early college students who want articles and stories that speak to their life experiences. All articles must be presented with a Christian worldview. *Young Salvationist* always needs interviews/profiles of Christian athletes, musicians, and entertainers. Other ongoing needs are manuscripts dealing with the eternal themes of adolescence: music, school, family/parents, dating/love/sex, preparing for college, and so forth. *Young Salvationist* also needs short (350 to 600 words) evangelistic pieces aimed at teens.

Accepts unsolicited/unagented: Yes.

Preferred articles: *Young Salvationist* does not publish games or puzzles. Although *Young Salvationist* occasionally uses poetry, it is rare. Also rare are essays and how-to articles. Almost all the fiction in *Young Salvationist* is contemporary and realistic, so please save your science fiction, fantasy, and historical stories for another magazine.

Preferred form of submission/contact: Query or manuscript. You may want to query first if you're not sure an article is right for *Young Salvationist*. Manuscripts will only be returned if accompanied by an SASE.

Submission guidelines: Manuscripts should be typed, double-spaced, and should include word count. Photocopies are fine. *Young Salvationist* reserves the right to edit all manuscripts as necessary for publication. Manuscripts will only be returned if accompanied by an SASE. Address all submissions to the youth editor.

Tips and comments: You can improve your chances of being published in *Young Salvationist* by asking for a theme list and sample issue (include SASE). Write with a real 16-year-old student in mind. Contributors should keep in mind that the Salvation Army is Wesleyan in perspective. You may want to query first if you're not sure an article is right for *Young Salvationist*.

Your Big Backyard

8925 Leesburg Pike
Vienna, VA 22184
(703) 790-4000
Web site: www.nwf.org/ybby

Corporate structure/parent: National Wildlife Federation.

Youth Update

1615 Republic Street
Cincinnati, OH 45210-1298
(513) 241-5615

Corporate structure/parent: Street Anthony Messenger Press.

Description: Christian magazine for high school–age teens. *Youth Update* is a four-page monthly publication that aims to support the growth of teenagers in faith through the application of Catholic/Christian principles to topics of timely interest.

Seeks: *Youth Update* deals with Church structure, good habits, World Youth Day, Advent, apostleship, abortion, death and resurrection, self-esteem, Mary, domestic violence, and communicating with the opposite sex. The *Youth Update* format requires the author to answer questions from advisers gathered by the editor and representing a cross-section of readers. These questions will be in response to the edited manuscript and need to be answered quickly. Answers are published in the same issue as the manuscript and are no more than 150 words each.

Accepts unsolicited/unagented: Please query first.

Preferred articles: Since you are not the same age as the readership, steer clear of inferring that you are "with it" in any superficial sense. Second-person plural is preferred. In other words, not *I* or *they* but *you*. Articles should be filled with examples, anecdotes, and references to the real world. Avoid citations from printed sources. Don't preach. Use inclusive language.

Preferred form of submission/contact: Please send a query letter and/or an outline before submitting a finished article.

Terms for writers: *Youth Update* pays $0.14 a published word following receipt of answers to the teenager's questions and the completion of a contractual agreement. Please provide a short bio for inclusion in *Youth Update*.

Submission guidelines: Write with an SASE for guidelines. Try for 2,300 words—roughly seven double-spaced pages of elite type. Guide the reader by dividing the material with lively subheads. Draft an involving quiz, checklist, inventory or table that relates to your topic. Consult samples. When citing the Bible, please refer to the New American Bible as your translation. *Youth Update* can work with PC files from an IBM compatible system, and will accept either 5.25- or 3.5-inch diskettes. Please be sure that the file is output using ASCII format (or in some cases, DOS format—depending on the particular word-processing program). Label the diskette noting the word-processing program and the level of software used (e.g., WordStar 4.0, WordPerfect 5.1, etc.). Always include a printed copy as well. *But please query first*—these are submission guidelines only for approved submissions.

Tips and comments: *Youth Update* is for high school–age teens who vary both in their religious education and in their reading ability. Write for a 15-year-old with a C+ average. Avoid glib phrases and clichés. Aim toward a more casual, conversational sound rather than an academic or erudite approach.

ZILLIONS

101 Truman Avenue
Yonkers, NY 10703
(914) 378-2551
(914) 378-2985 (fax)
Web site: www.zillions.org

Description: *Consumer Reports* for kids.

Key people:

Articles editor: Karen McNulty

Art director: Rob Jenter

Note: Zillions is now exclusively an online publication.

PART THREE

Literary Agents and Artist Representatives

Literary Agents and Artist Representatives

About the Directory of Literary Agents and Artist Representatives

ELLEN R. SHAPIRO

The universe of quality children's literary agents and artist representatives is small, especially when you consider how many children's books, magazines, and publishers are out there. Worse, the field is full of charlatans, so-called agents who are actually nothing of the sort: They charge a fee to read your manuscript and then offer to help you rework it for yet another fee. Their profits are not tied to selling your work—they derive their incomes from exploiting vulnerable aspiring talent. This isn't true of every agent who charges a reading fee (some are perfectly ethical, good people), but I and many others, including the Association of Authors' Representatives (AAR), find this practice objectionable as a matter of principle, and I therefore do not list any such agents.

The listing of agents in this part is correspondingly short, as I've only listed the best. Most are members of AAR, the Society of Children's Book Writers and Illustrators (SCBWI), the Graphic Artists Guild (GAG), or the Society of Photographers and Artists Representatives (SPAR) or have been specifically vouched for by other reliable sources. All of the agents listed here are excellent, but some are more receptive to new clients or are in other ways distinguished from the group (this doesn't necessarily mean they're better agents, but in a book such as this one there's little point to giving extensive coverage to an agent who, for example, is very resistant to establishing any new relationships). I have given these "featured agents" (indicated by a ★) more detailed entries, including their (mostly uncensored) answers to some personal questions. In other cases, I've included just the basic information. Please, these featured agents have given of their time, and I'd hate to think that by highlighting their listings here they'd be subjected to inappropriate submissions, so take the time to read carefully and submit only in a particular agent's area of expertise (and submit only the best possible work).

I've organized these listings by the name of the individual agent, not by the name of the agency, because it is the agent who is most important (though an established agency may have some special resources). I've listed agents and art reps together and sometimes use the term *agent* to refer to both, because there is some crossover and blurring of boundaries. (Please also see "Getting a Rep," in Part I of this book, which contains a listing of dedicated art reps.)

Please take the listings here as only a starting point. Almost every agent I spoke to in the process of researching this book made similar comments, and the most significant and emphatic comment by far (tracking a similar comment made by most publishers), was "Do your research." The good children's agents and art reps are well known and receive hundreds or even thousands of unsolicited submissions a year. They read these submissions with no compensation (I have listed here only agents who do not charge a reading fee, because those who do are not in my opinion worth listing), and they ask in return that you not waste their time with inappropriate material. Take the time to learn the types of authors an agent represents, and the types of illustrators an art rep handles, and make certain you fall into a relevant category before querying or making a submission. Anything else is a waste of postage.

It follows from this eminently sensible comment that, in seeking and finding an agent or art rep, there is no substitute for knowledge. And as much as I'd love to tell you that you can read this book and gain that knowledge, it would be a disservice for me to do so. Every author/illustrator–agent/art rep combination is so unique that it's virtually impossible to generalize. So what should you do?

Perhaps the best (and in many cases the only) way to find the best representation for you is to get recommendations from other authors and illustrators. To do that, you first have to be in contact with other authors and illustrators. So, as in many fields of human endeavor, before you take the huge step of establishing what might be a lifelong and very personal relationship with a single person, you may find that you benefit from "playing the field." That is, in this context, you need to build a network. And one of the best ways to do that is to participate in writer's conferences, take classes, and get involved with writer's groups (both in person and online). Your best chance of getting representation is to have a referral from one of an agent's or art rep's current clients.

Take a look at the appendixes to this book for lists of the best resources in this regard. I also think you'll gain a lot of valuable insight by reading the roundtable discussion presented here, as well as the personal profiles throughout this part and the rest of the book.

Somewhat counterintuitively (though not really once you think about it), editors can also be great sources of agent referrals. Many editors will be reluctant to refer you to agents, however, if an editor indicates interest in your work and you're on friendly terms, take the opportunity to ask, "Who are some really good agents you've worked with who represent this kind of work?" Obviously, if you're on the cusp of a deal with a publisher, you're more likely to gain representation with an agent. And, though your first instinct might be to think, "Why would an editor send me to a good agent?" most good editors actually want to work with good agents. Good agents aren't adversaries of the publishing companies. Their loyalties run to their clients, but ultimately through their expertise they create win–win–win situations for all three parties, and smart editors know this and act accordingly.

If you've found an agent who has offered to represent you, please be sure to do just a little more research before you allow your enthusiasm to get the better of you. First, ask a lot of questions: How long has the agent been in business, what other clients in your specific genre has the agency represented, what will be the exact nature of every important aspect of the relationship (how will payments be accounted for; what will happen if the agent leaves the agency; what expectations do you have of one another), and how many books has the agent sold (and to whom, and under what terms and circumstances)? For an excellent, hard-hitting list of questions to ask any prospective agent, see the AAR Web site (www.publishersweekly.com/aar/).

Second, before you commit to a relationship, I strongly encourage you to visit the brutally honest Web site of Agent Research & Evaluation (www.agentresearch.com), where you can verify the legitimacy of any agent for free and order—for a well-worth-it fee—a detailed report on almost any serious agent. Agent Research & Evaluation also publishes an excellent newsletter: *Talking Agents* (see its Web site for subscription information).

Please feel free to send comments or corrections to ellen@writechild.com and visit www.writechild.com for updates and further information.

SECTION ONE

A Roundtable Discussion on Agents and Art Reps

HOSTED BY ELLEN R. SHAPIRO

The most common question asked by aspiring authors is "Do I need representation?"

My own thoughts on the matter: A great agent or art rep is a great thing, but anything less than a great one is not worth having. Mathematically, given the number of top representatives versus the number of authors and illustrators in the world, it will always be the case that the vast majority of authors and illustrators will never gain representation. So, while writers and illustrators starting out would no doubt be well served by a top agent or art rep, at the same time they shouldn't devote all their time to finding one. The most important thing is to focus on the quality of your work because no agent is going to make you a good writer, and no art rep is going to make you a good illustrator, and if you're really good at either and persistent as all get-out, you'll sell something. It's so much easier to get representation once you've sold a first book that you should seriously consider flying solo on your first project. Though you should never allow yourself to be exploited, your priority as an unpublished author or illustrator is to get published—not to find representation. If you can secure representation, that's even better, but don't let that effort divert you from your real mission.

Still, there is no one right answer to the representation question, so, to present the most useful and complete answers and to present opinions from a variety of perspectives, I contacted two successful authors (one with an agent and one without), a first-rate agent, and a highly regarded editor, and I asked them to participate in a roundtable discussion on agents and art reps. The roundtable participants were as follows:

Jennie Dunham—agent and founder of Dunham Literary, Inc.

Emily van Beek—assistant editor, Hyperion Books for Children

Julie A. Peters—agented author (10 books for children and young adults; Web site: JulieAnnePeters.com)

Janet Wong—unagented author (nine books—five poetry collections and four picture books)

I asked each of these folks, "Do you think it's worthwhile for a prospective children's book author or illustrator to try to obtain representation by an agent or artist's representative?" I asked for, and I think I received, brutal honesty. Here's what they said:

Julie A. Peters: Depends on your reasons for wanting an agent. There's a common misperception among writers that acquiring an agent translates to immediate sales. Unfortunately, agents perpetuate this myth. I'm always leery of agents who are out there "selling" themselves, supposedly building their clientele, when they know perfectly well they rarely sign up new writers. They give people false hope by preying on their frustration and vulnerability. And I bristle when agents imply that writers don't have the intellectual capacity to read and understand contracts. We slog through tax forms, don't we? I think aspiring authors still have a better chance of connecting with an editor who recognizes their potential than finding an agent willing to take on an unpublished writer.

Agents should be thought of in terms of long-term career management. They can protect you from becoming the victim of unethical business practices. They have insider information into the publishing houses. They're up on marketing trends and evolving contractual standards. But you know what? There are enough resources out there that you could do these things effectively—if you wanted to. When you decide it's worth paying someone else to handle your business affairs, you should seek representation.

As far as marketing, remember; agents represent numerous clients. They may not have the time or inclination to market your work as aggressively as you could—and should. I believe with all my heart that if your work is good enough, it will sell itself.

Jennie Dunham: As an agent, I have numerous clients. Some are authors, some are illustrators, and some are both. I deal with a wide variety of publishers, so I know the particularities of each one. Because I have this wide perspective and because I am removed from the creative process, I can advise my clients about a situation in a way that might be more difficult for them on their own. An unagented author might call a few friends and ask for opinions. But of course these opinions vary widely in part because each author or publisher is different, and rarely does an author deal with numerous publishers regularly. It's hard for an unagented author to know what to do. Also, negotiations inherently put author and editor on either side of the fence, and an agent can prevent the relationship from deteriorating. When tricky situations arise—and inevitably at some point in an author's career they do—having an agent can help resolve the problem.

What can an agent do for you? Let's start with advances. One client came to me unagented. On his next book, I got his publisher to increase his advance five times higher than his previous book with them. He was ecstatic! I could also negotiate reasonable terms for him that previously he hadn't even known to ask for. Another author-illustrator had been dealing with a large company, and her editor kept telling her that she couldn't budge on the terms she was offering, that she didn't need an agent, and that the author-illustrator should only be publishing with her. But the editor didn't want to publish books that this author-illustrator wrote, just ones that she illustrated for another author's work. So the author-illustrator came to me. Not only did I double her advances, but I found two new publishers who were thrilled to be publishing books that she both wrote and illustrated! We still do business with that other company (with much improved advances and terms), but nowhere near as often.

Now, with all this talk about big advances, I should also say that I think it's always good to have a reasonable advance that earns out. If it doesn't earn out, nobody wins. The author won't have the sales to justify another big advance, and the publisher has lost money on the project and won't necessarily want to contract another one. Sometimes I have to explain to an author that a publisher's offer is actually quite fair and that I recommend accepting it. This frequently happens when a picture book author writes a first young adult novel or vice versa.

Finally, all publishers, even the more home-style, low-key ones, are getting more and more grabby about rights associated with the book. There are some rights that can be lucrative for authors that an author shouldn't have to share with a publisher. And some licenses, if made by the publisher on behalf of the author, could change the author's public image—for example by endorsing products. An author should have control of his or her image. Electronic rights also are constantly changing, and an agent is much more likely than most individual authors to know about what various terms mean and what terms are reasonable in the contract.

Some editors complain that agents are sharks trying to squeeze every penny from publishers. Some agents are. But most good agents that I know care tremendously about their clients, work hard to protect them, and provide a valuable service that benefits the client. And every once in a while, an editor will admit that he or she is glad an agent was there to explain what is industry standard or to help resolve a problem.

Janet Wong: To *try* to obtain representation, no. If you meet an agent at a conference, and she takes an interest in your work, and you like her, and you're not comfortable with contracts and negotiations, and you're not a cheapskate, like me—then I'd say yes. Otherwise, I think your energy should be spent on writing or illustrating your books, taking classes, going to conferences and book signings, and meeting as many editors and published authors and illustrators as you can. An agent will open the door for you, certainly, but you can do it yourself, too.

Emily van Beek: I do feel literary or artistic representation is a valuable pursuit for the first-time author or illustrator. An agent acts as a liaison between the writer/artist and the publishing house. Typically, an agent has established relationships with individual editors at the various houses and has the inside scoop on what types of projects a given editor seeks to acquire, including insight as to sought-after formats, genres, and audiences. With a given manuscript or portfolio in mind, an agent can hone in on certain houses and more successfully pair an author or artist with a suitable editor. Agents also act as a preliminary editorial filter. They may assist with the refining of a manuscript or guide an artist prior to the submission stage, thereby improving both the work and the likelihood that it will be given serious consideration by an editor. Moreover, an agent tends to have a more complete understanding of the complexities of the publishing industry. Not only is an agent fluent in the language of publishing contracts and negotiations, but she understands the ever-evolving nature of this business. Basically, an agent has his or her clients' best interests at heart. An agent's role is not only to support clients but to work for each client in the pursuit of a successful career.

Each roundtable participant then had the opportunity to respond to the others. (Note: Janet Wong felt the others said it so well that she refrained from further comment.)

Peters: I agree with Janet that your energies are better spent focusing on your work, which will ultimately (agent or no) open doors for you.

What Jennie says reinforces my beliefs about the value of an agent. She knows the industry and how each publisher works. Her example demonstrates that an agent is most effective with a client who already has a track record or comes to her with a particular problem.

Again, all this talk about doubling and quadrupling advances misleads beginning writers and illustrators, in my opinion. We're not talking tens of thousands of dollars here, the way we might in the adult industry. If, like Jennie, an agent prefers to negotiate an advance that always earns out, then the writer is going to get her or his money either way—through the advance or in royalties. Maybe I'm misinformed (which isn't inconceivable), but what I've been told is that even if your advance doesn't earn out, the publisher still makes money on your book. It's rarely a no-win situation.

Subsidiary rights expertise is where agents earn their weight in gold doubloons, I think. Not only are the contractual terms confusing and constantly changing, it does require in-depth knowledge of the book business to realize the best deal for yourself. Reputable publishers have standard contracts that they feel are fair, though. They aren't out to cheat their writers and illustrators. Why would they? We keep them employed.

And finally, I do agree with Emily that an agent serves a vital role as liaison. An agent is a valuable business partner in a writing career. But aspiring authors need to know—if they haven't already discovered this—that acquiring an agent is as difficult as connecting with an editor. My feeling is that your time is better spent aggressively marketing your own work to publishers. Once you've been offered a contract, you can decide whether you need an agent to deal with all the complexities. With contract in hand, you'll be amazed how eager agents will be to represent you.

van Beek: I appreciate everyone's perspective on this subject. I feel seeking representation is a personal choice, and every prospective writer and illustrator needs to make the decision that best suits him or her. Of course, if an artist or author feels comfortable with contracts and negotiations, and feels knowledgeable enough of the publishing industry, then perhaps representation would not best meet their needs. It has been my experience, however, that agents have had their clients' best interests at heart, and representation has been mutually beneficial to both the clients and the editors. It should also be noted that some houses will not consider any unsolicited submissions. Should authors and illustrators wish to have their work reviewed by these houses, then representation is a must.

Dunham: I think all authors and artists have the "to be or not to be represented" debate in mind when starting out. Here are my opinions: Does an author need an agent to sell a first book? No. Would life be easier with an agent? Almost certainly. Would the author or artist get a better deal by using an agent? Yes. Is it worth the hassle of finding an agent? Yes, if you find the right match for your individual needs.

As Janet Wong says, it is just as hard if not harder to find an agent than it is to find an editor. While an editor considers the commitment of one project, an agent considers handling all of an author's work, which is a much bigger commitment. An author typically makes lots of submissions to find an agent, and it takes time, persistence, and patience. I encourage all writers and artists, new and established, to go to conferences, classes, and signings in order to meet as many authors, illustrators, editors, and agents as possible. It's always good to meet people, and a connection may pay off years later. That said, it is true that perfecting the art or manuscript must be the first priority.

Janet Wong also brings up the cheapskate issue. Okay, a percentage is money, and that means the individual author or artist receives less of the profit. But a service is provided, a service that is worth the percentage. Most authors aren't making a living at writing when they start out. Beginning advances are not large. But authors and artists with agents consistently get higher advances and improved royalty rates. They also end up with more control over various other rights associated with the book. And consider the rate. Fifteen percent for a literary agent is not so huge when you compare it to artists' representatives' 25 to 30 percent, merchandising agents' 50 percent, and fine art galleries' 50 to 60 percent. When you look at it this way, that 15 percent seems reasonable. Also, remember the Superman story. Reportedly, the two creators of Superman sold the idea, image, copyright, and all other rights to Superman for $130. The publisher took the characters and created new comics that made Superman into an American hero and a huge financial success. But the publisher didn't compensate the creators, who in turn spent their lives trying to gain recognition and recompense. That would've been worth a 15 percent commission to them.

I also agree with Julie Peters that each person must know his or her individual reasons for wanting an agent. Some writers are too busy creating, some prefer to have someone else handling business affairs, and some want to make sure they're getting the best deal. Still others want someone to negotiate contracts so they maintain strong relationships with their editors. A tough negotiation isn't what an author or editor should be thinking about throughout the editing process.

Julie Peters points out that representation does not mean an immediate sale, and this is true. But an agent is more likely than an author to know a wide base of editors and the likes and dislikes of each one. If an agent knows the right editor, the manuscript can be matched with an editor much faster than if an author submitted on his or her own. One client called me and said that she wanted to submit her middle-grade novel to a particular editor who was her friend's daughter. She was very excited about this connection. Because I knew the editor, however, I informed my client that this editor specialized in picture books and that a submission to another editor at that publisher would be a more likely match. An author may have an "in," but it is not necessarily the right "in" to make a sale.

Authors and illustrators certainly are smart enough to read contracts, to understand what they say, and to negotiate them. But do they know from past experience what a publisher would be willing to change in a contract? Do they have the leverage of an established agent? Do they have a marketing team to sell any rights retained such as foreign, movie, or merchandising rights? Authors can look up information if they're willing to take the time; however, most prefer to spend their free time doing anything but slogging through legalese. An analogy would be someone starting to invest in the stock market.

Anyone can invest in the stock market without an agent, but most new investors choose to have an agent do it for them because of their invaluable experience.

Julie Peters also says that agents have numerous clients and may not market rights as aggressively as an author would think. Some agents don't. An author always needs to have reasonable expectations and should ask an agent about those up front. The agent should give a realistic response. But think about this perspective: A publisher may have hundreds of authors and thousands of books when all those front list and back list books from years of publishing are added together, and the subsidiary rights department must handle them all. Each agent usually has far fewer clients to concentrate on.

As Emily van Beek notes, agents and editors are inundated with literally hundreds of unsolicited requests each week. In an editor's eyes, an agent's opinion is different from an author's opinion of his or her own work because the agent has an objective, professional perspective. An agent can say to an editor that his or her best business guess is that the manuscript being submitted will be just as successful as the previous books the agent has represented. Editors, who have less and less time, value that prescreening process that an agent does for them. They open a package and know they will be reading a high-quality manuscript hoping it's right for them.

An agent can help an author prepare the manuscript or art samples so that an editor or art director will buy it. Sometimes this preparation is only about the presentation, but sometimes it's suggestions that focus the project to be more salable while still keeping creative integrity. Editors often don't have the time to do that. True, agents are also busy. But an agent will give editorial suggestions up front knowing that he or she can submit the project to numerous publishers. The editor might decide it would be too time-consuming because he or she must bring the project to an editorial board that might say no. If the project doesn't need work, there is less risk of investing an editor's time just to have it voted down in the acquisition meeting. And if it's that much stronger a project, chances are it's going to come through the acquisition meeting with an offer approved.

If your work is good, it will sell. No agent can sell work that isn't good. But wouldn't you prefer to have an advocate who isn't toting the corporate line because his or her paycheck comes from a publisher's pocket? Wouldn't it be nice to know that you got the sweetest deal possible? Wouldn't you like to speed up your sale by having someone who knows exactly which editors would love to read your manuscript?

SECTION TWO

Directory of Literary Agents and Artist Reps

★ Indicates a "Featured Agent."

★ Tracey Adams

McIntosh & Otis, Inc.
353 Lexington Avenue
New York, NY 10016
(212) 687-7400

Bio: Born Stamford, Connecticut; education, Mount Holyoke College.

Avoids: Activity and craft books.

Preferred form of contact: Send a well-thought-out query letter with a self-addressed stamped envelope.

Commission structure: 15 percent.

Percentage of submissions accepted: A *very* limited few.

Robert Allred

Allred & Allred Literary Agents
7834 Alabama Avenue
Canoga Park, CA 91304

Description: Particularly focused on dealing with previously unpublished clients.

★ Carol Bancroft

Carol Bancroft & Friends
121 Dodging Town Road
Bethel, CT 06801
(203) 748-4823
E-mail: artists@carolbancroft.com
Web site: www.carolcancroft.com

Meet Carol Bancroft

Artist Representative

Carol Bancroft is the principal in Carol Bancroft & Friends (121 Dodgingtown Road, Bethel, CT 06801). She hails from Philadelphia, Pennsylvania, and attended Lasell College (A.A.) and Rhode Island School of Design (B.F.A.). Before founding Carol Bancroft & Friends, she was art director of Junior Books at McGraw-Hill. She handles the K–12 audience.

As an art rep, what telltale signs or characteristics are you looking for in prospective clients?

Good draftsmanship, imagination, and energy and ability to take a character through a story.

Do you have any advice for an illustrator starting out in the children's publishing field, in terms of how to get representation?

Exposure: Their images should be seen through advertising in major sourcebooks and by sending mailers.

What is the most important key to getting your attention? To piquing the interest of any art rep? To turning an inquiry into representation?

Good artwork. Period.

What in your opinion makes an illustrator easy to work with?

Great attitude; respect; constantly experimenting with new examples; sending new artwork regularly.

What are key no-no's (or common mistakes) of illustrators who are trying to impress you?

Refuse to advertise/promote their work with us; have a bad attitude; want to promote their work themselves; are not making deadlines; are too choosy about the work that they take; want to do my job; have difficulty in letting go of the business aspects; make constant calls/e-mails; make issues.

Is there anything else you'd like to say to aspiring illustrators? Any words of encouragement or warning?

Publishers are very eager to, and very open to, using new artists to the field because hopefully they will bring a new, fresh approach and a different point of view to the industry.

Bio: Art director for Junior Books at McGraw-Hill. Attended Rhode Island School of Design. Born Philadelphia, 1930.

Hobbies and personal interests: Painting; animals; children.

Specializes in: Artists who bring energy and passion—specifically in art for children of all ages.

Preferred form of contact: Send me an e-mail, visit my Web site, or send a letter with an SASE.

Commission structure: 25 percent for artists within a 100-mile radius of Carol Bancroft & Friends; 30 percent outside that radius.

Number of titles sold in a recent year: 10.

Percentage of submissions accepted: 25 to 30 percent.

How would you describe what it is you actually do for a living? We represent artists who specialize in art for children of all ages.

★ Michael Brodie

Artists International
17 Wheaton Road
New Preston, CT 06777
(860) 868-1011
(860) 868-6655 (fax)
E-mail: artsitnl@javanet.com
Web site: www.artistsintl.com

Bio: Agent for 29 years. Born October 1937, United Kingdom.

Hobbies and personal interests: Race cars, rugby, cycling, and automobiles.

Specializes in: Children's books.

Avoids: Comics and fashion.

Commission structure: 30 percent.

Breakdown of clients: Fiction, 90 percent; nonfiction, 10 percent.

Percentage of submissions accepted: 1 percent.

Avoids clients who: Are amateur—someone who submits manuscripts blindly without doing any research.

Favors clients who: Are essentially the opposite of the amateur—the writer who takes the time to submit appropriate, well-thought-out work.

What might you be doing if you weren't an agent? Racing cars!

Jane Jordan Browne

Multimedia Product Development, Inc.
410 S. Michigan Avenue, Suite 724
Chicago, IL 60605

Description: Medium-sized agency, established 1981, handling fiction and nonfiction of all types, including children's. Member of AAR.

PEMA BROWNE

Pema Browne Ltd.
HCR Box 104B, Pine Road
Neversink, NY 12765
(914) 985-2936
Web site: www.geocities.com/~pemabrowneltd

Description: Pema (rhymes with Emma) Browne Limited, established in 1966, is a literary agency that also represents illustrators. The agency continues to grow and be an innovator going into the 21st century.

Representative titles:
The Pirate's Siren Song (horror/suspense) by Linda Cargill (Cora Verlag)
Koi's Python by Miriam Moore and Penny Taylor (Hyperion)
I Like a Snack on an Iceberg illustrated by John Sandford (HarperCollins)

RUTH COHEN

Ruth Cohen, Inc. Literary Agency
PO Box 2244
La Jolla, CA 92038-2244

Description: Children's book agent; member of AAR.

★ SUSAN COHEN

Writers House LLC
21 W. 26th Street
New York, NY 10010
(212) 685-2400
(212) 685-1781 (fax)
E-mail: scohen@writershouse.com

Bio: 20 years at Writers House. B.A. from Princeton. Born June 27, 1958, New York City.

Specializes in: Picture books, novels, and innovative nonfiction. Also illustrators.

Avoids: Nonbooks (e.g., plays, textbooks, film scripts, merchandising); activity books, inspirational books, joke books, and so forth.

Preferred form of contact: Send a good query letter with sufficient information about your background, describing or enclosing sample books if you're published, and the manuscripts (for picture books) or sample chapters (for picture books) or proposals (nonfiction) you want me to consider.

Commission structure: 15 percent.

Number of titles sold in a recent year: 100.

Breakdown of clients: Two-thirds, fiction and picture books; one-third, nonfiction.

Percentage of submissions accepted: So small at this point it's hard to put a number on it.

Representative titles:

Danny Dromedary and *Ouija Boy* by John Halliday (both titles pending, YA novel and middle grade to McElderry Books)

Untitled YA science fiction trilogy by Jennifer Armstrong and Nancy Butcher (Avon/Harper)

YA Harlem Renaissance book by Laban Hill (Megan Tingley Books, Little Brown)

Three deals for picture book illustrations (of other authors' texts) by Debbie Tilley (Harcourt, Clarion, and Orchard Books).

Avoids clients who: Are too pushy, with expectations too high.

Favors clients who: Are talented, reasonable, organized, patient—and have a good sense of humor.

Common client mistakes: Sending only published books and nothing current. Sending a photo of yourself. Calling after we've had a submission for two days!

Became an agent because: Seemed like such an interesting mix of roles (editor, salesperson, therapist, paralegal, etc.).

What might you be doing if you weren't an agent? Studying . . . traveling. . . .

How would you describe what it is you actually do for a living? Act as an author's advocate.

How did you become an agent? I apprenticed for an agent and gradually took on clients of my own.

What do you think about editors? I respect editors for their talents and feel badly for them for being so overworked and for having to deal with so much bureaucracy.

★ Jennie Dunham

Dunham Literary, Inc.
156 Fifth Avenue, Suite 625
New York, NY 10016
(212) 929-0994
(212) 929-0904 (fax)
Web site: www.dunhamlit.com

Bio: See "Meet Jennie Dunham" on page 468.

Hobbies and personal interests: Book arts and paper making, movies, photography, Old English, language and linguistics, feminist/women's studies, travel, science, history, health, religion, and collection of rare children's books.

Specializes in: Novelty (pop-up, pull the tab, lift the flap, board book, etc.), picture books, easy readers, chapter books, middle grade, young adult.

Avoids: Rarely do we handle sci-fi/fantasy or poetry for kids. No activity books. No textbooks. Also, we don't represent plays or screenplays (but we do represent books into movies and plays).

Preferred form of contact: Write a letter describing the project and the author's qualifications for the project, and enclose the customary self-addressed stamped envelope for a response. If the project piques our interest, we will request it. Please do not send sample material unless requested. We have a great deal of information on our Web site about submissions and what we're interested in (www.dunhamlit.com). Illustrators should not send original art.

Commission structure: 15 percent for domestic contracts and for dramatic rights contracts; 20 percent for foreign contracts. When we receive money for a client, we recover expenses we incur that specifically relate to projects by the author. For example, we will recover the cost of foreign postage, messenger fees, and photocopying, among others.

Number of titles sold in a recent year: 15 children's (we represent books for adults as well as children, and this figure represents children's book sales only).

Breakdown of clients: Fiction, 75 percent; nonfiction/poetry, 25 percent.

Percentage of submissions accepted: We reject the vast majority of query letters sent to us, but we read each one and respond usually within a week. So many people query us regarding books on subjects we don't handle. Doing a little research before querying will substantially increase a writer's chance of finding a match with the right agent.

Representative titles:

The Wonderful Wizard of Oz (pop-up) by Robert Sabuda (Little Simon)
A Little Princess retold and illustrated by Barbara McClintock (HarperCollins)
Clever Beatrice illustrated by Heather Solomon (Atheneum)
Lincoln illustrated by David Johnson (Scholastic)
Gauchada by C. Drew Lamm (Knopf)

Avoids clients who: Say one thing and does another, who don't trust an agent's advice, who don't know or pay attention to the market, and who try to tell an agent how to handle his or her business.

Favors clients who: Are productive, dedicated, talented, successful, interesting, and pleasant. It's also good if the client wins awards and is a self-promoter. A client may be a match for one agent but not another because of style.

Common client mistakes: In this day of computers, it's a mistake to send a form query letter without a specific person's name in the salutation. Also, writers sometimes address agents with familiarity, despite never having had any contact. This type of address should really be reserved for people who do know them personally. The grammar, spelling, and punctuation should all be correct. It's really best to send the query letter in writing rather than to call first and ask to send it. That does not constitute a solicited manuscript. We are less interested in a series of a number of mediocre books than in one very well-written book. Do not fax a request.

How to improve your chances: Professionalism, good writing, good ideas, and the willingness to work with an agent to manage the writer's career makes us enthusiastic about a client. More people try to write bestsellers than good books, and if they concentrated on writing a good book, they'd be closer to having a bestseller. We look closely at a writer's previous experience, especially in magazines and books.

Became an agent because: As an agent I like helping authors to bring their books to the world. In this sense I like to think of myself as a midwife of creativity or someone who can make a writer's dream come true. I like the variety of book projects I handle as an agent. I receive great satisfaction in protecting authors by negotiating contracts for them. Ever since my first job as an agent, I knew that this is what I wanted for a career. I also collect books.

What might you be doing if you weren't an agent? Maybe I would be an anthropologist or a professor of English, folklore, or communications. If I won the lottery, I'd build my own personal library and buy and read all the books I could. I'd also travel to faraway places.

How would you describe what it is you actually do for a living? As an agency, we handle three areas for clients: submissions, negotiating contracts, and collecting and distributing money. Basically, it boils down to handling the business affairs for authors and illustrators. It's also important to say what an agency doesn't do. We aren't accountants (we don't prepare tax returns for clients). We aren't bankers (we don't give loans). We aren't parents (we don't nag clients about delivery dates).

How did you become an agent? By accident, of course. After college, I had an internship with a publisher. Once the internship ended, they referred me to a publishing job placement agency. I was hired on the spot of my first interview at an agency. I didn't say specifically I wanted to be placed with an agency, but I loved the work I was doing and kept doing it.

What do you think about editors? Editors are a vital part of the creative process. A good editor responds to the author or illustrator's work and helps direct it, enables the author to see a character in a new way or an artist to stretch his or her creative abilities. An editor is also an author or illustrator's advocate at a particular publishing house. But at the end of the week when an editor gets his or her paycheck, it's the publisher who pays them. An agent is paid by the client and is the client's primary anchor. Many authors and illustrators have more than one publisher, and the agent oversees the entire career with various editors and publishers.

What do you think about publishers? Publishers must think of an entire list of books, both the new ones and the back list ones. They see the big picture of their business while the editor pays attention to the details of an artistic work. Publishers are also in business to make money (with all due respect), and sometimes they can try to demand more of authors and illustrators than is necessary. That said, publishers do a good job of getting books in bookstores and selling them.

Comments: Observe proper etiquette when submitting. If it's an exclusive submission, say so. If it's a multiple submission, say so. If one agent or editor makes an offer, thank him or her and say you need time to think about it and to contact the others who have the work (this will not be a problem if you've already stated that you made a multiple submission). Then call up the others who have the material, explain the situation, ask for a reasonable amount of time for them to get back to you, and wait that amount of time. Once you have all of the offers in front of you (or information that various editors or agents aren't interested), then you can make your best, informed decision.

People often ask what I look for when I'm considering a submission. First, I'm looking for a good story. Am I turning pages without realizing that time is passing? Do I care about the characters? Do I want to keep going just to find out what will happen next? Then I look for voice. Is the story told in a compelling way? Do the language and style give me insight to the characters and their situations? Finally, when I put the story down at the end, do I feel exhilarated? Do I know more about life than I did before? Do I think I spent my time well by reading the story? Do I want to call up friends and tell them they have to read the book?

★ ETHAN ELLENBERG

Ethan Ellenberg Literary Agency
548 Broadway, #5E
New York, NY 10012

Bio: Prior to 16 years as agent and owner of the Ethan Ellenberg Literary Agency, Ethan Ellenberg was contracts manager of Berkley/Jove and Associate Contracts Manager of Bantam.

Specializes in: Picture books, middle grade, and young adult fiction.

Avoids: Poetry.

Preferred form of contact: Send sample manuscripts, publishing history (if any), and an SASE.

Commission structure: 15 percent commission on all sales, except for most foreign sales, in which a foreign coagent is often employed, the commission is 10 percent.

Number of titles sold in a recent year: 100.

Breakdown of clients: Most clients write and/or illustrate picture books, middle grade, and YA fiction.

Percentage of submissions accepted: 5 percent.

Representative titles:

Puppy and Me by Julia Noonan (Scholastic)
Time Flies by Eric Rohmann (Crown, Caldecott Honor Book 1995)
Amber Spyglass by Eric Rohmann (cover illustration only, Crown)
The Invisible Enemy by Marthe Jocelyn (Dutton)
Hannah's Collections by Marthe Jocelyn (Dutton)

Avoids clients who: We don't work with unprofessional clients.

Favors clients who: We're happy to work with many different hardworking writers and illustrators. We do not have any one particular "dream client."

How to improve your chances: We only take on clients whom we truly believe in. Be professional and hardworking.

Became an agent because: I love books and enjoy business and working with people.

How would you describe what it is you actually do for a living? Cultivating and managing talent.

How did you become an agent? Left my second publishing job, as contracts manager, and opened my own agency.

Comments: We love books for children. We are always looking to work with talented people.

JENNIFER FLANNERY

Flannery Literary
1140 Wickfield Court
Naperville, IL 60563
(630) 428-2682

Description: Handles mostly children's books, fiction and nonfiction, from concept and picture books to YA.

★ Barry Goldblatt

Barry Goldblatt Literary Agency
PMB 266
320 7th Avenue
Brooklyn, NY 11215
(718) 832-8787
(718) 832-5558 (fax)
E-mail: bgliterary@earthlink.net

Bio: Started out as a rights assistant at Dutton Children's Books/Dial Books for Young Readers, then moved on to the Putnam & Grosset Group as rights associate/manager, and spent the last four years as the rights and contract director at Orchard Books, until leaving to open my agency in October 2000. B.S. journalism, B.A. English, University of Kansas. Born September 28, 1967, Topeka, Kansas (don't hold it against me).

Hobbies and personal interests: Needless to say, I'm a voracious reader, but I also like riding my bike, playing computer games (a longtime vice I can't seem to kick), and cooking with my two-year-old son, Josh.

Specializes in: I represent children's books exclusively at this time, and my primary interest is in cutting-edge young adult fiction with unique voices and settings. Genre doesn't matter—I like most everything—but I do have a taste for science fiction and fantasy. I also represent some picture book authors, and a few artists, too.

Avoids: I don't handle nonfiction, really, unless someone out there has written the YA equivalent of *Midnight in the Garden of Good and Evil* (i.e., great nonfiction that reads like a novel). I also am not handling adult books at this time.

Preferred form of contact: The best way is to send me work. For novels, a summary and five sample chapters will give me a good sense of what's there. For picture books, the whole manuscript is needed. If one has multiple picture books, please don't send me a dozen, just choose two or three that represent one's best work. I don't accept e-mail queries, and unless I'll know your name the instant you say it, telephone queries really aren't much good, either.

Commission structure: 15 percent for all domestic sales, 20 percent for foreign sales, 20 percent for dramatic/film/TV sales.

Approximately, what percentage of your clients fall into which categories (e.g., children's fiction, children's nonfiction, etc.): 100 percent children's, divided fairly evenly right now between novelists and picture book authors. I have two author/illustrator clients as well.

Percentage of submissions accepted: At this point it's pretty low, 5 percent at best.

Representative titles:

The Sea Chest by Toni Buzzeo (Dial Books for Young Readers)

Dawdle Duckling by Toni Buzzeo (Dial Books for Young Readers)

Delilah's Music by Angela Johnson (Dial Books for Young Readers) (sense a pattern here?)

The Monster in Me by Mette Harrison (Holiday House)

Avoids clients who: Anyone not open to the revision process is particularly unwelcome to me, as I consider revisions to be one of the most important steps in getting published and getting the best book published. I also don't want to work with anyone who isn't really open to my advice or someone who just wants me to negotiate contracts on their behalf. For me, my relationship with a client is a partnership.

Favors clients who: First and foremost, an amazing writer. After that, someone who writes in multiple genres (picture books, chapter books, novels) and writes quickly, someone willing to work with me to create the best possible long-term career.

Common client mistakes: Bad cover letters. Turns me off from the first moment, sometimes so much so that I can't really fairly evaluate the work. I also am not fond of being pitched over the phone; I can't read someone's work by phone, and that's the most important thing.

How to improve your chances: Be professional. Package your work in an organized, well-thought-out manner. Don't use silly gimmicks or send food or toys with a submission. All I care about initially is the work.

Became an agent because: I'd spent nearly 12 years selling rights for large publishers, and I finally decided I wanted to get more involved in selecting the work I got to sell. Agenting seemed like the natural next step.

What might you be doing if you weren't an agent? If I were independently wealthy, I'd be a full-time dad, traveling the world with my family. Since I'm not, hmm, let's see. Selling insurance is out; so is food service. I'd probably be a part of the dot-com craze in some way or another, I suppose.

How would you describe what it is you actually do for a living? I get to read for a living! How great is that? I also get to talk and negotiate daily with great editors, many of whom I consider friends, and I get to tell wonderful new struggling authors that I just sold their first (or second, or third) book. Sure, I also have to deal with lots of rejections, which is never fun, but overall, I couldn't be having more fun.

How did you become an agent? I called an author friend of mine, told her I was thinking about opening my own agency, and she said "where do I sign?" That gave me the confidence to set up shop.

What do you think about editors? I love editors—some more than others, of course. Without editors, I don't have a job. No need to find authors and artists if there aren't great craftspeople to make their work better and make sure the rest of the world sees it.

What do you think about publishers? As with editors, some are better than others, but they all have something to offer. I tend to concentrate on the editor first, the publisher second.

Comments: I've been thrilled to death with the enthusiastic response I've had from other agents with whom I'd worked over the years who cheer me on and give advice, and I've been thrilled at how welcome and open editors have been to seeing a fresh face out there, too. I love children's publishing, and I think it's a great time to be an agent.

★ JANET KOBOBEL GRANT

4788 Carissa Avenue
Santa Rosa, CA 95405
(707) 538-4184
E-mail: jkgbooks@aol.com

Bio: Imprint editor at Zondervan Publishing; managing editor at Focus on the Family Books; agent for five years. B.A. in English.

Specializes in: Nonfiction.

Avoids: Science fiction; fantasy; westerns.

Preferred form of contact: E-mail or query letter.

Commission structure: 15 percent.

Number of titles sold in a recent year: 28.

Breakdown of clients: 42 percent, children's fiction; 11 percent, nonfiction.

Percentage of submissions accepted: 5 percent.

Representative titles:

Hidden Diary Series by Sandra Byrd (Bethany House)

Lullaby by Jane Orcutt (Tyndale)

How to Make a Moose Run by Gary Stanley (Honor Books)

Avoids clients who: The one who is "tone-deaf" regarding the marketability of a manuscript but is confident every new idea is a gem—and asks about the status of each manuscript every week.

Favors clients who: Someone who consistently comes up with exciting approaches, a creative writer who meets deadlines and actively promotes all existing titles.

What are the most common mistakes prospective clients make when soliciting you to represent them? Not explaining why their work is unique—and salable to publishers and readers.

How to improve your chances: Establish yourself by writing for children's magazines.

Became an agent because: Helping authors break in and become successful brings me satisfaction.

What might you be doing if you weren't an agent? Writing or acquiring books for a publisher.

How would you describe what it is you actually do for a living? Make authors successful by helping them develop their careers.

How did you become an agent? By examining what part of the publishing process was most fulfilling to me—gave me the most satisfaction. Working with authors in developing their abilities in being successful.

What do you think about editors? Most of them are bright, interesting people.

What do you think about publishers? Most are well-intentioned but far too busy.

ASHLEY GRAYSON

Carolyn Grayson
Ashley Grayson Literary Agency
1342 18th Street
San Pedro, CA 90732

Description: Children's book agents; members of AAR.

Meet Jennie Dunham
Literary Agent

Jennie Dunham is the principal of Dunham Literary, Inc. (156 Fifth Avenue, Suite 625, New York, NY 10010-7002). Born in April 1969, she attended Princeton University, where she received a BA in anthropology, magna cum laude. Her studies at Princeton were in part focused on ideas of writing, presentation of books, how the look of a book influences a reader's interpretation and mind-set of the book, and the important role of the person who is literate in a mostly illiterate society. Before establishing Dunham Literary, she spent six years with Russell & Volkening and a year each with Mildred Marmur Associates and John Brockman Associates. She handles all ages of children's books, from novelty through young adult. She also handles literary fiction and nonfiction for adults and is an avid book collector.

As an agent, what telltale signs or characteristics are you looking for in prospective clients?

Someone who writes well. Someone who has interesting stories with characters I'd want to meet (or not meet!) in real life. Someone who listens to my ideas and suggestions and who is able to express desires and concerns to me. Someone who is organized and professional. Someone who knows his or her audience and knows about books already published in his or her area. Someone who has realistic expectations. Someone who is pleasant to work with. Someone who respects the ground rules of working with an agent (don't go behind an agent's back to submit projects or negotiate contractual terms, don't make promises to an editor, etc.).

I often find that writers either have a strong voice or are able to weave stories well. Not often do I find writers who can bring both of these together well, and it's very exciting to find a writer who combines these qualities seamlessly.

Do you have any advice for an author starting out in the children's publishing field, in terms of how to get an agent?

First have a complete manuscript that is ready for submission. When a writer submits to an agent or editor, it is always important to put the best foot forward. The manuscript should be in the appropriate format (single-sided, not bound, double-spaced, font size no smaller than 12, etc.) without spelling or grammatical errors.

Then find out as much as possible about various agents. Are you looking for an agent who specializes in one particular area? Are you looking for an agent who represents clients in a couple of areas such as both young adult and novelty or such as both adult and children's books? Do you want an AAR (Association of Authors' Representatives) member? Do you prefer a big agency or a small agency? The more you know about individual agents—for example, what specialty they have and what clients they represent—the better chance you have of finding the right match.

Then send query letters to the agents you've identified. Your cover letter should be clear and professional. Make sure the cover letter has a date, the author's name, address, phone number, and e-mail address. Make sure the query letter tells an agent enough about you and your project without being too long. Include a brief description of the project and a brief bio. Always enclose a self-addressed prestamped envelope for the response. Do not send original art or manuscripts as they will frequently not be returned.

What are some important "keys" to getting your attention? To piquing the interest of the agent? To turning an inquiry into a contract?

In a query letter, I look for someone who has some or all of these qualities: Has a story that sounds fresh or unusual, funny or edgy. Has written a concise letter that tells me everything I want to know and nothing I don't need to know.

In addition, I also look for these credentials: Has won prizes for writing in the same area as is being submitted to me—for instance, someone who has won a prize for technical articles about physics doesn't tell me anything about his or her writing picture books. Has already published books that have received star reviews and sold well.

Do you work with illustrators? What characteristics are you looking for in an artist's work?

Occasionally I work with illustrators. Usually I handle illustrators if they also write.

I like art that is more sophisticated than mass-market commercial in style. I like whimsical, energetic, fun illustrations for very young kids or older kids.

To submit art samples to me, I prefer color photocopies (no original art and preferably no slides), and I like to see several illustrations including a series of five to seven illustrations with the same character(s) from the same story. If you don't have a story, pick an old favorite that everyone will recognize.

What in your opinion makes an author easy to work with? Difficult to work with? How about for illustrators?

An author who is easy to work with works with me so that we are a team; trusts my judgment; is pleasant, appreciative, and professional; has good ideas; understands that it's better to have one really good manuscript than 10 mediocre ones; and self-promotes his or her books.

An author who is difficult to work with insists on his or her way of doing things; goes behind my back; is grumpy, cranky, and unappreciative; writes and deals with other people unprofessionally; and generally is the opposite of the author who is easy to work with

What are key no-no's (or common mistakes) of authors/illustrators who are trying to impress you?

Telling me how much a live audience (usually family or class at school) liked reading the book. Telling me it's a fictional novel. (If it's a novel, I already know it's fiction.) Giving me a "gift" to encourage me to read the material. Calling me on the phone to ask if I want to read a query letter or talk to me about a submission. Sending me an e-mail query. Telling me that he or she has written a 50-page picture book for 13-year-olds or a 20-page middle-grade novel for 5-year-olds so their parents will read it aloud. (Know the specifics for each age group.) Telling me that he or she has the next Harry Potter or other bestseller. Writing didactic, preachy, or moralized stories.

continues

What do you think are the key differences between writing for children and writing for adults?

In a children's book the protagonist tends to be younger and to have a child's view of events. The subjects can be edgy, but they must be portrayed in a way that makes a kid interested in the story, in a way that is relevant to kids' lives. Picture books have very little room for description because children have a shorter threshold for giving a book a chance. Even writers of middle-grade and young adult books should be wary that a child or young adult will put a book down if the story isn't keeping him or her interested. Also, philosophical treatises and didactic texts won't hold a child's attention.

Do you recommend formal training for children's writers, or do you think it's a question of practice or of natural ability?

Everyone writes differently. I think that both natural ability and practice are needed. Some people are most creative when alone in silence, some people when they're with a writing group, and some people when they are in a class setting. There is no right or wrong way to write. What's important is to come up with good writing, stories, and characters. Some writers will benefit greatly from formal training and some won't.

Is there anything else you'd like to say to aspiring authors and illustrators? Any words of encouragement or warning?

I've always found these two very basic formulas helpful. Here is the basic format for a book of fiction: A likeable character endures hardship as he or she struggles for a worthy reason. Here is the basic format for a book of nonfiction: Say that you are going to say it, say it, then say you said it.

Books are very important to young readers. A good story has meaning for a child in it and serves as a vicarious life experience for them. Stories give kids the information that they need in order to live their lives, and I believe that they carry those stories with them as inspiration for the rest of their lives.

Editor's note: Jennie Dunham is an unusually busy agent and was extremely generous with her time, both here and in participating in the roundtable. Please, just because she took the time to give advice and stuck her neck out, don't punish her for her magnanimity by sending inappropriate submissions.

★ Charlotte Gusay

The Charlotte Gusay Literary Agency
10532 Blythe Avenue
Los Angeles, CA 90064
(310) 559-0831
(310) 559-2639 (fax)
E-mail (for queries): gusay1@aol.com
Web site: www.mediastudio.com/gusay

Bio: Teacher/English and drama (3 years); filmmaker/owner of documentary film company (3 years); audio producer/audiocassette company (5 years); bookseller/George Sand, books in West Hollywood (11 years); literary agent/The Charlotte Gusay Literary Agency (10 years). BA in English Literature; master's in education.

Hobbies and personal interests: Reading, gardening, travel (Greece, France), and more reading.

Specializes in: Categorically, I don't rule out anything (much).

Avoids: Not particularly interested in science fiction/fantasy. Do not take on poetry or short stories (not because I don't like them, but because they don't sell).

Preferred form of contact: Query by mail. One page with two or three paragraphs describing the project succinctly. Provide a bit of pertinent information about yourself. Include a self-addressed stamped envelope (SASE).

Commission structure: 15 percent, books; 10 percent, screenplays.

Number of titles sold in a recent year: By way of example, I recently sold two books to film: *A Place Called Waco* to Fox and *Love, Groucho* to CBS.

Breakdown of clients: I represent very few children's books/writers. I am interested in young adult novels or nonfiction books that have film potential.

Percentage of submissions accepted: I accept for review approximately 10 percent of all queries that come into my office.

Representative titles:

A Visit to the Art Galaxy by Annie Reiner (Green Tiger Press/Simon & Schuster)

The Potty Chronicles by Annie Reiner (Magination Press)

The History of Christmas by Annie Reiner (Dove Books)

The Long Journey of the Little Seed by Annie Reiner (Dove Books)

This Nervous Breakdown Is Driving Me Crazy by Annie Reiner (Dove Books)

I'll Know What to Do: A Young Peoples' Guide to Natural Disasters by Drive Bonnie Mark and Aviva Layton (Magination Press)

Avoids clients who: One who is difficult, impatient, who doesn't understand the publishing or film business, and who expects me to send flowers and limousines.

Favors clients who: One who understands how the business of publishing and film works. One who has done his or her homework. One who knows that this does not happen by magic, that the publishing business is excruciatingly difficult, especially now with all the fast-moving changes happening every day. And one who understands how hard I work for my clients.

Common client mistakes: Making broad assumptions. Being hostile when given our instructions for submitting. Not following directions.

How to improve your chances: Be courteous, professional, patient, and knowledgeable.

Became an agent because: I love books and movies, and I know how to sell them.

What might you be doing if you weren't an agent? Reading. Producing movies. Developing books.

How would you describe what it is you actually do for a living? I read a lot of mail (lots and lots of mail). Too much. Then I read lots and lots of manuscripts. Too many. I'm on the phone a lot, talking to editors and producers.

How did you become an agent? I closed my bookstore and wanted to remain in the book business. So here I am.

What do you think about editors? Editors have a tough time. The publishing business is extremely skittish right now.

What do you think about publishers? I commend publishers for remaining in one of the most difficult businesses there is.

Comments: I can't wait to find the next great manuscript for a nonfiction book or novel (children's or adult) that I can then sell as a book and as a movie. That is one of my most favorite things to do!

Elizabeth Harding

Curtis Brown, Ltd.
Ten Astor Place
New York, NY 10003

Description: Children's book agent; member of AAR. For more information about Curtis Brown, Ltd., in general, please see the entry for agent Laura Blake Peterson.

★ Rosalie Grace Heacock

Heacock Literary Agency, Inc.
PO Box 927
Malibu, CA 90265-0927
(310) 589-1775
E-mail: gracebooks@aol.com

Bio: 1978 to present, Heacock Literary Agency, Inc. B.A. California State University, Northbridge (art/English); M.A. California State University, Dominguez Hills (humanities). Born Girard, Kansas.

Specializes in: Well-written, timely books.

Avoids: Horror, true crime, fantasy, commercial fiction.

Preferred form of contact: Query letter with self-addressed stamped return envelope.

Commission structure: 15 percent on domestic sales, 25 percent on international sales (10 percent of which goes to the international agent).

Number of titles sold in a recent year: 20.

Breakdown of clients: 10 percent, children's picture books; 5 percent, children's middle readers; 85 percent, adult general trade nonfiction.

Percentage of submissions accepted: Approximately 5 percent.

Representative titles:

Jubal's Wish by Don and Audrey Wood (Scholastic)

Baby Bear by Larry Dane Brimner (HarperCollins)

Rookie Choices Series by Larry Dane Brimner (Grolier)

Reading Group Journal: Notes in the Margin by Martha Burns and Alice Dillon (Abbeville Press)

Favors clients who: Mutual respect and courtesy are cherished qualities.

Common client mistakes: The most frequent mistake is soliciting representation for materials we specifically do not handle.

Became an agent because: My father introduced me to the world of books when I turned six—he took me to the library to get my first library card—and encouraged a love of good books, which endures to this day.

How did you become an agent? Because he lived abroad, a good friend asked me to submit his manuscripts to publishers for him. I never sold his manuscript but did learn the business and have sold over 1,000 other manuscripts in the 22 years of business.

What do you think about editors? I respect them and value their efforts.

What do you think about publishers? Publishing is in major transition today (like everything else in the world). As an optimist, I do believe we will see improvements in the world of publishing, but today it is more difficult than ever for new writers to get published. This will change, I am confident, and we will hear many new voices in the days ahead.

Emilie Jacobson

Curtis Brown, Ltd.
Ten Astor Place
New York, NY 10003

Description: Children's book agent; member of AAR. For more information about Curtis Brown, Ltd., in general, please see the entry for agent Laura Blake Peterson.

Ginger Knowlton

Curtis Brown, Ltd.
Ten Astor Place
New York, NY 10003

Description: Children's book agent; member of AAR. For more information about Curtis Brown, Ltd., in general, please see the entry for agent Laura Blake Peterson.

★ Barbara S. Kouts

PO Box 560
Bellport, NY 11713
(631) 286-1278

Bio: Agent for 20 years. Master's degree in English literature. Born October 1936, New York City.

Hobbies and personal interests: Reading; gardening; walking; spending time with family.

Specializes in: All areas of children's fiction and nonfiction projects.

Avoids: Violence and horror.

Preferred form of contact: Please write a query letter and enclose a self-addressed stamped return envelope.

Commission structure: 15 percent.

Number of titles sold in a recent year: 25 to 40.

Breakdown of clients: Fiction, 80 percent; nonfiction, 20 percent.

Percentage of submissions accepted: 10 percent.

Representative titles:

Froggy's First Christmas by Jonathan London

Cinderella Skeleton by Robert San Souci

Squanto's Journey and *Sacagawea* by Joseph Bruchac

Avoids clients who: Expect instant fame and success; are overdemanding and supercritical; nontrusting; who submit a manuscript that is not ready to be published; who call on the phone and ask questions when they should write first; who ignore the guidelines for new writers.

Favors clients who: Write well and rewrite well; are eager, cheerful, happy, and responsive to others; are upbeat and positive.

How to improve your chances: Be patient and considerate—and *write well.*

Became an agent because: I want to be a part of producing good literature for children—books with thoughtful and positive values.

What might you be doing if you weren't an agent? I would be a teacher or a librarian.

How would you describe what it is you actually do for a living? Work between the publisher and the writer; try to find good writing, writing that can be published.

How did you become an agent? I studied English literature and the editing process, whereupon I worked for magazine and then book publishers in editorial. It was a natural transition into agenting when I started reading for an established literary agency.

What do you think about editors? With writers, good editors create good books. Editors are the key to a talented writer's success. Good editors are priceless.

What do you think about publishers? Publishers think about the bottom line too much: Sales = money. Not as many are seeking out fine literature these days.

Fran Lebowitz

Writers House
21 W. 26th Street
New York, NY 10010

Description: Children's book agent; member of AAR. For more information about the Writers House agency in general, please see the entry for agent Susan Cohen.

Ray Lincoln

Ray Lincoln Literary Agency
Elkins Park House
7900 Old York Road, Suite 107-B
Elkins Park, PA 19027

Description: Established in 1974, this agency handles mostly children's fiction.

Dorothy Markinko

McIntosh & Otis, Inc.
353 Lexington Avenue
New York, NY 10016

Description: Children's book agent; member of AAR. For more information about the McIntosh & Otis agency in general, see the entry for agent Tracey Adams.

Marilyn Marlow

Curtis Brown, Ltd.
Ten Astor Place
New York, NY 10003

Description: Children's book agent; member of AAR. For more information about Curtis Brown, Ltd., in general, please see the entry for agent Laura Blake Peterson.

Leighton O'Connor

Leighton & Company, Inc.
7 Washington Street
Beverly, MA 01915
(978) 921-0887
Web site: www.leightonreps.com

Description: Art reps and literary agents; members of SCBWI and GAG.

Andrea Pedolsky

Altair Literary Agency
141 Fifth Avenue, Suite 8N
New York, NY 10010
Web site: www.altairliteraryagency.com

Description: Altair Literary Agency handles "authors with passion, books with a purpose." Member of AAR.

★ Laura Blake Peterson

Curtis Brown, Ltd.
Ten Astor Place
New York, NY 10003

Specializes in: The subject matter isn't as important as is the quality of the work—good stories written by good storytellers is the key to success.

Avoids: Science fiction and fantasy.

Preferred form of contact: Send a query letter with a self-addressed stamped envelope. Expect a reply within a month, or slightly longer depending on the caseload.

Commission structure: 15 percent for domestic sales and 20 percent for foreign.

Breakdown of clients: 90 percent, fiction; 10 percent, nonfiction.

Percentage of submissions accepted: 1 percent.

Avoids clients who: Someone who is sloppy, unprofessional, and unpleasant to work with.

Favors clients who: Someone who is a talented storyteller but also a real professional regarding his or her work.

Common client mistakes: Calling on the phone and not doing their homework are the two most common and problematic mistakes. These things are just a waste of everyone's time—theirs included.

How to improve your chances: As with anything, there is a manner in which we agents like to be approached. Take some time to research the objective and you'll have a much better chance of getting your foot in the door.

Became an agent because: I love books. What better way to make a living is there than to read for a living?

What might you be doing if you weren't an agent? Teaching; gardening; reading for fun.

★ William Reiss

John Hawkins and Associates
71 W. 23d Street, Suite 1600
New York, NY 10010
(212) 807-7040
(212) 807-9555 (fax)

Bio: Freelance researcher; editorial assistant to Lombard Johnes (a graphic designer and editor); encyclopedia editor at Funk & Wagnalls Standard Reference Library; literary agent. Kenyon College. Born September 1942, New York City.

Specializes in: Biography, nonfiction historical narratives, archaeology, science fiction and fantasy, mysteries and suspense, true crime narratives, natural history, children's fiction, and adult fiction.

Avoids: Romance novels, poetry, and plays.

Preferred form of contact: Telephone or send a letter describing the project with a few sample pages to provide a sense of the writing style.

Commission structure: 15 percent except on foreign rights, in which case the commission is 20 percent.

Breakdown of clients: About 45 percent are children's fiction writers, and about 5 percent write children's nonfiction. The rest write for adults.

Percentage of submissions accepted: 5 percent.

Representative titles:

Four Stupid Cupids by Gregory Maguire (Clarion)
A Spy among the Girls by Phyllis Reynolds Naylor (Delacorte Press)
Story Time for Little Porcupine by Joseph Slate (Marshall Cavendish)
The Copper Elephant by Adam Rapp (Front Street)

Laura Rennert

Andrea Brown Literary Agency, Inc.
PO Box 429
El Granada, CA 94018-0429

Description: Handles most types of children's books from concept books to YA. Focuses on sophisticated material.

Wendy Schmalz

Harold Ober Associates, Inc.
425 Madison Avenue
New York, NY 10017

Description: The agency considers all fiction and nonfiction subject areas, including nonfiction books, juvenile books, and novels. Member of AAR.

★ Nicholas Smith

Altair Literary Agency
141 Fifth Avenue, Suite 8N
New York, NY 10010
(212) 505-3320

Bio: Bookseller (1974–1976); editor; publisher; marketing and sales manager (publishing); director, new product development (packager/agency); Independent agent; agent/cofounder, Altair Literary Agency (1996–present). Born 1952, St. Louis, Missouri.

Hobbies and personal interests: Music, reading, museums (all, but especially art, science, and natural history exhibitions), travel, and history.

Specializes in: The only area of children's books that I am currently agenting is activity books, and only those in the areas of science, natural history, nature, technology, and, occasionally, art. Some of my clients are individuals, some are museums, and some are a combination/alliance of both. Almost all of these books have an active aspect to them, and all have some special format/production elements, such as pop-ups, mazes, pull-outs, reveals, or something that the reader can make/do based on the content of the book. I look for innovation, simplicity, accuracy of content, appropriate language level, interesting topics with realistically large potential audiences, and an author's clear knowledge of not only the subject matter but also the competition already available in the marketplace.

Preferred form of contact: The best way for a prospective author to initiate contact is via a query letter (with accompanying SASE), and, if appropriate, either a drawing or photograph of what they are proposing. This is especially important if the project is complex. (On occasion, I have paired a good concept with a different format, and I have also paired the creator of an interesting format with a better concept.)

Commission structure: 15 percent, domestic; 20 percent, international/rights.

Percentage of submissions accepted: At present, I accept about 2 percent of the total number. Although I see other projects I would like to take on, at present, it would be unfair to my current clients to do so.

Representative titles:

Jack in Search of Art by Arlene Boehm with the Delaware Art Museum (Court Wayne)

Amazing Bones by Elizabeth Carpenter with the American Museum of Natural History (Workman)

Planets and *Blue Whale* both by Christine Malloy with the American Museum of Natural History (Chronicle Children's Books)

Avoids clients who: Require too much hand holding, who expect that they are an agent's only client.

Favors clients who: Are knowledgeable, skillful, creative—someone who understands the collaborative process and the marketplace. Most important: someone who is responsible and understands the importance of meeting deadlines. Someone with a sense of humor and perspective.

How to improve your chances: Prospective clients whose books are a good fit with my very specific and defined interests will always receive first priority and a prompt reply. My practice is to call those who have queried with a possible fit for me—so, please do not forget your telephone number(s), with the best times to call. But don't call me on the telephone or, worse, send a fax. For the types of children's books I currently represent, an e-mail is not of much use.

Became an agent because: I love what I do—and I enjoy bringing good authors and editors together over a great book.

★ Rosemary B. Stimola

Stimola Literary Studio
210 Crescent Avenue
Leonia, NJ 07605
(201) 944-9886 (phone/fax)
E-mail: ltrystudio@aol.com

Bio: College professor, children's bookseller, editorial consultant, and agent. B.A. in elementary education and theoretical linguistics; M.A. in teaching English as a second language; Ph.D. in applied linguistics. Born November 1952, Queens, New York.

Hobbies and personal interests: Latin dance; beach combing.

Specializes in: Children's books for preschool through young adult in fiction and nonfiction subject areas.

Avoids: Educational books; adult fiction and nonfiction.

Preferred form of contact: E-mail.

Commission structure: 15 percent of all monies due the author/illustrator.

Number of titles sold in a recent year: 10.

Breakdown of clients: 90 percent, children's fiction; 10 percent, children's nonfiction.

Percentage of submissions accepted: 10 percent or less.

Representative titles:

Sweet Talkin' Series (four boardbook titles) by J. Reinach and J. Proimos (Random House)

The Beacon Hill Boys by K. Mochizuki (Scholastic Press)

The Secret to Freedom by M. Vaughan (Lee and How Books)

Johnny Mutton by J. Proimos (Harcourt)

Avoids clients who: "I read this story to my 4-year-old and she loved it!" "I've published for adults so I can *certainly* write for children!" "That advance doesn't begin to pay me for the emotional investment I've made in this book."

Favors clients who: A willing collaborator with a realistic view of publishing.

Common client mistakes: Making assumptions about how *easy* it is to write for a young audience.

How to improve your chances: Come through a referral by an editor, agent, or an existing client.

Became an agent because: Past work lives in teaching and children's bookselling have provided me with an excellent "feel" for good children's books, a sense of the market, and an editor network that naturally led me to agenting.

What might you be doing if you weren't an agent? Working at a publishing house as an editor.

How would you describe what it is that you actually do for a living? I shape and sell books to trade publishers of children's books.

How did you become an agent? Through the encouragement of children's book editors and one particularly convincing author who said, "I want you to represent me."

What do you think about editors? A mixed bag. Many talented, experienced individuals with distinctive tastes; a growing number of younger editors who haven't developed their identities and don't know what they want.

What do you think about publishers? Continued mergers are problematic for the industry. It's important to have a strong personal network, or agents risk falling into the black holes of lost or ignored submissions.

Comments: I prefer to work collaboratively rather than adversarially whenever possible. My goal is to strike a win–win deal for all parties involved.

Roslyn Targ

Roslyn Targ Literary Agency, Inc.
105 W. 13th Street, 15E
New York, NY 10011

Description: Roslyn Targ Literary Agency, Inc., has been in existence for over 35 years and has an eclectic list of authors. Member of AAR.

Scott Treimel

Scott Treimel New York
434 Lafayette Street
New York, NY 10003

Description: Established 1995. Has many previously unpublished clients. Handles everything from concept and picture books to YA. Scott Treimel often attends SCBWI conferences. Member of AAR.

James C. Vines

The Vines Agency
684 Broadway, Suite 901
New York, NY 10012

Description: Since 1989, James C. Vines and William Clark have become premier literary agents in New York, with nearly 900 properties under contract with domestic and foreign publishers or under contract for feature film or dramatic television productions. The agency handles work by published and unpublished writers from all over the world and seeks to maintain a diverse mix of projects. Dedicated to providing full-service representation and management for clients, and offering representation to a broad range of fiction and nonfiction literary properties. Member of AAR.

Mary Jack Wald

Mary Jack Wald Associates, Inc.
111 E. 14th Street
New York, NY 10003

Description: Medium-sized agency, established 1986, handling genre fiction and nonfiction. Mary Jack Wald was formerly an editor at Random House. Member of AAR.

Mitchell S. Waters

Curtis Brown, Ltd.
Ten Astor Place
New York, NY 10003

Description: Children's book agent; member of AAR. For more information about Curtis Brown, Ltd., in general, please see the entry for agent Laura Blake Peterson.

Eugene Winick

McIntosh and Otis, Inc.
353 Lexington Avenue, 15th Floor
New York, NY 10016

Description: Children's book agent; member of AAR. For more information about the McIntosh & Otis agency in general, see the entry for agent Tracey Adams.

Albert Zuckerman

Writers House
21 W. 26th Street
New York, NY 10010

Description: Children's book agent; member of AAR. For more information about the Writers House agency in general, please see the entry for agent Susan Cohen.

APPENDIX I

Internet Research and Resources

In the rapidly shifting world of Internet research and resources, there's only a limited extent to which a printed list of Web sites can be helpful. Here, I've listed the best sites for children's book writers and illustrators as of the date on which I finished this manuscript. But by the time you read this—even though we published this book on an extraordinarily tight schedule—there will no doubt have been many changes. Even more important than the list below, then, is that you be aware of a few basic elements of Internet research and resources:

- **It's out there.** The most important thing to remember about research on the Internet is that whatever you can think of is probably online somewhere, and most likely it's free. The days of the SASE are numbered: Most book and magazine publishers now place their latest guidelines on their Web sites. Nearly every children's writers and illustrators organization has a site. Many authors maintain their own sites. And most sites within a given subject area link to many other similar sites, and there are sites consisting exclusively of links to other sites, not to mention sites containing lists of links to sites that link to other sites.
- **Use the search engines and indices.** Whatever it is you want to find online, if it's not on one of the sites below, you can search for it. But it's important to understand the difference between a search engine and a Web index. A Web index, such as Yahoo.com, takes Web sites and categorizes them by subject, much like a gigantic cross-referenced Web encyclopedia. It is an orderly universe. A search engine, like Google.com, performs a raw search of millions of sites across the Internet. It is far less disciplined an approach than what Yahoo does, but at the same time it gets you deeper into the content you're trying to search. When searching for something online, it's always wise to use an index and a search engine in tandem—this gives you the best of both worlds. And remember, the more specific you make your query, the better your results will be. "Children's Publishers" isn't nearly as effective as "Children's Christian Magazine Publishers." (Assuming that's what you want to learn about!)
- **Remember your links.** When you find a useful site, it's imperative that you record it as a "bookmark" or "favorite" on your Web browser. Otherwise, you'll forget the Web address (URL) in no time and you'll have to go through the whole search process all over again to find it.
- **Get interactive.** Many people use the Web only as a passive resource for reading information. But this just begins to scratch the surface of what the Internet can do. It is also the greatest communication tool ever developed, bringing people together from all over the world. Be sure to seek advice from others like you in message boards and chat rooms. Some of the most

active and supportive message boards are on the www.write4kids.com site (see below for full description). But remember, netiquette requires that you take the time to learn the subject matter before you start posting messages on these interactive forums. So "lurk" a little bit (read and get to know the style of the group) before diving in.

- Finally: **Don't believe everything you read!** The Internet is a fantastically deep well of information, but at the same time few would say that online information is on the whole particularly reliable. Though the sites I've listed here tend to be professionally researched and maintained, many other Web sites—even some from major book and magazine publishers—haven't been updated in years but give no indication as to the currency or lack thereof of their information. Others are simply not well fact-checked. So be careful. Cross-reference, check dates, and if possible pick up the phone to confirm information. Take what you find online with a grain of salt and you'll easily separate the wheat from the chaff.

The Best Sites for Children's Writers and Illustrators

Note: Please also see the Organizations appendix. Each organization mentioned therein maintains its own Web site, many of which have tremendous resources (some for members only).

Agent Research & Evaluation

www.agentresearch.com

Especially useful for the agent verification section (which is free).

America Writes for Kids

www.usawrites4kids.cjb.net/

A great site chock full of resources. Scroll down to the bottom of the home page for an excellent list of useful links.

Authors and Illustrators for Children Webring

www.geocities.com/aicwebring/

Links to many of the best sites.

Bookseller Web sites

www.amazon.com
www.bn.com
www.borders.com

You don't have to buy a single book to get a lot out of these information-rich sites. The major bookseller sites are a great way to learn what's out there in the market, who's buying it, and what they're saying about it.

Children's Book Insider

www.write4kids.com

Online since 1995, the CBI Web site is a tremendous asset to both the aspiring author/ illustrator as well as to those who have already broken into the industry. The site features a library of how-to articles, publishing industry search tools, an active (and very supportive) message board, Write4Kids Radio, children's bestsellers, tips for beginners, etc. The site is maintained and presented by the *Children's Book Insider*, the newsletter for children's writers.

Children's Book Committee at Bank Street College

www.bnkst.edu/bookcom

Children's Book Council (CBC)

www.cbcbooks.org

Especially useful on this site is the FAQ (Frequently Asked Questions) section, under which is listed the "Publishing Process for New Writers" ("Learning About Children's Trade Book Publishing," "Presenting Your Work to a Publisher," etc.) and the "Publishing Process for New Illustrators" ("Illustrated Children's Trade Books," "How to Show Work to a Publisher," etc.) and the author/illustrator index.

Children's Literature Guide

www.nypl.org/research/chss/grd/intguides/children.html

An exhaustive listing of children's literature sites from the peerless New York Public Library.

The Drawing Board

www.members.aol.com/thedrawing

A useful resource with lots of helpful advice for illustrators

Illustrating Children's Books—A Student's Guide

www.mindspring.com/~amoss/teaching/1intro.html

From start to finish, learn about the process of illustrating a children's book.

Illustration for Children's Publishing

www.phylliscahill.com

An extremely useful Web site with listings of everything from children's agents (www.phylliscahill.com/greatsites/agents.html) to copyrights and legal information to other useful Web sites.

Picturebook Sourcebook

www.picture-book.com

Great articles, links and more.

The Purple Crayon

www.underdown.org

Useful articles, mostly for writers and illustrators, and selected links to online resources for writers, editors, teachers, librarians, parents, and others.

Vandergrift's Children's Literature Page

www.scils.rutgers.edu/special/kay/childlit.html

An A-to-Z listing of children's literature, along with the whys and wherefores of it all.

Writer's Digest

Conferences: www.writersdigest.com/conferences/index.htm

Guidelines: www.writersdigest.com/guidelines/

The Writer's Digest Web site is an excellent resource for listings of conferences and an equally worthwhile (and fairly extensive) listing of book and magazine publishers' guidelines online. Not all guidelines are 100% up-to-date, though. As always, there is no substitute for going directly to the source for the most current information.

Writing World

www.writing-world.com/

From the former Managing Editor of Inklings! Writing World is a comprehensive Web site for all aspects of the publishing field.

APPENDIX II

Conferences, Workshops, and Programs

The number of conferences, workshops and programs available to aspiring and established children's book writers and illustrators is extensive enough that an entire book could be written on the subject. Navigating your way through a massive list can be overwhelming and confusing: Some are better than others and many (especially the workshops) are more of a business for the organizers than they are a learning experience for participants. Fortunately, there are many organizations and annual and regional conferences and workshops that are ethical, economical, and specifically tailored to the aspiring and established children's book writer and illustrator.

The best place to start, with the most extensive and well-established offerings, is directly at the most indispensable source: The Society of Children's Book Writers and Illustrators (SCBWI). Though it is not necessary to be a member of SCBWI to attend all of these conferences and workshops, if you are considering attending, it would be worth your while to join too: You will receive mailings and updated calendars, have access to local meetings and support groups, and have better opportunities to get actively involved in the children's publishing network. SCBWI offers scores upon scores of regional conferences, as well as two annual national conferences (in New York City and Los Angeles). See the SCBWI Web site, www.scbwi.org, for the most complete and regularly updated listing of conferences. If you never have, I strongly encourage you to attend one.

Additionally, there are annual retreats, weeklong seminars, and Master's programs devoted to the needs of the children's writer and illustrator. Listed below are some of the most reputable, recognized, and beloved ones—but by no means is this an exhaustive list. If you're able to travel, you'll most likely want to attend some of the conferences listed here; they are the best of the lot. But there are local conferences and meetings most everywhere. To learn about them, the best strategy is to contact the local universities and colleges in your area, and to do a little online research (see the Internet Resources section).

For full descriptions of each of the programs listed below, please see the accompanying Web sites.

Note: A ★ indicates an exceptional resource.

SCBWI Conferences

★ SCBWI

8271 Beverly Boulevard
Los Angeles, CA 90048
(323) 782-1010
www.scbwi.org

National conferences in Los Angeles (August) and New York (February). See the Web site for details as well as a listing of local events, retreats, conferences and workshops.

Other Conferences

American Christian Writers Conference

P.O. Box 110390
Nashville, TN 37222
(615) 834-0450
(800) 21-WRITE
www.ecpa.org/acw

Annual 1, 2, and 3-day writers conferences throughout the U.S. Instruction, networking opportunities, and one-on-one time with editors and professional freelance writers.

The Bay Area Writers League

P.O. Box 728
Seabrook, Texas 77586
(281) 268-7500
www.angelfire.com/tx2/bawl

BAWL holds an annual writing conference at the University of Houston, Clear Lake. A manuscript competition for novice writers is held in conjunction with the conference.

★ Bootcamp

www.wemakewriters.com

Laura Backes, publisher of *Children's Book Insider*, and Linda Arms White, children's author (*Too Many Pumpkins*; *Comes a Wind*; *Cooking on a Stick*; *Author to Editor*, *Query Letter Secrets of the Pros*), teach an intensive two-day children's writing workshop—Children's Authors' Bootcamp. With Laura's editing and agenting background and Linda's story crafting expertise, attendees gain an in-depth view of the industry while working to develop and write a selling story. Bootcamps take place around the country. Check for their Web site for current events and details. Highly recommended.

Cape Cod Writer's Conference

Cape Cod Writers' Center
P.O. Box 186
Barnstable, MA 02630

(508) 375-0516
www.capecod.net/writers

Weeklong program for writers of different genres, including children's books.

Chattanooga Conference on Southern Literature

Arts & Education Council
P.O. Box 4203
Chattanooga, TN 37405
(423) 267-1218
(800) 267-4AEC (4232)
www.artsedcouncil.org

More observatory than participatory. Lectures and panels on Southern literature.

Children's Book Illustration/Writing

Taos Institute Of Arts
108 Civic Plaza Drive
Taos, New Mexico 87571
(800) 822-7183
www.tiataos.com

Multi-day courses specializing in either illustration or writing for children. Taught by Deborah Nourse Lattimore.

First Coast Writers' Festival

101 W. State Street
Jacksonville, FL 32202
(904) 633-8327
http://web.fccj.org/~ngardner/fr-main.htm

Glorieta Christian Writers' Conference

LifeWay Glorieta Conference Center
P.O. Box 8
Glorieta, NM 87535-0008
www.desertcritters.com

Highland Summer Conference

Box 7014 Radford University
Radford, VA 24142
(540) 831-5366
www.radford.edu/~arsc/programs.htm

★ Highlights Foundation Writers Workshop at Chautauqua

814 Court Street
Honesdale, PA 18431
(570) 253-1192
www.highlights.com/about/mediaKit.html

Week-long writer's workshop.

Kentucky Women Writers Conference

(859) 254-4175
www.carnegieliteracy.org/

Weekly sessions of manuscript critique.

Midland Writer's Conference

(517) 837-3435
www.gracedowlibrary.org/writers.html

MFA in Writing Post-Graduate Semester

Norwich University, Vermont College
Northfield, VT 05663
(800) 468-6679
www.norwich.edu/vermontcollege/

For those who want a serious, intensive education in writing.

Perspectives in Children's Literature Conference

226 Furcolo Hall
Box 3035
University of Massachusetts Amherst
Amherst, MA 01003
(413) 545-1116
www-unix.oit.umass.edu/~childlit/home.htm

★ Robert Quackenbush's Children's-Book Writing and Illustrating Workshops

P.O. Box 20651
New York, NY 10021
www.rquackenbush.com

A five-day children's-book writing and illustration workshop (held annually during the second week in July). Attracts participants of all experience levels, from all over the world. Authors and illustrators work with Robert Quackenbush, who has to his credit 170 fiction and non-fiction works for young readers including mysteries, biographies, and songbooks. The objective of the workshop (focusing on picture books) is to learn how to create books for children—from start to finish—and to help free participants from creative blocks. Workshop size is limited to 10 participants. Highly recommended.

Sage Hill Writing Experience

Box 1731
Saskatoon, Saskatchewan
Canada S7K 3S1
(306) 652 7395
www.lights.com/sagehill/programs.html

Sandhills Writers Conference

Augusta State University, Division of Continuing Education
2500 Walton Way
Augusta, GA 30904
www.aug.edu/langlitcom/sand_hills_conference

SouthWest Writers

8200 Mountain Road NE, Suite 106
Albuquerque, NM 87110
(505) 265-9485
www.southwestwriters.org

Taos Summer Writers' Conference

UNM Department of English
Humanities Building #255
Albuquerque, NM 87131
(505) 277-6248
www.unm.edu/~taosconf

The Writers' Program Summer Intensives

UW Educational Outreach
5001 25th Avenue Northeast
Seattle, Washington 98105
(206) 543-2320
(800) 543-2320
www.outreach.washington.edu/extinfo/certprog/wrt/wfc_ins.asp

Comprised of three individual certificate programs: Commercial Fiction, Literary Fiction, Narrative Nonfiction.

New York Area Programs

If you happen to live in or near New York City, there are many programs that are offered on a continuing basis throughout the year. These are two that stand out:

★ Gotham Writers' Workshop

1841 Broadway, Suite 809
New York, NY 10023
(212) WRITERS (212/974-8377)
(877) WRITERS
www.gothamwriters.com

Ten-week, day-long and intensive weekend courses are available from this well-regarded organization. Online courses are available too, so you don't even have to be local to take advantage of the offerings.

★ The New School Graduate Writing Program

Writing for Children Program
Office of Admissions
66 W. 12th Street, Room 401
New York, NY 10011
(212) 229-5630
www.nsu.newschool.edu

The New School Graduate Writing Program is designed as a two-year MFA in Writing for Children. Other classes available as well.

APPENDIX III

Awards & Contests

Although the primary goal of any author or illustrator is to get published and sell books (or articles), winning awards and contests (or even just placing) can be a valuable means of gaining recognition both for beginners and for those with a lifetime of credits to their names. By no means does this list constitute all of the contests and awards that are available but these are the most relevant for writers and illustrators starting out, and I've included some that will be of interest to established writers and illustrators as well. Please also see the book and magazine publisher listings. Many of the most prestigious publishers do not accept unsolicited or unagented manuscripts except through their annual contests. Winning one of these contests can catapult an author or illustrator from obscurity to recognition overnight. Contest rules change often, so please contact the organization for the latest details or visit the Web sites listed below.

Barbara Karlin Grant

Society of Children's Book Writers and Illustrators
345 North Maple Drive, Suite 296
Beverly Hills, CA 90210
www.scbwi.org

Grant awarded to an aspiring picture book writer. Winners receive $1,500, $500 to the runner up. For SCBWI members only.

Boston Globe-Horn Book Awards

56 Roland Street, Suite 200
Boston, MA 02129
(617) 628-0225
www.hbook.com

Annual award for children's and young adult books, both fiction and nonfiction. For books published in the U.S.

Brant Point Literary Prize

P.O. Box 18203
Beverly Hills, CA 90209
800-269-7757
www.brantpointprize.com

Sponsored by What's Inside Press, this annual award for excellence in children's (age 2-8) and young adult (age 12-17) writing is given to an author who conveys an original and moving story based upon the theme of the year. For previously unpublished works. Open to all writers—globally.

Previous themes include unconditional love and envy. Cash prize and a publishing contract with What's Inside Press (minimum first run printing of 10,000 books).

Calliope Fiction Contest

Calliope
P.O. Box 466
Moraga, CA 94556

Annual contest sponsored by the Writer's Special Interest Group of American Mensa. Original entries only. Maximum of 2,500 words. Winners receive cash prizes and likely publication in *Calliope*.

Dana Awards

Mary Elizabeth Parker, Chair
7207 Townsend Forest Court
Browns Summit, NC 27214
www.pipeline.com/~danaawards

The Dana Award is for a work of short fiction, a collection of five poems and a novel that is previously unpublished and not under consideration for publication or award at the time of submission. The award is $1,000 in each category. Work may be submitted elsewhere after submission for Dana Award.

Delacorte Press Contest

1540 Broadway
New York, NY 10036
www.randomhouse.com

The prize of a book contract for a hardcover and a paperback edition, including and royalties, will be awarded annually to encourage the writing of contemporary young adult fiction. The award consists of $1,500 in cash and a $6,000 advance.

Don Freeman Memorial Grant-in-Aid

Society of Children's Book Writers and Illustrators
8271 Beverly Boulevard
Los Angeles, CA 90048
(323) 782-1010
www.scbwi.org

Cash grant and award of $1,500 ($500 to the runner up) for picture book artists. SCBWI members only.

The Ezra Jack Keats New Writer Award

New York Public Library Early Childhood Resource and Information Center
66 Leroy Street
New York, NY 10014
(212) 929-0815
www.nypl.org

Annual award for new writers of children's picture books for ages nine and under that reflect the tradition of Ezra Jack Keats. Only for authors who have published fewer than five books.

Edgar Allen Poe Awards

Mystery Writers of America
17 E. 47th Street, 6th Floor
New York, NY 10017
www.mysterynet.com/awards

Prestigious mystery writers awards which include Best Young Adult Mystery and Best Juvenile Mystery. For entries that have been published in the U.S. within the last year.

Highlights for Children Fiction Contest

803 Church Street
Honesdale, PA 18431
(570) 253-1080
www.highlights.com

Contest winners will have their entries published in *Highlights* unpublished submissions only, $1,000 prize.

IRA Children's Book Awards

International Reading Association (IRA)
800 Barksdale Road
PO Box 8137
Newark, DE 19714
(302) 731-1600
www.reading.org

These awards are given for an author's first or second published book. Awards are for fiction and non-fiction in two age categories. Monetary award.

Lee Bennett Hopkins Promising Poet Award

International Reading Association (IRA)
800 Barksdale Road
PO Box 8137
Newark, DE 19714
(302) 731-1600
www.reading.org

Awarded every three years to a new author of children's poetry (for children up to Grade 12) who has published as many as (but not more than) two books of children's poetry. Monetary award.

Lorian Hemingway Short Story Competition

P.O. Box 993
Key West, FL 33041

Contest designed to recognize up-and-coming writers for short stories of up to 3,000 words in several categories. $1,000 cash award for the winner, $500 for the runner-up.

Margaret A. Edwards Awards

American Library Association
50 E. Huron Street
Chicago, IL 60611
(312) 944-6780
www.ala.org/yalsa

Award given by the Young Adult Library Services Association to recognize authors whose work has been especially meaningful to young adults. For books that have been in print five or more years.

Marguerite De Angeli Contest

Delacorte Press
1540 Broadway
New York, NY 10036
www.randomhouse.com

The prize of a book contract for a hardcover and a paperback edition, including and royalties, will be awarded annually to encourage the writing of contemporary or historical fiction in set in North American, for readers age 7-10. The award consists of $1,500 in cash and a $3,500 advance.

The McElderry Picture Book Prize

Margaret K. McElderry Books
Simon & Schuster Children's Publishing
1230 Avenue of the Americas
New York, NY 10020
www.simonsays.com

Picture book award for previously unpublished writers. The author must both write and illustrate the entry. The winner receives a book contract and $12,500 advance.

Milkweed Prize for Children's Literature

Milkweed Editions
1011 Washington Ave. South, Suite 300
Minneapolis, MN 55415
(612) 332-3192
www.milkweed.org

Award for an outstanding literary novel for ages 8-13. Unpublished submissions only. Winning submission will be published by Milkweed press with a $10,000 advance.

New Voices Award

Lee & Low Books
95 Madison Avenue
New York, NY 10016

(212) 779-4400
www.leeandlow.com

Award for children's writer of color who has not previously published a children's picture book. $1,000 prize and publication to the winner, $500 to the runner-up.

Paul A. Witty Short Story Award

International Reading Association (IRA)
800 Barksdale Road
PO Box 8137
Newark, DE 19714
(302) 731-1600
www.reading.org

Awarded to an author of a previously unpublished original short story published during the previous calendar year in a periodical for children.

PEN/Norma Klein Award for Children's Fiction

PEN American Center
568 Broadway
New York, NY 10012
(212) 334-1660
www.pen.org

Awarded to an emerging voice of literary merit among American writers of children's fiction. Awarded every three years. $3,000 prize.

The PEN/Phyllis Naylor Working Writer Fellowship

PEN American Center
568 Broadway
New York, NY 10012
(212) 334-1660
www.pen.org

Awarded annually to an author of children's or young-adult fiction. $5,000 prize.

Pleasant T. Rowland Prize for Fiction for Girls

Pleasant Company Publications
8400 Fairway Place
Middleton, WI 53562
www.americangirl.com

Award for literature for girls ages 8-12. Submissions must be previously unpublished with a female main character of the same age group. Winner receives a publishing contract and $10,000 advance.

Pockets Magazine Fiction Contest

The Upper Room
1908 Grand Avenue
P.O. Box 340004
Nashville, TN 37203
(615) 340-7333
www.upperroom.org/pockets

Contest for new freelance magazine writers. Unpublished submissions only. Winners will be published in *Pockets* and awarded $1,000.

SCBWI Work-In-Progress Grants

Society or Children's Book Writers and Illustrators
345 North Maple Drive, Suite 296
Beverly Hills, CA 90210
www.scbwi.org

Grants awarded in four categories including one for an unpublished author. Winners receive $1,500, runners-up, $500.

Young Adult Canadian Book Award

Canadian Library Association
328 Frank Street
Ottawa, Ontario K2P 0X8 Canada
(613) 232-9625

Annual award to recognize an outstanding Canadian book (English language) for young adults ages 13-18. Canadian only.

PRESTIGE AWARDS

These are the very most prestigious awards in the industry. If you win one of these, you certainly won't need this book—I'll be coming to you for advice! But, as in all things, it never hurts to try.

The Caldecott

www.ala.org/alsc/caldecott.html

The Newbery

www.ala.org/alsc/newbery.html

The Coretta Scott King Award

www.ala.org/srrt/csking

The Michael L. Printz

www.ala.org/yalsa/printz

The Golden Kite Award

www.scbwi.org/goldkite.htm

APPENDIX IV

Organizations

It's not strictly necessary to belong to any organizations in order to be a successful children's author or illustrator. Organizations, however, do serve important purposes for many writers and illustrators: They often present excellent networking opportunities, they can help you navigate legal and commercial obstacles, and some sponsor conferences, publications and awards. Some of the organizations listed below are for established writers and illustrators only; others accept all comers. If there is one organization that I believe it makes sense for any aspiring children's book writer or illustrator to join it is SCBWI (see below), which offers a dizzying array of excellent resources.

Authors Guild

330 W. 42nd Street
New York, NY 10036
(212) 563-5904
www.authorsguild.org

7000-member organization for established authors only. Offers terrific business and literary resources—especially in the contract area—but you'll need to publish a book with an established American publisher or three articles in general circulation magazines before you can be considered for membership.

Association of Authors' Representatives

10 Astor Place, 3rd Floor
New York, NY 10003
www.publishersweekly.com/AAR/

AAR is a highly regarded professional organization for agents. Agents who are members list their affiliation as a credential.

Canadian Society of Children's Authors, Illustrators and Performers (CANSCAIP)

c/o Northern District Library, Lower Level
40 Orchard View Boulevard
Toronto, Ontario M4R 1B9
CANADA

(416) 515-1559
www.canscaip.org

Major Canadian organization that supports creative work for children and young adults.

Graphic Artists Guild

90 John Street, Suite 403
New York, NY 10038
(212) 791-3400
www.gag.org

National union organization that advocates on behalf of graphic arts professionals. You must derive half your income from artwork to join, though student memberships are available.

International PEN

568 Broadway
New York, NY 10012
(212) 334-1660
www.pen.org

A fellowship of writers working for more than 75 years to advance literature, to promote a culture of reading, and to defend free expression. For established writers only.

International Reading Association (IRA)

Headquarters Office
800 Barksdale Road
PO Box 8137
Newark, DE 19714
(302) 731-1600
www.reading.org

Focuses on promotion of literacy and quality reading instruction. Sponsors numerous conferences, publications and awards.

Society of Children's Book Writers and Illustrators (SCBWI)

8271 Beverly Boulevard
Los Angeles, CA 90048
(323) 782-1010
www.scbwi.org

Arguably the most highly regarded and well recognized professional organization in the business, SCBWI is an international organization (of more than 15,000 authors, illustrators, editors and agents) in the field of children's literature dedicated to providing practical information and assistance to its membership. SCBWI sponsors conferences, workshops and critique groups in most regions of the country and many countries abroad. SCBWI gives out grants and awards, offers access to health insurance, and provides more than 20 publications on marketing and the writing process free to its membership. For more information on everything from the history of the organization to upcoming conferences and awards, check out the Web site.

Society of Illustrators

Museum of American Illustration
128 E. 63rd Street
New York, NY 10021
(212) 838-2560
www.societyillustrators.org

An extremely reputable organization offering prestige to members but not much in the way of conferences and the like. The annual publication is a worthwhile resource and should be available in larger bookstores.

APPENDIX V

Books & Periodicals

BOOKS ON WRITING

An Author's Guide to Children's Book Promotion by Susan Salzman Raab (Raab Associates)
Author to Editor: Query Letter Secrets of the Pros by Linda Arms White (Children's Book Insider)
A Basic Guide to Writing Selling and Promoting Children's Books by Betsy B. Lee (Learning Abilities Books)
Children's Writer Guide, Susan M. Tierney, editor (Institute of Children's Literature)
The Classic Guide to Better Writing by Rudolf Flesch, Ph.D., and A.H. Lass (HarperCollins)
Blood on the Forehead: What I Know About Writing by M.E. Kerr (HarperTrophy)
Children's Writer's & Illustrator's Market by Alice Pope (Writer's Digest Books)
Children's Writer's Word Book by Alijandra Mogilner (Writer's Digest Books)
The Complete Idiot's Guide to Publishing Children's Books by Harold D. Underdown and Lynne Rominger (Alpha Books)
Edit Yourself by Bruce Ross-Larson (Norton)
The Forest for the Trees: An Editor's Advice to Writers by Betsy Lerner (Riverhead Books)
Get Published: 100 Top Magazine Editors Tell You How by Diane Gage and Marcia Coppess (Owl Books)
Handbook for Proof Reading by Laura Killen Anderson (NTC Business Books)
How to Promote Your Children's Book: A Survival Guide by Evelyn Gallardo (Primate Production)
How to Sell Your Photographs and Illustrations by Elliot and Barbara Gordon (North Light Books)
How to Write a Children's Book & Get it Published by Barbara Seuling (Charles Scribner's Sons).
How to Write A Damn Good Novel by James N. Frey (St. Martin's Press)
How to Write, Illustrate, and Design Children's Books by Frieda Gates (Lloyd-Simone Publishing Company)
Networking at Writer's Conferences: From Contacts to Contracts by Steven D. Spratt and Lee G. Spratt (Wiley)
A Sense of Wonder: On Reading and Writing Books for Children by Katherine Peterson (Plume Books)
Ten Steps to Publishing Children's Books; How to Develop, Revise & Tell All Kinds of Books for Children by Berthe Amoss and Eric Suben (Writer's Digest Books)
The Ultimate Portfolio by Martha Metzdorf (North Light Books)
Transcending Boundaries: Writing for a Dual Audience of Children and Adults by Sandra L. Beckett, editor (Garland Publishing)
The Way to Write for Children by Joan Aiken (St. Martin's Griffin)
Wings Of An Artist: Children's Book Illustrators Talk About Their Art by Julie Cummins and Barbara Kiefer (Harry N Abrams)
The Business of Writing for Children: An Award-Winning Author's Tips on How to Write, Sell, and Promote Your Children's Books by Aaron Shepard (Shepard Publications)

Worlds of Childhood: The Art and Craft of Writing for Children edited by Maurice Sendak and William Zinsser (Houghton Mifflin)

Writing Books for Young People by James Cross Giblin (The Writer, Inc.)

Writing.Com: Creative Writing Strategies to Advance Your Writing Career by Moira Anderson Allen (Allworth Press)

Writing for Children and Getting Published by Allan Frewin Jones and Lesley Pollinger (NTC Publishing Group)

Writing for Children and Teenagers by Lee Wyndham and Arnold Madison (Writer's Digest Books)

Writing for Young Adults by Sherry Garland (Writer's Digest Books)

Writing with Pictures: How to Write and Illustrate Children's Books by Uri Shulevitz (Watson-Guptill Publications)

Books on Law/Contracts

Business and Legal Forms for Authors and Self-Publishers by Tad Crawford (Allworth Press)

The Copyright Permission and Libel Handbook: A Step-By-Step Guide for Writers, Editors, and Publishers by Lloyd J. Jassin and Steve C. Schecter, (Wiley)

Every Writer's Guide to Copyright and Publishing Law by Ellen M. Kozak (Owlet)

Kirsch's Guide to the Book Contract: For Authors, Publishers, Editors and Agents by Jonathan Kirsch (Acrobat Books)

Kirsch's Handbook of Publishing Law: For Author's, Publishers, Editors and Agents by Jonathan Kirsch (Acrobat Books)

Negotiating a Book Contract: A Guide for Authors, Agents and Lawyers by Mark L. Levine (Moyer Bell Ltd.)

The Writer's Legal Companion: The Complete Handbook for the Working Writer by Brad Bunnin and Peter Beren (Perseus Press)

The Writer's Legal Guide (2nd Edition) by Tad Crawford and Tony Lyons (Allworth Press)

Periodicals

Booklist
(888) 350-0949
www.ala.org/booklist

Published by the American Library Association (ALA), *Booklist* contains reviews of more than 2,500 titles for children per year, in addition to adult titles, reference books, and audiovisual materials. Essential reading for those who want to stay on top of the library market.

Children's Book Insider, the Newsletter for Children's Writers
901 Columbia Road
Fort Collins, CO 80525
(970) 495-0056
www.write4kids.com
Monthly "how-to" newsletter for children's writers covering all aspects of writing and submitting children's literature. Contains the latest market news, interviews with top authors, articles covering every step of the writing and submission process, tips about electronic publishing, copyright, legal issues, contract negotiation, etc. One year, 12 issue subscription: $29.95 (within US) or $26.95 for electronic edition (anywhere in world).

Children's Writer
(800) 443-6078
www.childrenswriter.com

Monthly newsletter devoted to writing and publishing children's books. First year introductory rate, $15 (13 issues). Regular subscription, $26.

The Horn Book
(800) 325-1170
www.hbook.com

The Horn Book Magazine is the nation's premier journal of record for children's literature.

The Lion and the Unicorn
(800) 548-1784
http://muse.jhu.edu/journals/lion_and_the_unicorn/

Published by Johns Hopkins University Press, this journal is devoted to serious discussion of children's literature. Published three times per year in January, April, and September.

Publishers Weekly (PW)
www.publishersweekly.com

A weekly magazine primarily utilized by the book industry.

School Library Journal
(800) 595-1066
www.slj.com

Journal directed towards librarians who work with young people in school and public libraries. Useful for authors looking to research this critical segment of the market.

Society of Children's Book Writers and Illustrators Bulletin
www.scbwi.org

Bimonthly publication with updates in the field of children's literature. Features include the market reports, articles on writing, illustrating, and publishing, information on contests and awards, SCBWI activities, etc. Included with membership to SCBWI ($50/year, $10 initiation fee).

APPENDIX VI

Other Useful Resources (Artists Directories, General Resources)

ARTIST DIRECTORIES

American Showcase
915 Broadway, 14th Floor
New York, NY 10010
(800) 894-7469
www.americanshowcase.com

Very highly regarded and extensive directory—and you pay for the privilege.

Picture Book
3911 Tenth Avenue South
Birmingham, AL 3522
(888) 490-0100
www.picturebk.com

Specifically devoted to children's book illustrators.

Stock Illustration Sourcebook
16 W. 19th Street
New York, NY 10003
(800) 4-IMAGES

A stock house with extensive listings.

GENERAL RESOURCES

Literary Marketplace
The LMP is an annual guide of the ins and outs of "who's who" in the business of book publishing. It's readily available in libraries and is an indispensable resource for tracking down anyone related to the industry.

Raab Associates
345 Millwood Road
Chappaqua, NY 10514
(914) 241-2117
E-mail: info@raabassociates.com
www.raabassociates.com

Raab Associates is an agency that specializes in marketing consulting and public relations for children's and parenting books and products. The company provides product consulting, marketing, publicity, and web content design services, as well as educational courses for children's authors and illustrators. The client list includes Angel Records, Briarpatch Games, Charlesbridge Publishing, Kids Can Press, Kingfisher Books, Listening Library, Penguin Putnam and Pleasant Company/ American Girls Collection, as well as individual authors and illustrators. The company's Web site serves as an industry resource for information, articles and tips related to children's publishing.

APPENDIX VII

Glossary of Terms

The following are key terms you'll often hear in the children's writing and illustrating business, as well as throughout this book.

Advance A negotiated amount of money paid to the author upon signing the book contract (or in installments as chapters of the book are delivered) that must be "earned out" (paid back) against royalties of the sale of the book. For example, an author signs a contract and gets a $10,000 advance against 7.5% royalties. When the book hits the shelves, depending on the price and the exact means of computing royalties, a number of copies (enough to cover $10,000 in royalties) will have to be sold before the author gets any more money. See *Earning out.*

Agent One who represents an author and negotiates on the author's behalf with publishers.

Anthology A collection of work by various authors, or of various work by one author.

Anthropomorphism Attributing human characteristics to animals and objects. The primary example in children's literature is animals that talk.

Art director One whose responsibilities within a publishing company or magazine include the selection of artistic talent, purchase of visual work, and supervision of execution of artistic projects. An art director can be in-house or freelance.

Artist representative (art rep) Essentially, the artist's/illustrator's version of a literary agent: Someone who represents and advocates on behalf of an artist (most commonly used to sell the artist's work to the publisher and handle the details of contracts, paperwork and legalities).

Backlist A publisher's list of titles that have been in print for more than one season.

Boilerplate Refers to the preprinted language of a publishing company's (or any other company's) standard contract. Reputable publishers usually have boilerplate that, though favorable to the company, is considered fair within the industry. Most authors and illustrators accept the boilerplate, though departures can be negotiated, as is especially likely when an agent or attorney is involved in the process.

Byline What it sounds like: The line that states who wrote something (that is to say, who it's by). Sometimes, especially in magazines, shorter articles are published without a byline. It is also possible for a byline to be shared. Though it is often not an issue, it is nonetheless important to negotiate the byline in writing whenever there is a potential question about what the byline will say.

Chapter book Often used to describe books for readers who are transitioning from concept and picture books to books that tell their stories through words. Chapter books may be illustrated, but the emphasis is on language.

Clips Samples of an author's work that have appeared in print. It is also possible to have online clips. Unpublished work is never properly referred to as a clip; it is more akin to a sample.

Copyright An author's or illustrator's legal rights to ownership of a work, as specified in the federal copyright laws.

Cover art The design of the book cover (jacket).

Cover letter A very short letter (rarely longer than a page) accompanying a submission or clips that indicates only the most essential information about what is enclosed. It is especially important to mention in a cover letter if the work was requested, and to remind the recipient of any other essential details.

Critique group A group of authors or illustrators that assembles periodically (either in person or, these days, online) to review and comment upon each other's work. Critique groups can have various rules and structures, but the essential purpose is to get another set of eyes on your work, and (hopefully) to lend moral support.

Dummy A model/demonstration book consisting of and used to showcase an illustrator's art (and possibly text) in the format that a book would ultimately take.

Earning out When enough copies of a book are sold such that the agreed royalties cover the amount of the advance. An author typically is not paid beyond the advance until the advance has been earned out. Specific contracts can of course vary. See *Advance*.

E-book (electronic book) A book published in electronic form that can be downloaded (usually via the Internet) to a computer or handheld device.

Electronic rights We are still in the early stages of electronic rights, and there are no uniform rules, but these are the rights pertaining to content published on the Internet.

First serial rights Permission given (for a price) to a newspaper or magazine to publish excerpts from the work prior to its volume publication.

Foreign rights The right to publish a work in countries other than that of the primary publisher. Sometimes referred to as translation rights, though this is not an entirely accurate description (especially not when between publishers in English-speaking nations).

Genre A term used simply to refer to a particular species of writing or art, for example, "Western," or "romance."

House style Most publishers have particular conventions with regard to spelling, gender-neutral language, punctuation, and other specifics of the writing process. These conventions are known, collectively, as the house style. When working with a specific publisher, it is always a plus (and sometimes absolutely essential) to be familiar with the house style.

Kill fee Many contracts, especially in magazine writing, will specify a kill fee. This is an amount that is paid in the event the work is never published, for whatever reason, even though it has been submitted on time and is of acceptable quality.

Middle grade See *Middle reader*.

Middle reader Refers to books for ages approximately 8 to 12. See also *Picture book*, *Young adult*, *Young reader*.

Multiple submission Submitting several pieces of work at one time to a single publisher. Often confused with simultaneous submission (see below), which means to submit one work to many publishers (or agents, etc.).

Over the transom See *Unsolicited manuscript*.

Payment on acceptance and **Payment on publication** In magazine publishing in particular, these terms describe when the author or illustrator will receive payment: Either when the publication accepts the work, or when the work actually appears in print. This can make a difference of many months in terms of when money will be received.

Pen name See *Pseudonym*.

Picture book Refers to illustrated books (with limited text) for ages approximately preschool to 8-years-old. See also *Middle reader*, *Young adult*, *Young reader*.

Portfolio An artist's showcase of his or her (hopefully) best work, assembled in a presentable and portable form.

Pseudonym An assumed name (one other than the author's real name) used by an author who, for whatever reason, wants to remain anonymous in a given context. For example, a children's author may also write material with mature content targeted at adults. In order to protect his or her reputation as a children's author he or she may use a pseudonym for the adult material.

Public domain Describes non-copyright work or work that is no longer copyrighted. Work that is in the public domain can be reproduced without any need for permission.

Query letter A short letter summarizing a proposed book or article, or, in the context of a publisher or agent who does not accept unsolicited submissions, asking for permission to submit a manuscript or full proposal. Many publishers and agents prefer queries to manuscripts because queries are so much more efficient. If a query seems attractive, a manuscript will often be requested—and the occasional deal is made based only on queries (though usually only for established authors, and this is more common with magazine articles than with book contracts).

Royalties Monies paid to an author or artist based on the percentage of dollars generated through book sales. There are a number of ways to compute royalties. See also *Advance*.

SASE Acronym for Self Addressed Stamped Envelope. In the publishing business, a SASE is most often used for return of manuscripts from publishers and agents who typically will not bear this cost. Guidelines and contest rules also often require a SASE. Make certain the SASE includes sufficient postage, as determined by a reliable postal scale and the most current postal rates. In addition to a SASE, when making submissions, it is also often helpful to include a self-addressed and preprinted post card that the publisher or agent can use simply to acknowledge receipt of your documents.

Second serial rights Permission given to a newspaper or magazine to publish excerpts after volume publication.

Simultaneous submission Sending a piece of work to several publishers (or agents, etc.) at once. Some refuse to accept simultaneous submissions; others welcome them.

Slush pile See *Unsolicited manuscript*.

Spec Sometimes a magazine editor will like an article idea as expressed in a query letter but perhaps not be familiar enough with an author to be willing to give a contract based just on the idea. Thus the author will be offered the opportunity to write the article on spec, and the editor has no legal obligation to purchase it. However, ethical editors will always publish articles requested on spec if those articles meet the publication's standards.

Talent directory (or **book**) A publication in which an artist can take out an ad featuring his or her work.

Tearsheet A sample of an artist's printed work.

Unsolicited manuscript A manuscript that has not been requested by a publisher or agent. Unsolicited manuscripts are often said to have come *over the transom*. They typically end up in the *slush pile*.

Work for hire In the context of writing and illustrating, and in the purest sense of the term, a work for hire is a piece of writing or an illustration where, once completed, all rights to the work will belong to the publication that hired the work. The writer or illustrator completely surrenders the copyright to the work and is not entitled to additional income from it, even if it is resold. Specific contractual arrangements can of course be more specific as to which party gets which rights.

YA See *Young adult*.

Young adult (YA) Refers to books for ages approximately 12 to 18. See also *Middle reader*, *Picture book*, *Young reader*.

Young reader Refers to books for ages approximately 5 to 8. See also *Middle reader*, *Young adult*, *Picture book*.

Index

C

D

E